Y0-BYZ-623

Networking
Essentials

Second Edition

Microsoft Press

PUBLISHED BY
Microsoft Press
A Division of Microsoft Corporation
One Microsoft Way
Redmond, Washington 98052-6399

Copyright © 1998 by Microsoft Corporation

Library of Congress Cataloging-in-Publication Data
Microsoft Certified Systems Engineer Core Requirements Training Kit /
   Microsoft Corporation.
       p. cm.
   Includes index.
   ISBN 1-57231-905-4
    1. Electronic data processing personnel--Certification.
  2. Microsoft software--Examinations--Study guides. 3. Microsoft
Windows NT. I. Microsoft Corporation.
QA76.3.M524   1998
005.3--dc21   98-6123
                                       CIP

Printed and bound in the United States of America.

2 3 4 5 6 7 8 9 WCWC 3 2 1 0 9 8

Distributed in Canada by ITP Nelson, a division of Thomson Canada Limited.

A CIP catalogue record for this book is available from the British Library.

Microsoft Press books are available through booksellers and distributors worldwide. For further information about international editions, contact your local Microsoft Corporation office or contact Microsoft Press International directly at fax (425) 936-7329. Visit our Web site at mspress.microsoft.com.

BackOffice, Microsoft, Microsoft Press, MS, MS-DOS, Visual Basic, Windows, the Windows Logo, and Windows NT are registered trademarks and MSN is a trademark of Microsoft Corporation. Other product and company names mentioned herein may be the trademarks of their respective owners.

Acquisitions Editor: Jeff Madden
Project Editor: Stuart J. Stuple

Part No. 097-0002010

Contents

About This Kit   **xxvii**

    The Intended Audience xxvii

    Hardware and Software Requirements xxviii

    The Compact Disc Setup xxviii

        Lab and Demonstration Files Setup xxix

        Running the Labs and Demonstrations xxix

    Content Overview xxix

    Kit Features xxxi

        At the Lesson Level xxxi

        At the Chapter Level xxxi

    Where Should You Start? xxxii

    Additional Information xxxiii

        The Microsoft Certified Professional Program xxxiii

        Authorized Technical Education Center (ATEC) xxxvi

    Support for Book Content and Companion Disc xxxvi

Chapter 1 Network Orientation   **1**

    The Case Study Problem 1

    The Troubleshooter 2

    The LAN Planner 2

    Lesson 1: What Is Networking? 3

        What This Lesson Does 3

        Objectives 3

    The Concept of Networking 4

        Local Area Networks 6

        The Expansion of Networks 6

    Q & A 7

    Why Use a Network? 8

        Printers and Other Peripherals 8

        Data 9

        Applications 10

    Q & A 11

    Summary 12

    Your Next Step 12

    Lesson 2: The Two Major Types of Networks 13

        What This Lesson Does 13

        Objectives 13

        Networking Overview 14

Peer-to-Peer Networks. 16
    Size 16
    Cost 16
    Peer-to-Peer Operating Systems 16
    Implementation. 17
    Where Peer-to-Peer Is Appropriate. 17
    Peer-to-Peer Considerations 17
Q & A 19
Server-Based Networks 20
    Specialized Servers. 21
    The Role of Software 23
    Server-Based Network Advantages 24
Q & A 27
Combination Networks 28
Server Hardware Considerations 29
Activity 30
Lab 2: Sharing Directories. 30
    What This Lab Does. 30
    Objectives 30
    Exercise 1: Sharing a Directory. 30
    Exercise 2: Stop Sharing a Directory 31
Summary. 32
Your Next Step. 32
Lesson 3: Network Design 33
    What This Lesson Does 33
    Objectives 33
Designing the Network's Layout 34
Standard Topologies 35
    Bus. 35
Q & A 40
    Star. 41
    Ring 42
Hubs 44
    Active Hubs 44
    Passive Hubs. 44
    Hybrid Hubs 45
    Hub Considerations 46

Q & A 47
Variations on the Major Topologies 48
    Star Bus 48
    Star Ring 49
Selecting a Topology 50
Q & A 51
Activity 52
Summary 52
Your Next Step 52
Chapter 1 Review 53
Checkup 54
    Checkup Answers 56
Case Study Problem 57
    The Setting 57
    The Problem 58
    Your Solution 58
    Suggested Solution 58
The Troubleshooter 59
    Potential Problems 59
    Can You Solve This Problem? 60
    Your Solution 62
    Suggested Solution 63
The LAN Planner 64
    Choosing the Type of Network 64
    Choosing the Network Topology 67
    Choosing the Right Topology 68
The LAN Planner Summary 70

Chapter 2 Connecting Network Components   71
The Case Study 72
The Troubleshooter 72
The LAN Planner 72
Lesson 1: Network Cabling—the Physical Media 73
What This Lesson Does 73
Objectives 73
Primary Cable Types 74
Coaxial 74
Q & A 84
    Twisted-Pair Cable 86

Q & A 91
   Fiber-Optic Cable 92
Q & A 94
Signal Transmission 95
   Baseband Transmission 95
   Broadband Transmission 96
Q & A 97
The IBM Cabling System 98
   IBM Cabling System 99
Selecting Cabling 100
   Cabling Considerations 100
   Cable Comparison Summary 102
Summary 103
Your Next Step 103
Lesson 2: Wireless Network Communications 104
   What This Lesson Does 104
   Objectives 104
The Wireless Environment 105
   Wireless Capabilities 105
   Uses for Wireless 105
Types of Wireless Networks 106
   Local Area Networks 106
   Extended Local Area Networks 111
Q & A 113
   Mobile Computing 114
Q & A 116
Summary 117
Your Next Step 117
Lesson 3: Network Adapter Cards 118
   What This Lesson Does 118
   Objectives 118
The Role of the Network Adapter Card 119
   Preparing the Data 120
   Sending and Controlling Data 122
Q & A 123
Configuration Options and Settings 124
   Interrupt (IRQ) 125
   Base I/O Port 126
   Base I/O Port Settings 127

Base Memory Address. 127
Selecting the Transceiver. 128
Q & A. 129
Network Adapter Card Compatibility 130
Data Bus Architecture 130
Network Cabling and Connectors. 132
Q & A. 135
Network Performance 138
Servers. 139
Workstations. 139
Specialized Network Adapter Cards 140
Wireless Network Adapter Cards. 140
Fiber Optic Network Adapter Cards. 140
Remote-Boot PROMs 140
Summary 141
Activity. 142
Your Next Step 142
Chapter 2 Review 143
Checkup 144
Checkup Answers. 146
Case Study Problem. 148
The Setting 148
The Problem 149
Your Solution 149
Suggested Solution. 150
The Troubleshooter 151
Two Important Troubleshooting Questions 151
Cabling 152
Adapter Cards. 153
Can You Solve This Problem? 154
Your Solution. 154
Suggested Solution. 155
The LAN Planner. 157
Choosing Your Networking Media. 157
Choosing Your Network Adapter Card 161
The LAN Planner Summary 162

Chapter 3 How a Network Functions   **163**

The Case Study Problem 164
The Troubleshooter 164
The LAN Planner 164
Lesson 1: The OSI and 802 Networking Models 165
What This Lesson Does 165
Objectives 165
Network Communications 166
The OSI Model 167
A Layered Architecture 168
Relationship of OSI Model Layers 169
Q & A 174
The 802 Project Model 175
IEEE 802 Categories 175
Enhancements to the OSI Model 176
Q & A 178
Activity 179
Summary 179
Your Next Step 179
Lesson 2: Drivers 180
What This Lesson Does 180
Objectives 180
The Role of Drivers 181
The Network Environment 182
Drivers and the OSI Model 182
Drivers and the Networking Software 183
Implementation 184
Installing 184
Configuring 185
Updating 185
Removing 185
Q & A 186
Activity 187
Lab 8: Installing Network Adapter Cards 187
What This Lab Does 187
Objectives 187
Exercise 1: Installing Network Adapter Cards 187
Exercise 2: Deleting a Network Adapter Card Driver 189

Summary 190
Your Next Step 190
Lesson 3: How Networks Send Data 191
    What This Lesson Does 191
    Objectives 191
The Function of Packets in Network Communications 192
Packet Structure 193
    Packet Components 194
    Creating Packets 196
Q & A 198
    Example: Packets in Printing 199
Summary 203
Your Next Step 203
Lesson 4: Protocols 204
    What This Lesson Does 204
    Objectives 204
The Function of Protocols 205
    How Protocols Work 205
    Routable vs. Nonroutable Protocols 206
Q & A 207
Protocols in a Layered Architecture 208
    Protocol Stacks 208
    The Binding Process 209
    Standard Stacks 209
    Protocol Standards 212
Q & A 215
Common Protocols 216
    TCP/IP 216
    NetBEUI 217
    X.25 217
    XNS 217
    IPX/SPX and NWLink 217
    APPC 218
    AppleTalk 218
    OSI Protocol Suite 218
    DECnet 218
Implementing and Removing Protocols 219
Q & A 220

Summary. 221
Your Next Step. 221
Lesson 5: Putting Data on the Cable 222
    What This Lesson Does 222
    Objectives 222
The Function of Access Methods 223
    Traffic Control on the Cable 223
Major Access Methods 224
    Carrier-Sense Multiple Access with Collision Detection 224
    Carrier-Sense Multiple Access with Collision Avoidance 226
Q & A 227
    Token Passing. 228
    Demand Priority 229
    Access Methods Summary. 230
Q & A 231
Activity 232
Summary. 232
Your Next Step. 232
Chapter 3 Review 233
Checkup 234
    Checkup Answers. 236
Case Study Problem. 237
    The Setting 237
    The Problem 237
    Your Solution 238
    Case Study Suggested Solution. 239
The Troubleshooter 240
    Drivers. 240
    Packets. 240
    Protocols 241
    Access Methods 241
    Can You Solve This Problem? 242
    Your Solution 242
    Suggested Troubleshooting Solution 242
The LAN Planner. 244
    Drivers. 244
    Protocols 244
    Access Methods 246
The LAN Planner Summary 247

Chapter 4 Network Architectures   249

The Case Study Problem 250
The Troubleshooter 250
The LAN Planner 250
Lesson 1: Ethernet 251
What This Lesson Does 251
Objectives 251
Overview 252
The Origin of Ethernet 252
Ethernet Features 252
Q & A 255
The 10 Mbps IEEE Standards 256
10BaseT 256
10Base2 258
10Base5 260
Combining Thicknet and Thinnet 263
10BaseFL 263
Q & A 264
The 100 Mbps IEEE Standard 265
100VG-AnyLAN 265
100BaseX Ethernet 267
Performance Considerations 268
Segmentation 268
Network Operating Systems on Ethernet 268
Q & A 269
Summary 270
Your Next Step 271
Lesson 2: Token Ring 272
What This Lesson Does 272
Objectives 272
Overview 273
Token Ring Features 273
Frame Formats 275
Q & A 276
How Token Ring Works 277
Q & A 279

Hardware Components 280
    The Hub. 280
    Cabling 282
    Media Filters. 284
    Patch Panels 284
    Repeaters. 284
    Network Adapter Cards 284
    Fiber-Optic Cable. 284
Q & A 285
Summary. 286
Your Next Step. 286
Lesson 3: AppleTalk and ArcNet. 287
    What This Lesson Does 287
    Objectives 287
The AppleTalk Environment. 288
    AppleTalk 288
    LocalTalk 289
    AppleShare 290
    EtherTalk. 291
    TokenTalk 291
    AppleTalk Considerations 291
Q & A 292
The ArcNet Environment 293
    How ArcNet Works 293
    Hardware. 295
Q & A 296
Summary. 297
Your Next Step. 298
Chapter 4 Review 299
Checkup 300
    Chapter 4 Checkup Answers 301
Case Study Problem. 302
    The Setting 302
    The Problem 302
    Your Solution 302
    Suggested Solution 303

The Troubleshooter 304
    Can You Solve This Problem? 304
    Your Solution. 304
    Suggested Troubleshooting Solution. 305
The LAN Planner 306
    Considerations for Implementing a Network Architecture 306
    Selecting a Network Architecture 307
The LAN Planner Summary 311

Chapter 5 Network Operations   **313**
    The Case Study Problem 314
    The Troubleshooter 314
    The LAN Planner. 314
Lesson 1: Network Operating System Setup 315
    What This Lesson Does. 315
    Objectives 315
Overview 316
    Hardware and Software Coordination. 316
    Multitasking. 317
Software Components 318
    Client Software 319
Q & A 322
    Server Software 323
Installing Windows NT Server 325
    Server Naming Information. 325
    Server Responsibilities 326
    Partitioning. 327
    Configuring the Network Adapter Card 328
    TCP/IP Installation. 328
    Your Server's Requirements 331
    The Hardware Compatibility List 332
Q & A 333
Network Services. 334
    Installing and Removing Network Services 334
    Binding Options for Services. 336
Q & A 337
Activity 338

Lab 15: Installing a Network Operating System 338
    What This Lab Does. 338
    Objectives. 338
    Exercise 1: Installing Windows NT Server 338
    Exercise 2: Windows NT Server Setup 340
  Summary 344
  Your Next Step 344
Lesson 2:   Network Printing. 345
    What This Lesson Does 345
    Objectives. 345
  The Network Printing Process. 346
    Sharing a Printer. 347
    Connecting to a Printer. 349
  Q & A. 350
  Managing a Shared Printer 351
    Printer Maintenance 351
    Managing Users 351
    Page Description Languages 352
    Managing the Printer Remotely 353
  Q & A. 354
  Sharing Fax Modems. 355
    Routing Faxes. 355
    Enhancements for the Fax Server 356
  Summary 357
  Your Next Step 357
Lesson 3:   Implementing Network Applications 358
    What This Lesson Does 358
    Objectives. 358
  Applications Specifically for Networks. 359
  E-mail. 360
    E-mail Functions 361
    Large System E-mail Providers 362
    E-mail Support 363
    E-mail Standards 363
    Communication Between Standards 367
    E-mail Considerations 368
  Q & A. 369

Scheduling 370
   Individual Scheduling 370
   Group Scheduling. 372
Groupware 373
   Uses for Groupware. 374
   Features. 374
   Groupware Products. 376
   Mixed Environments 380
Q & A 381
Shared Network Applications. 382
   Sharing the Application. 382
   Application Requirements. 383
   The Software Log. 383
Summary 384
Your Next Step 384
Lesson 4: Networks in Multivendor Environments 385
   What This Lesson Does. 385
   Objectives. 385
The Typical Network Environment 386
Implementing Multivendor Solutions 387
   The Client Solution 387
   The Server Solution 388
   Vendor Options 389
Q & A 393
Summary 394
Your Next Step 394
Lesson 5: The Client/Server Environment 395
   What This Lesson Does. 395
   Objectives. 395
Centralized vs. Client/Server 396
   Centralized Computing 396
   Client/Server Computing. 396
The Client/Server Model. 398
   The Client/Server Process 398
   The Client 399
   The Server. 401
Q & A 403
   Client/Server Architecture. 404

The Advantages of Working in a Client/Server Environment 406

Summary. 407

Your Next Step. 407

Chapter 5 Review 408

Checkup 409

Checkup Answers. 411

Case Study Problem. 412

The Setting 412

The Problem 412

Your Solution 413

Case Study Suggested Solution. 415

The Troubleshooter 417

Network Operations 417

Network Printing and Network Fax 418

Network Applications 419

Networks in a Multivendor Environment. 419

The Client/Server Environment. 420

Can You Solve This Problem? 421

Your Solution 421

Suggested Troubleshooting Solution 422

The LAN Planner. 423

Network Printing 423

Network Applications 425

Networks in a Multivendor Environment. 425

The Client/Server Environment. 426

The LAN Planner Summary 427

Chapter 6 Network Administration and Support   429

The Case Study Problem 430

The Troubleshooter 430

The LAN Planner 430

Lesson 1: Managing Network Accounts. 431

What This Lesson Does 431

Objectives 431

Network Management 432

Five Management Areas 432

Administrator Responsibilities 433

Creating User Accounts. 434

Entering User Information. 436

Setting User Parameters 437

Key User Accounts 438
Passwords 439
Q & A 440
Group Accounts 441
Planning for Groups 441
Creating Groups 442
Types of Groups 443
Granting Group Privileges 445
Disabling and Deleting User Accounts 446
Disabling an Account 446
Deleting an Account 448
Q & A 450
Activity 451
Lab 20A: Creating and Deleting User Accounts 451
What This Lab Does 451
Objectives 451
Exercise 1: Creating a User Account 451
Exercise 2: Deleting a User Account 453
Summary 454
Your Next Step 454
Lesson 2: Managing Network Performance 455
What This Lesson Does 455
Objectives 455
Network Management Overview 456
Monitoring Performance 457
Bottlenecks 457
Windows NT Performance Monitor 458
Windows NT Network Monitor 460
Simple Network Management Protocol (SNMP) 461
Q & A 463
Total System Management 464
Maintaining a Network History 468
Activity 469
Summary 469
Your Next Step 469
Lesson 3: Ensuring Network Data Security 470
What This Lesson Does 470
Objectives 470

Planning for Network Security 471
    Level of Security 471
    Setting Policies 471
    Training 472
    Physical Security of Equipment 473
Security Models 474
    Password-Protected Shares 474
    Access Permissions 475
    Q & A 480
Security Enhancements 481
    Auditing 481
    Diskless Computers 482
    Data Encryption 482
    Virus Protection 483
    Q & A 484
    Summary 485
    Your Next Step 485
Lesson 4: Avoiding Data Loss 486
    What This Lesson Does 486
    Objectives 486
Data Protection 487
Tape Backup 488
    Implementing a Backup System 488
    Testing and Storage 490
    Maintaining a Backup Log 490
    Installing the Backup System 491
    Q & A 492
The Uninterruptible Power Supply (UPS) 493
    Types of UPS Systems 494
    Implementing UPS 494
Fault Tolerant Systems 495
    Redundant Arrays of Inexpensive Disks (RAID) 495
    Sector Sparing 499
    Microsoft Clustering 500
    Implementing Fault Tolerance 500
    Q & A 502
    Summary 503

Chapter 6 Review 504
  Checkup 505
    Checkup Answers. 507
  Case Study Problem. 508
    The Setting 508
    The Problem 508
    Your Solution 511
    Case Study Suggested Solution. 514
  The Troubleshooter 517
    Troubleshooting Network Accounts. 517
    Troubleshooting Network Data Security 517
    Troubleshooting Unauthorized Access. 518
    Can You Solve This Problem? 520
    Your Solution. 520
    Suggested Troubleshooting Solution 521
  The LAN Planner. 522
    Planning Network Security 522
    Managing Network Performance 525
    Avoiding Data Loss 526
    Planning for Your Network. 526
  The LAN Planner Summary 528

Chapter 7 Larger Networks   **531**
    The Case Study. 532
    The Troubleshooter 532
    The LAN Planner 532
  Lesson 1: Modems in Network Communications 533
    What This Lesson Does. 533
    Objectives 533
  Modem Technology. 534
    Basic Modem Functions 534
    Modem Hardware. 535
    Modem Standards. 537
    Modem Performance 538
  Q & A 539
  Types of Modems 540
    Asynchronous Communications (Async). 540
    Synchronous Communication 542
  Q & A 544

Carriers 545
   Telephone Lines 545
   Remote Access 546
   Point-to-Point Tunneling Protocol 547
Q & A 548
Activity 549
Summary 549
Your Next Step 549
Lesson 2: Creating Larger Networks 550
   What This Lesson Does 550
   Objectives 550
LAN Expansion 551
Repeaters 552
   How Repeaters Work 552
   Repeater Considerations 554
   Summary 554
Q & A 555
Bridges 556
   How Bridges Work 557
   Remote Bridges 560
   Differentiating Between Bridges and Repeaters 561
   Bridge Considerations 561
   Summary 562
Q & A 563
Routers 564
   How Routers Work 564
   Types of Routers 568
   Distinguishing Between Bridges and Routers 569
   Brouters 572
   Summary 572
Q & A 573
Gateways 574
   How Gateways Work 574
   Mainframe Gateways 576
   Gateway Considerations 577
   Summary 577
Q & A 578
Summary 579
Your Next Step 579

Lesson 3: Wide Area Network (WAN) Transmission. 580
    What This Lesson Does. 580
    Objectives. 580
WAN Overview. 581
Analog Connectivity 582
    Dial-Up Lines. 582
    Dedicated Analog Lines 583
    Dial-Up or Dedicated?. 584
Q & A. 585
Digital Connectivity 586
    T1 587
    T3 588
    Switched 56 588
Q & A. 589
Packet-Switching Networks 590
    How Packet Switching Works. 590
    Virtual Circuits. 591
Q & A. 592
Summary 593
Your Next Step 593
Lesson 4: Advanced WAN Technologies. 594
    What This Lesson Does. 594
    Objectives. 594
Sending Data Across a WAN 595
X.25 595
Frame Relay. 597
Q & A. 598
Asynchronous Transfer Mode (ATM) 599
    ATM Technology. 599
    ATM Components 600
    ATM Considerations 602
Q & A. 603
Integrated Services Digital Network (ISDN). 604
Fiber Distributed Data Interface (FDDI) 605
    Token Passing. 605
    Topology. 606
    Beaconing. 608
    Media 609

Q & A 610

Synchronous Optical Network (SONET). 611

Switched Multimegabit Data Service (SMDS) 612

Summary. 613

Your Next Step. 613

Chapter 7 Review 614

Checkup 615

Checkup Answers. 618

Case Study Problem. 619

The Setting 619

The Problem 619

Your Solution 619

Case Study Suggested Solution 620

The Troubleshooter 622

Can You Solve This Problem? 624

Your Solution 625

Suggested Troubleshooting Solution 625

The LAN Planner. 626

Modems. 626

Creating Larger Networks 627

Choosing Advanced WAN Transmission Technologies. 630

The LAN Planner Summary 633

Chapter 8 Solving Network Problems   635

The Case Study Problem 635

The Troubleshooter 636

The LAN Planner 636

Lesson 1: Monitoring Network Behavior to Prevent Problems 637

What This Lesson Does 637

Objectives 637

Approaches to Network Management 638

Prevention Through Planning 639

Backing Up the Network 639

Security 640

Standardization 641

Upgrades 642

Documentation 642

Q & A 643

Network Management Utilities. 644
    Network Monitoring 644
    Establishing a Baseline 646
    Management Software and Preemptive Troubleshooting 648
Q & A. 649
Summary 650
Your Next Step 650
Lesson 2: Network Troubleshooting. 651
    What This Lesson Does. 651
    Objectives. 651
Troubleshooting Methodology 652
    The Structured Approach. 652
    Asking for Help 655
Q & A. 656
Special Tools 657
    Digital Volt Meters (DVM). 657
    Time-Domain Reflectometers (TDRs). 657
    Advanced Cable Testers 658
    Oscilloscopes 658
    Network Monitors 659
    Protocol Analyzers. 659
    Popular Analyzers 661
Q & A. 662
Network Support Resources 663
    TechNet. 663
    Bulletin Board Services (BBS) 664
    User Groups 665
    Periodicals. 665
Common Troubleshooting Situations. 666
    Cabling and Related Components. 666
    Power Fluctuations. 667
    Upgrades. 667
    Computers. 668
    Server Disk Crash 668
    Poor Network Performance. 669
Q & A. 670
Summary 671
Your Next Step 671

Lesson 3: The Internet: A Worldwide Resource 672
    What This Lesson Does 672
    Objectives 672
Overview 673
Internet Services 674
    World Wide Web 674
    File Transfer Protocol (FTP) 674
    E-mail 676
    News 676
    Gopher 677
    Telnet 678
    Internet Sites 678
The Microsoft Network (MSN) 679
Locating Resources 681
Making an Internet Connection 683
    Dial-Up 683
    ISDN 684
    Considerations 684
Summary 685
Your Next Step 685
Chapter 8 Review 686
Checkup 687
    Checkup Answers 689
Case Study Problem 691
    The Setting 691
    The Problem 691
    Your Solution 691
    Case Study Suggested Solution 692
The Troubleshooter 693
    The System 693
    Applications 694
    Vendors 694
    Users 694
    Timing 696
    Can You Solve This Problem? 697
    Your Solution 698
    Suggested Troubleshooting Solution 699
The LAN Planner 700
The LAN Planner Summary 704

Appendix A: Common Network Standards and Specifications   707

Appendix B: Network Planning and Implementation   721

Appendix C: Network Troubleshooter   753

Bibliography   759

Glossary   761

Index   807

About This Kit

Welcome to *Networking Essentials, Second Edition, Hands-On, Self-Paced Training for Supporting Local and Wide Area Networks*. This kit will provide you with the fundamentals of current networking technology. This is an interactive self-study kit designed with two primary goals in mind:

1. To serve as a general introduction to networking including local and wide area network technology.
2. To prepare Microsoft® Certified Professional (MCP) program candidates to successfully complete the MCP Networking Essentials examination.

The kit consists of this book and a compact disc containing both interactive simulations and demonstrations.

The book is divided into chapters and lessons, and features exercises at both the lesson and chapter levels. You can use the lesson exercises to help reinforce what you have read in the lesson. At the end of each chapter you will be able to apply what you have learned to different networking situations from implementation to problem solving.

The Intended Audience

The kit was designed primarily for students who are beginning the Microsoft Certified Systems Engineer certification program and need a foundation in networking skills and knowledge.

The kit is also for the ambitious professional seeking a general understanding of the technical concepts and components in a network environment.

Prerequisites

To get the most out of this kit, students should have the following:

1. A desire to learn the essentials of networking.
2. Working knowledge of the operation and support of hardware and software in stand-alone personal computers. This includes, but is not limited to, the following:

    Using an operating system with a graphical user interface such as Microsoft Windows® 3.1, Microsoft Windows NT™ 4.0, or Microsoft Windows 95

    Installing application software

    Familiarity with files including batch, Autoexec.bat, and Config.sys files

    Installing hardware such as memory, communication peripherals, and disk drives

Hardware and Software Requirements

Networking Essentials includes this book, which can be used without any other equipment. However, the kit does include a compact disc containing supplemental information and interactive exercises.

To run the compact disc, you will need a computer that supports a CD-ROM drive and any of the following operating systems:

Microsoft Windows NT 3.5, 3.51, or 4.0

Microsoft Windows 95

Hardware requirements vary widely depending on the operating system you have running. If you have a machine that supports one of the products listed above, then you can run the labs and demonstrations.

To ensure correct video display, the demonstrations should be run on computers having the ability to display 256 colors or more.

The Compact Disc Setup

The compact disc included with the kit contains supplemental instruction in two forms, hands-on labs and demonstrations. Lessons that contain labs or demonstrations will direct you to them under the heading of Activity.

The labs simulate interactive network tasks in a Windows NT Server 4.0 environment.

These activities will provide a chance to experience some of the major network activities, such as administrator tasks, presented in the lessons. For example, where the book describes the network administrator's job of creating users for the network, the corresponding activity simulates creating a network user in an actual network environment. One of the labs simulates a complete Windows NT Server installation.

The demonstrations illustrate selected concepts presented in the text.

These are multimedia presentations designed to supplement instruction in some of the important networking concepts.

Note The multimedia (*.AVI) files included with this book do not have an audio component. There is no soundtrack for these presentations.

Lab and Demonstration Files Setup

The Setup.exe program on the compact disc will do all of the necessary installation for the labs and the demonstrations. You can use the Setup program to install a copy of the files on your hard disk. The lab files must be installed on your hard disk to work. The demonstrations files can be copied to your hard disk or run from the CD-ROM.

To install the labs and demonstrations, double-click the Setup.exe program on the compact disc. For additional information about the setup, see the Readme.txt file included on the compact disc.

Running the Labs and Demonstrations

Once you have run the Setup program, there will be a Networking Essentials program group created on your computer. To run the labs or demonstrations installed on your hard disk, click the appropriate icon in this program group. For example, to run Lab 8, click the icon labeled Lab8. To run the demonstrations from the CD-ROM, view the contents of the Demos folder and double click on the appropriate icon.

Content Overview

This book is designed to be completed from beginning to end. The first chapter is presented with the assumption the student has no prior networking knowledge and subsequently, each chapter builds on information presented in previous chapters. This self-paced training is divided into eight chapters. A review of the chapters will provide a good overview of the major concepts presented in the kit.

- Chapter 1: Network Orientation (3 lessons). Chapter 1 introduces fundamental networking concepts, components, and functions and presents the three basic network designs.

- Chapter 2: Connecting Network Components (3 lessons). Chapter 2 describes how network components are linked either by physical media such as cable or by wireless methods such as infrared or radio transmission. It provides an overview of the major types of cable and the issues involved in selecting network adapter cards.

- Chapter 3: How a Network Functions (5 lessons). Chapter 3 begins by presenting the theoretical structure which forms the foundation of all network activity—the Open Systems Interconnection (OSI) reference model. Next, you will go on to learn where different network components such as drivers, packets, and protocols fit into a network operation. The last lesson explains how access methods control the flow of data across the network.

Chapter 4: Network Architectures (3 lessons). Chapter 4 presents the primary network architectures, or layouts, and describes their major components, features, and functions.

Chapter 5: Network Operations (5 lessons). Chapter 5 describes the operating systems, applications, utilities, and special languages that make it possible for networks to provide the services they do. It also presents an overview of a particular type of network environment (client/server).

Chapter 6: Network Administration and Support (4 lessons). Chapter 6 explains what is involved in managing and supporting a network in its day-to-day functions of providing services to its users. This involves creating users and controlling their access to network resources, keeping track of how the network performs, and ensuring that the network is not damaged by either natural or human forces.

Chapter 7: Larger Networks (4 lessons). Chapter 7 describes how networks grow from a local area network (LAN) into larger and wide area networks (WANs). It introduces the modem as an important network communications component and then presents the principles, components, and technologies involved in expanding a LAN into a much larger system.

Chapter 8: Solving Network Problems (3 lessons). Chapter 8 describes how to manage a network to keep it running smoothly. The chapter explains how to establish a baseline and then monitor network behavior to determine when the network is not performing properly. It also presents an overview of how to identify and correct network problems and then reviews several sources of help in maintaining a successful network, including the Internet.

Appendixes

Appendix A: Common Network Standards and Specifications

Appendix B: Network Planning and Implementation

Appendix C: Network Troubleshooter

Bibliography

Glossary. The glossary is geared toward the networking beginner and contains definitions of networking terms used in the kit.

Kit Features

Both the lessons and the chapters offer interactive features which make *Networking Essentials* a true self-study course rather than a primer or textbook.

At the Lesson Level

In addition to the topic content, each lesson has the following components:

What This Lesson Does—Provides a brief overview of the lesson content

Objectives—Lists the skills and knowledge you will have after completing the lesson

Q & A—Practice questions which give you an opportunity to reinforce what you have learned as you go through each lesson

Activity—The labs and demonstrations contained on the kit compact disc

Summary—A review the major points of the lesson

Your Next Step—Provides continuity between what you have just learned and what you will learn in the next lesson

At the Chapter Level

The chapters tie lessons together under a common theme. Each chapter will end with a Chapter Review. It contains the following components:

Each Review begins with a summary of major points presented in each lesson.

The Checkup contains a variety of knowledge-based exercises. Use them to reinforce what you have learned. They can help you determine what content in the lesson you may need to review before going on to the next chapter. Answers are included at the end of each Checkup.

Each Case Study will describe a network situation and then ask you to apply what you have learned in the chapter to solving a problem. The Case Study also provides a suggested solution to which you can compare you own answer.

Each Troubleshooter presents key points you should check if you find yourself facing problems in an actual network in the field. Each chapter's Troubleshooter addresses issues presented in that chapter. For example, the Troubleshooter for Chapter 2, Connecting Network Components, presents tips on troubleshooting network cable. The Troubleshooter also includes troubleshooting problems for you to solve based on information in one or more of the lessons in that chapter. As in the Case Study, there is a suggested solution.

The LAN Planner presents questions you need to address when planning a network, whether it be installing a brand new one, or upgrading an existing one. When combined with the information in Appendix B, "Network Planning and Implementation," they can be used as a complete guide for implementing a network on your site from the ground up.

Where Should You Start?

Where you begin *Networking Essentials* will depend on:

Your background

Your experience

What you want out of the kit

This is a self-paced study kit, so if you already have some networking expertise you may choose to skip some lessons, or you may find you need to go through lessons more than once. The interactive exercises and activities may be your focus. Read the objectives at the beginning of each lesson to find out whether you want to read that lesson or not. You can use the kit as you need to achieve your own goals.

If You Are New to Networking

If you are new to networking, you should begin at the beginning. Technical information presented in later lessons requires that you have a working knowledge of basic networking concepts. As you successfully complete the lessons and the chapter reviews, you will build on your networking knowledge, and be able to grasp more advanced topics.

If You Have Some Networking Experience

To determine where you should begin if you have some network experience, look through the table of contents to identify a subject with which you want to start. Then, turn to the end of that chapter and read through the Chapter Review. If the subjects are familiar, try the Checkup. If you answer all of the questions correctly, you may want to do a quick review of the lessons in that chapter and then go on to the Case Study, Troubleshooter, and LAN Planner. If you answer several questions in the Checkup incorrectly, you should spend more time studying the lessons.

If You are Preparing for the Networking Essentials Examination

If you are preparing for the Networking Essentials examination, you should consider going through the entire kit from the beginning regardless of how much networking experience you have. The Case Studies, Troubleshooters, and LAN Planners in the Chapter Reviews enable you to apply the information in the lessons to actual network situations. Therefore, they will be especially helpful in preparing for the examination.

Additional Information

The following sections describe various programs offered by Microsoft that you may find useful.

The Microsoft Certified Professional Program

The Microsoft Certified Professional (MCP) program provides the best method to prove your command of current Microsoft products and technologies. Microsoft, an industry leader in certification, is on the forefront of testing methodology. Our exams and corresponding certifications are developed to validate your mastery of critical competencies as you design and develop, or implement and support, solutions with Microsoft products and technologies. Computer professionals who become Microsoft Certified are recognized as experts and are sought after industry-wide.

The Microsoft Certified Professional program offers four certifications, based on specific areas of technical expertise:

- *Microsoft Certified Systems Engineers.* Qualified to effectively plan, implement, maintain, and support information systems with Microsoft Windows 95, Microsoft Windows NT, and the Microsoft BackOffice™ integrated family of server software.
- *Microsoft Certified Solution Developers.* Qualified to design and develop custom business solutions with Microsoft development tools, technologies, and platforms, including Microsoft Office and Microsoft BackOffice.
- *Microsoft Certified Product Specialists.* Demonstrated in-depth knowledge of at least one Microsoft operating system. Candidates may pass additional Microsoft certification exams to further qualify their skills with Microsoft BackOffice products, development tools, or desktop programs.
- *Microsoft Certified Trainers.* Instructionally and technically qualified to deliver Microsoft Official Curriculum through Microsoft authorized education sites.

Who Should Become a Microsoft Certified Professional?

Anyone who must prove their technical expertise with Microsoft products should consider the program, including systems engineers, professional developers, support technicians, system and network administrators, consultants, and trainers.

What Are the Benefits of Becoming a Microsoft Certified Professional?

The Microsoft Certified Professional program offers a number of immediate and long-term benefits, including the following[1]:

Recognition. Microsoft Certified Professionals are instantly recognized as experts with the technical knowledge and skills needed to design and develop, or implement and support, solutions with Microsoft products. Microsoft helps build this recognition by promoting the expertise of Microsoft Certified Professionals within the industry and to customers and potential clients.

Access to technical information. Microsoft Certified Professionals gain access to technical information directly from Microsoft and receive special invitations to Microsoft conferences and technical training events. Depending upon the certification, Microsoft Certified Professionals also receive a prepaid trial membership to the Microsoft TechNet Technical Information Network, or a discount for the Microsoft Developer Network; free incidents with Microsoft Product Support Services; and are eligible to participate in the Microsoft Beta Evaluation program.

Global community. Microsoft Certified Professionals join a worldwide community of technical professionals who have validated their expertise with Microsoft products. Microsoft Certified Professionals are brought together through a dedicated CompuServe® forum and local events; receive a free subscription to the *Microsoft Certified Professional Magazine*, a career and professional development magazine created especially for Microsoft Certified Professionals; and, depending on their certification, are eligible to join the Network Professional Association, a worldwide association of computer professionals.

---

[1] *Not all benefits are available worldwide. Please check with your local Microsoft office to confirm available benefits in your country.*

What Are the Requirements for Becoming a Microsoft Certified Professional?

The certification requirements differ for each certification and are specific to the products and job functions addressed by the certification.

To become a Microsoft Certified Professional, you must pass rigorous certification exams that provide a valid and reliable measure of technical proficiency and expertise. These exams are designed to test your expertise and ability to perform a role or task with a product, and are developed with the input of professionals in the industry. Questions in the exams reflect how Microsoft products are used in actual organizations, giving them real-world relevance.

Microsoft Certified Systems Engineers are required to pass four operating system exams and two elective exams.

Microsoft Certified Solution Developers are required to pass two core technology exams and two elective exams.

Microsoft Certified Product Specialists are required to pass one operating system exam. In addition, individuals seeking to validate their expertise in a program must pass the appropriate elective exam.

Microsoft Certified Trainers are required to meet instructional and technical requirements specific to each Microsoft Official Curriculum course they are certified to deliver.

How Does One Get More Information About the Microsoft Certified Professional Program?

Internet: http://www.microsoft.com/train_cert/

CompuServe: GO MECFORUM, Library #2, E&CMAP.ZIP

Microsoft: In the United States, call (800) 636-7544. Outside the United States, contact your local Microsoft office.

Authorized Technical Education Center (ATEC)

Authorized Technical Education Centers (ATECs) are the best source for instructor-led training that will help prepare you to become a Microsoft Certified Professional. The Microsoft ATEC program is a worldwide network of qualified technical training organizations that provide authorized delivery of Microsoft Official Curriculum courses by Microsoft Certified Trainers to computer professionals. These independent education centers deliver consistent, high-level, hands-on technical training on the full range of Microsoft productivity, networking, operating system, and application development products.

Microsoft Official Curriculum course materials, used by ATECs, come straight from the source—Microsoft. Our staff of course designers, product developers, support engineers, and market experts work to ensure that you get the industry's most timely and reliable courses related to Microsoft advanced technology products and integration techniques. Microsoft Certified Trainers undergo rigorous training and testing to become certified to deliver each Microsoft Official Curriculum course. They are experts in providing the highest quality professional instruction. For a listing of ATEC locations in the United States and Canada, call the Microsoft fax service at (800) 727-3351. Outside the United States and Canada, call the fax service at (206) 635-2233.

Support for Book Content and Companion Disc

Every effort has been made to ensure the accuracy of this book and the contents of the companion disc. Microsoft Press provides corrections for books through the World Wide Web at the following address:

> http://mspress.microsoft.com/support/

If you have comments, questions, or ideas regarding this book or the companion disc, please send them to Microsoft Press using either of the following methods:

E-mail:

> TKINPUT@MICROSOFT.COM

Postal Mail:

> Microsoft Press
> Attn: Editor, Networking Essentials, Second Edition
> One Microsoft Way
> Redmond, WA 98052-6399

Please note that product support is not offered through the above mail addresses. For further information regarding Microsoft software support options, please connect to http://www.microsoft.com/support/ or call Microsoft Technical Support Priority Support Sales at (800) 936-3500.

C H A P T E R   1

Network Orientation

Lesson 1   What Is Networking? . . . 3

Lesson 2   The Two Major Types of Networks . . . 13

Lesson 3   Network Design . . . 33

Chapter 1   Review . . . 53

Welcome to Chapter 1, Network Orientation. This chapter presents the concepts upon which all networking is based. In this chapter you will learn what networks are and why organizations use them. You will be introduced to the essential components common to every network and see how these components work together to deliver the benefits that have made networks an essential business tool.

You will also learn about the two primary types of networks, peer-to-peer and server-based, and the three basic ways to lay out a network.

The Case Study Problem

When you finish the lessons in Chapter 1 you will be able to apply your knowledge to determine the type of network which would be appropriate for a small insurance company that wants to install its first network.

The Troubleshooter

The Troubleshooter will point out potential problems you may encounter when a network has outgrown its initial implementation. You will then provide a possible solution for an existing network that needs a new design.

The LAN Planner

The LAN Planner will provide you with a complete check list that can help you determine your real-world needs when you design your first network.

Lesson 1: What Is Networking?

What This Lesson Does

This lesson introduces the idea of connecting computers to form a local area network (LAN).

Objectives

By the end of this lesson, you will be able to:

- Identify the components of a local area network.
- Describe the advantages of networking.

Estimated lesson time 20 minutes

The Concept of Networking

At its most elementary level, a network consists of two computers connected to each other by a cable so that they can share data. All networking, no matter how sophisticated, stems from that simple system. While the idea of two computers connected by a cable may not seem extraordinary, in retrospect, it was a major achievement in communications.

Networking arose from the need to share data in a timely fashion. Personal computers are wonderful business tools for producing data, spreadsheets, graphics, and other types of information, but do not allow you to quickly share the data you have produced. Without a network, the documents have to be printed out so that others can edit them or use them. At best, you give files on floppy disks to others to copy to their computers. If others make changes to the document there is no way to merge the changes. This was, and still is, called working in a stand-alone environment.

Figure 1.1 Stand-alone environment

If the worker shown in Figure 1.1 were to connect his computer to other computers, he could share the data on the other computers and the printers. A group of computers and other devices connected together is called a network, and the concept of connected computers sharing resources is called networking.

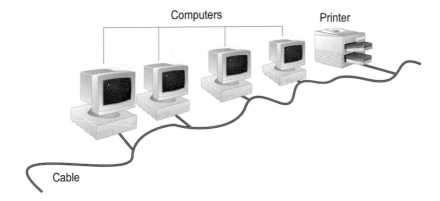

Figure 1.2 A simple network

Computers that are part of a network can share the following:

- Data
- Messages
- Graphics
- Printers
- Fax machines
- Modems
- Other hardware resources

This list is constantly growing as new ways are found to share and communicate by means of computers.

Local Area Networks

Networks started out small, with perhaps ten computers connected together with a printer. The technology limited the size of the network, including the number of computers connected as well as the physical distance that could be covered by the network. For example, in the early 1980's the most popular cabling method would allow about 30 users on a maximum cable length of just over 600 feet. Such a network might be on a single floor of a building, or within one small company. For very small companies today, this configuration is still adequate. This type of network, within a limited area, is known as a local area network (LAN).

The Expansion of Networks

Early LANs could not adequately support the network needs of a large business with offices in various locations. As the advantages of networking became known, and more applications were developed for the network environment, businesses saw the need to expand their networks to remain competitive. Today LANs have become the building blocks of larger systems.

As the geographical scope of the network grows by connecting users in different cities or different states, the LAN grows into a wide area network (WAN). The number of users in a company network can now grow from ten to thousands.

Today, most major businesses store and share vast amounts of crucial data in a network environment, which is why networks are currently as essential to businesses as typewriters and filing cabinets used to be.

Q & A

Using the information presented so far, determine which of the following are LANs. Circle Yes to indicate that it is a LAN, or circle No to indicate that it is not a LAN.

1. Three computers and a printer in the same office are all connected by a cable so that users can share the printer.   Yes   No

2. Two computers in Arizona and one in New York share the same documents and electronic mail (e-mail) program.   Yes   No

3. Over 150 stand-alone computers on the 47th floor of the World Trade Center in New York City all use Microsoft Word for word processing.   Yes   No

4. Over 200 computers on the 14th, 15th, and 16th floors of a large office building are cabled together to share files, printers, and other resources.   Yes   No

Answers

1. Yes. All components are in the same general vicinity and connected to each other.

2. No. The computers are too far apart to be a *local* area network.

3. No. The computers are stand-alone instead of connected.

4. Yes. There may be 500 computers, but they are cabled together and are located in one building.

Why Use a Network?

Organizations implement networks primarily to share resources and enable online communication. Resources include data, applications, and peripherals. A peripheral is a device such as an external disk drive, printer, mouse, modem, or joystick. Online communication includes sending messages back and forth, or e-mail.

Printers and Other Peripherals

Before the advent of networks, people needed their own individual printers, plotters, and other peripherals. Before networks existed, the only way to share a printer was for people to take turns sitting at the computer connected to the printer.

Figure 1.3 Sharing a printer in a stand-alone environment

Networks now make it possible for several people to share both data and
peripherals simultaneously. If many people need to use a printer, they can all use
the printer available on the network.

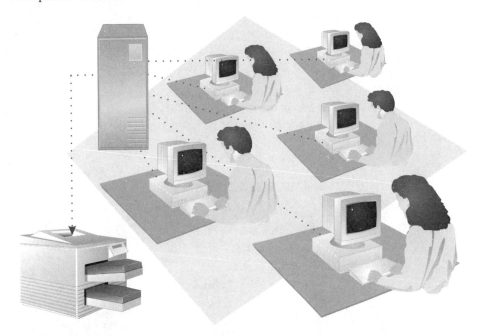

Figure 1.4 Sharing a printer in a networking environment

Data

Before networks existed, people who wanted to share information were limited to:

- Telling each other the information (voice communication).
- Writing memos.
- Putting the information on a floppy disk, physically taking the disk to another
  computer, and then copying the data onto that computer.

Networks can reduce the need for paper communication and make nearly any type
of data available to every user who needs it.

Applications

Networks can be used to standardize applications, such as a word processor, to ensure that everyone on the network is using the same application and the same version of that application. Standardizing on one application can simplify support. It is easier to know one application very well than to try to learn four or five different applications. It is also easier to deal with only one version of an application and to set up all computers in the same manner.

Some businesses invest in networks because of e-mail and scheduling programs. Managers can use these utilities to communicate quickly and effectively with large numbers of people and to organize and schedule an entire company far more easily than was previously possible.

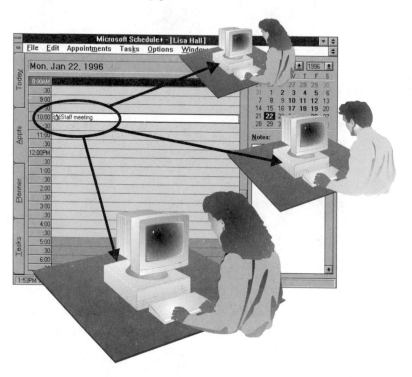

Figure 1.5 Scheduling a meeting with Microsoft Schedule+

Q & A

Fill in the blanks in the following sentences.

1. A primary reason for implementing a network is to _____ resources.

2. Key resources often shared on a network include _____ such as laser printers.

3. Applications such as _____ allow users to communicate quickly and effectively.

Answers

1. share

2. peripherals

3. e-mail

Summary

A local area network (LAN) consists of several computers and peripherals cabled together in a limited area, such as a department of a company or a single building. Networking allows people to share resources such as files and printers, and to use interactive applications such as scheduling and e-mail.

There are many benefits to networking, including:

- Cost cutting through sharing data and peripherals.
- Standardization of applications.
- Timely data acquisition.
- More efficient communications and scheduling.

Today, networks have expanded beyond the LAN to stretch across the country and around the world into wide area networks (WANs).

Your Next Step

Now that you have had an introduction to the networking environment, you are ready to begin taking a closer look at the major networking concepts. In the next lesson you will learn about the two basic, but completely different, approaches to networking.

Lesson 2: The Two Major Types of Networks

What This Lesson Does

This lesson describes two important approaches to networking: peer-to-peer and server-based networks. It presents the major features and advantages for each. It also outlines the considerations involved in implementing servers in peer-to-peer and server-based network environments.

Objectives

By the end of this lesson, you will be able to:

- Identify a peer-to-peer network.
- Identify a server-based network.
- Identify server functions and assign servers as needed.
- Determine which type of network would be appropriate for your site.

Estimated lesson time 45 minutes

Networking Overview

In general, all networks have certain components, functions, and features in common. These include:

- Servers—Computers that provide shared resources to network users.
- Clients—Computers that access shared network resources provided by a server.
- Media—The way that computers are connected.
- Shared data—Files provided by servers across the network.
- Shared printers and other peripherals—Other resources provided by servers.
- Resources—Files, printers, or other items to be used by network users.

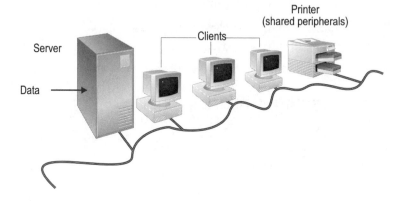

Figure 1.6 Common network elements

Even with these similarities, networks can be divided into two broad categories:

- Peer-to-peer
- Server-based

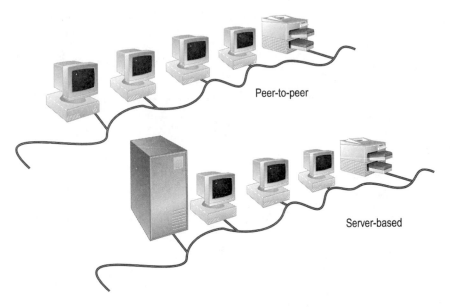

Figure 1.7 Typical peer-to-peer and server-based networks

The distinction between peer-to-peer and server-based networks is important because each has different capabilities. The type of network you implement will depend on numerous factors, including the:

- Size of the organization.
- Level of security required.
- Type of business.
- Level of administrative support available.
- Amount of network traffic.
- Needs of the network users.
- Network budget.

Peer-to-Peer Networks

In a peer-to-peer network, there are no dedicated servers or hierarchy among the computers. All of the computers are equal and therefore are known as peers. Normally, each computer functions as both a client and a server, and there is no one assigned to be an administrator responsible for the entire network. The user at each computer determines what data on their computer gets shared on the network.

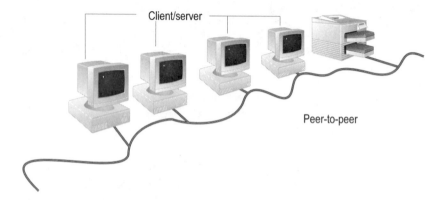

Figure 1.8 Peer-to-peer network computers act as both clients and servers

Size

Peer-to-peer networks are also called workgroups. The term workgroup implies a small group of people. In a peer-to-peer network, there are typically fewer than 10 computers in the network.

Cost

Peer-to-peer networks are relatively simple. Because each computer functions as a client and a server, there is no need for a powerful central server, or for the other components needed for a high-capacity network. Peer-to-peer networks can be less expensive than server-based networks.

Peer-to-Peer Operating Systems

In a peer-to-peer network, the networking software does not need the same level of performance and security as the networking software designed for dedicated servers. Dedicated servers function only as servers and are not used as a client or workstation. They are discussed in more detail later in this lesson.

In operating systems such as Microsoft Windows NT Workstation, Microsoft Windows for Workgroups, and Microsoft Windows 95, peer-to-peer networking is built into the operating system. No additional software is required to set up a peer-to-peer network.

Implementation

In a typical peer-to-peer environment, there are a number of networking issues that have standard solutions. These implementation solutions include:

- Computers located at the users' desks
- Users act as their own administrators and plan their own security
- A simple, easily visible cabling system is used, which connects computer to computer in the network

Where Peer-to-Peer Is Appropriate

Peer-to-peer networks are good choices for environments where:

- There are 10 users or fewer.
- The users are all located in the same general area.
- Security is not an issue.
- The organization and the network will have limited growth within the foreseeable future.

Considering these guidelines, there are times that a peer-to-peer network will be a better solution than a server-based network.

Peer-to-Peer Considerations

While a peer-to-peer network may meet the needs of small organizations, this type of approach may be inappropriate in certain environments. The following networking areas illustrate some peer-to-peer issues which a network planner will have to resolve before deciding upon which type of network to implement.

Administration

Network administration involves a variety of tasks including:

- Managing users and security.
- Making resources available.
- Maintaining applications and data.
- Installing and upgrading application software.

In a typical peer-to-peer network there is no system manager who oversees administration for the entire network. Each user administers their own computer.

Sharing Resources

All users can share any of their resources in any manner they choose. These resources include data in shared directories, printers, fax cards, and so on.

Server Requirements

In a peer-to-peer environment, each computer must:

- Use a large percentage of its resources to support the local user (the user at the computer).
- Use additional resources to support each remote user (a user accessing the server over the network) accessing its resources.

A server-based network needs more powerful, dedicated servers to meet the demands of all of the clients on the network.

Security

Security consists of setting a password on a resource, such as a directory that is shared on the network. Because all peer-to-peer users set their own security, and shares can exist on any computer rather only on a centralized server, centralized control is very difficult. This has a big impact on network security because some users may not implement any security at all. If security is an issue you should consider a server-based network.

Training

Because every computer in a peer-to-peer environment can act as both a server and a client, users will have to be trained before they will be able to function properly as both users and administrators of their computer.

Q & A

Fill in the blanks in the following sentences.

1. In a peer-to-peer network, each computer can act as both a server and a

   _____.

2. In a peer-to-peer network, there are no dedicated _____.

3. Each user in a peer-to-peer network shares their resources in place. For this reason, each user can be considered an _____.

4. Peer-to-peer networks are adequate if _____ is not an issue.

Answers

1. client
2. servers
3. administrator
4. security

Server-Based Networks

In an environment with more than 10 users, a peer-to-peer network—with computers acting as both servers and clients—will probably not be adequate. Therefore, most networks have dedicated servers. A dedicated server is one that only functions as a server and is not used as a client or workstation. Servers are "dedicated" because they are optimized to quickly service requests from network clients and to ensure the security of files and directories. Server-based networks have become the standard model for networking and will be used as the primary examples throughout the rest of this kit.

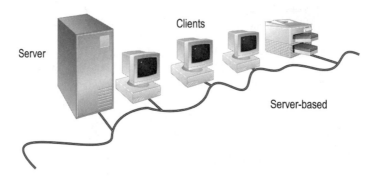

Figure 1.9 Server-based network

As networks increase in size and traffic, more than one server on the network is needed. Spreading the tasks among several servers ensures that each task will be performed in the most efficient manner possible.

Specialized Servers

The variety of tasks that servers must perform is varied and complex. Servers for large networks have become specialized to accommodate the expanding needs of users. For example, in a Windows NT Server network, the different types of servers include the following:

- File and print servers

  File and print servers manage user access and use of file and printer resources. For example, if you were running a word processing application, the word processing application would run on your computer. The word processing document stored on the file and print server is loaded into your computer's memory so that you can edit or use it locally. In other words, file and print servers are for file and data storage.

- Application servers

  Application servers make the server side of client/server applications, as well as the data, available to clients. For example, servers store vast amounts of data that is structured to make it easy to retrieve. This differs from a file and print server. With a file and print server, the data or file is downloaded to the computer making the request. With an application server, the database stays on the server and only the results of a request is downloaded to the computer making the request.

  A client application running locally would access the data on the application server. Instead of the entire database being downloaded from the server to your local computer, only the results of your query would be loaded onto your computer. For example, you could search the employee database for all employees who were born in November.

- Mail servers

  Mail servers manage electronic messaging between network users.

- Fax servers

  Fax servers manage fax traffic into and out of the network, by sharing one or more fax modem boards.

- Communication servers

  Communications servers handle data flow and e-mail messages between the server's own network and other networks, mainframe computers, or remote users using modems and telephone lines to dial in to the server.

  Directory services servers to enable users to locate, store, and secure information on the network. Windows NT Server combines computers into logical groupings, called domains, which allow any user on the network to be given access to any resource on the network.

Planning for various servers becomes important with an expanded network. The planner must take into account any anticipated network growth so that network use will not be disrupted if the role of a specific server needs to be changed.

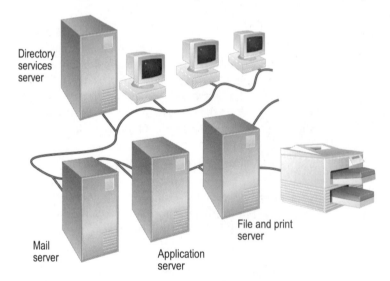

Figure 1.10 Specialized servers

The Role of Software

A network server and the operating system work together as a unit. No matter how powerful or advanced a server might be, it is useless without an operating system that can take advantage of its physical resources. Certain advanced operating systems, such as Microsoft Windows NT Server, were designed to take advantage of the most advanced server hardware.

For example, Windows NT Server can take advantage of server hardware in the following ways.

Category	Feature
Symmetric multiprocessing (SMP)	A multiprocessing system has more than one processor. SMP means that the system load and application needs are distributed evenly across all available processors.
Multiple-Platform Support	Faster processors from vendors such as Intel® 386/486 and Pentium®, MIPS® R4000®, RISC, and Digital Alpha AXP.
Filename/directory length	255 characters.
File size	16 EB (exabyte–2^{64} bytes).
Partition size	16 EB (exabyte–2^{64} bytes).

Note An exabyte is a big number, bigger than most of us can comprehend. One exabyte is a bit larger than one billion gigabytes. If every man, woman, and child on earth (about 5 billion people) had 2,000 pages of text, at 2K per page, every one of them could put their pages into a single Windows NT file. Even then, the file would be filled to only 1/16 (a little over 6 percent of its total capacity).

Server-Based Network Advantages

Sharing Resources

A server is designed to provide access to many files and printers while maintaining performance and security to the user.

Server-based sharing of data can be centrally administered and controlled. The resources are usually centrally located and are easier to locate and support than resources on random computers.

For example, in Windows NT Server, directory resources are shared through Windows NT Explorer, My Computer or by using the **net share** command from the command prompt.

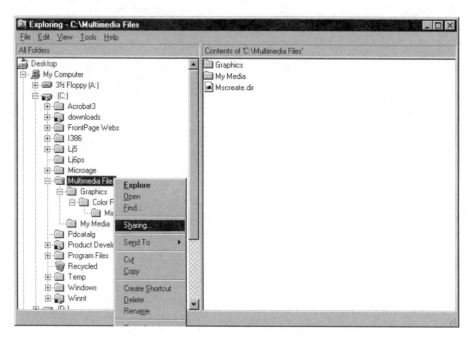

Figure 1.11 Windows NT Explorer

To share a directory, highlight it, and then **Right Click**, select the **Sharing…** option.

Security

Security is most often the primary reason for choosing a server-based approach to networking. In a server-based environment, such as a Windows NT Server network, security can be managed by one administrator who sets the policy and applies it to every user on the network.

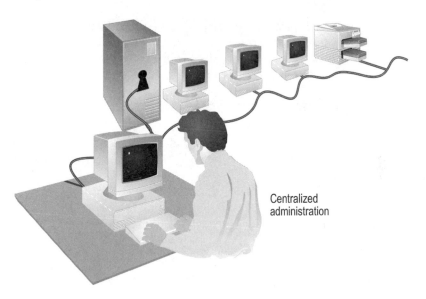

Centralized administration

Figure 1.12 One administrator handles Windows NT Server network security

Backup

Because crucial data is centralized on one or a few servers, it is easier to make sure that the data is backed up on a regular schedule.

Redundancy

Through redundancy systems, the data on any server can be duplicated and kept online so that even if something happens to the primary data storage area for the data, a backup copy of the data can be used to retrieve the data.

Number of Users

A server-based network can support thousands of users. This type of network would be impossible to manage as a peer-to-peer network, but current monitoring and network management utilities make it possible to operate a server-based network for large numbers of users.

Hardware Considerations

Client computer hardware can be limited to the needs of the user because clients do not need the additional RAM and disk storage needed to provide server services. A typical client computer has at least a 486 processor and 8 to 16 MB of RAM.

Q & A

Fill in the blanks in the following sentences.

1. The standard model for networking environments with more than 10 users involves _____-based networks.

2. A dedicated server is a computer not used as a _____.

3. Large network servers are _____ to accommodate growing user needs.

Answers

1. server

2. client

3. specialized

Combination Networks

It is not unusual for modern networks in business environments to combine the best features of both peer-to-peer and server-based approaches in one network.

In a combination network, two kinds of operating systems work together to provide what many administrators feel is the complete network.

A server-based operating system such as Microsoft Windows NT Server or Novell® NetWare® is responsible for sharing the major applications and data.

Client computers can run an operating system such as Microsoft Windows NT Workstation or Windows 95. They can both access resources on the designated server and, simultaneously, share their hard disks and make their personal data available as needed.

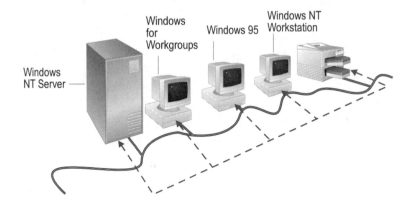

Figure 1.13 Combination networks have dedicated servers and computers

This type of network is common, but it requires extensive planning and training to implement properly and ensure adequate security.

Server Hardware Considerations

Shared resources are the foundation of both peer-to-peer and server-based networks. The differences between peer-to-peer servers and dedicated servers will have an impact on:

- Hardware requirements.
- How users are supported on the network.

The following server components require careful consideration.

Component	Peer-to-peer network	Server-based network
Location of the shared resource	On users' computers.	Dedicated servers.
RAM	Depends on user needs. Microsoft Windows NT Workstation requires a minimum of 12 MB, with 16 MB recommended. Windows 95 recommends at least 8 MB of RAM.	As much as possible. At least 12 MB. Super servers supporting thousands of users do not have less than 64 MB.
CPU	Depends on user needs. Should be at least a 386. Windows NT Workstation requires a 80386/25 or higher or a supported RISC processor. Windows 95 requires a 386DX or higher.	Depends on server usage. Should be at least a 486. High-performance servers support multiple processors.
Disk space	Varies with user needs.	Varies with organization's needs. As much as possible, but should plan for expansion. Suggest at least 1 GB for a small organization. Super servers no longer limit themselves to gigabyte figures. They refer to their capacity in terms of the number of drives they can accommodate.

Activity

Use the following steps to run Lab 2.

Lab 2: Sharing Directories

What This Lab Does

This lab teaches you how to set up a shared directory and how to stop sharing a shared directory. It is important to remember that this lab simulates a Windows NT Server 4.0 environment.

Objectives

By the end of this lab, you will be able to:

- Share a directory on Windows NT Server.
- Stop sharing a directory on Windows NT Server.

Exercise 1: Sharing a Directory

1. From the **Start** menu, point to **Programs**, then **Networking Essentials**, and click **Lab2**.

   The Networking Essentials - Lab2 window appears.

2. Right click **My Computer**, and select **Explore**.

   This opens a simulated Windows NT Explorer.

3. In the left pane, double click drive **C** (drive C is labeled **Cr112_c**).

   The contents of drive C should expand.

4. On drive **C**, right click the **Dos** folder.

   The **Dos** folder context menu appears.

5. Select **Sharing**.

   Note For purposes of this simulation, Dos is the only directory that can be shared.

   The **Dos Properties** dialog box appears.

6. Select **Shared As:**

   There are several options in the **Shared As:** section.

   Share Name—Shows the name users specify to connect to the shared directory in order for Microsoft MS-DOS–based computers to connect; the name must conform to the MS-DOS 8.3 naming convention. On a Windows NT–based network, the name can be up to 12 characters long.

By default, the share name is the name of the selected directory.

Note You can type a different name in the **Share Name:** box. However, if you change the default name of the share, when someone accesses the share, they will use the share name and not the folder name.

Comment—The comment is optional and is displayed with the share name in the Connect Network Drive dialog box.

User Limit—Sets the maximum number of users who can connect to the shared directory at one time. By default, no limit is set.

Permissions Button—You can control access to a shared directory by setting permissions on it. Permissions are covered in a later lesson.

7. Click **OK** to accept the default name DOS for the share.

   Notice the small hand holding the **Dos** folder. This indicates the folder is shared.

8. Click **OK** to close the Lab2 dialog box.

Exercise 2: Stop Sharing a Directory

1. Right click the **Dos** folder.

   The **Dos** folder context menu appears.

2. Select **Sharing**.

   The **Dos Properties** window appears.

3. Select **Not Shared:** and then click **OK.**

   Notice that the small hand holding the **Dos** folder has disappeared.

4. Click **OK** to close the Lab2 dialog box.

5. On the Explorer **File** menu, click **Exit.**

6. On the **File** menu, click **Exit Lab 2**.

Summary

There are two major types of networks: peer-to-peer and server-based.

In peer-to-peer networks each computer can act as both a client and a server. Peer-to-peer networks make sharing data and peripherals easy for small groups of people. Consistent, extensive security is difficult in a peer-to-peer environment because administration is not centralized.

Server-based networks are best for networks sharing many resources and data. An administrator oversees operation of the network and ensures that security is maintained. This type of network can have one or more servers, depending on the volume of traffic, number of peripherals, and so on. For example, there may need to be a print server, a communications server, and a database server all on the same network.

There are combination networks which have features of both peer-to-peer and served-based networks. This type of network is the most commonly used, but requires extensive planning and training for maximum productivity.

Features of the two major network types are summarized below.

Consideration	Peer-to-peer	Server-based
Size	Good for up to 10 computers.	Limited only by server and network hardware.
Security	Security established by the user of each computer.	Extensive, consistent resource, and user security.
Administration	Every user is responsible for their own administration. No full-time administrator necessary.	Centrally located for consistent network control. Requires at least one knowledgeable administrator.

Your Next Step

Now that you have an introduction to the differences between peer-to-peer and server-based networks, you are ready to learn how networks are designed and laid out. These network floor plans have a significant impact on the entire network environment, as you will see in the next lesson.

Lesson 3: Network Design

What This Lesson Does

This lesson introduces the different designs for connecting computers. It describes and illustrates:

- The standard topologies.
- The major components of each topology.
- Appropriate uses for each topology.

In addition to the standard topologies, you will learn about variations that are often used and what you need to consider when planning your network.

Objectives

By the end of this lesson, you will be able to:

- Identify the three standard topologies and their variations.
- Describe the advantages and disadvantages of each topology.
- Determine an appropriate topology for a given network plan.

Estimated lesson time 80 minutes

Designing the Network's Layout

The term topology, or more specifically, network topology, refers to the arrangement or physical layout of computers, cables, and other components on the network. Topology is the standard term that most network professionals use when they refer to the network's basic design. In addition to topology, these arrangements may be referred to as:

- Physical layout
- Design
- Diagram
- Map

A network's topology affects its capabilities. Choosing one topology over another can impact the:

- Type of equipment the network needs.
- Capabilities of the equipment.
- Network's growth.
- Way a network is managed.

Developing a sense of how the different topologies are used is one key to understanding the capabilities of the different types of networks.

Computers have to be connected in order to share resources or perform other communication tasks. Most networks use cable to connect one computer to another.

Note Wireless networks connect computers without using cable. This technology is discussed in Chapter 2 Lesson 2, "Wireless Network Communications."

However, it is not as simple as just plugging a computer into a cable connecting other computers. Different types of cable, combined with different network cards, network operating systems, and other components require different types of arrangements.

A network's topology implies a number of conditions. For example, a particular topology can determine not only the type of cable used but how the cabling is run through floors, ceilings, and walls.

Topology can also determine how computers communicate on the network. Different topologies require different communication methods, and these methods have a great influence on the network.

Standard Topologies

All network designs stem from three basic topologies:

- Bus
- Star
- Ring

If computers are connected in a row along a single cable (segment), the topology is referred to as a bus. If the computers are connected to cable segments that branch out from a single point or *hub*, the topology is known as a star. If the computers are connected to a cable that forms a loop, the topology is known as a ring.

While these three basic topologies are themselves simple, their real-world versions often combine features from more than one topology and can be complex.

Bus

The bus topology is also known as a linear bus. This is the simplest and most common method of networking computers. It consists of a single cable called a trunk (also backbone or segment) that connects all of the computers in the network in a single-line.

Figure 1.14 Bus topology network

Communication on the Bus

Computers on a bus topology network communicate by addressing data to a particular computer and putting that data on the cable in the form of electronic signals. To understand how computers communicate on a bus you need to be familiar with three concepts:

- Sending the signal
- Signal bounce
- The terminator

Sending the Signal

Network data in the form of electronic signals is sent to all of the computers on the network; however, the information is accepted only by the computer whose address matches the address encoded in the original signal. Only one computer at a time can send messages.

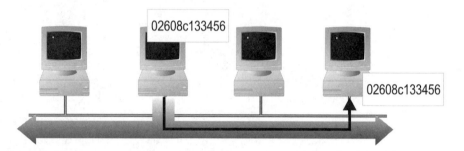

Figure 1.15 Data is sent to all computers, but only the destination computer accepts

Because only one computer at a time can send data on a bus network, network performance is affected by the number of computers attached to the bus. The more computers on a bus, the more computers there will be waiting to put data on the bus, and the slower the network.

There is no standard measure for the impact of numbers of computers on any given network. The amount the network slows down is not solely related to the number of computers on the network. It depends on numerous factors including:

- Hardware capabilities of computers on the network
- Number of times computers on the network transmit data
- Type of applications being run on the network
- Types of cable used on the network
- Distance between computers on the network

The bus is a passive topology. Computers on a bus only listen for data being sent on the network. They are not responsible for moving data from one computer to the next. If one computer fails, it does not affect the rest of the network. In an active topology computers regenerate signals and move data along the network.

Signal Bounce

Because the data, or electronic signal, is sent to the entire network, it will travel from one end of the cable to the other. If the signal were allowed to continue uninterrupted, it would keep bouncing back and forth along the cable and prevent other computers from sending signals. Therefore, the signal must be stopped after it has had a chance to reach the proper destination address.

The Terminator

To stop the signal from bouncing, a component called a terminator is placed at each end of the cable to absorb free signals. Absorbing the signal clears the cable so that other computers can send data.

Every cable end on the network must be plugged into something. For example, a cable end could be plugged into a computer or a connector to extend the cable length. Any open cable ends—ends not plugged into something—must be terminated to prevent signal bounce.

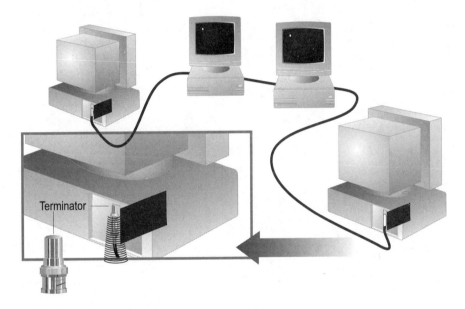

Figure 1.16 Terminators absorb free signals

Disrupting Network Communication

A break in the cable will occur if the cable is physically cut into two pieces or if one end of the cable becomes disconnected. In either case, one or more ends of the cable will not have a terminator, the signal will bounce, and all network activity will stop. This is referred to as the network being "down."

The computers on the network will still be able to function as stand-alone computers, but as long as the segment is broken, they will not be able to communicate with each other.

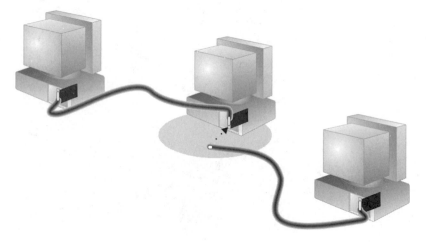

Figure 1.17 An unplugged cable is not terminated and will take down the network

LAN Expansion

As the network site gets bigger, the LAN will need to grow. Cable in the bus topology can be extended by one of the two following methods.

- A component called a barrel connector can connect two pieces of cable together to make a longer piece of cable. However, connectors weaken the signal and should be used sparingly. It is much better to purchase one continuous cable than to connect several smaller ones with connectors. In fact, using too many connectors can prevent the signal from being correctly received.

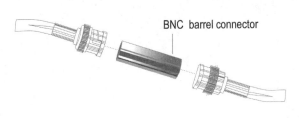

BNC barrel connector

Figure 1.18 Connectors can be used to combine cable segments

- A device called a repeater can be used to connect two cables. A repeater actually boosts the signal before it sends the signal on its way. A repeater is better than a connector or a longer piece of cable because it allows a signal to travel even farther and still be correctly received.

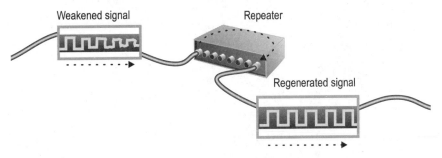

Weakened signal   Repeater

Regenerated signal

Figure 1.19 Repeaters connect cables and amplify the signal

Q & A

Fill in the blanks in the following sentences.

1. The primary term for the design or arrangement of a network is _____.

2. All network designs stem from the _____, _____, and _____ topologies.

3. When connecting cables to cover long distances, the distance the signals can travel is increased by using a _____ because it boosts the signals before it sends them on their way.

4. The bus is a _____ topology, which means that the computers are not responsible for moving the data from one computer to the next.

5. To absorb signals and prevent signal bounce, the ends of the cable in a bus topology must be connected to a _____.

Answers

1. topology
2. bus, ring, star
3. repeater
4. passive
5. terminator

Star

In the star topology, computers are connected by cable segments to a centralized component, called a hub. Signals are transmitted from the sending computer through the hub to all computers on the network. This topology originated in the early days of computing with computers connected to a centralized mainframe computer.

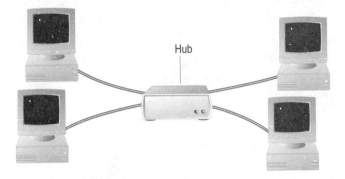

Figure 1.20 Simple star network

The star network offers centralized resources and management. However, because each computer is connected to a central point, this topology requires a great deal of cable in a large network installation. Also, if the central point fails, the entire network goes down.

If one computer, or the cable that connects it to the hub, fails on a star network, only the failed computer will not be able to send or receive network data. The rest of the network continues to function normally.

Ring

The ring topology connects computers on a single circle of cable. There are no terminated ends. The signals travel around the loop in one direction and pass through each computer. Unlike the passive bus topology, each computer acts like a repeater to boost the signal and send it on to the next computer. Because the signal passes through each computer, the failure of one computer can impact the entire network.

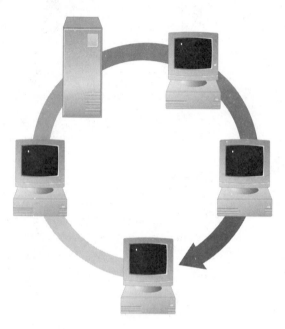

Figure 1.21 Simple ring network showing logical ring

Token Passing

One method of transmitting data around a ring is called token passing. The token is passed from computer to computer until it gets to a computer that has data to send. The sending computer modifies the token, puts an electronic address on the data, and sends it around the ring.

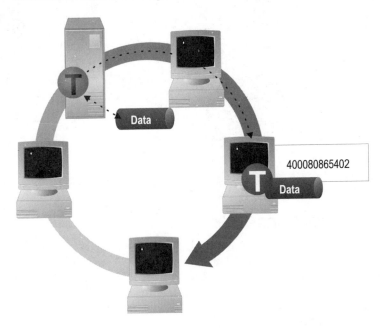

Figure 1.22 A computer grabs the token and passes it around the ring

The data passes by each computer until it finds the one with an address that matches the address on the data.

The receiving computer returns a message to the sending computer indicating that the data has been received. After verification, the sending computer creates a new token and releases it on the network.

It may seem that token passing would take a long time, but the token actually travels at roughly the speed of light. A token can circle a ring 200 meters in diameter at about 10,000 times a second.

Hubs

One network component that is becoming standard equipment in more and more networks is the hub. A hub is the central component in a star topology.

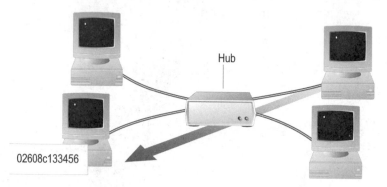

Figure 1.23 A hub is the central point in a star topology

Active Hubs

Most hubs are active in that they regenerate and retransmit the signals the same way a repeater does. In fact, because hubs usually have eight to twelve ports for network computers to connect to, they are sometimes called multiport repeaters. Active hubs require electrical power to run.

Passive Hubs

Some types of hubs are passive, for example, wiring panels or punchdown blocks. They act as connection points and do not amplify or regenerate the signal; the signal passes through the hub. Passive hubs do not require electrical power to run.

Hybrid Hubs

Advanced hubs that will accommodate several different types of cables are called hybrid hubs. A hub-based network can be expanded by connecting more than one hub.

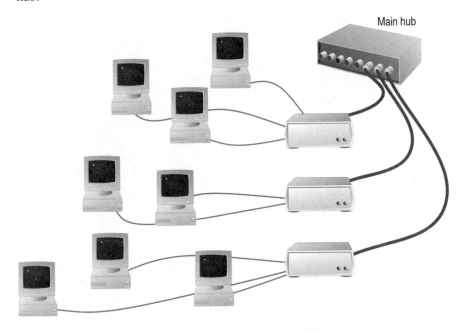

Figure 1.24 Hybrid hub

Hub Considerations

Hubs are versatile and offer several advantages over systems that do not use hubs.

In the standard linear bus topology, a break in the cable will take the network down. With hubs, however, a break in any of the cables attached to the hub affects only that segment. The rest of the network keeps functioning.

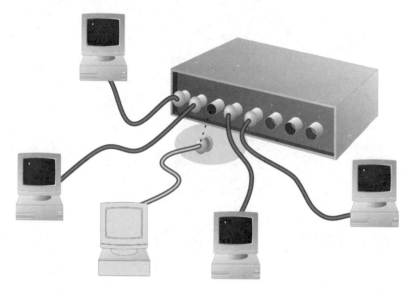

Figure 1.25 A break or unplugged cable takes down only the unplugged computer

Other benefits of hub-based topologies include:

- Changing or expanding wiring systems as needed. Simply plug in another computer or another hub.
- Using different ports to accommodate a variety of cabling types.
- Centralized monitoring of network activity and traffic. Many active hubs contain diagnostic capabilities to indicate whether or not a connection is working.

Q & A

Fill in the blanks for questions 1 through 3, and circle True or False for questions 4 through 7.

1. In the star topology, cables branch out from a _____.

2. In the ring topology, each computer acts as a _____ and boosts the signal before sending it on.

3. Hubs that regenerate and retransmit signals are _____.

4. In a star topology, if one computer goes down, it will take down the entire network. True   False

5. The ring topology is a passive topology.   True   False

6. A ring topology uses terminators.   True   False

7. In a star topology, if the central point that connects all of the computers goes down, the entire network will be down.   True   False

Answers

1. hub

2. repeater

3. active

4. False. The only computer on the star that will not be able to communicate is the one that is down.

5. False. The ring is an active topology in that each computer acts as a repeater to regenerate the signal and pass it on to the next computer.

6. False. The ring topology creates a single circle of cable, so there are no terminated ends.

7. True.

Variations on the Major Topologies

Today, many working topologies are combinations of the bus, the star, and the ring.

Star Bus

The star bus is a combination of the bus and star topologies. In a star bus topology, there are several star topology networks linked together with linear bus trunks.

If one computer goes down, it will not affect the rest of the network. The other computers will be able to continue to communicate. If a hub goes down, all computers on that hub are unable to communicate. If a hub is linked to other hubs, those connections will be broken as well.

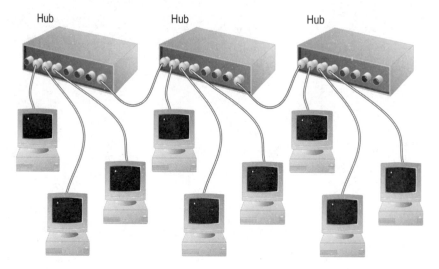

Figure 1.26 Star bus network

Star Ring

The star ring (sometimes called a star wired ring) appears similar to the star bus. Both the star ring and the star bus are centered in a hub which contains the actual ring or bus. The hubs in a star bus are connected by linear bus trunks, while the hubs in a star ring are connected in a star pattern by the main hub.

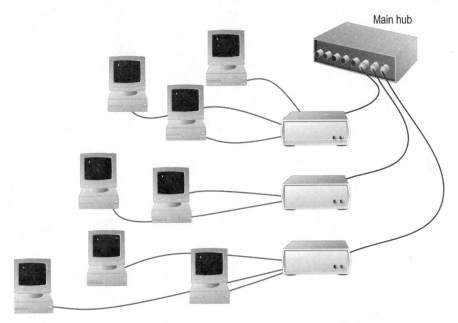

Figure 1.27 Star ring network

Selecting a Topology

There are many factors to consider when determining what topology best suits the needs of an organization. The following table provides some guidelines for selecting a topology.

Topology	Advantages	Disadvantages
Bus	Economical use of cable. Media is inexpensive and easy to work with. Simple, reliable. Easy to extend.	Network can slow down in heavy traffic. Problems are difficult to isolate. Cable break can affect many users.
Ring	Equal access for all computers. Even performance despite many users.	Failure of one computer can impact the rest of the network. Problems hard to isolate. Network reconfiguration disrupts operation.
Star	Easy to modify and add new computers. Centralized monitoring and management. Failure of one computer does not affect the rest of the network.	If the centralized point fails, the network fails.

Q & A

Fill in the blanks in the following sentences.

1. In a star bus topology, there are several star topology networks linked together with linear bus _____.

2. The star bus sends data like the _____ topology does.

3. The star bus and the star wired ring both connect computers through a central _____.

Answers

1. trunks

2. bus

3. hub

Activity

Run Demo 3.

Summary

The physical layout of computers on a network is called a topology. There are three primary topologies: bus, star, and ring. There are variations on these basic topologies, including the star bus and star wired ring.

The bus is the simplest and most commonly used topology. It is a linear configuration, with all computers connected by a single cable. On a bus, signals are sent to all of the computers on the network. To keep the signal from bouncing back and forth along the cable, a terminator is placed at the end of the cable. Only one computer can send data at a time. Therefore, the more computers on a bus, the slower the data transmission speed will be.

In a star topology each computer is directly connected to a central component called a hub. If the central component fails, the entire network goes down.

A Token Ring network connects computers in a logical circle. The signal, or token, passes around the ring through each computer in a clockwise direction. A computer takes the free token and sends data on the network. The receiving computer copies the data and marks it as having been received. Finally, the data continues around the ring back to the sending computer, which removes the data from the ring and releases a free token.

A hub is used to centralize LAN traffic through a single connection point. If a cable breaks on a network that uses a hub, the break will only affect that segment and not affect the rest of the network. Networks can be expanded easily using hubs; they allow for use of different types of cabling.

Your Next Step

With the completion of this lesson, you have learned about the basic network designs known as topologies. You are now familiar with the fundamental concepts of a basic network environment.

You are now ready to go on to the Unit 1 Review in which you will use the information presented in the first three lessons to:

- Test you knowledge of networking concepts.
- Solve example network problems based on what you have learned so far.

Chapter 1 Review

Chapter 1, Network Orientation, defined networking and provided an overview of the networking environment including the benefits of networking, its essential components, and the standard network designs, or topologies.

Networks connect computers in order to share resources including information and peripherals. This is done through:

- A peer-to-peer approach in which the networked computers can be both servers and clients.
- A server-based approach in which certain computers are designated as servers based on their power, storage capacity, and function in the network.
- A combination of both approaches in which some computers are dedicated servers but users can share their own resources.

The network is laid out according to one of three topologies: bus, star, or ring. Networks can also be created from a combination of topologies, resulting in either a star bus or a star ring.

Checkup

Follow the instructions for each exercise as indicated. All answers follow the last exercise.

Exercise 1: Matching

Match each item in Column A with the best choice from Column B. One item in Column B will not be used, and items will be used no more than once.

Column A	Column B
1. Client computer _____	A. Acts as both client and server.
2. Server _____	B. Accesses shared resources.
3. Peer computer _____	C. Connects the computers together.
4. Media _____	D. Acts as a file and print server.
5. Terminator _____	E. Stops signal bounce.
6. Repeater _____	F. Signal on cable ring.
7. Token _____	G. Centralizes network traffic.
8. Hub _____	H. Boosts the signal.
	I. Provides shared resources.

Exercise 2: Multiple Choice

Select the letter of the best answer for each of the following questions.

1. What is true for peer-to-peer networks?

    a. Provide greater security and more control than a server-based network.

    b. Recommended for networks with 10 or fewer users on the network.

    c. Require a powerful central server.

    d. Users are typically located in a large geographical area.

2. What best describes a ring topology network?

    a. Needs less cabling than other topologies.

    b. Media is inexpensive and easy to work with.

    c. Equal access for all computers.

    d. Requires terminators to function properly.

3. What best describes a bus topology network?

    a. Needs significantly more cabling than other topologies.

    b. Media is inexpensive and easy to work with.

    c. Easier to troubleshoot than other topologies.

    d. The number of computers on the network does not affect performance.

4. Which of the following statements best describes a star topology?

    a. Needs significantly less cabling than other topologies.

    b. Break in a single cable segment takes down entire network.

    c. More difficult to reconfigure than other topologies.

    d. Centralized monitoring and management.

5. Which of the following topologies is passive?

    a. Bus

    b. Token passing

    c. Ring

    d. Star ring

6. Cabling on a linear bus topology can be extended using which of the following?

    a. Network adapter card

    b. Terminator

    c. Barrel connector

    d. Medium attachment unit

Exercise 3: True or False

For the following sentences, circle True if the statement is true or False if the statement is false.

1. Server-based networks are also called workgroups.   True   False

2. A Microsoft peer-to-peer network requires both a stand-alone computer operating system and a network operating system.   True   False

3. Server-based networks always have a dedicated server.   True   False

4. If security is an issue, a company should choose a server-based environment. True   False

5. Because every computer on a bus has an address, several computers can send data at once over the bus with assurance that the data will get to the correct computer. True   False

Checkup Answers

Exercise 1: Matching

1. B
2. I
3. A
4. C
5. E
6. H
7. F
8. G

Exercise 2: Multiple Choice

1. What is true for peer-to-peer networks?

   b. Recommended for networks with 10 or fewer users on the network.

2. What best describes a ring topology network?

   c. Equal access for all computers.

3. What best describes a bus topology network?

   b. Media is inexpensive and easy to work with.

4. Which of the following statements best describes a star topology?

   d. Centralized monitoring and management.

5. Which of the following topologies is passive?

   a. Bus

6. Cabling on a linear bus topology can be extended using which of the following?

   c. Barrel connector

Exercise 3: True or False

1. False. Peer-to-peer networks are also called workgroups.
2. False. In a Microsoft peer-to-peer network the operating system includes peer-to-peer capabilities.
3. True. Server-based networks always have a dedicated server.
4. True. Server-based networks provide centralized security.
5. False. Only one computer at a time may send data on a bus.

Case Study Problem

The Setting

A small, independent, business/home/life insurance company consisting of an owner, a manager, an administrator, and five agents decides to implement a network. The company occupies half of a small building in an office park. Their volume of business has been stable for the past four years but has been increasing lately. To handle the increased volume of business, two new agents will be hired.

Figure 1.28 illustrates the current arrangement.

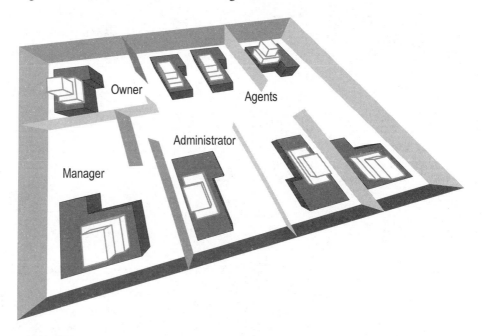

Figure 1.28

Everyone in the company has a computer. When the employees share information, they do it verbally or copy the information to floppies and swap disks. In general, agents handle only their specific clients, and the information their clients provide is confidential. The office administrator has an eight-year old laser printer. The agents all have their own dot matrix printers.

As part of the migration to a networking environment, the company has decided to purchase a high-speed laser printer.

The Problem

You are tasked with designing the network for this company. Answer the following questions to simplify your task of choosing a solution.

Your Solution

Underline the most appropriate answers to the following questions:

1. What type of network would you suggest for this company?
   - Peer-to-peer
   - Server-based

2. What network topology would be appropriate in this situation?
   - Bus
   - Ring
   - Star
   - Star bus
   - Star ring

Suggested Solution

There are no completely right or wrong answers to this problem. The suggested answers and explanations are only a guide.

1. Server-based

   Although there are only eight people in the entire company at present, and a peer-to-peer network would seem adequate, the company is experiencing growth. Some of the information to go on the network is confidential. It is better to invest in a server-based network which can accommodate growth and provide centralized security than have growth make a peer-to-peer network obsolete in a year or two.

2. There is no single correct answer. The most commonly installed networks currently are the star bus and the bus.

   A hub-centered star bus seems to be the best choice because of the ease of troubleshooting, and ease of reconfiguration.

   A bus network might be chosen because of cost or ease of installation considerations, although it does not offer the centralized troubleshooting or administrative advantages of a hub.

   A ring is probably more complex than necessary for this network.

The Troubleshooter

Use the information presented below to help you solve the troubleshooting problem which follows.

Potential Problems

Choosing a network that will not meet an organization's needs will lead directly to trouble. A common problem is choosing a peer-to-peer network when the situation calls for a server-based network.

Trouble in a Peer-to-Peer Environment

A peer-to-peer, or workgroup, network may begin to exhibit problems with changes in the network site. These will not be hardware or software problems as much as logistical or operational problems. Indicators that a peer-to-peer network is not up to the task include:

- Difficulties caused by lack of centralized security
- Users turning off computers which are servers

Topology Problems

A network's design can cause problems if the design limits the network so it cannot perform in some environments.

Bus Networks

There are a few situations that will cause a bus network to no longer be properly terminated and will usually take the network down. A cable on the network may:

- Break

  A break in the cable will cause both ends of the cable on either side of the break to no longer be terminated. Signals will start to bounce and this will take the network down.

- Lose a connection

  If a cable becomes loose and is disconnected, this will separate the computer from the network. It will also create an end that is not terminated, that will cause signals to bounce and the network to go down.

- Lose a terminator

  If a terminator is loose, it will create an end that is not terminated. Signals will start to bounce and the network will go down.

Hub-Based Networks

While problems with hubs are infrequent, they do occur. For example, they can:

- Drop a connection

  If a computer becomes disconnected from the hub, the computer will be off the network, but the rest of the network will continue to function normally.

- Lose power

  If an active hub loses power, the network will stop functioning.

Ring Networks

A ring network is usually very reliable, but problems can occur. For example, a cable on the network may:

- Break

  If one of the cables in the ring breaks, the network will temporarily stop functioning. In token-ring networks, restoring the cable will immediately restore the network. (*Note: this is true with a basic token-ring network. If the token-ring network uses multistation access units (MAUs), when a cable is cut the MAU will reroute the traffic in the opposite direction, using a redundant set of wires in the cable.)

- Lose a connection

  If one of the cables in the ring becomes disconnected, the network will temporarily stop functioning. In token-ring networks, restoring the cable will immediately restore the network. (*Note: this is true with a basic token-ring network. If the token-ring network uses multistation access units (MAUs), when a cable is cut the MAU will reroute the traffic in the opposite direction, using a redundant set of wires in the cable.)

Can You Solve This Problem?

Now you can use what you have just read to troubleshoot the situation described below.

The Situation

A small company with three departments recently began networking by installing peer-to-peer networks in each department. Four people in one department are working on a project. Each person has a different set of responsibilities, but they all produce documentation for their part of the project. Each person has made the hard drive on their own computer available to everyone else on the project.

The Available Facts

As the project grows, each user produces more documents, and there is some question about who has which documents and who was the last person to change the documents. Also, people who are not in the department but who have an interest in the project are asking to see some of the completed material.

Your Solution

Cause of the Problem

What is one reason there are problems concerning who has which document?

_____

_____

Possible Solution

What one thing could you change which would give you centralized control of the access to these documents?

_____

_____

Impact of Your Solution on Network Users

Describe one change which your solution will bring to the users' operating environment.

_____

_____

_____

_____

Suggested Solution

Cause of the Problem

What is one reason why there are problems concerning who has which document?

The network has clearly outgrown the friendly, trusting, give-and-take style of the workgroup. The number of new users, the politics involved in determining who has what responsibilities on the network, and the increased traffic of network-intensive applications makes the peer-to-peer approach inadequate.

Possible Solution

What one thing could you change which would give you centralized control of the access to these documents?

Add a dedicated server and implement a network operating system that can provide extensive, centralized security.

Impact of the Solution on Network Users

Describe one change which your solution will bring to the users' operating environment.

Changing from a peer-to-peer to a server-based network will disrupt the organization's routine and present everyone with the challenge of adjusting to a new communications environment. It will change the entire personality of the work environment, but it will have to be done if the organization wants to network successfully. This is why planning is so important in implementing a network. A good plan will take potential growth into account and identify factors which will reveal the short term solution for what it is—a temporary solution.

The LAN Planner

Now that you have reviewed the material covered in this unit and have looked at a case study and the troubleshooter, you are ready to apply this information to your site and your future network.

Choosing the Type of Network

The following section of the LAN Planner will not only help you determine whether a peer-to-peer environment or a centralized, server-based environment would be appropriate for your site, but will also help you form a generalized picture of the role servers should play in your LAN.

Note All of the LAN Planners assume there is no network on your site. If there is one, use these questions as a guide to applying the information in the text to the network on your site in order to help familiarize yourself with an actual network environment.

Determining the Type of LAN on Your Site

Put a check mark on the line next to the choice which applies to your site. To determine which type of network would be most appropriate for your site, simply add the number of peer-to-peer selections with check marks next to them, and compare it with the number of server-based selections with check marks next to them. The one with the most check marks should be your first consideration.

1. Approximately how many users does the network at your site serve?

    0–10 _____ Peer-to-peer

    10 + _____ Server-based

2. Is there data and resources on your network that need to be restricted or regulated?

    Yes _____ Server-based

    No _____ Peer-to-peer

3. Your computer will be used primarily as a:

   Client computer   _____   Server-based

   Server   _____   Server-based

   Both   _____   Peer-to-peer

   If your computer will be used as both a client and a server, you may be in a peer-to-peer environment, otherwise, you may be in a server-based environment. However, many networks are server-based with client computers also sharing in a peer-to-peer fashion. This type of combined network is the most common type of network used for new installations because the networking capabilities are now built-in to most client computer operating systems.

4. Can the users on your network take care of their own network administration and management needs?

   Yes _____ Peer-to-peer

   No _____ Server-based

5. Does your network need extensive data security?

   Yes _____ Server-based

   No _____ Peer-to-peer

6. Are you allowed to share your own resources and set other network policies for your computer?

   Yes _____ Peer-to-peer

   No _____ Server-based

7. Does your network use centralized servers?

   Yes _____ Server-based

   No _____ Peer-to-peer

8. Does your network have one central administrator who sets network policies?

   Yes _____ Server-based

   No _____ Peer-to-peer

9. Does your network have more than one server?

   Yes _____ Peer-to-peer or server-based depending on other issues

   No _____ Server-based

The following questions will help you identify and resolve issues with a server-based environment.

1. Approximately how many servers does your network have?

    0–5 _____

    5–10 _____

    10–50 _____

    50–100 _____

2. Will your network's servers be centrally located or spread out in different locations?

    Centrally located _____

    Spread out _____

3. Will some of your network's servers be in a secure location?

    Yes _____

    No _____

    If not, why not? _____

4. Are some of the servers designated for special tasks?

    Yes _____

    No _____

5. Check the tasks below which will apply to your servers:

    Communication _____

    Backup/redundancy _____

    Application _____

    Database _____

    E-mail _____

    Fax _____

    Print _____

    User directories _____

    General data storage _____

If some of your servers are supporting more than one of these applications and the number of users is large (25 users or more), you should consider adding more servers and dedicating them to specialized tasks.

Choosing the Network Topology

The following section of the LAN Planner will help you to choose an appropriate topology for your network. The answers to these questions can be used in conjunction with the advantages and disadvantages sections of Lesson 3, "Network Design."

Put a check mark on the line next to the choice which applies to your site. To determine which type of topology would be most appropriate for your site, simply add the number of bus selections with check marks next to them, the number of star bus selections with check marks next to them, and the number of star ring selections with check marks next to them. The one with the most check marks should be your first consideration.

Because the ring is more expensive than the bus, a star bus would be more economical than a star ring. In a case where both star bus and star ring would work, star bus would usually be the preferred choice.

1. Approximately how many users does the network at your site serve?

   0–10 _____ All

   10 + _____ Star bus, star ring

2. Is cost a consideration in choosing your network topology?

   Yes _____ Star bus

   No _____ All

3. Does your building have drop ceilings?

   Yes _____ All

   No _____ Star bus, star ring

4. Is there easy access to crawl spaces or wiring conduits?

   Yes _____ All

   No _____ Star bus, star ring

5. Is ease of troubleshooting important?

   Yes _____ Star bus, star ring

   No _____ All

6. Does the physical layout of the computers and office spaces naturally lend itself to a particular topology?

   Yes _____

   No _____

7. If the answer to question 6 is No, go on to question 8. If the answer to question 6 is Yes, which topology does it lend itself to using?

    Circle one: bus   star bus

8. Is ease of reconfiguration important?

    Yes _____ Star bus, star ring

    No _____ All

9. Is there existing wiring in the building which could be used for your new network?

    Yes _____

    No _____

10. If the answer to question is 9 is yes, what kind of topology could it be part of?

    Circle one: bus   star bus

Choosing the Right Topology

Choosing an appropriate topology for your network is often difficult. The most common network being installed today is the star bus, but that may not meet your needs. There are several criteria you can use, based on the information you generated in the LAN Planner, to help you with this decision. Again, there is no one completely right choice.

Reliability

If you need an extremely reliable network with redundancy built in, you might want to consider either a ring or a star wired ring network.

Cost

There are at least three considerations involved in estimating the cost of implementing a certain topology:

- Installation
- Troubleshooting
- Maintenance

Eventually, topology translates into cabling, and the installation phase is where theoretical topology meets the real world of the actual network. If cost is an overriding factor, then perhaps you should choose the topology which you can install with the lowest cost.

Ninety percent of the wiring cost is in labor. As a general rule, any time cabling has to be permanently installed in any kind of structure, the initial cost multiplies exponentially because of labor and expertise.

Once a network requires installing cable in a structure, a star bus usually becomes less expensive than a bus. To clarify this, imagine what it would take to wire a large building for a bus network. Then, imagine what it would take to reconfigure that network six months later to add eight new computers. Finally, imagine how much more economically and efficiently those same operations could be performed if the installation were a star bus.

For a small (5–10 users) network, a bus is usually economical to install initially but may be expensive to maintain because troubleshooting and reconfiguring take time. On a larger network (20 or more users), however, a star bus may cost more initially than a bus because of the equipment (a hub), but will be significantly less expensive to maintain in the long run.

Existing Cabling

Finally, if there is installed network cabling which you can reuse, you might choose the existing topology if it meets your needs.

The LAN Planner Summary

Based on the information generated in the LAN Planner, your network components should be:

Type of network: _____

Topology: _____

C H A P T E R   2

Connecting Network Components

Lesson 1   Network Cabling—the Physical Media . . . 73

Lesson 2   Wireless Network Communications . . . 104

Lesson 3   Network Adapter Cards . . . 118

Chapter 2   Review . . . 143

Welcome to Chapter 2, Connecting Network Components. In this chapter you will see how the hardware presented in Chapter 1—the servers, the client computers, and the peripherals—are physically connected.

You will learn about the different physical media, which connect computers. Though cable is the most common medium, people on the move who need to be connected to their networks cannot drag cable along with them. Wireless communications is filling this need, and this chapter will present an overview of the current wireless technology which allows mobile computers to remain part of cabled networks.

Ultimately, no matter what type of media a network uses, the data will have to actually leave and enter a computer. It does this through a network adapter card, which connects the computer to either cable or the wireless environment. As with cable, there are many types of cards available, and, as this unit explains, choosing the right one is critical to the success of the network.

The Case Study

In the case study for this unit you will evaluate the recommendations for a cabling scheme for your company's new office building.

The Troubleshooter

You will get a chance to troubleshoot a problem that arises when new client computers are added to an existing network.

The LAN Planner

The LAN Planner contains questions you need to ask when selecting cabling and network adapter cards for your network.

Lesson 1: Network Cabling—the Physical Media

What This Lesson Does

This lesson presents the essential LAN cabling concepts.

You will learn about the major cable types including their construction, features, and operation. This information will help you determine what type of cabling is best for any networking situation.

Objectives

By the end of this lesson, you will be able to:

- Define terms related to cabling including shielding, crosstalk, attenuation, and plenum.
- Identify the primary types of network cabling.
- Distinguish between baseband and broadband transmissions and identify appropriate uses for each.
- Determine which type of cabling and connection hardware would be appropriate for a particular network environment.

Estimated lesson time 50 minutes

Primary Cable Types

The vast majority of networks today are connected by some sort of wire or cabling, which act as the network transmission medium carrying signals between computers. There is a variety of cable that can meet the varying needs and sizes of networks, from small to large.

Cabling can be confusing. Belden, a leading cable manufacturer, publishes a catalog that lists more than 2,200 types of cabling. Fortunately, only three major groups of cabling connect the majority of networks:

- Coaxial
- Twisted-pair
    - Unshielded twisted-pair
    - Shielded twisted-pair
- Fiber-optic

The next part of this lesson will describe the features and components of these three major cable types. Understanding their differences will help you determine when to use each type of cabling.

Coaxial

At one time, coaxial cable was the most widely used network cabling. There were a couple of reasons for coaxial's wide usage. Coaxial was relatively inexpensive, and it was light, flexible, and easy to work with. It was so popular that it became a safe, easily supported installation.

In its simplest form, coaxial consists of a core made of solid copper surrounded by insulation, a braided metal shielding, and an outer cover. One layer of foil insulation and one layer of braided metal shielding is referred to as dual shielded. However, quad shielding is available for environments that are subject to higher interference. Quad shielding consists of two layers of foil insulation and two layers of braided metal shielding.

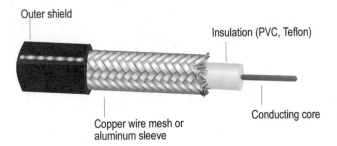

Figure 2.1 Coaxial cable showing various layers

Shielding refers to the woven or stranded metal mesh (or other material) that surrounds some types of cabling. Shielding protects transmitted data by absorbing stray electronic signals, called noise, so that they do not get onto the cable and distort the data.

The core of a coaxial cable carries the electronic signals which make up the data. This core wire can be either solid or stranded. If the core is solid, it is usually copper.

The core is surrounded by a *dielectric* insulating layer which separates it from the wire mesh. The braided wire mesh acts as a ground and protects the core from electrical noise and crosstalk. Crosstalk is signal overflow from an adjacent wire.

The conducting core and the wire mesh must always be separated from each other. If they touch, the cable will experience a short, and noise or stray signals on the mesh will flow onto the copper wire. This will destroy the data.

The entire cable is surrounded by a non-conducting outer shield, usually made of rubber, Teflon, or plastic.

Coaxial cable is more resistant to interference and attenuation than twisted-pair cabling. Attenuation is the loss of signal strength which begins to occur as the signal travels further along a copper cable.

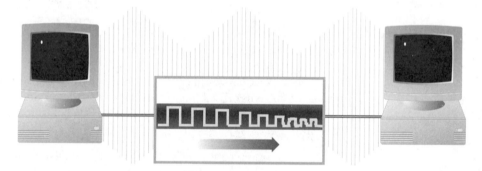

Figure 2.2 Attenuation causes signals to deteriorate

The stranded, protective sleeve can absorb stray electronic signals so they do not affect data being sent over the inner copper cable. For this reason, coaxial is a good choice for longer distances and for reliably supporting higher data rates with less sophisticated equipment.

Types of Coaxial Cable

There are two types of coaxial cable:

- Thin (thinnet)
- Thick (thicknet)

What type you select depends on the needs of your particular network.

Thinnet

Thinnet is a flexible coaxial cable about .25 inch thick. Because this type of coaxial is flexible and easy to work with, it can be used in almost any type of network installation. Networks that use thinnet have the cable connected directly to a computer's network adapter card.

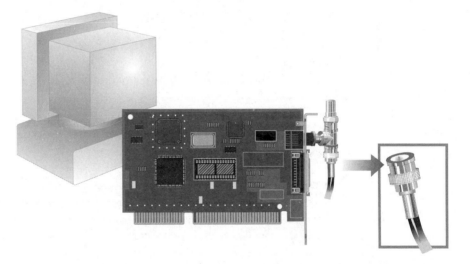

Figure 2.3 Close-up view of thinnet cable showing where it connects to a computer

Thinnet coaxial cable can carry a signal up to approximately 185 meters (about 607 feet) before the signal starts to suffer from attenuation.

Cable manufacturers have agreed upon certain designations for different types of cable. Thinnet is included in a group referred to as the RG-58 family and has a 50-ohm impedance. Impedance is the resistance, measured in ohms, to alternating current flowing in a wire. The main difference in the RG-58 family is the center core of copper. It can either be a stranded wire or solid copper core.

Figure 2.4 RG-58 coaxial showing stranded wire and the solid copper cores

Cable	Description
RG-58 /U	Solid copper core
RG-58 A/U	Stranded wire core
RG-58 C/U	Military specification of RG-58 A/U
RG-59	Broadband transmission such as cable television
RG-6	Larger in diameter and rated for higher frequencies than RG-59, but used for broadband transmissions as well
RG-62	ArcNet® networks

Thicknet

Thicknet is a relatively rigid coaxial cable about 0.5 inch in diameter. It is sometimes referred to as Standard Ethernet because it was the first type of cable used with the popular network architecture Ethernet. The copper core is thicker than a thinnet core.

Figure 2.5 Thicknet cable has a thicker core than thinnet

The thicker the copper core, the farther the cable can carry signals. This means that thicknet can carry signals farther than thinnet. Thicknet can carry a signal for 500 meters (about 1,640 feet). Therefore, because of thicknet's ability to support data transfer over longer distances, it is sometimes used as a backbone to connect several smaller thinnet-based networks.

A device called a transceiver connects the thinnet coaxial to the larger thicknet coaxial cable.

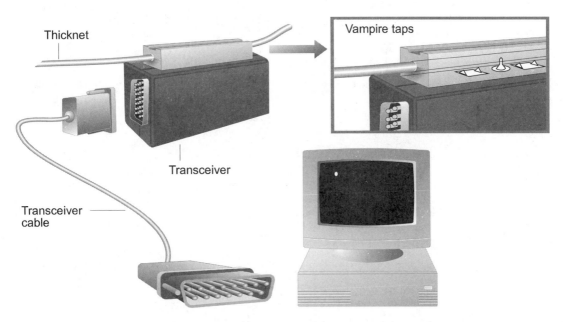

Figure 2.6 Thicknet cable transceiver with detail of a vampire tap piercing the core

A transceiver designed for thicknet Ethernet includes a connector known as a vampire tap or a piercing tap to make the actual physical connection to thicknet core. This connector is pierced through the insulating layer and makes direct contact with the conducting core. Connection from the transceiver to the network adapter card is made using a transceiver cable (drop cable) to connect to the attachment unit interface (AUI) port connector on the card. An AUI port connector for thicknet is also known as a *Digital Intel Xerox*® (DIX) connector after the three companies that developed it and its related standards, or as a DB-15 connector.

Thinnet vs. Thicknet

As a general rule, the thicker the cable, the more difficult it is to work with. Thin cable is flexible, easy to install, and relatively inexpensive. Thick cable does not bend easily and is, therefore, harder to install. This is a consideration when an installation calls for pulling cable through tight spaces such as conduits and troughs. Thick cable is more expensive than thin cable, but will carry a signal farther.

Coaxial Connection Hardware

Both thinnet and thicknet use connection components, known as a BNC (British Naval Connector), to make the connections between the cable and the computers. There are several important components in the BNC family, including the following:

- The BNC cable connector

  The BNC cable connector is either soldered or crimped to the end of a cable.

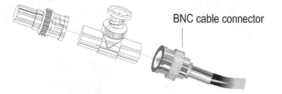

BNC cable connector

Figure 2.7 BNC cable connector

- The BNC T connector

  This connector joins the network interface card in the computer to the network cable.

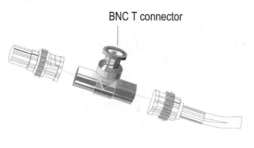

BNC T connector

Figure 2.8 BNC T connector

- The BNC barrel connector

  This connector is used to join two lengths of thinnet cable to make one longer length.

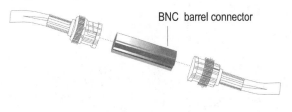

Figure 2.9 BNC barrel connector

- The BNC terminator

  A BNC terminator closes each end of the bus cable to absorb stray signals. Without BNC terminators, a bus network will not function.

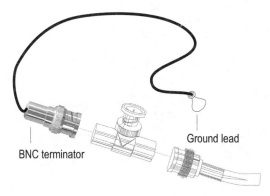

Figure 2.10 BNC terminator

Coaxial Cable Grades and Fire Codes

The type of cable grade that you should use depends on where the cables will be in your office. Coaxial cables come in two grades:

- Polyvinyl chloride
- Plenum

Polyvinyl chloride (PVC) is a type of plastic used to construct the insulation and the cable jacket for most types of coaxial cable. PVC coaxial cable is flexible and can be easily routed in the exposed areas of an office. However, when it burns, it gives off poisonous gases.

A plenum is the short space in many buildings between the false ceiling and the floor above; it is used to circulate warm and cold air through the building. Fire codes are very specific on the type of wiring that can be routed through this area, because any smoke or gas in the plenum will eventually become part of the air breathed by everyone in the building.

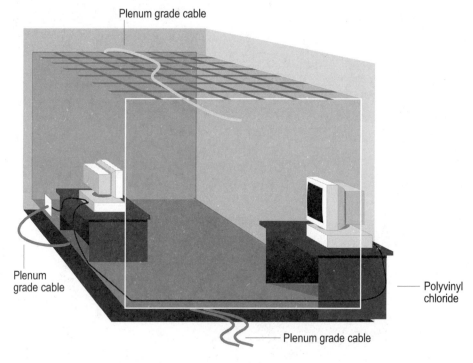

Figure 2.11 Plenum grade cabling is required by fire code in the plenum

Plenum cabling refers to coaxial that contains special materials in its insulation and cable jacket. These materials are certified to be fire resistant and produce a minimum amount of smoke. This reduces poisonous chemical fumes. Plenum cable can be used in the plenum area and in vertical runs (for example, in a wall) without conduit. However, plenum cabling is more expensive and less flexible than PVC cable.

Note Please consult your local fire and electrical codes for specific regulations about running networking cable in your office.

Coaxial Considerations

Consider these coaxial capabilities when making a decision on the type of cabling to use.

Use coaxial cable if you need:

- A medium that will transmit voice, video, and data.
- To transmit data longer distances than less expensive cabling can transmit.
- A familiar technology that offers reasonable data security.

Q & A

This is a two-part exercise. In the first part, supply the missing word(s) to complete the sentence. In the second part, identify the types of cable shown.

1. Coaxial consists of a core made of solid or stranded _____ _____.

2. If the coaxial conducting core and wire mesh touch, the cable will experience a _____.

3. The core of coaxial cable is surrounded by an _____ _____ which separates it from the wire mesh.

4. Thicknet is sometimes used as a _____ to connect thinnet segments.

5. Thinnet can carry a signal about 185 meters before the signal starts to suffer from _____.

6. The electronic signals which make up the data are actually carried by the _____ in a coaxial cable.

7. A flexible coaxial cable that is easily routed but should not go into crawl spaces is _____.

8. Coaxial that contains special materials in its insulation and cable jacket is called _____ cabling.

Answers

1. copper conductor
2. short
3. insulating layer
4. backbone
5. attenuation
6. core
7. PVC
8. plenum

Identify the following components.

1. _____

2. _____

Answers

1. terminator
2. BNC T connector

Twisted-Pair Cable

In its simplest form, twisted-pair cable consists of two insulated strands of copper wire twisted around each other. There are two types of twisted-pair cable: unshielded twisted-pair (UTP) and shielded twisted-pair (STP).

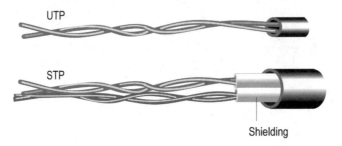

Figure 2.12 Unshielded twisted-pair and shielded twisted-pair cables

A number of twisted-pair wires are often grouped together and enclosed in a protective sheath to form a cable. The actual number of pairs in a cable varies. The twisting cancels out electrical noise from adjacent pairs and from other sources such as motors, relays, and transformers.

Unshielded Twisted-Pair (UTP)

UTP using the 10BaseT specification is the most popular type of twisted-pair cable and is fast becoming the most popular LAN cabling. The maximum cable length segment is 100 meters or about 328 feet.

UTP consists of two insulated copper wires. Depending on the particular purpose, there are UTP specifications which govern how many twists are permitted per foot of cable. In the North American continent, UTP cable is the most commonly used cable for existing telephone systems and is already installed in many office buildings.

Figure 2.13 UTP cable

UTP is specified in the Electronic Industries Association and the Telecommunications Industries Association (EIA/TIA) 568 Commercial Building Wiring Standard. EIA/TIA 568 used UTP in creating standards that apply to a variety of building and wiring situations and ensure consistency of products for customers. These standards include five categories of UTP:

- Category 1

    This refers to traditional UTP telephone cable which can carry voice but not data. Most telephone cable prior to 1983 was Category 1 cable.

- Category 2

    This category certifies UTP cable for data transmissions up to 4 Mbps (megabits per second). It consists of four twisted-pairs.

- Category 3

    This category certifies UTP cable for data transmissions up to 10 Mbps. It consists of four twisted-pairs with three twists per foot.

- Category 4

    This category certifies UTP cable for data transmissions up to 16 Mbps. It consists of four twisted-pairs.

- Category 5

    This category certifies UTP cable for data transmissions up to 100 Mbps. It consists of four twisted-pair of copper wire.

Most telephone systems use a type of UTP. In fact, one reason why UTP is so popular is because many buildings are prewired for twisted-pair telephone systems. As part of this prewiring, extra UTP is often installed to meet future cabling needs. If preinstalled twisted-pair cable is of sufficient grade to support data transmission, it can be used in a computer network. Caution is required, however, because common telephone wire may not have the twisting and other electrical characteristics required for clean, secure, computer data transmission.

One potential problem with all types of cabling is crosstalk. You may remember that crosstalk is defined as signals from one line getting mixed with signals from another line. UTP is particularly susceptible to crosstalk. Shielding is used to reduce crosstalk.

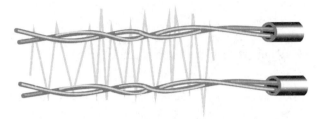

Figure 2.14 Crosstalk occurs when signals from one line mix into another line

Shielded Twisted-Pair (STP)

STP uses a woven copper braid jacket which is a higher-quality, more protective jacket than UTP has. STP also uses a foil wrap between and around the wire pairs, and internal twisting of the pairs. This gives STP excellent shielding to protect the transmitted data from outside interference.

What this means is that STP is less susceptible to electrical interference and supports higher transmission rates over longer distances than UTP.

Figure 2.15 STP cable

Twisted-Pair Cabling Components

- Connection hardware

  Twisted-pair uses RJ-45 telephone connectors to connect to a computer. This is similar to the RJ-11 telephone connector. Although they look alike at first glance, there are crucial differences between them.

  The RJ-45 is slightly larger, and will not fit into the RJ-11 telephone jack. The RJ-45 houses eight cable connections, while the RJ-11 only houses four.

Figure 2.16 RJ-45 connector and jack

Several components are available to help organize large UTP installations and make them easier to work with. These include:

- Distribution racks and rack shelves

  Distribution racks and rack shelves can create more room for cables where there isn't much floor space. They are a good way to centralized and organize a network that has a lot of connections.

- Expandable patch panels

  These come in various versions that support up to 96 ports and transmission speeds of 100 Mbps.

- Jack couplers

  These single or double RJ-45 jacks snap into patch panels and wall plates and support data rates to 100 Mbps.

- Wall plates

  These support two or more couplers.

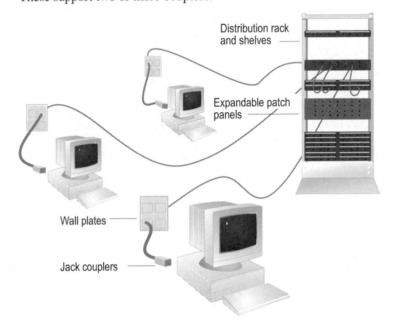

Figure 2.17 Various twisted-pair cabling components

Twisted-Pair Considerations

Use twisted-pair cable if:

- Your LAN is under budget constraints.
- You want a relatively easy installation where computer connections are simple.

Do not use twisted-pair cable if:

- You must be absolutely sure of data integrity transmitted over great distances at high speeds.

Q & A

Fill in the blanks in the following sentences.

1. The most popular type of twisted-pair cable is _____ (10BaseT).
2. UTP cable for data transmissions up to 10 Mbps is category _____.
3. UTP cable for data transmissions up to 100 Mbps is category _____.
4. STP uses a foil wrap for _____.
5. STP is less susceptible to electrical _____ and supports higher transmission rates over longer distances than UTP.
6. Twisted-pair uses _____ telephone connectors to connect to a computer.
7. The RJ-45 connection houses _____ cable connections while the RJ-11 only houses _____.

Answers

1. UTP
2. 3
3. 5
4. shielding
5. interference
6. RJ-45
7. 8, 4

Fiber-Optic Cable

In fiber-optic cable, optical fibers carry digital data signals in the form of modulated pulses of light. This is a relatively safe way to send data because no electrical impulses are carried over the fiber-optic cable. This means that fiber-optic cable cannot be tapped and the data stolen, which is possible with any copper-based cable carrying data in the form of electronic signals.

Fiber-optic cable is good for very high-speed, high-capacity data transmission because of the lack of attenuation and the purity of the signal.

Fiber-Optic Composition

Optical fibers consists of an extremely thin cylinder of glass, called the core, surrounded by a concentric layer of glass, known as the cladding. The fibers are sometimes made of plastic. Plastic is easier to install, but cannot carry the light pulses as far as glass.

Each glass strand passes signals in only one direction, so a cable consists of two strands in separate jackets. One strand transmits and one receives. A reinforcing layer of plastic surrounds each glass strand while kevlar fibers provide strength. See Figure 2.18 for an example of kevlar fibers. The kevlar fibers in the fiber-optic connector are placed between the two cables, which are encased in plastic.

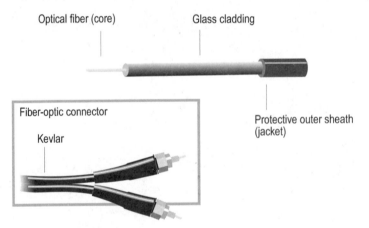

Figure 2.18 Fiber-optic cable

Fiber-optic cable transmissions are not subject to electrical interference and are extremely fast (currently transmitting about 100 Mbps with demonstrated rates of up to > 1Gbps). They can carry a signal—the light pulse—for many miles.

Fiber-Optic Considerations

Use fiber-optic cable if you:

- Need to transmit data at very high speeds over long distances in a very secure media.

Do not use fiber-optic cable if you:

- Are under a tight budget. (*Note: Pricing for fiber optic cable is competative to hi-end copper cabling.)
- Do not have the expertise available to properly install it and connect devices to it. (*Note: Fiber optic cable is increasingly easier to work with. Polishing and teminating techniques require fewer parts and less expertise.)

Q & A

Fill in the blanks in the following sentences.

1. Optical fibers carry _____ data signals in the form of light pulses.

2. Fiber-optic cable cannot be _____ and the data stolen.

3. Fiber-optic cable is better for very high speed, high-capacity data transmission than _____ cable because of the lack of attenuation and the purity of the signal.

4. Fiber-optic cable transmissions are not subject to electrical

    _____.

Answers

1. digital

2. tapped

3. copper

4. interference

Signal Transmission

Two techniques can be used to transmit the encoded signals over cable—baseband and broadband transmission.

Baseband Transmission

Baseband systems use digital signaling over a single frequency. Signals flow in the form of discrete pulses of electricity or light. With baseband transmission, the entire communication channel capacity is used to transmit a single data signal. The digital signal uses the complete bandwidth of the cable, which constitutes a single channel. A cable's total bandwidth is the difference between the highest and lowest frequencies that are carried over that cable.

Each device on a baseband network transmits bidirectionally, and some can transmit and receive at the same time.

Figure 2.19 Baseband transmission showing bidirectional digital wave

As the signal travels along the network cable, it gradually decreases in strength and can become distorted. If the cable length is too long, the result is a signal that is weak or distorted. The received signal may be unrecognizable or misinterpreted.

As a safeguard, baseband systems sometimes use repeaters to receive an incoming signal and retransmit it at its original strength and definition to increase the practical length of a cable.

Broadband Transmission

Broadband systems use analog signaling and a range of frequencies. With analog transmission, the signals are continuous and nondiscrete. Signals flow across the physical medium in the form of electromagnetic or optical waves. With broadband transmission, signal flow is unidirectional.

Figure 2.20 Broadband transmission showing unidirectional analog wave

If sufficient total bandwidth is available, multiple analog transmission systems such as cable television and network transmissions can be supported simultaneously on the same cable.

Each transmission system is allocated a part of the total bandwidth. All devices associated with a given transmission system, such as all computers using a LAN cable, must then be tuned so that they use only the frequencies that are within the allocated range.

While baseband systems use repeaters, broadband systems use amplifiers to regenerate analog signals at their original strength.

Because broadband transmission signal flow is unidirectional, there must be two paths for data flow in order for a signal to reach all devices. There are two common ways to do this:

- Mid-split broadband configuration divides the bandwidth into two channels, each using a different frequency or range of frequencies. One channel is used to transmit signals, the other to receive signals.
- In dual-cable broadband configuration, each device is attached to two cables. One cable is used to send and the other is used to receive.

Q & A

Fill in the blanks in the following sentences.

1. Baseband systems use _____ signaling over a single frequency.
2. Each device on a _____ network can transmit and receive at the same time.
3. Broadband systems use _____ signaling and a range of frequencies.
4. With _____ transmission, the signal flow is unidirectional.

Answers

1. digital
2. baseband
3. analog
4. broadband

The IBM Cabling System

IBM® developed its own cabling system, complete with its own numbers, standards, specifications, and designations. Many of these parameters, however, are similar to non-IBM specifications.

The IBM cabling system was introduced in 1984 in order to define these components:

- Cable connectors
- Face plates
- Distribution panels
- Cable types

The IBM cabling component that is unique is the IBM connector. The IBM connector is different from standard BNC or other connectors because it is neither male nor female but hermaphroditic in that two of them can be connected to each other. These IBM connectors required special face plates and distribution panels to accommodate their unique shape.

The IBM cabling system classifies cable as types. For example, Category 3 cable (voice grade UTP) is referred to by the IBM system as Type 3.

The cable definitions specify which cable would be appropriate for a given application or environment. The wire indicated in the system conforms to American Wire Gauge (AWG) standards.

AWG—the Standard Cable Measurement

In cable measurements you will often see the word gauge followed by the initials AWG. AWG is a measurement system for wire that specifies its thickness. As the thickness of the wire increases, the AWG number decreases. Telephone wire is often used as a reference point. It has a thickness of 22 AWG. A wire of 14 AWG would be thicker than telephone wire, and 26 AWG would be thinner than telephone wire.

IBM Cabling System

IBM type	Standard label	Description
Type 1	Shielded twisted-pair (STP)	Two pair of 22 AWG wires surrounded by an outer braided shield. Used for computers and MAUs.
Type 2	Voice and data cable	A voice and data shielded cable with two twisted-pairs of 22 AWG wires for data, an outer braided shield, and then four twisted-pairs of 26 AWG for voice.
Type 3	Voice grade cable	Consists of four solid, unshielded twisted-pair 22 or 24 AWG cables.
Type 4	Not yet defined	
Type 5	Fiber-optic cable	Two 62.5/125-micron multimode optical fibers—the industry standard.
Type 6	Data patch cable	Two 26 AWG twisted-pair stranded cables with a dual foil and braided shield.
Type 7	Not yet defined	
Type 8	Carpet cable	Housed in a flat jacket for use under carpets. Two shielded twisted-pair 26 AWG cables. Limited to one-half the distance of Type 1 cable.
Type 9	Plenum	Fire safe. Two shielded twisted-pair cables.

Selecting Cabling

To determine which cabling is the best for a particular site you need to answer the following questions:

- How heavy will the network traffic be?
- What are the security needs of the network?
- What are the distances the cable must cover?
- What are the cable options?
- What is the budget for cabling?

The more the cable protects against internal and external electrical noise, the farther and faster the cable will carry a clear signal. However, the better the speed, clarity, and security, the higher the cabling cost.

Cabling Considerations

As with most network components, there are trade-offs with the type of cable you purchase. If you work for a large organization and choose the least expensive cable, the accountants may initially be pleased, but you may soon notice that the LAN is inadequate in both transmission speed and data security.

Cabling depends on the needs of a particular site. The cabling you purchase to set up a LAN for a small business has different requirements than those of a larger organization, such as a major banking institution.

Some of the considerations which affect cabling price and performance include:

- Installation logistics

  How easy is the cable to install and work with? In a small installation where distances are short and security isn't a major issue, it does not make sense to choose thick, cumbersome, and expensive cable.

- Shielding

  The level of shielding required will be an added cost. Almost every network will be using some form of shielded cable. The noisier the area in which the cable is run, the more shielding will be required. Plenum grade cable is more expensive as well.

- Crosstalk

    Crosstalk and noise can cause serious problems in large networks where data
    security is crucial. Inexpensive cabling has low resistance to outside electrical
    fields generated by power lines, motors, relays, and radio transmitters. This
    makes it susceptible to both noise and crosstalk.

- Transmission speed (part of bandwidth)

    Transmission rates are measured in megabits per second (Mbps). A standard
    reference point for current LAN transmission over copper cable is 10 Mbps,
    however, recent standards now allow > 100 Mbps transmission speeds.

    Thick cable transmits data over a longer distance than thin cable. But thick
    cable, such as thicknet, is more difficult to work with than thinner cables such as
    thinnet.

    Fiber-optic cable transmits at more than 1 Gbps, so it is even faster than copper,
    but requires expertise to install and is relatively expensive.

- Cost

    Better cable, which transmits data securely over long distances, is more
    expensive than thin cable, which is easy to install and work with.

- Attenuation

    Attenuation is the reason for cable specifications that recommend certain length
    limits on different types of cabling. If a signal suffers too much attenuation, it
    will not be understood by the receiving computer. Most networks have error
    checking systems that will generate a retransmission if the signal is too weak to
    be understood, but retransmission takes time and slows down the network.

Cable Comparison Summary

Characteristics	Thinnet coaxial (10Base2)	Thicknet coaxial (10Base5)	Twisted-pair (10BaseT)	Fiber-optic
Cable cost	More than twisted-pair	More than thinnet	Least expensive	More expensive
Usable cable length*	185 meters or about 607 feet	500 meters or about 1640 feet	100 meters or about 328 feet	2 kilometers or 6562 feet
Transmission rates**	10 Mbps	10 Mbps	10 Mbps 4–100 Mbps	100 Mbps or more (> 1Gbps)
Flexibility	Fairly flexible	Less flexible	Most flexible	Very flexible
Ease of installation	Easy to install	Easy to install	Very easy; possibly already installed	Easy to install
Susceptibility to interference	Good resistance to interference	Good resistance to interference	Susceptible to interference	Not susceptible to interference
Special features	Electronic support components less expensive than twisted-pair	Electronic support components less expensive than twisted-pair	Same as telephone wire; often pre-installed in buildings	Supports voice, data, and video
Preferred uses	Medium to large sites with high security needs		UTP–smaller sites on budget STP–Token Ring in any size	Any size installation requiring speed and high data security and integrity

* Usable cable length can vary with specific network installations. As technology improves, usable cable length also increases.

**Transmission rates for specific cable types are beginning to blur. Again, technological advances are producing copper wire that can carry a signal faster than has ever been considered possible.

Summary

Choosing the appropriate network cable depends on several factors including installation logistics, shielding, security requirements, transmission speed (in Mbps), and attenuation. There are three primary types of cable: coaxial, twisted-pair, and fiber-optic.

There are two types of coaxial cable, thinnet and thicknet. Both have a copper core surrounded by wire mesh that absorbs noise and crosstalk. Coaxial cable is a good choice for data transmission of long distances.

Twisted-pair cable is available both unshielded and shielded. Unshielded twisted-pair (UTP) is available in five categories of which Category 5 is the most popular for network installations. Shielded twisted-pair (STP) supports higher transmission rates over longer distances than UTP.

Fiber-optic cable is faster and more secure than copper wire cable, but it is relatively expensive and requires some expertise to install.

Broadband and baseband are two transmission techniques. Broadband uses analog signaling to transmit multiple simultaneous transmissions on the same cable. Baseband sends single channel, digital signals.

IBM has its own cabling system complete with its own types. IBM Type 3 cabling, for example, is a voice grade, shielded twisted-pair cable otherwise known as STP.

Your Next Step

Cables are the most commonly used way to transmit data between computers. However, the wireless environment is an emerging collection of topologies that may someday do away with the need for physical connections. You will learn about the basics of wireless communication technology in the next lesson.

Lesson 2: Wireless Network Communications

What This Lesson Does

This lesson presents an overview of wireless network technology. In this lesson you will learn the differentiation between the various wireless environments and learn about the major wireless transmission and receiving components.

Objectives

By the end of this lesson, you will be able to:

- Identify the three types of wireless networks and the uses of each.
- Describe the four transmission techniques used in local area networking.
- Describe the three types of signal transmission used in mobile computing.

Estimated lesson time 25 minutes

The Wireless Environment

The wireless environment is emerging as a viable networking option. As the technology matures, vendors will be offering more products at attractive prices which, in turn, will mean increased sales and demand. As demand increases, the wireless environment will grow and improve.

The phrase wireless environment is misleading because it implies a network completely free of cabling. In most cases, this is not true. Most wireless networks actually consist of wireless components communicating with a network that uses cables in a mixed component network called a hybrid.

Wireless Capabilities

The idea of wireless networks is attracting attention because wireless components can:

- Provide temporary connections to an existing, cabled network.
- Help provide backup to an existing network.
- Provide a certain degree of portability.
- Extend networks beyond the limits of copper or even fiber-optic cables.

Uses for Wireless

Difficulty implementing cable is a factor which will continue to push wireless environments toward greater acceptance. Wireless can be especially useful for networking:

- Busy areas such as lobbies and reception areas.
- People who are constantly on the move such as doctors and nurses in hospitals.
- Isolated areas and buildings.
- Departments where the physical setting changes frequently.
- Structures, such as historical buildings, where cabling would be difficult.

Types of Wireless Networks

Wireless networks can be divided into three categories based on their technology:

- Local area networks
- Extended local area networks
- Mobile computing

The primary difference between these categories is the transmission facilities. Wireless LANs and extended LANs use transmitters and receivers owned by the company in which the network operates. Mobile computing uses public carriers such as AT&T®, MCI, Sprint and the local telephone companies and their public services, to transmit and receive signals.

Local Area Networks

A typical wireless network looks and acts almost like a cabled network except for the media. A wireless network adapter card with a transceiver is installed into each computer, and users communicate with the network just as if they were at cabled computers.

Access Points

The transceiver, sometimes called an access point, broadcasts and receives signals to and from the surrounding computers and passes data back and forth between the wireless computers and the cabled network.

These wireless LANs use small wall-mounted transceivers to connect to the wired network. The transceivers establish radio contact with portable networked devices. This is not a true wireless LAN because it uses a wall-mounted transceiver to connect to a standard cabled LAN.

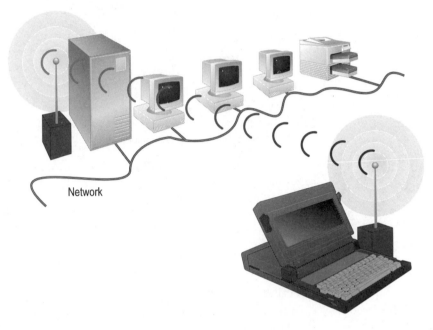

Network

Figure 2.21 Wireless portable computer connecting to a cabled network access point

Transmission Techniques

Wireless LANs use four techniques for transmitting data:

1. Infrared
2. Laser
3. Narrow-band (single-frequency) radio
4. Spread-spectrum radio

Infrared

All infrared wireless networks operate by using an infrared light beam to carry the data between devices. These systems need to generate very strong signals because weak transmission signals are susceptible to light from sources such as windows.

This method can transmit signals at high rates because of infrared light's high bandwidth. An infrared network can normally broadcast at 10 Mbps.

There are four types of infrared networks:

- Line-of-sight networks

  As the name implies, this version of infrared transmits only if the transmitter and receiver have a clear line of sight between them.

- Scatter infrared networks

  This technology broadcasts transmissions so they bounce off walls and ceilings and eventually hit the receiver. This has an effective area limited to about 100 feet and has a slow signal because of all of the signal bouncing.

- Reflective networks

  In this version of infrared networks, optical transceivers situated near the computers transmit toward a common location which redirects the transmissions to the appropriate computer.

- Broadband optical telepoint

    This version of infrared wireless LAN provides broadband services. This wireless network is capable of handling high quality multimedia requirements that can match those provided by a cabled network.

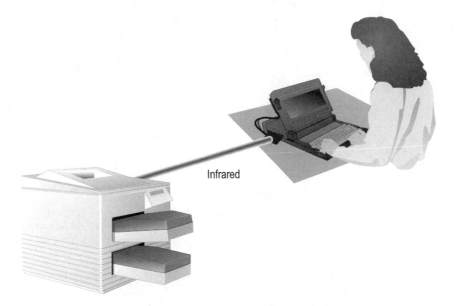

Figure 2.22 Wireless portable computer using an infrared light beam to print

While the speed of infrared and its conveniences are generating interest, infrared has difficulty transmitting distances greater than 100 feet. It is also subject to interference from the strong ambient light found in most business environments.

Laser
Laser technology is similar to infrared technology in that it requires a direct line of sight, and any person or thing that breaks the laser beam will block the transmission.

Narrow-Band (Single-Frequency) Radio
This approach is similar to broadcasting from a radio station. The user tunes both the transmitter and the receiver to a certain frequency. This does not require line of sight focusing because the broadcast range is 5000 meters square. However, because the signal is high frequency, it cannot go through steel or load-bearing walls.

Customers subscribe to this method from a service provider such as Motorola®. The service provider handles all of the Federal Communications Commission (FCC) licensing requirements. This method is relatively slow; transmission is in the 4.8 Mbps range.

Spread-Spectrum Radio

Spread-spectrum radio broadcasts signals over a range of frequencies. This helps it avoid narrow-band communication problems.

The available frequencies are divided into channels or hops. The spread-spectrum adapters tune in to a specific hop for a predetermined length of time and then switch to a different hop. A hopping sequence determines the timing. The computers in the network are all synchronized to the hop timing. This type of signaling provides some "built-in" security in that the frequency hopping algorithm of the network would have to be "known" in order to tap into the data stream.

To further enhance secuity and to keep unauthorized users from listening in to the broadcast, the sender and the receiver can encrypt (code) the transmission.

The typical speed of 250 Kbps (kilobits per second) makes this method much slower than the others. However, some implementations of spread-spectrum radio can offer transmission speeds of 4 Mbps over distances of two miles outdoors and > 800 feet indoors.

This is one area where the technology actually provides for a truly wireless network. For example, two or more computers equipped with Xircom CreditCard Netwave Adapters and an operating system such as Microsoft Windows 95 or Microsoft Windows NT can act as a peer-to-peer network with no connecting cables. However, if you have an existing Windows NT Server-based network, you can tie the above wireless network into it by adding a Netwave Access Point to one of the computers on the Windows NT Server-based network.

Point-to-Point Transmission

This method of data communication does not fall neatly into the present definitions of networking. It uses a point-to-point technology that transfers data from one computer to another as opposed to communicating among several computers and peripherals. However, additional components such as single and host transceivers are available. These can be implemented in either stand-alone computers or computers already on a network to form a wireless data transfer network.

This technology involves wireless serial data transfer that:

- Uses a point-to-point radio link for fast, error-free data transmission.
- Penetrates through walls, ceilings, and floors.
- Supports data rates from 1.2 to 38.4 Kbps up to 200 feet indoors or one-third of a mile with line-of-site transmission.

This type of system will transfer data between computers, and between computers and other devices such as printers or bar code readers.

Extended Local Area Networks

Other types of wireless components are able to do jobs in the extended LAN environment similar to their cabled counterparts. A wireless LAN bridge, for example, can connect networks up to three miles apart.

Multipoint Wireless Connectivity

A component called a wireless bridge offers an easy way to link buildings without using cable. As a foot bridge provides a path between two points for people, a wireless bridge provides a data path between two buildings. The AIRLAN/Bridge Plus, for example, uses spread-spectrum radio technology to create a wireless backbone to tie locations together over distances beyond the reach of LANs. Depending on conditions, this can be up to three miles.

The cost of such a component may be justified because it eliminates the expense of leased lines.

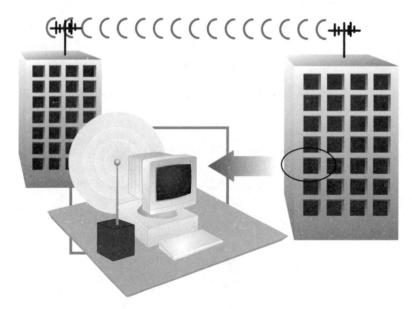

Figure 2.23 Wireless bridge connecting two LANs

The Long-Range Wireless Bridge

If the wireless bridge will not reach far enough, an organization might consider a long-range wireless bridge. These also use spread-spectrum radio technology to provide both Ethernet and Token Ring bridging for up to 25 miles.

As with the original wireless bridge, the cost of the long range bridge may be justified because it eliminates the need for T1 line or microwave connections. T1 is the standard digital line service and provides transmission rates of 1.544 Mbps. It can carry both voice and data.

Q & A

Fill in the blanks in the following sentences.

1. Wall mounted _____ connected to the wired LAN maintain and manage radio contact between portable devices and the cabled LAN.

2. Broadband optical telepoint transmission is a type of _____ network capable of handling high-quality multimedia requirements.

3. A component called a wireless _____ offers an easy way to link buildings without using cable.

4. Spread-spectrum broadcasts signals over a range of _____.

5. Point-to-point transmission involves wireless _____ data transfer.

6. In local area networks a transceiver, sometimes called an _____ _____, broadcasts and receives signals to and from the surrounding computers.

Answers

1. transceivers
2. infrared
3. bridge
4. frequencies
5. serial
6. access point

Mobile Computing

Wireless, mobile networks involve telephone carriers and public services to transmit and receive signals using:

- Packet-radio communication
- Cellular networks
- Satellite stations

Traveling employees can use this technology with portable computers or PDAs (Personal Digital Assistants) to exchange e-mail, files, or other information.

While this form of communication offers conveniences, it is slow. Transmission rates range from 8 Kbps to 19.2 Kbps. The rates get even slower when error correction is included.

Mobile computing incorporates wireless adapters that use cellular telephone technology to connect portable computers with the cabled network. Portable computers use small antennas to communicate with radio towers in the surrounding area. Satellites in near-earth orbit pick up low-powered signals from portable and mobile networked devices.

Packet-Radio Communication

This system breaks a transmission into packets, similar to other network packets, that include:

- The source address
- The destination address
- Error-correction information

The packets are uplinked to a satellite which broadcasts them. Only devices with the correct address can receive the broadcast packets.

Cellular Networks

Cellular Digital Packet Data (CDPD) uses the same technology and some of the same systems as cellular telephones. It offers computer data transmissions over existing analog voice networks between voice calls when the system is not busy. This is very fast technology that only suffers subsecond delays, which makes it reliable enough for real-time transmission.

As in other wireless networks, there must be a way to tie in to the existing cabled network. Nortel out of Mississauga, Ontario, Canada is one company that makes an Ethernet interface unit (EIU) that can provide this connection.

Satellite Stations

Microwave systems are good for interconnecting buildings in small, short-distance systems such as those on a campus or in an industrial park.

Microwave is currently the most widely used long distance transmission method in the United States. It is excellent for communicating between two line of sight points such as:

- Satellite to ground links.

- Between two buildings.

- Across large, flat, open areas such as bodies of water or deserts.

A microwave system consists of:

- Two radio transceivers—one to generate (transmitting station) and one to receive (receiving station) the broadcast.

- Two directional antennas pointed at each other to implement communication of the signals broadcast by the transceivers. These antennas are often installed on towers to give them more range and raise them above anything which might block their signals.

Q & A

Fill in the blanks in the following sentences.

1. Wireless _____ LANs involve telephone carriers and public services to transmit and receive signals.

2. CDPD uses the same technology and some of the same systems as _____ telephones.

3. Currently, the most widely used long-distance transmission method in the United States is _____.

Answers

1. mobile

2. cellular

3. microwave

Summary

Wireless networking is emerging as a transmission method for local area networks, extended local area networks, and mobile computing. A typical wireless network acts like a cabled network. A wireless network adapter card with a transceiver is installed into each computer, and users communicate with the network just as if they were at cabled computers.

Wireless networks use infrared, laser, narrow-band radio, and spread-spectrum radio transmission techniques. An additional type of technology is point-to-point. It transfers data from one computer to another as opposed to communicating among several computers and peripherals.

LANs can be extended using a component called a wireless bridge. It provides a way to link buildings separated by 25 miles or less without using cable.

Mobile computing involves telephone carriers and public services to transmit and receive signals using packet-radio communication, cellular networks, and satellite stations.

Your Next Step

Now that you have been introduced to the technology and the components that connect computers to each other, you are ready to learn about the component that acts as the point-of-data entry and exit between the computer and the network—the network adapter card. Knowing the key features of network adapter cards will help you select the appropriate one for your site.

Lesson 3: Network Adapter Cards

What This Lesson Does

This lesson introduces the basic features and functions of network adapter cards and how they can affect network performance. It describes the different cable media connector types as well as the configuration options for a network adapter card.

This lesson provides you with all of the information you need to select the right network adapter cards for your network.

Objectives

By the end of this lesson, you will be able to:

- Describe the role of the network adapter card in a network including preparing, sending, and controlling data.
- Describe the configurable options for network adapter cards.
- List the primary considerations for selecting a network adapter card.
- Describe at least two enhancements to network adapter cards that will improve network performance.

Estimated lesson time 85 minutes

The Role of the Network Adapter Card

Network adapter cards act as the physical interface or connection between the computer and the network cable. The cards are installed in an expansion slot in each computer and server on the network.

After the card has been installed, the network cable is attached to the card's port to make the actual physical connection between the computer and the rest of the network.

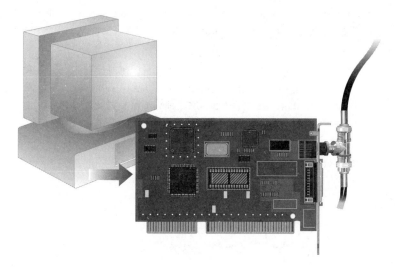

Figure 2.24 Sample network adapter card

The role of the network adapter card is to:

- Prepare data from the computer for the network cable.
- Send the data to another computer.
- Control the flow of data between the computer and the cabling system.

The network adapter card also receives incoming data from the cable and translates it into bytes the computer's CPU can understand.

Stated at a more technical level, the network adapter card contains the hardware and firmware (software routines stored in read-only memory) programming that implements the Logical Link Control and Media Access Control functions (in the Data Link layer function of the OSI model).

Preparing the Data

Before data can be sent over the network, the network adapter card must change it from a form the computer can understand to another form which can travel over a network cable.

Data moves through a computer along paths called busses. These are actually several data paths placed side by side. Because several paths are side by side (parallel), data can move along them in groups instead of a single (serial) data stream.

Older busses, such as those used in the original IBM personal computer, were known as 8-bit busses because they could move data 8 bits at a time. The IBM PC/AT® used a 16-bit bus, which means it could move data 16 bits at a time. Many computers use 32-bit buses. When data travels on a computer's bus, it is said to be traveling in parallel because the 16 or 32 bits are moving along side by side. Think of a 16-bit bus as being a 16-lane highway with 16 cars moving side by side (moving in parallel), each carrying one bit of data.

On the network cable, data must travel in a single bit stream. When data travels on a network cable it is said to be traveling as a serial transmission because one bit follows another. In other words, the cable is a one-lane highway. The data on these highways always travel in one direction. The computer is either sending or receiving data.

The network adapter card takes data traveling in parallel as a group and restructures it so that it will flow through the 1-bit wide serial path of the network cable. This is accomplished through the translation of the computer's digital signals into electrical and optical signals that can travel on the network's cables. The component responsible for this is the transceiver (transmitter/receiver).

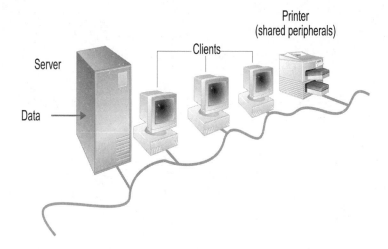

Figure 2.25 Parallel data stream converted to a serial data stream

Network Address

In addition to transforming data, the network adapter card also has to indicate its location, or address, to the rest of the network to distinguish it from all of the other cards on the network.

Network addresses are determined by the IEEE (Institute of Electrical and Electronics Engineers, Inc.) committee. The committee assigns blocks of addresses to each network adapter card manufacturer. The manufacturers hardwire these addresses into chips on the card by a process known as burning the address into the card. With this process each card, and therefore each computer, has a unique address on a network.

The network adapter card also participates in several other functions in taking data from the computer and getting it ready for the network cable.

1. The computer and network adapter card must communicate in order to move data from the computer to the card. On cards that can utilize direct memory access (DMA), the computer assigns some of its memory space to the network adapter card.

2. The network adapter card signals the computer requesting the computer's data.

3. The computer's bus moves the data from the computer's memory to the network adapter card.

Data can often move faster than the network adapter card can handle it, so the data is sent to the card's buffer (RAM) where it is held temporarily during both the transmission and reception of data.

Sending and Controlling Data

Before the sending network adapter card actually sends data over the network, it carries on an electronic dialog with the receiving card so that both cards agree on the following:

- Maximum size of the groups of data to be sent
- The amount of data to be sent before confirmation
- The time intervals between sending data chunks
- The amount of time to wait before confirmation is sent
- How much data each card can hold before it overflows
- The speed of the data transmission

If a newer, faster, more sophisticated card needs to communicate with an older, slower model, both cards need to find a common transmission speed each can accommodate. Some newer network adapter cards incorporate circuitry that allows the card to adjust to the rate of the slower card.

Each card signals to the other indicating its parameters and accepting or adjusting to the other card's parameters. When all of the communication details have been determined, the two cards begin sending and receiving data.

Q & A

For the following sentences, circle True if the statement is true or False if the statement is false.

1. The network adapter card converts serial data from the computer into parallel data for transmission over the network cable.   True   False

2. 16-bit and 32-bit are currently the two most popular bus widths.   True   False

3. To help move data onto the network cable, the computer assigns all of its memory to the network adapter card.   True   False

4. Data is temporarily held in the network adapter card's transceiver which acts as a buffer.   True   False

5. Both sending and receiving network adapter cards must agree on transmission speeds.   True   False

Answers

1. False. The reverse is true. The card converts parallel data to serial data.

2. True.

3. False. The computer can assign some of its memory to the card, but not all of it.

4. False. Only RAM acts as a buffer. The transceiver transmits and receives data.

5. True.

Configuration Options and Settings

Network adapter cards often have configurable options that must be set for the network adapter card to function properly. Examples include:

- Interrupt (IRQ)
- Base I/O port address
- Base memory address
- Transceiver

Note Sometimes it is possible to specify network adapter card settings in software, but these settings commonly must match jumper or dual inline package (DIP) switch settings configured on the network adapter card. See the network card product documentation for DIP switch settings. (*Note: Many newer network adapter cards use the Plug-and-Play (PnP) technology, which makes manually setting the network adapter card options obsolete).

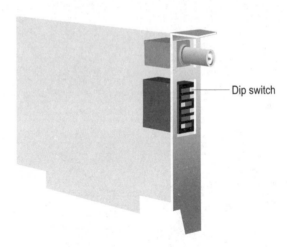

Dip switch

Figure 2.26 Older network adapter card with DIP switches

Interrupt (IRQ)

Interrupt request lines are hardware lines over which devices such as input/output ports, the keyboard, disk drives, and network adapter cards can send interrupts or requests for service to the computer's microprocessor.

Interrupt request lines are built into the computer's internal hardware and are assigned different levels of priority so that the microprocessor can determine the relative importance of incoming service requests.

When the network adapter card sends a request to the computer, it uses an interrupt—an electronic signal sent to the computer's CPU. Each device in the computer must use a different interrupt request line or interrupt (IRQ). The interrupt line is specified when the device is configured. See the examples in the following table.

In most cases, IRQ3 or IRQ5 can be used for the network adapter card. IRQ5 is the recommended setting if it is available, and it is the default for most systems. Use a system diagnostic tool such as Microsoft Diagnostic (MSD) to determine which IRQs are already being used.

If neither IRQ3 nor IRQ5 is available, you can refer to the following table for alternative values to use. The IRQs listed as available usually can be used for a network adapter card. If the computer does not have the hardware device listed for a specific IRQ, that IRQ should be available.

IRQ	Computer with an 80286 processor (or higher)
2 (9)	EGA/VGA (enhanced graphics adapter/video graphics adapter)
3	Available (unless used for second serial port [COM2, COM4] or bus mouse)
4	COM1, COM3
5	Available (unless used for second parallel port [LPT2] or sound card)
6	Floppy-disk controller
7	Parallel port (LPT1)
8	Real-time clock
10	Available
11	Available
12	Mouse (PS/2®)
13	Math coprocessor
14	Hard-disk controller
15	Available

Base I/O Port

The base input/output (I/O) port specifies a channel through which information flows between the computer's hardware (such as the network adapter card) and its CPU. The port appears to the CPU as an address.

Each hardware device in a system must have a different base I/O port number. The port numbers (in hexadecimal format) in the following table are usually available to assign to a network adapter card unless they are already in use. Those with a device listed next to them are addresses commonly used for the devices. Check the computer documentation to determine which addresses are already in use.

Base I/O Port Settings

Port	Device	Port	Device
200 to 20F	Game port	300 to 30F	Network adapter card
210 to 21F		310 to 31F	Network adapter card
220 to 22F		320 to 32F	Hard-disk controller (for PS/2 Model 30)
230 to 23F	Bus mouse	330 to 33F	
240 to 24F		340 to 34F	
250 to 25F		350 to 35F	
260 to 26F		360 to 36F	
270 to 27F	LPT3	370 to 37F	LPT2
280 to 28F		380 to 38F	
290 to 29F		390 to 39F	
2A0 to 2AF		3A0 to 3AF	
2B0 to 2BF		3B0 to 3BF	LPT1
2C0 to 2CF		3C0 to 3CF	EGA/VGA
2D0 to 2DF		3D0 to 3DF	CGA/MCGA (also EGA/VGA, in color video modes)
2E0 to 2EF		3E0 to 3EF	
2F0 to 2FF	COM2	3F0 to 3FF	Floppy-disk controller; COM1

Base Memory Address

The base memory address identifies a location in a computer's memory (RAM).
This location is used by the network adapter card as a buffer area to store the
incoming and outgoing data frames. This setting is sometimes called the RAM start
address.

Often, the base memory address for a network adapter card is D8000. (For some
network adapter cards, the final "0" is dropped from the base memory address—for
example, D8000 would become D800.) It is necessary to select a base memory
address that is not already being used by another device.

Note Some network adapter cards do not have a setting for the base memory
address because they do not use any system RAM addresses.

Some network adapter cards contain a setting that allows you to specify the amount of memory to be set aside for storing data frames. For example, for some cards you can specify either 16K or 32K of memory. Specifying more memory provides better network performance but leaves less memory available for other uses.

Selecting the Transceiver

The network adapter card may have other settings that need to be defined during configuration. For example, some cards come with an external and an on-board transceiver. In this case, you would have to determine which transceiver you want to use and then make the appropriate choice on your card.

The choice on the card is usually done with jumpers. Jumpers are small connectors that tie two pins together to determine which circuits the card will use.

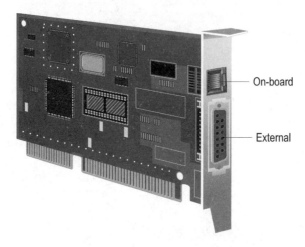

Figure 2.27 Network adapter card showing external and on-board transceivers

Q & A

Fill in the blanks in the following sentences.

1. In an 80386 computer, COM1 typically uses IRQ _____ and LPT1 typically uses IRQ _____.

2. IRQ lines are assigned different levels of _____ so that the CPU can determine how important the request is.

3. The recommended setting for a network adapter card is IRQ _____.

4. Every device on the computer must use a _____ IRQ line.

5. Each hardware device needs a default _____ ___/___ _____ number.

6. Choosing the appropriate transceiver on an adapter card that can use either an external or an on-board transceiver is usually done with _____.

Answers

1. 4, 7
2. priority
3. 5
4. different or separate
5. base I/O port
6. jumpers

Network Adapter Card Compatibility

To ensure compatibility between the computer and the network, the network adapter card must:

- Fit with the computer's internal structure (data bus architecture).
- Have the right type of cable connector for the cabling.

A card that would work in an Apple® computer communicating in a bus network, for example, would not work in an IBM computer in a ring environment. The ring requires cards that are physically different from those used in a bus, and Apple uses a different type of network communication method.

Data Bus Architecture

In the personal computer environment, there are four types of computer bus architectures: ISA, EISA, Micro Channel®, and PCI. Each type of bus is physically different from the others. It is essential that the network adapter card and the bus match.

- ISA (Industry Standard Architecture)

  ISA is the architecture used in the IBM PC, XT™ and AT computers and all of their clones. It allows various adapters to be added to the system by means of inserting plug-in cards in expansion slots. ISA was expanded from an 8-bit path to a 16-bit path in 1984 when IBM introduced the IBM PC/AT. ISA refers to the expansion slot itself (an 8-bit slot or a 16-bit slot). The 8-bit slots are shorter than the 16-bit slots which actually consist of two slots, one behind the other. An 8-bit card could fit into a 16-bit slot, but a 16-bit card could not fit into an 8-bit slot.

  ISA was the standard personal computer architecture until Compaq® and several other companies developed the EISA bus.

- EISA (Extended Industry Standard Architecture)

  This is the bus standard introduced in 1988 by a consortium of nine computer-industry companies: AST® Research, Inc., Compaq, Epson®, Hewlett-Packard®, NEC®, Olivetti®, Tandy®, Wyse® Technology, and Zenith®.

  EISA offers a 32-bit data path and maintains compatibility with ISA while providing for additional features introduced by IBM in its Micro Channel Architecture bus.

- Micro Channel Architecture

  IBM introduced this standard in 1988 as part of its PS/2 roll out. Micro Channel Architecture is electrically and physically incompatible with the ISA bus. Unlike the ISA bus, the Micro Channel functions as either a 16-bit or a 32-bit bus and can be driven independently by multiple bus master processors.

- PCI (peripheral component interconnect)

  This is a 32-bit local-bus used in most Pentium computers and in the Apple Power Macintosh®. The current PCI bus architecture meets most of the requirements for providing Plug and Play functionality. Plug and Play is both a design philosophy and a set of personal computer architecture specifications. The goal of Plug and Play is to enable changes to a personal computer configuration with no intervention by the user. The installation of any device should be a simple, fail-safe operation. Microsoft Windows 95 is a Plug and Play-compliant operating system.

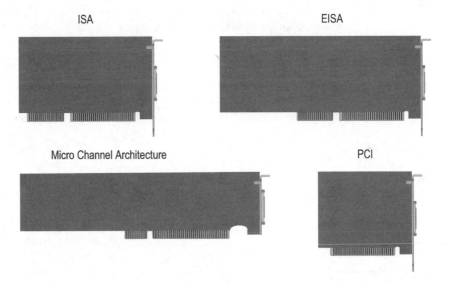

Figure 2.28 ISA, EISA, Micro Channel, and PCI network adapter cards

Network Cabling and Connectors

The network adapter card performs three important functions in coordinating activities between the computer and the cabling:

- Making the physical connection to the cable.
- Generating the electrical signals that travel over the cable.
- Following specific rules controlling access to the cable.

To select the appropriate card for your network, you need to determine the type of cabling and cabling connectors it will have.

Each type of cable has different physical characteristics which the network adapter card must accommodate. Therefore, each card is built to accept a particular type of cable such as coaxial, twisted-pair, or fiber-optic.

Some network adapter cards have more than one interface connector. For example, it is not uncommon for a network adapter card to have both a thinnet and thicknet connector, or a twisted-pair and a thicknet connector.

If a card has more than one interface connector, make a selection either by setting jumpers or DIP switches on the card itself, or by using a software-selectable option. Consult the network adapter card documentation for information on how to properly configure the card. Three examples of typical connectors found on network adapter cards follow.

A thinnet network connection uses a coaxial BNC connector as shown in Figure 2.29.

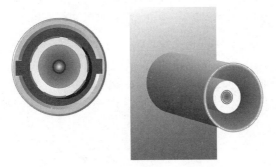

Figure 2.29 Thinnet network connection for a coaxial BNC connector

A thicknet network connection uses a 15-pin attachment unit interface (AUI) cable to connect the 15-pin (DB-15) connector on the back of the network adapter card to an external transceiver. As you may recall from Lesson 1, "Network Cabling—the Physical Media," the external transceiver uses a vampire tap to connect into the thicknet cable.

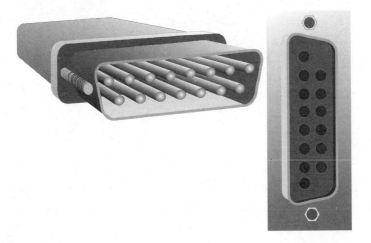

Figure 2.30 Thicknet network connection for a 15-pin AUI

Caution Be careful not to confuse a joystick port with an AUI network adapter port. They both look alike. You will need to be familiar with the specific hardware configuration in order to know whether the connector is for a network adapter card or a joystick.

An unshielded twisted-pair connection uses an RJ-45 connector, as shown in Figure 2.31. The RJ-45 connector is similar to an RJ-11 telephone connector but is larger in size because it has eight conductors; an RJ-11 only has 4 conductors.

Figure 2.31 RJ-45 connector

Some proprietary twisted-pair networking topologies use the RJ-11 connector. These topologies are sometimes referred to as pre-10BaseT. The RJ-11 connector is the same connector that is used on a telephone wire.

Q & A

Fill in the blanks for questions 1 through 4, and then identify the connectors illustrated for letters A through C.

1. ISA was the standard bus until Compaq and others developed the _____ bus.

2. The _____ bus functions as either a 16-bit or a 32-bit bus and can be driven independently by multiple bus master processors.

3. Telephone wire uses an _____ connector.

4. Plug and Play is both a design philosophy and a set of personal computer _____ specifications.

Answers

1. EISA

2. Micro Channel

3. RJ-11

4. architecture

Identify the Ethernet media connector types:

a. Connector:_____

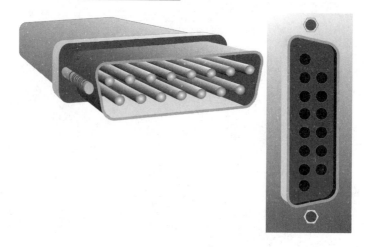

b. Connector:_____

c. Connector:_____

Answers
a. BNC
b. AUI or DIX
c. RJ-45

Network Performance

Because of the effect it has on data transmission, the network adapter card has a great affect on the performance of the entire network. If the card is slow, data will not pass to and from the network quickly. On a bus network, where no one can use the network until the cable is clear, a slow card can increase wait times for all users.

After identifying the physical requirements of the card—the type of connector it needs and the type of network in which it will be used—it will be necessary to consider several other factors which affect the capabilities of the card.

Although all network adapter cards conform to certain minimum standards and specifications, some cards feature enhancements which greatly improve server, client, and network performance.

You can speed up the movement of data through the card with the following:

- Direct memory access (DMA)

  With this method, the computer moves data directly from the network adapter card's buffer to the computer's memory, without using the computer's microprocessor.

- Shared adapter memory

  In this method, the network adapter card contains RAM which it shares with the computer. The computer identifies this RAM as if it is actually installed in the computer.

- Shared system memory

  In this system, the network adapter card's processor selects a section of the computer's memory and uses it to process data.

- Bus mastering

  With bus mastering, the network adapter card takes temporary control of the computer's bus, by-passes the computer's CPU, and moves data directly to the computer's system memory. This speeds up computer operations by freeing the computer's processor to concentrate on other tasks. These cards are expensive, but they can improve network performance by 20 to 70 percent.

  Both EISA and Micro Channel Architecture network adapter cards offer bus mastering.

- RAM buffering

  Current network traffic travels at a speed which is often too fast for most network adapter cards. RAM chips on the network adapter card form a buffer. When the card receives more data than it can process immediately, the RAM buffer holds some of the data until the adapter card can process it.

  This speeds up the card's performance and keeps the card from becoming a bottleneck.

- Onboard microprocessor

  With a microprocessor, the network adapter card does not need the computer to help process data. Most cards feature their own processors which speed network operations.

Servers

Because they handle such high volumes of network traffic, servers should be equipped with the highest-performance cards possible.

Workstations

Workstations can use less expensive cards if their main network activities are limited to applications that do not generate great volumes of network traffic, such as word processing. Other applications, such as databases or engineering applications, will quickly overwhelm inadequate network adapter cards.

Specialized Network Adapter Cards

Wireless Network Adapter Cards

There are wireless network adapter cards available that support the major network operating systems.

These cards often come with:

- Indoor omnidirectional antenna and antenna cable.
- Network software to make the adapter card work with a particular network.
- Diagnostic software for troubleshooting.
- Installation software.

These network adapter cards can be used to:

- Create an all wireless LAN.
- Add wireless stations to a cabled LAN.

Usually, these cards are used with a component called a wireless concentrator, which acts as a transceiver to send and receive signals.

Fiber Optic Network Adapter Cards

"Fiber to the desktop" has become a watch phrase for the computing industry. As transmission speeds increase to accommodate the "bandwidth" hungry applications and multi-media data streams, that are common on today's intranets, fiber optic network cards allow direct connections to the high speed fiber optic networks. These cards should be used in special cases only due to the high cost of these devices.

Remote-Boot PROMs

In some environments, security is such an important consideration that workstations do not have disk drives. Without disk drives, users are not able to copy information to either floppy or hard disks and, therefore, cannot take any data from the work site.

However, because computers normally start from either a floppy or hard disk, there has to be some other source for the software that initially starts the computer and connects it to a network. In these environments, the network adapter card can be equipped with a special chip called a remote-boot PROM (programmable read-only memory) which contains the hardwired code that starts the computer and connects the user to the network.

With remote-boot PROMs diskless workstations can join the network when they start.

Summary

Network adapter cards are the interface between the computer and the network cable. The function of the network adapter card is to prepare, send, and control data on the network. To prepare data for the network, the card uses a transceiver to reformat data from parallel to serial transmission. Each card has its own unique address which allows it to be distinguished from all of the other cards on the network.

Network adapter cards have configurable options that must be set. These options include the interrupt (IRQ), the base I/O port address, and the base memory address.

To ensure compatibility between the computer and network, the network adapter card must fit the computer's data bus architecture and have the right type of cable connector for the cabling.

The network adapter card has a great affect on the performance of the entire network. There are several ways to enhance network performance with the network adapter card. Some cards have enhancements designed into them. These include direct memory access, shared adapter memory, shared system memory, and bus mastering. Performance can also be enhanced through RAM buffering and with the use of an on-board microprocessor.

There are also network adapter cards for specialized environments, such as wireless and fiber optic networks, and workstations without disk drives in high-security environments.

A check list for buying a network adapter card includes:

- Bus width (32-bit is faster than 16-bit)
- Bus type (PCI, EISA and Micro Channel are faster than ISA)
- Memory transfer (shared memory is faster than I/O or DMA)
- Bus mastering
- Vendor considerations (stability, reliability, experience, and so on)

Activity

Run Demo 6.

Your Next Step

With the completion of this lesson, you now know the fundamentals of network adapter cards. So far in the kit, you have been introduced to the basic network components and design concepts common to most LANs.

You are now ready to go on to the Chapter 2 Review and apply what you have learned.

Chapter 2 Review

In Chapter 2 you learned how computers are connected to form networks. You started with cabling and related components, then moved to wireless communications, and finally learned about network adapter cards.

In today's environment, cable connects most networks. Coaxial has traditionally been the cable of choice. However, UTP and fiber-optic cable are currently replacing coaxial in many installations.

Wireless networks are also gaining popularity as prices fall and the technology matures. Today, most wireless installations actually connect to a cabled LAN. Three popular wireless technologies are:

- Infrared
- Narrow-band radio
- Spread-spectrum radio

Network adapter cards act as the interface between the computer and both cable and wireless connections. There are options that must be set correctly if network adapter cards are to function properly. These options include the following:

- Interrupt (IRQ)
- Base I/O port address
- Base memory address
- Transceiver selection

Some network adapter cards have features designed into them that can enhance network performance, such as direct memory access and shared system memory.

Checkup

Follow the instructions for each exercise as indicated. The answers for all of the exercises are after the last exercise.

Note To get the most out of the Checkup exercises, you may want to cover the answers with a piece of paper until you have answered the questions. If your answer differs from the one in the book, you should review the appropriate text.

Exercise 1: Matching

Match each item in the Column A with the best choice from Column B. One item in Column B will not be used, and items will be used no more than once.

Column A	Column B
1. Fiber-optic ____	A. Requires direct line-of-sight.
2. STP ____	B. The short space in buildings between the false ceiling and the floor above it.
3. Thinnet ____	C. Supports voice, data, and video.
4. Scatter infrared ____	D. Typically used as the backbone in a large Ethernet network.
5. Laser ____	E. Typically uses RJ-45 connectors.
6. Plenum ____	F. Signals bounce off walls and ceilings.
7. Thicknet ____	G. RG-58 family of cables that carries signal up to 185 meters.
8. Parallel port ____	H. Typically uses IRQ 3.
9. COM1 ____	I. Typically uses IRQ 4.
	J. Typically uses IRQ 5.
	K. Typically uses IRQ 7.

Exercise 2: True or False

For the following sentences, circle True if the statement is true or False if the statement is false.

1. Because thinnet is lighter and more flexible than thicknet, it can carry data farther, faster. True   False

2. The maximum distance for UTP (10BaseT) is about 100 meters (328 feet). True   False

3. Data often moves faster in a network adapter card than it does in the computer. True   False

4. Devices use the IRQ lines to send interrupts or requests for service to the computer's microprocessor. True   False

5. A Micro Channel adapter can be used in an EISA slot. True   False

6. Thicknet networks require an 8-pin RJ-11 plug to connect to a network adapter card. True   False

Exercise 3: Open-Ended

Supply the items for the lists below.

1. List three of the configuration options for a network adapter card.

    a. _____

    b. _____

    c. _____

2. List three types of enhancements to network adapter cards that can improve network performance.

    a. _____

    b. _____

    c. _____

Checkup Answers

Exercise 1: Matching

1. C
2. E
3. G
4. F
5. A
6. B
7. D
8. K
9. I

Exercise 2: True or False

1. False. Thick copper wire, with less resistance because of its diameter, carries more data farther, faster than thin wire.

2. True.

3. False. The opposite is true. Data moves from the computer to the adapter card faster than the card can handle it. This is why better cards are sold with on-board RAM, to act as a buffer for the incoming data until the card can take care of it.

4. True.

5. False. They are physically different and cannot be compatible. Network adapter cards are made specifically for one bus or the other.

6. False. Thicknet uses a 15-pin D connector. An RJ-11 is a 4-wire telephone connector.

Exercise 3: Open-Ended

1. List three of the configuration options for a network adapter card. (Four were discussed; any three of the following would be fine.)

    a. IRQ (Interrupt)

    b. Base I/O port address

    c. Base memory address

    d. Transceiver setting

2. List three types of enhancements to network adapter cards that can improve network performance.

    a. Direct memory address (DMA)

    b. Shared adapter memory

    c. Shared system memory

    d. Bus mastering

    e. RAM buffering

Case Study Problem

The Setting

You have been asked to review the proposals submitted by a consulting firm for the cabling scheme for your company's new office building.

Location	Distance	Location	Distance
A to B	50 feet	Hub to A	500 feet
B to C	50 feet	Hub to B	525 feet
C to D	50 feet	Hub to C	550 feet
D to E	200 feet	Hub to D	575 feet
E to F	75 feet	Hub to E	500 feet
F to G	75 feet	Hub to F	425 feet
G to H	75 feet	Hub to G	350 feet
H to I	75 feet	Hub to H	300 feet
I to J	200 feet	Hub to I	275 feet
J to K	50 feet	Hub to J	350 feet
K to L	50 feet	Hub to K	325 feet
L to M	50 feet	Hub to L	275 feet
A to M	725 feet	Hub to M	225 feet
D to M	800 feet	A to J	800 feet

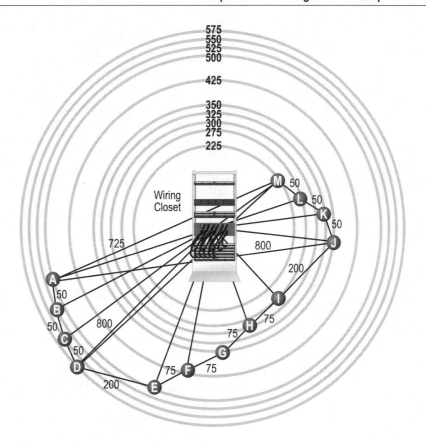

The Problem

The consulting firm has recommended that you implement 10BaseT Category 5 UTP wire for your company's network.

Your Solution

1. Where does this recommendation violate the UTP and 10BaseT specifications?

_____

_____

2. What type of cabling might you recommend instead?

_____

Suggested Solution

1. The distances for A, B, C, D, E, F, and G to the hub all exceed the maximum cable length of 328 feet specified by 10BaseT. Therefore this solution would not work.

2. You could use thinnet with a multiport repeater where the hub is in the picture. All of the cable lengths from the hub to individual computers are less than 185 meters, or 607 feet.

You could also use a star wired fiber-optic network for this situation, but it would cost significantly more than the coaxial solution.

The Troubleshooter

Listed below are questions you need to ask regarding cabling and network adapter cards when troubleshooting a variety of network problems. Use them to help you troubleshoot the problem which follows.

Two Important Troubleshooting Questions

The first troubleshooting question should always be: "Did the thing ever work correctly?"

Yes ____

No ____

The next question should be, "What has changed since then?"

Cabling

Most network engineers have learned to check cabling first because experience has taught them that the majority of network problems can be found in the cabling.

Is the cabling connected properly?

Yes _____

No _____

Is the cable broken or frayed?

Yes _____

No _____

Is the cable too long?

Yes _____

No _____

Does the cable conform to the specifications of the network adapters?

Yes _____

No _____

Is the cable crimped or bent too sharply?

Yes _____

No _____

Does the network cable run near a source of interference such as an air conditioner, transformer, or large electric motor?

Yes _____

No _____

Is the cabling terminated properly?

Yes _____

No _____

Adapter Cards

The most common network adapter problems are interrupt conflicts and transceiver settings. The following questions will help you determine if the network adapter card is the source of your problem.

Do the settings on the card match the settings in the network software you are using?

Yes _____

No _____

Is there an I/O address conflict between the network adapter card and another card installed in the computer?

Yes _____

No _____

Is there an interrupt conflict between the network adapter card and another card installed in the computer?

Yes _____

No _____

Is there a memory conflict between the network adapter card and another card installed in the computer?

Yes _____

No _____

Is the cable plugged into the correct interface (AUI, BNC, or RJ-45)?

Yes _____

No _____

Is the network adapter card set to the speed setting that your network is using?

Yes _____

No _____

Are you using the correct type of network card for your network? (That is, are you trying to use a Token Ring card in an Ethernet network?)

Yes _____

No _____

If you are you using more than one network adapter card in the computer, do their settings conflict?

Yes _____

No _____

Can You Solve This Problem?

Refer back to the questions to arrive at possible causes of the problem situation described below. Remember, there could be several causes and solutions.

The Situation

You have a 20-user, thinnet, coaxial bus network which has been in use for about a year. Three new client computers are going to be added to the network.

The Available Facts

Your vendor was in over the weekend adding the new computers, and when you came in Monday morning, nobody could access the server.

Your Solution

Cause of the Problem

List two things which could cause the network not to function.

1. _____

2. _____

Possible Solution

What could you do to resolve each of the two possible causes you listed above?

_____

_____

_____

_____

Impact of Your Solution on Network Users

What will be the impact of each of your solutions on network users (assuming that they repair the problem)?

_____

_____

_____

_____

Suggested Solution

Cause of the Problem

The answers you have written down might not be listed, but they could still be correct. This list is not exhaustive, it just lists some of the causes of the problem.

1. The network cable might not be correctly connected, that is, it might have a break in it caused by adding the new computers.

2. The new cable added to service the new computers might not be the correct type for your network.

3. The new cable added to your network might have a short in it.

4. The existing network cabling might have been damaged by rough handling during the installation of the new computers.

5. The addition of the new cable needed for the new computers might have made your total network cable length exceed the maximums specified for the type of network you have.

6. The bus network might be missing a terminator. It might have been removed or fallen off by accident during the installation of the new computers.

Possible Solution

What could you do to resolve the each of the two possible causes you listed above?

1. Find and repair the break or disconnection in the cable.

2. Check the cable type of the existing cable and make sure the new cables are of the same type. If they are different replace the new cables with cables of the correct type. For example, the original cable might be RG-58A/U and the new cables might be RG-62 /U. These two cable types are not compatible.

3. Test the new cables with an ohmmeter to see if they are shorted.

4. Check all of the cables in the new installation for shorts, frayed cables, breaks, and so on.

5. If the maximum coaxial cable length (185 meters) has been exceeded, you might have to add a repeater to your network so that you will have two network cable segments which are within specifications.

Impact of Your Solution on Network Users

What will be the impact of each of your solutions on network users (assuming that they repair the problem)?

The impact for each of the solutions listed above is very positive. Before the repair, the network did not function, and afterwards, it works.

With new users on the network, monitor the network's performance to ensure that it is not suffering from degradation.

The LAN Planner

Note This LAN Planner is only concerned with networking subjects presented in this unit. Appendix B, "Network Planning and Implementation," summarizes information from all of the LAN Planners in the kit to take you step-by-step through the complete LAN planning process. Therefore, the information you contribute here will be used in the last lesson as part of a complete LAN plan specifically for your site.

Choosing Your Networking Media

Research has shown that about 90 percent of all new network installations are using UTP cable in a star bus topology. Because most of the cost of cable installation is labor, there is often little cost difference between using Category 3 UTP cable and Category 5 UTP cable. Most new installations use Category 5 because it supports transmission speeds of up to 100 Mbps. Category 5 allows you to install a 10 Mbps solution now, and upgrade it later to a 100 Mbps solution.

However, UTP cable may not be suitable for all networking situations.

Each of the following sections will ask you several questions about your network cable needs. If you answer yes to most of the questions in a section, then that type of cable is probably the correct cable type to choose for your network.

Note UTP is currently the most popular cabling. Unless there is a compelling reason to use another type, UTP should be your first consideration.

Put a check mark on the line next to the choice which applies to your site. To determine which type of cabling would be most appropriate for your site, simply total the number of each type of cable indicator (UTP, coaxial, STP, fiber-optic). The indicator with the highest score is the candidate unless there is a specific requirement for particular type of cable such as fiber-optic (distance and security). In cases where more than one type of cable is indicated, choose UTP where possible.

Unshielded Twisted-Pair

Is ease of troubleshooting and long-term maintenance costs important?

Yes _____ UTP cable

No _____ Any of the discussed cable types

Are most of your computers within 100 meters of your wiring closet?

Yes _____ UTP cable

No _____ Coaxial or fiber-optic cable

Is ease of reconfiguration important?

Yes _____ UTP cable

No _____ Any of the discussed cable types

Does any of your staff have experience with UTP cable?

Yes _____ UTP cable

No _____ UTP, depends on other factors

Note Even if no one has experience with UTP, someone may have transferable experience with another type of cable such as coaxial, STP, or even fiber-optic.

Shielded Twisted-Pair

Does your network have any existing STP cabling?

Yes _____ STP cable

No _____ Any of the discussed cable types

Does the topology or network card you want to use require the use of STP cable?

Yes _____ STP

No _____ Depends on other factors

Do you have a need for cable which is more resistant to EMI (interference) than UTP?

Yes _____ STP, coaxial, or fiber-optic cable

No _____ Depends on other factors, UTP cable

Coaxial

Do you have existing coaxial cabling in your network?

Yes _____ Coaxial cable

No _____ Any of the discussed cable types

Is your network very small (less than ten computers)?

Yes _____ Coaxial cable (bus), UTP cable

No _____ Any of the discussed cable types, depends on other factors

Is your network going to be installed in an open area using cubicles to separate work areas?

Yes _____ Coaxial, or UTP cable

No _____ Depends on other factors

Do you have a need for cable which is more resistant to EMI than UTP?

Yes _____ Coaxial, fiber-optic, or STP cable

No _____ Depends on other factors, UTP cable

Fiber-Optic

Note Some situations require fiber-optic cable. This is especially true where other types of cable will not meet specific distance or security requirements. In such cases, fiber is the only type of cable that can be considered regardless of what the questions in the other areas indicate. In the questions below, "Any" means that UTP can be considered, depending on your other site considerations.

Do you have a need for network cabling which is immune to electromagnetic interference (EMI)?

Yes _____ Fiber-optic cable

No _____ Any of the discussed cable types, depends on other factors

Do you have a need for network cabling which is relatively secure from most eavesdropping or corporate intelligence gathering equipment?

Yes _____ Fiber-optic cable

No _____ Any of the discussed cable types, depends on other factors

Do you have a need for network transmission speeds which are higher than those supported by copper media?

Yes ____ Fiber-optic cable

No ____ Any of the discussed cable types, depends on other factors

Do you have a need for longer cabling distances than those supported by copper media?

Yes ____ Fiber-optic cable

No ____ Any of the discussed cable types, depends on other factors

Do you have a budget that can absorb the costs of implementing fiber?

Yes ____ Fiber-optic or any of the discussed cable types, depends on other factors

No ____ Any of the discussed cable types, depends on other factors

Wireless Network Communications

Note In the questions below, wireless, like fiber-optic, may be the only option in some cases regardless of what the questions in the other areas indicate. Keep in mind that wireless can also be used in combination with a cabled network.

Do users on your network need to physically move their computers in the course of their work day?

Yes ____ Wireless, depends on other factors

No ____ Any of the discussed cable types, depends on other factors

Are there limitations which make it very difficult or impossible to cable computers to the network?

Yes ____ Wireless

No ____ Any of the discussed cable types, depends on other factors

Does your network have unique needs which are best fulfilled by one or more of the features of current wireless technology, such as computer mobility, or the ability to have a network in a building in which it is very difficult or impossible to install cable?

Yes ____ Wireless

No ____ Any of the discussed cable types, depends on other factors

Choosing Your Network Adapter Card

There are dozens of manufacturers making each type of network adapter card, and each card has slightly different features, such as setup (using jumpers and switches, or on newer cards using a software setup program or Plug-and-Play, PnP), bus type, and so on. You should do some research to determine which card is best for you because the industry is constantly changing and updating. The best card this month might be superseded by another manufacturer's card next month.

If you can answer yes to each of the following questions, then the card you have chosen will probably work in your environment.

Note These questions are not designed to promote a particular card, but, rather, to ensure that the card you choose is compatible with the rest of your network.

Are there drivers available for the card that will work with the operating system you are using?

Yes _____

No _____

Is the card compatible with the cable type and topology you have chosen?

Yes _____

No _____

Is the card compatible with the bus type of the computer into which it will be installed?

Yes _____

No _____

The LAN Planner Summary

Note This information will be taken into account in the final lesson.

Based on the information generated in the LAN Planner, your network components should be:

Cable: _____

C H A P T E R   3

How a Network Functions

Lesson 1   The OSI and 802 Networking Models . . . 165

Lesson 2   Drivers . . . 180

Lesson 3   How Networks Send Data . . . 191

Lesson 4   Protocols . . . 204

Lesson 5   Putting Data on the Cable . . . 222

Chapter 3   Review . . . 233

Welcome to Chapter 3, How a Network Functions. This chapter will:

- Present the essential standard model upon which network communication is based.
- Explain how software utilities enable hardware functions.
- Describe how a network breaks data into manageable chunks before transmitting it.
- Introduce the special languages computers use in communicating with each other.
- Explain the different ways computers can put data onto the cable during transmission.

The chapter shows how networks are implemented with guidelines established by standards organizations. This enables all network components to function together regardless of the vendor.

You will learn why software utility programs called drivers are the key to hardware functionality. You will also learn how to implement drivers. This chapter also explains the basic package that carries data around a network. You will see how networks send large blocks of data, such as long files or extensive pieces of information, from a database across a network.

Just because a computer can put raw data on the network does not mean it will reach its destination successfully and be understood. Similar to the interaction of people who speak different languages, there may be no mutual understanding of the words and actions unless each person follows a common set of rules, or protocols. This chapter explains the role protocols play in network communications.

The chapter also shows how networks use different methods for actually putting the data on the cable for transmission. The different ways this can happen affect the type of network an organization will have.

The Case Study Problem

The case study at the end of this chapter describes how a small company that relies on its network functioning properly can suffer growing pains when the network is expanded and improved. You will be able to apply your troubleshooting skills to track down the cause of their network problems.

The Troubleshooter

The Troubleshooter includes methods for troubleshooting problems involving drivers, packets, and protocols. You will be called upon to use your knowledge of drivers to troubleshoot a printing problem.

The LAN Planner

This LAN Planner provides you with the key issues you need to address regarding drivers and protocols when you are planning or upgrading a network.

Lesson 1: The OSI and 802 Networking Models

What This Lesson Does

This lesson presents a description of the Open Systems Interconnection (OSI) networking model and the IEEE Project 802 model. Project 802 provides enhancements to the OSI model. You will learn the position and importance of each model in networking.

Objectives

By the end of the lesson, you will be able to:

- Describe the primary function of each OSI layer.
- Identify the OSI layer at which a particular network activity takes place.
- Identify the OSI layer at which a particular network component functions.
- Describe the Project 802 enhancements to the OSI model.

Estimated lesson time 45 minutes

Network Communications

Network activity involves sending data from one computer to another. This complex process can be broken into discrete tasks:

- Recognize the data
- Divide the data into manageable chunks
- Add information to each chunk of data to:
  - Determine the location of the data
  - Identify the receiver
- Add timing and error checking information
- Put the data on the network and send it on its way

The network operating system follows a strict set of procedures in performing each task. These procedures are called protocols, or rules of behavior. The protocols guide each activity to successful completion.

There arose a need for standard protocols to allow hardware and software from various vendors to communicate. There are two primary sets of standards: the OSI model and a modification of that standard called Project 802.

A clear understanding of these models is an important first step in understanding the technical aspects of how a network functions.

The OSI Model

In 1978, the International Standards Organization (ISO) released a set of specifications that described a network architecture for connecting dissimilar devices. The original document applied to systems that were open to each other because they could all use the same protocols and standards to exchange information.

Note Every networking professional needs to be aware of the major standards organizations and how their work affects network communications. A review of the most important standards bodies is presented in Appendix A, "Common Network Standards and Specifications."

In 1984, the ISO released a revision of this model and called it the Open Systems Interconnection (OSI) reference model. The 1984 revision has become an international standard and serves as a guide for networking.

This model is the best known and most widely used guide to describe networking environments. Vendors design network products based on the specifications of the OSI model. It provides a description of how network hardware and software work together in a layered fashion to make communications possible. It also helps with troubleshooting by providing a frame of reference that describes how components are supposed to function.

A Layered Architecture

The OSI model is an architecture that divides network communication into seven layers. Each layer covers different network activities, equipment, or protocols.

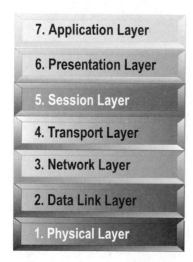

Figure 3.1 The seven-layer OSI model

Figure 3.1 represents the layered architecture of the OSI model. Layering specifies different functions and services at different levels. Each OSI layer has well-defined networking functions, and the functions of each layer communicate and work with the functions of the layers immediately above and below it. For example, the Session layer must communicate and work with the Presentation and Transport layers.

The lowest layers—1 and 2—define the network's physical media and related tasks, such as putting data bits onto the network adapter cards and cable. The highest layers define how applications access communication services. The higher the layer, the more complex its task.

Each layer provides some service or action that prepares the data for delivery over the network to another computer. The layers are separated from each other by boundaries called interfaces. All requests are passed from one layer, through the interface, to the next layer. Each layer builds upon the standards and activities of the layer below it.

Relationship of OSI Model Layers

The purpose of each layer is to provide services to the next higher layer and shield the upper layer from the details of how the services are actually implemented. The layers are set up in such a way that each layer acts as if it is communicating with its associated layer on the other computer. This is a logical or virtual communication between peer layers as shown in Figure 3.2. In reality, actual communication takes place between adjacent layers on one computer. At each layer there is software that implements certain network functions according to a set of protocols.

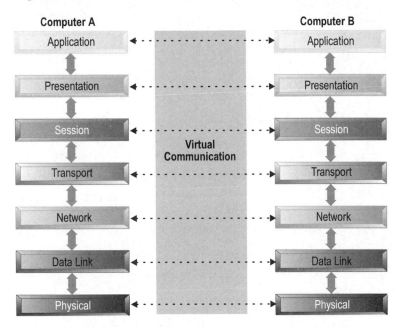

Figure 3.2 Relationships among OSI layers

Before data is passed from one layer to another it is broken down into packets. A packet is a unit of information transmitted as a whole from one device to another on a network. The network passes a packet from one software layer to another in the order of the layers. At each layer the software adds some additional formatting or addressing to the packet, which it needs to be successfully transmitted across the network.

At the receiving end, the packet passes through the layers in the reverse order. A software utility at each layer reads the information on the packet, strips it away, and passes the packet up to the next layer. When the packet finally gets passed up to the Application layer, the addressing information has been stripped away and the packet is in its original form, which is readable by the receiver.

Except for the lowest layer in the networking model, no layer can pass information directly to its counterpart on another computer. Information on the sending computer must be passed through all of the lower layers. The information then moves across the networking cable to the receiving computer and up that computer's networking layers until arriving at the same level that sent the information on the computer that sent the information. For example, if the Network layer sent information from computer A, it moves down through the Data Link and the Physical layers on the sending side, over the cable, and up the Physical and Data Link layers on the receiving side to its destination at the Network layer on computer B.

In a client/server environment, an example of the kind of information sent from the Network layer on computer A to the Network layer on computer B would be a network address and perhaps some error checking information added to the packet.

Interaction between adjacent layers occurs through an interface. The interface defines which services the lower networking layer offers to the upper one and how those services will be accessed. In addition, each layer on one computer acts as though it is communicating directly with the same layer on another computer.

The following sections describe the purpose of each of the seven layers of the OSI model and identify services that they provide to adjacent layers.

Application Layer

Layer 7, the topmost layer of the OSI model, is the Application layer. It serves as the window for application processes to access network services. This layer represents the services that directly support user applications, such as software for file transfers, for database access, and for e-mail. The lower levels support these tasks performed at the application level. The Application layer handles general network access, flow control, and error recovery.

Presentation Layer

Layer 6, the Presentation layer, determines the format used to exchange data among networked computers. It can be called the network's translator. At the sending computer, this layer translates data from a format sent down from the Application layer into a commonly recognized, intermediary format. At the receiving computer, this layer translates the intermediary format into a format useful to that computer's Application layer. The Presentation layer is responsible for protocol conversion, translating the data, encrypting the data, changing or converting the character set, and expanding graphics commands. The Presentation layer also manages data compression to reduce the number of bits that need to be transmitted.

A utility known as the redirector operates at this layer. The purpose of the redirector is to redirect input/output (I/O) operations to resources on a server.

Session Layer

Layer 5, the Session layer, allows two applications on different computers to establish, use, and end a connection called a session. This layer performs name recognition and the functions, such as security, needed to allow two applications to communicate over the network.

The Session layer provides synchronization between user tasks by placing checkpoints in the data stream. This way, if the network fails, only the data after the last checkpoint has to be retransmitted. This layer also implements dialog control between communicating processes, regulating which side transmits, when, for how long, and so on.

Transport Layer

Layer 4, the Transport layer, provides an additional connection level beneath the Session layer. The Transport layer ensures that packets are delivered error free, in sequence, and with no losses or duplications. This layer repackages messages, dividing long messages into several packets and collecting small packets together in one package. This allows the packets to be transmitted efficiently over the network. At the receiving end, the Transport layer unpacks the messages, reassembles the original messages, and typically sends an acknowledgment of receipt.

The Transport layer provides flow control, error handling, and is involved in solving problems concerned with the transmission and reception of packets.

Network Layer

Layer 3, the Network layer, is responsible for addressing messages and translating logical addresses and names into physical addresses. This layer also determines the route from the source to the destination computer. It determines which path the data should take based on network conditions, priority of service, and other factors. It also manages traffic problems on the network, such as packet switching, routing, and controlling the congestion of data.

If the network adapter on the router cannot transmit a data chunk as large as the source computer sends, the Network layer on the router compensates by breaking the data into smaller units. On the destination end, the Network layer reassembles the data.

Data Link Layer

Layer 2, the Data Link layer, sends data frames from the Network layer to the Physical layer. On the receiving end, it packages raw bits from the Physical layer into data frames. A data frame is an organized, logical structure in which data can be placed.

Figure 3.3 shows an example of a simple data frame. In this example, the sender ID represents the address of the computer that is sending the information; the destination ID represents the address of the computer to which the information is being sent. The control information is used for frame type, routing, and segmentation information. The data is the information itself. The cyclical redundancy check (CRC) represents error correction and verification information to ensure that the data frame is received properly.

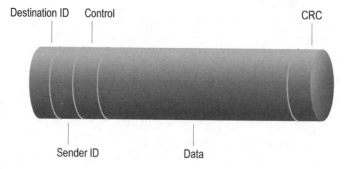

Figure 3.3 A simple data frame

The Data Link layer is responsible for providing the error-free transfer of these frames from one computer to another through the Physical layer. This allows the Network layer to assume virtually error-free transmission over the network connection.

Generally, when the Data Link layer sends a frame, it waits for an acknowledgment from the recipient. The recipient Data Link layer detects any problems with the frame that may have occurred during transmission. Frames that were not acknowledged, or frames that were damaged during transmission, are resent.

Note You will learn more about frames and packets in Lesson 3, "How Networks Send Data."

Physical Layer

Layer 1, the bottommost layer of the OSI model, is the Physical layer. This layer transmits the unstructured raw bit stream over a physical medium (such as the network cable). The Physical layer relates the electrical, optical, mechanical, and functional interfaces to the cable. The Physical layer also carries the signals that transmit data generated by all of the higher layers.

This layer defines how the cable is attached to the network adapter card. For example, it defines how many pins the connector has and each pin's function. It also defines which transmission technique will be used to send data over the network cable.

The Physical layer is responsible for transmitting bits (zeros and ones) from one computer to another. The bits themselves have no defined meaning at this level. This layer defines data encoding and bit synchronization, ensuring that when a transmitting host sends a 1 bit, it is received as a 1 bit, not a 0 bit. This layer also defines how long each bit lasts and how each bit is translated into the appropriate electrical or optical impulse for the network cable.

Q & A

Fill in the blanks in the following sentences.

1. The OSI model divides network activity into _____ layers.

2. The purpose of each layer is to provide services to the next _____ layer and shield the upper layer from the details of how the services are actually implemented.

3. At each layer the software adds some additional formatting or _____ to the packet.

4. Each layer on one computer acts as though it is communicating directly with the _____ layer on another computer.

5. The top, or _____, layer handles general network access, flow control and error recovery.

6. At the sending computer, the _____ layer translates data from a format sent down from the Application layer.

7. The _____ layer determines the route from the source to the destination computer.

8. The Data Link layer is responsible for sending _____ _____ from the Network layer to the Physical layer.

9. The _____ information in a data frame is used for frame type, routing, and segmentation information.

10. The _____ layer defines how the cable is attached to the network adapter card.

Answers

1. seven
2. higher
3. addressing
4. same
5. Application
6. Presentation
7. Network
8. data frames
9. control
10. Physical

The 802 Project Model

In the late 1970s, when LANs first began to emerge as a potential business tool, the IEEE realized that there was a need to define certain LAN standards. To accomplish this task, the IEEE launched what became known as Project 802, named for the year and month it began (1980, February).

Although the published IEEE 802 standards actually predated the ISO standards, both were in development at roughly the same time and both shared information which resulted in two compatible models.

Project 802 defined network standards for the physical components of a network—the interface card and the cabling—which are accounted for in the Physical and Data Link layers of the OSI model.

These standards, called the 802 specifications, have several areas of responsibility including:

- Network adapter cards.
- Wide area network components.
- Components used to create twisted-pair and coaxial cable networks.

The 802 specifications define the way network adapter cards access and transfer data over physical media. This includes connecting, maintaining, and disconnecting network devices.

IEEE 802 Categories

The LAN standards the 802 committees defined fall into 12 categories which can be identified by their 802 number as follows:

802.1   Internetworking

802.2   Logical Link Control (LLC)

802.3   Carrier-Sense Multiple Access with Collision Detection (CSMA/CD) LAN (Ethernet)

802.4   Token Bus LAN

802.5   Token Ring LAN

802.6   Metropolitan Area Network (MAN)

802.7   Broadband Technical Advisory Group

802.8   Fiber-Optic Technical Advisory Group

802.9   Integrated Voice/Data Networks

802.10   Network Security

802.11   Wireless Networks

802.12   Demand Priority Access LAN, 100BaseVG-AnyLAN

Enhancements to the OSI Model

The bottom two OSI layers, the Physical layer and the Data Link layer, define how multiple computers can simultaneously use the network without interfering with each other.

The IEEE 802 project worked with the specifications in those two layers to create specifications which have defined the dominant LAN environments.

The 802 standards committee decided that more detail was needed at the Data Link layer. They divided the Data Link layer into two sublayers:

- Logical Link Control (LLC)—establishing and terminating links, controlling frame traffic, sequencing frames and acknowledging frames
- Media Access Control (MAC)—managing media access, delimiting frames, checking frame errors and recognizing frame addresses

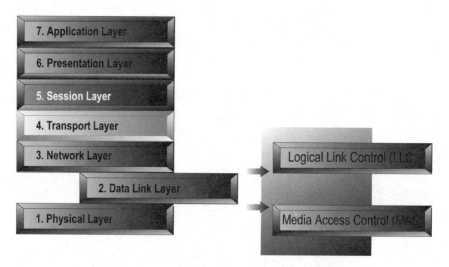

Figure 3.4 Project 802 Logical Link Control and Media Access Control sublayers

Logical Link Control Sublayer

The Logical Link Control sublayer manages data-link communication and defines the use of logical interface points, called service access points (SAPs). Other computers can refer to and use SAPs to transfer information from the Logical Link Control sublayer to the upper OSI layers. These standards are defined by 802.2.

Media Access Control Sublayer

As Figure 3.5 indicates, the Media Access Control sublayer is the lower of the two sublayers, providing shared access for the computers' network adapter cards to the Physical layer. The Media Access Control layer communicates directly with the network adapter card and is responsible for delivering error-free data between two computers on the network.

Categories 802.3, 802.4, 802.5, and 802.12 define standards for both this sublayer and OSI layer 1, the Physical layer.

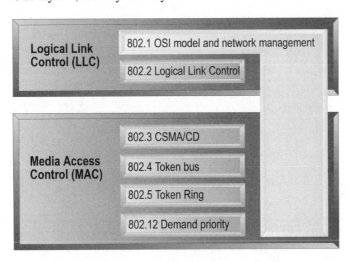

Figure 3.5 Project 802 Logical Link Control and Media Access Control standards

Q & A

Fill in the blanks in the following sentences.

1. The Project 802 specifications define the way _____ _____ _____ access and transfer data over physical media.

2. The 802 project divided the _____ layer of the OSI model into two sublayers, the Logical Link Control layer and Media Access Control layer.

3. The _____ sublayer communicates directly with the network adapter card and is responsible for delivering error-free data between two computers on the network.

4. The IEEE category _____ covers LAN standards for Ethernet.

5. The IEEE category _____ covers LAN standards for Token Ring.

Answers

1. network adapter cards
2. Data Link
3. Media Access Control
4. 802.3
5. 802.5

Activity

Run Demo 7.

Summary

The OSI and Project 802 models define the standard protocols used by networking hardware and software. These two models identify the way the complex process of sending data over a network is accomplished.

The OSI model has a layered architecture which divides network communications into seven layers. These layers are: Application, Presentation, Session, Transport, Network, Data Link, and Physical. Vendors design network products based on the specifications of the OSI layers.

The Project 802 model further defines standards for the physical components of a network. These standards address the Physical and Data Link layers of the OSI model and divide the Data Link layer into two sublayers: Logical Link Control (LLC) and Media Access Control (MAC).

Your Next Step

The OSI model is the operational foundation of networking. With an understanding of how the OSI layers work together to perform network communications, you can apply this knowledge to the real world of network functions. You will begin by learning about drivers—the software utility programs that make it possible for network hardware components to function.

Lesson 2: Drivers

What This Lesson Does

This lesson introduces the role of drivers in a network environment by explaining:

- The function of drivers.
- The importance of drivers in a network environment.
- How to implement and remove drivers.

Objectives

By the end of this lesson, you will be able to:

- Describe the role of drivers in a network environment, including their place in the OSI model.
- Identify sources for different drivers.
- Describe how to select and implement drivers given a networking situation.
- Install, update, and remove drivers.

Estimated lesson time 30 minutes

The Role of Drivers

A driver (sometimes called a device driver) is software that enables a computer to work with a particular device. Although a device might be installed on a computer, the computer's operating system cannot communicate with the device until the driver for that device has been installed and configured. It is the software driver that tells the computer how to drive or work with the device so that the device performs the job it is supposed to, the way it is supposed to.

There are drivers for nearly every type of computer device and peripheral including:

- Input devices, such as mouse devices.
- SCSI and IDE disk controllers.
- Both hard and floppy disk drives.
- Multimedia devices such as microphones, cameras, and recorders.
- Network adapter cards.
- Printers, plotters, tape drives, and so on.

Usually it is the computer's operating system that works with the driver in making the device perform. Printers provide a good illustration of how drivers are used. Printers built by various vendors all have different features and functions. It would be impossible for computer vendors to equip new computers with all of the software necessary to identify and work with every type of printer. Instead, printer manufacturers make drivers available for each printer. Before your computer can send documents to a printer, you must load the drivers for that particular printer so that your computer will be able to communicate with the printer.

As a general rule, manufacturers of components such as peripherals or cards that must be physically installed are responsible for supplying the drivers for their equipment. For example, network adapter card manufacturers are responsible for making drivers available for their cards. Drivers will come on a disk with the equipment when it is purchased, with the computer operating system, or they can be downloaded from a service such as The Microsoft Network (MSN), CompuServe, or other internet locations.

One other type of device that requires a driver and can cause a lot of confusion for users is the disk controller. Two types are the small computer system interface (SCSI) disk controllers and the integrated device electronics (IDE) disk controllers. SCSI controllers are multidevice chained interfaces used in many devices such as hard drives and CD-ROM drives. They require the correct driver to be installed and for the device to be correctly configured. If you replace a SCSI host adapter with one from a different company, you will need to install the correct driver and configure it correctly. The IDE disk drive is an interface in which the controller electronics reside on the drive itself, eliminating the need for a separate adapter card.

The Network Environment

Network drivers provide communication between a network adapter card and the network redirector running in the computer. The redirector is part of the networking software that accepts input/output (I/O) requests for remote files and then sends, or redirects, them over the network to another computer. The network administrator uses a utility commonly called a setup program to install the driver. During installation, the driver is stored on the computer's hard disk.

Drivers and the OSI Model

Network adapter card drivers reside in the Media Access Control sublayer of the Data Link layer of the OSI model. The Media Access Control sublayer is responsible for providing shared access for the computer's network adapter cards to the Physical layer. In other words, the network adapter card drivers ensure direct communication between the computer and the network adapter card. This, in turn, provides a link between the computer and the rest of the network.

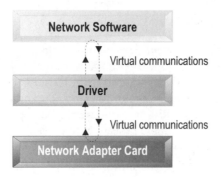

Figure 3.6 Communication between the network adapter card and network software

Drivers and the Networking Software

It is common for the network adapter card manufacturer to provide drivers to the networking software vendor so that the drivers can be included with the network operating software.

The operating system vendor's hardware compatibility list (HCL) lists the drivers they have tested and included with the operating system.

The HCL for Microsoft Windows NT Server, for example, lists more than 100 network adapter card drivers from various manufacturers that Microsoft has tested and included with Windows NT Server. This means that Windows NT Server, as it is shipped, includes drivers that will allow it to work with more than 100 different network adapter cards.

Even if the driver for a particular card has not been included with the network operating system, it is normal for the network adapter card manufacturer to include drivers for most popular network operating systems on a disk that is shipped with the card. Before buying a card, however, it is necessary to make sure that the card has a driver that will work with a particular network operating system.

Implementation

Implementing and managing drivers includes installing, configuring, updating, and removing them.

Installing

Each network operating system will have its own method for installing drivers, but current installation procedures in the popular network operating systems normally use an interactive graphical interface to lead the installer through the process.

Microsoft Windows NT Server, for example, features a utility called the Control Panel. It contains the interactive icons that lead the user through the steps involved in a network adapter card driver installation.

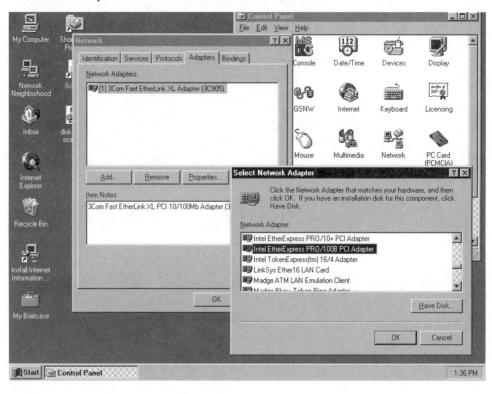

Figure 3.7 Installing a network adapter card on Windows NT Server

Configuring

Network adapter cards usually have configurable options that must be set correctly for the network adapter card to function properly. As was discussed in Chapter 2: Lesson 3, "Network Adapter Cards," this can be done through jumpers or DIP switches.

However, most of the newer network adapter cards are software configurable or are Plug-and-Play PnP bios compliant. There are no DIP switches or jumpers to configure. The configuration is done through the software during or after the installation of the drivers, or as with a Plug-and-Play compliant system, i.e. Microsoft Windows 95, the operating system will attempt to configure the hardware device automatically.

Updating

Occasionally, a vendor will write additions or changes to a driver that will improve a component's performance. Vendors can send these driver changes in the mail to registered users, post them on a bulletin board, or make them available through a service such as The Microsoft Network (MSN), CompuServe or other internet location. The user can then implement the updated driver.

The process of updating drivers is usually similar to installing them.

Removing

It may occasionally be necessary to remove drivers. This will happen, for example, when for some reason the original drivers conflict with newer drivers. In another case, if a piece of equipment is being removed, it would be a good idea to remove its drivers, if any, to ensure that no conflicts arise between the old drivers and any new drivers which may be installed later.

The process of removing drivers is similar to installing or updating them.

Q & A

Circle the letter of the best answer for each of the following sentences.

1. A driver is:
    a. hardware.
    b. a peripheral device.
    c. a card.
    d. software.

2. The HCL is:
    a. a list of network operating system vendors.
    b. a list of hardware the operating system vendor has approved for use.
    c. a list of all network adapter cards and their compatible drivers.
    d. a list of LAN drivers.

3. In the networking environment, a network adapter card driver is needed for:
    a. communication with other adapter cards on a network.
    b. communication between the adapter card and the computer's operating system.
    c. communication between the file server and the other computers on the network.
    d. communication between different types of computers on a network.

4. Select the statement which is most correct about printer drivers.
    a. There is one universal printer driver that will allow full functionality of all printers.
    b. All printers made by a specific printer manufacturer can always use the same printer driver and have full functionality.
    c. There is a specific printer driver designed for every model of printer that will allow the full functionality of that model of printer.
    d. A laser printer driver from one manufacturer will provide full functionality for all laser printers regardless of the manufacturer.

Answers

1. d. software.
2. b. a list of hardware the operating system vendor has approved for use.
3. b. communication between the adapter card and the computer's operating system.
4. c. There is a specific printer driver designed for every model of printer that will allow the full functionality of that model of printer.

Activity

Use the following steps to run Lab 8.

Lab 8: Installing Network Adapter Cards

What This Lab Does

This lab teaches you how to install the software for the network adapter cards in your computer, and how to configure the cards. Also, in case you change the network adapter card, it teaches you how to remove the software installed for the existing network adapter card. It is important to remember that this lab simulates a Windows NT Server 4.0 environment.

Objectives

By the end of this lab, you will be able to:

- Install the software to support network adapter cards in Windows NT Server-based computer.

- Configure network adapter cards installed in a Windows NT Server-based computer.

- Delete the software for network adapter cards in Windows NT Server-based computer.

Exercise 1: Installing Network Adapter Cards

1. From the **Start** menu, point to **Programs**, then **Networking Essentials**, and click **Lab8**.

   The **Networking Essentials – Lab8** window appears.

2. Click **Control Panel**.

   This opens **Control Panel**.

3. In **Control Panel**, double-click the **Network** icon.

4. Click the **Adapters** Tab.

   Notice that the **Network Adapters:** text box is empty.

5. Click **Add**.

   The **Select Network Adapter** window appears.

6. In the **Network Adapter Card** field, make sure that **Intel® EtherExpress PRO Ethernet Adapter** appears and is highlighted, and then click **OK.**

   The **Intel EtherExpress PRO Ethernet Adapter Setup** window appears.

7. Use the following settings for your card:

Parameter	Setting
Interrupt Number	5
I/O Port Address	0x300
I/O Channel Ready	Late
Transceiver Type	Thick Net (AUI/DIX)

8. Click **OK** to accept the default settings.

    If there is more than one type of bus available on the Windows NT Server computer, an **Intel EtherExpress PRO Ethernet Adapter Bus Location** window will appear. This window allows you to select the appropriate Bus (i.e., EISA or PCI) in the **Type** menu, and to select the appropriate number of the bus in the **Number** menu.

9. Click **OK** to accept the default settings.

    The Windows NT Setup dialog stating, "Setup needs to copy some Windows NT files" appears.

10. Type **C:\i386** and click **Continue**.

    The Network window appears.

    Notice that the Intel EtherExpress PRO Adapter card is now listed in the **Network Adapters:** text box.

11. Click the **Protocols** Tab.

12. Click **Add**.

    The **Select Network Protocol** dialog box appears.

13. Click **NetBEUI Protocol**, and then click **OK**.

14. To add another network adapter card, click the **Adapters** Tab and then click **Add**.

    The **Select Network Adapter** appears.

15. Select the **3Com 3C508 ISA 16-bit Ethernet Adapter**, and click **OK**.

16. Use the following settings for your card:

Parameter	Setting
Interrupt Number	3
I/O Port Address	0x300
I/O Channel Ready	Late
Transceiver Type	Thick Net (AUI/DIX)

17. Click **OK** to accept the default settings.

    If there is more than one type of bus available on the Windows NT Server, a **3Com 3C508 ISA 16-bit Adapter Bus Location** window will appear. This window allows you to select the appropriate Bus (i.e., EISA or PCI) in the **Type** menu and to select the appropriate number of the bus in the **Number** menu.

18. Click **OK** to accept the default settings.

    The **Windows NT Setup** dialog stating, "Setup needs to copy some Windows NT files" appears.

19. Type **C:\i386** and click **Continue**.

    The Network window appears.

    Notice that the **3Com 3C508 ISA Adapter** is now listed in the **Network Adapters:** text box.

Exercise 2: Deleting a Network Adapter Card Driver

1. In the Network window, select the 3Com 3C508 ISA Adapter in the **Network Adapters:** window.

2. Click **Remove**.

   A warning message appears indicating that, "This action will permanently remove the component from the system…"

3. Click **Yes**.

   Notice that the **3Com 3C508 ISA Adapter** is no longer in the list of installed adapter cards.

4. Click **Close**.

   A dialog box appears stating, "You must shut down and restart your computer before the new settings will take effect. Do you wish to restart now?"

5. Click **Yes**.

   A dialog box appears stating, "On the File menu, click Exit Lab 8"

6. Click **OK**.

7. On the File menu in the upper left hand corner of the screen, not on the Control Panel File menu, click **Exit Lab 8**.

Summary

A driver is a software utility that enables a computer to work with a particular device. Devices such as mouse devices, disk drives, network adapter cards, and printers each come with their own driver. The computer's operating system will not recognize a device until its associated driver has been installed, unless the operating system is Plug and Play-compliant. Microsoft Windows 95 is an example of a Plug and Play-compliant operating system.

Most drivers are provided by the operating system or network operating system vendor. If not, drivers are included on a disk with equipment when it is purchased. In some cases, drivers can be downloaded from a service such as The Microsoft Network (MSN), CompuServe, or other internet location.

In a networking environment, each computer has a network adapter card and its associated driver. Together they enable the computer to send data out onto the network. Current installation procedures, usually in the form of an interactive graphical interface, lead the installer through the process. Occasionally it may be necessary to update or remove a driver. These procedures are similar to installing the driver.

Your Next Step

Now that your computers and peripherals can communicate (because the correct drivers have been installed, of course) the network is ready to begin sending data from one computer to another. However, most files are too large to put onto a cable intact. They must be broken into manageable units called packets.

Packets are the building blocks of network communication. Understanding them is essential to understanding the functional aspects of LAN/WAN technology, as you will see in the next lesson.

Lesson 3: How Networks Send Data

What This Lesson Does

This lesson introduces the concept of packets as the basic building blocks of network data communications. It presents an overview of:

- The role and importance of packets in network communications.
- The basic parts of a packet.
- The origin and formation of packets.
- How packets are sent and received.
- How packets are joined with other packets to complete the transmission of data.

Objectives

By the end of this lesson, you will be able to:

- Define the term packet, including its function and components.
- Describe the contents and function of each packet component: header, data, and trailer.
- Describe how packets are sent across a network.

Estimated lesson time 35 minutes

The Function of Packets in Network Communications

Data tends to exist as rather large files. However, networks cannot operate if computers put large amounts of data on the cable at one time. There are two reasons why putting large chunks of data on the cable at one time slows down the network.

First, large amounts of data sent as one large unit ties up the network and makes timely interaction and communications impossible because one computer is flooding the cable with data.

The second reason networks reformat large chunks of data into smaller packages is in case there is an error in transmission. Only a small section of data is affected, so only a small amount of data must be resent, making it relatively easy to recover from the error.

Figure 3.8 Large continuous streams of data slow down the network

In order for many users at once to transmit data quickly and easily across the network, the data must be broken into small, manageable chunks. These chunks are called packets, or frames. Although the terms packet and frame are used interchangeably, there are some differences based on the type of network. This lesson will use the term packet.

Packets are the basic units of network communications. With data divided into packets, individual transmissions are speeded up so that every computer on the network will have more opportunities to transmit and receive data. At the target (receiving) computer, the packets are collected and reassembled in the proper order to form the original data.

Data

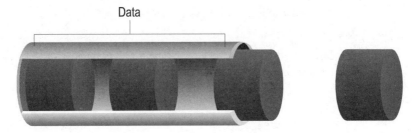

Figure 3.9 Breaking data in packets

When the network operating system at the sending computer breaks the data into packets, it adds special control information to each frame. This makes it possible to:

- Send the original, disassembled data in small chunks.
- Reassemble the data in the proper order at its destination.
- Check the data for errors after it has been reassembled.

Packet Structure

Packets may contain several types of data including:

- Information, such as messages or files.
- Certain types of computer control data and commands, such as service requests.
- Session control codes, such as error correction, that indicate the need for a retransmission.

Packet Components

All packets have certain components in common. These include:

- A source address identifying the sending computer.
- The data that is intended for transmission.
- A destination address identifying the recipient.
- Instructions that tell network components how to pass the data along.
- Information that tells the receiving computer how to connect the packet to other packets in order to reassemble the complete data package.
- Error checking information to ensure that the data arrives intact.

The components are grouped into three sections: header, data, and trailer.

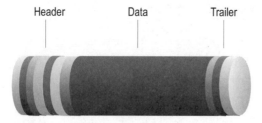

Figure 3.10 Packet components

Header

The header includes:

- An alert signal to indicate that the packet is being transmitted.
- The source address.
- The destination address.
- Clock information to synchronize transmission.

Data

This is the actual data being sent. This part of the packet can be of various sizes, depending on the network. The data section on most networks varies from 512 bytes (0.5k) to 4k.

Because most original data strings are much longer than 4k, data must be broken into chunks small enough to be put into packets. It takes many packets to complete the transmission of a large file.

Trailer

The exact content of the trailer varies depending on the communication method, or protocol. However, the trailer usually contains an error checking component called a cyclical redundancy check (CRC). The CRC is a number produced by a mathematical calculation on the packet at its source. When the packet arrives at its destination, the calculation is redone. If the results are the same, it indicates that the data in the packet has remained stable. If the calculation at the destination differs from the calculation at the source, it means the data has changed during the transmission. In that case, the CRC routine signals the source computer to retransmit the data.

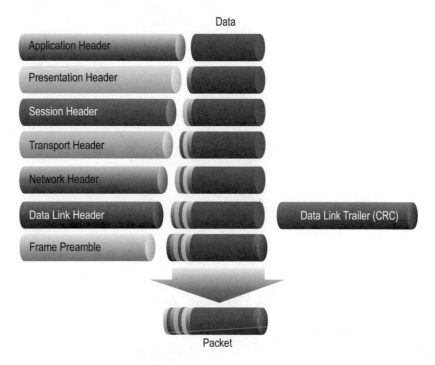

Figure 3.11 The complete packet

Different networks have different formats for the packets and allow different size packets. The packet size limits determine how many packets the network operating system will create from one large piece of data.

Creating Packets

The packet creation process begins at the Application layer of the OSI model, where the data is generated. Information to be sent across the network starts at the Application layer and descends through all seven layers.

At each layer, information relevant to that layer is added to the data. This information is for the corresponding layer in the receiving machine. Information added at the Data Link layer in the sending computer, for instance, will be read by the Data Link layer in the receiving computer.

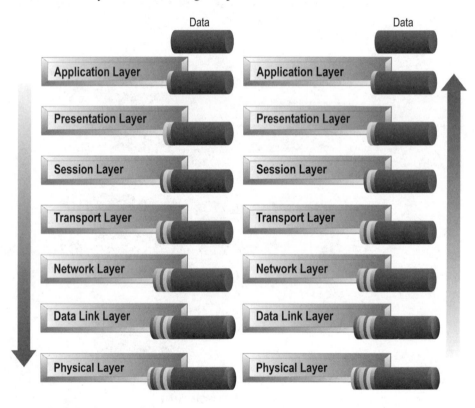

Figure 3.12 Packet creation process

At the Transport layer, the original block of data gets broken into the actual packets. The structure of the packets is defined by the protocol used by the two computers.

When the packet gets to the Transport layer, sequence information is added which will guide the receiving computer in reassembling the data from packets.

When the packets finally pass through the Physical layer on their way to the cable, they contain information from each of the other six layers.

Packet Addressing

Most packets on the network are addressed to a specific computer and, as a result, get the attention of only one computer. Every network adapter card sees all packets sent on its cable segment, but it only interrupts the computer if the packet's address matches its individual address. Alternatively, a broadcast type address may also be used. Packets sent with a broadcast type address can get the simultaneous attention of many computers on the network.

In situations involving large networks that cover states (or even countries) and offer several possible communication routes, the network's connectivity and switching components use the packet's addressing information to determine the best route for packet addressing.

Directing Packets

Network components use the addressing information in packets to direct the packets to their destinations, or keep them away from network locations where they do not belong. The following two functions play a key role in properly directing packets:

- Packet forwarding

  Computers can send a packet on to the next appropriate network component based on the address in the packet's header.

- Packet filtering

  This refers to the process of using criteria such as an address to select specific packets.

Q & A

Fill in the blanks for questions 1 through 4, and circle True or False for questions 5 through 8.

1. With data masses divided into _____, individual transmissions are speeded up so that every computer on the network will have more opportunities to transmit and receive data.

2. The packet creation process begins at the _____ layer of the OSI model.

3. Packets may contain session control codes, such as error correction that indicate the need for a _____.

4. A packet's components are grouped into three sections: _____, data, and trailer.

5. In a packet, the header usually contains an error checking component called a CRC.   True   False

6. The structure of the packets is defined by the communication method, known as a protocol, used by the two computers.   True   False

7. Every network adapter card sees all packets sent on its segment, but it only interrupts the computer if the packet's address matches its individual address.   True   False

8. The trailer of a packet contains the destination address.   True   False

Answers

1. packets
2. Application
3. retransmission
4. header
5. False. The trailer contains this component.
6. True.
7. True.
8. False. The header contains the destination address.

Example: Packets in Printing

The following example illustrates how, in step-by-step fashion, packets are used in network communications.

A large print job must be sent from a computer to a print server.

1. First, the sending computer establishes a connection with the print server.

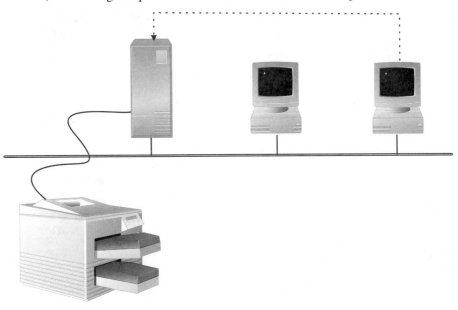

Figure 3.13 Establishing a connection with a print server

2. The computer then breaks the large print job into packets with each packet containing the destination address, the source address, the data, and control information.

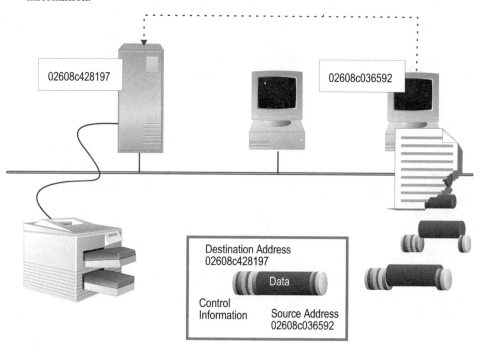

Figure 3.14 Creating packets

3. The network adapter card in each computer examines the receiver's address on all frames sent on its segment of the network. However, because each network adapter card has its own specific address, the card does not interrupt the computer until it detects a frame addressed specifically to it.

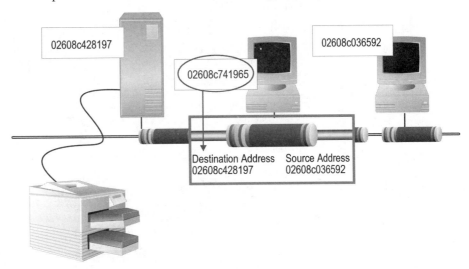

Figure 3.15 Examining the receiver's address

4. At the destination computer, in this example it is the print server, the packets enter through the cable into the network adapter card.

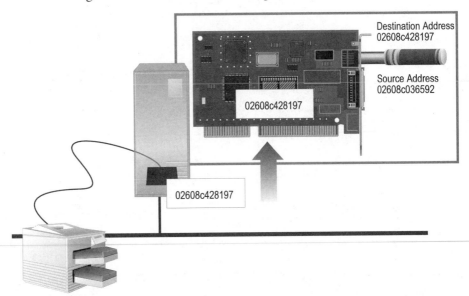

Figure 3.16 Network adapter card accepts packets addressed to the print server

5. The network software processes the frame stored in the network adapter card's receive buffer. Sufficient processing power to receive and examine each incoming frame is built into the network adapter card. This means that no computer resources are used until the adapter card identifies a frame addressed to the specific computer.

6. The network operating system in the receiving computer reassembles the packets back into the original text file and moves the file into the computer's memory. From there it is sent to the printer.

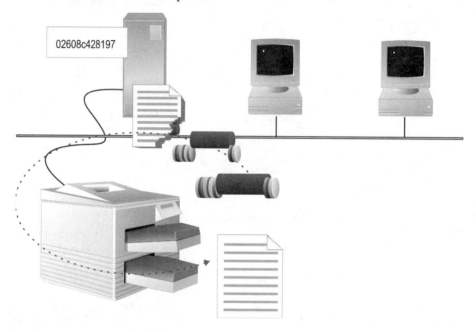

02608c428197

Figure 3.17 Reassembled packets sent to the printer

Summary

Before data is sent out onto the network, the sending computer divides it into small packages easily transmitted on the network cable. These packets, or chunks, of data are the basic units of network communications. They make timely interaction and communications on a network possible.

All packets have these basic components: source address, data, destination address, instructions, and error checking information. Each packet has three sections: a header which contains an alert signal, source and destination addresses, and clock information, the data, and a trailer which contains the error checking component (CRC).

Packet creation starts at the Application layer of the OSI model and descends through all of the layers of the model, with information added to the packet at each layer.

Your Next Step

Now that you are acquainted with the concept of packets, you are ready to begin learning how computers send packets back and forth on networks.

Computers, in a sense, are like international organizations when it comes to communicating with each other. There are a variety of languages and methods they can use. The important thing to remember is that everyone involved in the communication needs to be speaking the same language and following the same rules, or protocols, for the communication to be successful.

Computers, too, have their protocols which make it possible for two different types of machines to communicate. In the next lesson, you will be introduced to the major computer protocols.

Lesson 4: Protocols

What This Lesson Does

This lesson introduces the concept of protocols in a networking environment. It explains the role that protocols play in network communications and describes how different protocols work at various OSI levels.

You will learn:

- What protocols are.
- What protocols do.
- Where they come from.
- How they work together in stacks.
- How to implement and remove protocols.

Objectives

By the end of this lesson, you will be able to:

- Identify the function of protocols and protocol stacks.
- Describe the network processes which use protocols and how they use them.
- Map particular protocols to the appropriate OSI levels.

Estimated lesson time 45 minutes

The Function of Protocols

Protocols are rules and procedures for communicating. For example, diplomats from one country adhere to protocol to guide them in interacting with diplomats from other countries. The use of communication rules applies in the same way in the computer environment. When several computers are networked, the rules and technical procedures governing their communication and interaction are called protocols.

There are three points to keep in mind when thinking about protocols in a network environment:

1. There are many protocols. While each protocol allows basic communications, they have different purposes and accomplish different tasks. Each protocol has its own advantages and restrictions.

2. Some protocols work at various OSI layers. The layer at which a protocol works describes its function.

   For example, a certain protocol works at the Physical layer, meaning that the protocol at that layer ensures that the data packet passes through the network adapter card and out onto the network cable.

3. Several protocols may work together in what is known as a protocol stack, or suite.

   Just as a network incorporates functions at every layer of the OSI model, different protocols also work together at different levels in a single protocol stack. The levels in the protocol stack map or correspond to the layers of the OSI model. Taken together, the protocols describe the entire stack's functions and capabilities.

How Protocols Work

The entire technical operation of transmitting data over the network has to be broken down into discrete systematic steps. At each step, certain actions take place which cannot take place at any other step. Each step has its own rules and procedures, or protocol.

The steps must be carried out in a consistent order that is the same on every computer in the network. In the sending computer, these steps must be carried out from the top down. In the receiving machine, these steps must be carried out from the bottom up.

The Sending Computer

At the sending computer, the protocol:

- Breaks the data into smaller sections, called packets, that the protocol can handle.
- Adds addressing information to the packets so the destination computer on the network will know the data belongs to it.
- Prepares the data for actual transmission through the network adapter card and out onto the network cable.

The Receiving Computer

At the receiving computer, a protocol carries out the same series of steps in reverse order. The receiving computer:

- Takes the data packets off the cable.
- Brings the data packets into the computer through the network adapter card.
- Strips the data packets of all of the transmitting information added by the sending computer.
- Copies the data from the packets to a buffer for reassembly.
- Passes the reassembled data to the application in a usable form.

Both the sending and the receiving computers need to perform each step the same way so that the data will look the same when it is received as it did when it was sent.

For example, two protocols might both break data into packets and add on various sequencing, timing, and error checking information, but they will each do it differently. Therefore, a computer using one of these protocols will not be able to communicate successfully with a computer using the other protocol.

Routable vs. Nonroutable Protocols

Until the mid-1980s, most LANs were isolated. They served a single department or company and were rarely connected to any larger environments. As LAN technology matured, however, and the data communication needs of businesses expanded, LANs became components in larger data communication networks where LANs talked to each other.

Data being sent from one LAN to another along any of several available paths is routed. The protocols that support multipath LAN-to-LAN communications are known as routable protocols. Because routable protocols can be used to tie several LANs together and create new wide-area environments, they are becoming increasingly important.

Q & A

Fill in the blanks in the following sentences.

1. A sending computer breaks the data into smaller sections, called
   _____, that the protocol can handle.

2. Several protocols may work together in what is known as a protocol
   _____.

3. A receiving computer copies the data from the packets to a _____ for
   reassembly.

4. Protocols that support multipath LAN-to-LAN communications are known as
   _____ protocols.

5. The receiving computer passes the reassembled data to the
   _____ in a usable form.

Answers

1. packets
2. stack
3. buffer
4. routable
5. application

Protocols in a Layered Architecture

In a network, several protocols have to work together to ensure that the data is:

- Prepared
- Transferred
- Received
- Acted upon

The work of the various protocols must be coordinated so that there are no conflicts or incomplete operations. The answer to this coordination effort is called layering.

Protocol Stacks

A protocol stack is a combination of protocols. Each layer specifies a different protocol for handling a function or subsystem of the communication process. Each layer has its own set of rules.

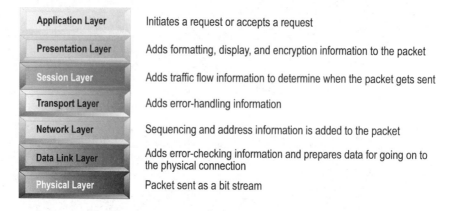

Figure 3.18 The OSI model showing the layers of protocols

As in the OSI model, the lower layers in the stack specify how vendors can make their equipment connect to equipment from other vendors. The upper layers specify rules for conducting communications sessions and the interpretation of applications. The higher in the stack, the more sophisticated the tasks and their associated protocols become.

The Binding Process

The binding process allows a great deal of flexibility in setting up a network. Protocols and network adapter cards can be mixed and matched on an as-needed basis. For example, two protocol stacks, such as IPX/SPX and TCP/IP, can be bound to one network adapter card. If there is more than one network adapter card in the computer, one protocol stack can be bound to either or both network adapter cards.

The binding order determines the order in which the operating system runs the protocol. If there are multiple protocols bound to a single adapter card, it indicates the order in which the protocols will be used to attempt a successful connection. Typically, the binding process occurs when either the operating system or the protocol is installed or initialized. For example, if TCP/IP is bound as the first protocol, TCP/IP will be used to attempt a network connection. If this network connection fails, your computer will transparently attempt to make a connection using the next protocol in the binding order.

Binding is not limited to the protocol stack being bound to the network adapter card. Protocol stacks need to be bound or associated with components above and below it, so data can proceed smoothly through the stack during execution. For example, TCP/IP may be bound to the NetBIOS Session layer above and the network adapter card driver below it. The network adapter card driver is also bound to the network adapter card.

Standard Stacks

The computer industry has designated several stacks as standard protocol models. The most important ones include:

- The ISO/OSI protocol suite
- The IBM Systems Network Architecture (SNA)
- Digital DECnet™
- Novell NetWare
- Apple AppleTalk®
- The Internet protocol suite, TCP/IP

Protocols exist at each level of these stacks doing the job specified by that level. However, the communication tasks networks need to perform are assigned to protocols working as one of three protocol types. These protocol types map roughly to the OSI model. They are:

- Application
- Transport
- Network

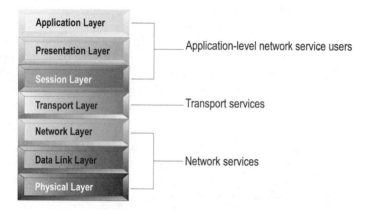

Figure 3.19 Communication tasks within the OSI model

Application Protocols

Application protocols work at the upper layer of the OSI model. They provide application-to-application interaction and data exchange. More popular application protocols include:

- APPC (advanced program-to-program communication)—IBM's peer-to-peer SNA protocol, mostly used on AS/400®s.
- FTAM (file transfer access and management)—An OSI file access protocol.
- X.400—A CCITT protocol for international e-mail transmissions.
- X.500—A CCITT protocol for file and directory services across several systems.
- SMTP (simple mail transfer protocol)—An Internet protocol for transferring e-mail.
- FTP (File Transfer Protocol)—An Internet file transfer protocol.
- SNMP (simple network management protocol)—An Internet protocol for monitoring networks and network components.

- Telnet—An Internet protocol for logging on to remote hosts and processing data locally.
- Microsoft SMBs (server message blocks) and client shells or redirectors.
- NCP (Novell NetWare Core Protocol) and Novell client shells or redirectors.
- AppleTalk and Apple Share®—Apple's networking protocol suite.
- AFP (AppleTalk filing protocol) Apple's protocol for remote file access.
- DAP (data access protocol)—A DECnet file access protocol.

Transport Protocols

Transport protocols provide for communication sessions between computers and ensure that data is able to move reliably between computers. Popular transport protocols include:

- TCP (Transmission Control Protocol)—The TCP/IP protocol for guaranteed delivery of sequenced data.
- SPX—Part of Novell's IPX/SPX (internetwork packet exchange/sequential packet exchange) protocol suite for sequenced data.
- NWLink is the Microsoft implementation of the IPX/SPX protocol.
- NetBEUI [NetBIOS (network basic input/output system) extended user interface)]—Establishes communication sessions between computers (NetBIOS) and provide the underlying data transport services (NetBEUI).
- ATP (AppleTalk transaction protocol), NBP (name binding protocol)—Apple's communication session and data transport protocols.

Network Protocols

Network protocols provide what are called link services. These protocols handle addressing and routing information, error checking, and retransmission requests. Network protocols also define rules for communicating in a particular networking environment such as Ethernet or Token Ring. The more popular network protocols include:

- IP (Internet Protocol)—The TCP/IP protocol for packet forwarding routing.
- IPX (internetwork packet exchange)—NetWare's protocol for packet forwarding and routing.
- NWLink—The Microsoft implementation of the IPX/SPX protocol.
- NetBEUI—A transport protocol that provides data transport services for NetBIOS sessions and applications.
- DDP (datagram delivery protocol)—An AppleTalk data transport protocol.

Protocol Standards

The OSI model is used to define what protocols should be used at each layer. Products from different vendors that subscribe to this model can communicate with each other.

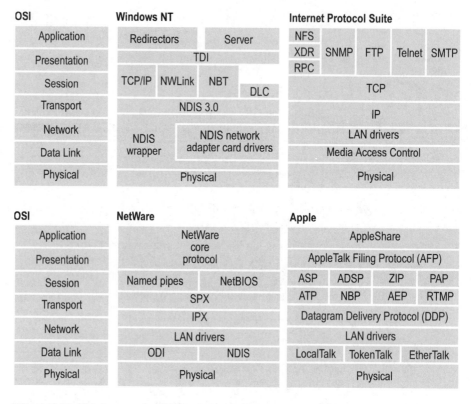

Figure 3.20 Vendor compatibility

The ISO, the IEEE, ANSI (American National Standards Institute), CCITT (Comité Consultatif Internationale de Télégraphie et Téléphonie), now called the ITU (International Telecommunications Union) and other standards bodies have developed protocols which map to some of the layers in the OSI model.

The IEEE protocols at the Physical layer are:

- 802.3 (Ethernet)

  This is a logical bus network that can transmit data at 10 Mbps. Data is transmitted on the wire to every computer. Only those meant to receive the data acknowledge the transmission. The CSMA/CD protocol regulates network traffic by allowing a transmission only when the wire is clear and no other computer is transmitting.

- 802.4 (token passing)

  This is a bus layout that uses a token passing scheme. Every computer receives all of the data but only the ones addressed respond. A token that travels the wire determines which computer is able to broadcast.

- 802.5 (Token Ring)

  This is a logical ring network that transmits at either 4 Mbps or 16 Mbps. Even though this is called a ring, it looks like a star with each computer branching off a hub. The ring is actually inside the hub. A token traveling around the ring determines which computer may send data.

Within the Data Link layer, the IEEE has further defined protocols to facilitate communications activity at the Media Access Control sublayer.

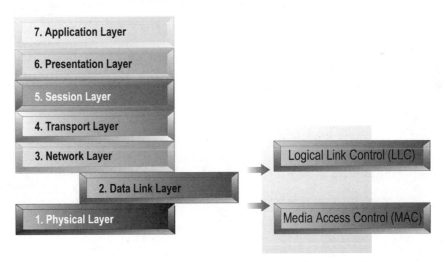

Figure 3.21 Media Access Control driver or network adapter card driver

214 Networking Essentials, Second Edition

A Media Access Control driver is the device driver located at the Media Access Control sublayer. This driver is also known as the network adapter card driver. It provides low-level access to network adapters by providing data transmission support and some basic adapter management functions.

A Media Access Control protocol determines which computer may use the network cable if several computers are trying to use it simultaneously. CSMA/CD, the 802.3 protocol, allows computers to transmit data if there is no other computer transmitting. If two hosts transmit simultaneously, a collision occurs. The protocol detects the collision and halts all transmission until the wire is clear. Then, each computer can begin transmitting again after waiting a random period of time.

Q & A

Fill in the blanks in the following sentences.

1. To avoid conflicts or incomplete operations, protocols are _____ in an orderly fashion.

2. The _____ order indicates where the protocol sits in the protocol stack.

3. Three protocol types which map roughly to the OSI model are application, _____, and network.

4. Application protocols work at the upper layer of the OSI model and provide _____ _____ between applications.

5. A network adapter card driver protocol resides in the _____ _____ _____ sublayer of the OSI model.

6. Rules for communicating in a particular LAN environment such as Ethernet or Token Ring are called _____ protocols.

Answers

1. layered
2. binding
3. transport
4. data exchange
5. Media Access Control
6. network

Common Protocols

This section looks at some of the most commonly used protocols. They are:

- TCP/IP
- NetBEUI
- X.25
- Xerox Network System (XNS™)
- IPX/SPX and NWLink
- APPC
- AppleTalk
- OSI protocol suite
- DECnet

TCP/IP

Transmission Control Protocol/Internet Protocol (TCP/IP) is an industry standard suite of protocols providing communications in a heterogeneous environment. In addition, TCP/IP provides a routable, enterprise networking protocol and access to the worldwide Internet and its resources.

It has become the standard protocol used for interoperability among many different types of computers. This interoperability is one of the primary advantages to TCP/IP. Almost all networks support TCP/IP as a protocol. TCP/IP also supports routing, and is commonly used as an internetworking protocol.

Because of its popularity, TCP/IP has become the de facto standard for internetworking.

Other protocols written specifically for the TCP/IP suite include:

- SMTP (simple mail transfer protocol)—E-mail
- FTP (File Transfer Protocol)—For exchanging files among computers running TCP/IP
- SNMP (simple network management protocol)—Network management

Historically, there were two primary disadvantages of TCP/IP: its size and speed. TCP/IP is a relatively large protocol stack which can cause problems in MS-DOS-based clients. However, on graphical user interface (GUI)-based operating systems, such as Windows NT or Windows 95, the size is not an issue and speed is about the same as IPX.

NetBEUI

NetBEUI is NetBIOS extended user interface. Originally, NetBIOS and NetBEUI were very tightly tied together, and considered one protocol. However, several network vendors separated NetBIOS, the Session layer protocol, out so that it could be used with other routable transport protocols. NetBIOS (network basic input/output system) is an IBM Session layer LAN interface that acts as an application interface to the network. It provides the tools for a program to establish a session with another program over the network. It is very popular because so many application programs support it.

NetBEUI is a small, fast, and efficient Transport layer protocol that is supplied with all Microsoft network products. It has been available since the mid-1980s and was supplied with the first networking product from Microsoft, MS®-NET.

NetBEUI advantages include its small stack size (important for MS-DOS-based computers), its speed of data transfer on the network medium, and its compatibility with all Microsoft-based networks.

The major disadvantage of NetBEUI is that it does not support routing. It is also limited to Microsoft-based networks.

X.25

X.25 is a set of protocols incorporated in a packet switching network made up of switching services. The switching services were originally established to connect remote terminals to main frame host systems.

XNS

Xerox Network System (XNS) was developed by Xerox for their Ethernet LANs. It became widely used in the 1980s, but has been slowly replaced by TCP/IP. It is a large, slow protocol, but produces more broadcasts, causing more network traffic.

IPX/SPX and NWLink

Internetwork packet exchange/sequenced packet exchange is a protocol stack that is used in Novell networks. Like NetBEUI, it is a relatively small and fast protocol on a LAN. But, unlike NetBEUI, it does support routing. IPX/SPX is a derivative of XNS.

Microsoft provides NWLink as its version of IPX/SPX. It is a transport protocol and is routable.

APPC

APPC (advanced program-to-program communication) is IBM's transport protocol developed as part of its systems network architecture (SNA). It was designed to enable application programs running on different computers to communicate and exchange data directly.

AppleTalk

AppleTalk is Apple Computer's proprietary protocol stack designed to enable Apple Macintosh® computers to share files and printers in a networked environment.

OSI Protocol Suite

The OSI protocol suite is a complete protocol stack. Each protocol maps directly to a single layer of the OSI model. The OSI protocol suite includes routing and transport protocols, IEEE 802 series protocols, a Session layer protocol, a Presentation layer protocol, and several Application layer protocols designed to provide full networking functionality, including file access, printing, and terminal emulation.

DECnet

DECnet is Digital Equipment Corporation's proprietary protocol stack. It is a set of hardware and software products that implement the Digital Network Architecture (DNA). It defines communication networks over Ethernet local area networks, fiber distributed data interface metropolitan area networks (FDDI MANs), and WANs that use private or public data transmission facilities. DECnet can also use TCP/IP and OSI protocols as well as its own protocols. It is a routable protocol.

DECnet has been updated several times; each update is called a phase. The current revision is DECnet Phase V, and the protocols used are both Digital proprietary and a fairly complete implementation of the OSI protocol suite.

Implementing and Removing Protocols

Protocols are implemented and removed in much the same way that drivers are added and removed. Depending on the operating system, the essential protocols will be installed automatically during the initial operating system installation. In Windows NT Server 4.0, for example, the default protocol is TCP/IP.

To install protocols such as NWLink after the initial installation, the network operating system will usually include a utility that leads the administrator through the process. In Windows NT Server, for example, the Setup program provides a series of graphical windows that lead the administrator through the process of:

- Installing a new protocol.
- Changing the order in which the installed protocols have been linked.
- Removing a protocol.

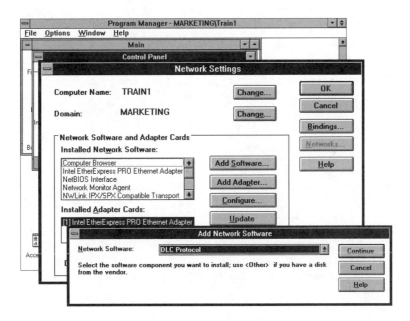

Figure 3.22 Windows NT Server Setup program

Q & A

Fill in the blanks in the following sentences.

1. TCP/IP supports routing, and is commonly used as an
   _____ protocol.

2. NetBIOS is an IBM Session layer LAN interface that acts as an
   _____ interface to the network.

3. APPC (advanced program-to-program communication) is IBM's
   _____ protocol.

4. To help the network administrator install a protocol after the initial system
   installation, a _____ is included with the operating system.

Answers

1. internetworking
2. application
3. transport
4. utility

Summary

Protocols in a networking environment define the rules and procedures for transmitting data. Sending data over the network involves discrete steps that must be carried out in a consistent fashion in order for communication to take place. The sending and receiving computers use protocols to:

- Break data into packets.
- Add addressing information to the packets.
- Prepare the packets for transmission.
- Take the packets off the cable.
- Copy the data from the packets for reassembly.
- Pass the reassembled data to the computer.

Many protocols work together for communication on a network. These protocols are layered into stacks. There are several stacks used as standard protocols, with the most prominent ones based on the OSI model layers.

Protocols are implemented and removed in the same manner as drivers. Most often they are installed automatically during operating system installation. However, there are times when you will want to either install a new protocol, change the order of protocols, or remove a protocol. Most often there is a utility to help you through these processes.

Your Next Step

As you've seen, the correct protocols are required to enable communications between users, departments, and large organizations. However, implementing the correct protocols will not, by itself, enable network activity. The data still needs to be put on the wire and transmitted. To do this, LANs use one of several methods to have the data get onto, or access, the cable. These are called access methods.

Choosing the access method that will work in a certain environment is just as important as choosing an appropriate protocol, as you will see in the next lesson, "Putting Data on the Cable."

Lesson 5: Putting Data on the Cable

What This Lesson Does

This lesson introduces the role of an access method in putting data on a network cable. It describes the major access methods including carrier-sense multiple access methods, token passing, and demand priority.

Objectives

By the end of this lesson, you will be able to:

- Define access method.
- Describe a primary feature of each of the major access methods:

  CSMA/CD

  CSMA/CA

  Token passing

  Demand priority

Estimated lesson time 55 minutes

The Function of Access Methods

The set of rules defining how a computer puts data onto the network cable and takes data from the cable is called an access method.

Traffic Control on the Cable

Multiple computers must share access to the cable. However, if two computers were to put data onto the cable at the same time, the data packets from one computer would collide with the packets from the other computer, and both sets of data packets would be destroyed.

Figure 3.23 Collision occurs if two computers put data on the cable at the same time

If data is to be sent over the network from one user to another, or accessed from a server, there must be some way for the data to:

- Access the cable without running into other data.
- Be accessed by the receiving computer with reasonable assurance that it has not been destroyed in a data collision during transmission.

Access methods need to be consistent in the way they handle data. If different computers used different access methods, the network would fail because some methods would dominate the cable.

Access methods prevent simultaneous access to the cable. By assuring that only one computer at a time can put data on the network cable, access methods keep the sending and receiving of network data an orderly process.

Major Access Methods

There are three ways to prevent simultaneous use of the cable:

- Carrier-sense multiple access methods

    With collision detection

    With collision avoidance

- A token passing method that allows only a single opportunity to send data
- A demand priority method

Carrier-Sense Multiple Access with Collision Detection

With the access method known as carrier-sense multiple access with collision detection (CSMA/CD), each computer on the network, including clients and servers, checks the cable for network traffic.

1. A computer "senses" that the cable is free, there is no traffic on the cable.

2. The computer can send data.

3. If there is data on the cable, no other computer may transmit until the data has reached its destination and the cable is free again.

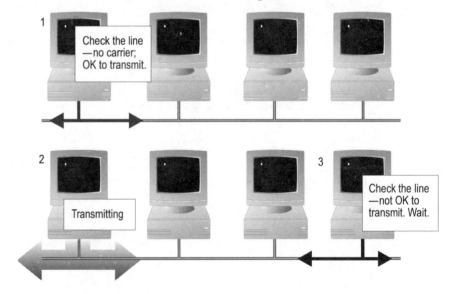

Figure 3.24 Computers can only transmit data if the cable is free

Remember, if two or more computers happen to send data at exactly the same time, there will be a data collision. When that happens, the two computers involved stop transmitting for a random period of time and then attempt to retransmit.

With these points in mind, the access method's name, carrier-sense multiple access with collision detection (CSMA/CD) makes sense. Computers listen or sense the cable (carrier-sense). There are usually many computers on the network attempting to transmit data (multiple access) while at the same time listening to see if any collisions occur that will cause them to wait before retransmitting (collision detection).

The collision detection capability is the parameter that imposes a distance limitation on CSMA/CD. Due to attenuation, the collision detection mechanism is not effective beyond 2,500 meters (1.5 miles). Segments cannot sense signals beyond that distance and, therefore, may not be aware that a computer at the far end of a large network is transmitting. If more than one computer transmits data on the network, a data collision will take place that will corrupt the data.

Contention Method

CSMA/CD is known as a contention method because computers on the network contend or compete for an opportunity to send data.

This might seem like a cumbersome way to put data on the cable, but current implementations of CSMA/CD are fast enough so that users are not even aware they are using a contention access method.

CSMA/CD Considerations

The more computers there are on the network, the greater the network traffic. With more traffic, collision avoidance and collisions tend to increase, which slows the network down, so CSMA/CD can be a slow access method.

After each collision, both computers will have to try to retransmit their data. If the network is very busy there is a chance the attempts by both computers will result in collisions with packets from other computers on the network. If this happens, four computers (the two original computers and the two computers that were the source of the packets colliding with the original computer's retransmitted packets) will have to attempt to retransmit. These proliferating retransmissions can bring the network to a near standstill.

The occurrence of this problem depends on the number of users attempting to use the network and the applications they are using. Database applications tend to put more traffic on the network than word processing applications.

Depending on the hardware components, the cabling, and the networking software, a CSMA/CD network with many users running several database applications may be very frustrating because of heavy network traffic.

Carrier-Sense Multiple Access with Collision Avoidance

Carrier-sense multiple access with collision avoidance (CSMA/CA) is not as popular as either CSMA/CD or token passing. In CSMA/CA, each computer signals its intent to transmit before it actually transmits data. In this way, computers sense when a collision might occur and may avoid transmission collisions.

However, broadcasting the intent to transmit data increases the amount of traffic on the cable and slows down network performance. Because CSMA/CA is a slower access method, it is less popular than CSMA/CD.

Q & A

Fill in the blanks in the following sentences.

1. Access methods prevent _____ access to the cable.

2. With CSMA/CD, if there is data on the cable, no other computer may _____ until the data has reached its destination and the cable is clear again.

3. CSMA/CD is known as a _____ method because computers on the network compete for an opportunity to send data.

4. With more traffic on a CSMA/CD network, _____ tend to increase, which slows the network down.

Answers

1. simultaneous
2. transmit
3. contention
4. collisions

Token Passing

In token passing, a special type of packet called a token circulates around a cable ring from computer to computer. When any computer on the ring wants to send data across the network, it must wait for a free token. When a free token is detected, the computer may take control of it.

The computer can now transmit data. Data is transmitted in frames, and additional information, such as addressing, is attached to the frame in the form of headers and trailers.

In Figure 3.25, the server is shown transmitting data. It takes control of the free token on the ring and sends data to the computer with the address 400080865402.

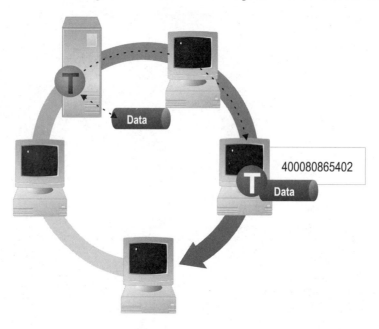

Figure 3.25 Token passing access method

While the token is in use by one computer, other computers cannot transmit data. Because only one computer at a time can use the token, there is no contention, no collision, and no time spent waiting for computers to resend tokens due to network traffic on the cable.

Demand Priority

Demand priority is a relatively new access method designed for the 100 Mbps Ethernet standard called 100VG-AnyLAN. It has been sanctioned and standardized by the IEEE in 802.12.

This access method is based on the fact that repeaters and end nodes are the two components that make up all 100VG-AnyLAN networks. The repeaters manage network access by doing round-robin searches for requests to send from all nodes on the network. The repeater, or hub, is responsible for noting all addresses, links and end nodes and verifying that they are all functioning. According to the 100VG-AnyLAN definition an end node could be a computer, bridge, router, or switch.

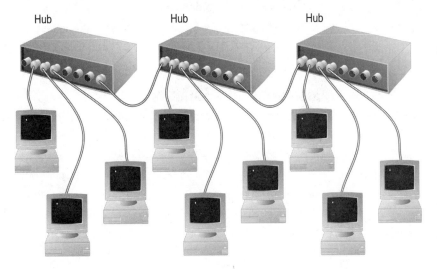

Figure 3.26 Star bus network access method for 100VG-AnyLAN is demand priority

Demand Priority Contention

As in CSMA/CD, two computers can cause contention by transmitting at exactly the same time. However, with demand priority, it is possible to implement a scheme where certain types of data will be given priority if there is contention. If two requests are received by the hub or repeater at the same time, the highest priority request is serviced first. If the two requests are of the same priority, both requests are serviced by alternating between the two.

In a demand priority network, computers can receive and transmit at the same time because of the cabling scheme defined for this access method. Four pairs of wires are used. The four wires enable quartet signaling, which transmits 25 MHz signals on each of the pairs of wire in the cable.

Demand Priority Considerations

In demand priority, there is only communication between the sending computer, the hub, and the destination computer. This is more efficient than CSMA/CD, which broadcasts transmissions to the entire network. In demand priority, each hub knows only about the end nodes and repeaters directly connected to it, whereas in a CSMA/CD environment each hub knows the address of every node in the network.

Demand priority offers several advantages over CSMA/CD including:

- The use of four pairs of wires.

  Four pairs of wires allows computers to transmit and receive at the same time.

- Transmissions through the hub.

  Transmissions are not broadcast to all other computers on the network. The computers are not contending on their own for access to the cable, but are under the centralized control of the hub.

Access Methods Summary

The table below summarizes the major points for each access method.

Feature or function	CSMA/CD	CSMA/CA	Token passing	Demand priority
Type of communication	Broadcast-based	Broadcast-based	Token-based	Hub-based
Type of access method	Contention	Contention	Non-contention	Contention
Type of network	Ethernet	LocalTalk®	Token Ring ArcNet	100VG-AnyLAN

Q & A

Fill in the blanks in the following sentences.

1. With token passing, only one computer at a time may use the token; therefore, there is no _____ or _____.

2. With demand priority the _____ manage network access by doing round-robin searches for requests to send from all nodes.

3. In demand priority, transmissions are not _____ to all other computers on the network.

4. A token is a special type of _____ that circulates around a cable ring.

Answers

1. contention, collisions

2. repeaters

3. broadcast

4. packet

Activity

Run Demo 11.

Summary

There is a need for traffic control on a network cable to prevent data packets from colliding and being destroyed. The set of rules that govern how a computer puts data on the cable is called an access method. Access methods prevent simultaneous access to the cable. Access methods use three basic approaches to achieve this:

- A sensing and collision detection method
- A token passing method
- A demand priority method

With CSMA/CD, computers listen to the cable and, when there is no traffic, send data. Collision detection is a contention method meaning computers compete for an opportunity to send data. CSMA/CD can be a slow access method when there is heavy network traffic. With collision avoidance (CSMA/CA) each computer signals its intent to transmit before it actually transmits data. This is a slower method than collision detection.

In a token passing network, a computer takes control of a token as it passes by, attaches data, and then sends the token on. Only one computer at a time may use the token; therefore, there are no collisions. In demand priority, there is only communication between the sending computer, the hub, and the destination computer. Transmissions are under the centralized control of the hub and are not broadcast to all other computers on the network.

Your Next Step

With the completion of this lesson, you are acquainted with many of the components that make it possible for a network to function.

You are now ready to go on to the Chapter 3 Review in which you will use the information presented in these lessons to confirm your knowledge about:

- Major network operating standards.
- How a network functions (OSI).
- The components involved in basic network operations (drivers, packets, and protocols).
- Network traffic control, or access methods.

Chapter 3 Review

In this chapter you learned about the inner workings of a network. Your learned the components and processes that make it possible for data to be transmitted from one computer to another. The ISO and the IEEE have created standards which guide manufacturers in creating network products. These standards include the OSI model, which covers nearly all network activity, and Project 802 which defines network standards for the physical components of a network.

Drivers permit a computer system to communicate with a device, such as network adapter cards, so that they can recognize each other and function together. Utilities such as the Microsoft Windows NT Control Panel and the Windows NT Setup program make drivers easy to install and remove.

To send data across a network it has to be broken into manageable chunks called packets, which are the basic data components of network communications.

Networks adhere to rules, or protocols to guide their communications. Windows NT provides a graphical user interface that allows you to easily install and remove protocols.

Access methods are responsible for regulating network traffic so that data can be put on the cable, transmitted, and received without being destroyed. The two primary network access methods are CSMA/CD and token passing.

Checkup

Follow the instructions for each exercise as indicated. All answers follow the last exercise.

Exercise 1: Matching

Match each item in Column A with the best choice from Column B. One item in Column B will not be used, and items will·be used no more than once.

Column A	Column B
1. Application layer _____	A. Ensures messages are delivered error free.
2. Data Link layer _____	B. Determines route from source to destination computer.
3. Network layer _____	C. Provides synchronization between user tasks by placing checkpoints in the data stream.
4. Presentation layer _____	D. Verifies that all addresses, links, and end nodes are functioning.
5. Transport layer _____	E. Represents services that directly support user applications.
6. Physical layer _____	F. Packages raw bits from the Physical layer into data frames.
7. Session layer _____	G. Responsible for translating the data format.
	H. Defines how cable is attached to network adapter cards.

Exercise 2: Multiple Choice

Select the letter of the best answer for each of the following questions.

1. Project 802 defines standards for which layers of the OSI model?

    a. Application and Presentation layers.

    b. Physical and Data Link layers.

    c. Network and Data Link layers.

    d. Transport and Network layers.

2. The Media Access Control sublayer resides in which OSI layer?

   a. Transport

   b. Physical

   c. Network

   d. Data Link

3. What enables a computer to work with a printer?

   a. Drivers

   b. HCL

   c. Packet processor

   d. Protocols

4. Which protocol is a Network layer protocol?

   a. IPX

   b. Telnet

   c. FTP

   d. SPX

5. Which of the following describes the NetBEUI protocol?

   a. Developed by the Department of Defense for their internal network.

   b. A small, fast, and efficient Transport layer protocol that is supplied with all Microsoft network products.

   c. IBM Session layer LAN interface that acts as an application interface to the network.

   d. The network protocol stack used in Novell networks.

6. What layer of the OSI model does data compression?

   a. Network

   b. Data Link

   c. Physical

   d. Presentation

7. Which of the following access methods listens to the cable for network traffic before sending data?

   a. CSMA/CD

   b. CSMA/CA

   c. Token passing

   d. Polling

8. Token passing prevents data collisions by:

    a. Using code to steer tokens around each other.

    b. Having multiple tokens take alternate routes.

    c. Allowing only one computer at a time to use the token.

    d. Using zones to control network traffic congestion.

Checkup Answers

Exercise 1: Matching

1. E

2. F

3. B

4. G

5. A

6. H

7. C

Exercise 2: Multiple Choice

1. Project 802 defines standards for which layers of the OSI model?

    b. Physical and Data Link layers.

2. The Media Access Control sublayer resides in which OSI layer?

    d. Data Link

3. What enables a computer to work with a printer?

    a. Drivers

4. Which protocol is a Network layer protocol?

    a. IPX

5. Which of the following describes the NetBEUI protocol?

    b. A small, fast, and efficient Transport layer protocol that is supplied with all Microsoft network products.

6. What layer of the OSI model does data compression?

    d. Presentation

7. Which of the following access methods listens to the cable for network traffic before sending data?

    a. CSMA/CD

8. Token passing prevents data collisions by:

    c. Allowing only one computer at a time to use the token.

Case Study Problem

The Setting

A small but growing mail order company has a staff of four people on telephones talking with customers and taking orders. As they talk and take orders, the customer service representatives type information across a network into the company's database.

The original network was designed with security, a powerful, centralized database, and expansion and reconfiguration in mind. Therefore, the company implemented a server-based, star bus network using UTP with a two-year old super server and 486-based computers.

Business has been so good that the original four customer service representatives are overworked, and management has decided to add three more representatives. The original customer service representatives will pass their computers on to the new workers. The new computers will be Pentium-based machines that are much faster, have bigger monitors, and faster network adapter cards than the original computers.

The network administrator set up the new computers next to the existing equipment and inventoried everything that came with the shipment. This included:

- Warranty cards and instruction manuals.
- Disks with drivers and special utility programs for both the monitors and the network adapter cards.

The network administrator installed network operating systems in the new computers making sure that both the operating systems and the protocols matched the ones in the existing equipment.

The network administrator instructed the customer service representatives in installing both the monitors and the network adapter cards. The workers used the network operating system's utility program to implement drivers for the network adapter cards. They accessed the list of drivers and saw a driver for the brand of card they were using and chose it.

The Problem

When the senior customer service representatives turned their new computers on, they saw beautiful graphics, but they couldn't communicate on the network. It was as if their computers had been turned into stand-alone computers. The older computers, on the other hand, functioned as they had before the new machines were installed.

The network administrator checked the cables. All were plugged in correctly.

Because the administrator had installed the network operating systems in the new computers herself, she assumed the operating systems and protocols were correct. The administrator asked the customer service representatives which network adapter drivers they had installed, and they told her the correct brand.

Your Solution

There is one detail the network administrator neglected because the obvious procedures and tools hid the real solution. Clues have been placed strategically in the case study. The following lists may help you isolate the problem and identify a solution.

Network Support Check List

What would make the network successful? Check the appropriate answers in the list below. The solution to the case study appears after the case study.

1. Are appropriate network protocols active on this network?

   Yes _____

   No _____

2. Do cables physically fit with network adapter cards?

   Yes _____

   No _____

3. Did the version of the network adapter card drivers match the version of the network adapter cards?

   Yes _____

   No _____

4. Were the new computers using the appropriate access method?

   Yes _____

   No _____

Case Study Suggested Solution

This answer to this particular problem may seem picky, but nearly every experienced network engineer has fallen into the trap illustrated in this case study. It has to do with the version of the network adapter card driver.

Are appropriate network protocols active on this network?

Yes _____ The administrator had installed the correct protocol when she installed the operating systems on the computer.

No _____

Do cables physically fit with network adapter cards?

Yes _____ The cards were of the correct type for the network, and all of the cables fit correctly.

No _____

Did the version of the network adapter card drivers match the version of the network adapter cards?

Yes _____ The administrator chose the driver from the list in the operating system's setup so they should have been correct, but in reality, the version of the driver which shipped with the operating system did not support the brand new cards that were installed.

No _____ Because the version of driver which shipped with the operating system did not support the brand new cards that were installed, the administrator should try the driver from the driver floppy disk which shipped with the card.

Were the new computers using the appropriate access method?

Yes _____ Yes, if the cards were the right ones, then the access method was correct also.

No _____

This happens frequently as manufacturers update their hardware and software. Always check the version of driver you are installing against the version of driver that the manufacturer shipped with the hardware.

The Troubleshooter

Drivers

If a piece of network equipment, including the network adapter card, does not work, drivers may be the problem. Lack of communication with the network can indicate problems with the adapter card. To further isolate the problem, the technician can ask a series of questions about the component in an attempt to identify when, where, how, and why the problem started.

The answers to the following questions will help determine if drivers are the problem.

How old is the equipment?

_____

What has changed since it last worked correctly?

_____

Has the hardware been moved?

Yes _____

No _____

Has new software been installed?

Yes _____

No _____

If the equipment is new, has the appropriate driver been installed or is the computer working with an old driver?

Yes _____ The appropriate driver is installed.

No _____ An old driver or the incorrect driver is being used.

Packets

When dealing with packets you will not have many choices to make during setup. Most protocols determine the packet type to be used, so it is normally not an issue.

The exception to this rule is NWLink IPX (or Novell IPX). The IPX protocol is not tied to any particular frame type. In an Ethernet environment, there are four frame types supported by IPX, and in the Token Ring environment there are two supported frame types. A frame type is simply the structure of the headers added by the Data Link layer to the data packet.

So, what you need to know for troubleshooting is:

Does the frame type for IPX on the computer you are adding to the network match the frame type for IPX used by the computers already on the network?

Yes _____

No _____

This is a very common issue currently, because several vendors have changed the default frame type for IPX from their older versions of network software to their more recent releases.

Protocols

If you are adding new computers to an existing network, answer the following question.

Does the protocol you are installing on the new computer match the protocol in use on the network you want it to access?

Yes _____

No _____

Access Methods

There is virtually no choice of access methods for the network administrator. The choice of access method is determined by the type of network adapter card you are installing.

Are all of the network cards you are installing of the same type?

Yes _____

No _____

Note Cards from different manufacturers will usually work. You just cannot mix cards of different types, or cards of the same type which use different signaling speeds.

Can You Solve This Problem?

With knowledge of drivers and troubleshooting in mind, read the following scenario and create a possible solution.

The Situation

Christine sent a document to the printer. The document printed only the top half of the page. No one else seemed to have this problem. Other people, printing similar documents, were getting their entire documents printed successfully.

The Available Facts

The printer was the same one Christine had used successfully in the past.

She used to use Microsoft Windows for Workgroups, but had recently upgraded to a newer operating system.

Your Solution

Cause of the Problem

List one thing which could be the cause of Christine's printing problem.

_____

Possible Solution

What could you do to help Christine restore her printing capabilities?

_____

_____

Suggested Troubleshooting Solution

Cause of the Problem

Christine did not use the correct printer driver.

Many technicians have set up an operating system or an application only to discover that they chose the wrong printer driver. Many types of printing problems can result from this issue including:

- Pages printed in the wrong fonts
- Pages full of printer information language
- Many pages printed with only one character per page

When performing an operating system upgrade, or installing a different operating system, sometimes the new operating system will not have drivers for the hardware already in use with the old operating system. Hardware vendors must write drivers for each operating system that their hardware is to be used with, and there is often a time delay in supporting new operating systems because of the time required to develop drivers to support the new operating system. Also, some vendors choose not to support all operating systems. They may choose only to support the most commonly installed operating systems.

Possible Solution

Investigate the driver issue for all hardware before upgrading to ensure that the operating system, the driver, and the hardware all work together to perform properly.

The LAN Planner

Drivers

The key issues in planning for drivers are:

Does the hardware you are planning to buy come with drivers for the type of computer and operating system you plan to use it with?

Yes ____

No ____

Has the vendor of the operating system software you want to use tested the card and driver you plan to purchase in the type of computer you plan to install it in?

Yes ____

No ____

Note Most network operating system vendors have a hardware compatibility list (HCL). To verify whether or not the card you are considering is compatible with your operating system, check the vendor's HCL before making a decision.

Protocols

Many networks have a need for more than one protocol to:

- Support different operating environments.
- Access different services.
- Support each different operating system vendor.

Answer the following questions to help you determine the appropriate protocol. If you answer yes to more than one question in a protocol section, it indicates that you should add that protocol to your network.

NWLink IPX (or Novell IPX)

Is IPX the default protocol for the network operating system you are installing?

Yes ____

No ____

Does the network software you are installing support IPX?

Yes ____

No ____

Does the network need to support routing?

Yes _____

No _____

Do you have to support network servers or clients running Novell NetWare server or client software?

Yes _____

No _____

If you answered yes to more than one of these questions, install IPX.

TCP/IP

Is TCP/IP the default protocol for the network operating system you are installing?

Yes _____

No _____

Does the network software you are installing support TCP/IP?

Yes _____

No _____

Does the network need to support routing?

Yes _____

No _____

Do the computers on the network need to access the Internet? (The primary supported protocol on the Internet is TCP/IP.)

Yes _____

No _____

Do you have to support network clients and servers from multiple vendors? (Most network software vendors support TCP/IP either in their base product, or as an add-on.)

Yes _____

No _____

If you answered yes to more than one of these questions, install TCP/IP.

AppleTalk

Is AppleTalk the default protocol for the network operating system you are installing?

Yes _____

No _____

Do any of the computers you are installing require support for AppleTalk? (Macintoshes have AppleTalk built in to the operating system.)

Yes _____

No _____

Does the network need to support routing?

Yes _____

No _____

Does the network software you are installing support AppleTalk?

Yes _____

No _____

Access Methods

There is virtually no choice of access methods for the network administrator because the access method is determined by the network architecture.

The LAN Planner Summary

Based on the information generated in the LAN Planner, your network protocols should be:

_____

_____

_____

_____

_____

C H A P T E R   4

Network Architectures

Lesson 1 Ethernet . . . 251

Lesson 2 Token Ring . . . 272

Lesson 3 AppleTalk and ArcNet . . . 287

Chapter 4 Review . . . 299

Welcome to Chapter 4, Network Architectures. This chapter will provide a functional description of the four major network architectures.

A network's architecture includes its overall structure and all components that makes it functional including hardware and system software.

For each of the network architectures, this chapter presents:

- The primary design features.
- The performance parameters.
- Hardware and software considerations.
- Designs for implementation.

This chapter will bring together what you have learned so far about network types, media, topologies, and the basics of how networks function, and will show you how all of these elements are combined in four ways to create networks.

The Case Study Problem

In this case study you will be able to incorporate what you have learned in the previous chapters with your newly acquired knowledge of network architectures to solve a problem. The Ferguson and Bardell public relations firm needs to expand beyond their existing network.

The Troubleshooter

You will be asked to troubleshoot a problem that arises after an Ethernet network is upgraded.

The LAN Planner

The LAN Planner will provide you with questions specific to each of the four architectures. If you are planning a network, answering these questions will lead you toward a selection of the best architecture and topology for your site.

It will help you form a better picture of the network architecture your organization has implemented or begin formulating plans to implement one yourself.

Lesson 1: Ethernet

What This Lesson Does

This lesson introduces the Ethernet network architecture and presents an overview of the major Ethernet components, features, and functions.

Specifically, you will learn about:

- IEEE standards that define Ethernet networks.
- Components associated with each IEEE standard.
- Considerations for implementing an Ethernet network.

Objectives

By the end of this lesson, you will be able to:

- Identify the standard Ethernet components.
- Describe the features of each IEEE Ethernet standard topology.
- Identify the cabling for a given IEEE Ethernet standard topology.
- Determine which Ethernet topology would be appropriate for a given site.

Estimated lesson time 50 minutes

Overview

Network architecture combines standards, topologies, and protocols to produce a working network. This lesson describes Ethernet, and is the first in a series of lessons covering network architectures.

The Origin of Ethernet

In the late 1960s, the University of Hawaii developed a WAN called ALOHA. As you may remember from an earlier lesson, a WAN extends LAN technology across a larger geographical area. The university had a large geographical area and they wanted to connect computers that were spread throughout its campus. One of the key features of the network that they designed was the use of CSMA/CD as the access method.

This early network was the foundation for today's Ethernet. In 1972, Robert Metcalfe and David Boggs invented a cabling and signaling scheme at the Xerox Palo Alto Research Center (PARC), and in 1975 introduced the first Ethernet product. The original version of Ethernet was designed as a 2.94-Mbps system to connect over 100 computers on a 1-kilometer cable.

Xerox Ethernet was so successful that Xerox, Intel Corporation, and Digital Equipment Corporation drew up a standard for a 10-Mbps Ethernet. Today it is a specification describing a method for computers and data systems to connect and share cabling.

The Ethernet specification performs the same functions as the OSI Physical and Data Link layers of data communications. This design is the basis for the IEEE's 802.3 specification.

Ethernet Features

Ethernet is currently the most popular network architecture. This baseband architecture uses a bus topology, usually transmits at 10 Mbps, and relies on CSMA/CD to regulate traffic on the main cable segment.

The Ethernet media is passive, which means it draws power from the computer and thus will not fail unless the media is physically cut or improperly terminated.

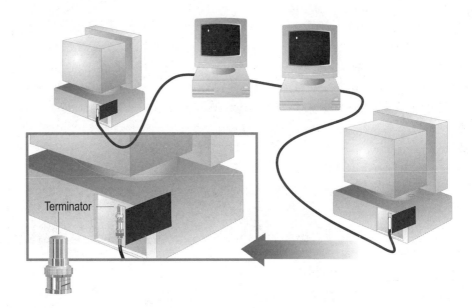

Terminator

Figure 4.1 Simple Ethernet bus network terminated at both ends

Ethernet Basics

The following list summarizes Ethernet features.

- Traditional topology   linear bus
- Other topologies   star bus
- Type of architecture   baseband
- Access method   CSMA/CD
- Specifications   IEEE 802.3
- Transfer speed   10 Mbps or 100 Mbps
- Cable types   thicknet, thinnet, UTP

The Ethernet Frame Format

Ethernet breaks data down into packages in a format that is different from the packet used in other networks. Ethernet breaks data down into frames. A frame is a package of information transmitted as a single unit. An Ethernet frame can be between 64 and 1,518 bytes long, but the Ethernet frame itself uses at least 18 bytes; therefore, the data in an Ethernet frame can be between 46 and 1,500 bytes long. Every frame contains control information and follows the same basic organization.

For example, the Ethernet II frame, used for TCP/IP, that gets transmitted across the network consists of the sections listed in the following table.

Frame field	Description
Preamble	Marks the start of the frame.
Destination and source	The origin and destination addresses.
Type	Used to identify the Network layer protocol (IP or IPX).
Cyclical redundancy check (CRC)	Error checking field to determine if the frame arrived without being corrupted.

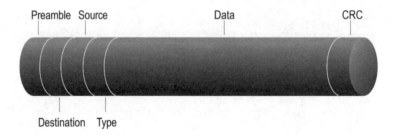

Figure 4.2 Sample Ethernet II frame

Ethernet networks include a variety of cabling and topology alternatives. The remaining sections of this lesson present these alternatives based on their IEEE specification.

Q & A

Fill in the blanks in the following sentences.

1. Typically, Ethernet is a baseband architecture that uses a _____ topology.

2. Ethernet relies on the _____ access method to regulate traffic on the main cable segment.

Answers

1. bus

2. CSMA/CD

The 10 Mbps IEEE Standards

This section looks at four different 10 Mbps Ethernet topologies:

- 10BaseT
- 10Base2
- 10Base5
- 10BaseFL

10BaseT

In 1990, the IEEE committee published the 802.3 specification for running Ethernet over twisted-pair wiring. 10BaseT (10 Mbps, baseband, over twisted-pair cable) is an Ethernet network that typically uses unshielded twisted-pair (UTP) cable to connect computers. While 10BaseT normally uses UTP, shielded twisted-pair (STP) will also work without changing any of the 10BaseT parameters.

Most networks of this type are configured in a star pattern but internally use a bus signaling system like other Ethernet configurations. Typically, the hub of a 10BaseT network serves as a multiport repeater and often is located in a wiring closet of the building. Each computer is located at the end point of a cable connected to the hub. Each computer has two pairs of wire—one pair is used to receive data and one pair is used to transmit data.

The maximum length of a 10BaseT segment is 100 meters (328 feet). Repeaters can be used to extend this maximum cable length. The minimum cable length between computers is 2.5 meters (about 8 feet). A 10BaseT LAN will serve 1,024 computers.

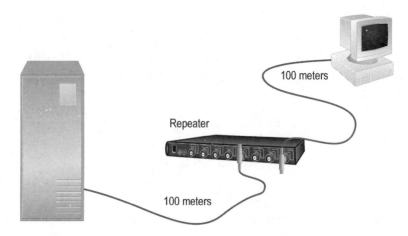

Figure 4.3 A multiport repeater (hub) can be used to extend an Ethernet LAN

Figure 4.4 shows how a 10BaseT solution provides the advantages of a star wired topology. The UTP cable features 10 Mbps data transmission. It is easy to make moves and changes by moving a modular patch cord on the patch panel. Other devices on the network will not be affected by a change at the patch panel, unlike in a traditional Ethernet bus network.

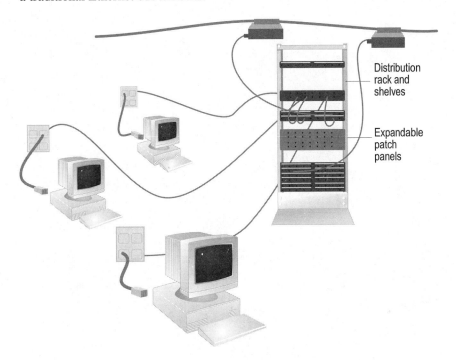

Distribution rack and shelves

Expandable patch panels

Figure 4.4 A patch panel makes moving computers easy

Patch panels should be tested for rates higher than 10 Mbps. The latest hubs can provide connections for both thick and thin Ethernet cable segments. In this implementation, it is also easy to convert thick Ethernet cable to 10BaseT cable by attaching a mini 10BaseT transceiver to the AUI port of any network adapter card.

10BaseT Summary

Category	Notes
Cable	Category 3, 4, or 5 UTP
Connectors	RJ-45 at cable ends
Transceiver	Each computer needs one; some cards have transceivers built in
Transceiver to hub distance	100 meters maximum
Backbones for hubs	Coaxial or fiber-optic to join a larger LAN
Total computers per LAN without connectivity components	1024 by specification

10Base2

This topology is called 10Base2 by the IEEE 802.3 specification because it transmits at 10 Mbps over a baseband wire and can carry a signal roughly two times 100 meters (the actual distance is 185 meters).

This type of network uses thin coaxial cable, or thinnet, which has a maximum segment length of 185 meters. There is also a minimum cable length of at least 0.5 meters (20 inches). There is also a 30 computer maximum per 185 meter segment.

Thinnet cabling components include:

- BNC barrel connectors
- BNC T connectors
- BNC terminators

Thinnet networks generally use a local bus topology. IEEE standards for thinnet do not allow a transceiver cable to be used from the bus T connector to a computer. Instead, a T connector fits directly on the network adapter card.

A BNC barrel connector may be used to connect thinnet cable segments together, thus extending a length of cable. For example, if you need a length of cable that is 30 feet long, but all you have is a 25-foot length and a 5-foot length of thinnet cable, a BNC barrel connector can be used to join the two cable segments together. However, the use of barrel connectors should be kept to a minimum because each connection in the cable reduces the signal quality.

A thinnet network is an economical way to support a small department or workgroup. The cable used for this type of network is:

- Relatively inexpensive.
- Easy to install.
- Easy to configure.

A single thinnet network can support a maximum of 30 nodes (computers and repeaters) per cable segment as per the IEEE 802.3 specification.

The 5-4-3 Rule

A thinnet network can combine as many as five cable segments connected by four repeaters, but only three segments can have stations attached. Thus, two segments are untapped and are often referred to as inter-repeater links. This is known as the 5-4-3 rule.

In Figure 4.5 there are five segments, four repeaters, and trunk segments 1, 2, and 5 are populated (have computers attached to them). Trunk segments 3 and 4 only exist to increase the total length of the network and to allow the computers on trunk segments 1 and 5 to be on the same network.

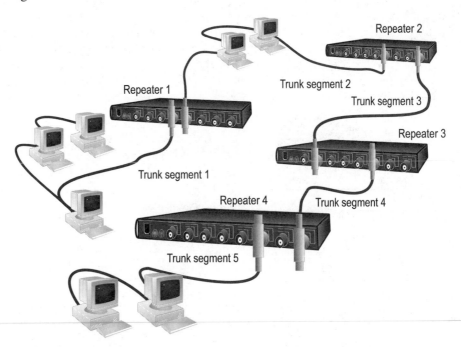

Figure 4.5 The thinnet 5-4-3 rule; 5 segments, 4 repeaters, and 3 populated segments

Because normal Ethernet limits would be too confining for a large business, repeaters can be used to join Ethernet segments and extend the network to a total length of 925 meters.

10Base2 Summary

Category	Notes
Maximum segment length	185 meters (607 feet)
Connection to network adapter card	BNC T connector
Trunk segments and repeaters	Five segments may be joined using four repeaters
Computers per segment	30 computers per segment by specification
Segments that can have computers	Three of the five segments may be populated
Maximum total network length	925 meters (3,035 feet)

10Base5

The IEEE specification for this topology is 10 Mbps, baseband, and 500-meter (five 100-meter) segments. It is also called standard Ethernet.

This topology makes use of thick coaxial, or thicknet. Thicknet generally uses a bus topology and can support as many as 100 nodes (stations, repeaters, and so on) per backbone segment. The backbone, or trunk segment, is the main cable from which transceiver cables are connected to stations and repeaters. A thicknet segment can be 500 meters long for a total network length of 2,500 meters (8,200 feet).

The distances and tolerances for thicknet are greater than those for thinnet.

Figure 4.6 Thicknet cable composition

The thicknet cabling components include:

- Transceivers.

  Transceivers (transmit and receive) provide communications between the computer and the main LAN cable and are located in the vampire taps attached to the cable.

- Transceiver cables.

  The transceiver cable (drop cable) connects the transceiver to the network adapter card.

- DIX or AUI connector.

  This is the connector on the transceiver cable.

- N-series connectors including N-series barrel connectors, and N-series terminators.

The thicknet components work the same way that the thinnet components do. Figure 4.7 shows a thicknet cable with a transceiver attached and a transceiver cable. It also shows the DIX or AUI connector on the transceiver cable.

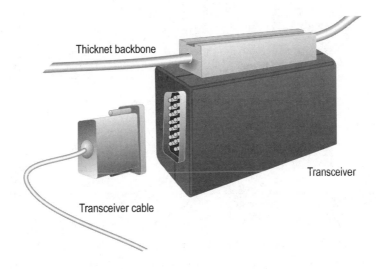

Figure 4.7 Thicknet backbone with attached transceiver and cable

The 5-4-3 Rule in Thicknet

One thicknet Ethernet network can have a maximum of five backbone segments connected using repeaters (based on the IEEE 802.3 specification), of which three can accommodate computers. The length of the transceiver cables is not used to measure the distance supported on the thicknet cable; only the end-to-end length of the thicknet cable segment itself is used.

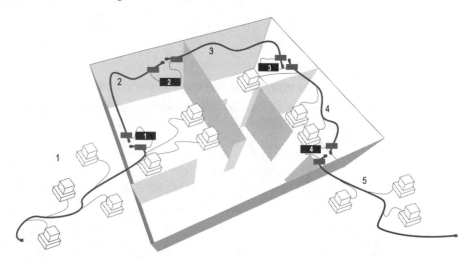

Figure 4.8 Thicknet 5-4-3 rule; 5 backbone segments, 4 repeaters, and 3 segments

Between connections, the minimum thicknet cable segment is 2.5 meters (about 8 feet). This measurement excludes transceiver cables. Thicknet was designed to support a backbone for a large department or an entire building.

10Base5 Summary

Category	Notes
Maximum segment length	500 meters
Transceivers	Connected to the segment (in the tap)
Maximum computer-to-transceiver distance	50 meters (164 feet)
Minimum distance between transceivers	2.5 meters (8 feet)
Trunk segments and repeaters	Five segments may be joined using four repeaters
Segments that can have computers	Three of the five segments may be populated
Maximum total length of joined segments	2,500 meters (8,200 feet)
Maximum number of computers per segment	100 by specification

Combining Thicknet and Thinnet

It is common for larger networks to combine thick and thin Ethernet. Thicknet is good for backbones with thinnet used for branch segments. What this means is that the thicknet cable is the main cable covering the long distances. You may remember that thicknet has a larger copper core and can therefore carry signals for a longer distance than thinnet. The transceiver attaches to the thicknet cable and the transceiver cable's AUI connector plugs into a repeater. The branching segments of thinnet plug into the repeater and connect the computers to the network.

10BaseFL

The IEEE committee published a specification for running Ethernet over fiber-optic cable. 10BaseFL (10Mbps, baseband, over fiber-optic cable) is an Ethernet network that typically uses fiber-optic cable to connect computers and repeaters.

The primary reason for using 10BaseFL is for long cable runs between repeaters, such as between buildings. The maximum distance for a 10BaseFL segment is 2000 meters.

Q & A

Fill in the blanks in the following sentences.

1. The maximum length of a 10BaseT segment is _____ meters.

2. 10BaseT is an Ethernet network that uses _____ cable to connect stations.

3. Typically, the hub of a 10BaseT network serves as a _____ _____.

4. A thinnet network can combine as many as _____ cable segments connected by four repeaters, but only three segments can have stations attached.

5. Because single segment 10Base2 Ethernet limits would be too confining for a large business, _____ can be used to join Ethernet segments and extend the network to a total length of 925 meters.

6. A 10Base5 topology is also referred to as _____.

Answers

1. 100
2. unshielded twisted-pair (UTP)
3. multiport repeater
4. five
5. repeaters
6. thicknet (or standard Ethernet)

The 100 Mbps IEEE Standard

New Ethernet standards are pushing the traditional Ethernet limits beyond the original 10 Mbps. These new capabilities are being developed to handle such high-bandwidth applications as:

- CAD (computer aided design)
- CAM (computer aided manufacturing)
- Video
- Imaging and document storage

Two emerging Ethernet standards that can meet the increased demands are:

- 100BaseVG-AnyLAN Ethernet
- 100BaseX Ethernet (Fast Ethernet)

Both Fast Ethernet and 100BaseVG-AnyLAN are about five to 10 times faster than standard Ethernet. They are also compatible with existing 10BaseT cabling systems. This means they will allow for Plug and Play upgrades from existing 10BaseT installations.

100VG-AnyLAN

100VG (Voice Grade) AnyLAN is an emerging networking technology that combines elements of both Ethernet and Token Ring. Originally developed by Hewlett-Packard, it is currently being refined and ratified by the IEEE 802.12 committee. The 802.12 specification is a standard for transmitting 802.3 Ethernet frames and 802.5 Token Ring packets.

This technology goes by any of the following names, all of which refer to the same type of network:

- 100VG-AnyLAN
- 100BaseVG
- VG
- AnyLAN

Specifications

Some of the current 100VG-AnyLAN specifications include:

- A minimum data rate of 100 Mbps.

- Ability to support a cascaded star topology over Category 3, 4, and 5 twisted-pair and fiber-optic cable.

- The demand priority access method which allows for two priority levels (low and high).

- Ability to support an option for filtering individually addressed frames at the hub to enhance privacy.

- Support for both Ethernet frames and Token Ring packets.

Topology

A 100VG-AnyLAN network is built on a star topology with all computers attached to a hub. The network can be expanded by adding child hubs to the central hub. The child hubs act as computers to their parent hubs. The parent hubs control transmission of computers attached to their children.

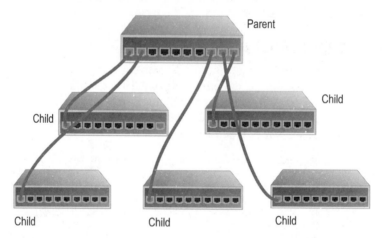

Figure 4.9 Parent hub with five attached child hubs

Considerations

This topology requires its own hubs and cards. Also, the cable distances of 100BaseVG are limited when compared to 10BaseT and other implementations of Ethernet. The two longest cables from the 100BaseT hub to a computer cannot exceed 250 meters. Extending this requires special equipment used to expand the size of a LAN. These cable length limits mean that 100BaseT will require more wiring closets than 10BaseT.

100BaseX Ethernet

This standard, sometimes called Fast Ethernet, is an extension to the existing Ethernet standard. It runs on UTP Category 5 data-grade cable and uses CSMA/CD in a star wired bus, similar to 10BaseT where all cables are attached to a hub.

Media Specifications

100BaseX incorporates three media specifications:

- 100BaseT4 (4-pair Category 3, 4, or 5 UTP)
- 100BaseTX (2-pair Category 5 UTP or STP)
- 100BaseFX (2-strand fiber-optic cable)

These media are described further in the following table.

Value	Represents	Actual meaning
100	Transmission speed	100 Mbps or 100 megabits per second
Base	Signal type	Baseband
T4	Cable type	Indicates twisted-pair cable using four telephone-grade pairs
TX	Cable type	Indicates twisted-pair cable using two data-grade pairs
FX	Cable type	Indicates fiber-optic link using two strands of fiber-optic cable

Performance Considerations

Ethernet can use several communication protocols including TCP/IP, which works well in the UNIX® environment. This makes Ethernet a favorite in the scientific and academic communities.

Segmentation

Ethernet performance can be improved by dividing a crowded segment into two less-populated segments and joining them with either a bridge or a router. This reduces traffic on each segment. Because there are fewer computers attempting to transmit onto the segment, access time improves.

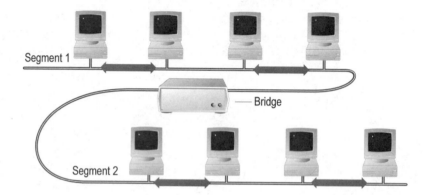

Figure 4.10 Using a bridge to segment a network and reduce network traffic

Segment division is a good tactic if large numbers of new users are joining the network or new, high-bandwidth applications such as database or video programs are being added to the network.

Network Operating Systems on Ethernet

Ethernet will work with most popular network operating systems including:

- Microsoft Windows 95
- Microsoft Windows NT Workstation
- Microsoft Windows NT Server
- Microsoft LAN Manager
- Microsoft Windows for Workgroups
- Novell NetWare
- IBM LAN Server
- AppleShare

Q & A

Fill in the blanks in the following sentences.

1. Fast Ethernet is another name for the _____ topology.

2. Ethernet can use several communication _____ including TCP/IP.

3. The 100BaseTX topology runs on UTP Category _____ data-grade cable.

4. A 100BaseVG network is built on a _____ topology with all computers attached to a hub.

Answers

1. 100BaseX
2. protocols
3. 5
4. star

Summary

The following table summarizes the specifications for Ethernet architecture discussed in this lesson. It outlines the minimum standards required to conform to IEEE specifications. A particular implementation of the network architecture may differ from the information in the following table.

Ethernet (IEEE 802.3)

	10Base2	10Base5	10BaseT
Topology	Bus	Bus	Star bus
Cable type	RG-58 (thinnet coaxial)	Thicknet; 3/8-inch shielded-pair transceiver cable	Category 3, 4, or 5 unshielded twisted-pair
Connection to network adapter card	BNC T connector	DIX or AUI connector	RJ-45
Terminator resistance, Ω (ohms)	50	50	Not applicable
Impedance, Ω	50 ± 2	50 ± 2	85–115 unshielded twisted-pair; 135–165 shielded twisted-pair
Distance in meters	0.5 between computers (about 23 inches)	2.5 between taps (about 8 feet) and maximum of 50 (about 164 feet) between the tap and the computer	100 between the transceiver (the computer) and the hub
Maximum cable segment length, meters	185 (about 607 feet)	500 (about 1640 feet)	100 (about 328 feet)
Maximum connected segments	5 (using 4 repeaters); only 3 segments can have computers connected	5 (using 4 repeaters); only 3 segments can have computers connected	5 (using 4 repeaters); only 3 segments can have computers connected
Maximum total network length, meters	925 (about 3,035 feet)	2,460 (about 8,200 feet)	Not applicable
Maximum computers per segment	30 (There can be a maximum of 1024 computers per network.)	100	1 (Each station has its own cable to the hub. There can be a maximum of 12 computers per hub. There can be a maximum of 1024 transceivers per LAN without some type of connectivity.)

Your Next Step

While Ethernet is a very popular architecture, there are others that are also widely used. There are many organizations that prefer Token Ring, not only because it was developed and marketed by IBM but because it offers several important features which Ethernet does not, as you will see in the next lesson.

Lesson 2: Token Ring

What This Lesson Does

In this lesson you will learn about the Token Ring architecture including its features, components, and how it works. There is also information that can help you implement a Token Ring network.

Objectives

By the end of this lesson, you will be able to:

- Describe the features of a Token Ring network.
- Identify the major components of a Token Ring network.
- Determine the components needed to implement a Token Ring network at a given site.

Estimated lesson time 25 minutes

Overview

IBM's version of Token Ring was introduced in 1984 as part of its connectivity solution for the entire range of IBM computers and computing environments including:

- Personal computers.
- Mid-range computers.
- Mainframes and the Systems Network Architecture environment (recall that SNA is IBM's networking architecture).

The goal of IBM's version of Token Ring was to allow for a simple wiring structure using twisted-pair cable that connected a computer to the network through a wall socket, with the main wiring located in a centralized location.

In 1985, the IBM Token Ring became an ANSI/IEEE standard.

Token Ring Features

A Token Ring network is an implementation of IEEE standard 802.5. The token-passing ring access method, more than the physical cable layout, distinguishes Token Ring networks from other networks.

Architecture

The architecture of a typical Token Ring network begins with a physical ring. However, in its IBM implementation, a star wired ring, computers on the network are connected to a central hub. The logical ring represents the token's path between computers. The actual physical ring of cable is in the hub. Users are part of a ring, but they connect to it through a hub.

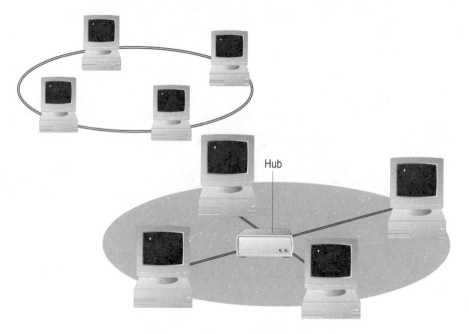

Figure 4.11 Logical ring, but the actual wiring scheme passes through the hub

Token Ring Basics

A Token Ring network includes the following features:

- Star wired ring topology
- Token passing for access method
- Shielded and unshielded twisted-pair (IBM Types 1, 2, and 3) cabling
- Transfer rates of 4 and 16 Mbps
- Baseband transmission
- 802.5 specifications

Frame Formats

The basic format of a Token Ring data frame is shown in Figure 4.12 and described in the following table. The sizes of the fields in Figure 4.12 are not representative of the sizes of the fields in an actual frame. The data field makes up the vast majority of the frame.

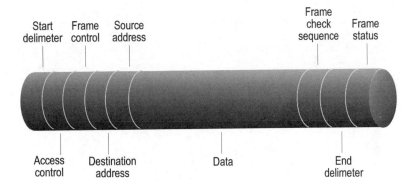

Figure 4.12 Token Ring data frame

Frame field	Description
Start delimiter	Indicates start of the frame.
Access control	Indicates the frame priority and whether it is a token or a data frame.
Frame control	Contains either Media Access Control information for all computers or "end station" information for only one computer.
Destination address	Indicates the address of the computer to receive the frame.
Source address	Indicates the computer that sent the frame.
Information, or data	The data being sent.
Frame check sequence	CRC error-checking information.
End delimiter	Indicates the end of the frame.
Frame status	Tells whether the frame was recognized, copied, or whether the destination address was available.

Q & A

Fill in the blanks in the following sentences.

1. A Token Ring network is an implementation of IEEE standard _____.

2. In the IBM implementation of Token Ring, a star wired ring, the actual physical ring of cable is in the _____.

3. In a Token Ring frame the Media Access Control field indicates whether the frame is a _____ frame or a _____ frame.

Answers

1. 802.5

2. hub

3. token or data

How Token Ring Works

When the first Token Ring computer comes online, the network generates a token. The token travels around the ring polling each computer until one of the computers signals that it wants to transmit data and takes control of the token. The token is a predetermined formation of bits (a stream of data) which permits a computer to put data on the cables. A computer may not transmit unless it has possession of the token; while the token is in use by a computer, no other computer can transmit data.

After the computer captures the token, it sends a data frame (such as the one shown in Figure 4.13) out on the network. The frame proceeds around the ring until it reaches the computer with an address that matches the destination address in the frame. The destination computer copies the frame into its receive buffer and marks the frame in the frame status field to indicate that the information was received.

The frame continues around the ring until it arrives at the sending computer where the transmission is acknowledged as successful. The sending computer then removes the frame from the ring and transmits a new token back on the ring.

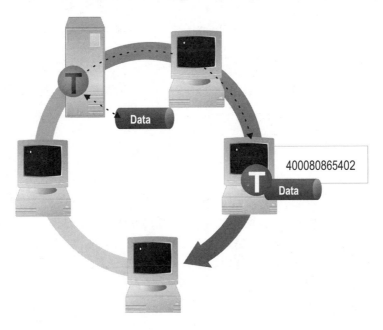

Figure 4.13 Clockwise flow of the token around the logical ring

Only one token at a time may be active on the network, and the token may only travel in one direction around the ring.

Token passing is deterministic, meaning that a computer cannot force its way on to the network as it can in a CSMA/CD environment. If the token is available the computer can use it to send data. Each computer acts as a unidirectional repeater, and regenerates the token and passes it along.

Monitoring the System

The first computer to come online is assigned by the Token Ring system to monitor network activity. The monitor checks to make sure that frames are being delivered and received correctly. It does this by checking for frames that have circulated the ring more than once, and ensuring that only one token is on the network at a time.

Recognizing a Computer

When a new computer comes online on the network, the Token Ring system initializes it so that it can become part of the ring. This includes:

- Checking for duplicate addresses.
- Notifying other computers on the network of its existence.

Q & A

Fill in the blanks in the following sentences.

1. When a frame reaches the destination computer, that computer copies the frame into its _____ _____.

2. Token passing is _____ , meaning that a computer cannot force its way onto the network as it can in a CSMA/CD environment.

3. When a frame returns to its sending computer, that computer _____ the frame and puts a new token back on the ring.

Answers

1. receive buffer

2. deterministic

3. removes

Hardware Components

The Hub

In a Token Ring network, the hub, which houses the actual ring, is known by several names that all mean the same thing. These include:

- MAU (Multistation Access Unit)
- MSAU (MultiStation Access Unit)
- SMAU (Smart Multistation Access Unit)

Cables attach the individual clients and servers to the MSAU, which works like other passive hubs. The internal ring converts to an external ring at each connection point when a computer is connected.

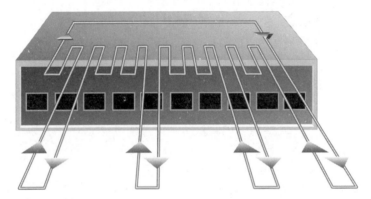

Figure 4.14 Hub showing the internal ring and clockwise token path

Hub Capacity

An IBM MSAU has 10 connection ports. It can connect up to eight computers. However, a Token Ring network is not limited to one ring (hub). Each ring can have as many as 33 hubs.

Each MSAU-based network can support as many as 72 computers that use unshielded wire or up to 260 computers that use shielded wire.

Other vendors offer hubs with more capacity, depending on the vendor and the hub model.

When one Token Ring is full, that is, when every port on an MSAU has a computer connected to it, the network can be enlarged by adding another ring (MSAU).

The only rule to follow is that each MSAU must be connected in such a way so that it becomes part of the ring. An MSAU's ring-in and ring-out connection points make it possible to use patch cables to connect many MSAUs on top of each other and still form a continuous ring inside the MSAUs. Up to 12 MSAU devices can be connected to each other.

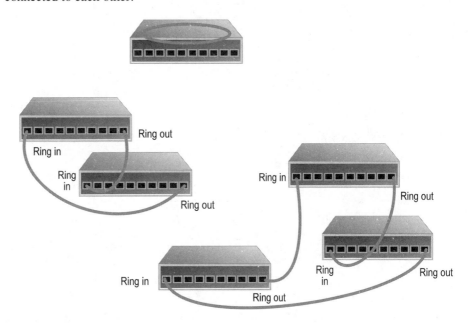

Figure 4.15 Adding hubs while maintaining the logical ring

Built-in Fault Tolerance

In a pure token passing network, a computer that fails will stop the token from continuing. This will bring down the network. MSAUs were designed to sense when a network adapter card fails and disconnect from it. This procedure by-passes the failed computer so that the token can continue.

In IBM's MSAUs, bad MSAU connections or computers are automatically by-passed and disconnected from the ring. Therefore, a faulty computer or connection will not affect the rest of the Token Ring network.

Cabling

Computers on a Token Ring network are connected by STP or UTP cable to a hub. Token Rings use IBM Type 1, 2, and 3 cabling. Most networks use IBM Cabling System Type 3 UTP cabling.

Each computer can only be 101 meters (330 feet) from an MSAU when using Type 1 cable. Each computer can be up to 100 meters (about 328 feet) from the MSAU using STP, or 45 meters (about 148 feet) using UTP. The minimum shielded or unshielded cable length is 2.5 meters (about 8 feet).

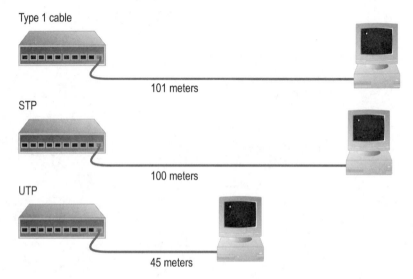

Figure 4.16 Maximum hub to computer distances on Type 1, STP, and UTP cables

According to IBM, the maximum cabling distance from an MSAU to a computer or a file server is 150 feet using Type 3 cabling. Some vendors, however, claim reliable data transmission of up to 500 feet between an MSAU and a computer.

The distance from one MSAU to another has a 500-foot limit. Each single Token Ring can only accommodate 260 computers using STP cable and 72 computers using UTP.

Patch Cables

Patch cables extend the connection between a computer and an MSAU. They can also join two MSAUs together. In the IBM cabling system, these are Type 6 cables and can be any length up to 150 feet. Patch cable will only allow 45 meters (150 feet) between a computer and an MSAU.

The IBM cabling system also specifies a Type 6 cable for patch cables for:

- Increasing the length of Type 3 cables.
- Directly connecting computers to MSAUs.

Connectors

Token Ring networks normally use the following types of connectors in joining cables to components:

- Media interface connector (MIC) for connecting Type 1 and 2 cable.

  These are IBM Type A connectors. They are hermaphroditic (or androgynous) in that you can connect one to another by flipping either one over.
- RJ-45 telephone connectors (8-pin) for Type 3 cable.
- RJ-11 telephone connectors (4-pin) for Type 3 cable.
- Media filters to make the connection between the Token Ring adapter card and a standard RJ-11/RJ-45 telephone jack (outlet).

Media Filters

Media filters are required in computers that use Type 3 telephone twisted-pair cabling because they convert cable connectors and reduce line noise.

Patch Panels

A patch panel is used to organize cable that runs between an MSAU and a telephone punchdown block.

Repeaters

All Token Ring cable distances can be increased by using repeaters. A repeater actively regenerates and retimes the Token Ring signal to extend distances between MSAUs on the network. Using one pair of repeaters, MSAUs can be located up to 1200 feet (365 meters) apart using Type 3 cable, or 2400 feet (730 meters) apart using Type 1 or 2 cable.

Network Adapter Cards

Token Ring network adapter cards are available in both 4 Mbps and 16 Mbps models. The 16 Mbps cards accommodate an increased frame length that requires fewer transmissions for the same amount of data.

Implementing Token Ring cards requires caution because a Token Ring network will only run at one of two possible speeds, 4 Mbps or 16 Mbps. If the network is a 4 Mbps network, the 16 Mbps cards can be used because they will revert back to 4 Mbps mode. A 16 Mbps network, however, will not accept the slower 4 Mbps cards because they cannot speed up.

Although several manufacturers make Token Ring network adapter cards and other Token Ring components, IBM currently sells the majority of them.

Fiber-Optic Cable

Because of the mix of data streaming, high speeds, and data traveling in one direction only, Token Ring networks are well suited to fiber-optic cable. Though more expensive, fiber-optic cable can greatly increase the range of a Token Ring network up to ten times what copper cabling allows.

Q & A

Fill in the blanks in the following sentences.

1. Cables attach the individual clients and servers to the MSAU which works like other _____ hubs.

2. When an IBM Token Ring network is full, the network can be enlarged by adding another _____.

3. MSAUs were designed to sense when a _____ _____ _____ fails and disconnect from it.

4. Each single Token Ring can accommodate _____ computers using STP cable.

5. Most Token Ring networks use IBM Cabling System Type _____ UTP cabling.

Answers

1. passive

2. MSAU

3. network adapter card

4. 260

5. 3

Summary

The following table summarizes the specifications for Token Ring architecture presented in this lesson. It outlines the minimum standards required to conform to IEEE specifications. A particular implementation of the network architecture may differ from the information in the following table.

IEEE specification	Token Ring
Topology	Star ring
Cable type	Shielded or unshielded twisted-pair cable
Terminator resistance, Ω (ohms)	Not applicable
Impedance, Ω	100–120 UTP, 150 STP
Maximum cable segment length, meters	From 45 to 200 (about 148 to 656 feet), depends on cable type
Minimum length between computers, meters	2.5 (about 8 feet)
Maximum connected segments	33 multistation access units (MSAUs)
Maximum computers per segment	Unshielded: 72 computers per concentrator; Shielded: 260 computers per hub

Your Next Step

To complete your overview of network architectures, you will look at two others that are not as popular as Ethernet and Token Ring, but have found strong support and a loyal following in certain segments of the business community. These will be presented in Lesson 3, "AppleTalk and ArcNet."

Lesson 3: AppleTalk and ArcNet

What This Lesson Does

This lesson introduces two more architectures you may encounter, AppleTalk and ArcNet. The AppleTalk architecture is used in the Apple Macintosh environment, while the ArcNet architecture is used in personal computer-based environments. Since the advent of Ethernet, the popularity of ArcNet has decreased.

Objectives

By the end of this lesson, you will be able to:

- Identify the components and features of AppleTalk.
- Identify the components and features of ArcNet.

Estimated lesson time 40 minutes

The AppleTalk Environment

Apple Computer, Inc. introduced AppleTalk in 1983 as a proprietary network architecture for small groups. Networking functions are built into Macintosh computers which makes the AppleTalk network very simple compared to other networks.

The primary terms used in the Apple environment can be confusing because they sound similar but relate to different aspects of a network. The following aspects of Apple networking will be addressed:

- AppleTalk
- LocalTalk
- AppleShare
- EtherTalk®
- TokenTalk®

AppleTalk

AppleTalk is the Apple network architecture and is included in the Macintosh operating system software. This means that network capabilities are built into every Macintosh. AppleTalk Phase2 is a later, enhanced release of AppleTalk. The architecture is a collection of protocols that correspond to the OSI model.

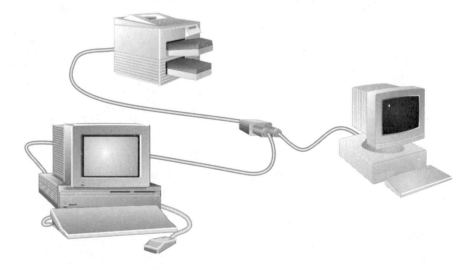

Figure 4.17 AppleTalk network

When a device attached to a LocalTalk network comes online, three crucial things happen in the following order:

1. The device assigns itself an address chosen at random from a range of allowable addresses.

2. The device broadcasts the address to see if any other device is using it.

3. If no other device is using the address, the device stores it to use the next time the device comes online.

LocalTalk

AppleTalk networks are commonly referred to as LocalTalk networks. LocalTalk uses CSMA/CA as an access method in a bus or tree topology with shielded, twisted-pair cabling, but will also accept fiber-optic cable and UTP. LocalTalk is inexpensive because it is built into Macintosh hardware. But, because of its comparatively modest performance, LocalTalk is not as widely used in large business networks as Ethernet or Token Ring.

LocalTalk also refers to the physical cabling components. These include:

- Cables
- Connector modules
- Cable extenders

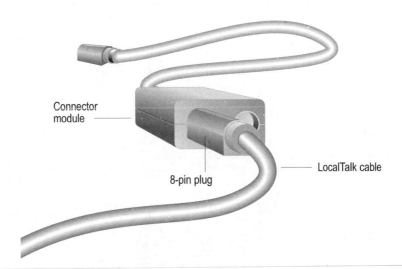

Connector module

8-pin plug

LocalTalk cable

Figure 4.18 LocalTalk connector module with a LocalTalk cable

STP cabling is most often used in a bus or tree topology. A LocalTalk network supports a maximum of 32 devices.

Because of LocalTalk's limitations, clients often turn to vendors other than Apple for cabling. Farallon® PhoneNet™, for example, can handle 254 devices. PhoneNet uses telephone cable and connectors and can be implemented as a bus network or plugged into a central wiring hub to form a star topology.

AppleShare

AppleShare is the file server on an AppleTalk network. The client-side software is included with every copy of the Apple operating system. There is also an AppleShare print server, which is a server-based print spooler.

Zones

Single LocalTalk networks can be joined together into one larger network through the use of zones. Each connected subnetwork is identified by a zone name. Users in one LocalTalk network can access the services in another network simply by selecting that zone. This is helpful for accessing file servers in a variety of small networks, thereby expanding the size of the network. Networks using other architectures, such as Token Ring, can also be joined to an AppleTalk network in this way.

Conversely, working groups on a single LocalTalk network can be divided into zones to relieve congestion on a busy network. Each zone, for example, could have its own print server.

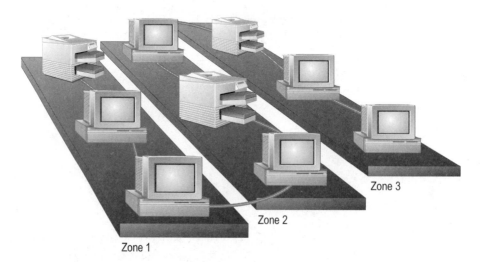

Figure 4.19 Three zones joined together to form a larger network

EtherTalk

EtherTalk allows the AppleTalk network protocols to run on Ethernet coaxial cable. As you may remember, there are two types of coaxial cable: thinnet and thicknet.

The EtherTalk NB card allows a Macintosh II to connect to an 802.3 Ethernet network. EtherTalk software is included with the card and is compatible with AppleTalk Phase2.

TokenTalk

The TokenTalk NB card is an expansion card that allows a Macintosh II to connect to an 802.5 Token Ring network. TokenTalk software is included with the card and is compatible with AppleTalk Phase2.

AppleTalk Considerations

Computers from companies other than Apple can also use AppleTalk. These include:

- IBM personal computers and compatibles
- IBM mainframes
- Digital Equipment Corporation VAX™ computers
- Some UNIX computers

Apple is open to third-party development. As a result, the AppleTalk environment facilitates products from a variety of vendors.

Q & A

Fill in the blanks in the following sentences.

1. LocalTalk uses _____ as an access method in a bus or tree topology.

2. When a device attached to an AppleTalk network comes online, the device broadcasts an _____ to see if any other device is using it.

3. A single LocalTalk network supports a maximum of _____ devices.

4. Single LocalTalk networks can be joined together into one larger network through the use of _____.

Answers

1. CSMA/CA

2. address

3. 32

4. zones

The ArcNet Environment

The Attached Resource Computer Network (ArcNet) was developed by Datapoint Corporation in 1977. It is a simple, inexpensive, flexible network architecture designed for workgroup-sized networks. The first ArcNet cards were shipped in 1983.

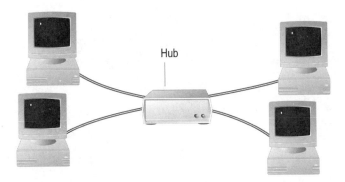

Figure 4.20 Simple star wired ArcNet network

ArcNet technology predates IEEE Project 802 standards, but loosely maps to the 802.4 document. This specifies the standards for token-passing bus networks using broadband cable. An ArcNet network can have a star bus or bus topology.

How ArcNet Works

ArcNet uses a token-passing access method in a star bus topology passing data at 2.5 Mbps. A successor to the original ArcNet, ArcNet Plus, supports data transmission rates of 20 Mbps.

Because ArcNet is a token-passing architecture, a computer in an ArcNet network must have the token in order to transmit data. The token moves from one computer to the next according to their numerical order regardless of how they are placed on the network. This means that the token moves from computer 1 to computer 2 in order even if computer 1 is at one end of the network and computer 2 is at the other end of the network.

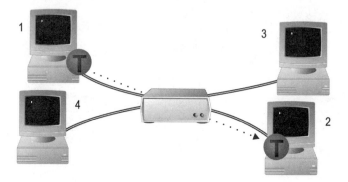

Figure 4.21 Token movement based on numerical order

The standard ArcNet packet contains:

- A destination address.
- A source address.
- Up to 508 bytes of data (or 4096 bytes of data in ArcNet Plus).

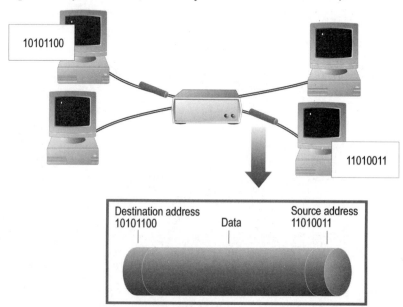

Figure 4.22 An ArcNet packet contains source and destination addresses

Hardware

Each computer is connected by cable to a hub. The hubs can be active, passive, or smart. As you may recall, passive hubs merely relay the signal. Active hubs can regenerate and relay signals. Smart hubs have all of the features of active hubs, and usually add diagnostic features such as reconfiguration detection and operator control-of-port connections.

The standard cabling used for ArcNet is 93 ohm RG-62 A/U, 93 Ohm coaxial cable. ArcNet also supports twisted-pair and fiber-optic media. The distances between computers varies, depending on the cabling and the topology.

Using coaxial cable with BNC connectors, using active hubs, a maximum cable distance of 610 meters (2,000 feet) from a workstation to the hub, can be achieved with a star topology, whereas the maximum distance drops to 305 meters (1,000 feet) on a linear bus segment.

Using unshielded twisted-pair cable with either RJ-11 or RJ-45 connectors, there is a maximum cable distance of 244 meters (800 feet) between devices on both star and bus topologies.

Q & A

Fill in the blanks in the following sentences.

1. ArcNet uses a token passing access method in a _____ topology.

2. An ArcNet token moves from one computer to the next according to their _____ order, regardless of how they are placed on the network.

3. Each computer in an ArcNet network is connected by cable to a _____.

Answers

1. star bus

2. numerical

3. hub

Summary

AppleTalk is the network architecture used in an Apple computer environment. LocalTalk refers to a single physical network. LocalTalk networks can be joined, with the use of zones, to create larger networks. AppleShare is the operating system that allows the sharing of files on the network. A LocalTalk network typically uses CSMA/CA as an access method in a bus or tree topology with shielded, twisted-pair cabling.

EtherTalk allows the AppleTalk network protocols to run on Ethernet coaxial cable. The EtherTalk NB card allows a Macintosh II to connect to an 802.3 Ethernet network. EtherTalk software is included with the card and is compatible with AppleTalk Phase2.

The TokenTalk NB card is an expansion card that allows a Macintosh II to connect to an 802.5 Token Ring network. TokenTalk software is included with the card and is compatible with AppleTalk Phase2.

ArcNet is a flexible network architecture designed for workgroup-sized LANs. It loosely maps to the IEEE 802.4 category which specifies standards for token-passing bus networks. It most often uses coaxial cable and can accommodate both active and passive hubs. The following table summarizes ArcNet specifications.

Note The following information gives the minimum standards required to conform to IEEE specifications. A particular implementation of the ArcNet network architecture may differ from the information in this table.

IEEE specification	ArcNet
Topology	Series of stars
Cable type	RG-62 or RG-59 (coaxial)
Terminator resistance, Ω (ohms)	Not applicable
Impedance, Ω	RG-62: 93 RG-59: 75
Maximum cable distance with coaxial cable, star topology in meters	610 (2,000 feet)
Maximum cable distance with coaxial cable, bus topology in meters	305 (1,000 feet)
Maximum cable distance with twisted-pair cable in meters	244 (800 feet)
Minimum length between computers in meters	Depends on cable
Maximum connected segments	Does not support connected segments
Maximum computers per segment	Depends on cable used

Your Next Step

You are now ready to go on to the Chapter 4 Review where you can test your knowledge of network architectures, and apply what you have learned to solve some network implementation problems.

Chapter 4 Review

Chapter 4 presented a detailed overview of the four major network architectures.

Today's most popular architecture is the IEEE 802.3 Ethernet standard. It can be implemented using one of three topologies: 10BaseT, 10Base2, or 10Base5. Additionally, there are new Ethernet standards developed to handle high-bandwidth applications, two of which are 100BaseVG-AnyLAN and 100BaseX Ethernet.

The token passing architecture is also commonly used, the most popular being based on the IBM Token Ring. A Token Ring network is built around a hub, sometimes called an MSAU. There are no data collisions on a Token Ring network because the only computer that can transmit data is the one with the token.

AppleTalk is built into Macintosh computers, which makes it easy to implement a network a Macintosh environment. The size of an AppleTalk network can be increased through the use of zones.

An early architecture, ArcNet, uses token passing in a star bus topology to transmit data at 2.5 Mbps in workgroup-sized LANs.

Checkup

Follow the instructions for each exercise as indicated. All answers follow the last exercise.

Exercise 1: Matching

Match each item in Column A with the best choice from Column B. One item from Column B will not be used, and items will be used no more than once.

Column A	Column B
1. ArcNet _____	A. Known as Fast Ethernet.
2. 10BaseT _____	B. Uses bus star topology with UTP.
3. 100BaseVG-AnyLAN _____	C. Used in the SNA environment.
4. Token Ring _____	D. Uses token passing in star bus topology.
5. 100BaseX _____	E. Combines Ethernet and Token Ring.
6. 10Base5 _____	F. Uses local bus topology with thinnet.
7. 10Base2 _____	G. Built-in networking for Macintosh.
8. LocalTalk _____	H. Uses bus topology with thicknet.
	I. Uses token passing in a bus topology.

Exercise 2: True or False

For the following sentences, circle True if the statement is true or False if the statement is false.

1. A 100BaseVG network is built on a star topology with all computers attached to a hub.   True   False

2. The ending delimiter on a packet tells its source.   True   False

3. An IBM Token Ring network is an implementation of IEEE standard 802.5.   True   False

4. To ensure rapid Token Ring broadcasts, all computers on a Token Ring network are assigned one address.   True   False

5. Because of their different sizes, construction, and abilities to carry data at different speeds, thicknet and thinnet should not be used in the same network.   True   False

Chapter 4 Checkup Answers

Exercise 1: Matching

1. D
2. B
3. E
4. C
5. A
6. H
7. F
8. G

Exercise 2: True or False

1. True.
2. False. A frame has a beginning and ending delimiter. Packets have only headers.
3. True.
4. False. Each computer must have a unique address. This is what makes it possible to send data to a particular computer. When a new computer comes online in a Token Ring network, it checks for duplicate addresses and notifies the network of its existence. Broadcasts go out to all addresses.
5. False. It is common for larger networks to combine thicknet and thinnet Ethernet. Thicknet is good for backbones with thinnet used for branch segments. They both carry data at 10 Mbps.

Case Study Problem

These problems will continue to focus primarily on the subject matter presented in Chapter 4, but they may occasionally draw on concepts and information presented in earlier chapters. This case study, for example, while focusing on a particular architecture described in this chapter, requires you to draw on information presented in earlier lessons to formulate a solution.

The Setting

Ferguson and Bardell, a small public relations firm, leases two groups of offices in building A and building G of a suburban office park. The business staff, including human resources and accounting, has 12 people and is located in two offices in building A. The creative staff, including copy writing, graphics, and production, with a total of 22 employees, is in building G. Building A and Building G are about 600 meters apart.

The business staff is networked with a four-year old coaxial bus that ties their 386- and 486-based computers together in a peer-to-peer workgroup.

The creative staff in building G has a conglomeration of computers including Apple Macintoshes and personal computer-compatibles. They are not networked.

The Problem

The owners of the company would like to network all of the computers for the creative staff, and connect the creative staff network to the business staff network. They would also like to standardize on the type of network used in both buildings to keep troubleshooting issues to a minimum.

Your Solution

1. What kind of network should they install?

   Server-based _____

   Peer-to-peer _____

2. What type of network should they standardize on within the offices?

   Fiber-optic Ethernet _____

   Fiber-optic Token Ring _____

   Fiber-optic ArcNet _____

   Ethernet 10BaseT _____

   Ethernet 10Base2 _____

   Token Ring _____

   LocalTalk _____

   ArcNet _____

3. What type of network should they install between the two buildings?

    Fiber-optic Ethernet ____

    Fiber-optic Token Ring ____

    Fiber-optic ArcNet ____

    Ethernet 10BaseT ____

    Ethernet 10Base2 ____

    Token Ring ____

    LocalTalk ____

    ArcNet ____

Note There is no single right answer to this case study. This is especially true because there are so many variables to take into account. You may find another solution that works better that the suggested solution.

Suggested Solution

This case study can be solved with several combinations of components and cable.

1. A server-based network is suggested because it is very hard to implement a peer-to-peer network which will service both Macintoshes and personal computers. The company needs a server-based operating system which serves both Macintoshes and personal computers, so you could choose Microsoft Windows NT Server, although there are several other server-based operating systems which could complete the same functions.

2. Within the offices, Ethernet 10BaseT is the suggested solution because it is supported on all platforms and is easy to troubleshoot and install. Token Ring and ArcNet solutions would have also worked, but LocalTalk would not have met the requirements because:

    ▪ It is slow.

    ▪ It is difficult to find LocalTalk cards for personal computers.

3. Between the two buildings a fiber-optic Ethernet solution called 10BaseF is suggested because only fiber-optic cable can offer the distance capabilities needed to cover 600 meters, and because with Ethernet all that is needed is a fiber-optic to 10BaseT repeater in each building.

The Troubleshooter

The information for troubleshooting Ethernet, Token Ring, ArcNet, and LocalTalk has already been covered in three other lessons. Use that information to solve the troubleshooting problem presented here.

Can You Solve This Problem?

Use your knowledge of network architectures to troubleshoot the situation described below and create a possible solution.

The Situation

You have a 500-node 10BaseT network. It started with 50 nodes five years ago, and you have been expanding it constantly since then. Recently the network has started to suffer from poor response time to the end users, and you have identified the network as the bottleneck in this situation. The vendor that you have been working with for the last two years recommends moving to 100BaseX. They said that all you should have to do is put the new 100BaseX network adapter cards in your computers, replace your hubs with 100BaseX hubs, and you will be up and running.

The Available Facts

You and several technicians from your vendor spent the entire weekend installing the new cards and replacing hubs on your network. When the staff started showing up for work on Monday morning, most were ecstatic with the performance of the new network, but about fifty staff members reported that they could not connect to the network. When you investigated further you noticed that all fifty were at stations which were cabled at least four to five years earlier.

Your Solution

Cause of the Problem

List at least two things which could cause those nodes not to function.

_____

_____

_____

Possible Solution

What could you do to resolve each of the two possible causes you listed above?

_____

_____

Suggested Troubleshooting Solution

Cause of the Problem

List two things which could cause the network not to function.

This list contains the most common errors which could be causing the problem, but they are not the only correct possibilities. Furthermore, you are not expected to provide this level of detail in your solutions.

1. The cables to the computers which are having problems might not be the correct category. Category 5 wire, which can handle the 100 Mbps network, is fairly new, and may have been too expensive when those older cable runs were installed.

2. The cables to the computers which are having problems could be the correct category, but might not have been installed to Category 5 specifications. The cable could work fine for 10BaseT, but fail for 100BaseX.

3. The patch cables used to connect each of the problem computers to the wall jack might not be Category 5 patch cables, and could work for 10BaseT but not for 100BaseX.

4. The existing network cabling might have been damaged by rough handling during the installation of the new computers.

Possible Solution

What could you do to resolve each of the two possible causes you listed above?

1. Upgrade to Category 5, and test the cable runs with appropriate test equipment (test equipment is discussed Chapter 8) to determine if it will support 100 Mbps networking. Replace all cables that will not support your new network.

2. Test the cable runs with appropriate test equipment to determine if it will support 100 Mbps networking. Replace all cables that will not support your new network.

3. Test the patch cables with appropriate test equipment to determine if it will support 100 Mbps networking. Replace all cables that will not support your new network.

4. Visually inspect all of the cables for damage, and replace any with obvious problems, and then test the rest to determine if there are any hidden problems. And of course, replace all cables that will not support your new network.

The LAN Planner

Considerations for Implementing a Network Architecture

Ethernet

Research has shown that about 90 percent of all new network installations are using Ethernet 10BaseT with Category 5 UTP. Category 5 allows you to install a 10 Mbps solution now, and upgrade it to a 100 Mbps solution later. However, despite its popularity, Ethernet 10BaseT may not be suitable for all situations.

Because most of the cost of cable installation is labor, there is little cost difference between using Category 3 UTP and Category 5 UTP cable. Most new installations use Category 5 because it supports transmission speeds up to 100 Mbps.

Token Ring

The IBM Cabling System is used in a Token Ring environment. The star wired topology makes moves, changes, and additions simple and easy. Changes can be made by moving a patch cable on the distribution panel.

Additionally, various minicomputer and mainframe systems have built-in Token Ring connections. Cable manufacturers other than IBM also make Token Ring cabling, with UTP being the most popular.

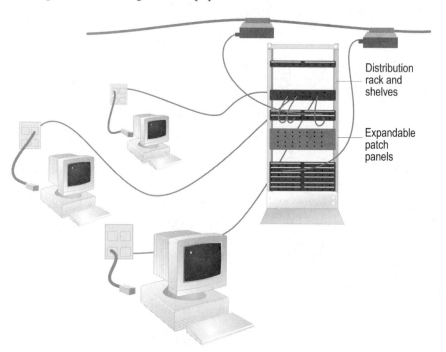

Distribution rack and shelves

Expandable patch panels

Figure 4.23 A patch panel makes moving computers easy

This UTP star wired Token Ring network transmits data at 16 Mbps. Changes can be made easily by simply moving a modular patch cord on the patch panel. This network simplifies management by using an intelligent MSAU. Some intelligent MSAUs allow distances of up to 100 meters to each network lobe (the cable distance between the MSAU and a computer). This cabling scheme follows AT&T wiring standards that make it fully compatible with all 10BaseT applications. It is also compatible with 4 Mbps Token Ring networks.

Selecting a Network Architecture

Note In the following questions, 10 indicates 10BaseT, T indicates Token Ring, F indicates fiber-optic, C indicates coaxial, A indicates that any will do, and D indicates that the appropriate choice depends on other factors.

Because 10BaseT is currently the most popular implementation of the Ethernet architecture, it should be chosen unless there is a compelling reason to choose something else. Therefore, in a case where any architecture will work, 10BaseT should be given first consideration.

Make a check mark on the line next to the choice which applies to your site. To determine which type of architecture would be most appropriate for your site, simply total the number of check marks for each indicator. The indicator with the most check marks should be your first consideration.

Ethernet 10BaseT

Are ease of troubleshooting and long-term maintenance costs important?

Yes _____ 10

No _____ A

Are most of your computers within 100 meters of your wiring closet?

Yes _____ 10

No _____ A

Is ease of reconfiguration important?

Yes _____ 10

No _____ A

Does any of your staff have experience with UTP cable?

Yes _____ 10

No _____ A, D

Note Even if no one has experience with UTP, someone may have transferable experience with another type of cable such as coaxial, STP, or even fiber-optic cable.

10Base2 (Thinnet) and 10Base5 (Thicknet) Ethernet

Note Technically, these are cables, but the Ethernet architecture can be implemented according to several preferences, one of which is the cabling type.

Do you have existing coaxial cabling in your network?

Yes _____ C, if existing cabling is extensive. Otherwise, switch to 10BaseT.

No _____ A

Is your network very small (less than ten computers)?

Yes _____ C

No _____ A

Is your network going to be installed in an open area using cubicles to separate work areas?

Yes _____ C, 10, D

No _____ A

Do you have a need for cable which is more resistant to EMI (electromagnetic interference) than UTP?

Yes _____ C, F, D

No _____ A

Do you have a need for longer cable runs than are supported by UTP?

Yes _____ C, F, D

No _____ A

10BaseF (Fiber)

Do you have a need for longer cabling distances than those supported by copper media? For example, do you need to connect two buildings in a campus environment, or connect two wiring closets in a single building which are more than 185 meters (607 feet) apart?

Yes _____ F

No _____ A, D

Do you have a need for network cabling which is relatively secure from most eavesdropping or corporate intelligence gathering equipment?

Yes _____ F

No _____ A

Token Ring

Does your network have any existing STP cabling?

Yes _____ T

No _____ A

Note While it is possible to use STP with more than one architecture, it is most closely associated with token passing, specifically with IBM's Token Ring implementation. IBM refers to it as Type 1. It is much more expensive than UTP.

Do you have any equipment which needs Token Ring cards (such as an IBM mainframe, and so on)?

Yes _____ T

No _____ A

Do you have any equipment already installed which uses Token Ring?

Yes _____ T

No _____ A

Do you have a need for a network cable system which has built-in redundancy?

Yes _____ T

No _____ A

Do you have a need for cable which is more resistant to EMI than UTP?

Yes _____ T

No _____ A

ArcNet

Do you have existing ArcNet infrastructure you need to connect to?

Yes _____ Use ArcNet

No _____ A

LocalTalk

Do you have an existing LocalTalk network?

Yes _____ Use LocalTalk or create a multivendor network (see Chapter 5: Lesson 4, "Networks in Multivendor Environments").

No _____ A

Do you have Macintosh computers which do not have an Ethernet or Token Ring interface?

Yes _____ Use LocalTalk or create a multivendor network.

No _____ A

The LAN Planner Summary

Based on the information generated in the LAN Planner, your network architecture should be: _____

CHAPTER 5

Network Operations

Lesson 1 Network Operating System Setup . . . 315

Lesson 2 Network Printing . . . 345

Lesson 3 Implementing Network Applications . . . 358

Lesson 4 Networks in Multivendor Environments . . . 385

Lesson 5 The Client/Server Environment . . . 395

Chapter 5 Review . . . 408

Welcome to Chapter 5, Network Operations. Network Operations encompasses several different aspects of networking including the kinds of applications and services networks provide to users, as well as how the network administrator installs and manages those applications and services.

Before anything else can happen on a network, the network operating system must be installed, and so this unit begins with the procedures for operating system installation. Next you will learn how to get network printing up and running, followed by other common network applications.

Because most networks today are made up of hardware and software from a variety of vendors, you will learn two different ways to ensure smooth network operations in a multivendor environment.

And finally, you will learn how the client/server model operates, and why it is the most common form of networking today.

The Case Study Problem

The case study will have you use not only what you learned in this unit, but also previous units to address the networking needs of the Lakes & Sons company. With a number of separate LANs, different applications, and computers, including Macintoshes and personal computers, the company decides it is time to connect all of their computers on a network.

The Troubleshooter

This Troubleshooter begins with some basic questions you need to ask when troubleshooting network operations and network printing and faxing. You will then use these questions to head off potential problems related to a network with Microsoft Windows NT servers and NetWare servers. Also, you will be able to use your knowledge regarding network faxing and e-mail to suggest ways for improving these services.

The LAN Planner

Here you will find considerations for planning and implementing network printing and e-mail, a multivendor network, and more.

Lesson 1: Network Operating System Setup

What This Lesson Does

This lesson serves as an introduction to network operating systems. It describes a network operating system's basic features and functions and contrasts these with the capabilities of a stand-alone operating system.

The lesson also introduces the process of installing a network operating system and provides an overview of major installation issues.

Objectives

By the end of this lesson, you will be able to:

- Identify essential network operating system components.
- Define preemptive and nonpreemptive multitasking.
- Describe the elements of client software.
- Describe the elements of server software.
- Define network services.
- Identify the major considerations in a network operating system installation.
- Install Windows NT Server.

Estimated lesson time 35 minutes

Overview

Until recently, personal computer network operating software was added to existing operating systems. A personal computer that was part of a network was actually running both a stand-alone and a network operating system.

Both operating systems needed to be installed in the same computer in order to handle all of the functions involved in both stand-alone and network activity. For example, Microsoft LAN Manager was sometimes referred to as a network operating system, but it really only provided networking capabilities to an operating system such as MS-DOS, UNIX, or OS/2®.

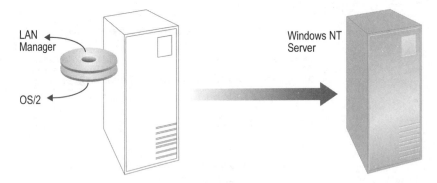

Figure 5.1 Microsoft Windows NT Server has built-in networking software

Now, in advanced network operating systems such as Windows NT Server, Windows NT Workstation, and Windows 95, the stand-alone and network operating systems have been combined into one operating system that runs both the stand-alone computer and the network. This operating system is the foundation for all computer hardware and software activity.

Hardware and Software Coordination

The operating system controls the allocation and use of hardware resources such as the following:

- Memory
- CPU time
- Disk space
- Peripheral devices

The operating system coordinates the interaction between the computer and the application programs it is running. It is also the base upon which applications such as word processing and spreadsheet programs are built. In fact, application programs are written with certain operating systems in mind. Vendors may point out that their applications have been written to take full advantage of advanced Windows NT Server 4.0 features.

Multitasking

Supporting a network operating system and network activity is a complex, demanding job. One consideration in choosing an operating system for a network environment is multitasking.

A multitasking operating system provides the means for a computer to process more than one task at a time. A true multitasking operating system can run as many tasks as there are processors. When there are more tasks than processors, the computer must time slice so that the available processors devote a certain amount of time to each task, alternating between tasks until they are all done. This system makes the computer appear to be working on several tasks at once.

There are two major types of multitasking:

- Preemptive

  In preemptive multitasking, the operating system can take control of the processor without the task's cooperation.

- Non-preemptive (cooperative)

  In non-preemptive multitasking, the processor is never taken from a task. The task itself decides when to give up the processor. Programs written for non-preemptive multitasking systems must include provisions for yielding control of the processor. No other program can run until the non-preemptive program gives up control of the processor.

Because of the constant interaction between the stand-alone operating system and the network operating system, a preemptive multitasking system offers certain advantages. For example, when the situation requires it, the preemptive system can shift CPU activity from a local task to a network task.

Software Components

All network operating systems used to be application programs that were loaded on top of a stand-alone operating system. A significant difference between the Microsoft Windows NT operating system and other operating systems is that the networking capabilities are built into Windows NT.

A network operating system:

- Ties together all of the computers and peripherals in the network.
- Coordinates the functions of all computers and peripherals in a network.
- Provides security for and access to data and peripherals in a network.

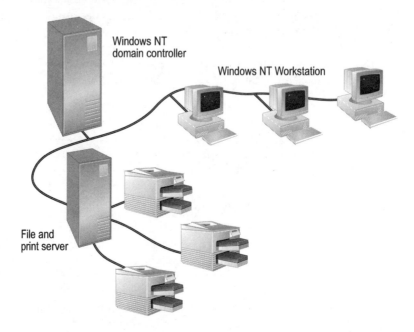

Figure 5.2 Windows NT Server domain controller ties the network together

There are two major components of network software:

- The network software that is installed on clients
- The network software that is installed on a server

For example, in Figure 5.2, the clients are the three computers with Windows NT Workstation installed. The two servers, the domain controller, and the file and print server have Windows NT Server installed on them.

Client Software

In a stand-alone system, when the user types a command which makes a request for the computer to perform some task, the request goes over the computer's local bus to the computer's CPU. For example, if you want to see a directory listing on one of the local hard disks, the CPU interprets the request and then displays a directory listing on the window.

Figure 5.3 Directory listing request on a local hard disk

In a network environment, however, when a user initiates a request to use a resource that exists on a server in another part of the network, the request has to be forwarded or redirected away from the local bus, out onto the network, to the server with the requested resource.

The Redirector

The process of forwarding requests is done by a redirector. Depending on the networking software, this redirector may also be referred to as a shell or a requester. The redirector is a small section of code in the network operating system that:

- Intercepts requests in the computer.

- Determines if they should be left alone to continue in the local computer's bus or redirected out to the network to another server.

Redirector activity originates in a client computer when the user issues a request for a network resource or service. The user's computer is referred to as a client because it is making a request of a server. The request is intercepted by the redirector and forwarded out onto the network.

In Windows NT, the server processes the connections requested by client redirectors and gives them access to the resources they request. In other words, the server services or fulfills the request made by the client.

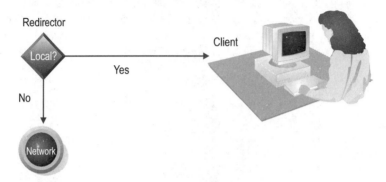

Figure 5.4 The redirector forwards requests for remote resources onto the network

Designators

The redirector needs to keep track of which drive designators are associated with which network resources.

If you need to access a shared directory and you have permission to access it, you have several choices depending on your operating system. For example, with Windows NT you could use File Manager to connect to the network drive you want to access. When you specify the server and shared directory name, File Manager assigns a letter of the alphabet as a designator, such as G. You can then refer to the shared directory on the remote computer as G and the redirector will locate it.

Peripherals

Redirectors can send requests to either computers or peripherals. With the redirector, LPT1 or COM1 can refer to network printers instead of local printers. The redirector will intercept any print job going to LPT1 and forward it out of the local machine to the specified network printer.

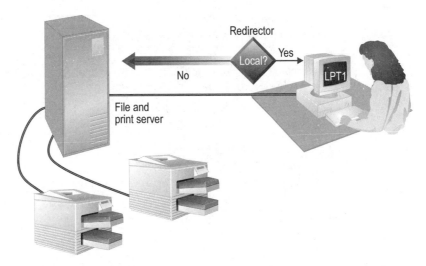

Figure 5.5 Request to print redirected out LPT1 to a printer on the network

The redirector makes it unnecessary for users to worry about the actual location of data or peripherals or the complexities involved in making a connection. To access data on a network computer, for example, a user only needs to type the drive designator assigned to the location of the resource, and the redirector does the rest.

In Figure 5.5, the original request is redirected away from the originating computer and sent over the network to the target computer. In this case, the target is the file and print server with the requested printer, where the file is printed.

Q & A

Fill in the blanks in the following sentences.

1. A true multitasking operating system can run as many tasks simultaneously as there are _____.

2. The operating system can take control of the processor without the task's cooperation in a multitasking operating system that uses _____ multitasking.

3. The process of forwarding requests is done by a _____, which is also commonly referred to as a shell or a requester.

4. Redirector activity originates in the _____ computer when the user issues a request for a network resource or service.

5. Redirectors can send requests to either computers or _____.

6. All network operating systems used to be _____ that were loaded on top of a stand-alone operating system.

Answers

1. processors

2. preemptive

3. redirector

4. client

5. peripherals

6. applications

Server Software

Server software makes it possible for users at other machines to share the server's data and peripherals including printers, plotters, and disks.

Typically, all computers in a Windows NT domain contain both client and server software. If Windows NT workstations are acting as your clients, they have the software built-in to act as both clients and servers.

In Figure 5.6, a user is requesting a directory listing on a shared remote hard disk. The request is forwarded by the redirector onto the network and is passed to the file and print server containing the shared directory. The request is granted and the directory listing is provided.

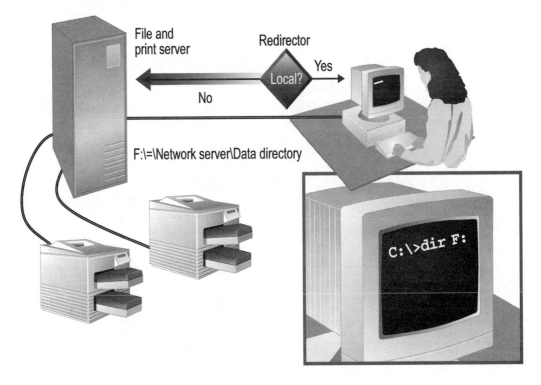

Figure 5.6 Directory listing request on a remote hard drive

Resource Sharing

Most network operating systems not only allow sharing, but they also determine the degree of sharing. The degree of sharing includes:

- Allowing different users different levels of access to the resources.

- Coordinating access to the resources to make sure that two users do not use the same resource at the same time.

For example, an office manager wants everyone on the network to be familiar with a certain document (a file), so she shares the document. However, she controls access to the document by sharing it so that:

- Some users will only be able to read it.
- Other users will be able to read it and make changes in it.

Managing Users

Network operating systems also make it possible for a network administrator to determine which people will be able to use the network. A network administrator can use the network operating system to:

- Create users privileges tracked by the network operating system, which indicates who gets to use the network.
- Grant or take away user privileges on the network.
- Remove users from the list of users that the network operating system tracks.

Managing the Network

Some advanced network operating systems contain management tools to help administrators keep track of network behavior.

If a problem develops on the network, management tools can detect signs of trouble and present these in charts or other formats. This allows the network manager to take corrective action before the problem halts the network.

Installing Windows NT Server

The installation program is an application that will do the work of installing the network operating system in a variety of ways, depending on:

- The environment into which it will be installed.
- The size of the network.
- The types of jobs the server will perform in the network.
- The type of file system the server will use.
- The identification of the server.
- Operating systems in the server.
- How the server's hard disk space is divided.

The installation program asks a series of questions to determine the installation parameters. The following text describes some of the key question areas.

Note Before trying to install a network operating system yourself, it is a good idea to discuss these parameters with a qualified systems engineer.

Server Naming Information

It is common for the installation program to ask for the following server and network identification information:

- A name you have given to your network segment, for example, a domain name or a workgroup name
- A name you have given to your server

This information helps the network operating system identify the particular server and its network environment and distinguish them from other computers and other network segments. This will be important when sending or receiving data over the network.

Server Responsibilities

You may be asked to supply information about the responsibilities your server will have in your network environment.

For example, a Microsoft NT Server network is divided into areas called domains. A domain is a logical grouping of computers to simplify administration. Certain servers in these domains are responsible for keeping track of all of the users, security policies, and other information about the domain. The first server installed in a domain must be installed as the primary domain controller (PDC). The PDC not only contains a master copy of domain information and validates users, but it can act as a file, print, and application server as well. Every domain is required to have one and only one PDC.

Some of the Windows NT servers installed after the PDC may be installed as backup domain controllers. A backup domain controller (BDC) refers to a computer that receives a copy of the domain's security policy and domain database, and authenticates network logons. It provides a backup in the event that the primary domain controller becomes unavailable. A domain is not required to have a BDC, but it is recommended to have at least one BDC to back up the PDC. A BDC can also function as a file, print, and application server.

Other servers can be installed that will function just as servers and not as domain controllers or backup domain controllers. These are referred to as "stand-alone servers," and can act as file, print, and application servers. This type of server can "never" be a PDC or a BDC unless the operating system is re-installed and the server is designated as a PDC or a BDC.

You need to determine if the server you are installing is a primary server (a domain controller), a backup to the primary server or just a file, print, and application server.

Partitioning

In order to install a network operating system, you will need to supply information about how space on the server's hard disks is being used.

The hard disk can be divided into areas called partitions. You can assign different partitions for different purposes. For example, you might create a partition for a certain type of program. Whatever is kept on that partition will usually be kept separate from anything stored on any other partition.

As part of the installation process you will need to either create a partition for the network operating system or identify the partition into which you will be installing the network operating system.

Figure 5.7 Server disk partitioning

Configuring the Network Adapter Card

During the installation of Windows NT Server, you will be asked to choose or configure the network adapter card installed in your computer. In addition to installing the network adapter card, you must also choose a protocol. Protocol choices include TCP/IP, NetBEUI, DLC, and IPX/SPX. If you are unsure which protocol to use, review Chapter 3: Lesson 4, "Protocols." The default protocol for a Windows NT Server installation is TCP/IP.

TCP/IP Installation

Microsoft TCP/IP on Windows NT enables enterprise networking and connectivity on your Windows NT-based computer. TCP/IP provides:

- A standard, routable, enterprise networking protocol for Windows NT.
- An architecture that facilitates connectivity in heterogeneous environments.
- Access to the worldwide Internet and organizational Intranets and their resources.

Installing TCP/IP is simple and straightforward. From the Control Panel, double-click the Network icon, then select the Protocols tab, select Add. Choose the TCP/IP protocol.

Installation Parameters

When you install Microsoft TCP/IP, you need the following three configuration parameters to use it in a routed network environment.

IP Address

An IP address is a logical 32-bit address used to identify a TCP/IP host. Each IP address has two parts: the network ID and the host ID. The network ID identifies all hosts that are on the same physical network. The ID identifies a specific host on a network. Each computer that runs TCP/IP requires a unique IP address. For example, the following is a valid IP address: 131.107.2.200.

Subnet Mask

A subnet mask is used to mask a portion of the IP address so that TCP/IP can distinguish the network ID from the host ID. TCP/IP hosts communicate by using the subnet mask to determine whether the destination host is located on a local or remote network. The following is a valid subnet mask: 255.255.0.0.

Default Gateway

For communication with a host on another network, an IP host must be configured with a route to the destination network. If a configured route is not found, the host uses the gateway (synonymous with a router) to transmit the traffic to the destination host. The default gateway is where the IP sends packets that are destined for remote networks. If a default gateway is not specified, communications are limited to the local network.

Configuring TCP/IP Manually

For manual configurations, assign an IP address, the subnet mask, and the default gateway in the Windows NT-based computer to use TCP/IP. Enter these parameters for each network adapter card in the computer that will use TCP/IP. If you are installing Windows NT Server on an existing network that contains computers with TCP/IP addresses, you should see your network administrator for details on installing TCP/IP.

Configuring TCP/IP Automatically

Microsoft Windows NT Server provides a service called the dynamic host configuration protocol (DHCP) server service. When a DHCP server is configured on the network, clients that support DHCP (including Windows NT Workstation and Windows NT Server) can request TCP/IP configuration information (IP address, subnet mask, default gateway, and so forth) from the DHCP server. This can greatly simplify the configuration of TCP/IP on the client computer.

If you have a DHCP server available, TCP/IP can be configured automatically by selecting the Obtain an IP address from a DHCP server check box when installing TCP/IP. With the Obtain an IP address from a DHCP server option selected, the DHCP Client contacts a DHCP Server for its configuration information, such as the IP address, subnet mask, and default gateway. This option can also be configured at a later time through the Network option, Protocols, TCP/IP Properties in Control Panel.

When you select Obtain an IP address from a DHCP server, DHCP configures TCP/IP on all of the network adapter cards in the computer. TCP/IP automatically binds to all network adapter cards in the computer.

After you select Obtain an IP address from a DHCP server, no further configuration of TCP/IP is necessary on the DHCP client.

TCP/IP Utilities

Microsoft Windows NT Server provides a few simple utilities that work with TCP/IP protocols to provide information and extended netowrk capabilities.

- ping (Packet Internet Groper) - Verifies config. and tests connections.

- ipconfig - Displays current TCP/IP config.

- nbtstat - Displays protocol stats & connections using NetBIOS over TCP/IP.

- netstat - Displays TCP/IP protocol stats & connections.

- Route - Displays or modifies the local routing table.

- Tracert - Checks the route to a remote system.

- ARP – Displays cache of locally resolved IP addresses to physical addresses.

Windows Internet Name Service (WINS)

Computers can very easily use the numeric method of identifying each other on a network, but computer users find it easier to use easily remembered computer names. A method to resolve these computer names (NetBIOS names) to IP addresses needs to be available. To ensure that the computer names and IP addresses are unique to the network, a computer running Microsoft Windows NT will register its computer name and IP address during system startup. Using WINS a computer can dynamically register their NetBIOS names and IP addresses into a database that will allow proper resolution of NetBIOS resources in a routed TCP/IP network.

Your Server's Requirements

It is important to understand what resources your server needs in order to work well with a network operating system. These system requirements can include parameters such as:

- Available disk space
- Type of Processor
- Memory (RAM)
- Type of file system
- Local and remote hosts and clients

Each of these will vary depending on the requirements of the network operating system. The requirements for Windows NT Server 4.0 are given in the following table as an example.

Category	Intel requirement	RISC requirement
Processor	32-bit *x*86-based (80486/33 or higher)	A supported RISC-based processor, such as the MIPS® R4000 and R4400, or Digital's Alpha
Display	VGA (or higher resolution) video display adapter	VGA (or higher resolution) video display adapter
Hard disk space	One or more hard disks, with approximately 125 MB minimum free disk space on the partition that will contain the Windows NT Server files	One or more hard disks, with approximately 160 MB minimum free disk space on the partition that will contain the Windows NT Server files
Other drivers	High-density 3.5-inch floppy disk drive, or a high-density 5.25-inch floppy drive plus a SCSI CD-ROM drive (for computers with only a 5.25-inch drive, you must install Windows NT Server over a network)	SCSI CD-ROM drive
Memory	16 MB minimum	16 MB minimum
Optional components	Mouse or other pointing device	Mouse or other pointing device
Other components	One or more network adapter cards	One or more network adapter cards

The Hardware Compatibility List

You should verify that your server and its associated hardware will work with your network operating system. To do this, check the HCL published by the network operating system vendor. The HCL is an important network tool that tells you which hardware has been tested with the network operating system.

Q & A

Fill in the blanks in the following sentences.

1. A logical grouping of computers in a Windows NT Server environment is called a _____.

2. The hard disk can be divided into areas called _____ into which you may install the operating system or simply store applications or data.

3. Most network operating systems determine the _____ of sharing of network resources.

4. The first server installed in a Windows NT domain must be installed as the
_____ _____ _____.

5. You verify that your server and its associated hardware will work with your network operating system by checking the _____
_____ _____ published by the network operating system vendor.

6. Using WINS will ensure that the _____ names and _____ addresses are unique to the network.

Answers

1. domain
2. partitions
3. degree
4. primary domain controller
5. hardware compatibility list
6. NetBIOS, IP

Network Services

Network services are network operating system application programs that run your network. In the Microsoft Windows NT Server environment, they are called services.

Your network operating system installation program will ensure that you have a minimum of network services installed by default. However, as the network expands its operations, you may need to install services and functions your network did not originally need.

Installing and Removing Network Services

Installing or removing a service is similar to installing or removing drivers. Most network operating systems include a utility which provides a graphical user interface to lead you through the procedure.

Figure 5.8 shows how the Control Panel Network icon can be used to add and remove network services. From the Network Settings window, you would select the **Services** tab, **Add**. Select the service you want to add, for example the Services for **Microsoft DHCP Server**, and then select the OK button. The service is added.

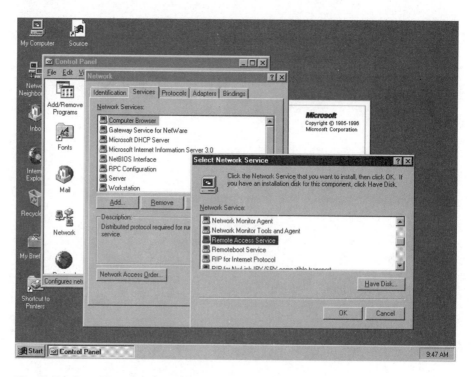

Figure 5.8 Installing services with Windows NT Server

By default, some services start automatically when you turn on your computer. Other services do not start automatically and must be manually started. To manually start services, select the Services icon in the Windows NT Server Control Panel. If the Startup column is Manual, you must select the service and then select the **Startup** button. The service will start.

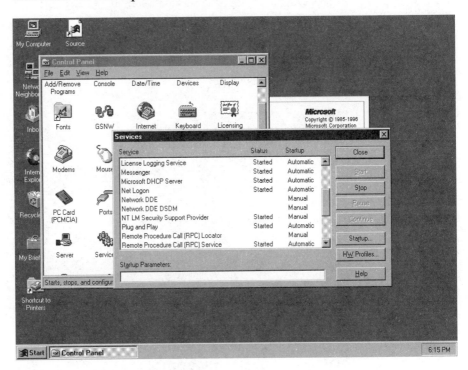

Figure 5.9 Starting services with Windows NT Server

For those services that are set to Manual startup, you can use the above window and the **Startup**... button to change them to start automatically.

Binding Options for Services

Bindings are a series of bound paths from the upper OSI layer network services and protocols to the lowest layer of network adapter card device drivers. Each network component can be bound to one or more network components preceding or following it to make the services available to any component that needs them. For example, the network operating system protocol needs to be attached to the network adapter card; this process is referred to as binding.

As shown in Figure 5.10, the protocol (TCP/IP) is bound to the 3Com Fast Etherlink XL Adapter card.

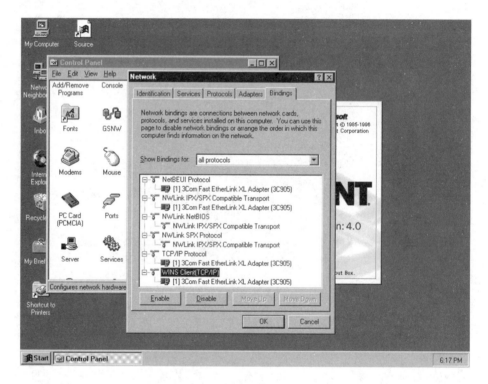

Figure 5.10 Protocol bindings

You can also use the Network Bindings dialog box to change the bindings path order. Binding paths are processed in the order listed. If the network protocol you use most frequently is first in the binding list, average connection time is lower. Some protocols are faster than others for certain network topologies. Putting the faster protocol first in the binding list improves performance.

Q & A

Fill in the blanks in the following sentences.

1. Installing or removing a service is similar to installing or removing a
   _____.

2. Attaching the network operating system protocol to the network adapter card is referred to as _____.

3. Network services are network operating system _____ programs that run your network by performing different network jobs.

4. You can change the bindings path order and put the faster _____ first in the binding list to improve performance.

Answers

1. driver
2. binding
3. application
4. protocol

Activity

Run Demo 15.

Use the following steps to run Lab 15.

Lab 15: Installing a Network Operating System

What This Lab Does

This lab simulates the installation of a network operating system. In going through the lab, you will experience the same process as if you were installing an actual network operating system.

It is important to remember that this lab simulates a Windows NT Server 4.0 installation. It is also important to remember that it is only a simulation. The choices and keystrokes you make in this lab will not affect your system. Therefore, feel free to explore all of the alternatives.

If you have a problem, try either Help for an explanation of the process in which you are involved, or Press **F3** to exit the simulation.

Objectives

By the end of this lab, you will be able to:

- Install Windows NT Server.

- Recognize the default options during an installation and determine whether or not they are appropriate for your network.

- Choose appropriate network options as needed during an installation of Windows NT Server.

Exercise 1: Installing Windows NT Server

1. From the **Start** menu, point to **Programs**, then **Networking Essentials**, and click **Lab15**.

   The **Welcome** dialog box appears with instructions on how to navigate through the simulation.

2. Click **Continue** to start the installation simulation.

Note When the blue screen titled Windows NT Server Setup appears, your mouse will not be active. Use the arrow keys to make selections.

---

3. Read the Setup screen. You can press the **F1** key for Help, **ENTER** to continue with the setup, **F3** to Exit, **R** for Repair of damaged installation (this option is inoperative)

Note To return to Setup from a Help screen, press **ESC**.

4. Press **ENTER** to continue the installation.

The next screen describes the procedures that Windows NT follows to detect mass storage devices.

The **S** option to skip (is inoperative). **F3** exits the setup routine.

5. Press **ENTER** to continue.

A screen asking you to insert the disk labeled Windows NT Server Setup Disk #3 appears. For this simulation, a diskette will not be needed.

6. Press **ENTER** to bypass the screen and continue with the installation.

A screen appears informing you that Setup has recognized an Adaptec® 274x/284x/AIC777x hard disk controller in your system (simulated).

It is common for advanced installation programs to advise you about certain components and their parameters in your system. In an actual installation, you might need a disk containing the drivers for certain components in your computer. Because this is only a simulation, you will not need any drivers.

However, this is a good opportunity to explore some of the hardware possibilities available during setup.

You can specify an additional device by pressing **S** (this is inoperative in the simulation) or you can press **F3** to exit the setup.

7. Press **ENTER** to continue.

This lab will proceed as if the installation were being done from a compact disc.

The Windows NT Server license agreement screen appears. Read the information.

8. Press **PAGE DOWN** to continue.

A new screen appears, stating that Setup has determined that your computer contains the following hardware and software components. Remember, this is a simulated list; it does not reflect what is actually on your computer. During an actual setup, you could change the various settings from this screen. For this simulation, accept the settings that are listed.

9. Press **ENTER** to continue.

A screen appears asking you to choose the partition on which you will install Windows NT Server.

The installation program gives you the opportunity to determine the type and size of the partition on which the network operating system will be installed.

In a normal installation, you could press **D** to delete the highlighted partition (inoperative in this simulation), press **F1** for help, or press **F3** to exit the setup.

For this simulation, you want to install Windows NT Server on drive D:

10. Use the arrow keys to select drive D: then press ENTER to install Windows NT on the highlighted partition.

    Windows NT Server Setup displays a window that allows you to format the partition (FAT or NTFS) or convert the partition to NTFS.

11. Select to leave the current file system intact and press ENTER.

    A screen appears showing you the default path **\WINNT** for the location of the network subdirectory. You can accept the entry made for you or change it. In an actual installation you could use this opportunity to determine where in your computer you would like to install the network operating system. You could also press **F3** to exit.

12. Accept the default location and press ENTER to continue.

    Setup examines your hard disks for corruption before it copies files on the drives. If no hard disk corruption is found, Setup will continue with the install.

13. Press ENTER to start the simulated drive check and installation of files.

    A screen appears telling you that a portion of the Setup has been completed successfully.

14. Press ENTER to simulate the computer restarting.

    The next portion of the installation process is covered in Exercise 2.

Exercise 2: Windows NT Server Setup

In the second part of the installation the Setup Wizard will guide you through the rest of the Setup process. Your mouse is active during this process.

The Windows NT Setup screen appears explaining the next three parts of the Setup process.

1. Click **Next** to continue.

   A window appears requesting your name and the name of your company.

   Note Use the TAB key to toggle between the **Name** and **Company** text boxes.

   ---

2. Enter the requested information.

   This helps identify you to the network operating system.

3. Click **Next** to continue.

   The **Licensing Modes** window appears. This is to ensure that your site is properly licensed for the network products from that vendor. There are two client licensing modes: Per Server and Per Seat.

4. Select the **Per Server** option.

5. Increment the counter to 10.

If you should select 0 as the number of concurrent connections, a dialog box informs you that basic network services will be disabled.

6. Click **Next** to continue.

A window appears asking for your computer name. The computer name identifies your computer to the rest of the network. This makes it possible for the network operating system to distinguish your computer from all of the others on the network.

7. Enter a name for your computer.

Your computer name may be up to 15 characters in length. You should use a name that is unique to the network.

8. Click **Next** to continue.

The Server Type window appears asking for the role your server will be playing in your network. You must determine how you are going to use your server in the network.

If this is the first server being installed in the network, you should select **Primary Domain Controller**. If it is not the first computer on your network, select either **Backup Domain Controller** or **Stand Alone Server**.

9. For this simulation, select **Primary Domain Controller** and click **Next** to continue.

The **Administrator Account** window displays. This window allows you to determine the password for the system administrator. The administrator has more privileges and permissions on the network than just about any other user, so be careful when selecting this password and make sure you keep this password secure.

10. Enter and confirm the Administrators Password.

The password can be up to 14 characters in length. You need to enter it identically in each text box.

11. Click **Next** to continue.

The Emergency Repair Disk window allows you to specify whether or not to create an Emergency Repair disk. These are very useful during normal operations.

12. Select **Yes**.

A diskette is not required for this simulation.

13. Click **Next** to continue.

The install components window appears. Select the components you wish to install. The simulation does not support every option.

14. Click **Next** to continue.

A window appears informing you that Setup is now starting the second part of the installation process and is ready to guide you through installation of Windows NT networking.

15. Click **Next** to continue.

A window requesting how the computer will participate on the network appears. You have the options of being wired directly to the network or accessing the network remotely.

16. Select **Wired to the Network**.

17. Click **Next** to continue.

A window is displayed asking if you want to install Internet Information Server (IIS).

18. Do not check this box and click **Next** to continue.

A window appears prompting you to begin a search for a network adapter.

19. Click **Start Search**.

The Setup simulation detects the **Intel EtherExpress PRO/100B adapter**.

In a normal installation, you could use the Find Next button if another adapter card is present. In this simulation, there is only one network adapter.

20. Click **Next** to continue.

Networking protocols selection appears. You can select any or all of the protocols listed. For this simulation, accept the defaults, TCP/IP and NWLink.

21. Click **Next** to continue.

A list of network services appears. You may select any or all of the services listed. For this simulation, accept the defaults as they are listed.

22. Click **Next** to continue.

This dialog gives you the opportunity to review and change any of your selected networking components. Click **Back** to review your selections. When satisfied that your selections are correct, click **Next** to install the components you selected.

23. Click **Next** to continue.

The **Intel PROSet** dialog box appears with the adapter cards I/O address, Interrupt, and Ethernet Address. During a normal installation, you may test or change any of these settings.

24. Click **OK** to continue.

The **TCP/IP Setup** dialog box appears. DHCP is a convenient tool for managing IP addresses.

25. Click **Yes**.

    The simulation works through the automated setup of networking components. A screen displays the current network bindings. During a normal installation, you may change these bindings if required.

26. Click **Next** to continue.

    Windows NT is now ready to start the network.

27. Click **Next** to start the network and continue.

    For this simulation, you requested that Windows NT create a Primary Domain Controller. Your computer name will be displayed and you need to enter a Domain name. The domain name should be unique to your network.

28. Enter a domain name.

29. Click **Next** to continue.

    The Setup process is ready to start the third and final part of setting up a Windows NT Server.

30. Click **Finish** to continue.

    The Date/Time Properties dialog appears.

31. From the dropdown list, select the geographic region where you are currently located.

32. Click **Close** to continue.

    For this simulation, the **Detected display** dialog appears indicating that an ATI compatible display adapter was detected. In a normal setup, the display adapter that is present on your computer would be listed.

33. The **Display Properties settings** dialog appears. You can use this dialog to select and test various display attributes.

34. Click **Test** to test the new display modes.

35. On the **Testing Mode** dialog, click **OK**.

    A test bitmap appears. It should disappear after about 15 seconds.

36. Click **Yes** to indicate that the test was concluded properly.

37. Click **OK** to save the new settings.

38. Click **OK** to continue with the installation.

    Windows NT Server continues the setup process. A simulation of the setup of the files is displayed.

    A message indicates that Windows NT has been installed successfully appears.

39. Click **Restart Computer** to continue.

    A message concluding the Windows NT 4.0 Setup Simulation appears.

40. Click **Exit** to exit the simulation.

You have completed the installation exercise.

Summary

The operating system is the foundation for all computer hardware and software activity. In setting up a network you need to consider the interaction between the operating system of each stand-alone computer on the network, and the operating system of the network. One primary consideration for choosing network operating system software is multitasking, the means for a computer to process more than one task at a time.

The network operating system software has two primary components: client software and server software. Client software includes the redirector, which intercepts requests in the computer and determines if they should stay in the local computer's bus, or be redirected out to the network. Server software provides resource sharing and coordinates different levels of access. The network administrator manages users and the network through the server.

When installing network system software you need to name the server(s) and assign server responsibilities. In the Windows NT environment there are three categories of servers: primary domain controllers, backup domain controllers, and servers that act as file, print, and application services. When you install the network system software a number of services that perform different network jobs are automatically installed. There are additional services that you may choose to install.

Your Next Step

Network operating systems are the software engines that make networks run. Once your operating system is installed, you are ready to provide resources to the network users. Next you will see what these resources are, and how they are shared, starting with printing.

Lesson 2: Network Printing

What This Lesson Does

This lesson presents an overview of how to print documents in the networking environment. Specifically, it covers:

- Sharing a printer
- Connecting to a printer
- Managing a printer

The lesson also briefly explains page description languages, dedicated print sharing devices, and sharing fax modems on the network.

Objectives

By the end of this lesson, you will be able to:

- Identify the steps for installing and using a shared printer.
- List the tasks included in managing a shared printer.
- Determine whether a sharing fax service would be appropriate for a given site.

Estimated lesson time 25 minutes

The Network Printing Process

When network users want to print data on a shared network printer, they send their data to a print server. The server then feeds the data to be printed to a shared printer.

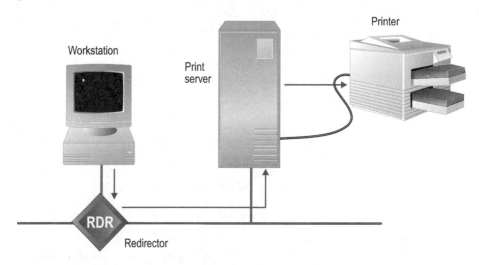

Figure 5.11 Data to be printed goes first to the printer server

Redirection plays a part in network printing because each network print job must be redirected away from a computer's local printer port and onto the network cable.

The printing process happens in two steps:

1. The computer's redirector puts the print job onto the network cable.
2. The print server's network software takes the print job from the cable and sends it into a queue with other items waiting for access to the shared printer.

In a busy environment, there may be many documents waiting to be printed. To facilitate the process of getting a job from the network into a printer, the network uses a spool (Simultaneous Peripheral Operation On Line).

A spooler is a memory buffer in the print server's RAM that holds the print job until the printer is ready to print. Because the spool is in RAM, it can move data to be printed faster than a hard disk can. However, if numerous documents are sent to the printer at once, and the spool overflows, the overflow documents will be sent to the print server's hard disk to await their turn in the spool.

Sharing a Printer

Simply connecting a printer to a network print server will not make the printer available to network users. This is because the printer, although physically part of the network, has not yet been given a network identification.

To send print jobs to a printer, users have to be able to identify or see the printer from their computers. In other words, the network operating system must provide a way for the printer to signal network computers to let them know its name and that it is available.

Essential Printer Information

Every network operating system has its own version of printer sharing, but they all require the administrator to provide printer drivers and supply the network operating system with information about the printer.

These procedures include:

- Loading printer drivers so the printer will work with the print server.
- Creating a share name for the printer so other network users will be able to recognize and access it.
- Identifying the destination of the output so the redirector will know where to send the print job.
- Setting information and output format parameters so the network operating system will know how to handle and format the print job.

The Print Sharing Utility

This process may seem complex, but most network operating systems have utilities to help administrators enter the information. In Windows NT Server, for example, a utility called the Print Manager presents the printer setup screen shown in Figure 5.12.

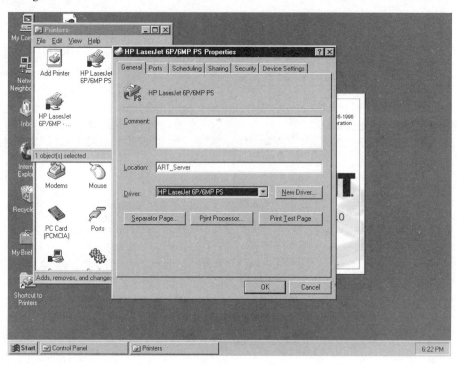

Figure 5.12 Windows NT Print Manager printer setup

Connecting to a Printer

After a printer has been shared, users must use the network operating system to connect to it. To do this, a user will need to know two things:

- The name of the server to which the printer has been connected.
- The name of the printer.

This explains why the administrator needs to supply a name for the printer during the sharing process. Current computer operating systems, such as Windows NT, provide a graphical user interface to help users connect to a printer.

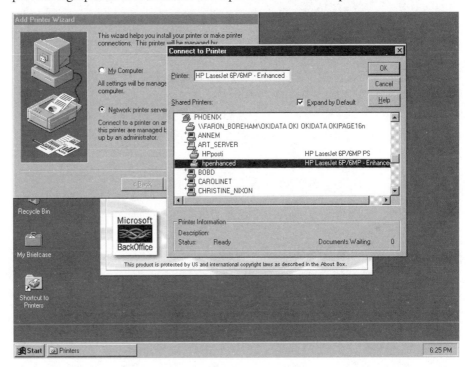

Figure 5.13 Windows NT Print Manager printer setup

As shown in Figure 5.13, you can double click on the server name and select the printer. For example, to connect to the printer hpenhanced on the server ART_SERVER, you would doubleclick the ART_SERVER icon then select the required printer.

Q & A

Fill in the blanks in the following sentences.

1. When network users want to print data on a shared network printer, the data is sent to a _____ which feeds the data the printer.

2. Each network print job must be _____ away from a computer's local printer port and onto the network cable.

3. A memory buffer in the print server's RAM that holds the print job until the printer is ready is called a _____.

4. In order for users to access a shared printer the printer must have a network _____.

Answers

1. server
2. redirected
3. spooler
4. identification

Managing a Shared Printer

After the network administrator has shared a printer, it needs to be managed and maintained. Printer management usually has two areas of responsibility:

- Maintenance of the printer itself
- Management of users who access the printer

Printer Maintenance

Maintenance tasks include:

- Supplying the printer with paper and toner.
- Clearing the printer if there is a paper jam.
- Monitoring the printer's output to ensure that print jobs do not back up and overflow the printer's output bin.
- Monitoring the printer's performance and notifying a technician if a serious problem develops.

Most of these are routine tasks that can be learned easily. Users generally do not mind doing jobs such as reloading an empty paper tray or even changing the toner if there are clear, step-by-step instructions for such tasks located near the printer.

However, problems can develop when no one person is responsible for the printer. It is not unusual for everyone who uses the printer to think someone else is taking care of any problems that arise. As a result, it sometimes happens that simple problems remain unsolved until a frustrated volunteer decides to take on the responsibility of remedying the situation.

Managing Users

The printer is like any other shared resource. Users must not only be given permission to use it, but they must also be assigned a level of permission.

For example, users can manipulate print jobs on shared printers. Users with the appropriate privileges can move their print jobs ahead of other users' print jobs in the print queue or delete another user's print job entirely. To avoid user conflicts, limit the number of users who have these privileges.

The range of printer privileges will vary with the network operating system. It is up to the administrator to determine which users will have which privileges. Network operating systems provide utilities the administrator can use to implement appropriate printing permissions.

The Windows NT Server Print Manager features a series of windows that guide the administrator through the user management process.

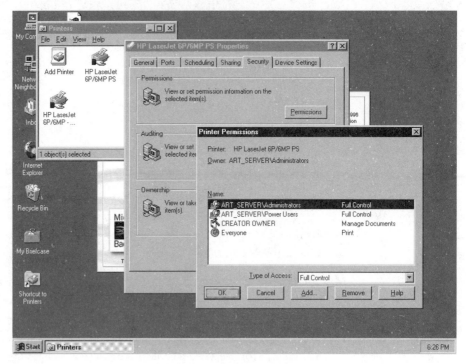

Figure 5.14 Setting user privileges with Windows NT Printer Properties

Page Description Languages

In addition to understanding network printer implementation and maintenance, network administrators should also be aware of any components which affect printer performance or behavior. One of these is called a page description language.

Page description languages (PDLs) tell a printer how printed output should look. The printer uses the PDL to construct text and graphics to create the page image. PDLs are like blueprints in that they set specifications for parameters and features such as type sizes and fonts, but they leave the drawing to the printer.

Because of their impact on printing, PDLs are important to administrators. PostScript®, for example, offers flexible font capability and high-quality graphics. Also, PostScript can create fonts of any size which allows creativity in producing documents.

Managing the Printer Remotely

The administrator does not have to be seated at the print server to manage a network printer. Most current network operating systems offer utilities which an administrator can use to manage a printer from any computer on the network.

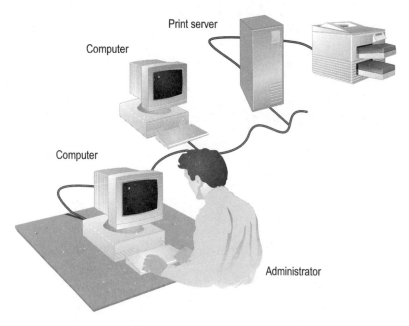

Figure 5.15 An administrator can manage the printer from any network computer

For example, from a remote computer, an administrator can:

- Pause the printer to stop it from printing.
- Delete jobs from the print queue.
- Reorder the jobs in the print queue.

In a small network where all of the servers and computers are relatively close together, this might not seem like an important feature. However, if the network is large and the printer is in one part of a building and the administrator's computer is in another part of the building, this feature can be very helpful.

The same utilities for local printer management are used for remote printer management. In Windows NT Server, for example, the administrator simply chooses the printer to be managed and the network operating system presents the screens which step the administrator through the process.

Q & A

Fill in the blanks in the following sentences.

1. The printer uses the _____ to construct text and graphics to create the page image.

2. Managing users with regard to printing means assigning _____, as with any other shared resource.

3. One task an administrator can do remotely is _____ print jobs in the queue.

4. Most current network operating systems offer utilities which allow an administrator to _____ manage a printer.

Answers

1. PDL
2. permissions
3. reorder
4. remotely

Sharing Fax Modems

The shared fax server does for fax communication what a shared printer does for printing. It makes fax capabilities available to all users on the network so that they do not have to leave their desks in order to send a fax. The ability to send a fax from the network can save time and frustration because users do not have to contend with the uncertainties of a stand-alone fax machine.

A good fax server service will allow an administrator to monitor incoming faxes and send appropriate ones to the proper people and discard others such as advertisements.

Some network fax utilities allow users to link their e-mail addresses to a fax number. This will automatically route their faxes to them.

Routing Faxes

Faxes arrive at a fax machine with no electronic addressing information; therefore, some thought has to be given to how they will be routed. Several methods can be used, including the following:

- Manual routing of the fax.
- Optical character recognition (OCR) software converts the cover sheet to text and searches for the name of the recipient of the fax.
- Intelligent character recognition (ICR) software converts the cover sheet to text and searches for the name of the recipient of the fax. ICR is slower, but more powerful than OCR.
- T.30 sub-addressing. The T.30 fax protocol has been modified to allow the sender of a fax to use an extension number which is used to route the fax.
- Novell embedded systems technology (NEST) is similar to T.30 sub-addressing. The sender of a fax adds an extension number when dialing the fax. The extension can be used to route the fax.
- Bar-code routing allows the sender of the fax to put a bar code on the cover sheet indicating the recipient of the fax.
- Transmission station identification (TSI) routing uses the number of the sender's fax machine to route the fax. The drawback is that all faxes from a certain machine go to one person.
- Received fax line routing uses multiple fax lines and modems. All faxes that are received on a given fax line are routed to a particular user or group.
- Direct inward dialing (DID) uses a special telephone line (trunk) provided by the telephone company which is associated with multiple telephone numbers. If any of these numbers is dialed, the call will come in on the same DID trunk. Before the ring signal is sent, the telephone company sends a special signal down the line identifying which of the numbers was dialed. In this manner, calls to different numbers can be routed and all calls go to the correct person.

Enhancements for the Fax Server

You can also purchase software to maximize your fax server. For example, Optus Software's FACSys product version 4.0 provides a fax-gateway for Windows NT. It allows applications to become a front-end for the fax server, so that users can send faxes from word processing packages, databases, spreadsheets, e-mail, and almost any other application. It also provides a dedicated fax server that gives all network users access to the fax server.

FACSys provides both Windows-based and MS-DOS-based interfaces for the client computers. It supports HP® PCL® (Hewlett-Packard Printer Control Language), PCL5, and PostScript with full text, font, and graphics. It also provides fully automatic routing of incoming faxes and provides comprehensive activity and status reports. It is compatible with GammaFax, Intel SatisFAXtion®, Hayes®, JTFax, and other leading fax boards.

FACSys provides complete diagnostics, detailed error reporting, and sophisticated accounting features to make fax servers easy to administer.

Summary

When setting up a printer to be shared on a network, the administrator needs to:

- Load printer drivers.
- Create a network name for the printer.
- Identify output destinations.
- Set output format parameters.

Most network operating systems have utilities that walk you through these steps. After the printer is set up, each user must individually connect to the printer.

The network administrator is responsible for maintenance of the printer and management of users. This includes a variety of tasks from loading printer paper to allocating printer privileges. Windows NT Server has a series of windows that guides you through the management process. Most current network operating systems allow the administrator to manage a printer from any computer on the network.

There are also fax servers for shared modems which allow network users to send faxes from their own computer. Various methods can be used for the routing of incoming faxes.

Your Next Step

At one time networks were often implemented solely for their print sharing capabilities. While a network's ability to make the most expensive printers available to everyone is a great attraction, emerging communications applications offer even more compelling reasons for networking. In fact, as you will see in Lesson 3, "Implementing Network Applications," some of these are changing the way companies do business.

Lesson 3: Implementing Network Applications

What This Lesson Does

This lesson introduces applications developed for the networking environment and describes their major characteristics. You will also learn how multiuser versions of applications originally developed for stand-alone computers can be shared on the network.

The lesson presents an overview of the three major categories of network applications:

- E-mail and messaging
- Scheduling
- Groupware

It describes the standards and protocols in each area and presents key points to consider in implementing these applications.

Objectives

By the end of this lesson, you will be able to:

- Identify the features and uses of e-mail.
- Identify the features and uses of scheduling.
- Describe the purpose of each of the four primary e-mail and messaging standards.
- Describe the considerations for sharing applications on a network.
- List steps the administrator needs to perform to share an application.
- Determine appropriate policies and procedures for implementing and managing an e-mail system.

Estimated lesson time 50 minutes

Applications Specifically for Networks

Many computer applications were originally developed for single users, such as word processing, spreadsheet, database, and drawing programs.

These programs were computerized versions of standard office equipment such as:

- Typewriters
- Calculators
- Rulers
- T-squares
- Notebooks
- Rolodex® systems

With the advent of networking, these applications were enhanced to take advantage of such networking capabilities as sharing and selective security. Nevertheless, underneath the improvements, they were still the same programs.

However, it wasn't long before software programmers recognized the powerful capabilities of networks and began developing programs specifically for multiple users. These include:

- E-mail and messaging
- Scheduling
- Groupware

In addition to the network applications previously listed, this lesson will look at how other applications can be shared on a network.

E-mail

Electronic mail, or e-mail, is a powerful, sophisticated tool that allows a user to send anything that can be created on a computer to anyone with an e-mail address. E-mail messages can include text, graphics, other attached files, audio, and video. E-mail communications can be:

- Read and discarded
- Read and saved
- Read and replied to
- Edited and saved or forwarded
- Printed in hard copy form

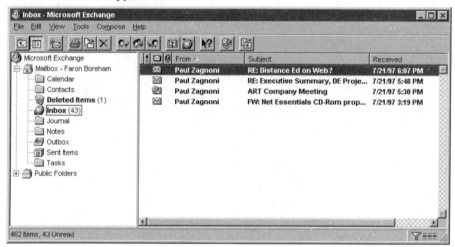

Figure 5.16 Microsoft Exchange is an example of an e-mail system

E-mail systems can provide instant communications between everyone in any organization, regardless of the size of the organization.

Unlike telephone communication with the nightmare of "telephone tag," e-mail correspondence takes place at the convenience of both the sender and the receiver. Messages can be sent at any time with the assurance that they will be available at the receiver's earliest convenience. E-mail can also provide a historical record of a series of communications on a particular topic.

E-mail Functions

E-mail functions include how e-mail works and its capabilities.

Mailboxes

In an e-mail environment, the network administrator creates a mailbox for each user on the system. A mailbox is the delivery location for all incoming e-mail for a designated owner.

Notification

E-mail systems can notify recipients when they have received messages. The receiver's computer uses sound, a visual cue, or a combination of sound and a visual cue to announce the arrival of new messages.

Return Receipt

An e-mail program can inform a user whether or not a message they sent was received and read.

Reply

Most e-mail systems offer a reply feature. Users can answer any e-mail communication by simply clicking a reply button instead of entering a complete e-mail address. Users can save messages from people they communicate with frequently and use the reply feature for future communications without having to be concerned with addressing details.

With an e-mail entrance to the Internet, many users save their incoming messages so that they can use the reply function to communicate with any number of people.

Attachments

Current e-mail systems allow users to attach more than just text files to messages. Attachments can include spreadsheets, databases, graphics, video, and sound clips.

E-mail Directories

Complete e-mail systems feature directories that list everyone on the e-mail system. These directories can include an extensive array of information including:

- Name
- Location
- Position
- Phone number
- Comments

These guides, available to anyone on the system, can be useful even in situations that do not involve communications. For example, finding a telephone number, a job title, or an office location in e-mail requires only a few keystrokes rather than a search through a paper-based directory.

Large System E-mail Providers

E-mail is also available through large service providers to provide communications and services for users around the country beyond any company affiliation. Five major online providers are:

- Microsoft
- CompuServe
- America Online®
- MCI MAIL®
- AT&T

These are becoming standard communication platforms through which subscribers can communicate with anyone else on the service who has a mail box. Typically, one service can communicate with another service. For example, CompuServe and MCI subscribers can send messages to each other. Subscriptions for these services are available from the vendors.

E-mail Support

When planning an e-mail system, the network administrator has to take support and training into consideration. Some sites select one person to act as the e-mail administrator whose responsibilities can include:

- Creating, modifying, and deleting users and groups.
- Setting default options for new users.
- Managing message and folder storage on the mail server.
- Managing the e-mail directory.
- Specifying new post offices, remote users, and other networks with which your e-mail system will have to communicate.
- Training new users.

E-mail Standards

The administrator who is considering implementing an e-mail system needs to be aware of the standards that have helped stabilize a rapidly expanding aspect of the networking products business. The most popular standards originated from the major standards sources.

The ISO locates electronic message handling activities at layer 7 (the Application layer) of the OSI model. This allows different networks running different network operating systems to communicate regardless of their operating system differences. Each standard is discussed on the following pages.

X.400

The CCITT (Comité Consultatif Internationale de Télégraphie et Téléphonie) which is also known as the International Telegraph and Telephone Consultative Committee, developed a set of message handling standards known collectively as X.400. X.400 is designed to be both hardware and software independent. Some of the X.400 standards include:

- User interfaces
- Encoding information
- Conversion rules
- Syntax
- Access protocols

The major parts of X.400 are:

- The User Agent (UA)

   This part of X.400 runs on the user's computer and serves as the connection to the actual X.400 MHS (message handling service). It features such e-mail utilities as message creation, read, and browse.

- The Message Transfer Agent (MTA)

   The MTA accepts messages, converts them to a form recipients can understand (if necessary), and then forwards them to other MTAs or to the destination UA.

- The Message Transfer System (MTS)

   The MTS is responsible for transferring messages of all types from the UA that creates the message to the destination UA. There are usually many MTAs to determine the screen display that network users will see. Groups of MTAs within the MTS are used to store and forward messages.

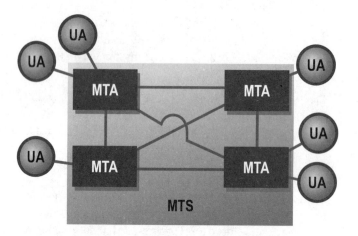

Figure 5.17 Major components of X.400: UAs, MTAs, and MTS

X.400 Features

X.400 can provide users with several useful features, including:

- Different levels of message priorities.
- Time and date stamping.
- Receipts to verify delivery.
- Multiple and alternate recipients.

X.400 Protocols

Within X.400 are several protocols developed by the CCITT to establish standards for:

- Routing information including message identifiers, display rules, destination address descriptions, and delivery and return receipt instructions.
- Specifications and definitions of X.400 services such as identifying authorized users, recipient notification, and indication of message subjects.
- Modifying routing and delivery parameters including passwords, message size, and testing to see if messages can be delivered.

X.500

On a large or distributed network, locating a particular person, server, or peripheral such as a printer can be frustrating. X.500 is the CCITT set of directory services developed to help users in distributed networks locate users on other networks to whom they want to send messages. With this in mind, X.500 may provide a global directory of e-mail users. To do this, X.500 relies on a hierarchical directory structure that uses agents to search for particular users or resources.

There are three pieces of information that X.500 uses to locate a particular resource:

- Name services to locate a network name.
- Electronic address books to identify a particular network address.
- Directory services which contain centrally managed electronic network names and addresses to help users search on an inter-network basis.

Simple Mail Transfer Protocol (SMTP)

SMTP was designed to transfer messages between two remote network computers. It is used on the Internet, in UNIX systems, and is part of the TCP/IP protocol stack.

SMTP works with other e-mail programs to provide both a client and a server function to send and receive e-mail messages.

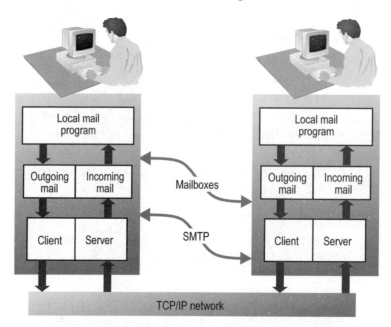

Figure 5.18 SMTP allows two remote computers to send and receive e-mail messages

SMTP provides the control signals two computers use in communicating (handshaking) including:

- Connection verification
- Message transmission
- Sender identification
- Transmission parameters

SMTP makes it possible for e-mail programs that use it to:

- Review message contents
- Print messages
- Forward messages
- Send messages to groups

SMTP also provides an address book feature.

Message Handling Service (MHS)

MHS is a de facto standard made popular by Novell. It is similar to X.400 in that one computer on a network, the MHS server, translates messages between computers that may be using different e-mail systems.

All products that are able to communicate with MHS servers can communicate with each other through e-mail.

Communication Between Standards

Networks that communicate over common carriers with other networks may run into the problem of having to communicate with an e-mail system that is different from theirs. In this situation, a network would have to translate incoming messages into an e-mail language its own system could understand. The device that does the translating is called a gateway, and is usually a computer dedicated to this purpose.

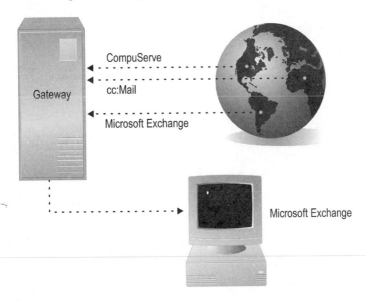

Figure 5.19 E-mail gateways allow e-mail packages to exchange messages

Advanced e-mail systems that include gateways are:

- Microsoft Exchange
- Microsoft Mail
- cc:Mail™

E-mail Considerations

In selecting an e-mail system, administrators should take the following features into account:

- Custom notification (Will it let you determine how it notifies you of incoming messages?)
- Reply (Will it let you respond automatically to received messages?)
- Return receipt (Can it notify you that your message has been received and read?)
- CC (Can you send the message to several selected people at once?)
- Attachments (Can you attach files to your messages?)
- Undelete (Can you recover messages you have accidentally deleted?)
- OOF (Out of Office—Can the system notify senders that recipients aren't available to receive messages, but will be at some future date?)

Q & A

Fill in the blanks in the following sentences.

1. An e-mail system associates a user's name with a _____ that stores the messages for the user.

2. The CCITT developed a set of directory services known as _____ to help users in distributed networks locate users on other networks to whom they wish to send messages.

3. A device that translates incoming messages into an e-mail language its own e-mail system could understand is called a _____.

Answers

1. mailbox
2. X.500
3. gateway

Scheduling

Network scheduling utilities can help users plan their time and avoid conflicts. They can be used for individual planning or in groups.

Individual Scheduling

Scheduling is an electronic version of paper-based schedulers that provide daily, monthly, and yearly planning. While schedulers differ depending on the vendor, they all provide standard functions. They help users schedule meetings, activities, appointments, or other events in an electronic tickler file that will automatically remind the user of a scheduled event. This frees the user from checking the schedule or having to remember schedule details.

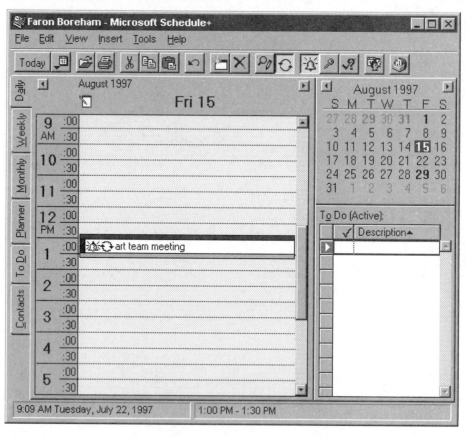

Figure 5.20 Microsoft Schedule+ is an example of a scheduling program

Most schedulers will monitor the calendar and flash a message on the user's screen as a reminder about an upcoming event.

When a user attempts to schedule an event such as a meeting, the scheduling utility automatically checks the user's electronic calendar for other events scheduled for that time period. If no other event is scheduled, the utility writes the event into the user's schedule. If the user later attempts to schedule something else in that time period, the scheduling utility will notify the user of the conflict.

Group Scheduling

Electronic scheduling at the network level solves the scheduling problem by automatically searching the calendars of all of the potential attendees and indicating to the meeting organizer which times are free and which are not. Based on the scheduler's information, the meeting organizer can choose a time when everyone is free, and the electronic scheduler will automatically put the event on everyone's calendar.

The electronic scheduler will then automatically follow up and remind everyone that the meeting is going to take place.

With products such as Microsoft Schedule+ you can look at another person's schedule provided that person has made their calendar available for viewing. This feature makes for the most efficient meeting and event planning. Electronic scheduling can also be used to provide historical information about schedules and activities in the past.

Groupware

Until recently, the term groupware was relatively unknown. Today, it is an emerging technology providing communications and work coordination beyond the capabilities of e-mail.

Groupware uses network communications technology to provide real-time document management in a centralized location. Groupware can facilitate several processes among multiple users including routing and tracking.

With groupware, teams will have simultaneous access to both information and each other. Team members do not all have to work for the same department or even the same company. These groups and teams can include:

- Employees
- Business partners
- Customers
- Suppliers

Bulletin boards and interactive conferences are also examples of groupware.

Uses for Groupware

Because groupware is a relatively new technology, its applications are still evolving. However, current groupware installations are used for:

- Routing and sharing information.
- Coordinating project and document development.
- Tracking projects.
- Managing group processes.
- Facilitating group discussions.
- Automating a variety of routine business tasks.
- Tracking customer inquiries.
- Managing customer relations.

Groupware is quickly being adapted as a primary network tool in many industries and agencies including manufacturing, research, construction, education, and the government.

Features

Features include the types of programs being defined as groupware today.

Groupware E-mail

Advanced groupware e-mail products have the capability to communicate with most standard e-mail systems. This means that people involved in a groupware project can communicate with other workers who are not involved in the project, but who do have access to a standard e-mail system.

Groupware Multimedia

Major groupware vendors are incorporating the newest technologies into their products in order to advance electronic communications into areas that didn't even exist a few years ago. For example, groupware multimedia features include:

- Scanned images
- Fax
- Voice
- Sound
- Optical character recognition (OCR)
- Graphics
- Video and video conferencing

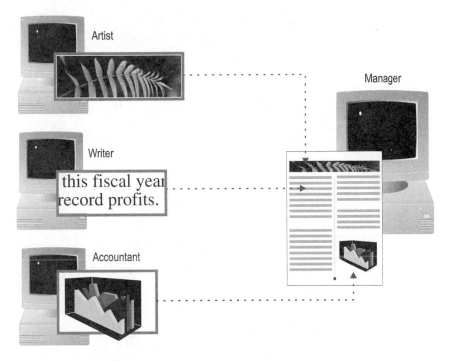

Figure 5.21 Groupware allows easy integration of several products

Groupware Products

The two major groupware products are Microsoft Exchange and Lotus Notes®.
There are also other programs that could be called groupware because they
incorporate some group communication features.

Microsoft Exchange

Microsoft incorporated the best features of information and e-mail communication
systems into a product designed to take advantage of client/server technology.

Microsoft Exchange Server is a messaging-based family of client/server products
designed to work with existing programs and networks to allow all users in an
organization to exchange and share a variety of information efficiently.

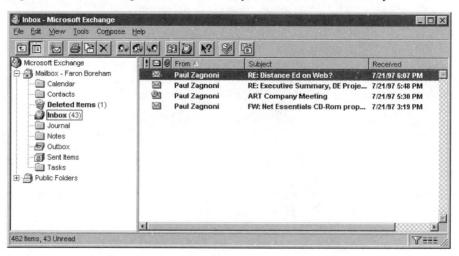

Figure 5.22 Microsoft Exchange client

Microsoft Exchange Server uses technology that has evolved from host-based systems to local area networks to provide five main client/server message-based functions:

- Scheduling

  With the scheduling features, users can manage personal time, organize tasks, and coordinate with others through scheduled meetings.

- Messaging services

  The messaging services include message transfer, delivery, routing, and directory services.

- Group information sharing

  In addition to communicating through the Microsoft Exchange Server e-mail system, users can also post information on a bulletin board, track customer accounts from a shared database, and access product information from a reference library.

- Forms

  Administrators can use the forms capabilities to create organized, custom views of information.

- Application design—with or without programming

  Application designers can develop applications that automate tasks and processes within an organization.

Lotus Notes

Designed for installations of nearly any size, Notes is a true groupware product family. The core services feature:

- Security
- Management
- Replication
- Directory services
- Connectivity services

These services will communicate across several connectivity and operating system environments including:

- Microsoft Windows NT
- LAN Server
- LAN Manager
- TCP/IP
- VINES®
- NetWare
- AppleTalk
- OS/2
- Microsoft Windows
- Macintosh
- UNIX

The Notes family is a group that offers three options: Lotus Notes, Lotus Notes Desktop, and Lotus Notes Express.

Microsoft Windows 95

Microsoft Windows 95 is a multitasking operating system that provides a workgroup environment which includes:

- OLE to create compound documents over the network
- Simple messaging that provides for conferencing
- E-mail
- Scheduling

Banyan® Intelligent Messaging Service

This product provides:

- Document storage, management, and routing
- E-mail
- Work-flow tracking

TeamLinks™ from Digital Equipment Corporation

The TeamLinks All-In-1™ office system offers:

- Connectivity to Digital's network operating system
- X.400 e-mail services
- File conversion
- Group conferencing software
- Work-flow tracking

Novell Groupwise

This integrated package provides:

- E-mail
- Scheduling
- Task management
- Work-flow tracking

Mixed Environments

Advanced groupware can incorporate a variety of computer platforms so that team members can continue using the equipment they already have, provided it has the communication capabilities required to network with others on the project.

Groupware can function in mixed operating system environments that include:

- Microsoft Windows NT
- Microsoft Windows 95
- Microsoft Windows 3.1
- OS/2
- UNIX
- Macintosh
- NetWare

Q & A

Fill in the blanks in the following sentences.

1. Groupware uses network communications technology to provide _____ _____ document management in a centralized location.

2. Microsoft Exchange Server is designed to work with existing _____ and _____ to allow all users in an organization to exchange and share a variety of information efficiently.

3. Microsoft Exchange Server uses technology that has evolved from host-based systems to local area networks to provide five main _____ message-based functions.

4. Advanced groupware can incorporate a variety of _____ _____ so that team members can continue using the equipment they already have.

Answers

1. real-time

2. applications, networks

3. client/server

4. computer platforms

Shared Network Applications

Applications such as word processors, databases, and spreadsheets can be shared on the network like any other resource. This offers at least two benefits:

- It makes application programs less expensive because buying a site license for 200 users on an application is usually cheaper than buying 200 individual copies of the application.
- It ensures that everyone will be using the same version of the product.

However, the network administrator should be aware of several considerations when sharing applications over a network. Companies that implement application sharing purchase a site license which makes it legal for network users to use the software. Otherwise, anyone other than the original purchaser who uses the shared application would be doing so illegally.

The network administrator will have to consider whether or not training is required. This will apply to upgrades of current applications as well as new applications. The administrator will need to let users know that new applications, upgrades, and training may impact productivity in the short term, but will provide long-term benefits.

Sharing the Application

To share an application, the administrator would perform these tasks:

1. Create a subdirectory on a server.
2. Install the application into the server's newly created subdirectory.
3. Share the subdirectory. This makes the application available to users.

Application Requirements

The network administrator should always be aware of the network's capacity to accept new resources. Does the server, for example, have enough hard disk space available to accommodate a new application and the data it will generate? Even if there is enough room on an existing server, will the server be able to handle the demand for the new application? Will the new application require peripheral support? A new word processing package, for example, may lead to the requirement for a new printer.

The Software Log

To avoid problems that might occur in any of these areas, the network administrator should keep a log of all software used on the network that indicates:

- Installation dates and procedures
- Version numbers
- Upgrade dates and version numbers
- Implementation procedures including batch files
- Configurations and modifications
- Access records describing levels of access provided to users and groups
- Training records

It is also wise for the network administrator to keep archived copies of the original software in case the system has to be recreated. This should include batch and configuration files.

Summary

Some applications designed specifically for the networking environment are e-mail and messaging, scheduling, and a group of interactive, real-time activities called groupware.

E-mail evolved from the original messaging capability of networks. E-mail messages can include text, graphics, audio, and video. E-mail users communicate through the use of mailboxes. E-mail features include notification to users they have messages, and a reply capability. Also, users can attach files of various types of messages. E-mail systems also have directories of all users.

E-mail and messaging standards include CCITT X.400 and X.500, simple mail transfer protocol (SMTP), and message handling service (MHS). Communication between networks using different standards is accomplished with the use of gateways. A gateway is a computer dedicated to translating the protocols.

Electronic scheduling utilities such as Microsoft Schedule+ provide individual or group scheduling. Features such as automatically reminding users of scheduled events and the capability to access others' calendars provide the most efficient way to plan meetings and other activities.

Groupware allows simultaneous, real-time document management by users at different locations, not necessarily on the same network. Groupware is an emerging networking capability that has many uses from routing and sharing information, to communicating through e-mail, to tracking customer inquiries. Groupware can be used in mixed operating system environments. Two of the major groupware products are Microsoft Exchange and Lotus Notes.

In addition to applications for networking in particular, applications originally designed for stand-alone use, such as databases or word processors, can be shared on a network. When implementing these applications for use on a network, there are various considerations for the network administrator to be aware of. These include network capacity, site licensing, keeping a software log, and training for users.

Your Next Step

You've seen how various applications and services allow users in a variety of networking environments to communicate. Networks also need to provide communication among different technologies and different vendor environments, often within the same LAN. You will see how network administrators can accomplish this in Lesson 4, "Networks in Multivendor Environments."

Lesson 4: Networks in Multivendor Environments

What This Lesson Does

This lesson presents an overview of the issues and problems involved in implementing a network that incorporates components from different vendors.

It describes some of the problems and solutions for achieving interoperability in a multivendor environment.

Objectives

By the end of this lesson, you will be able to:

- Define a client solution and a server solution for interoperability.
- Identify methods vendors use to integrate their products with those from other vendors.
- Determine which network operating systems and redirectors would be appropriate for a given site.

Estimated lesson time 25 minutes

The Typical Network Environment

Today, most networks are multivendor environments. While such a network can pose challenges, it will work well if it has been properly planned and implemented.

Problems arise when the network is running more than one type of network operating system, and the client operating systems and redirectors are from different vendors. The character of a network changes when software components from different vendors have to function in the same network.

The server's operating system, the client's operating system, and the redirector have to be compatible. For example, if you have a network where one client is running Microsoft Windows 95, another is running Novell NetWare, a third client is an Apple Macintosh, and the server is running Microsoft Windows NT Server, the server and the clients must find some common language so that each component can understand the other.

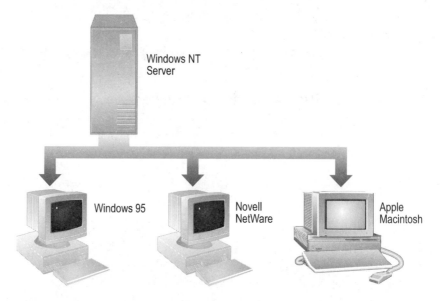

Figure 5.23 Windows NT Server supporting clients from multiple vendors

Implementing Multivendor Solutions

The solution for interoperability in multivendor environments is implemented at either the server end or the client end. The solution you choose depends on the vendors you are using.

The Client Solution

In most situations involving multiple network operating systems, the key to interoperability is the redirector. Just as your telephone can use more than one service provider to communicate with different people, computers can have more than one redirector to communicate over a network with different network servers.

Each redirector only handles the packets sent in the language or protocol that it can understand. If you know what your destination is, which resource you want to access, you implement the appropriate redirector, and the redirector forwards your request to the appropriate destination.

For example, if a Windows NT client needs to access a Novell server, the network administrator can accomplish this by loading the Microsoft redirector for accessing Novell servers on top of Windows NT in the client.

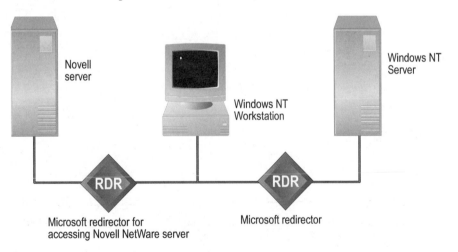

Figure 5.24 Windows NT Workstation using multiple redirectors

The Server Solution

The second way to implement communication between a client and a server is to install a service on the server. This is the approach when bringing Apple Macintoshes into a Windows NT environment. Microsoft supplies Services for Macintosh that allows a Windows NT Server-based server to communicate with the Apple client.

With the Services for Macintosh installed, Macintosh users can access resources on a Windows NT server. This service also converts files between Macintosh and Windows NT-based computers. This allows both Macintosh and Windows NT users to use their own interfaces to share the same files.

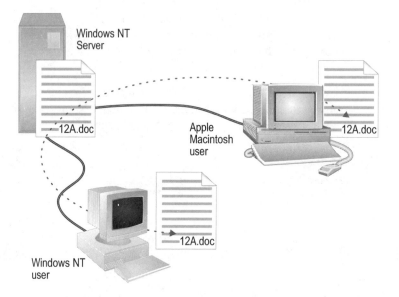

Figure 5.25 Services for Macintosh loaded on Windows NT Server

The Macintosh user still follows standard Macintosh procedures and sees the Macintosh icons such as the Chooser and Finder, even though that user is accessing resources on a Windows NT server.

Vendor Options

The three major networking products vendors are:

- Microsoft
- Novell
- Apple

These three vendors realized long ago that it would be to their advantage if their products worked with each other. Therefore, each vendor provides utilities that:

- Make it possible for its operating systems to communicate with servers from the other two vendors.
- Help its servers recognize clients from the other two vendors.

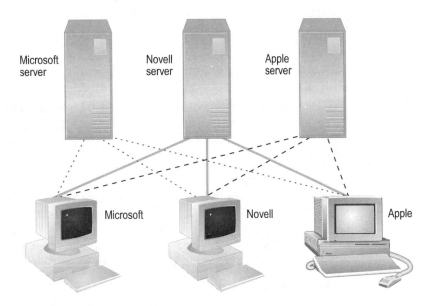

Figure 5.26 Multiple vendor connectivity

Microsoft

Microsoft has built the redirector that recognizes Microsoft networks into the following Microsoft operating systems:

- Windows NT
- Windows 95
- Windows for Workgroups

These are automatically implemented during the operating system's installation. A setup utility loads the required drivers and then edits the startup files so that the redirector will function when the user turns on the computer.

Microsoft redirector software not only makes it possible for clients to access resources, but it also provides each Windows for Workgroups and Windows NT client with the capability to share its own resources.

Microsoft in a Novell Environment

Connecting a Windows NT Workstation-based client to a Novell NetWare network requires NWLink and Client Service for NetWare (CSNW). Connecting a Windows NT Server-based server to a NetWare network requires NWLink and Gateway Service for NetWare (GSNW). NWLink is the Microsoft implementation of the IPX/SPX protocol. CSNW is the Microsoft implementation of a NetWare requester (Novell's term for redirector). Together they compose the Microsoft Windows NT solution for connecting to Novell NetWare servers.

Connecting a Windows 95-based client to a NetWare network requires IPX/SPX and Microsoft Client for NetWare Networks. Microsoft Service for NetWare Directory Services (NDS) is an enhanced client software for NetWare that incorporates support for Novell Network 4.x Directory Services. Microsoft NDS provides users with logon and browsing support for NetWare 2.x, 3.x, and 4.x bindery services as NetWare 4.x NDS servers.

MS-DOS-Based Clients

Server operating system vendors offer utilities that allow MS-DOS-based clients to access servers from the three vendors. All of these utilities can reside on one machine so that one MS-DOS-based client can access servers from all three environments.

Novell

Novell servers recognize the following clients for file and print services.

NetWare character-based clients running MS-DOS or DR-DOS® can connect to:

- Novell NetWare servers.
- Windows NT Server-based computers.

Windows NT clients running Novell's NetWare requester and the Windows NT redirector can connect to:

- Novell NetWare servers.
- Windows NT Workstation-based and Windows NT Server-based computers.

Novell provides requesters for the following client operating systems:

- MS-DOS
- OS/2
- NetWare Client for Windows NT

Apple

In the Macintosh environment, the Apple redirector is included with the Macintosh operating system. AppleShare is the Apple network operating system; it provides the file sharing function. The client-side software is included with every copy of the Apple operating system. There is also an AppleShare print server, which is a server-based print spooler. This means that Macintoshes come equipped to participate in Apple networks.

MS-DOS-Based Client

AppleShare personal computer software offers MS-DOS-based clients access to an AppleShare file server or print server. With AppleShare personal computer software and a LocalTalk personal computer card installed, personal computer users can access file server volumes (file storage) and printers on an AppleTalk network. The LocalTalk personal computer card contains firmware to control the link between the AppleTalk network and the personal computer. The LocalTalk personal computer driver software implements many of the Apple Talk protocols and interacts with the card to send and receive packets.

Services for Macintosh

With Services for Macintosh, a Windows NT server becomes available to Macintosh clients. This product makes it possible for MS-DOS-based and Macintosh clients to share files and printers. Services for Macintosh includes AppleTalk Protocol versions 2.0 and 2.1, LocalTalk, EtherTalk, TokenTalk, and FDDITalk. In addition, Services for Macintosh supports version 5.2 or later of the LaserWriter® printer.

Q & A

Fill in the blanks in the following sentences.

1. In most situations involving multiple network operating systems, the key to interoperability is the _____.

2. Each redirector only handles the packets sent in the _____ that it can understand.

3. One way to implement communication between a client and a server is to install a _____ in the server which makes the server appear to a client as if it were running the client's network operating system.

4. Microsoft has built the redirector that recognizes Microsoft networks into the major Microsoft operating systems, and it is automatically implemented during the operating system's _____.

5. Novell refers to its client software (the redirector) as the _____.

6. In the Macintosh environment, the Apple _____ is included with the Macintosh operating system.

Answers

1. redirector
2. protocol
3. service
4. installation
5. requester
6. redirector

Summary

Interoperability in multivendor environments can be achieved at the client or server end. You can install a redirector in the client. The redirector will intercept requests for service and forward them across the network to the appropriate network component. At the server end you can install a service to make the server appear to be running the operating system of the client.

Which method is implemented depends on the vendors you are using. There are three major networking products vendors: Microsoft, Novell, and Apple.

The server solution is used for incorporating Macintoshes into a personal computer environment. The client solution is used for most multivendor environments. With the client solution, you need to consider if there are redirectors available that will:

- Run on the computers in the network.
- Communicate with the network operating system.

Your Next Step

Achieving interoperability is a primary challenge for the network administrator. However, doing some research on compatibility between network operating systems and redirectors before committing to a major systems purchase can produce a successful network.

If the network must support extensive database activities, the administrator should consider implementing a client/server approach which will be introduced in Lesson 5, "The Client/Server Environment."

Lesson 5: The Client/Server Environment

What This Lesson Does

This lesson describes setting up and working on a network that has servers and clients. You will learn related concepts, features, and components that will enable you to implement this type of network.

The advantages of client/server over centralized computing are also presented.

Objectives

By the end of this lesson, you will be able to:

- Describe the differences between client/server and centralized computing.
- List the six steps of the client/server process.
- Identify client functions.
- Identify server functions.
- Determine if a client/server approach is appropriate for a given networking environment.

Estimated lesson time 30 minutes

Centralized vs. Client/Server

One of the reasons the client/server networking model is so popular is because of the advances in technology that allowed a shift from using dumb terminals as clients to using powerful computers.

Centralized Computing

In the traditional mainframe environment, an application such as a database runs on a large and very powerful centralized computer and is accessed by terminals. The terminal sends a request for information to the mainframe, the mainframe retrieves the information and then displays it on the terminal.

The entire database travels in message-sized pieces from the server across the network and is downloaded to the client that made the request. The file activity takes place through the network operating system and the cable. There is not much coordination between the client, or computer, and the server to determine what data to retrieve and send.

The data transfer between the client and the server causes a large increase in network traffic and slows down requests from other clients.

In centralized computing, when a client requests data from a database, the system moves all of the data across the network to the client. If it is a large database, moving what could be vast amounts of data takes time and ties up the network.

Client/Server Computing

The term client/server refers to the concept of sharing the work involved in processing data between the client computer and the more powerful server computer.

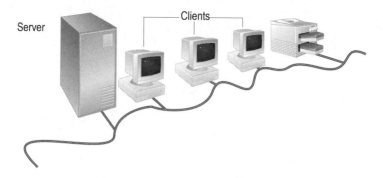

Figure 5.27 A simple client/server network

The client/server approach can benefit any organization where great numbers of people need constant access to large amounts of data.

The client/server network is the most efficient way to provide:

- Database access and management for applications such as:
  - Spreadsheets
  - Accounting
  - Communications
  - Document management
- Network management
- Centralized file storage

Database management is the most common application used in a client/server environment, therefore, this lesson focuses on how database management systems (DBMS) function.

The Client/Server Model

Most networks operate in the client/server model. Simply stated, a client/server network is a networking environment in which the client computer makes a request and a computer acting as the server fulfills the request. Typically, even in a peer-to-peer network, any computer is both a client and a server. This discussion presents the database management application as an example of how the client/server model operates.

In the client/server model the client software uses the Structured Query Language (SQL) to translate what the user sees into a request that the database can understand. SQL is an English-like database query language originally developed by IBM to provide a relatively simple way to manipulate data. Manipulating data means entering it, retrieving it, or editing it.

Other database vendors realized that a common database language would make it easier to develop database applications. Therefore, they supported SQL and it became a standard. Most database management systems use SQL.

The Client/Server Process

The database query is sent from the client but processed on the server. Only the results are sent across the network back to the client. The whole process of requesting and receiving information consists of six steps:

1. The client requests data.
2. The request is translated into SQL.
3. The SQL request is sent over the network to the server.
4. The database server carries out a search on the computer where the data exists.
5. The requested records are returned to the client.
6. The data is presented to the user.

In the client/server environment, there are two main components:

- The application, which is often referred to as the client or the front end
- The database server, which is often referred to as the server or the back end

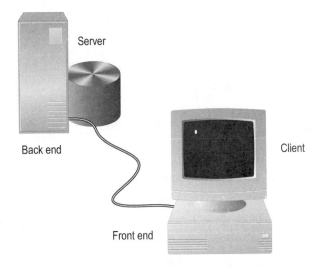

Figure 5.28 **The client is the front end and the server is the back end**

The Client

The user generates a request at the front end. The client runs an application that:

- Presents an interface to the user.
- Formats requests for data.
- Displays data it receives back from the server.

In a client/server environment, the server does not contain the user interface software. The client is responsible for presenting the data in a useful form, such as with user interfaces and report writing.

The client computer accepts instructions from the user, prepares them for the server, and then sends a request for specific information over the network to the server. The server processes the request, locates the appropriate information, and sends it across the network back to the client. The client then feeds the information to the interface which presents the information to the user.

In a client/server environment, the person at the client end uses an on-screen form, called a search key, to specify what information they are looking for.

Using the Front End

Front ends can present the same information to users in different ways depending on the request. For example, data that states Columbus crossed an ocean in 1492 can be presented in several ways including:

- Ocean crossings
- Columbus' achievements
- Events of 1492
- Bodies of water crossed by Columbus

In another example, in a manufacturing company, all customer and product information is kept in one database. But this information can be retrieved and presented through the front end in a number of ways:

- Marketing can send promotional mailings to customers in a certain zip code.
- Distributors can find out which products are in stock.
- The service department can find out which customers are due for service.
- The ordering department can see each customer's buying history.
- The accounts receivable department can stop a client who is behind on his payments from ordering.

Each department needs a front end designed to access the one common database and retrieve information for a particular need.

Front-End Tools

A number of tools, applications, and utilities for the front end make the client/server process more functional. These include:

- Query tools

  Query tools use predefined queries and built-in reporting capabilities to help users access back-end data.
- User applications

  Many common applications programs such as Microsoft Excel can provide front-end access to back-end databases. Others, such as Microsoft Access, include their own SQL to provide an interface to multivendor database management systems.
- Program development tools

  Many client/server installations need special, customized front-end applications for their particular data retrieval tasks. Program development tools, such as Microsoft Visual Basic®, are available to help programmers and information systems managers develop front-end tools to access back-end data.

The Server

The server in a client/server environment is usually dedicated to storing and managing data. This is where most of the actual database activity occurs. The server is also referred to as the back end of the client/server model because it fulfills the requests of the client. The server receives the structured requests from the clients, processes them, and sends the requested information back over the network to the client.

The database software on the file server reacts to client queries by running searches. As part of a client/server system, it only returns the results of the searches.

Back-end processing includes sorting data, extracting the requested data, and sending that data back to the user.

Also, database server software manages the data in a database including:

- Updates
- Deletions
- Additions
- Protection

Stored Procedures

Stored procedures are short, prewritten data-processing routines that help with certain details of data processing. They are stored in the server and can be used by any client.

They help process data and save on computer code and hard disk space on the client computers. One stored process can be called by any number of clients instead of having to incorporate the same routine into the code of each program.

These stored procedures:

- Perform some of the processing normally performed by the client.
- Reduce network traffic because a single call from the client to the server can begin a series of stored procedures that normally would require several requests.
- Can contain security controls to prevent unauthorized users from running some of the procedures.

Server Hardware

The servers in a typical client/server environment should be more powerful than the clients. These computers must be able to handle:

- Multiple and simultaneous requests
- Security
- Network management tasks

Any organization that implements a client/server network should use dedicated servers to handle the back-end functions.

Q & A

Fill in the blanks in the following sentences.

1. In the client computer, the _____ _____ presents data in a useful manner.

2. In most cases, the client software uses the _____ _____ _____ to translate what the user sees into a request that the database can understand.

3. The server in a client/server environment is usually dedicated to _____ and _____ data.

4. As part of the front-end process the client computer _____ requests for data.

Answers

1. front end
2. Structured Query Language (or SQL)
3. storing, managing
4. formats

Client/Server Architecture

There are several possible client/server arrangements. The two primary arrangements are illustrated in Figure 5.29.

- The data can be placed on a single server.
- The data can be distributed across several database servers, depending on the location of the users and the nature of the data.

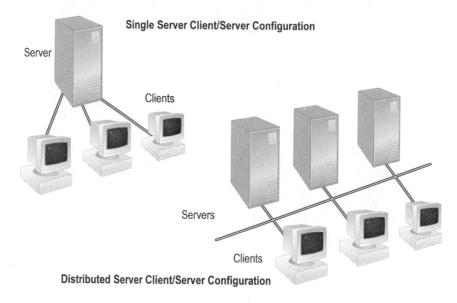

Figure 5.29 Data can be localized on one server or distributed over several servers

Two possible variations on the distributed server arrangement are:

- Having servers over a WAN periodically synchronize to ensure that they all have the same data in common.
- Using a data warehouse to store large amounts of data and forward the most sought-after data to an intermediate system that can also format the data into its most requested form. This off-loads some of the processing from the main server.

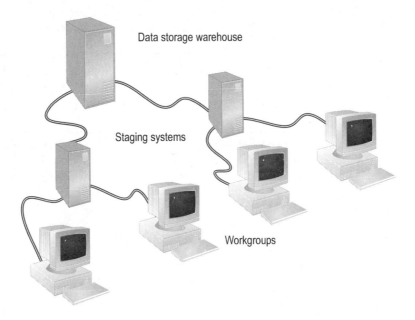

Figure 5.30 Data storage warehouse server off-loads data to other servers

The Advantages of Working in a Client/Server Environment

Client/server technology creates a powerful environment that offers many real benefits to organizations. Well-planned client/server systems provide relatively inexpensive platforms that provide mainframe computing capacity while being easy to customize for specific applications. Because client/server processing only sends the results of a query across the network, it cuts down on network traffic.

It puts the file search burden on a computer that is more powerful than the client, and is better able to handle the request. On a busy network, this means that the processing will be distributed more evenly than in a traditional server-based system.

The client/server network also saves RAM in the client computer because all of the data and the file I/O logic is on the application in the server. The servers in client/server systems are capable of storing large amounts of data. This allows more space on client computers for other applications.

Because the file services and the data are on the back-end server, the servers are easier to secure and maintain in one location. Data is more secure in a client/server environment because it is centrally located on one server or on a small number of servers. When the data is in one location and managed by one authority, backups are simplified.

Summary

The client/server approach to networking has several advantages over the traditional centralized network. Tasks are divided between the client and the server for more efficient running of the network. The most common client/server application is a database management system using SQL. In a client/server environment, the database query is sent from the client but processed on the server. Only the results are sent across the network back to the client.

The client is responsible for presenting the data in a useful form, such as user interfaces, and report writing. The server is usually dedicated to storing and managing data. With this division of labor only one or a few powerful servers are needed in a network to process data.

There are two basic ways to arrange client/server networks: data is on a single server, or data is distributed across several servers. The client/server environment provides for easier data security because the data is on one or a limited number of servers.

Your Next Step

Now that you've completed the "how" of network operations you can go on to the chapter Review to check up on your knowledge of setting up a network operating system, implementing a network using multiple vendors, implementing network printing, and using network applications such as databases.

Chapter 5 Review

Chapter 5, Network Operations, presented an overview of how networks function in several key areas.

The foundation of all network activity is the network operating system which coordinates the functions of the computers and peripherals on the network so they work together as one system. The redirector, a crucial networking software component, works with the network operating system by intercepting requests in the client computers and forwarding them across the network to the server.

Installing a network operating system requires information about the network, such as the server's name, which the installer needs to identify before the installation.

A network printer is managed just like any other resource on the network. It must be installed and shared, and then access privileges must be assigned to users. These operations are usually simplified for the network administrator with network printing utilities that are user-friendly.

A dedicated print sharing device can make network printing available economically. However, such devices do not always offer the management features that network printing services do. Fax machines can be shared in a manner similar to printers.

Applications designed specifically for networks have been partially responsible for the spread of networks as key business systems. E-mail is perhaps the most popular network application because it facilitates communication of practically any type of computer data, including multimedia.

Network applications such as scheduling and groupware products such as Microsoft Exchange are providing organizations with tools for coordinating teams and projects across departments, companies, and businesses.

Networks are commonly multivendor environments. Products make use of a variety of solutions for incorporating devices made by different vendors into one network. They use redirectors, shells, and other services to incorporate different network operating systems and clients into one functioning system.

The client/server networking approach is an advancement over traditional centralized computing. The client/server process divides one large task into several parts and uses multisystem parallel processing to work on the different parts simultaneously. The processing is divided between a client (front end) at the user's computer and a server (back end) which processes and returns only requested information across the network. Most client/server systems applications are database management systems.

Checkup

Follow the instructions for each exercise as indicated. All answers follow the last exercise.

Exercise 1: Matching

Match each item in Column A with the best choice from Column B. One item in Column B will not be used, and items will be used no more than once.

Column A	Column B
1. Forwards requests from one computer to another. ____	A. PDL
2. Memory buffer in a print server's RAM. ____	B. Bindings
3. Network system application programs that run a network. ____	C. SQL
4. Protocol paths from the upper OSI layers to the lower layers. ____	D. X.500
5. Standards that include a user agent and a message transfer agent. ____	E. Redirector
6. Directory services to help locate users on distributed networks to send them e-mail messages. ____	F. Spooler
7. Part of the TCP/IP protocol stack that is used to transfer messages between two remote network computers. ____	G. Services
8. Tells printer how output should look. ____	H. X.400
9. Developed by IBM to provide a way to manipulate data. ____	I. SMTP
	J. MHS

Exercise 2: True or False

For the following sentences, circle True if the statement is true or False if the statement is false.

1. When there are more tasks than processors, a computer must timeslice to balance the tasks with the available processors.   True   False

2. Because some protocols are faster than others, it is important to put the slower protocols higher in the binding list so they can begin working ahead of the faster protocols which will soon catch up.   True   False

3. After a printer has been shared, users at their computers will need to use the network operating system to connect to the printer.   True   False

4. A network printer must be installed near the network administrator so the administrator can manage the network's printing needs easily.   True   False

5. The higher-end e-mail systems can include both voice and video in messages.   True   False

6. Groupware may be used to track a project development process so that it can be monitored, edited, shared, and managed by all team members regardless of their locations.   True   False

7. In multivendor environments, a good network operating system will be able to understand a request regardless of the redirector that sent it.   True   False

8. In the client/server environment, the server sends the entire database across the network so the client computer can have access to all of it at once, which will speed up the search for information.   True   False

9. Clients in a client/server environment must have their own processing power in order to take some of the load off the server.   True   False

Checkup Answers

Exercise 1: Matching

1. E
2. F
3. G
4. B
5. H
6. D
7. I
8. A
9. C

Exercise 2: True or False

1. True.
2. False. Putting the faster protocol first in the binding list improves performance.
3. True.
4. False. With a good network operating system, an administrator can use nearly any computer on the network to manage a printer.
5. True.
6. True.
7. False. In multivendor environments, for the server to recognize and act on requests coming in over the network, the network operating system must be able to understand the redirector that sent the request.
8. False. In a client/server system, a server searches for data and returns only the data which the client requested.
9. True.

Case Study Problem

The Setting

The Lakes & Sons company makes custom-built rock crushing equipment for construction companies involved in building roads.

The owners realize that even though their company has computers and even one or two networks, their current information system cannot keep up with their business. The clerical staff uses a dedicated word processing system. The drafting department uses a CAD program. The purchasing department uses a database to track business activity. The accounting department has a Windows NT Server LAN. Another department has a workgroup running on Windows for Workgroups. The drafting department uses Apple Macintoshes. The publications department is networked with Novell.

The Problem

On Monday, the expediter got a call from a construction company manager in Chicago who needed to know the status of a rock crusher that was being built. The expediter recognized the job and knew the ship date wasn't for another month, but he told the Chicago contact that he'd find out the status and get back to him. The expediter asked the head of purchasing about it, because purchasing kept track of all outstanding parts for all projects. The director of purchasing sent him across the street to the assembly shop.

The assembly shop was a long warehouse where the machines were actually put together before shipping. The foreman knew he was missing some parts, but didn't know exactly where they were in the pipeline. The expediter took the list of missing parts and went back to purchasing.

This went on for an hour. At the end of the hour, the expediter had to call the construction company manager in Chicago and fill in some important blanks with imaginative excuses. The manager believed the expediter, but not without leaving some hard questions about more exact dates.

It was at that point that the expediter told his boss that they needed to implement a system for keeping track of all orders, projects, parts, and customers. The head of international business agreed that they needed a system which would allow anyone at any time to look up the status of any order for any customer. After some meetings with various company officers, the Lakes & Sons company decided to network with a complete system.

To define just what a complete system was, they hired a team of consultants to study their the situation and tell them what kind of network they should implement.

The project budget is always a consideration. The company is not rich, but the finance manager believes that quality, up to a practical point, is worth investing in. He knows that a system that will do the job adequately for the next few years will not be inexpensive.

Your Solution

Use the information in the case study and the lessons in this unit to answer the questions in the following survey. After you finish, compare your solutions with the network engineer's suggested solutions.

Remember, there may be several correct answers. The solution here is only one of many that could work.

The Operating System

List four capabilities the network operating system should have that will contribute to supporting the operation described in the case study.

1. _____

2. _____

3. _____

4. _____

A Multivendor Environment

List at least two operating systems functioning in the company:

1. _____

2. _____

What would be a workable solution to incorporating the various operating systems into a single network so that everyone in the company could access all shared resources?

_____

_____

Security

Network security in this system should be (check one):

Based on the resource (share-level) _____

Based on the individual user (user-level) _____

What is one good reason for your choice?

_____

Printing

List at least three locations that will need a high-quality networked printer.

1. _____
2. _____
3. _____

Network Applications

List two applications developed for networks that would improve the productivity of the company.

1. _____
2. _____

Topology

Which topology would be most appropriate for this environment?

_____

Architecture and Cabling

Which architecture and cabling would best fit the immediate and future networking needs of this company?

_____

Case Study Suggested Solution

The Operating System

The company needed one operating system that would accommodate all of the other network operating systems either through redirectors or a shell. The operating system would include advanced, centralized security so that information could be available to everyone but not abused by anyone.

The operating system should:

1. Be server-based.

    A peer-to-peer system would be inadequate in this environment.

2. Accommodate extensive security.

    The different departments will use data differently. Some of the data, such as human resource and payroll information, will be sensitive.

3. Support groupware applications such as Microsoft Exchange or Lotus Notes.

    The company should implement this type of application to accommodate everyone who needs information about the status of a project.

4. Support redirectors and shells in order to accommodate a multivendor environment.

    This is a multivendor environment.

5. The network operating system should be able to manage printing.

A Multivendor Environment

The operating systems in this environment are:

1. AppleTalk
2. Windows for Workgroups
3. Windows NT
4. Novell NetWare

Center the network around a network operating system that supports redirectors for each of the other operating systems. Or, in the case of AppleTalk, install a shell on a server that appears to the Macintoshes to be an AppleShare file server.

Security

The company should incorporate user-level security because many files are confidential and therefore need restricted access.

Printing

This company probably has many areas which could use a printer. However, good printers should be assigned to at least the following departments:

- Drafting
- Purchasing
- Accounting

Network Applications

This company could use the benefits of:

- Scheduling
- E-mail
- Groupware

Topology

The star bus is common and accommodates easy reconfiguration and upgrading as new technologies appear.

Architecture and Cabling

Ethernet (100BaseT using Category 5 cable) is the best choice. This is a large installation with a variety of needs. Use fiber-optic cable to connect the hubs in different departments, and you will not need repeaters. Use repeaters as needed within buildings.

The Troubleshooter

Network Operations

Is your server hardware on the hardware compatibility list?

Yes _____

No _____

Do you have correct (current) drivers for all of the hardware in your server?

Yes _____

No _____

Do you have the minimum amount of memory in your server to support your current network operating system?

Yes _____

No _____

Does your server have the minimum hard disk space recommended to support all of your storage needs?

Yes _____

No _____

Does your server have the minimum processing power to support your network?

Yes _____

No _____

Do you have all of your network bindings implemented correctly, and are the most used bindings listed first?

Yes _____

No _____

Do your client computers have the correct client software loaded (redirector)?

Yes _____

No _____

Network Printing and Network Fax

Do all of the computers which are using the shared printer have the correct printer driver configured?

Yes _____

No _____

Are the client computers selecting the appropriate shared printer for the driver they are using?

Yes _____

No _____

Do the users and printer managers have the appropriate permissions for the shared printer?

Yes _____

No _____

Are all of the cables to the shared printer in good repair, and properly connected?

Yes _____

No _____

Is the shared printer turned on?

Yes _____

No _____

Is the shared fax software configured correctly?

Yes _____

No _____

Is the shared fax turned on?

Yes _____

No _____

Are all of the cables to the shared fax in good repair, and properly connected?

Yes _____

No _____

Are all of the client computers configured with the correct driver software for the shared fax?

Yes _____

No _____

Network Applications

Are all of the users' e-mail and scheduling programs configured correctly?

Yes _____

No _____

Are each of the messaging gateways configured appropriately and working properly?

Yes _____

No _____

Networks in a Multivendor Environment

Troubleshooting networks in a multivendor environment is very difficult. The key point is almost always the configuration of the server and client. Here are a few questions which should help you start off in the right direction, but there is no substitute for in-depth understanding of the multiple servers and clients involved.

Is the client computer configured with redirectors for each of the server operating systems it needs to access, and are each of those redirectors configured correctly and working?

Yes _____

No _____

Are each of the servers configured with all of the network services needed by its clients, and are those services configured correctly and working?

Yes _____

No _____

Are all of the gateway computers which allow access between environments configured correctly and working?

Yes _____

No _____

The Client/Server Environment

Is the client front end configured correctly and working?

Yes _____

No _____

Is the server software configured correctly and working?

Yes _____

No _____

Is the network application performing as desired?

Yes _____

No _____

Does the server running the network application have enough capacity in terms of processing power, RAM, and hard disk space?

Yes _____

No _____

Are the end users trained in and using the appropriate procedures to get the most out of the network application?

Yes _____

No _____

Can You Solve This Problem?

With your new knowledge of network operations, and the preceding troubleshooter questions in mind, read the following scenario and then create a possible solution.

The Situation

Your network currently consists of 200 client computers and five servers. The two newer servers run Microsoft Windows NT Server, and the three older servers run NetWare 3.12. All users are connected to Microsoft Mail. There is a very large database on one of the NetWare servers. When users need to fax a document, they must first print it out, and then stand in line to use the fax machine.

Modifications

1. Your company would like all users to be able to access all five servers.

2. You need to speed up access to the corporate database and ensure that everyone can access it.

3. Your boss wants to everyone to be able to send faxes from their desktop instead of printing their faxes out and standing in line. He also wants to be able to route incoming faxes to individuals based on their extension number.

4. Your company needs to be able to exchange e-mail messages with another company which uses Lotus Notes for their e-mail.

Your Solution

1. What would you do to allow all of the NetWare clients access to the Windows NT Server servers?

   _____

2. What would you do to allow the Windows NT Server clients to access the NetWare servers?

   _____

3. How would you improve database access?

   _____

4. What faxing solution would you recommend?

   _____

5. What e-mail solution would you recommend?

   _____

Suggested Troubleshooting Solution

1. To allow the NetWare clients to access the Windows NT Server servers, there are two options:

   - Install an additional redirector on the NetWare clients which would also allow them to access the Windows NT Server servers.

   - Install a Server service on the Windows NT Server servers which will allow the NetWare clients to directly access the Windows NT Server servers.

2. To allow the Windows NT Server clients to access the NetWare servers, load the Microsoft redirector for accessing Novell servers on top of Windows NT in the client.

3. The best way to improve access to a large database is usually to implement a client/server SQL solution such as Microsoft SQL Server™. This also allows client computers from other server-based operating systems to access the same database without new client software, all they need is a common protocol such as IPX or TCP/IP.

4. To improve the network fax situation you could install a fax server which implemented T.30 subaddressing. This would allow both sending and receiving of faxes from the client computer. Any fax server such as FACSys would work well.

5. To allow e-mail communications with the other company, an e-mail gateway that would convert the different e-mail headers and allow some type of dial-up communications between the two companies would work.

The LAN Planner

Network Printing

Planning for printer networking primarily involves answering three questions:

1. Where should your printers be located?
2. How many printers will you need?
3. To what will you attach your printer(s) at that location(s)?

To answer the first question you need to know which users will need printed output and where it would be best for those users to pick it up. While this question may seem simple at first, it will take some research to answer properly in a large organization. The correct answer to this question will also help determine an answer to the second question. For example, if your organization has more than one building, it would not be prudent to have only one networked printer. It does not matter which building the printer is located in. It will still be an inadequate solution.

The Printing Survey

The following survey is designed to help answer the three questions.

Draw a Map

This may seem like an elementary step, but when placing printers, it may help to plot out everything on a map of your organization. If you do produce a map, save it as part of the network documentation.

Locating the Printers

Everyone on the network will have printed output of one kind or another. The trick is to identify which users or groups of users will produce more output than others and locate the printers near them.

Are there particular users or groups of users who will produce an exceptional amount of printed output?

Yes ____

No ____

If the answer is yes, identify a suitable printer location as close as possible to that person or group.

If the answer is no, determine a location as close to the middle of the users as possible location that would be suitable for a printer. Remember that time spent walking to and from the printer is time away from work.

Printer locations also need storage space for supplies such as paper and toner.

Determining the Number of Printers

The true answer to this question may have to wait until the network has been operational long enough to correctly judge user satisfaction. For example, if you have 30 or 40 users and only one printer, it will soon become obvious that you need more printers. The answer will also depend on a number of other variables.

The following questions should help you determine the appropriate number of printers.

Are there printers for each group that has been identified as producing a lot of printer output?

Yes _____

No _____

If the answer is no, consider buying more printers.

Are print jobs at certain printers spending too much time in print queues?

Yes _____

No _____

Users are the key to this answer. They will usually make their feelings known.

Based on the number of locations and the estimate of printer output, how many printers will your organization need? _____

Attaching Your Printers

At the locations you have chosen, how will your printers connect to the network? Make a check mark in the following list for each printer at each location. This will help you determine what you need in addition to printers.

A print server: _____

A computer (through peer-to-peer sharing): _____

A direct connection (a network card in the server): _____

A dedicated print server device: _____

Note One of your next steps will be to do the market research required to match your organization's network printing needs with the features of a particular vendor's printer. A printer survey is beyond the scope of this kit.

Network Applications

Most organizations implement some form of e-mail. The crucial e-mail planning question is not whether the organization will use e-mail, but, rather, what other e-mail systems it will have to communicate with.

Do you have to share e-mail with other users outside of your company?

Yes _____ What type of e-mail do they use? _____

No _____

If your answer is yes, you need to identify a gateway which will translate between the two environments. This may require some consulting with a network engineer.

Your e-mail gateway is: _____

Networks in a Multivendor Environment

Is there a need for more than one network operating system in your environment?

Yes _____

No _____

If your answer is yes, list the operating systems on the following lines:

_____

_____

_____

_____

The next steps are to identify which client computers have to communicate with which operating systems, and then determine if there are appropriate redirectors available for those client computers. The alternative is to determine if there is a service or a shell that can be installed on the server in question to enable communication with the client computer.

Does each client computer have the redirectors required to communicate with the appropriate servers?

Yes ____

No ____

If the answer is no, is a shell or other service available for that server which will enable communication between the client and that server?

Yes ____

No ____

If the answer is still no, then the administrator should consider moving the resources on the server in question to a server for which appropriate redirectors or shells are available.

The Client/Server Environment

Are you currently running the following applications in a non-client/server environment? (Check any that apply.)

Database ____

Groupware ____

If you checked either choice, are there more than 10 people using that application?

Yes ____

No ____

If the answer is yes, you should consider implementing a client/server version of that application.

Note If this LAN Planner indicated a need for a product or service, your next step is to do the market research required to match your organization's needs with the features of a particular vendor's products.

The LAN Planner Summary

Note This information will be taken into account in Appendix B, "Network Planning and Implementation."

Number of printers your organization will need: _____

Locations of these printers:

        Printer A: _____

        Printer B: _____

        Printer C: _____

        Printer D: _____

        Other printers: _____

Additional printing equipment (enter the number of each you will need):

Print servers: _____

Direct connections (a network card in the printer): _____

Dedicated print server devices: _____

Your e-mail gateway is: _____

CHAPTER 6

Network Administration and Support

Lesson 1   Managing Network Accounts . . . 431

Lesson 2   Managing Network Performance . . . 455

Lesson 3   Ensuring Network Data Security . . . 470

Lesson 4   Avoiding Data Loss . . . 486

Chapter 6   Review . . . 504

Welcome to Chapter 6, Network Administration and Support. So far you have learned what a network is and the basics of how to implement one. In this chapter you will learn how to keep a network going after it has been started. This chapter will take you through all of the essential areas of basic network management and support.

You will see how to provide users with access to the network and how to maintain a user's appropriate network status. This includes everything from initially entering the user's name on the network to deleting user accounts.

The chapter will describe the fundamentals of monitoring a network's performance. You will learn about several tools and methods for keeping track of important network functions.

Because organizations send sensitive data over the network, the network administrator must also ensure that any data on the network is not misused or destroyed. This chapter presents an overview of the common methods for ensuring network data security.

In the last lesson of this chapter you will learn how you can protect data with methods such as a backup system, power source protection, and redundancy systems.

The Case Study Problem

You will be able to put yourself into the role of the new network administrator for a small credit investigation company, Fitch & Mather. Their small peer-to-peer network needs to be upgraded to a server-based LAN. But that is only where the problems begin for Fitch & Mather.

The Troubleshooter

This Troubleshooter will provide you with questions to ask when there is a problem on any network with user accounts, data security, or unauthorized access. You can then use these questions to help you determine why a user cannot log on to the Windows NT Server network when she arrives at work one morning.

The LAN Planner

The LAN Planner will help you determine how extensive security on your network should be. In addition, it will focus on setting up a network monitoring program appropriate for your site, and guide you through issues to address regarding performance monitoring tools and record keeping. The LAN Planner will also lead you through considerations for implementing a backup policy and redundancy system to avoid loss of data.

Lesson 1: Managing Network Accounts

What This Lesson Does

This lesson provides an overview of essential network account administration areas including:

- Administrator tasks and responsibilities
- Types of accounts
- Passwords
- Groups

Administrator tasks include creating user and group accounts, granting rights and permissions, and deleting accounts.

Objectives

By the end of this lesson, you will be able to:

- Describe the process for creating a user account.
- List and define the four types of group accounts.
- Determine the appropriate types of accounts for a given network environment.
- Create a user account and a group account.

Estimated lesson time 45 minutes

Network Management

The network that will run itself has not been invented. New users will need to be added. Existing users will need to be deleted. New resources will need to be installed, shared, and given the appropriate access permissions. Access permissions are rules associated with a resource, usually a directory file or printer. Permissions regulate the users' access to the resource.

What all this means is that after a network has been installed, it needs to be managed. All of the network management tools have been consolidated in the Start Menu, Programs, Administrative Tools area.

Five Management Areas

There are five major areas of network management a network administrator needs to be familiar with:

- User administration—Creating and maintaining user accounts and appropriate access to resources.

- Resource management—The implementation and support of network resources.

- Configuration management—Planning the original configuration, expanding it, and maintaining the configuration information and documentation.

- Performance management—Monitoring and tracking network activity to maintain and enhance the system's performance.

- Maintenance—The prevention, detection, and solution of network problems.

Administrator Responsibilities

From the five management areas, it is possible to create a check list of network administration duties for which an administrator is responsible. These include:

- Creating and managing user accounts
- Security
- Training and supporting users as needed
- Updating existing software and implementing new software
- Archiving
- Preventing data loss
- Monitoring and regulating server storage space
- Tuning the network to achieve maximum performance
- Data backup
- Protecting the network against viruses
- Troubleshooting
- Upgrading and replacing network components as needed
- Adding new computers to the network

This lesson focuses on tasks related to user management. The remaining subjects are covered in subsequent lessons.

Creating User Accounts

Everyone working on the network needs a user account. An account is composed of a user name and logon parameters established for that user. This information is entered by the administrator and stored on the network by the operating system. The network uses this name to verify the account when the user attempts to log on.

All networks have a utility which the administrator can use to enter a new account name into the network security database. This process is sometimes referred to as creating a user. The Microsoft Windows NT Server network's utility for creating accounts is called the User Manager for Domains, and is found in the Start Menu, Programs, Administrative Tools (Common) area.

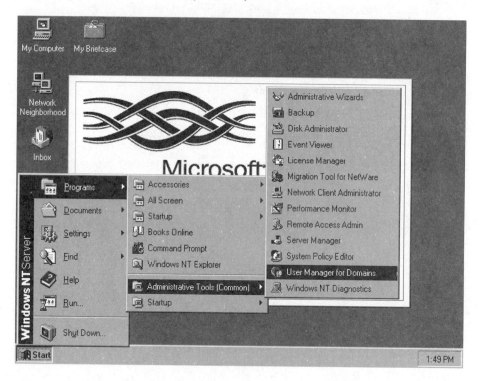

Figure 6.1 Windows NT Administrative Tools area

Once you open User Manager, on the **User** menu, select the menu option **New User**... as shown in Figure 6.2. A window appears for entering the information to create a new user.

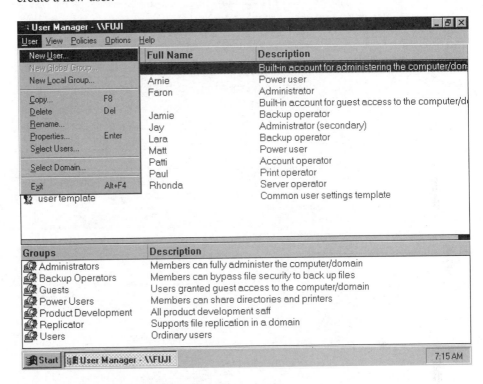

Figure 6.2 Menu showing the New User... selection

Entering User Information

The new account contains information that defines a user to the network security system. This includes:

- The user name and password.
- Rights the user has for accessing the system and using its resources.
- Administrative groups to which the account belongs and other groups to which it has been assigned.

This is essential information which the administrator will need in order to create the account.

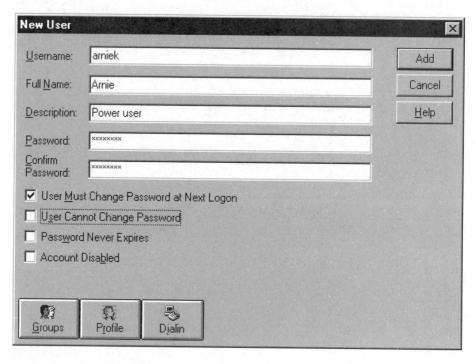

Figure 6.3 New User dialog box

Some of the fields used to create a new user are explained in the following text.

- **Username** This identifies the user account. A user name cannot be identical to any other user or group name of the domain or computer being administered. It can contain up to 20 characters and any uppercase or lowercase characters except the following: " / \ : ; | = , + * ? < >

- **Full Name** The user's complete name.

- **Description** Any text describing the account or the user.

- **Password** and **Confirm Password** A password can be up to 14 characters in length. It is case-sensitive. You must type the identical password in both fields.

Windows NT Server, like most network account management utilities, offers an account copying feature with which an administrator can create a template user having certain characteristics and parameters that are common among multiple users. To create a new account with those characteristics, the administrator highlights the template account, selects User, Copy (F8), then enters the new username and other identifying information (full name, description, etc.).

Setting User Parameters

Most networks will allow administrators to set a number of parameters for users including:

- Logon times—To restrict when users can log on.

- The home directory—To give the user a storage area for private files.

- The expiration date—To limit a temporary user's life on the network.

Profiles

It may be advantageous for an administrator to be able to structure a network environment for certain users. This might be necessary, for example, to maintain some level of security, or if the users are not familiar enough with computers and networks to be able to use the technology on their own. The administrator can use user profiles to control the user's logon environment.

Profiles are used to configure and maintain a user's logon environment including network connections and the appearance of the desktop when the user logs on. These can include:

- Printer connections
- Regional settings
- Sound settings
- Mouse settings
- Display settings
- Any other user-definable settings

The profile parameters may also include special logon conditions and information about where the user may store personal files.

Key User Accounts

Network operating systems come with certain types of user accounts already created and which are automatically activated during installation.

The Administrator—the Initial Account

When a network operating system is installed, the installation program automatically creates an account with complete network authority. Someone has to be able to:

- Start the network.
- Set the initial security parameters.
- Create other user accounts.

In the Microsoft networking environment, this account is called Administrator. In the Novell environment, this account is known as a Supervisor.

The first person to log on to the network is normally the person installing the network operating system. After logging on as administrator, that person has full control over all network functions.

The Guest Account

Another default account created by the installation program is an account called Guest. This is an account for people who do not have a valid user account but need temporary access to the network. Microsoft Windows NT Server disables the Guest account by default after installation. The network administrator must enable the account if it will be used.

Passwords

Passwords help ensure the security of a network environment. The first thing the administrator needs to do when setting up the initial account is enter a password. This will prevent unauthorized users from logging on as administrator and creating accounts.

Users should develop unique passwords and store them in a secure place. In particularly sensitive situations, it is a good idea to have users change their passwords periodically. Many networks offer password features that require users to do this automatically at a time interval set by the administrator.

In situations where security is not an issue, or when access needs to be limited (as in a Guest account), it is possible to modify an account so that it no longer uses a password.

The administrator must be alert to situations such as when a user is no longer employed by the company. In this case, the administrator should disable the account as soon as possible.

There are certain traditional suggestions governing the use of passwords including:

- Do not use obvious passwords such as your birth date, your social security number, or the name of your spouse, children, a pet, and so on.
- Memorize your password instead of writing it down and taping it to your monitor.
- Be conscious of your password expiration date—if there is one—so that you can change your password before it expires and you are locked out of your system.

After a few experiences with users who need the administrator to help them with their passwords, the administrator may determine that some kind of password policy is in order.

Q & A

Fill in the blanks in the following sentences.

1. The first person to log on to a network will use the _____ account.

2. The user account contains information that defines a user to the network's _____ system.

3. Most network account management utilities offer an account _____ feature with which an administrator can create a template user having certain characteristics and parameters that are common among multiple users.

4. An administrator can use a _____ to configure and maintain a user's logon environment.

5. Two key pieces of information that should be entered when creating a user account are account name and _____.

6. The _____ account is for people who do not have a valid user account but need temporary access to the network.

Answers

1. Administrator
2. security
3. copying
4. profile
5. password
6. Guest

Group Accounts

Networks can support thousands of accounts. There will be occasions when the administrator needs to conduct network business with each of these accounts or at least a certain percentage of all of the network accounts.

There may be times when the administrator needs to send messages to large numbers of users notifying them about an event or network policy, or perhaps determine which users should have access to certain resources. The administrator needs to identify each particular account that will have access. If 100 users needed permission to use a particular resource, the administrator has to implement that security 100 separate times.

Nearly every network has solved this problem by offering a way to gather many separate user accounts into one type of account called a group. A group is an account that contains other accounts. The primary reason for implementing groups is the ease of administration. Groups make it possible for an administrator to treat large numbers of users as one account.

If the 100 accounts were put in one group, the administrator could simply send one message to the group account, and all of the members of the group would automatically get the message. Permissions would be set for the group, and all of the members of the group would automatically receive and inherit those permissions.

Planning for Groups

Because groups are such a powerful network administration tool, they should be considered when planning a network. In fact, experienced administrators feel that there should not be any individual network accounts. All accounts will have certain access rights and activities in common. Access rights authorize a user to perform certain actions on the system. Rights apply to the system as a whole and are different from permissions. For example, a user may have the right to back up the system. Permissions and rights should be assigned to groups so that the administrator can treat them as a single account.

Groups are used to:

- Grant access to resources, such as files, directories, and printers. The permissions granted to a group are automatically granted to its members.
- Give rights to perform system tasks, such as to back up and restore files or change the system time. By default, user accounts have no rights. They obtain rights through group membership.
- Simplify communications by reducing the number of messages that need to be created and sent.

Creating Groups

Creating groups is similar to creating individual user accounts. Most networks feature a utility with which the administrator can implement new groups. In Microsoft Windows NT Server, this utility is called User Manager for Domains and is located in the Start Menu, Programs, Administrative Tools (Common) area.

In User Manager, click **New Local Group**… on the **User** menu. This selection presents you with a dialog box for entering the information to create a new local group, as shown in Figure 6.4.

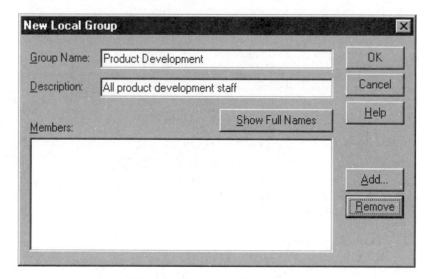

Figure 6.4 New local group dialog box

The fields used to create a new local group are explained in the following text.

- **Group Name** This field identifies the local group. A group name cannot be identical to any other group or user name of the domain or computer being administered. It can contain any uppercase or lowercase characters except for the following: " / \ : ; \ = + * ? < >

- **Description** This field contains text describing the group or the users in the group.

- **Members** This field displays the user names of the group members.

The major difference between creating a group and creating an individual user account is that the group will have users accounts assigned to it as members. The administrator needs to select the appropriate user accounts and assign them to the group. The administrator does this by selecting Add, from the New Local Group dialog box, then selecting the user account to be added.

Types of Groups

Microsoft Windows NT uses four types of groups.

- Local Groups

  This type of group is implemented in each local computer's account database. Local groups contain user accounts and other global groups that need to have access, rights and permissions assigned, to a resource on a local computer. Remember that, although local groups can contain user accounts and global groups from any domain (depending on the trust relationships that are established), local groups cannot contain other local groups.

- Global Groups

  This type of group is used across an entire domain. Global groups are always created on a primary domain controller (PDC) in the domain where the user accounts reside. Global groups can contain only user accounts from the domain where the global group is created. Global groups cannot contain local groups or other global groups. Although permissions to resources can be assigned to a global group, global groups should only be used to gather domain user accounts. Members of the global groups obtain resource permissions when the global group is added to a local group.

- System Groups

  These groups automatically organize users for system use. Administrators do not assign users to them, rather, users are either members by default or become members during network activity. Membership cannot be changed.

- Built-in Groups

  Certain functions are common to all networks. These include most administration and maintenance tasks. Administrators could create accounts and groups with the appropriate permissions to perform these standard tasks, but many network vendors have saved network administrators the trouble of creating those groups and accounts by offering them as built-in local or global groups created during the initial installation.

  Built-in groups are divided into three categories:

  - Administrators—Members of this group have full capabilities on a computer.
  - Operator-type groups—Members of these groups have limited administrative capabilities to perform specific tasks.
  - Other—Members of these groups have capabilities to perform limited tasks.

  Microsoft Windows NT Server, for example, offers the built-in groups shown in the table on the following pages.

Group	Initially contains	Who can modify?	Capabilities
Administrators	Domain Admins (global group) Administrator (user account)	Administrators	Create, delete, and manage user accounts, global groups, and local groups.
			Share directories and printers, grant resource permissions and rights.
			Install operating system files and programs.
Users	Domain users (global group)	Administrators, Account Operators	Perform tasks for which they have been given rights.
			Access resources to which they have been given permissions.
Guests	Guest (user account)	Administrators, Account Operators	Perform tasks for which they have been given rights.
			Access resources to which they have been given permissions.
Server Operators	None	Administrators	Share and stop sharing resources.
			Lock or override the lock of a server.
			Format the server's disks.
			Log on at servers.
			Back up and restore server.
			Shut down servers.
Print Operators	None	Administrators	Share and stop sharing printers.
			Manage printers.
			Log on locally at servers and shut servers down.

(continued)

Group	Initially contains	Who can modify?	Capabilities
Backup Operators	None	Administrators	Back up and restore servers. Log on locally. Shut down the server.
Account Operators	None	Administrators	Create, delete, and modify users, global groups, and local groups. Cannot modify administrator or server operator groups.
Replicator	None	Administrators, Account Operators, Server Operators	Used in conjunction with the Directory Replicator Service.

Granting Group Privileges

The easiest way to grant a large number of users similar permissions is to assign these permissions to a group. The users are then added to the group. The same process applies to adding users to the built-in group. For example, if the administrator wanted a certain user to have administrative capabilities on the network, the administrator would make that user a member of the Administrators group.

Disabling and Deleting User Accounts

Occasionally, an administrator will have to keep an account from being active on the network. This can be done by either disabling the account or deleting it.

Disabling an Account

If an account has only been disabled, it still exists in the network's account database, but no one can use the account to log on to the network. A disabled account will appear not to exist.

It is best if the administrator disables the account as soon as it has been established that the user will no longer be using the account. Once it has been determined that the account will never be needed again, it can be deleted.

Windows NT Server uses the User Properties window in User Manager to disable users. To disable a user, double-click the name of the account, select the **Account Disabled** check box, and then click **OK**. The account is now disabled, as shown in Figure 6.5.

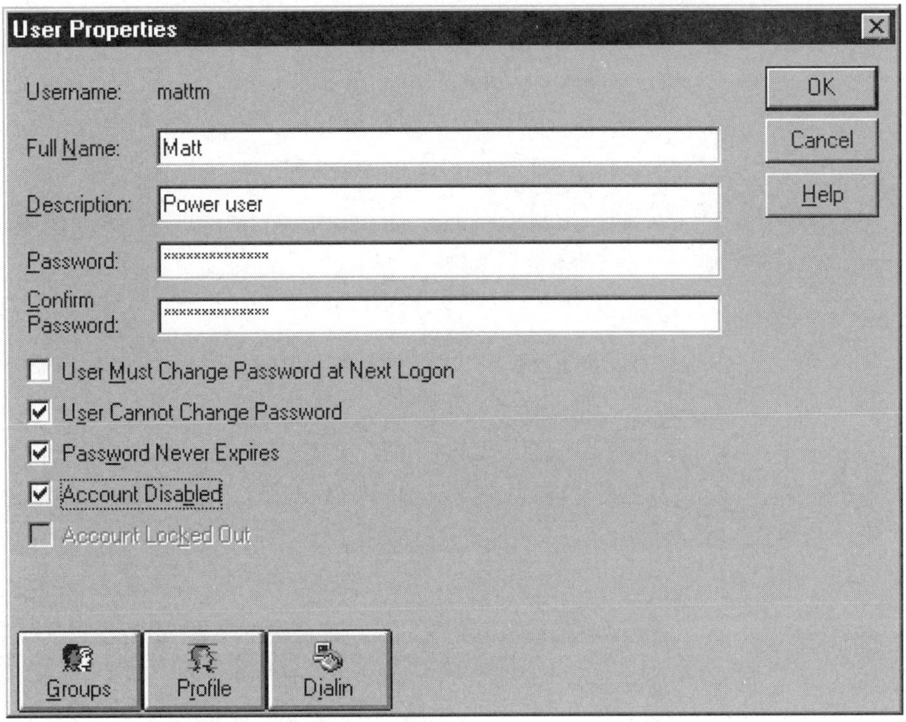

Figure 6.5 Disabling an account

Deleting an Account

Deleting an account erases the user's information from the network's user account database; the user no longer has access to the network.

A user account should be deleted when:

- The user has left the organization and will no longer have a business reason to use the network.
- The user's employment has been terminated.
- The user has moved within the organization and no longer needs access to that network.

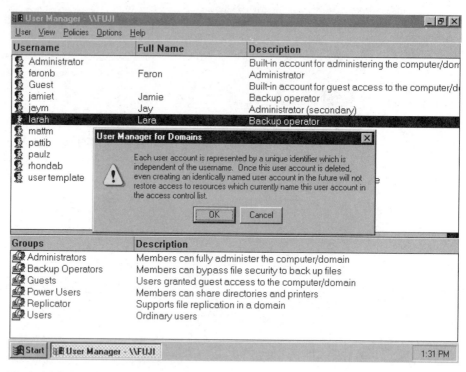

Figure 6.6 Deleting an account

The actual process of deleting a user is usually a simple matter of making a choice and clicking the selection in a dialog box. Microsoft Windows NT Server, for example, uses the User Manager utility for deleting user accounts. In User Manager, select the account to be deleted, and then press the DELETE key. A dialog box is displayed stating that, "Each user account is represented by a unique identifier which is independent of the username. Once the user account is deleted, even creating an identically named user account in the future will not restore access to resources which currently name this user account in the access control list." If you click **OK**, another dialog box will be displayed asking for confirmation that the specified user account will be deleted. Clicking **Yes** will delete the account, clicking **No** will cancel the operation.

Note Deleting an account permanently removes the account and the permissions and rights associated with it. Recreating the user account with the same name will not restore the users rights or permissions, this is because, upon initial creation a user account is assigned a unique security identifier (SID). Deleting and recreating a user will generate a new SID. Internal processes in Windows NT refer to the account's SID rather than the account's user or group name.

Q & A

Fill in the blanks in the following sentences.

1. An administrator can create a _____ account in order to simplify administrative tasks when dealing with a large numbers of users.

2. A global group is used across an entire _____.

3. One way groups are used is to give _____ to perform system tasks such as to back up and restore files.

4. The network administrator assigns _____ to groups to access resources, such as files, directories, and printers.

5. After being deleted, a user cannot use the network anymore because the network _____ database will have no record or description of the user.

Answers

1. group
2. domain
3. rights
4. permissions
5. security

Activity

Use the following steps to run Lab 20A.

Lab 20A: Creating and Deleting User Accounts

What This Lab Does

In this lab you will learn how to create and delete user accounts.

In this simulation of Windows NT Server, you will only be able to create one user and then delete the user you created. However, you may use the lab as many times as you like to practice creating and deleting users.

Objectives

By the end of this lab, you will be able to:

- Create a user account on Windows NT Server.
- Delete a user account on Windows NT Server.

Exercise 1: Creating a User Account

1. From the **Start** menu, point to **Programs**, then **Networking Essentials**, and click **Lab20a**.

   The Networking Essentials - Lab20a window appears.

2. In the **Start** menu, click **Programs, Administrative Tools**, and then **User Manager for Domains**.

   The User Manager for Domains dialog box opens. Two windows are displayed. The top window displays the names of existing user accounts on the system. The bottom window displays the existing groups on the system.

3. On the menu bar, click **User** (to select the user pull down menu).

   Because this is a simulation, most options appear dimmed on the menu except the **New User** and **Delete** options. (Dimmed options are unavailable and cannot be used at this time.)

4. Click **New User**.

   The New User window is displayed.

5. Add yourself as a user, use the following directions as a guideline:

   Username—Type the first **four** letters of your first name followed by your last initial. For example, if your name is David Jones, you would type **Davij**.

Note This new user naming system is for demonstration purposes only. Please follow the naming conventions of your network or contact the network administrator for guidance.

Full Name—Type your full name.

Description—Type information that will help identify the user (job description, or position). For example, President or Marketing Representative.

Password—Type a password that is easy to remember, however, the password you choose should be difficult to discover by anyone other than the valid user.

Confirm Password—Type the same password you typed in the **Password** field.

The following fields are used to enhance user security. You can click **Help** to display the function performed by each field:

User Must Change Password at Next Logon

User Cannot Change Password

Password Never Expires

Account Disabled

Note Checking both "User Must Change Password at Next Logon" and "User Cannot Change Password" will display a warning.

The **Groups** and **Profile** buttons will not be discussed at this time.

6. Click **OK** to create the user account.

The new account is added to **User Manager for Domains**.

Exercise 2: Deleting a User Account

1. Click the user name that you created in Exercise 1.

2. On the **User** menu, click **Delete**.

   You receive a dialog box warning you of the consequences of deleting a user.

3. Click **OK**.

   You receive a dialog box asking you to verify that you want to delete this user.

4. Click **Yes**.

   The user account you created has been deleted.

5. On the **File** menu in the upper left-hand corner of the screen, not on the User menu, click **Exit Lab 20a,** or select **Restart Lab 20a** to exit or restart the lab.

You have completed the installation exercise.

Summary

One very important aspect of a network administrator's job is creating user accounts. User accounts are created for individuals and groups. When the administrator first logs on to a network, an Administrator account and Guest account are automatically created. Passwords are an essential component of all accounts and are necessary for maintaining network security.

When setting up a user account, various types of information need to be included such as user name and password, rights for accessing the system and its resources, and administrative groups to which the user belongs. Profiles can be created for users to configure their logon environment. A profile can include printer connections, icons, desktop, the start menu, mouse settings, and more.

When planning a network, it is a good idea to consider the types of group accounts that may be needed. Creating groups can help make the administrator's job easier. The types of groups are local, global, special (for Windows NT Server), and built-in. Many network systems set up built-in local or global groups automatically during network installation.

Your Next Step

Managing user accounts, while necessary, is only one aspect of making sure a network does its job. If a network administrator plans the network well and follows up on the planning, account administration should not consume extensive time or other resources.

Ensuring that the network performs as expected and provides a consistent level of service, however, can develop into a full-time job as you will see in Lesson 2, "Managing Network Performance."

Lesson 2: Managing Network Performance

What This Lesson Does

This lesson focuses on the administrator management task of monitoring the performance of a network. It presents an overview of network performance problems, with an emphasis on network bottlenecks.

You will also learn about the Windows NT performance monitoring tool and a wide area network systems management application. The lesson also discusses the importance of documentation in keeping a thorough, accurate network history.

Objectives

By the end of this lesson, you will be able to:

- Identify major sources of network problems.
- List potential bottlenecks in network performance.
- Describe the simple network management protocol (SNMP).
- Develop a network performance monitoring plan.
- Describe the functions of the network monitor utility.
- Create appropriate network documentation.

Estimated lesson time 30 minutes

Network Management Overview

After a network has been installed and is up and running, the administrator will have to make sure that it continues to perform effectively. To do this, the administrator will need to manage and keep track of every aspect of the network's performance.

The scope of a network management program will depend on:

- The size of the network.
- The size and capabilities of the network support staff.
- The organization operating budget for the network.
- The organization's expectations of the network.

Small peer-to-peer networks consisting of 10 or 12 computers can be monitored visually by one support person, while a large network or WAN may need a dedicated staff and sophisticated equipment to perform proper network monitoring.

One way to ensure that the network does not fail is to watch certain aspects of its day-to-day behavior. By consistently monitoring the network you will notice if any areas begin to show a decline in performance.

Monitoring Performance

Administrators monitor network performance for various reasons:

- To improve performance based on the existing configuration
- To provide for capacity planning and forecasting
- To provide essential information for bottleneck detection

Bottlenecks

Most network activities involve the coordinated activity of several devices. Each device takes a certain amount of time to perform its part of the transaction. Poor performance results when one of these devices uses noticeably more CPU time than the others. The problem device is usually referred to as a bottleneck. Most performance monitoring is involved with identifying and eliminating bottlenecks.

To solve bottleneck problems, an administrator must be able to identify the devices that are taking more time than they should to perform their tasks.

These devices tend to become bottlenecks:

- CPUs
- Memory
- Network cards
- Disk controllers
- Network media

A device becomes a bottleneck due to one of the following reasons:

- It is not being used as efficiently as it could
- It is using other resources or CPU time more than it should
- It is too slow
- It does not have the capacity to handle the load placed on it

Proper monitoring will recognize these situations and provide information to help identify the problem component or components.

Windows NT Performance Monitor

Most current network operating systems include a monitoring utility that will help a network administrator track different aspects of a network server's performance.

Windows NT Server, for example, includes a utility called Performance Monitor which helps a network administrator view operations in both real time and recorded time for:

- Processors
- Hard disks
- Memory
- Network utilization
- Network as a whole

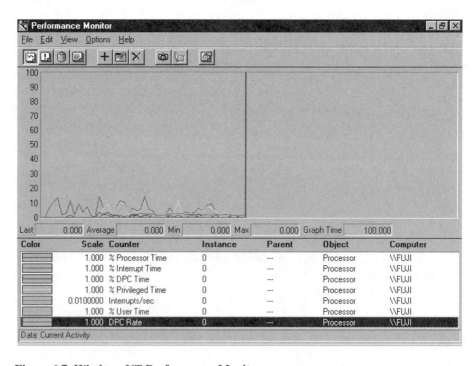

Figure 6.7 Windows NT Performance Monitor

Windows NT Performance Monitor can:

- Record the performance data.
- Send an alert to the network manager.
- Start another program that may adjust the system back into acceptable ranges.

When using a tool such as Performance Monitor, the first thing you need to do is establish a baseline of system performance. By maintaining a record of system performance in normal operation, you can build an understanding of reasonable performance values. With this record, you have a baseline for comparison when things change or when something has to be upgraded or replaced. Without this baseline, determining and maintaining acceptable levels of performance can be difficult.

Once you have established your baseline, you can monitor system performance and compare results with your baseline. The results of your analysis will help you determine the need to improve a specific performance area.

Monitoring your system over time will also let you study trends. By studying trends you will be able to detect problems before they reach a critical stage. This will make planning for the future and maintaining an acceptable level of performance an easier task. For example, if the network is slowing down you will be able to determine where the bottleneck is occurring and take corrective action.

Windows NT Network Monitor

Windows NT Server also includes another diagnostic tool called, Network Monitor. Network Monitor allows the administrator the ability to capture and analyze network data-streams to and from the server, making it easier to troubleshoot potential network problems.

Before transmission the data-stream is divided by the network software into smaller pieces, called frames or packets. Each frame contains the following information:

- The source address of the computer that sent the message.
- The destination address of the computer that received the frame.
- Headers from each protocol used to send the frame.
- The data or a portion of the information being sent.

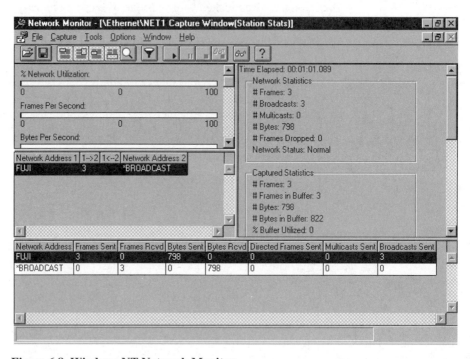

Figure 6.8 Windows NT Network Monitor

Network Monitor is installed as a service through the **Network** program in Control Panel. To do this select, **Start, Settings, Control Panel.** Double click on the **Network** icon. Click **Services,** then click **Add.** In the Network Services box, click, **Network Monitor Tools and Agent,** click **OK.** A dialog box requesting the location of the files to be copied will be displayed. After copying the files click Close. When prompted, click **Yes** to shut down and then restart the computer. This process will install Network Monitor. Network Monitor will appear on the **Administrative Tools (Common)** area.

Simple Network Management Protocol (SNMP)

Like most network components, network management software follows standards created by network equipment vendors. One of these standards is simple network management protocol (SNMP).

In an SNMP environment, programs called agents are loaded onto each managed device. The agents monitor network traffic and behavior in these key network components in order to gather statistical data. This data is stored in a management information base (MIB).

SNMP components include:

- Hubs
- Servers
- Interface cards
- Routers and bridges
- Other specialized network equipment

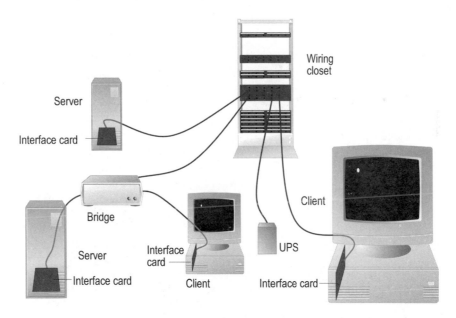

Figure 6.9 SNMP environment showing components

To collect the information in a usable form, a special management program console regularly polls these agents and downloads the information from their MIBs. Once the raw information has been collected, the management program can perform two more tasks:

- It presents the information in the form of graphs, maps, and charts.
- It sends the information to designated database programs to be analyzed.

If any of the data falls either above or below thresholds set by the manager, the management program can notify the administrator by means of alerts on the computer, or even by automatically dialing a pager number. The support staff can then use the management console program to implement changes in the network, depending on the component.

Q & A

Fill in the blanks in the following sentences.

1. One reason it is important to monitor network performance is to provide essential information for _____ detection.

2. Windows NT Server Performance Monitor helps a network administrator view operations in both _____ time and _____ time.

3. In an SNMP environment, programs called _____ monitor network traffic.

4. Windows NT Performance Monitor has the ability to send an _____ to the network manager when there is a problem.

5. Windows NT Server Network Monitor allows the administrator the ability to _____ and _____ network data-streams to and from the server.

Answers

1. bottleneck

2. real, recorded

3. agents

4. alert

5. capture, analyze

Total System Management

As networks have grown in size and complexity, keeping track of an entire system has become more taxing. Because of this, vendors have developed utilities that do for system management what performance monitors have done for system monitoring. An example of one of these system-wide management applications is the Microsoft Systems Management Server (SMS) centralized management for distributed systems program.

Systems Management Server provides centralized administration of computers in a WAN. This includes:

- Collecting hardware and software inventory information.
- Distributing and installing software.
- Sharing network applications.
- Troubleshooting hardware and software problems.

Systems Management Server complements other system management utilities found in Microsoft operating systems such as Windows NT Explorer, User Manager, Registry Editor, Event Viewer, and Server Manager.

Systems Management Server provides the functions listed in the following text.

- Inventory Management

  Systems Management Server collects and maintains an inventory of hardware and software for each computer. The inventory is stored in a SQL Server database. Typical inventory includes the type of CPU, amount of RAM, hard disk size, operating system, and application software.

- Software Distribution

  After a computer's inventory has become part of the database, Systems Management Server can install and configure new software, or upgrade previously installed software directly on a client. This distribution mechanism can also be used to run commands, such as virus scans, on clients.

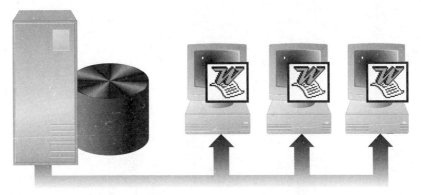

Figure 6.10 Systems Management Server distributes software

- Shared Application Management

  Shared applications can also be distributed to a server for clients to access. When a user logs on to the network, Systems Management Server builds a program folder on each client, these program folders contain more folders that contain the program icons that are the shared applications available to the user. To start the shared application, the user selects an icon from the program folder that is displayed on the local workstation, (the application is actually stored on the server's hard disk).

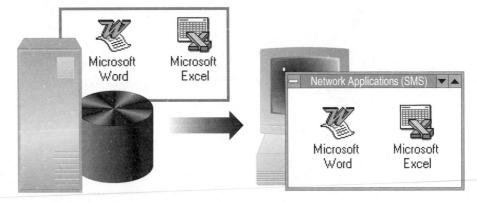

Figure 6.11 Systems Management Server simplifies application sharing

- Remote Control and Network Monitor

  Systems Management Server provides Help Desk and diagnostics utilities which allow you to control and monitor remote clients directly. The diagnostics utilities let you view the client's current configuration. The Help Desk utilities provide direct access to a remote client. Systems Management Server also includes a more advanced version Microsoft Network Monitor, which enables you to analyze network traffic and identify problem areas in your network.

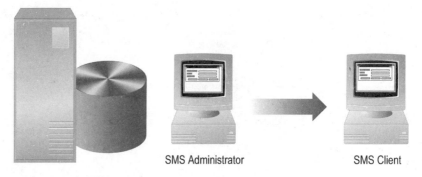

SMS Administrator   SMS Client

Figure 6.12 Systems Management Server simplifies remote client maintenance

Systems Management Server supports the following environments:

Environment	Supported
Network operating systems	Windows NT Server 3.51 and later, LAN Manager 2.1 and later, Novell® NetWare 3.1x and 4.x, IBM LAN Server 3.0 and 4.0, any network protocol supported by Windows NT Server, including TCP/IP and IPX.
Client computers	Windows 3.1, Windows 95, Windows for Workgroups 3.11, Windows NT Workstation 3.5 and later, MS-DOS 5.0 and later, IBM OS/2 2.x, and OS/2 WARP, Apple® Macintosh (System 7).

Maintaining a Network History

Documenting a network's history is as important as monitoring its real-time performance. A network's written record can:

- Indicate significant performance or equipment issues that real-time monitoring may miss.
- Provide a background against which current information may be compared.

If there is more than one administrator, it is important that they all record in only one log. This can be an invaluable guide to future administrators who may need to trace a performance problem or resolve one of these network issues:

- Growth
- Equipment
- Maintenance
- System configuration changes

This document should record:

- Purchase and installation dates and descriptions.
- Complete information on key people such as any contractors responsible for installation.
- Vendor, model, and warranty information, including serial numbers.
- The installation process and results.
- The initial and subsequent network configurations.
- Policies and procedures.
- Network resources and drive assignments.
- Copies of crucial network configuration files, such as Config.sys and .bat files.
- Any unusual application program configurations.
- Any particular computer, board, or peripheral settings.
- Any problems and their solutions.
- Hardware or software changes.
- Any activities affecting the topology or architecture.

It is important that all network historical documentation be easy to access and easy to read. Graphics, or even hand-drawn sketches, can be very helpful.

A network's history can be either online or in a notebook. Keeping the log in a computer file can cause difficulties, especially if the file is kept on a hard disk and the computer or disk crashes. This is exactly the type of behavior the log should record.

Activity

Run Demo 21.

Summary

Network management includes many responsibilities, one of the most important being network performance management. The administrator monitors network performance for bottlenecks and to see how performance can be improved. Monitoring performance also aids in planning and forecasting future network needs. The primary devices or software which can become bottlenecks are the CPU, memory, network adapter cards, and the disk controller.

Microsoft has three tools that help the network administrator in these tasks. Windows NT Server has Performance Monitor, which provides real-time and recorded viewing of network operations. Systems Management Server provides a broader scope of network system management with centralized administration of all computers in a wide area network. Network Monitor provides the ability to watch over server performance and overall network traffic.

An essential part of managing the network is maintaining a performance log. A network history is an invaluable tool for tracing system problems.

Your Next Step

Maintaining records of network performance and managing its daily activities are necessary to maintain an acceptable level of network performance. However, performance problems and equipment failures are not the only misfortunes which can transform the network from a productive business tool into a drain on the organization's resources. Unauthorized access to, or misuse of, sensitive data on the network can actually turn the network into a threat to the organization.

Next you will learn how to prevent these types of events by maintaining the security of your network.

Lesson 3: Ensuring Network Data Security

What This Lesson Does

This lesson presents an overview of network security, including security considerations for network planning. It presents two primary models for ensuring data security, as well as how to secure the physical components of a network.

Objectives

By the end of this lesson, you will be able to:

- List the basic security requirements for any network.
- Describe the primary components to be considered for physical security.
- Describe the features of password-protected shares.
- Describe the features of access permissions.

Estimated lesson time 35 minutes

Planning for Network Security

In a networking environment there must be assurance that sensitive data will remain private so that only authorized users can access it. Not only is it important to secure sensitive information, it is equally important to protect network operations.

Every network needs to be kept safe from deliberate or unintentional damage.

However, a good network administrator will remember that security requires a balance. A network does not need to be so secure that people have difficulty using it to get their work done. They should not be frustrated trying to get into their own files.

Even though networks handle the most sensitive and valuable business data, data security is sometimes an afterthought. Four major threats to the security of a network are:

- Unauthorized access
- Electronic tampering
- Theft
- Intentional or unintentional damage

Despite the reality of these threats, data security is not always understood or supported properly. It is the administrator's job to ensure that the network remains a reliable, secure business tool free from those threats.

Level of Security

The extent and level of the network security system will depend on the type of environment in which the network is running. A network that stores data for a major bank, for example, requires more extensive security than a LAN which links the computers in a small community volunteer organization.

Setting Policies

Network security requires a set of rules, regulations, and policies so that nothing is left to chance.

A security policy may be a company's first step toward ensuring data security. Policies set the tone and offer guidelines which can help the administrator and users through changes and unplanned situations in their network's development. They are an essential step toward maintaining a successful network.

Prevention

The best data security policies take a proactive, preventive approach. By preventing unauthorized access or behavior, data will remain secure. A prevention-based system requires that the administrator understand the tools and methods available with which to keep data safe.

Authentication

Before you can access a network, you must enter a valid user name and password. Because passwords are linked to user accounts, a password authentication system is your first line of security against unauthorized users.

Training

A well-trained network user is less likely to accidentally ruin a resource.

Figure 6.13 Training helps reduce costly user errors

The administrator should ensure that everyone who uses the network is familiar with its operating and security procedures. To accomplish this, the administrator can develop a short, clear guide to what users need to know as well as have new users attend appropriate training classes.

Physical Security of Equipment

The first consideration in keeping data safe is the physical security of the network hardware. The degree of this security will depend on:

- The size of the company.
- The sensitivity of the data.
- The available resources.

In a peer-to-peer situation, there may be no organized hardware security policy. The users are responsible for the security of their own computers and data.

Securing the Servers

In a larger, centralized system where much individual user and company data is sensitive, the servers should be physically safe from accidental or deliberate tampering.

There are always individuals in every group who want to demonstrate their technical abilities when the servers have problems. They may or may not know what they are doing. It is best to tactfully prevent these people from "fixing" the server.

The simple solution is to lock the servers in a computer room with limited access. Depending on the size of the company, this may not be practical. However, locking the servers in an office or even a large storage closet is a step in the right direction to securing the servers.

Securing the Cable

Copper cable, such as coaxial, acts like a radio in that it emits electronic signals which mimic the information it carries. This information can be monitored with the proper electronic listening equipment. Copper cable can also be tapped into so that information can be stolen directly from the original cable.

Cable runs that handle sensitive data should be accessible only to authorized people. Proper planning will make such cable runs inaccessible to unauthorized people. For example, they can be run inside the building structure, through the ceiling, walls, and floors.

Security Models

After implementing security for the network's physical components, the administrator will have to ensure that the network resources will be safe from both unauthorized access and accidental or deliberate damage. Policies for assigning permissions and rights to network resources are the heart of making the network a successful business tool.

Two different security models have evolved for keeping data and hardware resources safe:

- Password-protected shares
- Access permissions

These models are also called share-level security (for password-protected shares) and user-level security (for access permissions).

Password-Protected Shares

Implementing password-protected shares involves assigning a password to each shared resource. Access to the shared resource is granted when a user enters the appropriate password.

In many systems, resources can be shared with different types of permissions. For example, with Windows 95, directories can be shared as Read Only, Full, or Depends On Password.

- Read Only

    If a share is set up as Read Only, users who know the password have Read access to the files in that directory. They can view the documents, copy them to their machine, and print them, but they cannot change the original document.

- Full

    With Full access, users who know the password have complete access to the files in that directory. In other words, they can view, modify, add, and delete the shared directory's files.

- Depends On Password

    Depends On Password involves setting up a share that uses two levels of passwords: Read access and Full access. The users who know the Read access password have Read access and those who know the Full access password have Full access.

The password-protected share system is a simple security method that allows anyone who knows the password to obtain access to that particular resource.

Access Permissions

Access permission security involves assigning certain rights on a user-by-user basis. A user types a password when he or she logs on to the network. The server validates this user name and password combination and uses it to grant or deny access to shared resources by checking access to the resource against a user-access database on the server.

Access permission security provides a higher level of control over access rights, as well as tighter security on the system, than password-protected shares do. It is much easier for one person to give another person a printer password, as in share-level security. It is less likely for that person to give away their personal password.

Because user-level security is more extensive and can determine various levels of security, it is usually the preferred model in larger organizations.

Resource Security

After the user has been authenticated and allowed on the network, the security system gives the user access to the appropriate resources.

Users have passwords, but resources have permissions. In a sense, each resource is guarded by a security fence. The fence has several gates through which users may pass to access the resource. Certain gates allow users to do more to the resource than other gates. Certain gates, in other words, allow the user more privileges with the resource.

It is up to the administrator to determine which users should be allowed through which gates. One gate grants the user full access or full control of the resource. Another gate grants the user read-only access.

Each shared resource or file is stored with a list of users or groups and their associated permissions (gates).

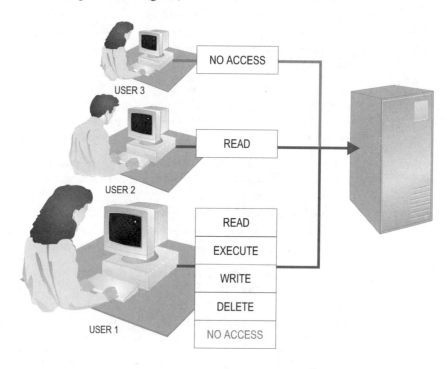

Figure 6.14 Permissions control the type of access to a resource

The following list contains common access permissions assigned to shared directories or files.

Note Different network operating systems give different names to these permissions. The following table shows some of the typical permissions that can be set on Windows NT Server directories.

Permission	Functionality
Read	Read and copy files in the shared directory.
Execute	Run (execute) the files in the directory.
Write	Create new files in the directory.
Delete	Delete files in the directory.
No Access	Prevents the user from gaining access to the directory, file, or resource.

Group Permissions

It is the administrator's job to assign each user the appropriate permissions to each resource. The most efficient way to accomplish this is through groups, especially in a large organization with many users and resources. Windows NT Server allows the user to select the file or folder that they want to set group permissions for. To set group permissions, select a file or folder from Windows NT Explorer, Click the File pull down menu, select Properties, the Properties screen is displayed with the tabs General, Sharing, and Security (available only on NTFS formatted partitions). The General tab displays information about the file or folder. The Sharing tab displays share level security options. The Security tab displays NTFS level security options.

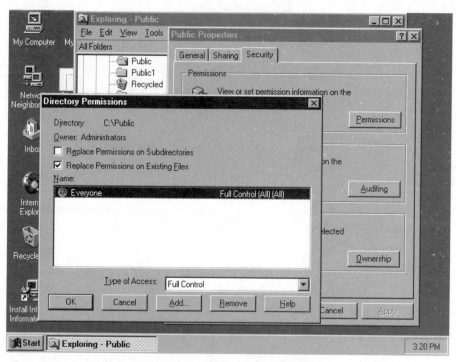

Figure 6.15 Windows NT Explorer is used to set permissions

Permissions for groups work the same way they do for individuals. The administrator reviews which permissions are required by each account and assigns the accounts to the proper groups. This is the preferred way to assign permissions, instead of assigning each account's permissions individually.

Assigning users to appropriate groups is far more convenient than having to assign separate permissions to every individual user. For example, in Figure 6.15 the group Everyone has Full Control to the PUBLIC directory. Typically, this may not be the best choice. Full access would allow anyone to delete or modify the contents of the files in the PUBLIC directory.

In Figure 6.16, the group Everyone has been granted Read access to the directory PUBLIC. This will allow members of the group Everyone to read but not delete or modify the files in PUBLIC.

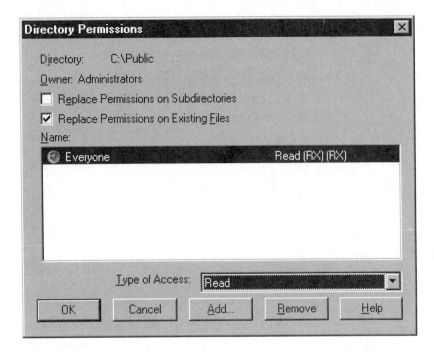

Figure 6.16 Modifying group permissions

As another example of how this might work, think of faculty access to student files in a college. The members of the academic review board might need complete access to student files while other faculty might only need Read access to the files. The administrator could create a group called Reviewers, grant complete access permissions to the student files to that group, and assign staff to the Reviewers group as needed. Another group, called Faculty, would only have Read permissions in the student files. Faculty members assigned to the Faculty group would be able to read the student files, but not change them.

Q & A

Fill in the blanks in the following sentences.

1. The first consideration in keeping data safe is the security of the network
   _____.

2. Another term for access permissions is _____ _____
   _____.

3. Implementing password-protected shares involves assigning a password to each
   shared _____.

4. If a share is set up as _____ _____, users can look at the documents
   or copy them to their machine, but they cannot change the original document.

5. Access permission security involves assigning certain _____ on a user-
   by-user basis.

6. The most efficient way to assign permissions is through the use of
   _____.

Answers

1. hardware
2. user-level security
3. resource
4. Read Only
5. rights
6. groups

Security Enhancements

There are various ways the network administrator can increase the level of security on a network. This section explores some of the options.

Auditing

Auditing records selected types of events in the security log of a server. This process tracks network activities by user accounts. Auditing should be part of network security because the audit records show the users that have accessed or attempted to access specific resources. Auditing helps administrators identify unauthorized or unintended activity. It can also provide usage information in situations where departments charge for making certain network resources available and need some way to determine the cost of those resources.

Auditing creates activity trails for functions such as:

- Log on/log off attempts
- Connecting and disconnecting from designated resources
- Connection termination
- Disabling accounts
- Opening or closing files
- Changes to files
- Directory creation or deletion
- Directory modification
- Server events and modifications
- Password changes
- Logon parameter changes

The audit records can indicate how the network is being used. The administrator can use the audit records to produce reports which show any number of specific activities and their date and time ranges. For example, repeated failed logon attempts or attempts to log on at odd hours may indicate that an unauthorized user is attempting to gain access to the network.

Diskless Computers

Diskless computers, as the name implies, have no floppy drives or hard disks. They can do everything a computer with disk drives can do except store data on a local floppy or hard disk. These computers are ideal for security because users cannot download data and take it away. Also, some companies use diskless computers because they are inexpensive compared to fully-equipped computers.

Diskless computers do not need boot disks. They are able to communicate with the server and log on because of a special ROM boot chip installed on the computer's network adapter card. When the diskless computer is turned on, the ROM boot chip signals the server that it wants to start. The server responds by downloading boot software into the diskless computer's RAM and automatically presents the user with a logon screen as part of the boot process. Once the user logs on, the computer is connected to the network.

Data Encryption

A data encryption utility scrambles data before it goes out onto the network. This makes the data unreadable even if someone taps the cable and reads the data as it passes over the network. When the data gets to the proper computer, a key, the code for deciphering encrypted data, decodes the bits into understandable information. Advanced data encryption schemes automate both encryption and the keys. The best encryption systems are hardware-based and can be expensive.

The traditional standard for encryption is the data encryption standard (DES). This system describes how the data should be encrypted and the specifications for the key. DES is currently specified by the U.S. Government. Both the sender and the receiver need access to the key. Problems arise because the only way to get the key from one location to another is to transmit it, which makes DES vulnerable.

However, the government is also using a newer standard called the Commercial COMSEC Endorsement Program (CCEP) which may replace DES. The National Security Agency (NSA) introduced CCEP and allows vendors to join CCEP, with the proper security clearances. Vendors are authorized to incorporate classified algorithms into communications systems. NSA has proposed that they themselves would actually provide the keys to end-users of such systems.

Virus Protection

Disastrous viruses are becoming more common place. They must be taken into account when developing network security procedures. Although no virus protection program can prevent all viruses, they can do some of the following:

- Keep the virus from activating.
- Remove the virus
- Repair the damage that a virus has caused to some extent.
- Keep the virus in check after it activates.

Preventing unauthorized access is one of the best ways to avoid a virus. Because prevention is the key, the network administrator needs to be sure all of the standard measures are in place. These include:

- Passwords to reduce the chance of unauthorized access.
- Well-planned access and privilege assignments for all users.
- Profiles to structure the network environment for users to configure and maintain a user's logon environment, including network connections and program items which appear when the user logs on.
- A policy determining what software can be loaded.
- A policy for implementing virus protection on the client workstations and network servers.

Q & A

Fill in the blanks in the following sentences.

1. Auditing records selected types of events in the _____ _____ of a server in order to track network activities by user accounts.

2. A data _____ utility scrambles data before it goes out onto the network.

3. The Commercial COMSEC Endorsement Program (CCEP) authorizes vendors to incorporate classified _____ into communication systems.

4. Diskless computers communicate with the server and log on through the use of a special ROM boot chip installed on the computer _____ _____ _____.

Answers

1. security log
2. encryption
3. algorithms
4. network adapter card

Summary

Planning a network includes planning for security. The level of security you need depends on a variety of factors including size of the organization and sensitivity of data. The network administrator must assess the needs of the network and determine security policies.

Two security models to choose from are password-protected shares and access permissions. Many companies use both. Password-protected shares focus on shared resources. A user must enter a password to access a particular resource. With access permissions, certain rights are assigned to users. The user enters a name and password combination when logging on. This logon determines access to shared resources.

The most efficient way to assign permissions is through groups. The administrator assigns permissions to groups of users, rather than individually.

Other ways to enhance network security are through auditing, diskless computers, data encryption, and virus protection.

Your Next Step

As illustrated in this lesson, there are many threats to network data security. This lesson primarily covered the kinds of threats that humans create. At least as important, however, are the unexpected events which can be so catastrophic they are called disasters. An unexpected event such as a fire can destroy the most thorough and carefully maintained security and support program. In fact, unexpected disasters can ruin not only the network's records, but the entire system as well.

You will begin learning how to keep your network resources safe from loss caused by natural disasters or equipment failure in Lesson 4, "Avoiding Data Loss."

Lesson 4: Avoiding Data Loss

What This Lesson Does

This lesson presents an overview of the possible causes of data loss and how to protect the network against them. You will learn about systems and processes for preventing data loss.

Objectives

By the end of this lesson, you will be able to:

- List the considerations for implementing a backup system.
- Determine a backup approach appropriate for a given site including the method and schedule.
- List the considerations for implementing an uninterruptible power supply.
- Describe each of the following types of fault tolerant systems: disk striping, disk mirroring, sector sparing, mirrored drive arrays, and clustering.

Estimated lesson time 60 minutes

Data Protection

A site disaster is defined as anything that causes you to lose your data. The causes of a network disaster range from the human kind to the natural kind, including:

- Arson
- Data deletion and corruption
- Theft or vandalism
- Fire
- Power supply failure and surges
- Component failure
- Natural disasters such as lightning, floods, tornadoes, and earthquakes

In the event of a site disaster, the downtime spent recovering data from backup storage (if you have backups) could result in a serious loss of productivity. Without backups the consequences are more severe, with probable financial losses resulting. Several ways to ensure against data loss are

- Tape backup
- Uninterruptible power supply (UPS)
- Fault tolerance

Any or all of these systems can be used, depending on how valuable the data is to the organization, and on the organization's budget constraints.

Tape Backup

Perhaps the simplest, most inexpensive way to avoid disastrous loss of data is to implement a schedule of periodic backups with storage off-site. Using a tape backup is still one of the few simple and economical ways to ensure that data remains safe and usable.

Experienced network engineers advise that a backup system should be the first line of defense. A secure backup strategy minimizes the risk of losing data by maintaining a current backup so that files can be recovered if something happens to the original data.

Backing up data involves:

- Equipment
- A schedule
- A person assigned to make sure that the schedule is carried out

The equipment will normally consist of one or more tape drives and tapes, or some other mass storage media. Any expense incurred in this area is considered minimal compared to what will potentially be saved.

Implementing a Backup System

The general rule is, if you cannot get along without it, back it up. Whether you back up entire disks, selected directories, or files will depend on how fast you need to get up and running after losing important data. Complete backups will make restoring disk configurations much easier, but can require multiple tapes if there are large amounts of data. Backing up individual files and directories might require fewer tapes, but may require the administrator to manually restore disk configurations.

Critical data should be backed up according to daily, weekly, or monthly schedules, depending on how critical the data is and how frequently it is updated. It is best to schedule backup operations during periods of low system use. Users should be notified when the backup will be performed so that they will not be using the servers during server backup.

Selecting a Tape Drive

Because the majority of backing up is done with tape drives, the first step is to choose a tape drive. The administrator should consider:

- How much data is involved
- Reliability
- Capacity
- Speed
- Cost of the drive and related media
- Hardware compatibility with the operating system

Ideally, a tape drive should have more than enough capacity to back up a network's largest server. It should also provide error detection and correction during backup and restore operations.

Backup Methods

An efficient backup policy will use a combination of the methods listed in the following table.

Method	Description
Full backup	Backs up and marks selected files, whether or not they have changed since the last backup.
Copy	Backs up all selected files without marking them as being backed up.
Incremental backup	Backs up and marks selected files only if they have changed since the last time they were backed up.
Daily copy	Backs up only those files that have been modified that day, without marking them as being backed up.
Differential backup	Backs up selected files only if they have changed since the last time they were backed up, without marking them as being backed up.

Backup methods normally involve tape drives. Experienced network administrators have found that using several tapes in a revolving schedule is the best approach to backing up large amounts of data.

Tapes can be backed up based on a multiple-week cycle, depending on how many tapes are available. There is no rigid rule about the length of the cycle. The principle is that on the first day of the cycle, the administrator performs a full backup and follows up with an incremental backup on succeeding days. When the entire cycle has finished, the process begins again. Some administrators have found through experience that it is wise to perform several incremental backups each day at specific times.

Testing and Storage

Experienced administrators will test the backup system before committing to it. They will perform a backup, delete the information, restore the data, and attempt to use the data.

The administrator should test the backup procedures regularly to verify that what is expected to be backed up is actually being backed up. Additionally, the restore procedure should be tested to ensure that important files can be restored quickly.

Ideally, an administrator will make two copies of each tape. One will be kept on site, and the other will be stored off-site in a safe place. Remember, storing tapes in a fireproof safe may keep them from actually burning, but the heat from a fire will ruin the data stored on them.

Maintaining a Backup Log

Maintaining a log of all backups is critical for later file recovery. A copy of the log should be kept both with the backup tapes and at the computer site. The log should record the following information:

- Date of backup
- Tape-set number
- Type of backup performed
- Computer backed up
- Files backed up
- Who performed the backup
- Location of the backup tapes

Installing the Backup System

Tape drives can be connected to a server or a computer with backups initiated from the computer to which the tape drive is attached. If you run backups from a server, backup and restore operations can occur very quickly because the data does not have to travel across the network.

Backing up across the network is the most efficient way of backing up multiple systems; however, it creates a great deal of network traffic and slows the network down considerably. Network traffic can also cause performance degradation. This is one reason why it is important to perform backups during periods of low server use.

If multiple servers reside in one location, backup traffic can be reduced by placing a backup computer on an isolated segment. The backup computer is then connected to a separate network adapter card on each server.

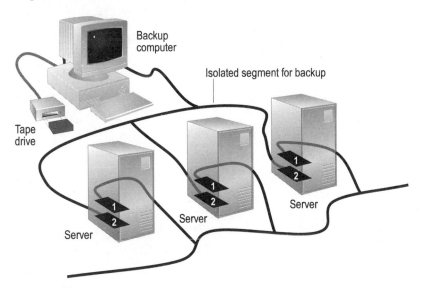

Figure 6.17 Network traffic is reduced by backing up to a separate segment

Q & A

Fill in the blanks in the following sentences.

1. The first line of defense against loss of data is usually a _____ _____ system.

2. It is important to have a regular _____ for backing up data.

3. Maintaining a _____ of all backups is important for later file recovery.

4. When backing up across a network, network traffic can be reduced by placing the backup computer on an isolated _____.

Answers

1. tape backup
2. schedule
3. log
4. segment

The Uninterruptible Power Supply (UPS)

The UPS is an automated external power supply that will keep a server or other device running in the event of a power failure. The UPS system takes advantage of uninterruptible power supplies that can interface with an operating system such as Microsoft Windows NT. The standard UPS provides a network with two crucial components:

- A power source to run the server for a short time.
- A safe shutdown management service.

The power source is usually a battery, but a UPS can also be a rotary system generating power from the action of a large flywheel, or a gasoline engine running an AC power supply.

If the power fails, users are notified of the failure and warned by the UPS to finish their tasks. The UPS then waits a predetermined amount of time and performs an orderly system shutdown.

A good UPS system will:

- Prevent any more users from accessing the server.
- Send an alert message to the network administrator through the server.

The UPS is usually located between the server and a power source.

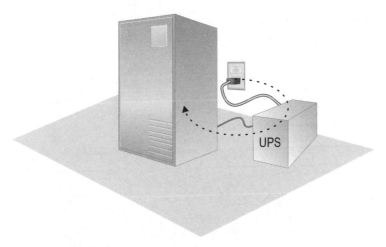

Figure 6.18 Uninterruptible power supply as a backup power source

If power is restored while the UPS is active, the UPS will notify users that the power has returned.

Types of UPS Systems

The best UPS systems perform online. When the normal power source fails, the UPS batteries automatically take over. The process is invisible to users.

There are also stand-by UPS systems that start when power fails. These are less expensive than online systems, but they are not as reliable.

Implementing UPS

The following questions will help the network administrator determine how to implement a UPS system.

- Will the UPS meet the basic power requirements of the network? How many components can it support?
- Does the UPS communicate with the server to notify it when a power failure has occurred and the server is running on batteries?
- Does the UPS feature surge protection to guard against power spikes?
- What is the life span of the UPS battery? How long can it be inactive before it starts to degrade?
- Will the UPS warn the administrator and users that it is running out of power?

Fault Tolerant Systems

Fault tolerant systems protect data by duplicating data or placing data in different physical sources, such as different partitions or different disks. Data redundancy allows access to data even if part of the data system fails. Redundancy is a prominent feature common to most fault tolerant systems.

Fault tolerant systems should never be used as a replacement for regular back up of servers and local hard disks. A carefully planned backup strategy is the best insurance for recovering lost or damaged data.

Fault tolerant systems offer these alternatives for data redundancy:

- Disk striping
- Disk mirroring
- Sector sparing
- Mirrored Drive Arrays
- Clustering

Redundant Arrays of Inexpensive Disks (RAID)

Fault tolerance options are standardized and categorized into levels. These levels are known as redundant arrays of inexpensive disks (RAID). The levels offer various combinations of performance, reliability, and cost. Microsoft Windows NT Server RAID solutions are software-based. Windows NT Server supports RAID levels 0, 1, and 5. Microsoft chose to support the redundant disk striping level 5, as opposed to levels 2, 3, and 4, because level 5 evolved from levels 2, 3, and 4 and is therefore a later, more current version of redundant level disk striping. RAID level 10, mirrored drive arrays, is also not supported by Microsoft Windows NT Server, and is only described in this section for information purposes only.

Level 0—Disk Striping

Disk striping divides data into 64K blocks and spreads it equally in a fixed rate and order among all disks in an array. However, disk striping does not provide any fault tolerance because there is no data redundancy. If any partition in the set fails, all data is lost.

A stripe set combines multiple areas of unformatted free space into one large logical drive, distributing data storage across all drives simultaneously. In Windows NT, a stripe set requires at least two physical drives and can use up to 32 physical drives. Stripe sets can combine areas on different types of drives, such as SCSI, enhanced small device interface (ESDI), and IDE drives.

Figure 6.19 shows three hard disks being used to create a stripe set. In this case the data consists of 192K of data. The first 64K of data is written to a stripe on disk 1, the second 64K is written to a stripe on disk 2, and the third 64K is written to the stripe on disk 3.

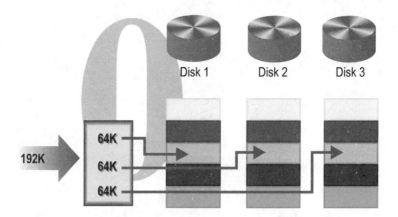

Figure 6.19 Disk striping combines areas on multiple drives

Disk striping has a couple of advantages. First of all, it makes one large partition out of several small partitions, which offers better use of disk space. Second, multiple disk controllers will result in better performance.

Level 1—Disk Mirroring

Disk mirroring actually duplicates a partition and moves the duplication onto another physical disk. There are always two copies of the data, with each copy on a separate disk. Any partition can be mirrored. This strategy is the simplest way of protecting a single disk against failure. Disk mirroring can be considered a form of continual backup because it maintains a fully redundant copy of a partition on another disk.

Duplexing

Disk duplexing is a mirrored pair of disks with an additional disk controller on the second drive. This reduces channel traffic and potentially improves performance. Duplexing is intended to protect against controller failures as well as media failures.

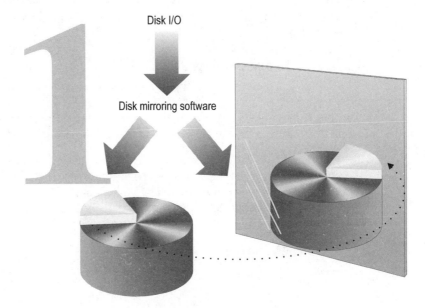

Figure 6.20 Disk mirroring duplicates a partition on another physical disk

Level 2—Disk Striping with ECC

When a block of data is written, the block is broken up and distributed (interleaved) across all data drives. Error correction code (ECC) requires a larger amount of disk space than parity-checking methods. While this method offers marginal improvement in disk utilization, it compares poorly with level 5.

Level 3—ECC Stored As Parity

Disk striping with ECC stored as parity is similar to level 2. Parity refers to an error-checking procedure in which the number of 1s must always be the same— either odd or even—for each group of bits transmitted without error. In this strategy the ECC method is replaced with a parity-checking scheme that requires only one disk to store parity data. This results in about 85 percent of usable disk space.

Level 4—Disk Striping with Large Blocks

This strategy moves away from data interleaving by writing complete blocks of data to each disk in the array. The process is still known as disk striping, but is done with large blocks. A separate check disk is still used to store parity information. Each time a write operation occurs, the associated parity information must be read from the check disk and modified. Because of this overhead, the block-interleaving method works better for large block operations than for transaction-based processing.

Level 5—Striping with Parity

Striping with parity is currently the most popular approach to fault tolerance design. It supports a minimum of three, to a maximum of 32, drives and writes the parity information across all of the disks in the array (the entire stripe set). The data and parity information are arranged so that the two are always on different disks.

A parity stripe block exists for each stripe (row) across the disk. The parity stripe block is used to reconstruct data for a failed physical disk. If a single drive fails, enough information is spread across the remaining disks to allow the data to be completely reconstructed.

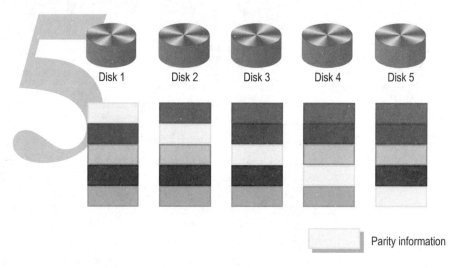

Parity information

Figure 6.21 Striping with parity allows data reconstruction if a drive fails

The parity stripe block is used to reconstruct data for a failed physical disk. A parity stripe block exists for each stripe (row) across the disk. RAID 4 stores the parity stripe block on one physical disk, while RAID 5 distributes parity evenly across all disks.

Level 10—Mirrored Drive Arrays

RAID level 10 duplicates data across two identical RAID 0 drive arrays. Data that is contained on a physical drive in one array is mirrored on a drive in the second array.

Sector Sparing

Some advanced network operating systems, such as Windows NT Server, offer an additional fault tolerance feature called sector sparing, also called hot fixing. This feature automatically adds sector-recovery capabilities to the file system while the computer is running.

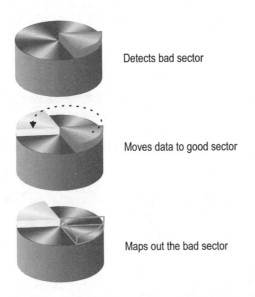

Detects bad sector

Moves data to good sector

Maps out the bad sector

Figure 6.22 Sector sparing or hot fixing steps

If bad sectors are found during disk I/O (input/output), the fault tolerance driver will attempt to move the data to a good sector and map out the bad sector. If the mapping is successful, the file system is not alerted.

It is possible for SCSI devices to perform sector sparing, but ESDI and IDE devices cannot.

Some network operating systems, such as Windows NT Server, have a utility that notifies the administrator of all sector failures and of the potential for data loss if the redundant copy also fails.

Microsoft Clustering

Microsoft Clustering is Microsoft's implementation of server clustering. In broader terms, "clustering" is a group of independent systems working together as a single system. Fault tolerance is built into the clustering technology. Should a system within the cluster fail, the cluster software will disperse the work from the failed system to the remaining systems in the cluster. Clustering is not intended to replace current implementations of fault tolerance solutions, although it does provide an excellent enhancement.

Implementing Fault Tolerance

Most advanced network operating systems will offer a utility for implementing fault tolerance. In Windows NT Server, for example, the Disk Administrator program is used to configure Windows NT Server fault tolerance. The graphical interface of Disk Administrator makes it easy to configure and manage disk partitioning and fault tolerance options.

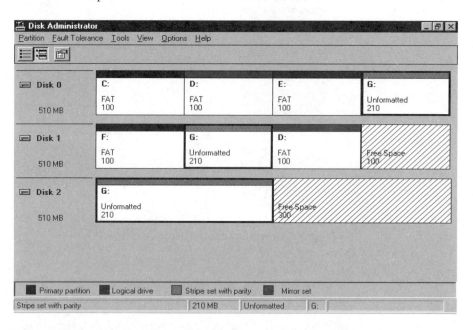

Figure 6.23 Disk Administrator allows you to set up fault tolerance

If you move the disk to a different controller, or change its ID, Windows NT will still recognize it as the original disk.

Note In Figure 6.23, drive G is a stripe set with parity, and drive D is mirrored.

Disk Administrator is used to create various disk configurations, including:

- Stripe sets with parity, which accumulate multiple disk areas into one large partition, distributing data storage across all drives simultaneously, adding fault tolerance parity information.

- Mirror sets, which make a duplicate of one partition and place it onto a separate physical disk.

- Volume sets, which accumulate multiple disk areas into one large partition, filling the areas in sequence.

- Stripe sets, which accumulate multiple disk areas into one large partition, distributing data storage across all drives simultaneously.

Q & A

Fill in the blanks in the following sentences.

1. Fault tolerant systems protect data by duplicating data or placing data in different _____ sources.

2. RAID level 0, called _____ _____ divides data into 64K blocks and spreads it equally, in a fixed rate and order among all disks in an array.

3. Level 0 disk striping does not offer data _____.

4. Disk _____ actually duplicates a partition and moves the duplication onto another physical disk so that there are always two copies of the data.

5. Duplexing is intended to protect against disk _____ failures as well as media failures.

6. Writing complete blocks of data to each disk in the array is known as disk

   _____.

7. In Windows NT Server, the _____ _____ program is used to configure Windows NT Server fault tolerance.

8. In RAID level 10, data that is contained on a physical drive in one array is _____ on a drive in the second array.

9. "Clustering" is a group of _____ systems working together as a single system.

Answers

1. physical
2. disk striping
3. protection
4. mirroring
5. controller
6. striping
7. Disk Administrator
8. mirrored
9. independent

Summary

There are various ways to head off disaster to a network with strategies for preventing data loss. The strategies are tape backup, uninterruptible power supply, and fault tolerant systems. Network administrators need to assess the needs of their network and choose from these accordingly.

The most common way to prevent data loss is to regularly use tape drives to back up files. This should be planned for and done on a regular schedule. There are a variety of backup methods to choose from. A backup log should be included in the process.

The uninterruptible power supply is an external power supply that keeps a server or other network devices running in the event of a power failure. The power source can be a battery or a rotary system.

Fault tolerant systems duplicate data or place data in different physical sources. These systems are used in addition to tape backup. Most fault tolerant strategies have been classified in the RAID system, including disk striping and disk mirroring. Some advanced network operating systems also make use of sector sparing. Most network operating systems, such as Windows NT Server, offer a utility for implementing fault tolerance. Microsoft has also implemented a new fault tolerance enhancement strategy called, server clustering.

Chapter 6 Review

In this chapter you learned what is involved in the day-to-day management and support of network operations.

One primary task is creating user accounts. These can be created individually or, if there are many users whose accounts are similar, they can be copied from a standard user model. Parameters can be assigned to users during account creation to structure their network environments. Key accounts, such as the administrator and guest accounts, are automatically activated when the network is installed. Account passwords, especially the administrator's, play an important part in system security.

Group accounts make managing large numbers of accounts as easy as managing single accounts. Advanced network operating systems feature built-in groups that meet most network administrative needs, but network administrators can create new groups as required. Also, deleting and disabling accounts when necessary is as important to secure network operations as creating accounts.

Another important network management task is managing network performance. Primary considerations in this area are identifying and eliminating bottlenecks. Advanced network operating systems include performance monitor and network monitors which can help a network administrator identify bottlenecks and troubleshoot potential network problems. Network management software standards such as SNMP help administrators create a global picture of large system performance, and products such as Microsoft Systems Management Server provide centralized management of these systems. In addition to using management tools, the administrator should keep a log of the system's history.

An administrator also needs to implement policies and take action to ensure the security of both the data and the equipment on the network. Resource security involves implementing password-protected shares and assigning appropriate access permissions to both individual accounts and groups. Auditing, profiles, diskless computers, virus protection, and data encryption can help keep network security intact. Training will ensure user awareness of policies and procedures.

The primary defense against lost data is an aggressive backup schedule with tapes rotated regularly and stored in different locations. An uninterruptible power supply can keep a system running in the event of a power failure.

Fault tolerant systems involving an appropriate RAID level will ensure that data remains available despite accidental hardware failures or other catastrophes. RAID level 5, striping with parity, is currently the most popular RAID implementation. Disk mirroring, disk duplexing, drive array mirroring, and sector sparing are also popular data-protection strategies. An enhancement to enterprise network fault tolerance is Microsoft's implementation of server clustering. This technology will allow uninterrupted availability of data even if a system within the cluster fails.

Checkup

Follow the instructions for each exercise as indicated. All answers follow the last exercise.

Exercise 1: True or False

For the following sentences, circle True if the statement is true or False if the statement is false.

1. The user account contains information about how groups are shared.
   True   False

2. The primary reason for implementing groups is ease of administration.
   True   False

3. Network monitoring programs set thresholds of performance and report the results to the network administrator.   True   False

4. It is best to keep the network log as a file on the network server.   True   False

5. Groups can be given the same access permissions as individual users.
   True   False

Exercise 2: Multiple Choice

Select the letter of the best answer for each of the following questions.

1. Which of the following describes password-protected shares?

   a. Passwords are assigned to resources on a network.

   b. Passwords are assigned on a user-by-user basis.

   c. Provides the highest level of security on a network.

   d. Easiest way to assign group privileges.

2. Which of the following describes the fault tolerant system striping with parity, RAID level 5?

   a. It is also called hot fixing.

   b. Data and parity information are always on different disks.

   c. When a 64K block of data is written, the block is broken up and distributed across all data drives.

   d. It is a form of continual backup because it maintains a fully redundant copy of a partition on another disk.

3. Which of the following statements describes SNMP (simple network management protocol)?

    a. Agents monitor users activity for efficiency ratings.

    b. Agents monitor network traffic and behavior in key network components.

    c. Agents monitor incoming and outgoing telephone call activity.

    d. Agents monitor database access activity.

4. What is the first account that must be set up on a Windows NT Server network?

    a. Guest

    b. Special

    c. Administrator

    d. Global

Exercise 3: Short Answer

Write short sentences or phrases to answer the following:

1. List the three primary ways to prevent loss of data.

    _____

    _____

    _____

2. Windows NT Server uses four types of group accounts. They are listed below. Write a short description of each type of account.

    Global: _____

    _____

    Local: _____

    _____

    Special: _____

    _____

    Built-in: _____

    _____

3. List three devices that tend to become bottlenecks on a network.

    _____

    _____

    _____

Checkup Answers

Exercise 1: True or False

1. False. The user account contains information that defines a user to the network's security system. Groups are not shared; resources are shared.

2. True.

3. False. The network administrator sets the network performance thresholds. This is why network monitoring programs are so helpful. They can indicate when network performance is straying from what the administrator determines is acceptable.

4. False. The log is supposed to record network problems. If the server goes down and the log is on the server, it defeats the purpose of keeping a log.

5. True.

Exercise 2: Multiple Choice

1. Which of the following describes password-protected shares?

   a. Passwords are assigned to resources on a network.

2. Which of the following describes the fault tolerant system striping with parity, RAID level 5?

   b. Data and parity information are always on different disks.

3. Which of the following statements describes SNMP (simple network management protocol)?

   b. Agents monitor network traffic and behavior in key network components.

4. What is the first account that must be set up on a Windows NT Server network?

   c. Administrator

Exercise 3: Short Answer

1. Tape backup, UPS, and fault tolerance.

2. Global groups are created on a primary domain controller and can contain user accounts only from their own domain account database.

   Local groups consists of individual user accounts that have rights and permissions on the local computer and other group accounts.

   Special groups are used for internal system access to resources and permissions.

   Built-in groups perform common network administration and maintenance tasks.

3. Any three of the following:

   CPU, memory, network adapter card, disk controller, or network media.

Case Study Problem

This case study involves a transition from a peer-to-peer environment to a server-based environment managed by an administrator who might not have been prepared to properly complete the transition.

The Setting

A credit investigation company, Fitch & Mather, was founded 10 years ago with 15 employees. Their first network was a peer-to-peer workgroup. There was no administrator to take care of operations, so everyone took care of their own networking needs.

By the time the company was four years old, it had grown to 28 employees. Not only had business increased, but the type of business had changed. Fitch & Mather was now serving a more sophisticated clientele which demanded absolute privacy. It became obvious to the owners that they could no longer use a system where the employees had unlimited access to each other's files. In 1995 the owners decided to upgrade to a server-based LAN so they could take advantage of the security it offered.

The Problem

Soon after the upgrade, the owners realized that would take more than new hardware and software to achieve their goals.

Declining Performance

Network performance was unreliable. The network was particularly slow during business reporting periods because everyone was constantly using the network.

Accounts

As soon as the administrator had to begin creating accounts, he realized that he missed the peer-to-peer environment where all users took care of themselves. There were so many details to pay attention to in creating accounts that sometimes these extra tasks, as the administrator thought of them, never happened. There are accounts that still exist for employees who have not been with the company in months.

Administration

The person selected to be the network administrator was chosen because he told everyone he knew more about computers than anyone else. He decided that in order to make things easier, several people should have administrative privileges. Also, he told just about everyone his administrator account password. Anyone who wanted to change anything on the network simply logged on as the administrator and made changes.

Regulating Permissions

The concept of a centralized server was confusing at first. The employees were used to working with information on their own computers. Having to access commonly shared information caused some problems. All users were getting into each other's files, sometimes deleting and copying sensitive material.

Unauthorized Use

At times, people would come in to work on Monday and find that some of their files had been changed. No one admitted to using the network on the weekends except for one person who said he only used his own computer and sent one document to the printer.

Repairs

Once, when a computer crashed, a technician replaced a part, but the replacement did not work. After replacing several more parts, someone recalled that the same problem had happened several months earlier with the same computer, but they could not remember what the solution was.

Computer Skills

Some of the computers contained job aids to help the users through basic functions, but most of the procedures were passed along verbally from one user to another.

Temporary Access

In especially busy times, Fitch & Mather would bring in contract workers to help with the extra workload. The network administrator had several computers standing by for just this purpose.

Sometimes, a contract worker would be with the company for a week or so, and the administrator would have to create a special temporary account just for this worker. When the worker left, the administrator would delete the account. Occasionally, a contractor would copy client information to a floppy disk and leave the building with it.

Data Security

Most of the equipment was several years old. The server was a super server, but it was installed in 1995. That server contained a tremendous amount of data, and even though the system was backed up periodically, any crash would be chaotic because of productivity lost while the data was being restored and the system was being brought back online.

Power

The building was old. There was even some aluminum cabling still present, so electrical shorts were not uncommon.

Server and Backup Security

A building repairman fixing the air conditioner put a heavy piece of equipment down on the server where someone had left Thursday's backup tape. The backup system is four years old. The backup process intrudes into everyone's workday, and users are getting angry because of the daily interruption in server service. When the system had been peer-to-peer, everyone backed up their own computer when time permitted, and in many ways that was easier.

A New Administrator

Fortunately for all concerned, the network administrator left the company to work for a competitor. The new administrator, Susan, is an individual who has closely observed all of these network activities and now and then would quietly suggest a change. When the position opened, she applied and was soon deep in network problem solving tasks.

Susan knows she has much to do to clean up the network operation. See if you and she make the same decisions.

Your Solution

Network Performance Issues

1. Identify two tools or utilities which could help the administrator keep track of key network and component activities.

   _____

2. List two areas the administrator should look at in isolating and identifying network problems.

   _____

   _____

3. Identify two server components which the administrator should track the performance of to gather information about total system health.

   _____

   _____

4. List two types of applications, utilities, or programs the administrator could use to gather information about the components and functions mentioned earlier.

   _____

   _____

Network Accounts

The administrator realized she needed to implement several account policies to bring order to the situation.

1. What is one common security measure she could require of every user? This simple security step would act as a gateway at the network's entrance to keep unauthorized users from logging on.

   _____

2. Describe one problem associated with this security measure and indicate how the administrator could allow for it.

   _____

   _____

3. What simple extra measure could the administrator attach to this security device to further ensure that only authorized workers had access to sensitive data for periods of time longer than a few days?

_____

_____

4. What action should the administrator take to ensure that people who have no business on the network would not be able to use it?

_____

5. The network administrator discovered that nearly anyone who had ever wanted to have administrator privileges had gotten them. She also saw that there were too many users to treat each account separately. What account management device could she use to help organize and manage both present and future accounts?

_____

6. What could she do about the number of users who had administrator privileges?

_____

_____

7. How could the administrator ensure that each account was given appropriate network and resource privileges?

_____

_____

8. What network management utility could the administrator use to create consistent accounts for users who were either nervous about the computer environment or needed their access to be restricted?

_____

9. What could the administrator implement to help her identify which users had accessed which resources over various periods of time?

_____

Tracking Problems and Solutions

Identify at least one action the administrator could take that would help technicians repair a computer which has had similar problems before.

Computer Awareness

Describe two actions the administrator could take to help acquaint new and experienced users with both the computer environment and her new policies and procedures.

Protecting Against Stolen Data

1. Describe at least one action the administrator could take to keep contract workers from copying sensitive client data and leaving the building with it.

2. What could the administrator do to provide for people who need to use the network temporarily?

Protecting Against Destroyed Data

Explain two measures the administrator could take to make sure the data was easily and quickly available in the event of a server crash.

Power Fluctuations

Identify one option available to the administrator to keep the system, or at least the server, running during electrical power outages.

Server and Backup Security

1. Describe one action the administrator could take to keep the server physically secure.

2. What is one thing that she could do to make sure the backup tapes were both safe and easily available?

Case Study Suggested Solution

Network Performance Issues

1. The two tools or utilities which could help the administrator keep track of key network and component activities is Microsoft Performance Monitor and Microsoft Network Monitor.

2. Three areas of network behavior which can reveal problems are:

   - Trends

   - Bottlenecks

   - Capacities

3. The administrator should pay particular attention to at least these three component behaviors:

   - CPU performance

   - Memory use

   - Disk controller activity

4. To track network activity and identify conditions and components that needed attention, the administrator could use three types of programs:

   - A performance monitor that comes with the network operating system

   - SNMP, with its use of agents to map performance and behavior

   - Microsoft Systems Management Server

Network Accounts

1. The administrator required everyone to have a password.

2. She did not record the passwords because she knew that if anyone forgot theirs she could simply remove their old password and let them create a new one.

3. She implemented an account policy that required anyone working with sensitive data to automatically change their password every 30 days.

4. She deleted any accounts that were no longer active or should not have access to the network.

5. The administrator created several groups including:

   - General office staff—The members of this group will have no access to sensitive material, and read-only privileges on most other directories.

   - Specialized office staff—The members of this group will have read, write, and create permissions on most directories. They will also be granted backup rights to help with network maintenance.

   - Administrators—For the two other people who will back up the administrator and will therefore need complete access to all network resources. These users were carefully chosen.

6. The administrator revoked administrator privileges for all but the two people that needed them to help her manage the network.

7. She assigned different access privileges to groups and then assigned appropriate groups to the various resources.

8. Profiles were used in creating user accounts. This gave the administrator an extra measure of account control and simplified things for the newer accounts. The new accounts had their computer options limited to just what was necessary for performing their jobs.

9. The network administrator implemented auditing on the network and for all of the resources in order to generate a record of who was using the network and accessing resources.

Tracking Problems and Solutions

The administrator began a log in a loose-leaf notebook which she kept on top of a bookshelf in her office. The log contained dates and details of all significant network activity. During a staff meeting, she made a point of telling everyone where the log was stored.

Computer Awareness

The administrator created two self-study courses designed to acquaint old and new users with standard computer policies and procedures. The first course was for beginners and the second was for experienced users and computer administrator assistants.

She gave everyone copies of the courses as appropriate, but she presented introductory computer networking training for newly hired employees.

Protecting Against Stolen Data

1. The administrator installed several diskless computers for contract workers to ensure that no sensitive data could be copied and taken out of the building. Also, she implemented data encryption for especially sensitive data communications.

2. The new network system came with a guest account. The administrator instructed temporary workers to use that account to log on.

Protecting Against Destroyed Data

The administrator chose to set up disk mirroring to protect against the data being destroyed. Disk mirroring or disk duplication would ensure that if one server disk went bad, the other server disk would continue to make the data available.

Power Fluctuations

The administrator installed a UPS for each server to ensure that they would still function even if the power failed.

Server and Backup Security

1. The network administrator found a closet, installed a lock on it, and secured the server in it.

2. She collected the backup tapes and stored one set in her office and another set in another secure building the company owns.

The Troubleshooter

Use the following information to help you solve the troubleshooting problems.

Troubleshooting Network Accounts

Problem: A user is unable to log on using a particular account.

1. Is the user typing their user name correctly?

   Yes _____

   No _____

2. Is the user logging on to the correct server or network location?

   Yes _____

   No _____

3. Is the user typing the password correctly? (Passwords are case-sensitive.)

   Yes _____

   No _____

4. Is the user account disabled? (Use User Manager.)

   Yes _____

   No _____

Troubleshooting Network Data Security

Problem: A user is unable to access a resource, or a user is able to access a resource which should be inaccessible.

1. Does the individual user have rights to the resource?

   Yes _____

   No _____

2. Does the user belong to a group which has access to the resource?

   Yes _____

   No _____

3. Does the user have conflicting permissions (share-level permissions versus user-level permissions) to the resource?

   Yes _____

   No _____

4. Does the user belong to any group which has been assigned "No Access"?

   Yes _____

   No _____

Troubleshooting Unauthorized Access

1. Is the server in a locked room?

   Yes _____

   No _____

   If the answer is yes, who has access to the server?

   _____

2. Are any computers left on and logged in unattended?

   Yes _____

   No _____

   If the answer is yes, perhaps a policy and proper notification sent to the system administrator would be appropriate.

Problem: Passwords

1. Are there passwords written down and left in obvious places such as under the keyboard, on the monitor, or in a desk drawer?

   Yes _____

   No _____

   If the answer to this question is yes, you need to send out a reminder that this is against company policy. (If this policy has not been implemented, have it implemented.) After a couple of days, check the computers for violators and disable their accounts. (Depending on the size of the company, you may have to get department managers or others to help check for violators.)

   If the answers to either of the following two questions is yes, you need to implement a password policy.

2. Do any users have obvious passwords, such as spouse, children, or pet names?

   Yes _____

   No _____

3. Do any users continually use the same password with a revision number (Wilma1, Wilma2, Wilma3, and so forth)?

   Yes _____

   No _____

Miscellaneous Security Problems

1. Do any users have a regular logon name which has super-user (administrator) equivalence?

   Yes _____

   No _____

   If the answer is yes, you need to make some changes. Everyone, including the system administrator should have a normal account. You only log on as an administrator (with an account which is a member of the administrators group) when you need to do administration.

2. Do any users store confidential data on their local hard disks?

   Yes _____

   No _____

   Confidential data stored on local hard disk is a security risk. The obvious question is, how sensitive is the data? Is it in an executive office that is normally locked?

3. Do any users have their operating system set up to automatically log them in and bypass the user name and password process?

   Yes _____

   No _____

   If the answer is yes, this is also a security risk. What level of access permissions does the account have assigned to it? In other words, how much of the system is accessible with that logon account?

Can You Solve This Problem?

Use your knowledge of troubleshooting, the troubleshooter you just completed, and the lessons in this chapter to help you with this troubleshooting situation.

The Situation

You are the administrator of your organization's Microsoft Windows NT Server network. You set all of the security options for your network.

The Available Facts

Patty came to you this morning, and she was very frustrated. She has been on vacation for the last 10 days. This morning, when she tried to log on to the network, she was not able to do so.

Your Solution

1. Which utility could you use to verify Patty's account information?

   _____

2. What is one thing which could cause Patty to be unable to log in?

   _____

3. What should you do, as the administrator, to fix the problem?

   _____

   _____

Suggested Troubleshooting Solution

1. Patty's account information could be verified in the account management utility (User Manager in Microsoft Windows NT Server).

2. Any of the following:

   The CAPS LOCK key could be activated.

   She is typing in the wrong password.

   Her password has expired.

3. As the administrator, you would have to use the account management utility (User Manager) to delete the password so that Patty could log in and create a new password.

The LAN Planner

Planning Network Security

The following questions will help you determine how extensive your network security should be. The key is the sensitivity of your data. If your network will be sharing very sensitive data, you should consider a centralized, server-based system regardless of the number of users it will serve.

1. Does your organization work with some data that should not be accessed by everyone on the network?

   Yes _____

   No _____

   If the answer is yes, it indicates the need for a centralized system with dedicated servers.

2. Do you want to put most shared resources on dedicated servers, but leave some to be shared in a peer-to-peer fashion?

   Yes _____

   No _____

   If the answer is yes, it indicates that you should probably implement a combination of centralized and peer-to-peer security.

3. Do you want to give permissions to resources by group membership? (Many administrators prefer to give users individual rights to their personal network storage, and to use groups to give permissions to all other shared network resources.)

   Yes _____

   No _____

4. Will everyone in your organization leave the server alone if it is left out and accessible, or will some users be tempted to tinker with it if there is a network problem or they feel it needs adjusting?

   Yes _____

   No _____

   If the answer to this question is yes, the server cannot be left out and should be kept in a closet or other secure place.

5. Are there people in your organization or visitors who should not have access to any of the network resources?

   Yes _____

   No _____

   If the answer is yes, it indicates the need to implement passwords and develop a password policy.

6. Is the environment in your organization such that passwords could get passed around, borrowed, or even stolen?

   Yes _____

   No _____

   If the answer is yes, it indicates that you may need to implement passwords that require renewal after a specified period of time.

7. Are there users working with sensitive data?

   Yes _____

   No _____

   If the answer is yes, it indicates that you should consider implementing passwords with a minimum length, that maintain a history of passwords already used, and that force users to periodically create new, unique passwords.

8. Is there a possibility that some of the users at your site would attempt to use someone else's computer without permission or log on to the network under someone else's name without permission?

   Yes _____

   No _____

   If the answer is yes, it may indicate a need to lock accounts if an incorrect password is entered several successive times.

9. Is there a possibility that users at your site may not understand how to implement passwords properly or not understand the importance of appropriate password use?

   Yes _____

   No _____

   If the answer is yes, it may indicate a need for password selection training so that users will avoid obvious passwords and not write them down or store them in accessible places.

10. Does your company use temporary, contract, or other non-permanent employees?

Yes _____

No _____

If the answer is yes, you may want to limit their access to the system to what the Guest account provides.

11. Is there a need to monitor or restrict access to any particularly sensitive network resources or peripherals, or a need to identify which users have accessed which resources over given periods of time?

Yes _____

No _____

If the answer is yes, it indicates that you should consider implementing auditing.

12. Is there a concern that non-permanent employees or permanent employees will intentionally copy data to disks and take it off the premises or download data and misuse it?

Yes _____

No _____

If the answer is yes, it indicates that you should consider using diskless computers for selected employees.

13. Will any of your data be so sensitive that it could be used against your organization if it were to become the property of the wrong person or organization?

Yes _____

No _____

If the answer is yes, it indicates that you should consider encryption. However, this is a major step in that encryption is complex, expensive, and requires a lot of homework and planning if it is to be successfully implemented.

14. Is your network currently protected from viruses?

Yes _____

No _____

If the answer is no, it indicates that you have a planning problem, and there is a serious threat to your system. Implement virus protection as soon as possible.

Managing Network Performance

1. Do any users in your organization ever experience erratic or inconsistent network performance?

   Yes _____

   No _____

   If the answer is yes, it indicates that you should consider implementing a network monitoring system. It could alert the administrator when the network requires attention to ensure that it continues to provide acceptable service.

2. Are any network monitoring tools either built-in to your network operating system or available as closely-linked add-ons such as Windows NT Performance Monitor, which is built-in to Windows NT, or Systems Management Server, which is available as an add-on?

   Yes _____

   No _____

   If the answer is no, you may want to do some research to identify one suitable for your environment.

   Note: You will have to allow for both the time and budget to properly implement a monitoring program.

   ---

3. Does your network have a written history that is easily accessible?

   Yes _____

   No _____

   If the answer is no, it indicates that there is a gap in your network support program and that you may need to begin a log.

4. Are you currently keeping a record of your network's behavior, or have you established and recorded a baseline based on monitoring information?

   Yes _____

   No _____

   If the answer is no, it indicates that you may need to develop a baseline that is part of your network's log.

Avoiding Data Loss

The three primary factors in determining a backup policy are:

- Data

  Do you need it backed up or can you afford to rebuild it from scratch when there is a server crash?

- Time

  Can you afford the time it takes to either rebuild the data from scratch or even restore it from tape?

- Budget

  A question at the core of the backup issue is which would be more expensive to your organization, lost data or a backup program?

Planning for Your Network

The following questions will help you determine how to plan for your network.

1. Is any of your data sensitive enough or valuable enough that it would irreparably damage your organization if it were lost?

   Yes _____

   No _____

   If the answer is yes, it indicates that reliable data backup is an essential part of your network.

2. Is someone primarily responsible for backing up the system?

   Yes _____

   No _____

   If the answer is no, you should choose someone who will assume that responsibility so they can be involved in implementing and supporting the system.

3. Can you afford the time required to back up to floppy disks?

   Yes _____

   No _____

   If the answer is no, it indicates that you need an efficient backup method such as tape.

4. Have you identified a backup system that will accommodate your network?

   Yes _____

   No _____

   If the answer is no, it means that you will have to do the homework and research necessary to determine which product's features best support your system.

5. If you determine that you will implement a tape system, will that system be able to hold an entire backup on a single tape?

   Yes _____

   No _____

   If the answer is no, it indicates that you will have to create a manual backup plan that incorporates switching tapes.

6. Have you established a backup schedule that includes rotating tapes as part of complete and incremental backups?

   Yes _____

   No _____

   If the answer is no, it indicates that the person responsible for backups needs to develop a backup schedule.

7. Does your facility have any type of power conditioning to prevent blackouts and brownouts or any type of online power backup?

   Yes _____

   No _____

   If the answer is no, it indicates that you should consider a UPS.

8. Can your organization afford to have any network downtime when the server fails?

   Yes _____

   No _____

   If the answer is no, it indicates that you should consider a redundancy (RAID) system.

   Note: A RAID system should be used in addition to, not instead of, a tape backup system.

9. Is the fastest possible performance more important than budget in a redundancy system?

   Yes _____

   No _____

   If the answer is yes, then you should consider RAID 5, striping with parity. This is the fastest redundancy system. Otherwise, consider either disk mirroring or disk duplexing. Disk duplexing may be more expensive because it involves an additional hard disk controller card.

The LAN Planner Summary

General Network and Server Security

Based on the information generated in the LAN Planner, your network security should include:

1. Type of security (centralized or peer-to-peer)
2. Type of servers (dedicated or peer-to-peer)
3. Location of servers:

Server name	Location
_____	_____
_____	_____
_____	_____
_____	_____

Groups

You will need to determine the role of groups in your network. Fill in the following chart with group names you create, the resources to which those groups will have permissions, and the types of permissions they will be assigned. This list is not meant to be exhaustive but only to serve as an example. It is probable that your network will need more groups than you can list here. In that case, create a more inclusive chart and include it in your network log.

Group name	Resources	Levels of permission
_____	_____	_____
	_____	_____
	_____	_____
	_____	_____
_____	_____	_____
	_____	_____
	_____	_____
	_____	_____
_____	_____	_____
	_____	_____
	_____	_____

Passwords and Encryption

1. Password training (Yes or No)

2. Password renewal period: _____

3. Password attempts allowed: _____

4. Other password parameters: _____

5. Encryption (Yes or No)

Guest Accounts

- Guest account parameters: _____

Auditing

1. Implement auditing (Yes or No)

2. Audit which resources? _____

_____

Diskless Computers

1. Implement diskless computers (Yes or No)

2. Which computers? _____

Other Security Considerations

- Location of the log: _____

C H A P T E R   7

Larger Networks

Lesson 1 Modems in Network Communications . . . 533

Lesson 2 Creating Larger Networks . . . 550

Lesson 3 Wide Area Network (WAN) Transmission . . . 580

Lesson 4 Advanced WAN Technologies . . . 594

Chapter 7 Review . . . 614

Welcome to Chapter 7, Larger Networks. In this chapter you will learn about devices and technologies that enable you to expand a network across the street or around the world.

Larger Networks, as the title implies, shifts the focus of the kit from LANs to wide area networks (WANs). Most current business networks would not properly support their organizations if they could not communicate with other organizations and other networks across the country and the world. Chapter 7 looks at the network concepts and components which make this possible.

You will first learn about the basic communication building block—the modem. You will see how modems operate, what different types of modems can do, and what the different modem standards mean.

Lesson 2, "Creating Larger Networks," presents an overview of the components essential for expanding a LAN into a larger LAN, several LANs, or even a WAN. The discussion begins with repeaters and moves on to bridges, routers, brouters, gateways, and more.

After learning the "what" of connectivity, you will go on to the "how" with lessons on the various ways data can be transmitted across wide area networks. The chapter ends with a presentation of the most advanced WAN transmission methods such as asynchronous transfer mode (ATM), and explains how the newest technologies can be implemented into present networks.

The Case Study

You will be able to help a company with offices in Seattle, New York, and Ft. Lauderdale expand their networking capabilities to create a WAN. But that is not all; local sites are having their own problems. See if you can find the solutions.

The Troubleshooter

As the network administrator for a computer firm you arrive at work one Monday morning and immediately begin hearing complaints. People are not able to access resources at remote sites. Your network uses a digital T1 communications link and your check for all of the obvious possible problems does not provide any answers. What can you do next?

The LAN Planner

This LAN Planner will help you determine how to expand a LAN on your site. It will provide you with questions to address regarding modems and connectivity devices such as repeaters and bridges.

If you are considering creating a wide area network it will also help you identify WAN transmission services which would best be suited to your site.

Lesson 1: Modems in Network Communications

What This Lesson Does

This lesson presents an overview of modem technology. It reviews basic modem functions and standards and describes the primary modem communication environments.

Objectives

By the end of this lesson, you will be able to:

- Define asynchronous and synchronous communications.
- Identify modem standards.
- Describe the two types of carriers for modem communications.
- Determine which type of modem would be appropriate for a given site.

Estimated lesson time 40 minutes

Modem Technology

A modem is a device that makes it possible for computers to communicate over a telephone line.

When computers are too far apart to be joined by a standard computer cable, a modem can enable communication between them. In a network environment, modems serve as a means of communicating between networks or connecting to the world beyond the local network.

Basic Modem Functions

Computers cannot simply connect over a telephone line because the computer communicates in digital electronic pulses (electronic signals) and a telephone line can only send analog pulses (sound).

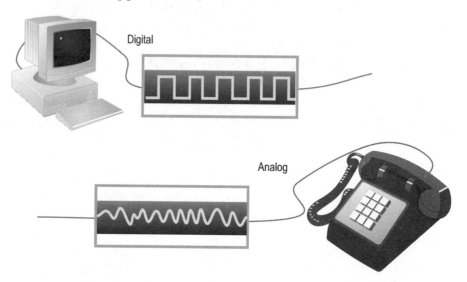

Figure 7.1 Digital waves versus analog waves

A digital signal is synonymous with binary, and the signal can only have a value of 0 or 1. An analog signal is a smooth curve which can represent an infinite range of values.

A modem at the sending end converts the computer's digital signals into analog and transmits the analog signals onto the telephone line. A modem at the receiving end converts the incoming analog signals back into digital signals for the receiving computer.

In other words, a sending modem <u>MO</u>dulates digital signals into analog signals, and a receiving modem <u>DEM</u>odulates analog signals back into digital signals.

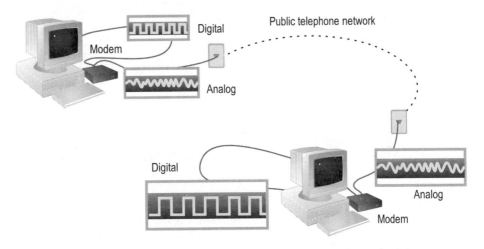

Figure 7.2 Modems convert digital waves to analog waves, and analog to digital

---

Note Using digital lines requires a special digital card to be installed in the computers.

Modem Hardware

Modems are known as data communications equipment (DCE) and share the following characteristics:

- A serial (RS-232) communications interface
- An RJ-11 telephone-line interface (a four-wire telephone plug)

Modems are available in both internal and external models. The internal models are installed in an expansion slot like any other circuit board.

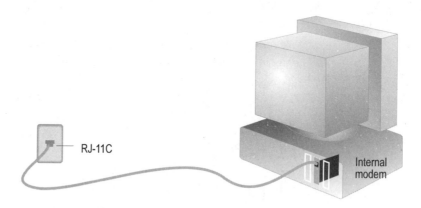

Figure 7.3 Internal modem installed in an expansion slot

An external modem is a small box that is connected to the computer by a serial (RS-232) cable running from the computer's serial port to the modem's computer cable connection. The modem uses a cable with an RJ-11C connector to connect to the wall.

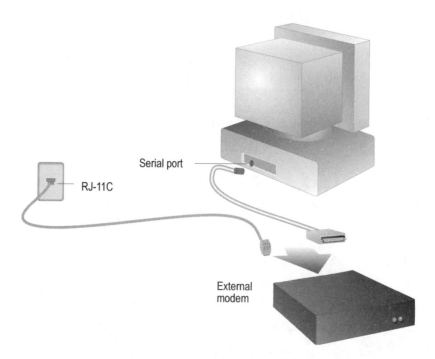

Figure 7.4 External modem connects with RS-232 cable to the computer serial port

Modem Standards

There are industry standards for just about every area of networking, and modems are no exception. Standards are necessary so that modems from one manufacturer can communicate with modems from another manufacturer. This section explains some of the common industry standards for modems.

Hayes

In the early 1980s, a company called Hayes Microcomputer Products, Inc. developed a modem called the Hayes Smartmodem™. It was called smart because it could automatically dial a number through a telephone which was hung up. The Smartmodem became the standard against which other modems were measured and generated the phrase "Hayes-compatible" just as IBM's personal computer generated the term "IBM-compatible." Because most vendors conformed to the Hayes standards, nearly all LAN modems could talk to each other.

The early Hayes Smartmodems sent and received data at 300 bits per second (bps). Improvements soon boosted that speed by four times to 1200 bps. Hayes currently offers modems with speeds of 28,800 bps or more.

International Standards

Since the late 1980s, the International Telecommunications Union (ITU) has developed standards for modems.

These specifications, known as the V series include a number which indicates the standard. Sometimes it also includes the word "bis," which means second in French. This indicates that the standard is a revision of an earlier standard. If the standard also contains the word "terbo," which is French for third, it indicates that the second, or bis, standard was also modified. As a reference point, the V.22bis modem would take 25 seconds to send a 1,000 word letter. The V.34 modem would only take two seconds to send the same letter, and the V.42bis compression standard in a 14,400 bps modem can send the same letter in only one second.

The following chart presents the compression standards and their parameters since 1984. The compression standard and the bps are not necessarily related. The standard could be used with any speed of modem.

Standard	bps	Introduced	Notes
V.22bis	2400	1984	An old standard. Sometimes included with the purchase of a computer.
V.32	9600	1984	Sometimes included with the purchase of a computer.
V.32bis	14,400	1991	The current standard model.
V.32terbo	19,200	1993	Not officially a standard yet. Will only communicate with another V.32terbo.
V.FastClass (V.FC)	28,800	1993	Not official.
V.34	28,800	1994	Improved V.FastClass. Backwards compatible with earlier V. modems.
V.42	57,600	1995	Backwards compatible with earlier V. modems.

Modem Performance

Initially, a modem's speed was measured in either bps or something called the baud rate, and most people confused the two thinking they were the same.

Baud refers to the speed of the oscillation of the sound wave on which a bit of data is carried over the telephone lines. It comes from the name of a French signal corps officer named Jean-Maurice-Emile Baudot. The baud rate did equal the transmission speed of modems in the early 1980s. At that time 300 baud equaled 300 bits per second.

But communications engineers learned how to compress and encode data so that each modulation of sound can now carry more than one bit of data. This means that the bps can be greater than the baud rate. For example, a modem that modulates at 28,800 baud can actually send at 115,200 bps. Therefore, the current parameter to look for is bps.

Several of the newer modems feature industry standards such as V.42bis/MNP5 data compression and have transmission speeds of 57,600 bps with some of them going up to 76,800 bps.

Q & A

Fill in the blanks in the following sentences.

1. An external modem is a small box that is connected to the computer by a
   _____ cable running from the computer's port to the modem's
   computer cable connection.

2. The modem at the _____ end converts digital signals into analog
   signals.

3. Baud refers to the speed of oscillation of the _____ _____
   on which a bit of data is carried.

4. The bps can be greater than the _____ rate.

Answers

1. serial

2. sending

3. sound wave

4. baud

Types of Modems

There are different types of modems because there are different types of communication environments which require different methods of sending data. These environments can be divided roughly into two areas related to the timing of communications:

- Asynchronous
- Synchronous

The type of modem a network uses will depend on the environment and what the network needs to do.

Asynchronous Communications (Async)

Asynchronous, or async, may be the most widespread form of connectivity in the world. This is because async was developed so it could use common telephone lines.

In the asynchronous environment, data is transmitted in a serial stream.

Figure 7.5 Asynchronous data stream

Each character—letter, number, or symbol—is turned into a string of bits. Each of these strings is separated from the other strings by a start-of-character bit and a stop bit. Both the sending and receiving devices must agree on the start and stop bit sequence. The receiving computer uses the start and stop bit markers to schedule its timing functions so it is ready to receive the next byte of data.

Communication is not synchronized. There is no clocking device or method to coordinate transmission between the sender and the receiver. The sending computer just sends data, and the receiving computer just receives data. The receiving computer then checks to make sure that the received data matches what was sent. Twenty-five percent of the data traffic in async communications consists of data traffic control and coordination.

Asynchronous transmission over telephone lines can happen at up to 28,800 bps. However, the latest data compression methods can boost the 28,800 bps to 115,200 bps over directly connected systems.

Error Control

Because of the potential for error, async can include a special bit, called a parity bit, which is used in an error checking and correction scheme called parity checking. In parity checking, the number of bits sent must match the number of bits received.

The original V.32 modem standard did not provide for error control. To help remedy the problem of generating errors during data transmission, a company called Microcom® developed its own standard for asynchronous data error control, the Microcom Network Protocol (MNP®). The method worked so well that other companies adopted not only the initial version of the protocol but different versions, called classes, as well. Currently, several modem vendors incorporate MNP Classes 2, 3, and 4.

In 1989, the CCITT published an asynchronous error-control scheme called V.42. This hardware-implemented standard featured two error-control protocols. The primary error control scheme is link access procedure for modems (LAPM), but it also uses MNP Class 4. The LAPM protocol is used in communications between two modems that are V.42-compliant. If one or the other modem is MNP 4-compliant, the correct protocol would be MNP 4.

Improving Transmission Performance

Communication performance depends on two elements:

- Signaling or channel speed

  This parameter describes how fast the bits are encoded onto the communications channel.

- Throughput

  This is a measure of the amount of useful information going across the channel.

Channel speed and throughput are easily confused, but they can be modified separately to improve performance. For example, it is possible to double the throughput by using compression without having to pay for a faster channel speed.

Compression improves the time required to send data by removing redundant elements or empty sections. One current data compression standard is Microcom's MNP Class 5 data compression protocol.

When both ends of a communication link use the MNP Class 5 protocol, data transmission time can be cut in half.

Even greater performance is possible with the V.42bis standard because it describes how to implement impressive data compression on the fly in hardware. For example, a 9,600 bps modem using V.42bis can achieve a throughput of 38,400 bps.

Coordinating the Standards

Because different standards address different areas of performance, it is possible for one modem to improve performance by using combinations of signaling and error-checking protocols.

For example, for modems over an async LAN-to-LAN link over analog circuits, the following combination will give fast, reliable service:

- V.32bis signaling
- V.42 error control
- V.42bis compression

Async, or serial, modems are less expensive than synchronous modems because the async modem does not need the circuitry and the components to handle the timing involved in synchronous transmission.

Synchronous Communication

Synchronous communication relies on a timing scheme coordinated between two devices to separate groups of bits and transmit them in blocks known as frames. Special characters are used to begin the synchronization and check its accuracy periodically.

Because the bits are sent and received in a timed, controlled (synchronized) fashion, start and stop bits are not required. Transmission stops at the end of one frame and starts again with a new one. This start and stop approach is much more efficient than asynchronous transmission.

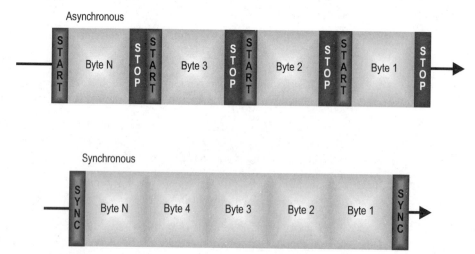

Figure 7.6 Asynchronous versus synchronous data stream

If there is an error, the synchronous error detection and correction scheme simply implements a retransmission.

Synchronous protocols perform a number of jobs that asynchronous protocols do not. Synchronous protocols:

- Format data into blocks.
- Add control information.
- Check the information to provide error control.

The primary protocols in synchronous communications are:

- Synchronous data link control (SDLC)
- High-level data link control (HDLC)
- Binary synchronous communications protocol (bisync)

Synchronous communications are used in almost all digital and network communications. For example, if you are using digital lines to connect your remote computers, you would use synchronous modems rather than asynchronous modems to connect the computer to the digital line. Generally, their higher cost and complexity have kept them out of the home market.

Q & A

Fill in the blanks in the following sentences.

1. Asynchronous transmission occurs over _____ _____.
2. The Microcom Network Protocol (MNP) is a standard for asynchronous _____ _____ control.
3. In asynchronous communications it is possible to double throughput by using _____ without having to pay for a faster channel speed.
4. Synchronous communication relies on a _____ scheme coordinated between two devices.

Answers

1. telephone lines
2. data error
3. compression
4. timing

Carriers

A modem is useless unless it can communicate with another component. All modem communications take place over some kind of communication line or cable. What type of cable it is, and who provides it and its related services, makes a difference in network performance and cost.

The general principle at work is that it is difficult and expensive to move data quickly over long distances. The three factors an administrator must take into account when considering how to implement modem communications are:

- Throughput
- Distance
- Cost

You need to apply these factors when considering the type of telephone lines you will install for your network.

Telephone Lines

There are two types of telephone lines available for modem communications.

- Public dial network lines (dial-up lines)

  These are common telephone lines. They require users to manually make a connection for each communication session, and are slow and not totally reliable for transmitting data.

  However, for some companies it may be practical to temporarily dial up a communication link between sites for a certain amount of time each day to transfer files or update databases.

  Carriers are continually improving their dial-up line service. Some digital lines claim data transmission speeds up to 56 Kbps can be achieved using error correction, data compression, and synchronous modems.

- Leased (dedicated) lines

  These provide full-time dedicated connections that do not use a series of switches to complete the connection. The quality of the line is often higher than the quality of a telephone line which was only designed for voice transmissions. They typically range in speed from 56 Kbps to 45 Mbps or more.

In reality, most long distance carriers use switched circuits to provide what appears to be a dedicated line. These are called virtual private networks (VPNs).

Remote Access

Dial-up telephone lines can be used to link networks. A modem at one end dials the modem at the other end, and the two networks are connected. However, even with a fast modem and data compression, this method can still create a large telephone bill for a temporary connection. Leased lines, which offer more permanent connections, are probably a better solution for companies which are constantly communicating between networks.

Most networks offer some kind of remote access capability for users who need to connect to their network while away from the network site. Microsoft Windows NT Server, for example, offers the Windows NT remote access service (RAS). The Windows NT Server RAS permits up to 256 remote clients to dial in.

RAS connects users over telephone lines through a remote access server to a Windows NT network. Once a user has made a connection, the telephone lines become transparent and the user can access all network resources as if they were sitting at a computer at the network site.

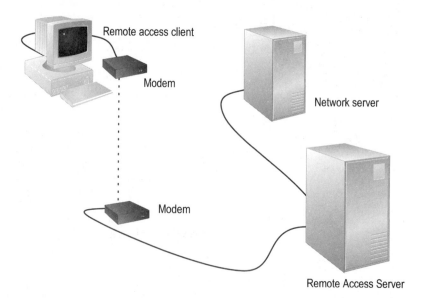

Figure 7.7 RAS allows remote users to access the network

Point-to-Point Tunneling Protocol

With the inception of Windows NT 4.0 RAS has been coupled with a new protocol called PPTP or Point-to-Point Tunneling Protocol. This protocol is a technology that supports multiprotocol VPNs or Virtual Private Networks. This support allows remote clients to connect and access the organizations network securely via the Internet. Using the Point-toPoint Tunneling Protocol, PPTP, the remote client would establish a connection to the Internet and then establish a connection to the RAS serveron the internet using PPTP.

PPTP provides a way to route IP, IPX, or NetBEUI PPP pckets over a TCP/IP network. PPTP allows for multiprotocol encapsulation that enable any of these packets to be sent over the TCP/IP network. The existing corporate or organizational LAN is treated as if it were a PSTN, ISDN, or X.25 network. This virtual WAN is supported through the public networks such as the Internet.

Q & A

Fill in the blanks in the following sentences.

1. Public telephone lines require users to _____ make a connection for each communication session.

2. The three factors an administrator must take into account when considering how to best implement communications between two modems are _____, _____, and _____.

3. Leased lines provide _____ connections that do not use a series of switches to complete the connection.

4. A good remote access solution that offers stable lines for companies which are constantly communicating between networks is _____ lines.

5. The _____allows the remote client to establish a secure connection to their corporate LAN via the Internet and RAS.

Answers

1. manually

2. throughput, distance, and cost

3. dedicated

4. leased (dedicated)

5. Point-to-Point Tunneling Protocol

Activity

Run Demo 24.

Summary

Modems make it possible for computers to communicate over telephone lines. They do this by taking the computer's digital signal and converting it to an analog signal (sound wave) that can travel over the telephone lines, and then reversing the process at the receiving end. Modems can be installed both internally and externally.

There are two types of telephone lines that can be used for modem communications: public dial-up network lines and leased lines. With dial-up lines a user must manually make a connection each time they use the modem. Leased lines are full-time, dedicated connections.

Modem performance has been improved by compressing data. The International Telecommunications Union (ITU) has created compression standards for modems.

There are two types of modems: synchronous and asynchronous. Asynchronous is the most widely used form of connectivity, where data is transmitted in a serial stream over telephone lines. With synchronous communication bits are sent in a timed, controlled fashion. This is a more efficient way to send data, but is more costly than async.

Your Next Step

While modems are an essential building block in extending network communications beyond the LAN, they are only one of many components used to create both large LANs and WANs. You will be introduced to these components when you begin to explore the WAN environment in Lesson 2, "Creating Larger Networks."

Lesson 2: Creating Larger Networks

What This Lesson Does

This lesson presents an introduction to the basic building blocks of network expansion. These building blocks are components such as repeaters, bridges, and routers.

You will learn the role of each component in LAN-to-LAN and LAN-to-WAN communications, including how they work and their uses and limitations.

Objectives

By the end of this lesson, you will be able to:

- Describe the function of each of the following:
  - Repeaters
  - Bridges
  - Routers
  - Brouters
  - Gateways
- Determine when to expand a LAN.
- Determine which components would be appropriate in a given network expansion situation.

Estimated lesson time 75 minutes

LAN Expansion

As companies grow, so do their networks. LANs tend to outgrow their original designs. This becomes evident when:

- The cable begins to get crowded with network traffic.
- Print jobs require longer wait times.
- Traffic-generating applications, such as databases, have increased response times.

There will come a time when every administrator will need to expand the size or improve the performance of the network. Networks cannot be made larger by simply adding new computers and more cable. Each topology or architecture has its limits. There are, however, components an engineer can install which will increase the size of the network within the existing environment. These components can:

- Segment existing LANs so that each segment becomes its own LAN.
- Join two separate LANs.
- Connect to other LANs and computing environments to join them into a larger comprehensive network.

The components that enable engineers to accomplish these goals are:

- Repeaters
- Bridges
- Routers
- Brouters
- Gateways

This lesson will take a close look at each of these LAN expansion components.

Repeaters

As signals travel along a cable, they degrade and become distorted in a process that is called attenuation. If a cable is long enough, attenuation will finally make a signal unrecognizable. A repeater enables signals to travel farther.

How Repeaters Work

A repeater works at the OSI Physical layer to regenerate the network's signals and resend them out on other segments.

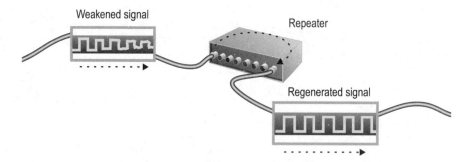

Figure 7.8 Repeaters regenerate weakened signals

A repeater takes a weak signal from one segment, regenerates it, and passes it to the next segment. To pass data through the repeater in a usable fashion from one segment to the next, the packets and the Logical Link Control (LLC) protocols must be the same on each segment. This means that a repeater will not enable communication, for example, between an 802.3 LAN (Ethernet) and an 802.5 LAN (Token Ring).

Repeaters do not translate or filter anything. For a repeater to work, both segments that the repeater joins must have the same access method. The two most common access methods are CSMA/CD and token passing. A repeater cannot connect a segment using CSMA/CD to a segment using token passing. That is, they cannot translate an Ethernet packet into a Token Ring packet.

Repeaters can move packets from one physical media to another. They can take an Ethernet packet coming from a thinnet coax segment and pass it on to a fiber-optic segment if the repeater is capable of accepting the physical connections.

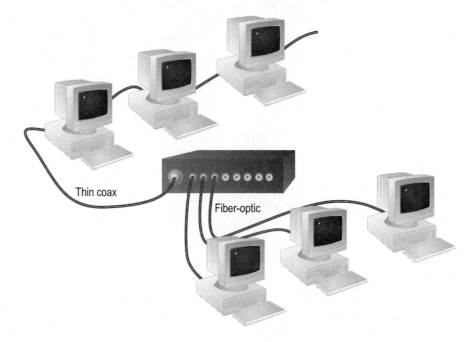

Figure 7.9 Repeaters can connect different types of media

Some multiport repeaters act as multiport hubs and connect different types of media. The same segment limits discussed in Chapter 4, "Network Architectures," apply to networks using hubs, but the limits now refer to each segment extending from a hub rather than the entire network.

Repeater Considerations

Repeaters are the least expensive way of expanding a network. While they are a good initial solution, they are at the low end of network expansion components. When the need arises to extend the physical network beyond its distance or node limitations, consider using a repeater to link segments when neither segment is generating much traffic and when cost is a major consideration.

No Isolation or Filtering

Repeaters send every bit of data from one cable segment to another, even if the data consists of malformed packets or packets not destined for use on the network. This means that a problem with one segment can disrupt every other segment. Repeaters do not act as a filter to restrict the flow of problem traffic.

Repeaters will also pass a broadcast storm along from one segment to the next, back and forth along the network. A broadcast storm occurs when there are so many broadcast messages on the network that the number is approaching the network bandwidth. If a device is responding to a packet that is continuously circulating on the network, or a packet is continuously attempting to contact a system that never replies, network performance will be degraded.

Summary

This section summarizes what you need to consider for implementing repeaters in your network. A repeater:

- Connects two segments of similar or dissimilar media.
- Regenerates the signal to increase the distance transmitted.
- Functions in the Physical layer of the OSI model.
- Passes all traffic in both directions.

Use a repeater when you want to connect two segments in the most cost-effective manner. Repeaters improve performance by dividing the network into segments, thus reducing the number of computers per segment.

Do not use a repeater when:

- There is heavy network traffic.
- Segments are using different access methods.
- You need any kind of data filtering.

Q & A

Fill in the blanks in the following sentences.

1. More advanced, complex repeaters can act as multiport _____ to connect different types of media.

2. Repeaters do not have a _____ function and so will pass along all data from one segment to the next.

3. A repeater takes a weak signal and _____ it.

4. A repeater functions at the _____ layer of the OSI model.

Answers

1. hubs
2. filtering
3. regenerates
4. Physical

Bridges

Like a repeater, a bridge can join segments or workgroup LANs. However, a bridge can also divide a network to isolate traffic or problems. For example, if the volume of traffic from one or two computers or a single department is flooding the network with data and slowing down the entire operation, a bridge could isolate those computers or that department.

Bridges can be used to:

- Expand the distance of a segment.
- Provide for an increased number of computers on the network.
- Reduce traffic bottlenecks resulting from an excessive number of attached computers.

    A bridge can take an overloaded network and split it into two separate networks, reducing the amount of traffic on each segment and making each network more efficient.

- Link unlike physical media such as twisted-pair and coaxial Ethernet.
- Link unlike network segments such as Ethernet and Token Ring, and forward packets between them.

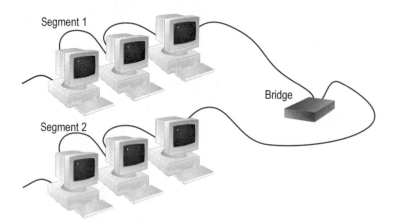

Figure 7.10 A bridge connecting two networks

How Bridges Work

Bridges work at the Data Link layer of the OSI model. Because they work at this layer, all information contained in the higher levels of the OSI model is unavailable to them. Therefore, they do not distinguish between one protocol and another. Bridges simply pass all protocols along the network. Because all protocols pass across bridges, it is up to the individual computers to determine which protocols they can recognize.

You may remember that the Data Link layer has two sublayers, the Logical Link Control sublayer and the Media Access Control sublayer. Bridges work at the Media Access Control sublayer and are sometimes referred to as Media Access Control layer bridges.

A Media Access Control layer bridge:

- Listens to all traffic.
- Checks the source and destination addresses of each packet.
- Builds a routing table as information becomes available.
- Forwards packets in the following manner:

  If the destination is not listed in the routing table, the bridge forwards the packets to all segments, or

  If the destination is listed in the routing table, the bridge forwards the packets to that segment (unless it is the same segment as the source).

A bridge works on the principle that each network node has its own address. A bridge forwards packets based on the address of the destination node.

Bridges actually have some degree of intelligence in that they learn where to forward data. As traffic passes through the bridge, information about the computer addresses is stored in the bridge's RAM. The bridge uses this RAM to build a routing table based on source addresses.

Initially, the bridge's routing table is empty. As nodes transmit packets, the source address is copied to the routing table. With this address information, the bridge learns which computers are on which segment of the network.

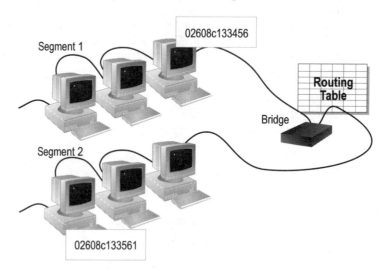

Figure 7.11 The routing table keeps track of addresses

Creating the Routing Table

Bridges build their routing tables based on the addresses of computers that have transmitted data on the network. Specifically, bridges use source addresses—the address of the device that initiates the transmission—to create a routing table.

When the bridge receives a packet, the source address is compared to the routing table. If the source address is not there, it is added to the table. The bridge then compares the destination address with the routing table database.

- If the destination address is in the routing table and is on the same segment as the source address, the packet is discarded. This filtering helps to reduce network traffic and isolate segments of the network.
- If the destination address is in the routing table and not in the same segment as the source address, the bridge forwards the packet out of the appropriate port to reach the destination address.
- If the destination address is not in the routing table, the bridge forwards the packet to all of its ports, except the one on which it originated.

In summary, if a bridge knows the location of the destination node, it forwards the packet to it. If it does not know the destination, it forwards the packet to all segments.

Segmenting Network Traffic

A bridge can segment traffic because of its routing table. A computer on segment 1 (the source), sends data to another computer (the destination) also located in segment 1. If the destination address is in the routing table, the bridge can determine that the destination computer is also on segment 1. Because the source and destination computers are both on segment 1, the packet does not get forwarded across the bridge to segment 2.

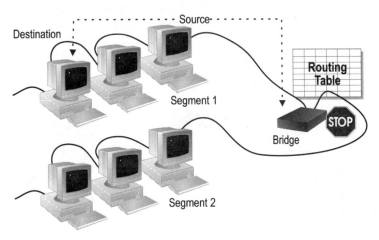

Figure 7.12 The routing table allows bridges to segment networks

Therefore, bridges can use routing tables to reduce the traffic on the network by controlling which packets get forwarded to other segments. This controlling (or restricting) of the flow of network traffic is known as segmenting network traffic.

A large network is not limited to one bridge. Multiple bridges can be used to combine several small networks into one large network.

Remote Bridges

Because bridges can be such powerful tools in expanding and segmenting a network, they are often used in large networks that have widely dispersed segments joined by telephone lines.

Only one bridge is necessary to link two cable segments. However, in a situation where two separate LANs are located great distances from each other, they may be joined into a single network. This can be done by implementing two remote bridges connected with synchronous modems to a dedicated, data-grade telephone line.

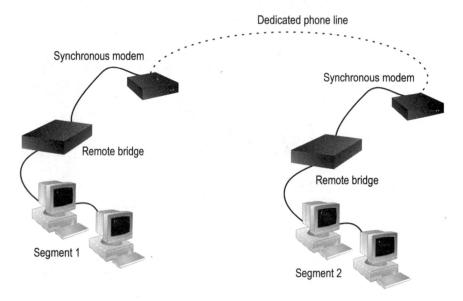

Figure 7.13 Remote bridges can be used to connect remote segments

Because remote LAN segments can be joined over telephone lines, there may be a situation where multiple LANs are joined by more than one path. In this situation, it is possible that data might get into a continuous loop. To handle this possibility, the IEEE 802.1 Network Management Committee has implemented the spanning tree algorithm (STA). Under STA, software can sense the existence of more than one route, determine which would be the most efficient, and then configure the bridge to use that one. Other paths are disconnected using software, though the disconnected routes can be reactivated if the primary route becomes unavailable.

Differentiating Between Bridges and Repeaters

Bridges work at a higher OSI layer than repeaters. This means that bridges have more intelligence than repeaters and can take more data features into account.

Bridges are like repeaters in that they can regenerate data, but bridges regenerate data at the packet level. This means that bridges can send packets over long distances using a variety of long distance media.

Bridge Considerations

Bridges have all of the features of a repeater, but also accommodate more nodes. They provide better network performance than a repeater. Because the network has been divided, there will be fewer computers competing for available resources on each segment.

To look at it another way, if a large Ethernet network were divided into two segments connected by a bridge, each new network would carry fewer packets, have fewer collisions, and operate more efficiently. Although each of the networks was separate, the bridge would pass appropriate traffic between them.

Implementing Bridges

A bridge can be either a stand-alone, separate piece of equipment (an external bridge) or it can be installed in a server. If the network operating system supports it, one or more network cards (an internal bridge) can be installed.

Network administrators like bridges because they are:

- Simple to install and transparent to users.
- Flexible and adaptable.
- Relatively inexpensive.

Summary

Consider the following when you are thinking about using bridges to expand your network.

- Bridges have all of the features of a repeater.
- They connect two segments and regenerate the signal at the packet level.
- They function at the Data Link layer of the OSI model.
- Bridges are not suited to WANs slower than 56K.
- They cannot take advantage of multiple paths simultaneously.
- They pass all broadcasts, possibly creating broadcast storms.
- Bridges read the source and destination of every packet.
- They pass packets with unknown destinations.

Use bridges to:

- Connect two segments to expand the length or number of nodes on the network.
- Reduce traffic by segmenting the network.
- Connect dissimilar networks.

Q & A

Fill in the blanks in the following sentences.

1. If the volume of traffic from one or two computers or a single department is flooding the network with data and slowing down the entire operation, a _____ could isolate those computers or that department.

2. The bridge builds a routing table based on the _____ addresses of computers that have sent traffic through the bridge.

3. Bridges work at the OSI _____ _____ layer and specifically, the _____ _____ _____ sublayer.

4. Bridges are often used in large networks that have widely dispersed segments joined by _____ _____.

5. Under STA, software can sense the existence of more than one _____, determines which would be the most efficient, and then configures the bridge to use that one.

6. Bridges connect two segments and regenerate the signal at the _____ level.

Answers

1. bridge
2. source
3. Data Link, Media Access Control
4. telephone lines
5. route
6. packet

Routers

In an environment consisting of several network segments with differing protocols and architectures, a bridge may not be adequate for ensuring fast communication among all of the segments. A network this complex needs a device which not only knows the address of each segment, but can also determine the best path for sending data and filtering broadcast traffic to the local segment. Such a device is called a router.

Routers work at the Network layer of the OSI model. This means they can switch and route packets across multiple networks. They do this by exchanging protocol-specific information between separate networks. Routers read complex network addressing information in the packet and, because they function at a higher layer in the OSI model than bridges, they have access to additional information.

Routers can provide the following functions of a bridge:

- Filtering and isolating traffic
- Connecting network segments

Routers have access to more information in packets than bridges, and use this information to improve packet deliveries. Routers are used in complex network situations because they provide better traffic management than bridges and do not pass broadcast traffic. Routers can share status and routing information with one another and use this information to bypass slow or malfunctioning connections.

How Routers Work

The routing table found in routers contains network addresses. However, host addresses may be kept depending on the protocol the network is running. A router uses a table to determine the destination address for incoming data. The table lists the following information:

- All known network addresses
- How to connect to other networks
- The possible paths between those routers
- The costs of sending data over those paths

The router selects the best route for the data based on costs and available paths.

Note Remember that routing tables were also discussed with bridges. The routing table maintained by a bridge contains Media Access Control sublayer addresses for each node, while the routing table maintained by a router contains network numbers. Even though manufacturers of these two different types of equipment have chosen to use the term routing table, it has a different meaning for bridges than it does for routers.

Routers require specific addresses. They only understand network numbers which allow them to talk to other routers and local network adapter card addresses. Routers do not talk to remote computers.

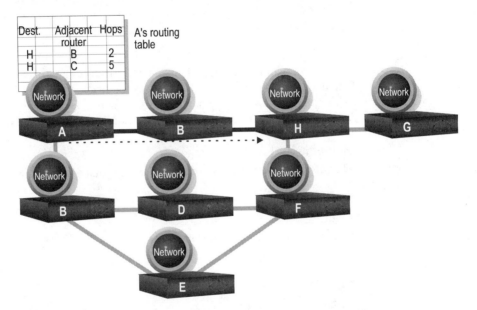

Figure 7.14 Routers talk to other routers, but not to remote computers

When routers receive packets destined for a remote network, they send them to the router that manages the destination network. In some ways this is an advantage because it means routers can:

- Segment large networks into smaller ones.

- Act as a safety barrier between segments.

- Prohibit broadcast storms, because broadcasts are not forwarded.

Because routers must perform complex functions on each packet, routers are slower than most bridges. As packets are passed from router to router, Data Link layer source and destination addresses are stripped off and then recreated. This enables a router to route a packet from a TCP/IP Ethernet network to a server on a TCP/IP Token Ring network.

Because routers only read addressed network packets, they will not allow bad data to get passed onto the network. Because they do not pass bad data or broadcast data storms, routers put little stress on networks.

Routers do not look at the destination node address; they only look at the network address. Routers will only pass information if the network address is known. This ability to control the data passing through the router reduces the amount of traffic between networks and allows routers to use these links more efficiently than bridges.

Using the router addressing scheme, administrators can break one large network into many separate networks, and because routers do not pass or even handle every packet, they act as a safety barrier between network segments. This can greatly reduce the amount of traffic on the network and the wait time experienced by users.

Routable Protocols

Not all protocols work with routers. The ones that are routable include:

- DECnet
- IP
- IPX
- OSI
- XNS
- DDP (AppleTalk)

Protocols which are not routable include:

- LAT (local area transport, a protocol from Digital Equipment Corporation.)
- NetBEUI

There are routers available which can accommodate multiple protocols such as IP and DECnet in the same network.

Choosing Paths

Unlike bridges, routers can accommodate multiple active paths between LAN segments and choose among redundant paths. Because routers can link segments which use completely different data packaging and media access schemes, there will often be several paths available for the router to use. This means that if one router will not function, the data can still be passed over alternate routes.

A router can listen to a network and identify which parts are the busiest. It uses this information in determining which path to send data over. If one path is very busy, the router will identify an alternative path and send data over that one.

A router decides the path the data packet will follow by determining the number of hops between internetwork segments. Like bridges, routers build routing tables and use these in routing algorithms such as those described below.

- OSPF (open shortest path first) is a link-state routing algorithm. Link-state algorithms control the routing process and allow routers to respond quickly to changes in the network. Link-state routing uses the Dijkstra algorithm to calculate routes based on the number of hops, the line speed, traffic, and cost. Link-state algorithms are more efficient, and create less network traffic than distance-vector algorithms. This can be crucial in a large routed environment with multiple WAN links. TCP/IP supports OSPF.

- RIP (routing information protocol) uses distance-vector algorithms to determine routes. TCP/IP and IPX support RIP.

- NLSP (NetWare link services protocol) is a link-state algorithm for use with IPX.

Types of Routers

The two major types of routers are:

- Static

  Static routers require an administrator to manually set up and configure the routing table and to specify each route.

- Dynamic

  Dynamic routers do an automatic discovery of routes and therefore have a minimal amount of set up and configuration. They are more sophisticated in that they examine information from other routers and make packet-by-packet decisions about how to send data across the network.

Static routers	Dynamic routers
Manual set up and configuration of all routes.	Manual configuration of the first route. Automatic discovery of additional networks and routes.
Always uses the same route which is determined by a routing table entry.	Can choose a route based on factors such as cost and amount of link traffic.
The route used is hard-coded and is not necessarily the shortest route.	Can decide to send packets over alternate routes.
Static routers are considered more secure because the administrator specifies each route.	Security can be improved in dynamic routers by manually configuring the router to filter out network addresses discovered and prevent traffic from going there.

Distinguishing Between Bridges and Routers

Bridges and routers can be confusing even to engineers with LAN/WAN experience because they appear to do the same things. They both:

- Forward packets between networks.
- Send data across WAN links.

How do you determine when to use a bridge and when to use a router?

The bridge, which works at the Media Access Control sublayer of the OSI Data Link layer, only sees a node address. To be more specific, a bridge looks for a node's Media Access Control sublayer address in each packet. If the bridge recognizes the address, it keeps the packet local or forwards it to the appropriate segment. If the bridge does not recognize the address, it forwards the packet to all segments, except the one through which the packet arrived.

It is really that simple. The bridge either recognizes the packet's Media Access Control sublayer address or it does not, and then it forwards the packet appropriately.

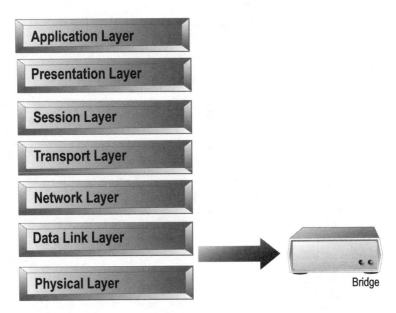

Figure 7.15 Bridges work at the Data Link layer Media Access Control sublayer

Broadcasting

Forwarding the packet is the key to understanding bridges and distinguishing them from routers. With bridges, forwarded broadcast data goes to every computer out all ports of the bridge except the one through which the packet arrived. That is, each computer on all networks (except the local network from which the broadcast originated) receives a broadcast packet. In small networks this may not have much of an impact, but a large network can generate enough broadcast traffic to slow down a network despite filtering for network addresses.

The router, which works at the Network layer, takes more information into account than the bridge in determining not only what to forward but where to forward it. The router recognizes not only an address, as the bridge did, but a type of protocol as well. In addition, the router can identify addresses of other routers and determine which packets to forward to which routers.

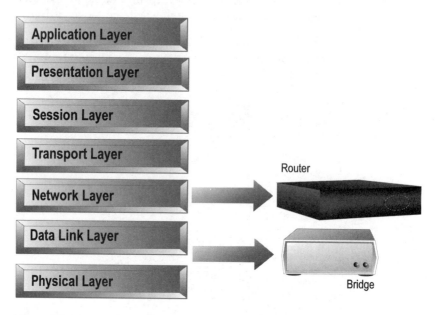

Figure 7.16 Routers work at the Network layer

Multiple Paths

A bridge can only recognize one path between networks. A router can search among multiple active paths and determine the best path for that particular moment.

As illustrated in Figure 7.17, if router A had a transmission that needed to be sent to router D, it could send the message to router C or to router B and the message would be forwarded to router D. Routers have the ability to evaluate both paths and determine which would be the best route for that transmission.

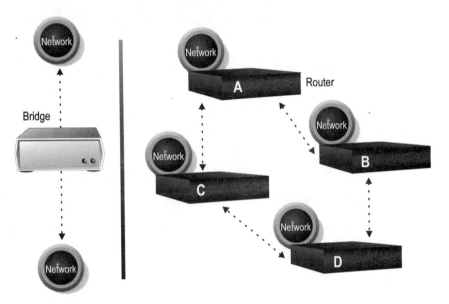

Figure 7.17 Routers recognize and use multiple paths between destinations

Conclusion

There are four key pieces of information you can use to distinguish between a bridge and a router, and to determine which would be appropriate in a given situation.

- The bridge only recognizes local Media Access Control sublayer addresses (the addresses of network cards in its own segment). Routers recognize network addresses.
- The bridge broadcasts (forwards) everything it does not recognize and forwards all addresses it knows, but only out the appropriate port.
- The router only works with routable protocols.
- The router filters addresses. It forwards particular protocols to particular addresses (other routers).

Brouters

A brouter, as the name implies, combines the best qualities of both a bridge and a router. A brouter can act like a router for one protocol and bridge all of the others.

Brouters can:

- Route selected routable protocols.
- Bridge nonroutable protocols.
- Deliver more cost-effective and more manageable internetworking than separate bridges and routers.

Summary

Routers interconnect networks and provide a filtering function. They also determine the best route for the data to take. Routers function at the Network layer of the OSI model.

Use routers to:

- Connect two networks and limit unnecessary traffic.
- Separate administrative networks.

If you are considering using routers be sure there are no nonroutable network protocols.

Q & A

Fill in the blanks in the following sentences.

1. Routers work at the _____ layer of the OSI model.

2. Because they must perform complex functions on each packet, routers are _____ than most bridges.

3. Routers do not look at the destination node address; they only look at the _____ address.

4. Unlike bridges, routers can accommodate multiple active _____ between LAN segments and choose among them.

5. The two major types of routers are _____ and _____.

6. A brouter will _____ nonroutable protocols.

Answers

1. Network

2. slower

3. network

4. paths

5. static, dynamic

6. bridge

Gateways

Gateways make communication possible between different architectures and environments. They repackage and convert data going from one environment to another so that each environment can understand the other environment's data. A gateway repackages information to match the requirements of the destination system. Gateways can change the format of a message so that it will conform to the application program at the receiving end of the transfer. For example, electronic mail gateways, such as the X.400 gateway, receive messages in a one format, translate it, and forward in X.400 format used by the receiver, and vice versa.

A gateway links two systems that do not use the same:

- Communication protocols
- Data formatting structures
- Languages
- Architecture

Gateways interconnect heterogeneous networks, for example, Microsoft Windows NT Server to SNA (IBM's Systems Network Architecture). They change the format of the data to make it conform to the application program at the receiving end.

How Gateways Work

Gateways are task-specific, which means that they are dedicated to a particular type of transfer. They are often referred to by their particular task name (Windows NT Server to SNA gateway).

The gateway takes the data from one environment, strips off its old protocol stack, and repackages it in the protocol stack from the destination network.

To process the data, the gateway:

- Decapsulates incoming data through the network's complete protocol stack.
- Encapsulates the outgoing data in the complete protocol stack of the other network to allow transmission.

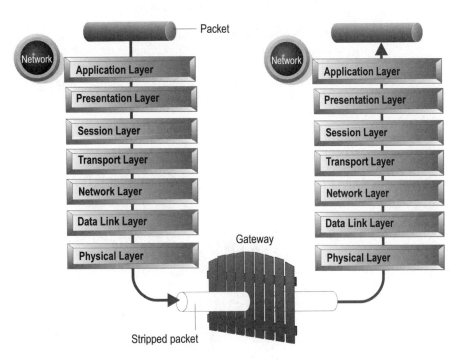

Figure 7.18 Gateways strip off an old protocol stack and add a new protocol stack

Some gateways use all seven layers of the OSI model, but gateways typically perform protocol conversion at the Application layer. However, the level of functionality varies widely between types of gateways.

Mainframe Gateways

One common use for gateways is to translate between personal computers and minicomputer or mainframe environments. A host gateway connects LAN computers with mainframe and minicomputer systems that do not recognize intelligent computers attached to LANs.

In a LAN environment, one computer is usually designated as the gateway computer. Special application programs in the desktop computers access the mainframe by communicating with the mainframe environment through the gateway computer. Users can access resources on the mainframe just as if these resources were on their own desktop computers.

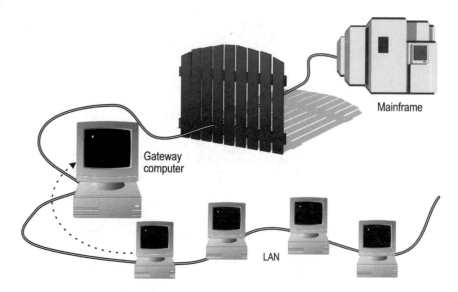

Figure 7.19 Mainframe gateways connect personal computers to mainframes

Gateway Considerations

Gateways are typically dedicated servers on a network. They can use a significant percentage of a server's available bandwidth because they are doing resource-intensive tasks such as protocol conversion. If a gateway server is used for multiple tasks, adequate RAM and CPU bandwidth should be allocated or performance of the server functions will be degraded.

Some considerations for implementing gateways are:

- They do not put a heavy load on internetwork communication circuits.
- They perform specific tasks efficiently.

Summary

Gateways perform protocol and data conversion. Some limitations of gateways are:

- They are task-specific.
- They can be slow.
- They are expensive.

Use gateways when different environments need to communicate.

Q & A

Fill in the blanks in the following sentences.

1. Most often, gateways are dedicated _____ on a network.

2. The gateway takes the data from one environment, strips it, and repackages it in the _____ _____ from the destination system.

3. Gateways are _____ specific, which means that they are dedicated to a particular type of transfer.

Answers

1. servers

2. protocol stack

3. task

Summary

A network administrator needs to consider many factors when it comes time to expand a LAN. It is not simply a matter of adding more cable and more computers, printers, and so on. Each topology has its limitations. Depending on the type of network and expansion needs, there is a variety of components that can be used to increase the size and performance of a network.

Repeaters are the least expensive way to expand a network, but they are limited to connecting two segments. You do not want to use repeaters if there is heavy network traffic. Bridges can perform the same functions as repeaters, but they reduce traffic by segmenting the network. You can use bridges to connect dissimilar networks.

Routers interconnect networks and provide filtering functions. They can determine the best route for data to take. But not all protocols are routable. They are best used to connect to networks at remote sites and pass only traffic destined for those sites.

Brouters combine the qualities of bridges and routers. They can route selected routable protocols and bridge nonroutable protocols.

Gateways are used to link two different environments. They link systems that have different communication protocols, data formatting structures, languages, and architectures. Gateways are dedicated to a particular type of transfer and are usually dedicated servers on a network.

Your Next Step

The components introduced in this lesson are used in both LAN and WAN environments. In fact, components such as routers enable LANs to become part of WANs. However, the WAN environment offers challenges of its own that require knowledge not only of expansion components, but also of the sophisticated communications technology presented in Lesson 3, "Wide Area Network (WAN) Transmission."

Lesson 3: Wide Area Network (WAN) Transmission

What This Lesson Does

This lesson presents an overview of WAN transmission technology. The lesson explains common WAN concepts and terminology including:

- Analog and digital services.
- Packet-switching networks.
- Virtual circuits.

Objectives

By the end of this lesson, you will be able to:

- Identify the features of analog connectivity.
- Identify the features of digital connectivity.
- Identify the features of packet-switching networks.
- Identify the major transmission components necessary for a simple, single-protocol WAN.
- Distinguish between the major data carriers (common carriers) and determine which would be most appropriate in a given WAN.

Estimated lesson time 50 minutes

WAN Overview

Local area networks work well, but have physical and distance limitations. Because they are not adequate for all business communication, there must be connectivity between LANs and other types of environments.

Using components such as bridges and routers, and communications service providers, the LAN can be expanded from an operation that serves a local area to one that can support data communications over a state, a country, or even the globe. When a network does this, it is called a wide area network (WAN).

To the user, the WAN appears to function in the same way as a local area network. In fact, if the WAN has been properly implemented, there will appear to be no difference between a LAN and a WAN.

Most WANs are combinations of LANs and other types of communications components connected by communication links called WAN links. WAN links can include the following:

- Packet-switching networks
- Fiber-optic cable
- Microwave transmitters
- Satellite links
- Cable television coaxial systems

WAN links, such as wide-area telephone connections, are too expensive and complex for most private companies to purchase, implement, and maintain on their own. Therefore, they are usually leased from service providers.

Communication between LANs will involve one of the following transmission technologies:

- Analog
- Digital
- Packet switching

Each of these technologies is described in detail in this lesson.

Analog Connectivity

The same network that your telephone uses is available to computers. One name for this world-wide network is the public switched telephone network (PSTN). In the computing environment, the PSTN, offering voice-grade dial-up telephone lines, can be thought of as one large WAN link.

Dial-Up Lines

The fact that the PSTN was designed primarily for voice-grade communication makes it slow and, as you learned earlier, dial-up analog lines require modems which can make them even slower. Because the PSTN is a circuit-switched network, the connections do not have consistent quality. Any single communication session will only be as good as the circuits linked for that particular session. Over long distances, country to country, for example, there may not be much consistency in the circuits from one session to the next.

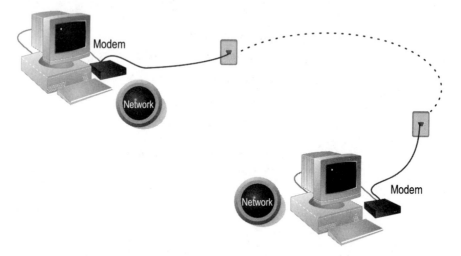

Figure 7.20 An analog telephone line can connect two computers using modems

Dial-Up Line Types

Telephone service providers offer a variety of telephone line types and quality. These include:

Line type	Description
1	Basic voice
2	Voice with some quality control
3	Voice/radio with tone conditioning
4	Data applications below 1200 bps
5	Basic data
6	Voice and data over trunk circuits
7	Voice and data over private lines
8	Voice and data over trunks between computers
9	Voice and video
10	Application relays

Dedicated Analog Lines

Unlike dial-up lines which must be reopened each time they are used, dedicated (or leased) analog lines provide a ready communication link. A leased analog line is faster and more reliable than a dial-up connection. It is also relatively expensive because the carrier is dedicating resources to the leased connection whether or not the line is being used.

Line Conditioning

In addition to providing a dedicated line, a service company will also implement line conditioning to improve the communications. Various types of conditioning are available, and are designated by letters and numbers. They include:

- C-conditioning, offering eight levels (C1–C8)
- D-conditioning

For example, an environment that requires a certain level of reliability could use a Type 5/C3 line. Individual service providers can provide the details of their designations.

Dial-Up or Dedicated?

There is no best type of service. The choice will depend on a number of factors including:

- The amount of time the connection is used.
- The cost for the service.
- The ability to have higher or more reliable data rates from a conditioned line.
- The need for a 24-hour a day connection.

If the need is infrequent, dial-up lines will work well. If the connection needs a high level of reliability and is fairly continuous over the month, then the quality of a dial-up line may not be adequate.

Q & A

Fill in the blanks in the following sentences.

1. Because the PSTN was designed primarily for voice, _____ lines do not have the consistent quality required for secure data communications.

2. A dedicated line is _____ and more _____ than a dial-up connection.

3. One advantage dedicated lines offer over dial-up lines is the ability to ensure the quality of the lines by having the service company implement _____ _____ to improve communications.

Answers

1. dial-up
2. faster, reliable
3. line conditioning

Digital Connectivity

In some cases, analog lines will provide sufficient connectivity. But when an organization generates so much WAN traffic that the transmission time makes an analog connection inefficient and expensive, it may be time to consider alternatives.

Organizations that need a faster, more secure transmission environment than analog lines can turn to digital data service (DDS) lines. DDS provides point-to-point synchronous communications at 2.4, 4.8, 9.6, or 56 Kbps. Point-to-point digital circuits are dedicated circuits which several telecommunications carriers can provide. The carrier guarantees full-duplex bandwidth by setting up a permanent link from each endpoint.

The primary reason customers use digital lines is because it provides transmission that is nearly 99 percent error free. Digital lines are available in several forms, including DDS, T1, T3, T4, and switched 56.

Because DDS uses digital communication, it does not require modems. Instead, DDS sends data from a bridge or router through a device called a CSU/DSU (channel service unit/data service unit). This device converts the standard digital signals the computer generates into the type of digital signals (bipolar) that are part of the synchronous communications environment. It also contains electronics to protect the DDS service provider's network.

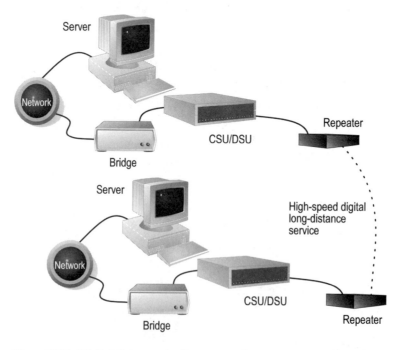

Figure 7.21 Digital data service line connecting two remote networks

T1

T1 is perhaps the most widely used type of digital line at higher data speeds. It is a point-to-point transmission technology that uses two-wire pairs (one pair to send and the other to receive) to transmit a full-duplex signal at a rate of 1.544 Mbps. T1 is used to transmit digital voice, data, and video signals.

T1 lines are among the most costly of all WAN links. Subscribers who do not need or cannot afford the bandwidth of an entire T1 line can subscribe to one or more T1 channels in 64 Kbps increments known as Fractional T-1 (FT-1).

In other countries, T1 service may not be available, but a similar service called E1 often is. E1 is very similar to T1, but has a signaling rate of 2.048 Mbps.

Multiplexing

Developed by Bell Labs, T1 uses technology called multiplexing, or muxing. Several signals from different sources are collected into a component called a multiplexer and fed into one cable for transmission. At the receiving end, the data is de-multiplexed back into its original form. This approach emerged when telephone cables, which only carried one conversation per cable, became overcrowded. The answer, called a T-Carrier network, enabled Bell Labs to carry many calls over one cable.

Dividing the Channel

A T1 channel can carry 1.544 megabits of data per second, the basic unit of T-Carrier service. T1 divides this into 24 channels and samples each channel 8,000 times a second. Using this method, T1 can accommodate 24 simultaneous data transmissions over each two-wire pair.

Each channel sample incorporates eight bits. Because each channel is sampled 8,000 times a second, each of the 24 channels can transmit at 64 Kbps. This data rate standard is known as DS-0. The 1.544 Mbps rate is known as DS-1.

DS-1 rates can be multiplexed to provide even greater transmission rates known as DS-1C, DS-2, DS-3, and DS-4. These have the transmission rates listed in the following table.

Signal level	Carrier system	T-1 channels	Voice channels	Data rate (Mbps)
DS-0	N/A	N/A	1	0.064
DS-1	T1	1	24	1.544
DS-1C	T-1C	2	48	3.152
DS-2	T2	4	96	6.312
DS-3	T3	28	672	44.736
DS-4	T4	168	4032	274.760

Copper wire will accommodate T1 and T2. However, T3 and T4 require a high-frequency medium such as microwave or fiber-optic.

T3

T3 and Fractional T-3 leased line service provides voice and data-grade service from 6 Mbps to 45 Mbps. They are the highest capacity leased line service commonly available today. T3 and FT-3 are designed for transporting large amounts of data at high speed between two fixed points. A T3 line can be used to replace several T1 lines.

Switched 56

Both local and long distance telephone companies offer this LAN-to-LAN digital dial-up service that transmits data at 56 Kbps. Switched 56 is merely a circuit-switched version of a 56 Kbps DDS line. The advantage of Switched 56 is that it is used on demand, thereby eliminating the cost of a dedicated line. Each computer using the service must be equipped with a CSU/DSU that can dial up another Switched 56 site.

Q & A

Fill in the blanks in the following sentences.

1. Digital lines provide _____ synchronous communications.

2. Because DDS uses _____ communication, it does not require modems.

3. T1 uses a technology called _____ , in which several signals from different sources are collected into a component and fed into one cable for transmission.

4. T1 can accommodate 24 _____ data transmissions over each two-wire pair.

5. Subscribers who do not need or cannot afford the bandwidth of an entire T1 line can subscribe to one or more T1 _____.

Answers

1. point-to-point

2. digital

3. multiplexing

4. simultaneous

5. channels

Packet-Switching Networks

Because packet technology is fast, convenient, and reliable, it is used in transmitting data over wide areas such as between cities, states, or countries. Networks that send packets from many different users over many different possible paths are called packet-switching networks because of the way they package and route data.

How Packet Switching Works

The original data package is broken into packets and each packet is tagged with a destination address and other information. This makes it possible to send each packet separately over the network.

In packet switching, packets are relayed through stations in a computer network along the best route currently available between the source and the destination.

Each packet is switched separately. Two packets from the same original data package may follow completely different paths to reach the same destination. The data paths for individual packets depend on the best route open at any given instant.

Even though each packet may travel along a different path, and the packets composing a message may arrive at different times or out of sequence, the receiving computer is still able to reassemble the original message.

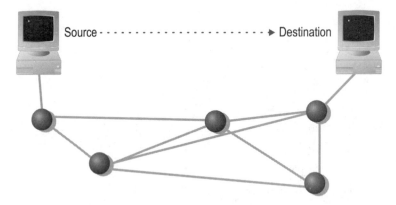

Figure 7.22 Simple packet-switching network

Switches direct the packets over the possible connections and pathways. These networks are sometimes called any-to-any connections. Exchanges in the network read each packet and forward them along the best route available at that moment.

Packet size is kept small. If there is an error in transmission, a small packet retransmission will be easier than the retransmission of a large packet. Also, small packets tie up switches for only short periods of time.

Using packet-switching networks to send data is similar to shipping vast quantities of merchandise by trucks instead of loading it all onto one train. If something should happen to the merchandise on one truck, it is easier to fix or reload than cleaning up the mess if a train runs off the track. Also, single trucks do not tie up crossings and intersections (switches) as trains do.

Packet-switching networks are fast and efficient. To manage the tasks of routing traffic and assembling and disassembling packets, such networks require some intelligence from the computers and software that control delivery.

Packet-switching networks are economical because they feature high-speed lines on a per-transaction basis instead of a flat fee rate.

Virtual Circuits

Many packet-switching networks use virtual circuits. These are circuits composed of a series of logical connections between the sending computer and the receiving computer. The circuit is not an actual cable, but bandwidth allocated on demand as opposed to a permanent, physical link between two stations. The connection is made after both computers exchange information and agree on communication parameters which establish and maintain the connection. These parameters include the maximum message size and the path the data will take.

Virtual circuits incorporate communication parameters to ensure reliability. These include:

- Acknowledgments
- Flow control
- Error control

Virtual circuits can last either as long as the conversation (temporary) or as long as the two communicating computers are up and running (permanent).

Switched Virtual Circuits (SVCs)

In SVCs, the connection between end computers uses a specific route across the network. Network resources are dedicated to the circuit, and the route is maintained until the connection is terminated. These are also known as point-to-many-point connections.

Permanent Virtual Circuits (PVCs)

PVCs are similar to leased lines that are permanent and virtual, except that the customer only pays for the time the line is used.

Q & A

Fill in the blanks in the following sentences.

1. With packet switching the data is broken down into packets, and each packet is tagged with a _____ _____ and other information.

2. At the destination, the packets are _____ into the original message.

3. Two packets from the same original data package may arrive out of sequence because they followed different _____ to reach the same destination.

4. Virtual circuits are composed of a series of _____ connections between the sending computer and the receiving computer.

Answers

1. destination address

2. reassembled

3. paths

4. logical

Summary

With components such as bridges and routers, and communications service providers, local area networks can be connected to create WANs. Communications services make use of three types of transmission technologies: analog, digital, and packet switching.

Analog transmission refers to telephone lines used with modems. These can be dial-up lines for infrequent data transmission, or dedicated lines for a ready communication link.

Organizations that need faster, more secure transmission than with telephone lines can use digital lines. Digital transmission does not require the use of modems. There are several forms of digital lines: DDS, T1, T3, and Switched 56. T1 and T3 use point-to-point transmission that can transmit voice, data, and video signals. T3 is the highest capacity leased (dedicated) line service available today. Switched 56 is a digital dial-up service. With this service, a CSU/DSU must be installed in or with each computer on the network.

Packet-switching networks are a fast and efficient way to transmit data over wide areas. With packet switching, data is divided into packets and transmitted over a common transmission line using virtual circuits. There is no single, dedicated line. A virtual circuit is not an actual cable, but bandwidth allocated on demand.

Your Next Step

Now that you have been introduced to the basic components of WAN transmission technology, you will see how it is implemented in several popular types of advanced WAN environments in Lesson 4, "Advanced WAN Technologies."

Lesson 4: Advanced WAN Technologies

What This Lesson Does

This lesson presents an overview of seven key advanced WAN transmission technologies. For each technology, the lesson describes the general characteristics, the advantages and disadvantages, and factors affecting implementation.

Objectives

By the end of this lesson, you will be able to:

- Identify the primary features of each of the following technologies:
  - X.25
  - Frame relay
  - ATM (asynchronous transfer mode)
  - ISDN (integrated services digital network)
  - FDDI (fiber distributed data interface)
  - SONET (synchronous optical network)
  - SMDS (switched multimegabit data service)
- Determine which technologies would be appropriate for a given network site.

Estimated lesson time 75 minutes

Sending Data Across a WAN

If the technologies discussed in previous lessons do not deliver the speed or bandwidth an organization needs, the network administrator should consider several advanced WAN environments which are becoming more popular as their technology matures. These include:

- X.25
- Frame relay
- ATM
- ISDN
- FDDI
- SONET
- SMDS

X.25

X.25 is a set of protocols incorporated in a packet-switching network. The packet-switching network is made up of switching services that were originally established to connect remote terminals to mainframe host systems.

An X.25 packet-switching network uses switches, circuits, and routes as available to provide the best routing at any particular time. Because these components (switches, circuits, and routes) change rapidly depending on the need and what is available, they are sometimes pictured as clouds. The clouds indicate an ever-changing situation, or that there is no standard set of circuits.

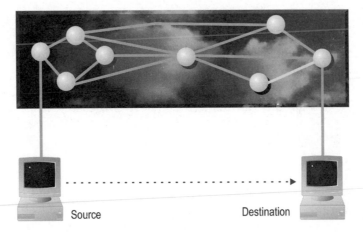

Figure 7.23 X.25 packet switching uses the best routing for each transmission

The early X.25 networks used telephone lines to transmit data. This was an unreliable medium which resulted in a lot of errors, so X.25 incorporated extensive error checking. Because of all of the error checking and retransmission, X.25 can appear to be slow.

Today's X.25 protocol suite defines the interface between a synchronous packet-mode host or other device and the public data network (PDN) over a dedicated or leased-line circuit. This interface is in reality a data terminal equipment/data communications equipment (DTE/DCE) interface.

Examples of DTEs include the following:

- A host computer with an X.25 interface
- A packet assembler/disassembler (PAD) which receives asynchronous characters input from a low-speed terminal and assembles them into packets to be transmitted over the network. The PAD also disassembles packets received from the network so the data can be delivered as characters to the terminals.
- A gateway between the PDN and a LAN or WAN.

For all three of these DTE examples, the DCE half of the DTE/DCE is the PDN. See Figure 7.24 for examples of DTEs.

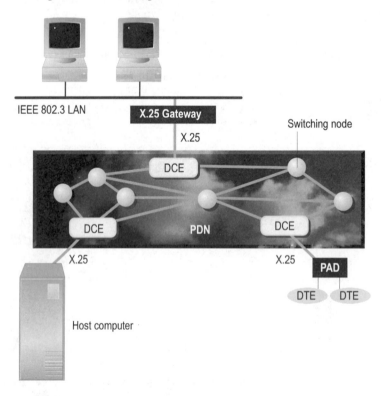

Figure 7.24 Examples of DTEs

Frame Relay

As network communications move toward digital and fiber-optic environments, new technologies will appear that require less error checking than earlier analog packet-switching methods.

Frame relay is an advanced fast packet variable-length, digital, packet-switching technology. With this technology designers have stripped away many of X.25's accounting and checking functions that are not necessary in a reliable, secure, fiber-optic circuit environment.

Frame relay is a point-to-point system that uses a PVC to transmit variable length frames at the Data Link layer. The data travels from a network over a digital leased line to a data switch into the frame relay network. It passes through the frame relay network and arrives at the destination network.

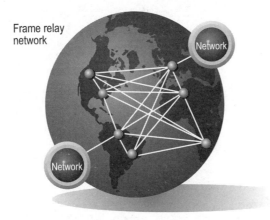

Frame relay
network

Figure 7.25 Frame relay uses a point-to-point system

Frame relay networks are gaining popularity because they are much faster than other switching systems at performing basic packet-switching operations. This is because frame relay uses a PVC so the entire path from end-to-end is known. There is no need for frame relay devices to perform fragmentation and reassembly, or to provide best-path routing.

Frame relay networks can also provide subscribers with bandwidth as needed, which lets the customer make nearly any type of transmission.

Frame relay technology requires a frame-relay capable router or bridge to successfully transmit data over the network. A frame relay router will need at least one WAN port for a connection to the frame relay network and another port for the LAN.

Q & A

Fill in the blanks in the following sentences.

1. Because of extensive _____ _____ , X.25 can appear to be slow.

2. X.25 was originally developed for the _____ environment.

3. Frame relay data travels from a network over a _____ _____ line to a data switch into the frame relay network.

4. Frame relay networks can also provide subscribers with _____ as needed, which lets the customer make nearly any type of transmission.

5. Frame relay networks are faster at performing basic _____ _____ operations than X.25 networks.

Answers

1. error checking
2. mainframe
3. digital leased
4. bandwidth
5. packet switching

Asynchronous Transfer Mode (ATM)

Asynchronous transfer mode is an advanced implementation of packet switching that provides high-speed data transmission rates to send fixed-size packets over broadband and baseband LANs or WANs. ATM can accommodate:

- Voice
- Data
- Fax
- Real-time video
- CD-quality audio
- Imaging
- Multimegabit data transmission

The CCITT defined ATM in 1988 as part of the broadband integrated services digital network (BISDN). Because of ATM's power and versatility, it will influence the future of network communications. It is equally adaptable to both LAN and WAN environments, and it can transmit data at very high speeds (155 Mbps to 622 Mbps or more).

ATM Technology

ATM is a broadband cell relay method that transmits data in 53-byte cells rather than in variable-length frames. These cells consist of 48 bytes of application information with five additional bytes of ATM header data. For example, ATM would divide a 1000-byte packet into 21 data frames and put each data frame into a cell. The result is a technology that transmits a consistent, uniform packet.

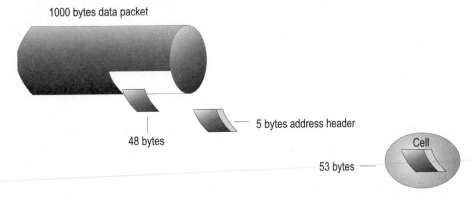

Figure 7.26 ATM cells have 48 bytes of data and a 5-byte header

Network equipment can switch, route, and move uniform-sized frames much more quickly than it can random-sized frames. The consistent, standard size cell uses buffers efficiently and reduces the work required to process incoming data. The uniform cell size also helps in planning application bandwidth.

Theoretically, ATM can offer throughput rates of up to 1.2 gigabits per second. Currently, however, ATM measures its speed against fiber-optic speeds that can reach as high as 622 Mbps. Most commercial ATM boards will transmit data at about 155 Mbps.

As a reference point, 622 Mbps ATM can transmit the entire contents of the latest edition of The Encyclopedia Britannica, including graphics, in less than one second. If the same transfer were tried using a 2400 baud modem, the operation would take more than two days.

ATM can be used in both LANs and WANs at approximately the same speed. ATM relies on carriers such as AT&T and US Sprint™ for implementation over a wide area. This will create a consistent environment that will do away with the concept of the slow WAN and the differing technologies used in the LAN and WAN environments.

ATM Components

ATM components are currently available only through a limited number of vendors. All hardware in an ATM network has to be ATM compatible. The implication is that implementing ATM in an existing facility will require extensive equipment replacement. This is one reason why ATM has not been adopted more quickly.

However, as the ATM market matures, various vendors will be able to provide:

- Routers and switches to connect carrier services on a global basis.
- Backbone devices to connect all of the LANs within a large organization.
- Switches and adapters which link desktop computers to high-speed ATM connections for running multimedia applications.

ATM Media

ATM does not restrict itself to any particular media type. It can be used with existing media designed for other communications systems including:

- Coaxial
- Twisted-pair
- Fiber- optic

However, these traditional network media in their present forms do not support all of ATM's capabilities. An organization called the ATM Forum is recommending the following physical interfaces for ATM:

- FDDI (100 Mbps)
- Fiber Channel (155 Mbps)
- OC3 SONET (155 Mbps)
- T3 (45 Mbps)

Other interfaces include frame relay and X.25.

ATM Switches

ATM switches are multiport devices that can act as either of the following:

- Hubs to forward data from one computer to another within a network.
- Router-like devices to forward data at high speeds to remote networks.

In some network architectures, such as Ethernet and Token Ring, only one computer at a time may transmit. ATM, however, uses switches as multiplexers to permit several computers to put data on a network simultaneously. In Figure 7.27, three routers are feeding data into the ATM switch and onto the ATM network at the same time.

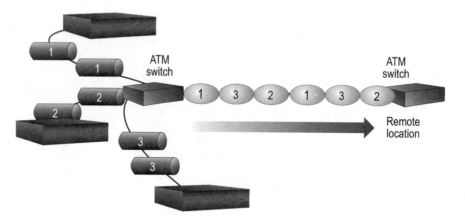

Figure 7.27 ATM switches act as multiplexers allowing multiple data input

ATM Considerations

ATM is a relatively new technology that requires special hardware and exceptional bandwidth to reach its potential. Current WAN technology does not have the bandwidth to support ATM in real time. Applications that support video or voice would overwhelm most current network environments and frustrate users trying to use the network for normal business. Also, implementing and supporting ATM requires expertise which is not widely available.

Q & A

Fill in the blanks in the following sentences.

1. ATM is an advanced implementation of _____ _____ that provides high-speed data transmission rates.

2. ATM transmits data in 53 byte _____ rather than variable-length frames.

3. ATM switches are multiport devices that can act as either _____ to forward data from one computer to another within a network or _____ to forward data at high speeds to remote networks.

4. ATM uses switches as _____ to permit several computers to put data on a network simultaneously.

5. ATM can be used with existing _____ designed for other communications systems.

Answers

1. packet switching
2. cells
3. hubs, routers
4. multiplexers
5. media

Integrated Services Digital Network (ISDN)

ISDN is an inter-LAN digital connectivity specification that accommodates:

- Voice
- Data
- Imaging

One of the original goals of ISDN developers was to link homes and businesses over copper telephone wires. The early ISDN implementation plan called for converting existing telephone circuits from analog into digital. This plan is being implemented world-wide.

Basic Rate ISDN divides its available bandwidth into three data channels. Two of these move data at 64 Kbps, and the third transmits at 16 Kbps.

The 64 Kbps channels are known as B channels. These can carry voice, data, or images. The slower 16 Kbps channel is called the D channel. The D channel carries signaling and link management data. ISDN basic rate desktop service is called 2B+D.

A computer connected to an ISDN service can use both B channels together for a combined 128 Kbps data stream. If both end stations also support compression, much higher throughput can be achieved.

Primary Rate ISDN uses the entire bandwidth of a T1 link by providing 23 B channels at 64 Kbps and one D channel at 64 Kbps. The D channel is only used for signaling and link management.

Networks which plan to use ISDN services should consider whether to use Basic Rate or Primary Rate, based on their need for data throughput. ISDN is the digital replacement for the public switched telephone network (PSTN), and as such is a dial-up service only. It is not designed to be a 24-hour (like T1), or bandwidth on demand (like frame relay) service.

Fiber Distributed Data Interface (FDDI)

FDDI is a specification that describes a high-speed (100 Mbps) token-passing ring network that uses fiber-optic media. It was produced by the ANSI X3T9.5 committee, and released in 1986. FDDI was designed for high-end computers that did not find enough bandwidth in existing 10 Mbps Ethernet or 4 Mbps Token Ring architectures.

FDDI is used to provide high-speed connections for various types of networks. FDDI can be used for metropolitan area networks (MANs) to connect networks in the same city with a high-speed fiber-optic cable connection. It is limited to a maximum ring length of 100 Kilometers (62 miles), so it is not really designed to be used as a WAN technology.

Networks in high-end environments use FDDI to connect components such as large and minicomputers in a traditional computer room. These are sometimes called back-end networks. These networks typically handle file transfer far more than interactive communication. When communicating with a mainframe, the minicomputer or personal computer often requires constant, real-time use of the media. They may even need exclusive use of the media for extended periods of time.

FDDI works with backbone networks to which other low-capacity LANs can connect. It is not wise to connect all of the data-processing equipment in a company to a single LAN because the traffic may overload the network, and a failure can halt the company's entire data processing operation.

LANs that require high data rates and fairly large bandwidth can use FDDI connections. These are networks composed of engineering computers or other computers that must support high bandwidth applications such as video, computer aided design (CAD), and computer aided manufacturing (CAM).

Any office requiring high-speed network operations may consider using FDDI. Even in business offices, producing graphics for presentations and other documentation can saturate and slow a network.

Token Passing

While FDDI uses a standard token passing system, there are differences between FDDI and 802.5. A computer on an FDDI network can transmit as many frames as it can produce within a predetermined time before letting the token go. As soon as a computer is through transmitting, it releases the token.

Because a computer releases the token when it is finished transmitting, there may be several frames circulating on the ring at once. This explains why FDDI offers higher throughput than a Token Ring network, which only allows one frame at a time to circulate.

Topology

FDDI operates at 100 Mbps over a dual-ring topology which supports 500 computers over a distance of 100 kilometers (62 miles).

FDDI uses shared network technology. This means that more than one computer at a time can transmit. Although FDDI can provide 100 Mbps service, the shared network approach can still become saturated. For example, if ten computers all transmit at 10 Mbps, the total transmission will equal 100 Mbps. In transmitting video or multimedia, even the 100 Mbps transmit rate can become a bottleneck.

FDDI uses the token passing system in a dual-ring setting. Traffic in an FDDI network consists of two similar streams flowing in opposite directions around two counter-rotating rings. One ring is called the primary ring and the other is called the secondary ring.

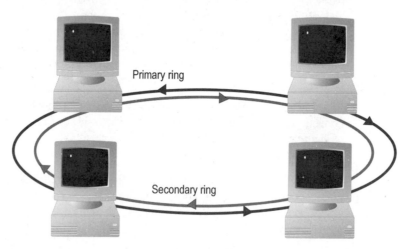

Primary ring

Secondary ring

Figure 7.28 FDDI uses a dual-ring topology

Traffic usually flows only on the primary ring. If the primary ring fails, FDDI automatically reconfigures the network so the data flows onto the secondary ring in the opposite direction.

One of the advantages of the dual-ring topology is redundancy. One of the rings is used for transmission, and the other is used for backup. If there is a problem, such as a ring failure or a cable break, the ring reconfigures itself and continues transmitting.

The total cable length of both rings combined must not exceed 200 kilometers, and it cannot hold more than 1000 computers. However, because the second, redundant ring protects against ring failure, the total capacities should be divided in half. Therefore, each FDDI network should be limited to 500 computers and 100 kilometers of cable. Also, there must be a repeater every two kilometers or less.

Computers may connect to one or both FDDI cables in a ring. Those that connect with both cables are known as Class A stations, and those that connect to only one ring are called Class B stations.

If there is a network failure, Class A stations can help reconfigure the network; Class B stations cannot.

FDDI in a Star

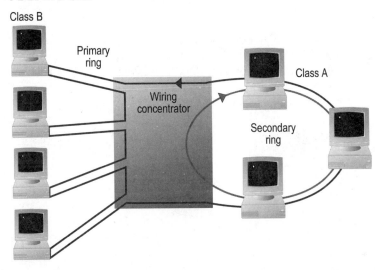

Figure 7.29 Class A computers connect to both rings; Class B connect to only one

FDDI computers can accommodate point-to-point links to a hub. This means that FDDI can be implemented using the star ring topology. This is an advantage in that it can:

- Help in troubleshooting.
- Take advantage of the management and troubleshooting capabilities of advanced hubs.

Beaconing

All computers in an FDDI network are responsible for monitoring the token passing process. To isolate serious failures in the ring, FDDI uses a system called beaconing. With beaconing, the computer that detects a fault sends a signal called a beacon onto the network. The computer will continue to send the beacon until it notices a beacon from its upstream neighbor, and then it stops. This process continues until the only computer sending a beacon is the one directly downstream of the failure.

As illustrated in Figure 7.30, computer 1 faults. Computer 3 detects the fault, starts to beacon, and continues to do so until it receives a beacon from computer 2. Computer 2 will continue to beacon until it receives a beacon from 1. Because computer 1 is the one with the fault, computer 2 will continue to beacon and pinpoint the fault being on computer 1.

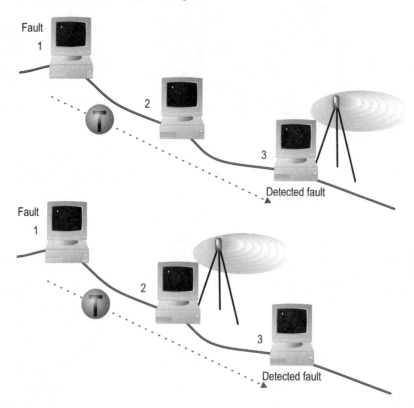

Figure 7.30 FDDI uses beaconing to isolate problems

When the beaconing computer finally receives its own beacon, it assumes the problem has been fixed, it regenerates a token, and the network returns to normal operation.

Media

FDDI's primary medium is fiber-optic cable. This means that FDDI is:

- Immune to electromagnetic interference or noise.

- Secure because fiber-optic cable does not emit a signal that can be monitored and cannot be tapped.

- Able to transmit long distances before needing a repeater.

FDDI can also be used on copper wire, known as copper distributed data interface (CDDI), but this will seriously limit its distance capabilities.

Q & A

Fill in the blanks in the following sentences.

1. Basic rate ISDN divides its available _____ into three data channels.

2. FDDI is a specification that describes a high-speed (100 Mbps) token-passing ring LAN that uses _____ - _____ media.

3. FDDI can be used for _____ networks to which other, low-capacity LANs can connect.

4. A computer on an FDDI network can transmit as many frames as it can produce within a predetermined time before letting the _____ go.

5. Traffic in an FDDI network consists of two similar streams flowing in opposite directions around two counter-rotating _____.

6. An advantage of the dual-ring topology is _____.

7. To isolate serious failures in the ring, FDDI uses a system called _____ in which a computer that detects a fault sends a signal onto the network.

Answers

1. bandwidth
2. fiber-optic
3. backbone
4. token
5. rings
6. redundancy
7. beaconing

Synchronous Optical Network (SONET)

Synchronous optical network (SONET) is one of several emerging systems that take advantage of fiber-optic technology. It can transmit data at more than one gigabit per second. Networks based on this technology are capable of delivering voice, data, and video.

SONET is a standard for optical transport formulated by the Exchange Carriers Standards Association (ECSA) for the American National Standards Institute (ANSI). SONET has also been incorporated into the Synchronous Digital Hierarchy recommendations of the CCITT, also known as the International Telecommunications Union (ITU), which sets the standards for international telecommunications.

SONET defines optical carrier (OC) levels and electrical equivalent synchronous transport signals (STSs) for the fiber-optic based transmission hierarchy.

SONET uses a basic transmission rate of STS-1, which is equivalent to 51.84 Mbps. However, higher-level signals are achievable and are integer multiples of the base rate. For example, STS-3 is three times the rate of STS-1 (3 X 51.84 = 155.52 Mbps) An STS-12 would be a rate of 12 x 51.84 = 622.08 Mbps.

SONET provides sufficient payload flexibility that it will be used as the underlying transport layer for BISDN ATM cells. BISDN is a single ISDN network that can handle voice, data, and video services. ATM is the CCITT standard that supports cell-based voice, data, video, and multimedia communication in a public network under BISDN. The ATM Forum is aligning with SONET as the transport layer for cell-based traffic.

Switched Multimegabit Data Service (SMDS)

Switched multimegabit data service is a switching service provided by some local exchange carrier services. Transmission speeds range from 1 Mbps to 34 Mbps with many-to-many connectivity. Unlike a dedicated mesh network (network with multiple active paths), this connectionless service can offer high bandwidth at reduced network costs.

SMDS uses the same fixed-length cell relay technology as ATM. One SMDS line with the appropriate bandwidth connects into the local carrier and can provide connections between all sites without a call set up or tear down procedure. SMDS does not perform error checking or flow control; that is left up to the sites being connected.

SMDS is compatible with the IEEE 802.6 metropolitan area network (MAN) standard as well as BISDN, but SMDS provides management and billing services not specified in the IEEE 802.6 specification.

SMDS uses the distributed queue dual bus (DQDB) as the interface and access method for the network. SMDS is a dual-bus topology that forms a ring that is not closed.

Summary

There are several new transmission technologies that can enhance the performance of a wide area network.

X.25 is a set of protocols incorporated in a packet-switching network. An X.25 packet-switching network uses switches, circuits, and routes as available to provide the best routing at any particular time.

Frame relay is a packet-switching technology that evolved from X.25. It performs much faster than X.25, due to reduced overhead. It requires a frame relay-capable router.

ATM is also an advanced form of packet-switching. It is a broadband method that transmits data in 53 byte cells rather than variable-length frames. It produces uniform frames that network equipment can switch, route, and move more quickly than frames of different sizes. ATM can be used with any media that includes the necessary physical interfaces.

Basic Rate ISDN employs digital transmission that divides its available bandwidth into two 64-Kbps B channels and one 16-Kbps D channel. Primary Rate ISDN has 23 64-Kbps B channels and one 64-Kbps D channel.

FDDI is a high-speed token-passing ring network that uses fiber-optic media and was developed for high-end computers. It is used in environments that connect components such as large and minicomputers in a traditional computer room, for backbone networks, for networks that require high data rates and fairly large bandwidth, and in high-speed office networks in general.

SONET is an emerging fiber-optic technology that can transmit data at more than one gigabit per second.

SMDS is a switching service provided by some local exchange carrier services. SMDS uses the same fixed-length cell relay technology as ATM.

Your Next Step

You are now ready to go on to the Chapter 7 Review in which you will use the information presented in this chapter to:

- Check your knowledge of LAN/WAN communication technology.
- Solve problems related to planning, implementing, and supporting LAN/WAN connectivity.

Chapter 7 Review

Chapter 7, "Larger Networks," presented an overview of the technology involved in expanding the network environment from a self-contained LAN to a large communications system linking WANs and LANs around the globe.

Modems make it possible to transmit data over dial-up or leased analog (telephone) lines. There are two types of modems: asynchronous and synchronous. Synchronous is used for digital and network communications. Modems can be installed externally or internally to a computer using a free expansion slot. When used with a dial-in service such as Microsoft RAS, they can link remote workers to their networks.

Networks, like the companies they serve, tend to grow. In this chapter you learned about the components you can use to expand a network. Repeaters are the simplest components used to expand a LAN. They work at the OSI Physical layer to boost signals and pass them along. More advanced repeaters act as multiport hubs.

Bridges work at the Data Link layer to extend a network's distance and segregate network traffic based on computer addresses. The bridge forwards data that is not addressed to a computer on its own segment. Bridges can also join, unlike architectures such as Ethernet and Token Ring.

Routers work at the Network layer to route packets across multiple networks based on specific network addresses. Routers forward packets to other routers. They can be used to break a large network into smaller, more manageable ones. Most protocols, including IP, IPX, DECnet, and AFP are routable. But some, like NetBEUI, are not. Routers can maintain multiple paths and will route along the best path at the moment based on the number of hops and the cost. Brouters combine the best features of both bridges and routers. For example, they will route selected protocols and bridge all others.

Gateways are another way to expand the size of a network. They are dedicated servers that enable communication between different network environments. Gateways strip the original protocol stack from data and repackage it in the destination network's protocol stack.

You also learned about transmission technology used in WANs. Most WANs are combinations of LANs and other types of communications components connected by WAN links. These links include analog and digital types of connections and packet switching networks. Analog technology can be used in WAN communications over dial-up or dedicated (leased) lines. Digital technology, such as a T1 connection, however, is more efficient.

Packet-switching technology is most efficient for transmitting data over very large distances such as city-to-city or between countries. Finally, you learned that there are emerging technologies that improve upon current analog, digital, and packet-switching transmission methods. Several were discussed, including FDDI, ISDN, and SONET. FDDI is a token-passing, dual-ring technology that transmits high-bandwidth applications such as video over fiber-optic cable at 100 Mbps. ISDN is digital connectivity that divides bandwidth into three channels to transmit voice, data, and imaging at about 150 Kbps. SONET is one of the newest systems to employ fiber-optic technology to transmit data at more than one gigabit per second.

Checkup

Follow the instructions for each exercise as indicated. All answers follow the last exercise.

Exercise 1: Multiple Choice

Select the letter of the best answer for each of the following sentences.

1. Analog lines, the standard voice lines used in telephone communications, are also known as _____ lines.
   a. dial-up
   b. direct digital
   c. any-to-any
   d. dedicated lines

2. Compression improves the time required to send data by _____.
   a. decreasing the possible routes
   b. removing the redundant elements
   c. removing the line noise
   d. decreasing time between transmissions

3. A routing table _____.
   a. supports broadcasts directed at particular addresses
   b. stores computer and network addresses
   c. sends packets to correctly addressed repeaters
   d. supplies an address for each newly activated computer

4. As packets are passed from router to router, Data Link layer source and destination addresses are stripped off and _____.

   a. then recreated

   b. sent on separately to be reformatted at the destination

   c. the packets are forwarded based on their lengths in bytes

   d. the packets are forwarded based on their priority level

5. An important difference between bridges and routers is that _____.

   a. bridges can choose between multiple paths

   b. bridges support Ethernet but not Token Ring environments

   c. routers support Ethernet but not Token Ring environments

   d. routers can choose between multiple paths

6. Voice-grade dial-up lines _____.

   a. are popular because they are almost as fast as private fiber-optic lines and less expensive

   b. are in short supply and are, therefore, expensive

   c. are widely used but do not provide consistent circuits from session to session

   d. use synchronous modems to provide access to computers

7. T1 technology offers _____.

   a. point-to-point, full-duplex transmission at 1.544 Mbps

   b. an inexpensive way to replace multiple T3 lines

   c. a permanent link to copper-based ATM and SONET carriers

   d. transmission speeds of 45 Mbps

8. Frame relay is a point-to-point system that transmits _____ _____ through the most cost-effective path.

   a. fixed-length packets at the Physical layer

   b. variable-length packets at the Physical layer

   c. fixed-length frames at the Data Link layer

   d. variable-length frames at the Data Link layer

Exercise 2: Matching

Match each description in column A with the best choice from Column B. One item in Column B will not be used, and items will be used no more than once.

Column A	Column B
1. Forwards packets based on Media Access Control sublayer address. ____	A. Repeaters
2. Dial-up service providing inter-LAN digital connectivity. ____	B. Gateways
3. Set of packet-switching network protocols. ____	C. SONET
4. Link networks that use different protocols. ____	D. SMDS
5. Prohibit broadcast storms and works at the Network layer. ____	E. Bridges
6. Works at the Physical layer and joins segments having same access method. ____	F. X.25
7. High-speed token-passing network that uses fiber-optic cable. ____	G. Routers
8. Function as repeaters with multiple ports. ____	H. ATM
9. The CCITT defined it as part of BISDN, capable of transmitting data at 155 Mbps to 622 Mbps or more. ____	I. Hubs
10. Uses a basic transmission rate or STS-1 which is equivalent to 52.84 Mbps. ____	J. FDDI
	K. SDN

Checkup Answers

Exercise 1: Multiple Choice

1. Analog lines, the standard voice lines used in telephone communications, are also known as _____ lines.

    a. dial-up

2. Compression improves the time required to send data by _____.

    b. removing the redundant elements

3. A routing table _____.

    b. stores computer and network addresses

4. As packets are passed from router to router, Data Link layer source and destination addresses are stripped off and _____.

    a. then recreated

5. An important difference between bridges and routers is that _____.

    d. routers can choose between multiple paths

6. Voice-grade dial-up lines _____.

    c. are widely used but do not provide consistent circuits from session to session

7. T1 technology offers _____.

    a. point-to-point, full-duplex transmission at 1.544 Mbps

8. Frame relay is a point-to-point system that transmits _____ _____ through the most cost-effective path.

    d. variable-length frames at the Data Link layer

Exercise 2: Matching

1. E
2. K
3. F
4. B
5. G
6. A
7. J
8. I
9. H
10. C

Case Study Problem

The Setting

A magazine publisher based in Seattle has a branch office in Ft. Lauderdale, Florida, and one in New York City. This company used to stay in touch by telephone and Federal Express®.

Each office is networked. The networks were implemented five years ago and each has a coaxial linear bus supporting Ethernet 10 Mbps traffic.

Lately, the company has been developing projects that involve teams consisting of members from more than one office. Each office has resources that the others do not; the current projects require all of these resources.

The networks have had frequent cable problems, and each time they have one, the entire network goes down until the problem is resolved.

The Problem

The management team would like a networking solution which would offer easier troubleshooting, less downtime, and WAN communications between sites. They would like the WAN connection to support about 256 Kbps of data, and several analog telephone conversations between sites (the long distance bills alone have been tremendous). The combination of long distance and Federal Express charges should be eliminated by the WAN. Management would like the WAN to be able to continue operations even if one of the WAN links should fail.

Your Solution

Local Fixes

Identify at least two items every site has that needs upgrading.

_____

_____

WAN Install—At Each Site

The offices need to maintain voice and data communications with each other.

1. What type of WAN connection (link) might you use to connect the three sites to each other?

   _____

2. How many WAN connections will it take to connect the three sites? Draw the links on the diagram below.

   Seattle ◎   ◎ New York

                                                      ◎ Fort
                                                        Lauderdale

3. What type of device could be used to collect the multiple signals from both voice and data and put them on the same WAN link?

   _____

4. What type of connectivity device should be used to connect the LAN to the multiple paths in the WAN illustrated in the diagram above?

   _____

Case Study Suggested Solution

Local Fixes

- Each site could use:
  - New cabling (from Ethernet to Category 5).
  - New cards (from Ethernet to 10BaseT).
  - New architecture (from linear bus to star bus (10BaseT) with hubs).

WAN Install—At Each Site

1. Use a T1 link, because it can carry both voice and data simultaneously. (T1 is available through a carrier such as AT&T, MCI, Sprint, and so forth).

Note E1 is a rough equivalent of T1 and it is used outside the U.S.

2. Three connections link the three sites (see following diagram). Note the redundancy built into the design. If any one link fails, each site can communicate with any other site by going through an intermediate site.

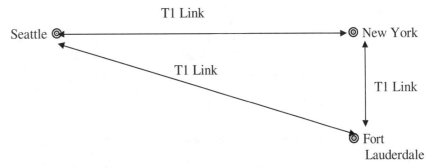

3. A multiplexer mixes both types of signals and places them on the same WAN link.

4. A router is the ideal device to connect the LAN to the multiple WAN paths. Routers can use multiple paths and can use best-path algorithms to determine the best path for each transmission.

The Troubleshooter

Use the information below to help you solve the troubleshooting problem which follows.

One of the key troubleshooting resources for communications is the vendor. Telecommunications is such a narrow field that most system administrators do not have extensive knowledge in this area. Usually telecommunications vendors have this type of expertise on staff.

1. Is the communications system a brand new installation?

   Yes _____

   No _____

   If the answer is yes, you should revisit the plans for the communication system and see if it was properly installed.

2. Has the present configuration worked in the past?

   Yes _____

   No _____

3. If it was a working system, when did it stop working?

   _____

4. What has changed since it last worked?

   _____

5. Did your vendor or service provider, including communications services vendors, change anything? (For example, during a weekend check of a leased line did the vendor change the data framing on your line from the one your equipment is set to use to a different type of frame format, that is, from pure 1.544 Mbps data to multiplexed multiple 56 Kbps inputs?)

   _____

6. Is there power to the modem, repeater, bridge, router, gateway, and CSU/DSU?

   Yes _____

   No _____

7. Are all sources of power backup and redundant sources of power, such as surge protectors, either supplying power or at least allowing the equipment to function properly?

   Yes _____

   No _____

8. Is the modem, repeater, bridge, router, gateway, or CSU/DSU turned on?

   Yes _____

   No _____

9. Are all of the cables to the modem, repeater, bridge, router, gateway, and CSU/DSU connected correctly and in good repair?

   Yes _____

   No _____

10. Is your modem, repeater, bridge, router, gateway, and CSU/DSU compatible with the communications medium and with the communications device on the other end of the link?

    Yes _____

    No _____

11. Is the software for your bridge, router, and or gateway configured correctly, and does it match the configuration of the communications equipment to which it is connected?

    Yes _____

    No _____

12. Do any of the network troubleshooting tools you have available point to any specific piece of equipment or configuration as a possible problem? For example, does your protocol analyzer indicate that two or more routers on the same segment are configured differently? Or does the analyzer indicate that two routers on the same segment think they are on different segments?

    Yes _____

    No _____

Can You Solve This Problem?

Often, actual problems are not nearly as difficult as they first appear to be. For example, a medium-sized computer firm lost its telephone service every Monday morning for nearly six months. Each Monday morning, employees would arrive at work to find that the telephone system was not working. No one in the company had the expertise to work on the problem, so they contacted their telephone vendor who sent someone out to fix the system. The telephone company sent a different technician each time, but each time it only took the technician about 15 minutes to fix the system.

One Monday, one of the computer firm's own technicians went to watch the telephone vendor's technician bring the system back up. The technician simply located the telephone system's surge suppresser and hit the reset switch. That was the total fix, and anyone who knew how to reset the surge suppresser (simply by pressing a Reset button) could now fix the telephone system.

The point is that even in a complex environment, problems and their solutions do not necessarily have to be complex.

While the answer was ultimately simple, the telephone company's technician was the only person who had the initial expertise necessary to locate and eliminate the problem. If you have WAN communication problems, and you have eliminated the LAN's local components as a source of trouble, do not hesitate to call the service provider to ask for help. There may be an initial expense, but time and money will be saved in the long run.

With that in mind, forge ahead and work through the troubleshooting problem.

The Situation

You are the multitalented network administrator and technician for this computer firm. Your LAN is connected to another LAN in a city 500 miles away. The communications link is a digital T1 with a multiplexer to allow you to send telephone conversations and data simultaneously on the same link.

The Available Facts

Monday morning when you came into work, you immediately began hearing complaints from people who could not use the WAN to access resources at the other site. After some checking you discover that you can use the T1 for the telephone conversations, but no data is being sent over the link. You examine all of the equipment and connectors, and you cannot see any obvious loose or frayed connections, and all of the equipment appears to be plugged in and turned on.

Your Solution

What can you do to start the troubleshooting process?

_____

_____

_____

Suggested Troubleshooting Solution

The first thing to do is a simple test on your hardware. Many pieces of complex equipment are microprocessor-driven hardware with built-in software. Simply going through the shut down and restart procedure for these devices (sometimes this is just an on-off switch) can restart the equipment and get it functioning properly again.

If shutting down and restarting the entire system does not get the system running, call the service provider and have them test the T1 line and verify that it is properly configured.

Finally, if neither of those two options solve the problem, you will need to contact your vendor for help troubleshooting the WAN equipment you have. Very few experienced systems engineers have the expertise needed to do this kind of troubleshooting.

The LAN Planner

The following questions will help you determine which, if any, WAN or advanced transmission components you should consider.

Modems

1. Do you need to communicate with bulletin board services and information services such as The Microsoft Network or CompuServe?

   Yes _____

   No _____

2. Do you need individual connectivity to the Internet?

   Yes _____

   No _____

3. Do you need to periodically transfer files with another user at a different location?

   Yes _____

   No _____

   If any of the answers to the first three questions was yes, it indicates that you need a modem. Your next step is to do the homework and research to determine which vendor's modem best fits your needs.

4. Do several users at once ever need to communicate with an online service or any remote resource?

   Yes _____

   No _____

   If the answer is yes, it indicates that you should consider a modem pool.

5. Do you have users who periodically need to access the network from home or on the road?

   Yes _____

   No _____

   If the answer is yes, it indicates that you may need a dial-in service. To implement this, you will also need a dial-in server.

Creating Larger Networks

You should consider one or several WAN connectivity devices if:

- Your network is getting too large and difficult to manage.
- You have added dozens of new users.
- The performance is degenerating.
- You need to connect multiple networks.
- You need to connect multiple sites.

If you are connecting multiple sites, then you probably need one of the advanced WAN transmission technologies discussed in Lesson 4, "Advanced WAN Technologies."

The determining factors in choosing a WAN connection service are:

- What services are available in your area?
- What do you need in the way of services?

The following questions will help you identify which connectivity devices would be appropriate for your system.

Repeaters

1. Do you need to extend the cable length of your network to accommodate new users located farther from the server?

   Yes _____

   No _____

2. If you extend the length of your network cable, will the newly extended cable length exceed the specifications for that type of cable?

   Yes _____

   No _____

3. Do you need to transmit signals on a different type of media than you are already using for your network? (For example, do you need to connect a thinnet segment to an Ethernet 10BaseT network?)

   Yes _____

   No _____

   If the answer to any of the above questions is yes, you should consider using a repeater to expand your network.

Bridges

Note A rule of thumb among many experienced network professionals is to use a bridge when dealing with non-routable protocols. Otherwise, use a router.

---

1. Do you need to connect two or more network segments?

   Yes _____

   No _____

2. Do you need to connect two networks of different network architectures (that is, Ethernet to Token Ring)?

   Yes _____

   No _____

3. Is your network performance slower than you would like it to be?

   Yes _____

   No _____

   If the answer is yes, keep that in mind while you answer the next question.

4. Does your network serve different departments that normally transmit network traffic only within their own department?

   Yes _____

   No _____

   If you answered yes to any of the questions, consider using bridges to either segment a single network or join two different networks.

Routers

Note Many network professionals prefer to use routers when either a bridge or a router will solve the problem. Their general rule is to use a bridge only with non-routable protocols. Otherwise, use a router. The cost difference between a bridge and a router is small considering the capabilities of a router.

1. Do you need to join several LAN segments into a single network?

    Yes _____

    No _____

2. Do you need to connect different network architectures (that is, Ethernet to Token Ring)?

    Yes _____

    No _____

3. Do you need to isolate or filter traffic between multiple segments?

    Yes _____

    No _____

4. Are network performance and data important enough to maintain redundant paths between multiple segments simultaneously?

    Yes _____

    No _____

5. If you have multiple paths, do you want packets routed on a "best path" algorithm?

    Yes _____

    No _____

    If the answer to any of these questions is yes, you should consider implementing routers between the different segments.

Gateways

Do you need to allow communications between unlike systems? (For example, do any users need to access a mainframe computer? Do users of Microsoft network software need to access servers running network software from Novell? Do users of network software from Novell need to access files on a UNIX computer?)

Yes _____

No _____

If your answer is yes, you should consider a gateway.

Choosing Advanced WAN Transmission Technologies

Choosing a WAN connection service varies from location to location based on available services and your network needs. You will have to do some market research to determine which service provider can best meet your system needs. The following questions will help you identify some of the services you will need.

1. Do you only have two sites to link?

    Yes _____

    No _____

    If the answer is yes, it indicates that you need point-to-point service.

2. Does your system need to link multiple sites to a central location?

    Yes _____

    No _____

    If the answer is yes, it indicates that you need a point-to-multipoint service.

3. Does your system need to link many sites simultaneously?

    Yes _____

    No _____

    If the answer is yes, it indicates that you need a multipoint-to-multipoint service.

4. Is the data that you transmit critical enough so that you require multiple links between sites to provide redundancy in case of link failure?

Yes _____

No _____

If the answer is yes, it indicates you may need multiple links.

Note Frame relay and other switching technologies provide redundancy but not at the transmission or receiving site. Also, because service providers bill packet switching by the packet, switching technology may be more or less expensive than T1, depending on the type of data and frequency of transmission. The service provider is the best source of information about costs.

---

5. What kind of network traffic will be on the link? (Check all that apply.)

- Voice _____

- E-mail _____

- Light file transfer _____

- Heavy file transfer _____

- Client/server database activity (should be fairly light network traffic) _____

- Client computer database activity with the data files stored on a remote server (can be very heavy traffic) _____

6. Based on the amount of network traffic identified in the previous question, approximately how much network bandwidth do you need? (Your WAN vendor might be able to help you determine this.)

- Less than 56 Kbps _____
- 56/64 Kbps _____
- 128 Kbps _____
- 256 Kbps _____
- 1 Mbps _____
- More than 1 Mbps _____

7. What types and speeds of WAN connection services (service providers) are available in your area?

_____

Note You will have to do some homework and service provider research to answer this.

_____

_____

_____

_____

8. Which of the above services can meet your requirements as determined by the questions above?

_____

9. Which service that can meet your requirements provides the best price and performance for your WAN needs?

_____

The LAN Planner Summary

Put a check mark next to the component you will need, indicate how many you will need, and note the parameters. To do this, it may help to draw a map of the network and place the components on the map.

Note Before filling out this chart, you will need to research different vendors and products to identify those which best fit your system's needs.

Component	Number	Notes and parameters
Modem	_____	_____
Repeater	_____	_____
Bridge	_____	_____
Router	_____	_____
Gateway	_____	_____

Service Providers

Service	Provider	Cost/notes
1. Point-to-point	_____	_____
2. Point-to-multipoint	_____	_____
3. Multipoint-to-multipoint	_____	_____
4. T1	_____	_____
5. Multiple T1	_____	_____

C H A P T E R   8

Solving Network Problems

Lesson 1   Monitoring Network Behavior to Prevent Problems . . . 637

Lesson 2   Network Troubleshooting . . . 651

Lesson 3   The Internet: A Worldwide Resource . . . 672

Chapter 8 Review . . . 686

Welcome to Chapter 8, Solving Network Problems. Now that you have learned about planning and implementing a network, it is time to move on to maintaining the network once it is installed.

The chapter begins by introducing the concept of avoiding problems through planning and management. You will learn about monitoring network behavior to develop a baseline of activity. This baseline of normal activity can be used as an aid in troubleshooting.

Lesson 2, "Network Troubleshooting," presents several troubleshooting tools and techniques, and resources for troubleshooting help including network support products and online services.

Finally, the chapter ends with an introduction to the Internet. You will learn the types of services the Internet provides, as well as how to access them.

The Case Study Problem

The case study problem walks you through upgrading your network server with a new operating system and a faster network adapter card. You decide to do this over the weekend to avoid disrupting the users, but a problem arises.

The Troubleshooter

The Troubleshooter will begin with a list of general troubleshooting questions that address the entire network system, applications, vendors, users, and more. You can use these as a focal point in troubleshooting a variety of network problems.

You will then be given a situation where you get to prepare a wish list of everything you would need to assume responsibilities for network troubleshooting.

The LAN Planner

The LAN Planner will help you identify sources of network support. You can use it to determine the tools, training, and other essentials you will need to be an effective network troubleshooter.

Lesson 1: Monitoring Network Behavior to Prevent Problems

What This Lesson Does

This lesson presents network monitoring and management from a preventive maintenance standpoint with the idea that it is better to plan and monitor for potential problems than wait until they happen. It will present some concepts and strategies that you have learned in earlier lessons, but in a different context. That is, planning and management strategies that will help you avoid network problems.

The lesson identifies several areas which should receive special attention during planning. It also introduces network monitoring and management programs and presents the concept of the baseline in determining acceptable network behavior.

Objectives

By the end of this lesson, you will be able to:

- List five strategies that are part of a network management plan for avoiding problems.
- Describe how establishing a baseline aids in preventing problems.
- Describe how documentation aids in troubleshooting.
- Incorporate a preemptive troubleshooting approach into a network plan.

Estimated lesson time 35 minutes

Approaches to Network Management

Part of managing a network is monitoring the network to avoid problems, and when necessary, troubleshooting problems that do eventually occur. The best way to avoid problems is through prevention with a proactive program that includes:

- Planning
- Monitoring
- Training
- Identifying, locating, and eliminating bottlenecks
- Ensuring adequate bandwidth
- Performing regular backups
- Identifying the key people who can help

If planning, prevention, and monitoring are carried out properly, people will not even know the administrator and the engineer are doing their jobs. As a network administrator, it is to your advantage to continuously monitor network components and activity to ensure continuous smooth, efficient operation and prevent problems before they occur.

This lesson and Lesson 2, "Network Troubleshooting," look at solving network problems from two different angles:

- Planning and management
- Damage repair and control

Network management and troubleshooting should work together as part of a plan. The plan must change and grow as the network changes and grows. The plan should include:

- Cable diagrams
- Cable layout
- Network capacity
- Protocols
- Equipment standards
- Forecasting for future needs and upgrades

Prevention Through Planning

Policies and procedures designed to avoid problems before they appear should be determined in the network planning stage. They are also part of the initial network plan. They include:

- Backups
- Security
- Standardization
- Upgrades
- Documentation

Backing Up the Network

Include a thorough backup system in your network plan. If someone questions the cost, explain it as an insurance policy and ask how much lost data would cost the company. The cost of replacing data is almost always more expensive than investing in a reliable backup system.

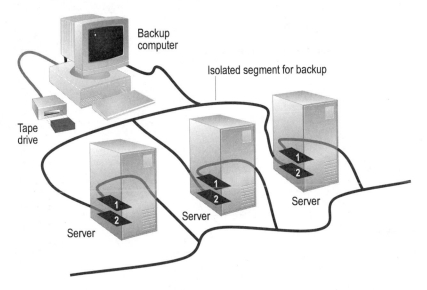

Figure 8.1 A reliable backup system is a critical part of every network

Security

Security in a server-based environment needs careful planning. The extent of your security policy will depend on:

- The size of your network.
- The sensitivity of the data.
- The business environment of your site.

Some of the security and password areas to be aware of are:

- User passwords.

  What is the minimum and maximum length?

  What type of characters (alphabetic, numeric, special) are allowed?

  How often are the users required to change their passwords?

  Is there a password history to prevent frequent repetition of passwords?

- Resource access.

  Granted only to those who have a need to access the resource.

  Grant the minimum access required.

- Security for remote (dial-in) users.

  Is there a guest account and does it have a password?

  What type of access is the guest account granted?

Keep the number of people who can perform administrator-level tasks very small. You do not want many people being able to access server functions.

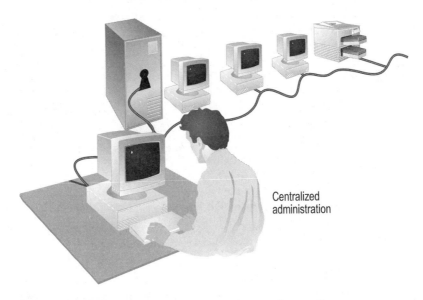

Centralized
administration

Figure 8.2 The administrator implements network security

Standardization

This subject is almost always overlooked in planning. Because the network administrator and engineer will be the ones responsible for supporting the network, they should be influential in deciding what hardware and software components will make up the network. The goal is to keep everything on the network as uniform as possible because it is easier to manage, upgrade, and, if necessary, repair.

With file standardization, an administrator can test and support the batch, configuration, and utility files which do so much of the LAN's work. Supporting these files would be difficult if there were as many different types of files as there were users. Also, the fewer types of applications on the network, the easier the support will be.

Upgrades

Vendors are continually upgrading products and introducing new ones. An administrator can spend a lot of time upgrading operating systems and applications for users. There are some guidelines which can help make the process go smoothly:

- Plan and announce upgrades well in advance. If the administrator stays late one evening to do the upgrades when no one else is at the site, the upgrades will not be disruptive to the users, and they will appreciate that fact.

- Test the upgrade or new installation on a small group of users before exposing the entire network to the upgrade. Also, it is a good idea to have a recovery procedure in place in case problems arise.

If the company and the network are successful, both will continue to grow. Periodically review network functions and components to ensure that they are adequate. If the network needs to expand in order to support more users or applications, plan the expansion as thoroughly as if it were a new network.

Documentation

Preparing and maintaining network documentation are essential tasks that will pay off when you need to troubleshoot a network problem. Up-to-date documentation provides information about how the network should look and perform, and where to find resources if there are problems. Documentation developed for maintenance and troubleshooting should contain:

- A map of the entire network including the locations of all hardware and details of the cabling.

- Server information including the data on each server and the schedule and locations of backups.

- Software information such as licensing and support details.

- Critical telephone numbers including vendors, suppliers, contractors, and other helpful contacts.

- Copies of all service agreements and the names and telephone numbers of contacts.

- A record of all problems and their symptoms, solutions, dates, contacts, procedures, and results.

Documentation should be thorough, well organized, and kept where it is readily available. This may seem obvious, but documentation can be lost or the person responsible for the documentation may leave the organization without properly orienting the next person to have that responsibility.

Q & A

Fill in the blanks in the following sentences.

1. Effective network troubleshooting begins in the _____ stage.

2. The best troubleshooting policy is _____ through a proactive monitoring program.

3. Documentation developed for prevention and troubleshooting should contain a _____ of the entire network including the locations of all machines and details of the cabling.

Answers

1. planning

2. prevention

3. map

Network Management Utilities

The best network monitoring and management programs will help an administrator or technician to:

- Identify conditions that lead to problems.
- Troubleshoot network problems.
- Help prevent the network from failing.

Because of the time, money, equipment, data, and frustration this approach saves, it is a more valuable troubleshooting method in the long run than identifying the cause of a failure after it appears.

If done correctly, network management can be considered preemptive troubleshooting. In fact, the ISO has identified five network management categories that relate directly to preemptive troubleshooting. These are:

1. Accounting management to record and report the use of network resources.
2. Configuration management to define and control the network components and their parameters.
3. Fault management to detect and isolate network problems.
4. Performance management to monitor, analyze, and control network data production.
5. Security management to monitor and control access to network resources.

Management tools are long-term troubleshooting tools. It takes time to learn which statistics you should be gathering. You must collect data over a period of time to learn about the typical network performance. Once you know how the network normally performs, you can watch for changes that would indicate a potential problem on the network.

Network Monitoring

Advanced network operating systems feature a built-in network monitoring utility. These can be used to track network behavior and establish a baseline as part of a preemptive troubleshooting program. Such tools make use of three types of information:

- Event logs that record errors, security audits, and other significant events for problem diagnosis.
- Usage statistics that tell who is accessing resources and how they are accessing them.
- Performance statistics that indicate such things as processor utilization, memory usage, and server throughput.

Microsoft Windows NT Server, for example, includes Performance Monitor to help present a picture of total system activity and health. A network administrator can use Performance Monitor to:

- Analyze network operation in both real time and recorded time.
- Identify trends over time.
- Identify bottlenecks.
- Monitor the effects of system and configuration changes.
- Determine system capacity.
- Monitor local or remote computers.
- Notify administrators of significant monitored events that exceed threshold values.
- Track the performance of isolated processors, hard disks, memory, and processes.
- View key system parameters as a whole.
- Perform monitoring functions separately or simultaneously.

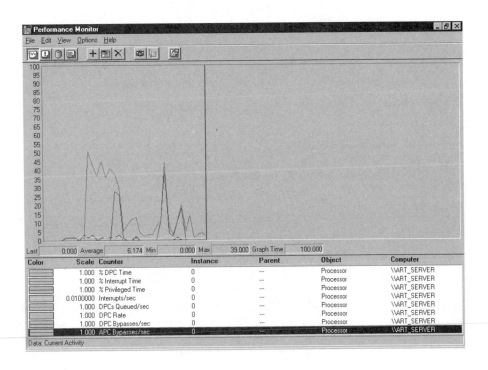

Figure 8.3 Performance Monitor helps you track system performance

Establishing a Baseline

Understanding how a network acts when it is healthy is as important as knowing how to solve problems after the network has failed. Monitoring and documenting the network when it is performing well will provide a baseline against which non-normal behavior can be compared.

The baseline must be established over time before anything goes wrong. Once a baseline exists, all network behavior can be compared to it as part of the on-going monitoring process.

The baseline is especially helpful in establishing and identifying:

- Daily network utilization patterns
- Bottlenecks
- Heavy user patterns
- Different protocol traffic patterns

The Performance Monitor tool is designed to track real-time computer activity to identify most performance bottlenecks. Figure 8.4 shows the %Processor Time approaching 100 percent. If this is a frequent occurrence or the duration is at or near 100 percent for a extended period, the processor could be a bottleneck.

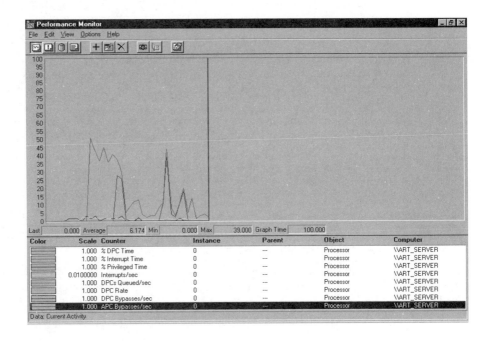

Figure 8.4 Performance Monitor will identify potential bottlenecks

Analysis of normal traffic patterns can head off potential problems by indicating whether:

- The network needs to be partitioned into multiple segments.
- More file servers should be added.
- Network adapters need to be upgraded for better performance.

Management Software and Preemptive Troubleshooting

Following is an overview of some of the areas in which an advanced network management software program can add much to preemptive troubleshooting.

- Cross checking and consistency monitoring of interacting network components to ensure that a fault in one component does not appear to be a problem in another healthy component.
- Identifying invalid or faulty message packets.
- Performing a regular inventory of network components, testing interfaces, and tracing network activities.
- Taking growth into account such as the addition of new computers or other components and technologies.
- Recording problems originating in adapters, cables, or other components, logging these in an error file, and notifying the administrator. Advanced management programs may even offer solutions to such problems.
- Monitoring server activity including print servers and gateways, logging the results and notifying an administrator in the event of a problem.
- Maintaining a history of network traffic activity and error statistics. This includes the status of paths between computers and between LANs.

The management program can log all relevant information and import that data into other files or databases. The administrator can use other application programs to access and present this information in any number of ways.

In a larger network, a good network management program will forward all of this information to a centralized computer which the administrator can use to maintain a detailed history of the remote LANs.

Q & A

Fill in the blanks in the following sentences.

1. Network management programs can maintain a history of network traffic and error statistics and forward all this information to a _____ computer which the administrator can use to manage the network.

2. One thing analysis of normal traffic patterns can help you determine is whether more file _____ should be added.

3. One area where management software can help in troubleshooting is identifying invalid or faulty message _____.

4. Once a _____ of normal network activity exists, all network behavior can be compared to it as part of the monitoring process.

5. One of the five ISO network management categories that apply to troubleshooting is _____ management to detect and isolate network problems.

Answers

1. centralized
2. servers
3. packets
4. baseline
5. fault

Summary

Network management includes monitoring network behavior as part of a preemptive approach to troubleshooting. If planning, monitoring, and management are done properly, there will be little need for troubleshooting. When planning a network, the administrator should implement policies and procedures designed to avoid problems before they appear. These plans include backups, standardization, regular upgrades, and documentation.

There are utilities available to help the network administrator with these tasks. Windows NT has built-in network monitoring and management programs which provide usage and performance statistics, and event logs.

As part of network management it is important to establish a baseline of typical network behavior. This is done over time and should be well documented. If problems do arise, the baseline is the first resource the administrator can turn to for comparison with daily utilization patterns, potential bottlenecks, error counts, and general performance statistics.

Your Next Step

In this lesson you were introduced to some tools and methods designed to help a network administrator recognize and solve potential network problems before they bring the network down. But not even the most effective, proactive management program can prevent every type of network problem. There are ways to isolate and solve even the most serious problems, as you will see in Lesson 2, "Network Troubleshooting."

Lesson 2: Network Troubleshooting

What This Lesson Does

This lesson takes troubleshooting from the baseline monitoring stage presented in Lesson 1, "Monitoring Network Behavior to Prevent Problems," to isolating the cause of a problem.

It introduces several troubleshooting tools, such as network or protocol analyzers, and describes various methods used by experienced administrators and support engineers to solve network problems. The lesson also includes a variety of resources you can use to aid in troubleshooting.

Objectives

By the end of this lesson, you will be able to:

- List the five steps that comprise a structured troubleshooting approach.
- Describe how a terminator is used in troubleshooting.
- Identify the capabilities of a protocol analyzer.
- Identify sources of up-to-date networking and troubleshooting information.
- Install Microsoft Technical Information Network (TechNet).
- Access the Microsoft Download Library (MSDL).
- Determine how to approach a given network problem in order to isolate and identify the cause.
- Identify any special equipment which would make it easier to solve a given network problem.

Estimated lesson time 40 minutes

Troubleshooting Methodology

Despite the most intricate plans, monitoring, and maintenance, network problems will still occur. When a problem occurs, the network administrator or support engineer will usually be able to determine and resolve the problem more efficiently by using a structured approach rather by trying random solutions.

The Structured Approach

The structured approach involves five steps which will lead to the solution of the problem:

1. Set the problem's priority.

2. Collect information to identify the symptoms.

3. Develop a list of possible causes.

4. Test to isolate the cause.

5. Study the results of the test to identify a solution.

Setting Priorities

The structured approach begins with scheduling the work. Everyone wants their computer fixed first. Therefore, the initial step an administrator or support engineer should take after receiving a problem call is to establish its priority.

Setting priorities in network problem solving is done by assessing the problem's impact. For example, if a board in a monitor has failed, and the monitor will not work, it is a simple replacement procedure and not as fun for the administrator or support engineer as tinkering with someone's CD-ROM sound system. But the user probably needs the monitor more than the game player needs his CD-ROM drive.

Network support cannot get to everything at once. Is everything a true emergency? Which types of problems take precedence over others?

Collecting Information

Collecting information will provide the foundation for isolating the problem. An administrator should have baseline information to compare with current network behavior.

Information gathering involves scanning the network looking for an obvious cause and a possible solution. A quick scan should include a review of the documented history of the network to see if the problem has occurred before and if there is a recorded solution.

Question the Users

Users can be very helpful in collecting information if they are questioned correctly. The engineer needs to ask: What is the network doing that makes the user think it is not performing correctly? Other user observations that can be clues are:

- "The network is really slow."
- "I cannot connect to the server."
- "I was connected to the server but I lost the connection."
- "One of my applications will not run."
- "I cannot print."

The experienced administrator or support engineer takes the user's initial comments into account and develops a series of either/or, yes/no questions to help isolate the problem. For example:

- Were many users affected or only one, or were users affected randomly?
- Is the whole network down or just one computer?
- Was the problem there before the upgrade?
- Does the problem occur constantly or is it intermittent?
- Does the problem appear with all applications or only one?
- Is this problem similar to a previous problem?
- Are there new users on the network?
- Is there new equipment on the network?
- Was a new application installed before the problem occurred?
- Has any of the equipment been moved lately?
- Which vendors' products were involved?
- Is there a pattern among certain vendors and certain components such as cards, hubs, disk drives, software, or network operating software?
- Has anyone else attempted to fix the problem?

Other areas the network administrator or support engineer should consider include:

- Versions of applications, operating systems, or other software.
- Reconfigurations of network components or the network operating system.

As a network administrator or support engineer you will become familiar with your own network components and applications and know where to look first for possible causes.

Divide the Network into Its Parts

If the initial network scan does not reveal the problem, the administrator or support engineer should consider mentally dividing the network into as many segments as possible in order to troubleshoot a small segment, rather than one large network.

After isolating the problem down to a specific segment, the administrator or support engineer can look separately at each network component. These can include:

- Clients
- Adapters
- Hubs
- Cabling and connectors
- Servers
- Connectivity components such as repeaters, bridges, routers, brouters, and gateways
- Protocols

  Network protocols require special attention because they are designed to bypass network problems and attempt to overcome any network faults.

  This is because most protocols incorporate retry logic that attempts to have the network automatically recover from whatever problem it is having. The only way this becomes noticeable is through slow network performance as the network makes new attempts to perform correctly.

  Retries increase network reliability, but they also make it difficult to isolate some network problems by masking several possible causes behind one symptom.

Here again, it might be a good idea to develop a list of questions designed to narrow down the possibilities and isolate the problem. It is important during this phase to understand both how each component is supposed to work and how each component can fail. Information from the baseline can be useful during this stage.

Questions at this stage can include:

- Which computers are able to function on the network?
- If a computer cannot function on the network, can it function as a stand-alone computer?
- If the computer cannot function on the network, is the computer's network adapter card working?
- Is there a normal amount of traffic on the network?

Possible Causes

Once you have gathered all of the information you can find, develop a list of possible causes of your problem. Try to rank them in order of most likely to cause the problem to least likely to cause the problem.

Isolate the Problem

After selecting the most likely candidate from the list of possible causes, test it and see if that is the problem. For example, if you expect that there is a faulty network adapter card in one of the computers, try replacing it with a network adapter card that is known to be good.

Study the Results

If your test resolves the problem, you have succeeded in identifying the problem. If your testing did not isolate the problem, you must go back to your list of possible solutions. If you have tested all problems on your list of possible causes, you may have to go back to the information gathering stage or you may want to ask for help.

Asking for Help

Most network administrators and support engineers take pride in being able to identify and solve network problems alone. Administrators and support engineers aspire to be respected as technical authorities. However, there are times when you will need some help in resolving the problem.

Perhaps there are other technical resources in your company that can assist you. If not, you may need to check with the hardware or software manufacturer's technical support line. Another good source is the vendor who sold you the network components.

Ironically, the best administrators and support engineers—the ones that customers appreciate the most—develop a knack for knowing where and when to call for help.

Q & A

Fill in the blanks in the following sentences.

1. To isolate a network problem the engineer can divide the network into _____.

2. Because they are designed to bypass network problems and attempt to overcome any network faults, special attention must be paid to network _____.

3. Collecting information will provide a _____ for isolating a problem.

Answers

1. segments
2. protocols
3. baseline

Special Tools

To help with troubleshooting, an administrator or support engineer has a variety of tools from which to choose. This section describes the most common ones.

Digital Volt Meters (DVM)

The volt meter (volt-ohm meter) is the most basic, all-purpose electronic measuring tool. In skillful hands, it can reveal far more than just the amount of voltage passing through a resistance. In network cable checking, it can measure continuity to determine if the cable is:

- Continuous and can carry network traffic, or
- Broken (has an open) and will bring the network down.

A continuity check can also reveal a short where:

- Two parts of the same cable are exposed and touching.
- An exposed part of the cable is touching another conductor such as a metal surface.

Time-Domain Reflectometers (TDRs)

These send sonar-like pulses along a cable looking for any kind of a break, short, or imperfection that might affect performance. If the pulse finds a problem, the TDR analyzes it and displays the result. A good TDR can locate a break within a few feet of the actual separation in the cable. These are used heavily during the installation of a new network, but are also invaluable in troubleshooting and maintaining existing networks.

Figure 8.5 Time-domain reflectometer

Advanced Cable Testers

These work beyond the OSI Physical layer in layers 2, 3, and even 4. They can display information about the condition of the physical cable as well as:

- Message frame counts
- Excess collisions
- Late collisions
- Error frame counts
- Congestion errors
- Beaconing

These testers can monitor overall network traffic, certain kinds of error situations, or traffic to and from a particular computer. They will indicate if a particular cable or network adapter card is causing problems.

Oscilloscopes

Oscilloscopes are electronic instruments that measure the amount of signal voltage per unit of time and display the results on a monitor. When used with TDRs, an oscilloscope can display:

- Shorts
- Sharp bends or crimps in the cable
- Opens (breaks in the cable)
- Voltage data that can indicate attenuation (loss of signal power)

Network Monitors

Network monitors are software that tracks all or a selected part of network traffic. They examine packets and gather information about packet types, errors, and packet traffic to and from each computer.

Figure 8.6 HP Network Advisor is an example of a network monitor

Protocol Analyzers

Protocol analyzers, also called network analyzers, perform a number of functions in real-time network traffic analysis, as well as packet capture, decoding, and transmission. Many experienced network administrators and support engineers responsible for larger networks rely heavily on the protocol analyzer. It is the tool they use most often to monitor the network interactively.

Protocol analyzers look inside the packet to identify the cause of a problem. They can also generate statistics based on the network traffic to help create a picture of the network:

- Cabling
- Software
- File server
- Workstations
- Interface cards

Most protocol analyzers have a built-in time-domain reflectometer.

The analyzer can provide insights into the network's behavior including:

- Faulty network components
- Configuration or connection errors
- LAN bottlenecks
- Traffic fluctuations
- Protocol problems
- Applications that may conflict
- Unusual server traffic

Because protocol analyzers can identify such a wide range of network behavior, they can be used to:

- Identify the most active computers and identify those which are sending error-filled packets. If one computer is sending so much traffic it is slowing down the network for other users, the administrator or support engineer might consider moving that computer to another network segment. The computer which is generating bad packets can be either fixed or removed.
- Identify, view, and filter certain types of packets. This becomes important where routing and internetwork traffic are concerned. Because the analyzer can distinguish protocols, it can determine what type of traffic is passing across a given network segment or component.

- Track network performance for a given period of time to identify trends. Recognizing trends can help an administrator better plan and configure the network based on the actual usage to accommodate peak periods and demanding applications.

- Check various components, connections, and cabling by generating test packets and tracking the results.

- Identify problem conditions by setting parameters in the analyzer to generate alerts if network traffic falls outside the parameters.

Popular Analyzers

- Hewlett-Packard Network Advisor

  The Network Advisor is actually a 386-based computer that includes a monochrome or color LCD screen, a LAN interface designed for data acquisition, and an artificial intelligence (AI) portion called Fault Finder.

- Network General Sniffer

  Sniffer, which is part of a family of analyzers from Network General, can decode and interpret frames from more than 14 protocols including AppleTalk, Windows NT, NetWare, SNA, TCP/IP, VINES, and X.25. Sniffer measures network traffic in kilobytes per second, frames per second, or as a percentage of available bandwidth. It will gather LAN traffic statistics, detect faults such as beaconing, and present this information in a profile of the LAN. Sniffer can also identify bottlenecks by capturing frames between computers and displaying the results.

- Novell's LANalyzer®

  The LANalyzer does much the same job as Sniffer but is only available on a NetWare LAN. It comes as a computer board and software to be installed in a computer on the network.

Q & A

Fill in the blanks in the following sentences.

1. A TDR sends _____ -like pulses along a cable looking for any kind of a break, short, or imperfection that might affect network performance.

2. Network monitors examine _____.

3. Protocol analyzers look inside the _____ to determine the cause of a problem.

4. Advanced cable testers will tell you if a particular cable or _____ _____ _____ is causing problems.

Answers

1. sonar
2. packets
3. packet
4. network adapter card

Network Support Resources

There is a variety of networking support software products, online support services, print materials, and other resources you can buy or subscribe to. These resources provide many different types of information, some of which can aid you in troubleshooting. This section describes some of them.

TechNet

Microsoft Technical Information Network (TechNet) provides information for supporting all aspects of networking with emphasis on Microsoft products. With the Microsoft Knowledge Base you can find up-do-date articles on many topics and learn about the latest software releases, updates, and revisions.

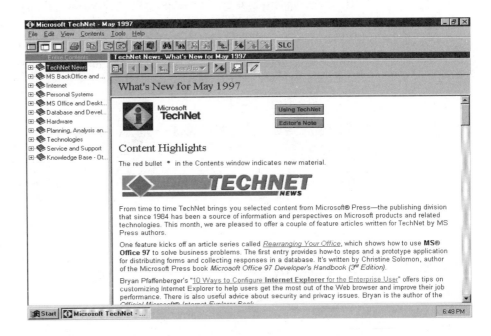

Figure 8.7 Sample TechNet content screen

Installing TechNet

The compact disc installs just like any other program. When installed, it adds icons to the appropriate program group for easy access.

There are several methods of locating the information you need on TechNet. The TechNet Find tool is an efficient choice. Refer to the Help menu for more information on using the various features of TechNet.

Subscribing to TechNet

You can subscribe to TechNet by calling:

(800) 344-2121

–or–

Mail your request for a subscription to:

Microsoft Corporation
PO Box 10296
Des Moines, IA 50336–0296

Bulletin Board Services (BBS)

There are numerous electronic bulletin board services (BBS) devoted to technical subjects such as networking. You can access the knowledge of experienced networking professionals by posting troubleshooting questions you may have.

For the latest information on Microsoft networking products there is the Microsoft Download Library (MSDL) through which the latest drivers and other software are available.

Note This service is for downloading only. It will not support uploading or questions.

This library can be accessed by dialing (206) 936-6735. The modem settings are:

- 8 data bits
- 1 stop bit
- No parity
- No flow control

User Groups

User groups are also a good way to interact with others who face many of the same challenges that installing, administrating, and supporting a network presents. There is a wealth of knowledge available at group meetings that cannot be found anywhere else. While these are a good source of knowledge, they tend to be focused on a specific aspect of technology.

Information about user groups for a particular subject or technology located in a particular area can be found through vendors, manufacturers, local publications, and solution providers.

Periodicals

After acquiring a foundation of knowledge, you will discover that the networking technology you have just learned is continually changing and advancing. There are many books available on networking, but they quickly become outdated. Periodicals are a better resource because they provide you with the most current information available. You can subscribe to several industry periodicals such as LAN Magazine, Data Communications, or PC Week. Many periodicals are available through the Internet.

LAN Magazine, published monthly, features a regular section called Tutorial. Each Tutorial focuses on some important network topic and presents it as an instructional guide to the subject rather than as a news story.

Common Troubleshooting Situations

With a structured approach it can take time to gather the information that finally isolates the problem and leads to a solution. This section includes some common network problems and ways to approach them. Each situation is affected by a number of factors including:

- The size of the network.
- The number of users.
- The types of applications.
- The age of the equipment.

For example, a WAN will present problems that a 12-workstation departmental network would never exhibit. These are traditional troubleshooting approaches collected by administrators and support engineers with years of hands-on experience.

Cabling and Related Components

Most network problems occur and are solved at the OSI Physical layer.

The Problem

- Cable breaks
- Cable shorts
- Breaks elsewhere in the circuit
- Malfunctioning network adapter card
- Faulty connections or connectors

Cabling is usually one of the first components that experienced network troubleshooters check because it is one of the most common causes of network failure. For example, if a segment of thinnet Ethernet breaks loose from the backbone or loses a terminator, the entire segment goes down.

The Approach

Network administrators and support engineers have to learn how to distinguish between computer problems and cable problems. One approach to this is to bring a portable computer equipped with a network adapter card on the trouble call. You can detach the questionable computer from the network and attach the portable. If the portable can "see" the network, then the cable can be eliminated as the cause of trouble. If, however, the portable exhibits the same symptoms as the questionable computer, then the cable should be checked.

If it is practical to check the cable on the site, you can scan the cable for obvious problems first. Ask people if they have moved anything or changed anything before the problem started.

Most experienced network administrators and support engineers have found they can save a great deal of time and money in the long run if they use either a TDR or a network analyzer to solve cable problems.

To start narrowing down the possibilities you can use a terminator. Find a computer at approximately the midpoint in the network and unhook or "break" the network cable. Attach a terminator first to one side and then to the other side and check to see which side fails when the terminator is in place. After determining which is the bad half of the network, repeat the previous steps at approximately the midpoint of the bad segment. Keep splitting the network in half until the cable problem is located.

Power Fluctuations

If the power in the building has gone off and then come on again, it is important to check the servers to make sure they are operating properly. All users should be notified before a power outage occurs that it may take some time after the power returns to ensure that the servers are back online.

To prevent this problem, an investment in an uninterruptible power supply (UPS) for each server will pay great dividends. Most UPS units will provide enough time to shut down operations in an orderly fashion after a power outage. Some will even shut a server down properly by themselves.

Upgrades

Because network operating systems are constantly being revised, an administrator will probably have to put the network through several operating system upgrades. During these upgrades, it is normal for some of the servers to be running on the old operating system while some will be running on the new system.

There are at least two key ideas to keep in mind during these transitions:

- Do a test upgrade on an isolated part of the network to test for failures or incompatibilities with the equipment, the operating system, or the applications.

- Make sure everyone knows that the upgrade is taking place so that if their applications or equipment fails or causes problems, they will understand why they are having problems.

Computers

When computers exhibit problems, the administrator or support engineer must first determine if it is a network problem or a computer problem. Are other computers having the same problems? If not, has anything changed in the computer since it was working properly? Did the user at that computer attempt to install any new software or even a simple utility? Was anyone other than the authorized user working at the computer?

Check the creation dates of any system files such as the Autoexec.bat and Config.sys files in the computer to verify that these were the same ones that were running before the problems occurred.

Server Disk Crash

Depending on the size and use of the network, a server disk crash is usually recognized as a catastrophic failure.

Once the crash occurs, it may be too late for traditional troubleshooting. Even if the administrator or support engineer announces that the problem has been discovered, and it is a faulty hard disk, there may be no way to get the data back. In a serious hard disk crash, the only remedy may be to replace the disk. If that happens, any data on the disk will be gone. No troubleshooting can bring it back.

The solution to this problem is avoidance through initial network planning. The primary question to be answered in this area is how much is the information on the network worth? If the information is essential to the life of the company, then it makes sense to invest in a redundant server system with complete backup.

Poor Network Performance

The network seems to get slower and slower. Sometimes this will happen during a short period of time, and sometimes the degradation occurs over days or weeks. The first question to ask is did the network ever work well? If it did not, then the administrator should start reviewing the planning and installation phases and asking the following questions:

- If the network did work properly at one time, what has changed since then?

- Has anyone added any new applications or equipment?

- Is someone playing a game that runs across the network?

- Is someone taking a new approach to any network procedures?

- Are there new users on the network?

- Is there a new cleaning service that moves things around at night?

- Is any new equipment, such as a generator, operating near the network?

If there are new users or new applications and there seems to be a relationship between degenerating network performance and the new users, perhaps it is time to think about expanding the network.

Q & A

Fill in the blanks in the following sentences.

1. Most network problems occur and are solved at the OSI _____ layer.

2. It is recommended that you start looking for the source of a cable problem using a _____ to isolate the problem.

3. Poor network performance may indicate you need to _____ the network.

4. Do a test upgrade on an _____ part of the network to test for failures or incompatibilities with the equipment, the operating system, or the applications.

5. When networked computers exhibit problems, the administrator or support engineer must first determine if it is a network problem or a _____ problem.

Answers

1. Physical
2. terminator
3. expand
4. isolated
5. computer

Summary

A troubleshooting methodology involves a structured approach to problem solving that begins with setting priorities and collecting information. The administrator or support engineer then develops a list of possible causes and performs the appropriate tests to isolate the cause. Once the cause is determined, a solution can be proposed.

If questioning users does not help isolate the cause of the problem, the administrator or support engineer can begin to look at segments of the network and what comprises those segments. There is a variety of troubleshooting tools, one of the most advanced being the network or protocol analyzer. Protocol analyzers can perform real-time network traffic analysis and provide statistics to help create a snapshot of various network components.

There are many network support resources the administrator or support engineer can access to help in troubleshooting, such as Microsoft TechNet and bulletin board services.

The most common network problems deal with cabling. It is one of the first components the administrator or support engineer should check. A time-domain reflectometer (TDR) or network analyzer will help locate cable problems.

Your Next Step

In this lesson you were introduced to several tools and methods that administrators and support engineers use to keep networks operational. Experience with the network at your site, and good record-keeping, are also important factors in troubleshooting.

Lesson 3: The Internet: A Worldwide Resource

What This Lesson Does

This lesson presents the Internet as a source for all types of information that can aid you, the network administrator or support engineer, in the performance of your job, from the latest technologies to product information to troubleshooting help. It provides an overview of what the Internet is and how you can access its many resources.

Objectives

By the end of this lesson, you will be able to:

- Identify Internet services.
- Access The Microsoft Network (MSN).
- Access the Microsoft FTP site.

Estimated lesson time 30 minutes

Overview

The Internet is a worldwide collection of networks, gateways, servers, and computers using a common set of telecommunications protocols to link them together.

The Internet provides worldwide access to information and resources. Without leaving your home or office, you can visit Ireland, Australia, or any other country in the world. There are vast stores of resource information that are easily accessible from universities, government organizations, the military, or libraries.

The Internet evolved from a U.S. Department of Defense project, the Advanced Research Projects Agency Network (ARPANET), which was designed as a test for packet-switching networks. The protocol used for ARPANET was TCP/IP, which continues to be used on the Internet today.

Over the last few years the primary uses of the Internet have shifted from research-based to commerce-based. Consumer and business use of the Internet is increasing by thousands of users monthly. People are discovering Internet-based resources and businesses are finding new ways to promote and sell their products on the Internet. As a network administrator you can use the Internet as a resource for current topics related to networking products, technologies, tools, and troubleshooting, and you can also find up-to-the-minute news, weather, sports, and information about the stock market. You have access to the Internet mall, as well as businesses, catalogues, and forums covering anything you can imagine. Microsoft believes this growth will continue, so it is important for our customers to be able to easily use the Internet.

Internet Services

Today the Internet is growing tremendously and is known mainly for the services it provides. Some of the best known services available on the Internet include the following:

- World Wide Web (WWW)
- File Transfer Protocol (FTP) servers
- Electronic mail
- News
- Gopher
- Telnet

World Wide Web

The World Wide Web (the Web) is the Internet's multimedia service that contains a vast storehouse of hypertext documents written using the Hypertext Markup Language (HTML). Hypertext is a method for presenting text, images, sound, and videos that are linked together in a non-sequential web of associations. The hypertext format allows the user to browse through topics in any order. There are tools and protocols that help you explore the Internet. These tools help you locate and transport resources between computers.

File Transfer Protocol (FTP)

File Transfer Protocol (FTP) support is one method of supporting remote networks. It is a protocol which allows simple file transfers of documents. There are FTP servers which provide vast amounts of information stored as files. The data in these files cannot be accessed directly, rather the entire file must be transferred from the FTP server to the local servers. It is a file transfer program for TCP/IP environments and is implemented at the Application layer of the OSI model.

The most common protocol used for sending files between computers is the File Transfer Protocol (FTP). FTP allows for transferring both text and binary files.

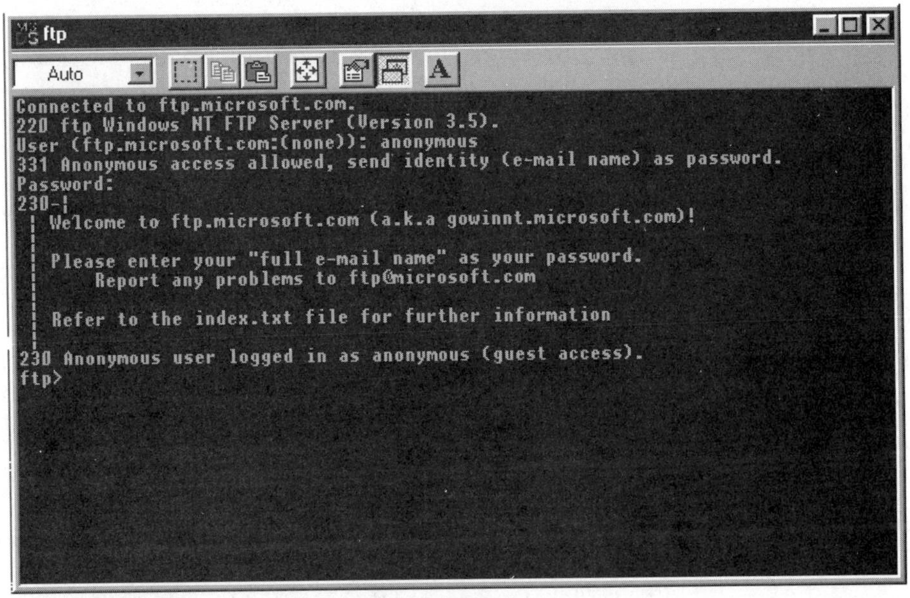

```
Connected to ftp.microsoft.com.
220 ftp Windows NT FTP Server (Version 3.5).
User (ftp.microsoft.com:(none)): anonymous
331 Anonymous access allowed, send identity (e-mail name) as password.
Password:
230-!
  | Welcome to ftp.microsoft.com (a.k.a gowinnt.microsoft.com)!
  |
  | Please enter your "full e-mail name" as your password.
  |     Report any problems to ftp@microsoft.com
  |
  | Refer to the index.txt file for further information
  |
230 Anonymous user logged in as anonymous (guest access).
ftp>
```

Figure 8.8 Character-based FTP client screen

Both Microsoft Windows NT and Windows 95 include the traditional character-based FTP client. This is one of the utilities that is copied onto the system when the TCP/IP protocol suite is installed. In addition, most Internet browsers such as Mosaic, Netscape™, or the Microsoft Internet Explorer support FTP and use it behind the scenes when transferring files.

Because of the large number of sites that support file transfer using FTP, it has become difficult to keep track of which computer has which files. A protocol named *Archie* is commonly used to act as an interactive search facility.

E-mail

Electronic mail, the sending and receiving of electronic messages, is currently one of the most popular activities on the Internet. E-mail is used on most commercial online services, and for many people, is the primary reason for getting onto the Internet or an online service.

To send e-mail, you must know the recipient's e-mail address. These addresses are composed of the user's identification, followed by the @ sign, followed by the location of the recipient's computer. For example, the e-mail address of the President of the United States is president@whitehouse.gov. The last three letters indicate this location is a government-sponsored domain on the Internet.

When you access the Internet through a local service provider or one of the large commercial online services, you can exchange e-mail without incurring the long-distance charges of a telephone call. E-mail has the added advantage of allowing you to access messages at your convenience. You can also send an identical message to any number of people at one time.

News

Network News Transfer Protocol (NNTP) is an Internet standard protocol defined for distribution, inquiry, retrieval, and posting of news articles. Network News (USENET) is a popular use of NNTP. It offers bulletin boards, chat rooms, and Network News. Network News is a massive system with over 5,000 ongoing conferences, called newsgroups, conducted 24 hours a day, 365 days a year. To access these newsgroups, download a special program from the Internet that allows you to participate in any newsgroup you want. Most commercial browsers, including the Microsoft Internet Explorer, have this capability built in. You then "subscribe" to the newsgroups that interests you and communicate through a message system similar to e-mail. The difference between Network News and e-mail is that with Network News conversations take place in a public forum called a news group.

You can simply view an ongoing dialog without participating; this is called lurking and is encouraged for newcomers. To enter the conversation, you post an article in the newsgroup and you become part of the forum. As with e-mail, Network News is usually informal communication with little distillation of content. However, some newsgroups are managed by a monitor who may elect not to post responses that are deemed inappropriate for that forum. Network News operates at a very high speed, with posting appearing quickly and constantly. Group administrators set the length of time that messages remain posted before being deleted from the system. Most do not keep postings longer than a week.

Discussion groups and chat rooms can be excellent sources of information and assistance on technical issues. They can also be sources for information on hobbies, entertainment, and travel, places for lively political debate, and provide an opportunity to meet people with shared interests.

Gopher

While FTP works well for transferring files, it does not provide a good means of dealing with file systems spread over multiple computers. An updated file transfer system called *Gopher* was developed in response to this issue.

Gopher is a widely-used tool on the Internet. It is a menu-based program that enables you to browse for information without having to know where the material is specifically located. It allows you to search lists of resources and then helps send the material to you. Gopher is one of the most comprehensive browser systems and is integrated to allow you access to other programs such as FTP and Telnet.

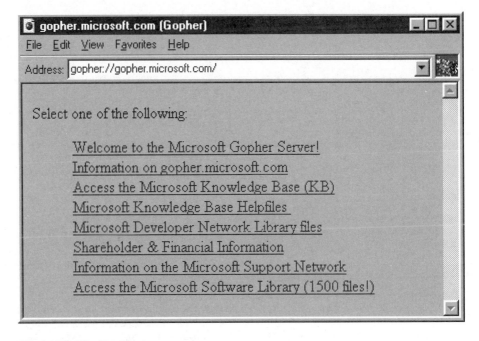

Figure 8.9 Gopher screen

Gopher computers are linked together with distributed indexes into a searchable system called a "Gopherspace." Gopherspaces typically offer a menu-driven system for access and are searchable with several search engines. The most common of these are the Gopher counterpart to Archie (named *Veronica*) and the wide area information server (WAIS) index search system.

Telnet

Telnet was one of the first Internet protocols. You can use Telnet to act as a remote terminal to an Internet host. When you connect to an Internet host, your computer acts as if your keyboard is attached to the remote computer. You can run programs on a computer on the other side of the world, just as if you were sitting in front of it.

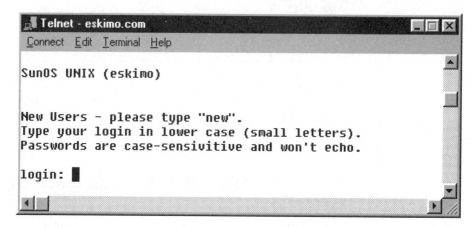

Figure 8.10 Telnet screen

This terminal/host system evolved from UNIX character-based systems in the early days of the Internet. Microsoft Windows NT and Windows 95 install a Telnet program as part of the TCP/IP utilities. This program allows you to act as either a VT-52 or VT-100 terminal to a system accessible by means of TCP/IP, including computers reached by means of the Internet.

Internet Sites

Many companies offer various types of support through Internet sites. For example, Microsoft maintains an Internet server that recognizes FTP. The FTP server contains product information, drivers, and other features for the network administrator or technician.

There are a number of sources to which an administrator or support engineer can turn for help with network problems before calling a technician. These include services that often provide information that will help you solve your particular network problem. These subscription support services are available through companies such as Microsoft.

The Microsoft Network (MSN)

Microsoft is one of the largest Internet access providers with The Microsoft Network (MSN). However, MSN is more than an Internet access provider or an online service. MSN presents MSN members with content from Microsoft, independent content providers (ICPs), and the Internet with a single, consistent, and integrated interface. To MSN members, MSN and the Internet are one service.

Figure 8.11 The Microsoft Network Sign In screen

Microsoft and ICPs create content exclusively for MSN. Microsoft works with MSN ICPs, such as the National Broadcasting Company, Inc. (NBC™), to develop unique programming that takes full advantage of the online medium. The Microsoft Consumer group will also be creating content that is unique to MSN. Some of the content that the Microsoft Consumer group has created for MSN includes Microsoft Encarta® multimedia encyclopedia and Microsoft Bookshelf® CD-ROM reference library.

The Microsoft Network e-mail client lets MSN members manage all of their messages and faxes in one place, regardless of which e-mail system originated the message. The version of Microsoft Exchange provided with MSN supports Rich Text Format (RTF), letting MSN members mix fonts, sizes, styles, colors, and even embedded graphics in messages for maximum impact. MSN mail also supports drag-and-drop attachments, making it easy for MSN members to include multiple objects within their e-mail messages, such as shortcuts, documents, pictures, and other files.

When MSN members are connected to the Internet, the Internet Explorer makes navigating and using the Internet easy. The Internet Explorer uses the same interface as Microsoft Windows 95. Folders and icons on MSN look and work just as they do on the Windows 95 desktop. MSN members use the Internet Explorer for all of their Internet access, so they do not have to learn new and different ways of working every time they explore a new Internet site.

Locating Resources

Locating resources on the Internet is possible because each resource on the Internet has an address. There are special programs called browsers that use these resource addresses and search engines to help users find information on a specific topic.

Internet Names

Every resource on the Internet has its own location identifier or Uniform Resource Locator (URL). The URLs specify the server to access as well as the access method and the location.

A URL consists of several parts. The simplest version contains:

- The protocol to be used
- A colon
- The address of the resource

The address begins with two forward slashes. Aside from using forward slashes rather than backslashes, this is very similar to the universal naming convention (UNC) format. The address below is the entry for accessing the Microsoft World Wide Web server. The http: indicates the protocol you use. The rest of the entry, //www.microsoft.com, is the address of the computer.

```
http://www.microsoft.com
```

The entry below shows how to access the Microsoft FTP server. In this case, you are using the FTP protocol.

```
ftp://ftp.microsoft.com
```

Use the following URL to access the Microsoft Gopher server:

```
gopher://gopher.microsoft.com
```

Domain Name System (DNS)

In addition to URLs, every computer on the Internet has a unique IP address. The IP address is four sets of digits separated by dots: 198.46.8.34.

Because these strings of numbers are hard to remember and difficult to accurately type, the domain name system (DNS) was created. Domain names enable short, alphabetical names to be assigned to IP addresses to describe where a computer is located. In the example, http://www.microsoft.com, the domain name is www.microsoft.com.

The last three characters of the DNS or UNC address indicate the type of domain. Some domain types you might see with U.S. addresses:

com   Commercial organizations

edu   Educational institutions

gov   Government organizations (except the military)

mil   Military organizations

net   Network service providers

org   Organizations

Here are some examples of international domain designations:

au   Australia

fr   France

uk   United Kingdom

us   United States

Browsers

To browse the Web you need a graphical interface, called a Web browser. Some Web browsers are Mosaic, Netscape, and the Microsoft Internet Explorer. Once you have your browser and an Internet connection, accessing the Internet is fairly straightforward. The only problem is that there is so much information on so many sites. To solve this, several sites have been set up as Internet search sites. To access them all you need is their URL. Some of the more common search sites are:

Escapes   http://home.mcom.com/escapes/index.html

GNN Subscriber Info   http://www.gnn.com/

Netscape Search   http://home.netscape.com/home/internet-search.html

Open Text Web Index   http://www.opentext.com:8080/

Starting Point   http://www.stp.com/

Yahoo Search Server   http://www.yahoo.com/

Note Be sure to type the URL exactly as shown.

Making an Internet Connection

In order to access servers on the Internet, your computer needs to be connected to the Internet WAN.

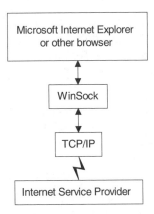

Figure 8.12 Making an Internet connection

There are currently two basic ways to physically connect to the Internet. The first is through dial-up lines, which you learned about in Chapter 7: Lesson 3, "Wide Area Network (WAN) Transmission." This is the most widely-used method. The second method for connecting to the Internet is an ISDN connection, which was discussed in Chapter7: Lesson 4, "Advanced WAN Technologies."

Dial-Up

There are several variations to the dial-up account which provide different capabilities, depending on the protocols used. All of these connections require the Internet Protocol, and are therefore called IP accounts. The three types of IP accounts are: point-to-point protocol (PPP), serial line Internet protocol (SLIP), and CSLIP, which is a compressed version of SLIP. PPP is the emerging connection of choice because it is faster and more reliable than other IP account types. But PPP is also more complex, so many computer platforms still only have built-in support for SLIP. Supplemental programs are being developed to enable most platforms to support PPP accounts. In addition to the increased flexibility of PPP, it also offers a dynamic allocation of IP addresses similar to dynamic host configuration protocol (DHCP), which makes logging on to the service simpler than having you provide a valid IP address. With a SLIP account an automated script is generally used to make logging on more automatic.

With both SLIP and PPP, the provider gives you a temporary IP address on the Internet and you can run any WinSock program (a program written to follow the Windows sockets specifications) on it. This includes graphical Web browsers such as Mosaic, Netscape, or the Microsoft Internet Explorer.

Commercial online services such as The Microsoft Network, CompuServe, America Online, and Prodigy™ often make a WinSock/PPP access method available either as part of their service or as an additional fee supplemental service.

ISDN

Integrated services digital network (ISDN) is a telecommunications service that connects networks through digital lines using a terminal adapter. ISDN provides a faster connection and can be more economical than dial-up service, if it is available in your local area code. In the future, ISDN boards designed to support ISDN connections through the personal computer will be commonplace.

Considerations

Theoretically, both the dial-up and the ISDN methods can connect single-user accounts or multiple-user accounts to the Internet. Dial-up accounts are probably most affordable for single-users, but ISDN provides a more economical solution (where available) for LANs, which connect multiple users at a specific location to the Internet.

If you connect directly to the Internet or are directly connected to a service provider, the computers on the Internet are essentially a part of your WAN, which means that you can access them directly. One issue with this is that you are also accessible to them, which may lead to potential security issues. For this reason, it is common for companies using a direct connection to set up a special machine, called a proxy agent, to act as a gateway between their local network and the Internet. The proxy agent filters requests over the gateway and makes it more difficult for unauthorized requests to reach the local network.

Summary

The Internet provides a wealth of information available through Internet providers and online services such as The Microsoft Network (MSN). Through these services you can access information in the World Wide Web and FTP servers. The WWW is a storehouse of hypertext documents through which you can browse for topics of interest. FTP servers are a good way of supporting remote networks. FTP servers allow access to files in a TCP/IP environment.

You can connect to these services either through dial-up lines or ISDN. Dial-up accounts are most affordable for single-users, but ISDN provides a more economical solution for local area networks.

Your Next Step

With your introduction to the Internet and all of the online help you will need to keep a network running smoothly, you have completed all of the lessons in this course. But you are not quite done yet. Do your last Checkup, Case Study, Troubleshooter, and LAN Planner to help reinforce what you have learned.

Chapter 8 Review

In Chapter 8, "Solving Network Problems," you learned how to manage and troubleshoot a network to keep it running in as trouble-free a condition as possible.

The best troubleshooting policy is prevention through planning and monitoring. Many potential problems can be avoided when the right strategies are incorporated into the planning stage of a network. These strategies deal with security, standardization, upgrades, and documentation.

Administrators can use a network operating system's built-in monitoring and management utilities. Microsoft Performance Monitor can help the administrator establish a performance baseline for use as a reference point in identifying network problems. It can also help identify bottlenecks that slow a network down.

When troubleshooting becomes necessary, the network technician can use a structured approach to isolate and solve a problem. The best network administrators and support engineers know they have to prioritize problems, collect information, identify possible causes, test, and study the results. Most network troubleshooting is performed on cabling problems.

There is a variety of tools the engineer can use to help solve network problems. These include TDRs, cable testers, network monitors, and network analyzers. Such tools are indispensable, but the new technician needs to be trained in their use.

There are many resources available to help with network management and troubleshooting. Microsoft TechNet, a compact disc and subscription service, provides technical information about all aspects of networking. Other resources for troubleshooting help include online bulletin board services, user groups, and periodicals.

The Internet is a vast storehouse of information where the network administrator or support engineer can access any topic of interest. The Internet provides services such as the World Wide Web and FTP servers. These resources can be accessed through an Internet provider such as The Microsoft Network (MSN).

Checkup

Follow the instructions for each exercise as indicated. All answers follow the last exercise.

Exercise 1: True or False

For the following sentences, circle True if the statement is true or False if the statement is false.

1. A performance monitoring program such as Performance Monitor can be used to identify trends over time. True   False

2. Most network problems occur at the OSI Physical layer. True   False

3. Network analyzers work at the Physical layer because that is where most network problems occur. True   False

4. The FTP utility acts as an agent to help users locate specific documents on the Internet. True   False

5. Network protocols can mask network problems because they attempt to overcome faults. True   False

6. The function of a TDR is to analyze and display information about packets. True   False

7. Microsoft TechNet is a service that provides access to the Internet. True   False

8. MSN is both an Internet access provider and an online service. True   False

9. Hypertext is a text-only method for presenting files that are linked together in a non-sequential web of associations. True   False

Exercise 2: Short Answer

Write a word or brief phrase to answer the following questions.

1. What are five areas that should be addressed in the network planning stage that will help keep network problems to a minimum?

   _____

   _____

2. Name three capabilities of Microsoft Performance Monitor.

   _____

   _____

3. What does a network administrator need to establish as a point of reference to aid in troubleshooting?

   _____

4. Name three Internet search sites.

   _____

   _____

   _____

5. What are three of the best known services available on the Internet that were covered in this self-paced training kit?

   _____

   _____

   _____

Checkup Answers

Exercise 1: True or False

1. True.

2. True.

3. False. Protocol analyzers, sometimes called network analyzers, perform a number of functions in real-time network traffic analysis as well as packet capture, decoding, and transmission. This means they work at a number of upper OSI model layers.

4. False. FTP (File Transfer Protocol) is a utility used to transfer files.

5. True.

6. False. A TDR (time-domain reflectometer) is a network troubleshooting tool that analyzes and displays problems related to cabling.

7. False. TechNet is a compact disc and subscription support service that provides help with network management.

8. True.

9. False. Hypertext is a method for presenting text, images, sound, and videos that are linked together in a non-sequential web of associations.

Exercise 2: Short Answer

1. Backups, security, standardization, upgrades, and documentation.

2. Any three of the following:
   - Analyze operation in both real time and recorded time.
   - Identify trends over time.
   - Identify bottlenecks.
   - Monitor the effects of system and configuration changes.
   - Determine system capacity.
   - Monitor local or remote computers.
   - Notify administrators of significant monitored events that exceed threshold values.
   - Track the performance of isolated processors, hard disks, memory, and processes.
   - View key system parameters as a whole.
   - Perform monitoring functions separately or simultaneously.

3. A baseline.

4. Any three of the following:

Escapes	http://home.mcom.com/escapes/index.html
GNN Subscriber Info	http://www.gnn.com/
Netscape Search	http://home.netscape.com/home/internet-search.html
Open Text Web Index	http://www.opentext.com:8080/
Starting Point	http://www.stp.com/
Yahoo Search Server	http://www.yahoo.com/

5. Any three of the following:

   World Wide Web

   File Transfer Protocol servers

   E-mail

   USENET

   Gopher

   Telnet

Case Study Problem

The Setting

You are upgrading your network server with a new operating system and a faster network adapter card.

The Problem

You do not want to disrupt network operations with the upgrade process, so you have decided to do it over the weekend. In the middle of performing the upgrade, you discover that the new network card does not have drivers for the new operating system you are installing.

Also, your boss has told you he wants some colorful, creative charts and graphs to help him show management that all of the money that was spent on the upgrade process was worthwhile.

Your Solution

1. What important task should be accomplished before making any changes to a network server?

   _____

2. List at least two important documents which you should have on hand for the upgrade process.

   _____

   _____

   _____

3. Once you discover that the new network card does not have drivers for the new operating system you are installing, where can you get the drivers? List two sources could you turn to for the necessary drivers late Saturday afternoon.

   _____

   _____

4. What type of data will you use to compare your new installation against the previous installation?

   _____

5. What tools can you use to gather performance data?

   _____

   _____

Case Study Suggested Solution

1. Before making any changes to a network server, a network administrator or support engineer should back up the data. Many engineers perform two backups just in case.

2. Important documents which should be available during an upgrade include:

   - Documentation for the original server hardware.
   - Documentation from the original installation.
   - Documentation for the new hardware.
   - Documentation for the new operating system.

3. Some sources to turn to for drivers late on a Saturday afternoon include:

   - The Internet
   - The Microsoft Network (MSN)
   - The manufacturer's BBS

4. The original baseline report can be compared with a baseline created for the new configuration. Hopefully the new installation will reflect improved performance.

5. Tools for gathering performance data include:

   - Performance Monitor
   - Network Analyzer
   - Other tools associated with your server's operating system, or third-party monitoring tools.

The Troubleshooter

The following troubleshooting questions are general in nature. You can use them to start your analysis of any network problem.

The System

1. Is this a brand new system which is untested or has the system been up and running for a while?

   Yes ____

   No ____

2. If the system did work correctly at one time, what has changed since then? (Any change to almost any part of the network hardware or software including configurations should be included here.)

   _____

   _____

   _____

3. Is the entire network down?

   Yes ____

   No ____

4. Is the problem isolated to just one computer?

   Yes ____

   No ____

5. Is this problem similar to a previous problem you have already solved?

   Yes ____

   No ____

   If the answer is yes, check the system's log.

6. Is there new equipment on the network?

   Yes ____

   No ____

7. Has any equipment been moved lately?

   Yes ____

   No ____

Applications

1. Was a new application program installed before the problem occurred?

   Yes _____

   No _____

2. Does the problem appear with all applications?

   Yes _____

   No _____

3. Do you have different revisions of anything including applications, operating systems, or other software on the network?

   Yes _____

   No _____

Vendors

1. Which vendors' products are involved?

   _____

   _____

   _____

2. Does the problem seem to be specific to certain vendors, certain versions or certain components such as cards, hubs, disk drives, application software, or network operating software?

   Yes _____

   No _____

Users

1. Is the problem limited to one user?

   Yes _____

   No _____

2. Is the problem limited to one group of users?

   Yes _____

   No _____

   If the answer is yes, which group of users is affected?

   _____

3. Were users affected randomly?

   Yes _____

   No _____

4. Are there new users on the network?

   Yes _____

   No _____

   If the answer is yes, how long have they been on the network, and how are they configured?

   _____

   _____

5. Are all of the new users affected?

   Yes _____

   No _____

   If the answer is no, what is the difference between the users who are affected and those who are not?

   _____

   _____

6. Has anyone else attempted to "fix" the network?

   Yes _____

   No _____

   If the answer is yes, who is it and what did they do?

   _____

   _____

7. Was the system working before they "fixed" it?

   Yes _____

   No _____

8. Has anyone reconfigured anything including components and the network operating system?

   Yes _____

   No _____

Timing

1. Does the problem occur only during certain times?

   Yes _____

   No _____

   If the answer is yes, what other events occur at that time that might affect the system?

   _____

   _____

2. Is the problem intermittent?

   Yes _____

   No _____

   If the answer is yes, do any other intermittent events occur at the same time?

   _____

   _____

3. Did the problem appear right after a change, such as an upgrade or the installation of a new network adapter card or printer?

   Yes _____

   No _____

   If the answer is yes, what changed?

   _____

   _____

Can You Solve This Problem?

Refer to the Chapter 8 lessons and the preceding questions to help you with the following situation.

The Situation

You are one of three network administrators responsible for a LAN that incorporates the following computers:

- 300 Microsoft Windows 95 client computers
- 5 Microsoft Windows NT Server-based computers
- 3 UNIX hosts

The Available Facts

Your supervisor is tired of paying for expensive consultants each time there is a problem with the network. She wants you to prepare a "wish list" of everything you would need to assume responsibilities for troubleshooting the network yourself.

Your Solution

1. What additional equipment will you need? List at least one type of troubleshooting and management equipment which would be helpful.

   _____

   _____

   _____

   _____

2. Attending training classes is a good means of learning technical information. In what areas of the system would it be good to receive some additional training? (List at least one type of course you might need.)

   _____

   _____

3. What additional periodicals will you need to help you stay on top of the issues concerning your network? (List any that you currently know of.)

   _____

   _____

   _____

   _____

4. What kind of network support services will you want to access?

   _____

   _____

   _____

Suggested Troubleshooting Solution

Planning for network troubleshooting is a complex task. The situation used here was designed to help you think through some of the issues involved, but it is not designed to be an exhaustive list.

The solution provided here is only a suggested list, but it includes the most common and essential items that should be part of every administrator's network resource kit.

1. Helpful troubleshooting and management equipment would include:

   - Microsoft Systems Management Server (SMS).
   - A protocol analyzer.
   - A time-domain reflectometer for your cable type.

2. Essential training would include:

   - Installation, troubleshooting, and maintenance courses for each operating system you are maintaining and troubleshooting.

     You might also want to pursue certifications in those operating systems.

   - Courses and certification for monitoring and troubleshooting equipment.

3. There are many periodicals which can help you keep up with the networking industry including:

   - PC Week
   - LAN Magazine
   - LAN Times
   - Data Communications
   - Windows NT Magazine

4. Some places where network support can be found include:

   - The Internet
   - The Microsoft Network (MSN)
   - Microsoft TechNet
   - Bulletin boards (BBSs)

The LAN Planner

This LAN Planner presents a list of questions which will help you decide on the documentation, the tools, and the training you will need to be an effective network troubleshooter. Some of the questions will not apply to all situations but are included here so that you can select what you need for your specific environment.

1. Do you have documentation for all of the operating systems and applications you will maintain, and is that documentation easily accessible to you?

   Yes _____

   No _____

   If the answer is yes, where is it located?

   _____

   If the answer is no, what is missing?

   _____

   _____

   _____

2. Do you have documentation and driver disks for all of the hardware platforms and additional hardware on your network, and is that documentation easily available?

   Yes _____

   No _____

   If the answer is yes, where is it located?

   _____

   If the answer is no, what is missing?

   _____

   _____

   _____

3. Do you have all of the training and expertise you need to support all of the hardware and software on your network?

   Yes _____

   No _____

   If the answer is no, can you schedule the training?

   Yes _____

   No _____

4. Do you have access to Internet providers such as MSN so that you can find help and download new drivers?

   Yes _____

   No _____

5. Do you have subscriptions to several industry periodicals?

   Yes _____

   No _____

6. Do you have subscriptions to a troubleshooting knowledge base (such as Microsoft TechNet, or the NetWare Support Encyclopedia) for all of the operating systems and hardware vendors that you support?

   Yes _____

   No _____

   If the answer is no, list the subscriptions you need:

   _____

   _____

7. Which troubleshooting and management tools are included in your network software?

   _____

   _____

8. What other troubleshooting and management tools are available to you?

   _____

   _____

9. Which important troubleshooting and management tools are you missing?

   _____

   _____

10. Do you know how to use the troubleshooting and management tools included in your network operating systems, as well as any others you might have?

    Yes _____

    No _____

    If the answer is no, how do you plan to gain this knowledge? (Check all that apply.)

    - Formal instructor-led, classroom training: _____
    - For which tools?

Tool	Training provider	Location	Dates
_____	_____	_____	_____
_____	_____	_____	_____
_____	_____	_____	_____

    - Self-paced training: _____
      For which tools? _____
      Source of training: _____
    - Hands-on field experience: _____
      For which tools? _____

11. Do you have a list of technical support telephone numbers for all of the hardware and software on your network?

    Yes ＿＿＿＿

    No ＿＿＿＿

    If the answer is yes, where is it located?

    ＿＿＿＿＿＿＿＿＿＿＿＿＿＿＿＿＿＿＿＿＿＿＿＿＿＿＿＿＿＿

    If the answer is no, which ones are you missing?

    ＿＿＿＿＿＿＿＿＿＿＿＿＿＿＿＿＿＿＿＿＿＿＿＿＿＿＿＿＿＿

    ＿＿＿＿＿＿＿＿＿＿＿＿＿＿＿＿＿＿＿＿＿＿＿＿＿＿＿＿＿＿

    ＿＿＿＿＿＿＿＿＿＿＿＿＿＿＿＿＿＿＿＿＿＿＿＿＿＿＿＿＿＿

12. Do you have a consultant or vendor you trust who will be available to help you when you cannot solve the problem on your own?

    Yes ＿＿＿＿

    No ＿＿＿＿

    If the answer is yes, what is the consultant's name and contact number?

    ＿＿＿＿＿＿＿＿＿＿＿＿＿＿＿＿＿＿＿＿＿＿＿＿＿＿＿＿＿＿

The LAN Planner Summary

1. Documentation location: _____

2. Network adapter card driver location: _____

3. Documentation and drivers you need:

Operating system/application	Vendor
_____	_____
_____	_____
_____	_____

Equipment	Vendor
_____	_____
_____	_____
_____	_____

4. Online services to which you have access:

Service	Access procedure
_____	_____
	_____
_____	_____
	_____
_____	_____
	_____
_____	_____
	_____

5. Location of the documentation for the services:

_____

6. Contact numbers:

Consultant or vendor	Product or area of expertise	Contact number
_____	_____	_____
_____	_____	_____
_____	_____	_____
_____	_____	_____
_____	_____	_____

To help you bridge the gap between this kit and an actual networking environment, this kit includes Appendix B, "Network Planning and Implementation." It draws concepts from the entire kit and applies them to implementing a LAN. Actually, you have been doing something similar in small pieces at the end of each chapter in each LAN Planner. Appendix B ties it all together and acts as a transition from learning about LANs in a book to getting involved with networking on a real site.

Appendix A: Common Network Standards and Specifications

The Role of Standards in Networking

Most networks are a combination of hardware and software from a variety of vendors. The ability to combine these products from different vendors is the result of industry standards.

Standards are guidelines vendors voluntarily adhere to in order to make their products compatible with products from other vendors. In general those standards address:

- Size
- Shape
- Material
- Function
- Speed
- Distance

More specifically, the standards define physical and operational characteristics of:

- Personal computing equipment
- Networking and communication equipment
- Operating systems
- Software

For example, standards make it possible to buy a network adapter card from one vendor for a computer from another vendor with reasonable assurance that card will:

- Fit into your computer.
- Work with your network cabling.
- Translate signals from your computer and send them out onto the network.
- Receive data from the network and deliver it to your computer.

When a vendor subscribes to a set of standards, it means that the vendor will make equipment that conforms to the specifications of the standard.

Standards have, in fact, been responsible for the success and growth of both the computer and networking products industries.

The Origin of Standards

Standards have grown primarily from two sources:

- Popular acceptance (customer driven)
- Organization recommendations

Customer-driven standards emerge from popular acceptance. The best example of this is the term "PC compatible," which means that a product will work with an IBM PC or clone. As the networking business grew in the mid- and late-1980s, it became apparent that customer-driven popularity was not adequate for creating and imposing standards.

The Influence of the Business Community

In the early years of networking, several large companies, including IBM, Honeywell, and Digital Equipment Corporation, had their own proprietary standards for how computers could be connected.

These standards described how to move data from one computer to another, but the standards only applied if all of the computers were made by the same company. There were real problems getting equipment from one vendor to communicate with equipment from another vendor.

For example, networks adhering to IBM's complex networking architecture called Systems Network Architecture (SNA) could not directly communicate with networks using Digital's Digital Network Architecture (DNA).

As networking technology matured, businesses began to trust crucial data to networking. But in the mid-1980s, the same communication problems existed between network vendors that had existed earlier among mainframe vendors. The increasing need for businesses to interact and share data was inescapable.

Computer manufacturers saw this as a business opportunity. They realized that networking technology which enabled communication by conforming to standards would be far more profitable in the long run than equipment which would only work in a single-vendor environment. As a result, standards gradually became a part of the computer and network environment.

The Influence of the Technical Community

Today, certain domestic and international organizations, rather than customers, create and define nearly all networking technical standards.

Some of these organizations have existed for many years and some, like the SQL Access Group, recently evolved out of necessity as new applications appeared. These in turn created new networking environments that required new guidelines.

Although there are probably dozens of organizations currently advocating standards of every description, only a few have gained the recognition required to enlist the support of major computing vendors. These associations and organizations have become the foundation upon which network acceptance is based. Therefore, network engineers need to be familiar with the names of the organizations and the networking areas they influence.

Standards Organizations

There is no one source for standards. Usually, a standards organization will coordinate the specifications for various pieces of equipment or set the parameters for features or functions. However, sometimes a need will set events in motion which result in a standard through consensus or through the action of the market place.

Most local and international network standards originate with ten organizations. Each of these organizations defines standards for a different area of network activity. The organizations are:

1. American National Standards Institute (ANSI)

2. Common Open Software Environment (COSE)

3. Comité Consultatif Internationale de Télégraphie et Téléphonie (CCITT)

4. Corporation for Open Systems (COS)

5. Electronics Industries Association (EIA)

6. Institute of Electrical and Electronics Engineers, Inc. (IEEE)

7. International Standards Organization (ISO)

8. Object Management Group (OMG)

9. Open Software Foundation (OSF)

10. SQL Access Group (SAG)

It is important to be aware of these organizations because their acronyms have become part of the common network vocabulary.

American National Standards Institute (ANSI)

ANSI is an organization of United States industry and business groups dedicated to the development of trade and communication standards. ANSI defines and publishes standards for:

- Codes
- Alphabets
- Signaling schemes

ANSI also represents the United States in the International Standards Organization (ISO) and the Comité Consultatif Internationale de Télégraphie et Téléphonie (CCITT).

ANSI in Microcomputers

In the microcomputer field, ANSI is commonly encountered in three areas:

- Programming languages
- The SCSI interface
- The Ansi.sys device driver

Network languages such as FORTRAN, COBOL, and C conform to ANSI recommendations to eliminate problems in transporting a program from one type of computer system or environment to another.

ANSI Specifications

Major ANSI specifications and standards include:

- ANSI 802.1–1985/IEEE 802.5—Token Ring access, protocols, cabling, and interface.
- ANSI/IEEE 802.3—Coaxial cable carrier sense, multiple access/collision detection (CSMA/CD) for Ethernet networks.
- ANSI X3.135—Structured Query Language (SQL) database query methods for front-end clients and back-end database services.
- ANSI X3.92—A privacy and security encryption algorithm.
- ANSI X12—Electronic data interchange (EDI) defining the exchange of purchase orders, bills of lading, invoices, and other business forms.
- ANSI X3T9.5—Fiber distributed data interface (FDDI) specification for voice and data transmission over fiber-optic cable at 100 Mbps.
- SONET—Fiber-optic specification defining a global infrastructure for the transmission of synchronous and isochronous (time-sensitive data such as real-time video) information.

Common Open Software Environment (COSE)

The goal of this consortium of vendors is to develop a common UNIX desktop environment (CDE). The vendors include:

- IBM
- Hewlett-Packard
- SunSoft™
- Novell

COSE Objectives

The COSE objectives are:

- Develop a specification that provides application program interfaces (APIs) for a common desktop graphical environment that is supported on the vendor's systems.
- Adopt common networking environments.
- Identify graphics, multimedia, and object technology for endorsement.
- Define system management and administration for distributed systems.

The COSE Specification

The COSE specification addresses:

- Communication and message passing among applications
- Data display
- Editing
- Object management
- Window management
- Desktop integration
- Cut and paste
- Drag and drop

To realize its goals, COSE incorporates a variety of elements and features from the following vendors and technologies:

- Hewlett-Packard
- IBM
- Open Software Foundation
- SunSoft
- UNIX System Laboratories
- Sun®
- Standard Generalized Markup Language (SGML)
- Multipurpose Internet Mail Extension (MIME)

A set of COSE specifications defines programming interfaces that promote the portability of applications between operating systems.

Comité Consultatif Internationale de Télégraphie et Téléphonie (CCITT)

The CCITT, which is also known as the International Telegraph and Telephone Consultative Committee, is based in Geneva, Switzerland. It was established as part of the United Nations International Telecommunications Union (ITU). The CCITT studies and recommends use of communications standards that are recognized throughout the world, and publishes these recommendations every four years.

Each update is distinguished by the color of its cover. The 1988 edition is known as the Blue Book. The 1992 edition is known as the White Book.

CCITT Protocols

CCITT protocols apply to:

- Modems
- Networks
- Facsimile transmission

The CCITT Study Groups

The CCITT has been divided into 15 study groups with each group preparing recommendations for standards in a different subject area. These subject areas include:

- A and B   Working procedures, terms, and definitions
- D and E   Tariffs
- F   Telegraph, telemetric, and mobile services
- G and H   Transmissions
- I   Integrated services digital network (ISDN)
- J   Television transmission
- K and L   Protection of facilities
- M and N   Maintenance
- P   Telephone transmission
- R–U   Terminal and telegraph services
- V   Data communication over telephone networks
- X   Data communication networks

The V Series

The recommendations for standardizing modem design and operations (transmission over telephone networks) are collectively called the V series. These include:

- V.22   1200 bps full-duplex modem standard
- V.22bis   2400 bps full-duplex modem standard
- V.28   Defines circuits in RS-232 interface
- V.32   Asynchronous and synchronous 4800/9600 bps standard
- V.32bis   Asynchronous and synchronous standard up to 14,400 bps
- V.35   Defines high data-rates over combined circuits
- V.42   Defines error-checking standards
- V.42bis   Defines modem compression using Lempel Ziv method
- V.terbo   An emerging standard that provides 19.2 Kbps rates

The X Series

The X series covers Open Systems Interconnection (OSI) standards including:

- X.200 (ISO 7498) OSI reference model
- X.25 (ISO 7776)   Packet-switching network interface
- X.400 (ISO10021) Message handling (e-mail)
- X.500 (ISO 9594) Directory services
- X.700 (ISO 9595) Common management information protocol (CMIP)

Corporation for Open Systems (COS)

COS attempts to ensure interoperability among vendors subscribing to standards for:

- OSI
- ISDN

COS also provides the following for OSI products:

- Conformance testing
- Certification
- Promotion of OSI products

Electronics Industries Association (EIA)

The EIA is an organization founded in 1924 of U.S. manufacturers of electronic parts and equipment. It develops industry standards for the interface between data processing and communications equipment, and has published many standards associated with telecommunication and computer communication. The EIA works closely with other associations such as ANSI and CCITT.

EIA Serial Interface Standards

The EIA standards for the serial interface between modems and computers include:

- RS-232—A standard for serial connections using DB-9 or DB-25 connectors and maximum cable lengths of 50 feet. It defines the serial connections between DTE (data terminal equipment—transmitting equipment) devices and DCE (data communications equipment—receiving equipment) devices.

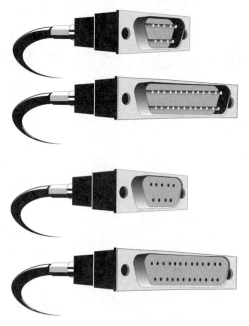

Appendix Figure 1: RS-232, DB-9, and DB-25 connectors

- RS-449—A serial interface with DB-37 connections that defines the RS-422 and RS-423 as subsets.
- RS-422—Defines a balanced multipoint interface.
- RS-423—Defines an unbalanced digital interface.

CCITT Equivalents

EIA standards often have CCITT equivalents. RS-232, for example, is also the CCITT V.24 standard.

Institute of Electrical and Electronics Engineers, Inc. (IEEE)

The Institute of Electrical and Electronics Engineers, Inc. (IEEE) is a United States-based society that publishes a variety of standards including those for data communications.

The 802 Committees

A subgroup of the IEEE, the 802 committees began developing network specifications in 1980 to ensure low-cost interfaces. These specifications are passed on to the ANSI for approval and standardization within the United States. They are also forwarded to the ISO.

Shortly after the 802 project began, the IEEE realized that a single network standard would be inadequate because it would not be able to account for the diverse hardware and emerging architectures. To adequately cover the wide range of subjects, the society established 12 committees that would be responsible for defining standards in different networking areas.

The 802 Committees

The twelve 802 committees are as follows:

802.1	Internetworking
802.2	Logical Link Control (LLC)
802.3	CSMA/CD NETWORK (Ethernet)
802.4	Token Bus NETWORK
802.5	Token Ring NETWORK
802.6	Metropolitan Area Network (MAN)
802.7	Broadband Technical Advisory Group
802.8	Fiber-Optic Technical Advisory Group
802.9	Integrated Voice/Data Networks
802.10	Network Security
802.11	Wireless Networks
802.12	Demand Priority Access NETWORK (100VG-AnyLAN)

International Standards Organization (ISO)

The International Standards Organization (ISO) is a Paris-based international organization of member countries, each of which is represented by its leading standard-setting organization. For example, ANSI represents the United States, and the British Standards Institution (BSI) represents the United Kingdom. Other organizations represented at the ISO include:

- Government bodies such as the U.S. State Department
- Businesses
- Educational institutes
- Research organizations
- CCITT

The ISO works to establish international standardization of all services and manufactured products.

ISO Computer Communication Goals

In the area of computers, the ISO's goal is to establish global standards for communications and information exchange. The standards will promote open networking environments that let multivendor computer systems communicate with one another using protocols that have been accepted internationally by the ISO members.

The ISO Model

The ISO's major achievement in the area of networks and communications was to define a set of standards, known as the OSI (Open Systems Interconnection) model which defines standards for the interaction of computers connected by communications networks.

Object Management Group (OMG)

The OMG consists of almost 300 organizations involved in developing a suite of languages, interfaces, and protocol standards that vendors can use to create applications that will operate in multivendor environments.

The OMG certifies products designed to meet the standards and specifications agreed upon by the OMG members.

In working toward its goals, the OMG developed the Object Management Architecture (OMA), a model for object-oriented applications and environments.

The OMG architecture has been adopted by the Open Software Foundation (OSF), which is developing portable software environments called the distributed computing environment (DCE) and the distributed management environment (DME).

The OMG standards are similar to elements in Microsoft OLE. OMG members include:

- Digital Equipment Corporation
- Hewlett-Packard
- HyperDesk Corporation
- SunSoft

Open Software Foundation (OSF)

The OSF creates computing environments by acquiring and combining technologies from other vendors and then distributing the results to interested parties.

These vendor-neutral environments, referred to as the Open System Software Environment, can be used to create a collection of open systems technologies in which users can incorporate software and hardware from several sources.

The following components comprise the OSF software environment:

- Distributed Computing Environment (DCE)

  This platform simplifies the development of products in a mixed environment.

- Distributed Management Environment (DME)

  The DME makes tools available for managing systems in distributed and mixed-vendor environments.

- The Open Software Foundation/1 (OSF/1)

  This is a UNIX operating system, based on the Mach kernel, which supports symmetric multiprocessing, enhanced security features, and dynamic configuration.

- OSF/Motif

  This is a graphical user interface that creates a common environment with links to IBM's Common User Access (CUA).

- OSF Architecture-Neutral Distribution Format (ANDF)

  Developers can use this environment to create a single version of an application that can be used on different hardware architectures.

SQL Access Group (SAG)

SAG is a consortium of 39 companies that was founded in 1989 by Hewlett-Packard, Digital, Oracle Corporation, and Sun Microsystems. Its charter is to work with the ISO to create standards covering the interoperability of front- and back-end systems.

SAG's purpose is to promote interoperability among structured query language (SQL) standards so that several SQL-based relational databases and tools can work together in a multivendor database environment. This will make it possible for different database applications running on different platforms to share and exchange data.

SAG Technical Specifications

SAG has developed three technical specifications:

- Structured Query Language

    This is a specification that follows international specifications in implementing the SQL language.

- SQL Remote Database Access

    This specification defines communication between a remote database server and an SQL-based client.

- SQL Access Call-Level Interface (CLI)

    This group of APIs provides interfacing with SQL-based products.

Appendix B: Network Planning and Implementation

This appendix combines information from all of the LAN Planners presented throughout the kit. You can use it as a guide when you plan and implement your first network.

In this document planning and implementation are divided into the following phases:

- Planning concerns
- The plan
- Implementation
- Expanding the network
- Post-installation support

Planning Concerns

This section explores some of the issues you should consider before proceeding with the actual plan.

Establishing the Need for a Network

You may examine several factors and realize your organization does not need a network. If, for example, the only reason you believe you need a network is to share a printer, there may be alternatives such as print switch boxes.

Identifying the Benefits

What are the benefits you think a network can provide? Are those achievable, and are they worth the effort and expense? Will they make your organization more efficient? You should be able to present the need for a network in terms of how it will help the organization.

Your organization could probably benefit from a network if:

- Coworkers exchange files by swapping disks more than once a day.
- Several users need a high-quality printer.
- People are having trouble finding, sharing, and copying data.
- Employees share physical filing cabinets or manually access data in any kind of shared filing cabinet.

Uses for the Network

It is important to identify the uses your organization may have for a network. The possibilities include: (Check any that apply to your organization).

- Communication ____
- Information sharing ____
- File sharing ____
- File sharing between environments (Macintosh and PC) ____
- Minicomputer or mainframe access ____
- Better computer management ____
- Centralized backup of all data ____
- Controlled access to sensitive data ____
- Localized control of information as opposed to having it on the company's mainframe ____

Planning for the Whole Network

To thoroughly plan for a network you need to consider more than the hardware, cabling, and operating system. Be sure to include the following in your network plan:

- Training
- Documentation
- Transitioning from a stand-alone environment to the LAN

The Role of a Consultant

If you are facing anything more challenging than a 10-user peer-to-peer installation, you should consider hiring some expertise. However, some organizations believe they can simply turn over the entire project to a consultant and trust that it will work out correctly.

While a consultant or some kind of expert help will probably be necessary, it is a good idea to do preliminary network planning before bringing in a consultant. This is because the act of planning will present information that will be important in discussions with the consultant. This appendix will provide you with the background you can use when meeting with a consultant to review the project.

The LAN Planning Workbook

It is common for vendors to offer some kind of workbook-style exercise that will take you step-by-step through selecting the appropriate hardware, software, installation, training, and support.

This workbook may take as long as a day to fill out completely and correctly. The completed information should be reviewed by a certified, experienced systems engineer. You will then sit down with one of their engineers to review your plan.

If your vendor does not offer a detailed, structured, written proposal, but rather prefers to simply go ahead with starting the installation, stop the process. You need to have a qualified professional first review the vendor's plans.

The Network Staff

Identify the people who will be involved in implementing and managing the network. You need to bring those who will be responsible for supporting the network into the planning stages.

If the LAN will consist of more than 20 computers, there will be more than enough planning work for several people to do. The planning can be divided into several areas of responsibility, and the LAN project leader can assign people to appropriate tasks.

Your Organization

Understanding and preparing for the human side of a network installation, especially a large one, can affect the success of the system just as much as the hardware and software can.

You should gather information that takes into account your organization's:

- History

   Has the organization welcomed change?

- Projected growth

   This will have a direct effect on the network.

- Operating policies

   How difficult will it be to appropriate the necessary hardware and software?

- Working environment

   Are they afraid of the coming network? Will they accept it as an opportunity to learn? This will affect how the network is implemented.

- Office systems and procedures

   This will affect support.

The Plan

Traditional LAN planning consists of three steps:

1. Gather as much data as possible.
2. Explore all possible implementations for your site.
3. Choose the best price and performance component combination available.

However, this type of research and planning is not usually successful because it:

- Takes an enormous amount of time.
- Is expensive.
- Does not always result in the best possible LAN implementation.

This is because there are so many variables involved in every aspect of a LAN.

The Default Network Plan

Networking professionals usually plan a network by starting with a preplanned LAN.

Instead of researching every possible component which might be appropriate for their network and narrowing the list down, networking professionals start with a predetermined "good for most situations" network plan which they alter to fit each individual situation. It is much easier to develop a plan from this perspective than to choose each component from scratch.

These are generic configurations that will work in many environments. If they work for your site, you can use the default plan and will not have to do much further design work for your network.

The following chart outlines what is probably the most common LAN configuration being implemented today for networks serving up to 50 users. It is a combination network, meaning it has elements of both peer-to-peer and server-based networks.

Component/feature	Implementation
Topology	Star bus
Cable	Category 5 UTP
Network adapters	Ethernet 10BaseT
Hubs	Ethernet 10BaseT

(continued)

Component/feature	Implementation
Resource sharing	Combination server-based with computers that can share resources in a peer-to-peer fashion. All resources that need any type of centralized control are shared from the server, and all others are shared from a few client computers.
Printer sharing	Most customers prefer to connect their publicly shared printers directly to the network cable using one of the network direct printing cards, and share it using software which allows the network server to function as a spooler for the printer. (This software is usually included in either the server operating system, or with the direct connect printing device.)
Other specialized services/servers	Implemented as needed for faxing, e-mail, modem pooling, network dial-in, database, and so on. Many of these specialty servers can be implemented as add-on software to a dedicated network server, although as the LAN grows in size it may be advantageous to dedicate individual servers to each task.

This default configuration was chosen because it is the most common and easy to implement. Also, finding resources for supporting this type of network is not difficult. As you gain experience you may develop your own default configuration which might differ from what is here. Because changing market conditions and many other factors affect what is installed, keeping up with current technology is a must for a networking professional.

The Map

As the plans materialize, draw a picture of the network. It will help you visualize what your system will need.

It may be a good idea to draw an actual picture of the physical layout of the company including different departments. This will help clarify the topology and any cabling challenges. If nothing else, this will help create a realistic picture of the implementation.

For example, if the organization occupies more than one building, you may have to start thinking in terms of a WAN.

Is the Preplanned LAN Adequate?

The preplanned network is adequate for most networks. However, there may be reasons why it will not work for your site including:

- Speed
- Security
- The number of servers
- The number and type of printers
- Non-standard software requirements
- Cost

If the preplanned network does not provide the specifications or the detail your site needs, continue to the following section.

Choosing Network Components

If the preplanned network configuration is not adequate, the following sections will help identify the appropriate components for your site.

Type of Network

If the combination network will not work, you may change to:

- Peer-to-peer only
- Server-based only

The following questions will help you to determine which type of network is appropriate for your site.

1. Is there a need for security on your network such that it would be inappropriate to share any resources which are not centrally controlled by user name, password authentication, and user-level security?

   Yes _____ You should have only server-based sharing on your network

   No _____ Use the default combination-based network

2. Is your network:
   - Small (less than 10 users)
   - Without a need for centralized security
   - Unlikely to grow

   Yes to all _____ Change design to peer-to-peer only

   No to any _____ Use the default combination-based network

Network Architecture

If Ethernet will not work, you may want to change your network architecture. The following questions will help you determine which is appropriate for your environment.

1. Do you have a need for 100 Mbps networking?

   Yes _____ Use 100baseTX or 100BaseVG-AnyLAN

   No _____ Use the default network plan

2. Do you have a need to use a specific topology other than 10BaseT because of connectivity, or existing network or cable issues?

   Yes _____ Use the required network architecture

   No _____ Use the default network plan architecture

Cabling

If Category 5 UTP is not adequate, you may need to change cabling. The following questions will help determine which cable is appropriate for your environment.

1. Do you have a need for network cabling which is immune to electromagnetic interference (EMI)?

   Yes _____ Fiber-optic cable

   No _____ Use the default network plan cabling

2. Do you have a need for network cabling which is relatively secure from most eavesdropping or corporate intelligence gathering equipment?

   Yes _____ Fiber-optic cable

   No _____ Use the default network plan cabling

3. Do you have a need for network transmission speeds which are higher than those supported by copper media?

   Yes _____ Fiber-optic cable

   No _____ Use the default network plan cabling

4. Do you have a need for longer cabling distances than those supported by UTP?

   Yes _____ Fiber-optic cable or maybe coaxial cable

   No _____ Use the default network plan cabling

5. Do you have some cable runs which exceed the 10BaseT specifications?

   Yes _____ Consider using 10BaseF (fiber-optic Ethernet) for those runs

   No _____ Use the default network plan cabling

6. Do users on your network need to work at remote sites away from their networked computer?

Yes _____ Wireless, depends on other factors

No _____ Use the default network plan

7. Is usable cable already in place, and would it be worth the savings to use it?

Yes _____

No _____ Use the default network plan cabling

The Network Adapter Card

The following questions will help you determine if the network adapter card you have chosen will work with your other choices.

1. Is the card compatible with the cable type and topology you have chosen?

Yes _____

No _____

2. Does the hardware you are planning to buy come with drivers for the type of computer, operating system, and network adapter card you plan to use with it?

Yes _____

No _____

3. Has the vendor of the operating system software you want to use tested the card and driver you plan to purchase in the type of computer you want to install it in?

Yes _____

No _____

4. Is the card compatible with the bus type of the computer into which it will be installed?

Yes _____

No _____ Find a card that is

5. Do any of the computers in your organization ever need to communicate with any other equipment that requires a specific type of architecture? In older mainframe and minicomputer environments, for example, it easier to implement Token Ring than trying to make Ethernet communicate. Digital Equipment hosts, however, traditionally accept Ethernet.

Yes _____ You may have to use that as a default

No _____

The Network Protocol(s)

The following questions will help you determine the appropriate protocol(s). If you answer yes to more than one question in a protocol section, it indicates that you should add that protocol to your network.

NWLink IPX (or Novell IPX)

1. Is IPX the default protocol for the network operating system you are installing?

   Yes _____

   No _____

2. Does the network software you are installing support IPX?

   Yes _____

   No _____

3. Does the network need to support routing?

   Yes _____

   No _____

4. Do you have to support network servers or clients running Novell NetWare server or client software?

   Yes _____

   No _____

   If you answered yes to more than one of these questions, install IPX.

TCP/IP

1. Is TCP/IP the default protocol for the network operating system you are installing?

   Yes _____

   No _____

2. Does the network software you are installing support TCP/IP?

   Yes _____

   No _____

3. Does the network need to support routing?

   Yes _____

   No _____

4. Do the computers on the network need to access the Internet? (The primary supported protocol on the Internet is TCP/IP.)

   Yes _____

   No _____

5. Do you have to support network clients and servers from multiple vendors? (Most network software vendors support TCP/IP either in their base product, or as an add-on.)

   Yes _____

   No _____

   If you answered yes to more than one of these questions, install TCP/IP.

AppleTalk

1. Is AppleTalk the default protocol for the network operating system you are installing?

   Yes _____

   No _____

2. Do any of the computers you are installing require support for AppleTalk? (Macintoshes have AppleTalk built in to the operating system.)

   Yes _____

   No _____

3. Does the network need to support routing?

   Yes _____

   No _____

4. Does the network software you are installing support AppleTalk?

   Yes _____

   No _____

Based on the information generated in the LAN Planner, your network protocols should be: (list all that apply)

_____

_____

_____

_____

Network Printing

1. Are there particular users or groups of users who will produce an exceptional amount of printed output?

   Yes _____

   No _____

   If the answer is yes, identify a suitable printer location as close as possible to that person or group.

   Printer locations:

   Printer A: _____

   Printer B: _____

   Printer C: _____

   Printer D: _____

   Other printers: _____

   If the answer is no, determine a location as close to the middle of the users as possible. Printer locations will also need storage space for printer supplies such as paper and toner.

2. Are print jobs at certain printers spending too much time in print queues?

   Yes _____ Consider buying more printers

   No _____

3. Are there printers for each group that has been identified as producing a lot of printer output?

   Yes _____

   No _____ Consider buying more printers

   Based on the number of locations and the estimate of printer output, how many printers will your organization need? _____

4. How many of each of the following components do you already have, and how many will you need to add to your network?

Device	Number on hand	Number needed
Print servers	_____	_____
Computers (for peer-to-peer)	_____	_____
Direct connections	_____	_____
Dedicated print server devices	_____	_____

E-mail

1. Do you plan to share e-mail with other users outside of your company?

   Yes _____ Identify an e-mail vendor

   No _____

   If your answer was yes, you will need to identify a gateway which will translate between the two environments. This may require some consulting with a network engineer.

2. Your e-mail gateway is: _____

The Client/Server Environment

1. Are you planning on running the following applications in a non-client/server environment?

   Database _____

   Groupware _____

2. If you checked either choice, are there more than 10 people using that application?

   Yes _____ Consider implementing a client/server version of that application

   No _____ Use a stand-alone application

Planning Network and Data Security

The following questions will help you determine what kind of security your network will need. The key is the sensitivity of your data. If your network will be sharing very sensitive data, you should consider a centralized, server-based system regardless of the number of users it will serve. There are also questions related to keeping your data safe.

Security Issues

1. Does your organization work with sensitive data?

    Yes _____ You need centralized security

    No _____

2. Do you want to put most shared resources on dedicated servers, but leave some to be shared in a peer-to-peer fashion?

    Yes _____ Implement a combination of centralized and peer-to-peer security

    No _____

3. Do you want to give permissions to resources by group membership? (Many administrators prefer to give users individual rights to their personal network storage, and to use groups to give permissions to all other shared network resources.)

    Yes _____

    No _____

Fill in the following chart to help you organize network accounts into groups.

If your network needs more groups, create a larger chart and include it in your network log.

Group name	Resources	Levels of permission
_____	_____	_____
	_____	_____
	_____	_____
	_____	_____
_____	_____	_____
	_____	_____
	_____	_____
	_____	_____
_____	_____	_____
	_____	_____
	_____	_____
	_____	_____

4. Where will your network's servers be located? If there is sensitive data on the network, the servers should be in secure locations.

Server name or designation	Location

5. Are there people in your organization or visitors who should not have access to any of the network resources?

Yes _____ Implement passwords and develop a password policy

No _____

6. Is the environment in your organization such that passwords could get passed around, borrowed, or even stolen?

Yes _____ Implement passwords that require renewal after a specified period of time

No _____

7. Is there sensitive data so that easily discovered passwords, such as obvious names, obvious personal dates such as birthdays, or social security numbers, need to be prevented?

Yes _____ Consider implementing passwords that maintain a history and force users to periodically create new, unique passwords

No _____

8. Is there a possibility that some of the users at your site would attempt to use someone else's computer without permission or log on to the network under someone else's name without permission?

Yes _____ Lock accounts if an incorrect password is entered several successive times

No _____

9. Is there a need to monitor or restrict access to any particularly sensitive network resources or peripherals or a need to identify which users have accessed which resources over given periods of time?

Yes _____ Implement auditing

No _____

10. Is there a concern that non-permanent employees, or even permanent employees, will intentionally copy data to disks and take it off the premises or download data and misuse it?

    Yes _____ Consider diskless computers

    No _____

11. Will any of your data be so sensitive that it could be used against your organization if were to become the property of the wrong person or organization?

    Yes _____ Implement encryption

    No _____

Avoiding Data Loss

1. Are your computers currently protected from viruses?

    Yes _____

    No _____ Be sure to include virus protection in your network

2. Who will be primarily responsible for backing up the system?

    _____

3. Where are the backup tapes and the backup schedule located?

    _____

4. Does your facility have power conditioning and online power backup?

    Yes _____

    No _____ Consider a UPS

5. Can your organization afford to have any network downtime when the server fails?

    Yes _____

    No _____ Consider a redundancy (RAID) system

6. Is the fastest possible performance more important than budget in a redundancy system?

    Yes _____ Consider RAID 5, striping with parity

    No _____

Network Performance

The following questions will help you implement appropriate network monitoring.

1. Are any network monitoring tools built in to the network operating system you are considering?

   Yes _____

   No _____ Identify a monitoring tool or tools for your environment

2. Who will be responsible for monitoring your network's behavior?

   _____

3. Where is your network's log located and who keeps it?

   _____

4. Who is responsible for creating and monitoring a performance baseline?

   _____

Implementation

The Installation

The installation process is the critical factor in having a smooth running network. The network planners should also oversee installation.

Questions you will need to address regarding this phase of the process include:

- How will the transition from the old environment to the new network be made?
- How long will this take?
- What types of events, such as strategy meetings and training, will occur during the transition, and when?

Vendor Installation

If your organization has decided to have a vendor install the network, there are several questions that need to be answered before proceeding with the actual installation:

- How will be vendor be chosen?
- Who will do the research on pricing and other vendor policies?
- Who will be the vendor liaison?

After choosing a vendor, it is a good idea to clarify three points before the installation starts.

1. Both your organization and the vendor need to identify contact people.
2. Both you and the vendor should agree on the installation's goals, deliverables, and schedule.
3. The major equipment, such as the server, should be tested before and after the installation. Some vendors prefer to configure and test the systems at their facilities before installing it at the customer's site.

Testing the Installation

This phase is crucial because it can uncover problems before your organization trusts data to the system.

Isolate a segment and test all of the elements of the network. This isolated test-case network should contain a representative of each type of component that will be on the entire network including:

- Servers
- Computers
- Cables
- Peripherals
- Hubs

After testing an isolated segment, it might be a good idea to phase or step the plan into the actual environment if implementing the entire network all at once would cause too much disruption.

Transition Plan for Users

Planning should take into account all of the issues involved in transitioning users from their current system into the new environment.

How will the transition be made? (Check all that apply.)

Orientation session _____

Training session _____

Job aids _____

Each user manages on their own _____

If the plan calls for each user managing on their own, are support resources ready? Will there be adequate time allowed for the learning curve?

One approach to determining what should be included in the transition is to envision each step new users take in sitting down at their terminals, turning them on, and running an application. What will they see and what will happen? Will they be able to do this successfully? Have a user test this on an isolated segment.

Training

Organizations have to realize that no network will be successful unless users are trained to work with it. Training is as important as selecting the server, and it needs to be built into the implementation as part of the original plan.

Training the Administrators

The first people trained should be the network administrator and a backup administrator who will assist with all of the network tasks.

This training should actually begin at the planning stage. The administrator and the backup administrator should be included in all phases of network activity so they can learn the network from the ground up. They should also be enrolled in the initial round of formal classes.

Training Alternatives

There are several ways an organization can train people for networking.

Most network vendors offer formal, instructor-led classes on their products. Often, these are for certification. Where time and resources permit, hands-on training that uses the actual LAN on the site usually offers a good return on investment even though the initial cost may seem prohibitive.

Increasingly, independent training companies and even vendors such as Microsoft are offering self-paced versions of their classroom training.

Regardless of the type of training selected, the organization needs to support user training. What may be the major obstacle to effective training is lack of time. If users are not given the appropriate time to learn how to use the network correctly, then they will not use it properly. This will have a major impact on network productivity and support, and will produce a poor return on investment.

Job Aids

The job aid outlines essential steps in an operation. If they are done well, job aids can be an excellent follow-up to training. These can be in the form of a loose-leaf notebook which the user can keep next to the computer.

The effort of creating adequate job aids for 25 people will be rewarded by saving the technician from having to respond to 25 calls. For example, a maintenance job aid can be placed by the printer to help users through situations such as loading paper or changing the toner cartridge.

Expanding the Network

> **Note** This section of the LAN Planner is only meant to provide an indication of what WAN planning involves. It is beyond the scope of this kit to provide anyone with the technical expertise and experience necessary for implementing WAN technology.

Modems

1. Do you need to communicate with Bulletin Board Services and information services such as The Microsoft Network or CompuServe?

   Yes _____ You need a modem

   No _____

2. Do you need individual connectivity to the Internet?

   Yes _____ You need a modem

   No _____

3. Do you need to periodically transfer files with another user at a different location?

   Yes _____ You need a modem

   No _____

4. Do several users at once ever need to communicate with an online service or any remote resource?

   Yes _____ Consider a modem pool

   No _____

5. Do you have users who periodically need to access the network from home or on the road?

   Yes _____ You should consider a dial-in service. To implement this, you will also need a dial-in server.

   No _____

Large Network Components

The following questions will help you identify which advanced connectivity devices would be appropriate for your system.

Repeaters

1. Do you need to extend the cable length of your network to accommodate new users located farther from the server than a single cable can run?

   Yes _____ Consider implementing a repeater

   No _____

2. If you extend the length of your network cable, will the newly extended cable length exceed the specifications for that type of cable?

   Yes _____ Consider implementing a repeater

   No _____

3. Do you need to transmit signals on a different type of media than you are already using for your network?

   Yes _____ Consider implementing a repeater

   No _____

Bridges

1. Do you need to connect two or more network segments?

   Yes _____ Consider implementing a bridge

   No _____

2. Do you need to connect two networks of different network architectures (that is, Ethernet to Token Ring)?

   Yes _____ Consider implementing a bridge, but first look into routers

   No _____

3. Is your network performance slower than you would like it to be?

   Yes _____ Keep this in mind while you answer the following question

   No _____

4. Does your network serve different departments that normally transmit network traffic only within their own department?

   Yes _____ Consider implementing a bridge

   No _____

Routers

1. Do you need to join several LAN segments into a single network?

    Yes _____ Consider implementing routers between the different segments

    No _____

2. Do you need to connect different network architectures (that is, Ethernet to Token Ring)?

    Yes _____ Consider implementing routers between the different segments

    No _____

3. Do you need to isolate or filter traffic between multiple segments?

    Yes _____ Consider implementing routers between the different segments

    No _____

4. Are network performance and data important enough to maintain redundant paths between multiple segments simultaneously?

    Yes _____ Consider implementing routers between the different segments

    No _____

Gateways

Do you need to allow communications between unlike systems?

Yes _____ Consider a gateway

No _____

Advanced WAN Transmission Technologies

1. Do you only have two sites to link?

    Yes _____ You need point-to-point service

    No _____

2. Does your system need to link multiple sites to a central location?

    Yes _____ You need a point-to-multipoint service

    No _____

3. Does your system need to link many sites simultaneously?

    Yes _____ You need a multipoint-to-multipoint service

    No _____

4. Is the data that you transmit critical enough so that you require multiple links between sites to provide redundancy in case of link failure?

   Yes _____ You should consider multiple links

   No _____

5. What kind of network traffic will be on the link? (Check all that apply.)

   • Voice _____

   • E-mail _____

   • Light file transfer _____

   • Heavy file transfer _____

   • Client/server database activity (should be fairly light network traffic) _____

   • Client computer database activity with the data files stored on a remote server (can be very heavy traffic) _____

6. Based on the amount of network traffic identified in the previous question, approximately how much network bandwidth do you need? (Your WAN vendor might be able to help you determine this.)

   • Less than 56 Kbps _____

   • 56/64 Kbps _____

   • 128 Kbps _____

   • 256 Kbps _____

   • 1 Mbps _____

   • More than 1 Mbps _____

7. What types and speeds of WAN connection services (service providers) are available in your area?

   _____

   _____

   _____

8. Which service that can meet your requirements provides the best price and performance for your WAN needs?

   _____

Post-Installation Support

No network has ever been able to support itself, and things will go wrong at the worst times. There are several solutions to the support problem.

On-Site Support

Unless your organization possesses the expertise and the parts to fix your network, you should consider contracting with a company that provides on-site service. It is not likely that anyone in the organization will want to take the system apart and take it to a computer repair shop when the system fails.

The level of on-site support your organization requires will depend on:

- The expertise of your organization's support staff.
- The value of the data in your system.
- The impact down-time has on your organization.

An on-site support contract is another consideration that should be built into the original budget.

1. Your network administrator(s) will be: _____

2. The network support staff in your organization will include:

_____

_____

_____

_____

_____

_____

Vendor Support

If you convert the time users spend guessing at solutions to network problems into money, you could probably pay for the finest unlimited telephone support. It is very smart to build professional third-party telephone support into the budget.

Contact numbers outside your organization:

Consultant/vendor	Product/area of expertise	Contact number
_____	_____	_____
_____	_____	_____
_____	_____	_____
_____	_____	_____
_____	_____	_____
_____	_____	_____

Remote Diagnostics

Remote diagnostics, which can usually be contracted for as part of a complete support program, allow an engineer to work on the customer's computer through the telephone system. The remote feature will let the engineer operate the customer's computer from a remote site and see, on the remote screen, exactly what he would see if he were sitting in front of the computer at the customer's site.

The engineer can use this type of program to ensure that the user has not disabled a valuable file, or simply made a mistake or forgotten a procedure.

Identifying Qualified Support

Enough time needs to be scheduled into the original plan to research which companies provide what range of services. Fortunately, many vendors now require technicians to become certified before authorizing them to work on their products. Microsoft, for example, features the MCSE (Microsoft Certified Systems Engineer) program. The MCSE certification is an indication to the customer that the engineer is qualified to work on the network. Novell, too, offers certification through its CNE (Certified NetWare Engineer) program.

Documentation

Do you have documentation for all of the operating systems and applications you will maintain, and is that documentation easily accessible to you?

Yes _____ Where is it located? _____

No _____ What is missing?

_____

_____

_____

Do you have documentation and driver disks for all of the hardware platforms and additional hardware on your network, and is that documentation easily available?

Yes _____ Where is it located? _____

No _____ What is missing?

_____

_____

_____

Additional Resources

Do you have access to online services such as CompuServe, MSN, and the Internet so that you can find help and download new drivers?

Yes _____

No _____

Do you have subscriptions to industry periodicals?

Yes _____

No _____ Which ones would you like to have?

_____

_____

Do you have subscriptions to a troubleshooting knowledge base (such as Microsoft TechNet, or the NetWare Support Encyclopedia) for all of the operating systems and hardware vendors that you support?

Yes _____

No _____ Which ones do you need to subscribe to?

_____

_____

Do you have a list of technical support telephone numbers for all of the hardware and software on your network?

Yes _____ Where is it located? _____

No _____ Which ones are you missing?

_____

_____

Do you have a consultant or vendor you trust who will be available to help you when you cannot solve the problem on your own?

Yes _____ What is the consultant's name and contact number?

_____

No _____ You might consider finding one

Your Network Components

1. Type of network (combination, peer-to-peer, server-based):

   _____

2. Topology: _____

3. Architecture: _____

4. Cable type: _____

5. Access method: _____

6. Adapter cards (brand and type):

Vendor/contact	Specifications	Quantity
_____	_____	_____
_____	_____	_____
_____	_____	_____
_____	_____	_____

7. Hubs (number and locations):

   _____

   _____

8. Your network operating systems:

   _____

   _____

   _____

9. Your network redirectors:

   _____

   _____

   _____

10. Your network protocol(s):

   _____

   _____

   _____

11. Printers:

Printer (vendor and type)	Number	Locations and attachment methods
_____	_____	_____
		_____
		_____
_____	_____	_____
		_____
		_____
		_____
_____	_____	_____
		_____
		_____
_____	_____	_____
		_____
		_____

12. Additional equipment and services (enter the number of each):
    - Print servers: _____
    - Direct connections (a network card in the printer): _____
    - Dedicated print server devices: _____

13. Your e-mail type (vendor and specifications): _____

14. Your e-mail gateway: _____

15. Client/server applications:

    _____
    _____

16. Applications:

Application/vendor	Server (name/number)	Server location
_____	_____	_____
_____	_____	_____
_____	_____	_____
_____	_____	_____
_____	_____	_____
_____	_____	_____

Security and Data Protection

1. What security measures are in place? Check those that apply:

   - Centralized: _____
   - Peer-to-peer: _____
   - Combination: _____
   - Auditing: _____
   - Diskless computers: _____
   - Encryption: _____

2. Virus protection: _____ Type: _____

3. Your network monitoring system is: _____

4. Your network monitor (the person responsible) is: _____

5. Log location and keeper: _____

6. Your backup system specifications: _____

   - Tape location(s): _____
   - Person responsible for backup: _____

7. Your UPS type: _____

8. Your RAID level is: _____

Network Performance

1. Person responsible for monitoring performance: _____

2. Your primary monitoring tool(s): _____

3. Other monitoring tools: _____

4. Baseline information location and keeper: _____

Network Expansion

1. Your modem(s) is (specifications): _____

2. Wide area network components (repeaters, bridges, routers, gateways):

Component	Vendor/model	Quantity	Locations
_____	_____	_____	_____
			_____
			_____
			_____
			_____
_____	_____	_____	_____
			_____
			_____
			_____
			_____
_____	_____	_____	_____
			_____
			_____
			_____
			_____
_____	_____	_____	_____
			_____
			_____
			_____

Your type of WAN service is: _____

Your carrier is: _____

Contact number: _____

Appendix C: Network Troubleshooter

This appendix summarizes the troubleshooting tips and techniques presented in the Troubleshooter section of each unit review.

General Questions

This section presents basic questions that you can initially use to approach a variety of network problems.

The first troubleshooting question should always be: "Did it ever work correctly?"

If the answer is yes, it did work correctly at one time, the next question should be: "What has changed since then?"

Other useful questions include:

- Were many users affected or only one, or were users affected randomly?
- Is the entire network down or just one computer?
- Was the problem there before the upgrade?
- Does the problem occur constantly or only during certain times?
- Does the problem appear with all applications or only one?
- Is this problem similar to a previous problem?
- Are there new users on the network?
- Is there new equipment on the network?
- Was a new application program installed before the problem occurred?
- Has any of the equipment been moved lately?
- Which vendors' products were involved?
- Do the symptoms occur among certain vendors and certain components such as cards, hubs, disk drives, application software, or network operating software?
- Has an anyone attempted to "fix" the network?
- If a computer cannot function on the network, can it function as a stand-alone computer?
- If the computer cannot function on the network, is the computer's network adapter card working?
- Is there a normal amount of traffic on the network?

Cabling Problems

Check the cabling for:

- Loose or lost connections
- Breaks or frayed sections
- Proper length (is the cable too long?)
- Proper resistance (ohms)
- Specifications of the network adapter cards
- Crimps or sharp bends
- Routing near a source of interference such as an air conditioner, transformer, or large electric motor
- Proper termination on bus topologies

Adapter Card Problems

Check the adapter cards for:

- Settings that match the settings in the network operating system software
- I/O address conflicts
- Interrupt conflicts
- Memory conflicts
- The correct interface (AUI, BNC, or RJ-45)
- The network speed setting
- The correct type of network card for the network? (such as a Token Ring card in an Ethernet network)
- Setting conflicts if there is more than one network adapter card in a computer
- Type and signaling speed

Driver Problems

Check the following to isolate driver problems:

- The age of the equipment
- Changes since the equipment worked correctly
- Hardware moves
- Software installations
- Old drivers being used with new equipment

Network Operations Problems

1. Make sure the hardware in your server:
   - Is on the hardware compatibility list (HCL).
   - Has the correct (current) drivers.
   - Has enough memory to support your current network operations.
   - Has enough hard disk space to support all your storage needs.
   - Has enough processing power to support your network.

2. Make sure all of your network bindings are done correctly and the most used bindings are listed first.

3. Ensure that your client computers have the correct client software (redirectors) loaded.

4. Make sure the frame types match. For example, the IPX frame type on a computer you are adding to the network must match the frame type for IPX used by the computers already on the network.

5. Make sure the protocol you are installing matches the protocol in use on the network.

Network Printing and Fax Problems

- Is the shared printer or fax turned on?
- Are client computers selecting the appropriate shared printer and fax machine for the drivers they are using?
- Do users and printer/fax managers have the appropriate permissions for the shared printer or fax?
- Are all of the cables to the shared printer or fax in good repair and properly connected?

Network Application Problems

- Are all of the users' e-mail and scheduling programs configured correctly?
- Are each of the messaging gateways configured appropriately and working properly?

Multivendor Environment Problems

- Has the client computer been configured with redirectors for each of the types of server operating systems it needs to access, and is each of those redirectors configured correctly and working?

- Are the servers configured with all of the network services needed by clients, and are those services configured correctly and working?

- Are all of the gateway computers which allow access between environments configured correctly and working?

Client/Server Problems

- The client front-end is configured correctly and working.

- The server software is configured correctly and working.

- The network application is performing as desired.

- The server running the network application has enough processing power, RAM, and hard disk space.

- The end users are trained in and using the appropriate procedures to get the most out of the network application.

Network Account Problems

If the user is unable to log on using a particular account, make sure that:

- The person is typing their user name correctly.

- The entry in the From box correctly reflects the location of the user account.

- The person is typing their password correctly (passwords are case-sensitive).

- The user account is not disabled.

Data Security Problems

1. If the user is unable to access a resource, or the user is able to access a resource which should be inaccessible to them, make sure:

   - The individual user has appropriate rights to the resource.

   - The user belongs to a group which has appropriate access to the resource.

   - There are no conflicting trustee assignments to the resource (share-level permissions versus user-level permissions).

2. Determine if the user belongs to any group which has been specifically granted the No Access permission.

3. If there are problems with access to previously secured data, or data theft, contamination or alteration, determine:

   - If the server is in a locked room, and who has access.

   - Whether there are computers left on and logged on unattended.

   - Whether there are passwords written down and left in obvious places such as under the keyboard, on the monitor, or in a desk drawer.

   - If any users have obvious passwords such as spouse, children's, or pet names.

   - If any users continually use the same password with a revision number (Wilma1, Wilma2, Wilma3, and so on).

   - If any users have a regular logon name which has super-user (administrator) equivalence.

   - If any users store confidential data on their local hard disks.

   - If any users have their operating system set up to automatically log them in and bypass the user name and password process.

Large Network Communications Problems

You can begin your troubleshooting of a WAN in the same manner you would with a LAN. The questions listed here are specific to larger network communications problems. For these types of problems you most often would require help from vendors or service providers.

1. The first, most obvious question would be "Did a vendor, including communications services vendors, add, remove, or replace anything?"

2. Determine if there is power to the following components and they are turned on:

   - Modem
   - Repeater
   - Bridge
   - Router
   - Gateway
   - CSU/DSU

3. Also, for the same components, determine if:

   - All of the cables are connected correctly and are in good repair.

   - The component is compatible with the communications medium and with the communications device on the other end of the link.

   - The software is configured correctly and matches the configuration of the communications equipment to which it is connected.

Bibliography

Cooper, Edward. *Broadband Network Technology*. Mountain View: Sytek Press, 1984.

Derfler, Frank J. and Freed, Les. *How Networks Work*. Emeryville: Ziff-Davis Press, 1993.

Derfler, Frank J. Jr. *Guide to Connectivity*. Berkeley: Ziff-Davis Press, 1990.

Derfler, Frank J. Jr. *Guide to Linking LANs*. Emeryville: Ziff-Davis Press, 1992.

Dyson, Peter. *Novell's Dictionary of Networking*. Alameda: Novell Press, 1994.

Kee, Eddie. *Networking Illustrated*. Indianapolis: Que Corporation, 1994.

Levy, Joseph. *Welcome to Networks: A Guide to LANs*. New York: MIS Press, 1993.

Lowe, Doug. *Networking For Dummies*. Foster City: IDG Books, 1994.

Martin, James. *Local Area Networks*. Englewood Cliffs: Prentice Hall, 1989.

Miller, Mark A. *Internetworking, A Guide to Network Communications, LAN to LAN; LAN to WAN*. Redwood City: M&T Publishing, Inc., 1991.

Miller, Mark A. *LAN Protocol Handbook*. Redwood City: M&T Publishing, Inc., 1990.

Miller, Mark A. *LAN Troubleshooting Handbook*. Redwood City: M&T Publishing, Inc., 1989.

Naugle, Matthew G. *Local Area Networking*. McGraw-Hill, Inc., 1991.

Nunemacher, Greg. *LAN Primer: Second Edition*. New York: M&T Books, 1992.

O'Dell, Peter. *The Computer Networking Book*. Chapel Hill: Ventana Press, 1989.

Schatt, Stan. *Linking LANs, Second Edition*. New York: McGraw-Hill, Inc., 1995.

Schnaidt, Patricia. *LAN Tutorial*. San Francisco: Miller Freeman Publications, 1990.

Sheldon, Tom, ed. *LAN Times Encyclopedia of Networking*. New York: Osborne McGraw-Hill, 1994.

Sheldon, Tom, ed. *LAN Times Guide to Interoperability*. New York: Osborne McGraw-Hill, 1994.

Tannenbaum, Andrew S. *Computer Networks, Second Edition*. Englewood Cliffs: Prentice Hall, 1989.

Wong, William. *Remote LAN Connections*. New York: M&T Books, 1995.

Glossary

A

access permissions

When setting up shares in Microsoft Windows NT Server, access to the share can be controlled through permissions. These permissions control the type of access to the share, and include the following:

No Access—Prevents any access to the shared directory, its subdirectories, and its files.

Read—Allows viewing file names and subdirectory names, changing to the shared directory's subdirectory, viewing data in files, and running applications.

Change—Allows viewing the file names and subdirectory names, changing to the shared directory's subdirectories, viewing data in files and running application files, adding files and subdirectories to the shared directory, changing data in files, and deleting subdirectories and files.

Full Control—Includes the same permissions as Change plus changing permissions (taking ownership of the Windows NT file system [NTFS] files and directories only).

account

See user account.

account policy

Controls the way passwords must be used by all user accounts in a domain, or in an individual computer.

ACK

An acknowledgment signal.

acknowledgment

The process used to guarantee reliable end-to-end message delivery.

active window

The window in which the user is currently working. An active window is typically at the top of the window order and is distinguished by the color of its title bar.

advanced cable testers

Advanced cable testers work beyond the OSI Physical layer up into layers 2, 3, and even 4. They can display information about the condition of the physical cable as well as message frame counts, excess collisions, late collisions, error frame counts, congestion errors, and beaconing. These testers can monitor overall network traffic, certain kinds of error situations, or traffic to and from a particular computer. They will indicate if a particular cable or network adapter card is causing problems.

advanced program-to-program communication (APPC)

A protocol developed by IBM as part of its Systems Network Architecture (SNA). It provides programs with a set of rules and a generic language to converse with one another without having to deal with either lower-level network functions or a master-slave arrangement that assumes the communicating machines have no intelligence (processing power) of their own and must therefore rely on a host computer to act as an intermediary.

Advanced RISC Computing (ARC)

A standard developed by a consortium of hardware and software manufacturers. This standard specifies a computer that is similar to a personal computer, but is based on a RISC processor.

AFP

See AppleTalk filing protocol (AFP).

agent

Software that runs on a client computer for use by administrative software running on a server. Agents are typically used to support administrative actions, such as detecting system information or running services.

American National Standards Institute (ANSI)

An organization of American industry and business groups dedicated to the development of trade and communications standards.

amplifier

A device such as a repeater or bridge that amplifies or increases the power of electrical signals so they can travel on additional cable segments at their original strength. Amplifiers strengthen signals that are weakened by attenuation.

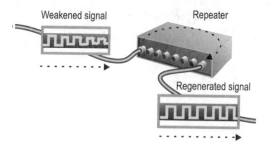

Weakened signal   Repeater

Regenerated signal

analog

Related to a continuously variable physical property, such as voltage, pressure, or rotation. An analog device can represent an infinite number of values within the range the device can handle. *See also* digital.

analog line

A communications line, such as a telephone line, that carries information in analog (continuously variable) form. To minimize distortion and noise interference, an analog line uses amplifiers to strengthen the signal periodically during transmission.

ANSI

See American National Standards Institute (ANSI).

APPC

See advanced program-to-program communication (APPC).

AppleShare

AppleShare is the Apple network operating system. AppleShare provides file sharing. The client-side software is included with every copy of the Apple operating system. There is also an AppleShare print server, which is a server-based print spooler.

AppleTalk

AppleTalk is the Apple network architecture included in the Macintosh operating system software. It is a collection of protocols that correspond to the OSI model. This means that network capabilities are built in to every Macintosh. The AppleTalk protocols support LocalTalk, Ethernet (EtherTalk), and Token Ring (TokenTalk).

AppleTalk filing protocol (AFP)

AFP describes how files are stored and accessed on the network. It is responsible for the Apple hierarchical filing structure of volumes, folders, and files. AFP also provides for file sharing between Macintoshes and MS-DOS-based computers. It provides an interface for communication between AppleTalk and other network operating systems. This means that Macintoshes can be integrated into any network that uses an operating system that recognizes AFP.

Application layer

The top (seventh) layer of the OSI model. This layer serves as the window which application processes use to access network services. This layer represents the services that directly support the user applications such as software for file transfers, database access, and e-mail.

application programming interface (API)

A set of routines that an application program uses to request and carry out lower-level services performed by the operating system.

application protocols

These protocols work at the higher end of the OSI model. They provide application-to-application interaction and data exchange. More popular application protocols include:

FTAM (file transfer access and management)—A file access protocol.

SMTP (simple mail transfer protocol)—A TCP/IP protocol for transferring e-mail.

Telnet—A TCP/IP protocol for logging on to remote hosts and processing data locally.

NCP (NetWare core protocol)—The primary protocol used to transmit information between a NetWare server and its clients.

archive

To store copies of computer programs and data to guard against loss in the event that the original materials are deleted or damaged. Archived files can be sent to tape, floppy disk, or another computer system.

ARC
See Advanced RISC Computing (ARC).

ArcNet (Attached Resource Computer Network)
ArcNet, developed by Datapoint Corporation in 1977, was designed as a baseband, token-passing, bus architecture, transmitting at 2.5 Mbps. A successor to the original ArcNet, *ArcNetplus*, supports data transmission rates of 20 Mbps. ArcNet is a simple, inexpensive, flexible network architecture designed for workgroup-sized LANs. ArcNet runs on coaxial cable, twisted-pair cable, and fiber-optic cable and supports up to 255 nodes. ArcNet technology predates IEEE Project 802 standards but loosely maps to the 802.4 document.

ASCII (American Standard Code for Information Interchange)
A coding scheme that assigns numeric values to letters, numbers, punctuation marks, and certain other characters. By standardizing the values used for these characters, ASCII enables computers and computer programs to exchange information.

asynchronous transfer mode (ATM)
ATM is an advanced implementation of packet switching that provides high-speed data transmission rates to send fixed-size cells over broadband LANs or WANs. Cells are 53 bytes; 48 bytes of data with five additional bytes of address. ATM can accommodate voice, data, fax, real-time video, CD-quality audio, imaging, and multimegabit data transmission. ATM uses switches as multiplexers to permit several computers to put data on a network simultaneously. Most commercial ATM boards will transmit data at about 155 Mbps, but theoretically 1.2 gigabits per second is possible.

asynchronous transmission
A form of data transmission in which information is sent one character at a time, with variable time intervals between characters. Asynchronous transmission does not rely on a shared timer that would enable the sending and receiving units to separate characters by specific time periods. Therefore, each transmitted character consists of a number of data bits (the character itself) preceded by a start bit and ends in an optional parity bit followed by a 1-, 1.5-, or 2-stop bit.

ATM
See asynchronous transfer mode (ATM).

attachment unit interface (AUI)
The connector used with standard Ethernet that often includes a cable running off the main, or backbone, coaxial cable. This is also known as a DIX connector.

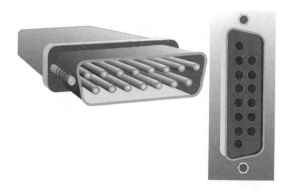

attenuation

The weakening or degrading (distorting) of a transmitted signal as it travels farther from its point of origin. This could be a digital signal on a cable or the reduction in amplitude of an electrical signal, without the appreciable modification of the waveform. Attenuation is usually measured in decibels. Attenuation of a signal transmitted over a long cable is corrected by a repeater, which amplifies and cleans up an incoming signal before sending it farther along the cable.

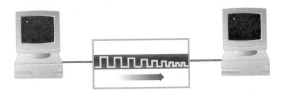

AUI

See attachment unit interface (AUI).

AWG (American Wire Gauge)

A standard for determining wire diameter. The diameter varies inversely to the gauge number.

B

back end

In a client/server application, back end refers to the part of the program running on the server.

backbone

The backbone, or trunk segment, is the main cable from which transceiver cables are connected to computers, repeaters, and bridges.

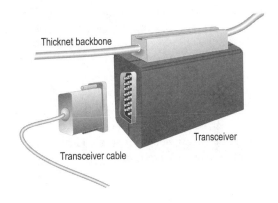

Thicknet backbone

Transceiver

Transceiver cable

backup

A duplicate copy of a program, a disk, or data, made either for archiving purposes or for safeguarding valuable files from loss.

backup domain controller (BDC)

In a Windows NT Server domain, a BDC refers to a computer that receives a copy of the domain's security policy and domain database, and authenticates network logons. It provides a backup in the event the primary domain controller becomes unavailable. A domain is not required to have a BDC, but it is recommended to have a BDC to back up the PDC. *See also* domain, domain controller, primary domain controller.

bandwidth

In communications, the difference between the highest and lowest frequencies in a given range. For example, a telephone accommodates a bandwidth of 3000 Hz, or the difference between the lowest (300 Hz) and highest (3300 Hz) frequencies it can carry. In computer networks, greater bandwidth indicates faster or greater data-transfer capability.

base I/O port

Specifies a channel through which information is transferred between your computer's hardware (such as your network card) and its CPU.

base memory address

Defines the address of the location in your computer's memory (RAM) that is used by the network adapter card. This setting is sometimes called the RAM start address.

baseband

A system used to transmit the encoded signals over cable. Baseband uses digital signaling over a single frequency. Signals flow in the form of discrete pulses of electricity or light. With baseband transmission, the entire communication-channel capacity is used to transmit a single data signal.

baud

A measure of data-transmission speed named after the French engineer and telegrapher Jean-Maurice-Emile Baudot. It is a measure of the speed of the oscillation of the sound wave on which a bit of data is carried over telephone lines. Originally used to measure the transmission speed of telegraph equipment, the term sometimes refers to the data-transmission speed of a modem. However, current modems can send at a speed higher than one bit per oscillation, so baud is being replaced by the more accurate bps (bits per second) as a measure of modem speed.

baud rate

A reference to the speed at which a modem can transmit data. Often confused with bps (the number of bits per second transmitted), baud rate actually measures the number of events, or signal changes, that occur in 1 second. Because one event can actually encode more than 1 bit in high-speed digital communications, baud rate and bps are not always synonymous, and the latter is the more accurate term to apply to modems. For example the 9600-baud modem that encodes 4-bits per event actually operates at 2400 baud, but transmits at 9600 bps (2400 events times 4-bits per event), and thus should be called a 9600-bps modem.

BDC
See backup domain controller (BDC).

beaconing
The process of signaling computers on a ring system that token passing has been interrupted by a serious error. All computers in an FDDI or Token Ring network are responsible for monitoring the token passing process. To isolate serious failures in the ring, FDDI and Token Ring use a system called beaconing in which a computer that detects a fault sends a signal called a beacon onto the network. The computer will continue to send the beacon until it notices a beacon from its upstream neighbor. This process continues until the only computer sending a beacon is the one directly downstream of the failure. When the beaconing computer finally receives its own beacon, it assumes the problem has been fixed and regenerates a token.

bind
To associate two pieces of information with one another.

binding
A process that establishes the communication channel between a protocol driver and a network adapter driver.

BISDN
See broadband ISDN (BISDN).

bisync (binary synchronous communications protocol)
A communications protocol developed by IBM. Bisync transmissions are encoded in either ASCII or EBCDIC. Messages can be of any length and are sent in units called frames, optionally preceded by a message header. Because bisync uses synchronous transmission, in which message elements are separated by a specific time interval, each frame is preceded and followed by special characters that enable the sending and receiving machines to synchronize their clocks.

bit
Short for binary digit: either 1 or 0 in the binary number system. In processing and storage, a bit is the smallest unit of information handled by a computer. It is represented physically by an element such as a single pulse sent through a circuit, or small spot on a magnetic disk capable of storing either a 1 or 0. Eight bits make a byte.

bit time
The time it takes each station to receive and store a bit.

bits per second (bps)

A measure of the speed at which a device can transfer data. *See also* baud rate.

BNC (British Naval Connector)

A connector for coaxial cable that locks when one connector is inserted into another and is rotated 90 degrees.

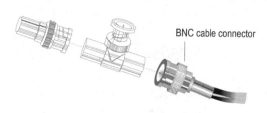

BNC cable connector

bottleneck

A device or program that significantly degrades network performance. Most network activities involve the coordinated activity of several devices. Each device takes a certain amount of time to perform its part of the transaction. Poor performance results when one of these devices uses noticeably more CPU time, some other resource than the others, or does not have the capacity to handle the load. Potential bottlenecks could be the CPU, memory, the network adapter card, and so on.

bounce

See signal bounce.

bps

See bits per second (bps).

bridge

A device used to join two LANs. It allows stations on either network to access resources on the other. Bridges can be used to increase the length or number of nodes for a network. The bridge makes connections at the Data Link layer of the OSI model.

broadband ISDN (BISDN)

Broadband integrated services digital network is a Consultative Committee for the CCITT that makes recommendations that define voice, data, and video in the megabit-gigabit range. BISDN is also a single ISDN network that can handle voice, data, and video services. BISDN works with an optical cable transport network called synchronous optical network (SONET) and an asynchronous transfer mode (ATM) switching service. SMDS (switched multimegabit data services) is also a BISDN service that can offer high bandwidth to WANs.

broadband network

A type of LAN on which transmissions travel as analog (radio-frequency) signals over separate inbound and outbound channels. Devices on a broadband network are connected by coaxial or fiber-optic cable, so signals flow across the physical medium in the form of electromagnetic or optical waves. A broadband system uses a large portion of the electromagnetic spectrum; for example, the range of frequencies from 50 Mbps to 600 Mbps. These networks can simultaneously accommodate television, voice, data, and many other services over multiple transmission channels.

broadcast

A transmission sent simultaneously to more than one recipient. In communications and on networks, a broadcast message is one distributed to all stations or computers on the network.

broadcast storm

A broadcast storm occurs when there are so many broadcast messages on the network that they approach or surpass the capacity of the network bandwidth. This can happen when one computer on the network transmits a flood of frames saturating the network with traffic so it can no longer carry messages from any other computer. Such a broadcast storm can shut down a network.

brouter

A network component that combines the best qualities of both a bridge and a router. A brouter can act like a router for one protocol and a bridge all the others. Brouters can route selected routable protocols, bridge nonroutable protocols, and deliver more cost-effective and more manageable internetworking than separate bridges and routers. A brouter is a good choice in an environment that mixes several homogeneous LAN segments with two different segments.

buffer

A reserved portion of RAM in which data is temporarily held pending an opportunity to complete its transfer to or from a storage device or another location in memory.

built-in groups

The default groups provided with Windows NT and Windows NT Server. Built-in groups have been granted useful collections of rights and built-in abilities.

In most cases, a built-in group provides all the capabilities needed by a particular user. For example, if a domain user account belongs to the built-in Administrators group, logging on with that account gives a user administrative capabilities over the domain and the servers in the domain.

bus topology

This topology connects each computer, or station, to a single cable. At each end of the cable is a terminating resistor, or terminator. A transmission is passed back and forth along the cable, past the stations and between the two terminators, carrying a message from one end of the network to the other. As the message passes each station, the station checks its destination address. If the address in the message matches the station's address, the station receives the message. If the addresses do not match, the bus carries the message to the next station, and so on.

byte

A unit of information consisting of 8 bits. In computer processing or storage, a byte is the equivalent to a single character, such as a letter, numeral, or punctuation mark. Because a byte represents only a small amount of information, amounts of computer memory are usually given in kilobytes (1024 bytes or 2 raised to the 10th power), megabytes (1,048,576 bytes or 2 raised to the 20th power), gigabytes (1024 megabytes), terabyte (1024 gigabytes), petabyte (1024 terabytes), or exabyte (1024 petabytes).

C

cable tester
See advanced cable testers.

cache
A special memory subsystem or part of RAM in which frequently used data values are duplicated for quick access. A memory cache stores the contents of frequently accessed RAM locations and the addresses where these data items are stored. When the processor references an address in memory, the cache checks to see whether it holds that address. If it does hold the address, the data is returned to the processor; if it does not, a regular memory access occurs. A cache is useful when RAM accesses are slow compared with the microprocessor speed.

carrier-sense multiple access with collision detection (CSMA/CD)
A type of access control generally used with bus topologies. Using CSMA/CD, a station "listens" to the physical medium to determine whether another station is currently transmitting a data frame. If no other station is transmitting, the station sends its data. A station "listens" to the medium by testing the medium for the presence of a carrier, a specific level of voltage or light, thus the term carrier-sense. The multiple access indicates that there are multiple stations attempting to access or put data on the cable at the same time. The collision detection indicates that the stations are also listening for collisions. If two stations attempt to transmit at the same time and a collision occurs, the stations must wait a random period of time before attempting to transmit.

CCEP (Commercial COMSEC Endorsement Program)
A data encryption standard introduced by the National Security Agency. Vendors can join CCEP (with the proper security clearances) and be authorized to incorporate classified algorithms into communications systems. *See also* encryption.

CCITT (Comité Consultatif Internationale de Télégraphie et Téléphonie)
An organization based in Geneva, Switzerland and established as part of the United Nations International Telecommunications Union (ITU). The CCITT recommends use of communications standards that are recognized throughout the world. Protocols established by the CCITT are applied to modems, networks, and facsimile transmission.

central file server
A network in which specific computers take on the role of a server with other computers on the network sharing the resources. *See also* client/server.

central processing unit (CPU)
The computational and control unit of a computer; the device that interprets and carries out instructions. Single-chip CPUs, called microprocessors, made personal computers possible. Examples include the 80286, 80386, 80486, and Pentium.

client
A computer that accesses shared network resources provided by another computer, called a server.

client/server
A network architecture designed around the concept of distributed processing in which a task is divided between a back end (server), which stores and distributes data, and a front end (client) which requests specific data from the server. *See also* central file server.

coaxial cable (coax)
A conductive center wire surrounded by an insulating layer, a layer of wire mesh (shielding), and a nonconductive outer layer. Coaxial cable is resistant to interference and signal weakening that other cabling, such as unshielded twisted-pair cable, can experience.

codec (compression/decompression)
Compression/decompression technology for digital video and stereo audio.

contention
On a network, competition among stations for the opportunity to use a communications line or network resource is called contention. Two or more computers attempt to transmit over the same cable at the same time, thus causing a collision on the cable. Such a system needs regulation to eliminate data collisions on the cable which can destroy data and bring network traffic to a halt. *See also* carrier-sense multiple access with collision detection (CSMA/CD).

CPU
See central processing unit (CPU).

CRC
See cyclical redundancy check (CRC).

crosstalk
Signal overflow from an adjacent wire. For example, if you are talking on the telephone and can hear someone else's faint conversation occurring in the background on your telephone, your telephone line is being affected by crosstalk.

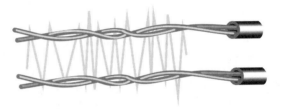

CSMA/CD
See carrier-sense multiple access with collision detection (CSMA/CD).

cyclical redundancy check (CRC)
The cyclical redundancy check is a number produced by a mathematical calculation on a packet at its source. When the packet arrives at its destination, the calculation is redone. If the results are the same, it indicates that the data in the packet has remained stable. If the calculation at the destination differs from the calculation at the source, it means the data has changed during the transmission. In that case, the CRC routine signals the source computer to retransmit the data.

D

daisy chain

A set of devices connected in a series. When devices are daisy-chained to a microcomputer, the first device is connected to the computer, the second device is connected to the first, and so on down the line. Signals are passed through the chain from one device to the next.

data communications equipment (DCE)

One of two types of hardware connected by an RS-232 serial connection, the other being a DTE (data terminal equipment) device. A DCE device takes input from a DTE device and often acts as an intermediary device, transforming the input signal in some way before sending it to the actual recipient. For example, an external modem is a DCE device that accepts data from a microcomputer (DTE), modulates it, and then sends the data along a telephone connection. In communications, an RS-232 DCE device receives data over line 2 and transmits over line 3. In contrast, a DTE device receives over line 3 and transmits over line 2. *See also* data terminal equipment (DTE).

data encryption

See encryption.

data encryption standard (DES)

A commonly used, highly-sophisticated algorithm developed by the U.S. National Bureau of Standards for encrypting and decrypting data. *See also* encryption.

data frame

Logical structured packages in which data can be placed. Data that is being transmitted is segmented into small units and combined with control information such as message start and message end indicators. Each package of information is transmitted as a single unit called a frame. The Data Link layer packages raw bits from the Physical layer into data frames. The exact format of the frame used by the network depends on the topology. *See also* frame.

Data Link layer

The second layer in the OSI model. This layer packages raw bits from the Physical layer into data frames. *See also* Open Systems Interconnection (OSI) reference model.

data stream

An undifferentiated, byte-by-byte flow of data.

data terminal equipment (DTE)

According to the RS-232 hardware standard, a DTE is any device, such as a microcomputer or a terminal, that has the ability to transmit information in digital form over a cable or a communications line. A DTE is one of two types of hardware connected by an RS-232 serial connection, the other being a DCE (data communications equipment) device, such as a modem, which normally connects the DTE to the communication line itself. In communications, an RS-232 DTE device transmits data over line 2 and receives it over line 3. A DCE receives over line 2 and transmits over line 3. *See also* data communications equipment (DCE).

database management systems (DBMS)

A layer of software between the physical database and the user. The DBMS manages all requests for database action from the user, including keeping track of the physical details of file locations and formats, indexing schemes, and so on. In addition, a DBMS permits centralized control of security and data integrity requirements.

DBMS

See database management systems (DBMS).

DCE

See data communications equipment (DCE).

DECnet

Digital Equipment Corporation hardware and software products that implement the Digital Network Architecture (DNA). DECnet defines communication networks over Ethernet LANs, fiber distributed data interface metropolitan area networks (FDDI MANs), and WANs that use private or public data transmission facilities. It can use TCP/IP and OSI protocols as well as Digital's DECnet protocols.

dedicated server

A dedicated server is a computer on a network that only functions as a server and is not also used as a client.

DES

See data encryption standard (DES).

DHCP

See dynamic host configuration protocol (DHCP).

digital

A system that encodes information in a binary state, such as 0 and 1. Computers use digital encoding to process data. A digital signal is a discrete binary state, either on or off. *See also* analog.

digital line

A communication line that carries information only in binary-encoded (digital) form. To minimize distortion and noise interference, a digital line uses repeaters to regenerate the signal periodically during transmission. *See also* analog line.

digital volt meter (DVM)

The volt meter is a basic, all-purpose electronic measuring tool. It can reveal more than just the amount of voltage passing through a resistance. In network cable testing, it can measure continuity to determine if the cable can carry network traffic or is broken (has an open) and will bring the network down.

DIP (dual inline package) switch

One or more small rocker or sliding type switches that can be set to one of two states—closed or open—to control options on a circuit board.

direct memory access (DMA)

Memory access that does not involve the microprocessor, frequently employed for data transfer directly between memory and an "intelligent" peripheral device such as a disk drive.

direct memory access (DMA) channel

A channel for direct memory access that does not involve the microprocessor, providing data transfer directly between memory and a disk drive.

disk duplicating

See disk mirroring.

disk mirroring

A technique, also known as disk duplicating, in which all or part of a hard disk is duplicated onto one or more hard disks, each of which ideally is attached to its own controller. With disk mirroring, any change made to the original disk is simultaneously made to the other disk(s). Disk mirroring is used in situations in which a backup copy of current data must be maintained at all times.

diskless computers

Computers that have neither a floppy disk nor a hard disk. Diskless computers depend on special ROM in order to provide users with an interface through which they can log on to the network.

DIX (Digital, Intel, Xerox) connector

The connector used with standard Ethernet that often includes a cable running off the main, or backbone, coaxial cable. This is also known as an AUI connector. *See also* attachment unit interface (AUI).

DMA

See direct memory access (DMA).

DMA channel

See direct memory access (DMA) channel.

domain

For Microsoft networking, a domain is a collection of computers and users that share a common database and security policy that is stored on a Windows NT Server domain controller. Each domain has a unique name. *See also* workgroup.

domain controller

For Microsoft networking, the Windows NT Server-based computer that authenticates domain logons, and maintains the security policy and the master database for a domain. *See also* backup domain controller (BDC), primary domain controller (PDC).

downtime

The amount of time a computer system or associated hardware remains nonfunctioning. Although downtime can occur because hardware fails unexpectedly, it can also be a scheduled event, such as when a network is shut down to allow time for maintaining the system, changing hardware, or archiving files.

driver

Specifically, a device driver is a software component that permits a computer system to communicate with a device. A printer driver is a device driver that translates computer data into a form understood by the target printer. In most cases, the driver also manipulates the hardware in order to transmit the data to the device.

DTE

See data terminal equipment (DTE).

dumb terminal

A device used for obtaining or entering data on a network that does not contain any "intelligence" or processing power provided by a CPU.

duplex transmission

Also called full-duplex transmission. Communication that takes place simultaneously, in both directions, between the sender and the receiver. Alternative methods of transmission are simplex, which is one-way only, and half-duplex, which is two-way communication occurring in only one direction at a time.

dynamic host configuration protocol (DHCP)

A protocol for automatic TCP/IP configuration that provides static and dynamic address allocation and management.

E

EBCDIC

See extended binary coded decimal interchange code (EBCDIC).

EISA

See Enhanced Industry Standard Architecture (EISA).

Enhanced Industry Standard Architecture (EISA)

A 32-bit bus design for *x*86-based computers introduced in 1988. EISA was specified by an industry consortium of nine computer-industry companies (AST Research, Compaq, Epson, Hewlett-Packard, NEC, Olivetti, Tandy, Wyse, and Zenith). An EISA device uses cards that are upwardly compatible from ISA. *See also* Industry Standard Architecture (ISA).

encryption

The process of making information indecipherable to protect it from unauthorized viewing or use, especially during transmission or when the data is stored on a transportable magnetic medium. A key is required to decode the information. *See also* CCEP, data encryption standard (DES).

enhanced small device interface (ESDI)

A standard that can be used with high-capacity hard disks and tape drives to enable high-speed communications with a computer. ESDI drivers typically transfer data at about 10 Mbps.

ESDI

See enhanced small device interface (ESDI).

Ethernet

A LAN developed by Xerox in 1976. Ethernet became a widely implemented network from which the IEEE 802.3 standard for contention networks was developed. It uses a bus topology and the original Ethernet relies on CSMA/CD to regulate traffic on the main communication line.

event

1. An action or occurrence to which a program might respond. Examples of events are mouse clicks, key presses, and mouse movements.
2. Any significant occurrence in the system or in a program that requires users to be notified or an entry to be added to a log.

exabyte

See byte.

extended binary coded decimal interchange code (EBCDIC)

A coding scheme developed by IBM for use with IBM mainframes and personal computers as a standard method of assigning binary (numeric) values to alphabetic, numeric, punctuation, and transmission-control characters.

F

fiber distributed data interface (FDDI)

A standard developed by the ANSI for high-speed fiber-optic local area networks. FDDI provides specification for transmission rates of 100 Mbps on networks based on the Token Ring standard.

file transfer access and management (FTAM)

A file access protocol. *See also* application protocols.

File Transfer Protocol (FTP)

A process that provides file transfers between local and remote computers. FTP supports several commands that allow bidirectional transfer of binary and ASCII files between computers. The FTP client is installed with the TCP/IP connectivity utilities.

fire wall

Fire walls are barriers set up in bridges, routers, or gateways to filter packets based on the type of packet (TCP/IP, IPX, and so on) or destination address. Fire walls control traffic between the network and the environment beyond it by controlling which packets pass through them. Fire walls also accommodate auditing.

firmware
Software routines stored in ROM. Unlike RAM, ROM stays intact even in the absence of electrical power. Startup routines and low-level I/O instructions are stored in firmware.

flow control
In networking, flow control refers to regulating the flow of data through routers to ensure that no segment becomes overloaded with transmissions.

frame
A package of information transmitted on a network as a single unit. Frame is a term most often used with Ethernet networks. A frame is similar to the packet used in other networks.
See also data frame, packet.

frame preamble
Header information, added to the beginning of a data frame in the OSI Physical layer.

frame relay
An advanced fast packet variable-length, digital, packet-switching technology. It is a point-to-point system that uses a private virtual circuit (PVC) to transmit variable length frames at the OSI Data Link layer. Frame relay networks can also provide subscribers with bandwidth as needed that allows the customer to make nearly any type of transmission.

front end
In a client/server application, front end refers to the part of the program carried out on the client computer.

FTAM
See file transfer access and management (FTAM).

FTP
See File Transfer Protocol (FTP).

full duplex transmission
See duplex transmission.

G

G
Abbreviation for giga-, meaning 1 billion, or 10^9. *See also* gigabyte.

gateway
A device which is used to connect networks using different protocols so that information can be passed from one system to the other. Gateways functions at the Network layer of the OSI model.

GB
See gigabyte.

gigabyte
Commonly, a thousand megabytes. However, the precise meaning often varies with the context. A gigabyte is 1 billion bytes. In reference to computers, bytes are often expressed in multiples of powers of two. Therefore, a gigabyte can also be either 1000 megabytes or 1024 megabytes, where a megabyte is considered to be 1,048,576 bytes (2 raised to the 20th power).

global group

Used in Windows NT Server for managing users. Global groups are created on a primary domain controller (PDC) and can be used in its own domain as well as in trusting domains. In all these places it can be granted rights and permissions and can become a member of local groups. However, it can contain user accounts only from its own domain. *See also* group.

gopher

The University of Minnesota developed gopher as a distributed document search and retrieval system. It can be used to both publish and retrieve information in a distributed network of host computers, such as the Internet. Gopher has the ability to collect data from several source computers and display it as one piece of information. *See also* Telnet.

group

In networking, an account containing other accounts that are called members. The permissions and rights granted to a group are also provided to its members, which makes groups a convenient way to grant common capabilities to collections of user accounts. For Windows NT, groups are managed with User Manager. For Windows NT Server, groups are managed with User Manger for Domains.

groupware

Groupware facilitates several processes among multiple users working simultaneously on a network. It enables users to perform the following tasks: routing and sharing information, coordinating project and document development, tracking projects, managing group processes, facilitating group discussions, automating a variety of routine business tasks, tracking customer inquiries, and managing customer relations.

H

handshaking

Handshaking, usually exchanged during modem-to-modem types of communication, consists of actual information transmitted between the sending and receiving devices to maintain and coordinate data flow between them. Proper handshaking ensures that the receiving device will be ready to accept data before the sending device transmits.

hard disk

One or more inflexible platters coated with material that allows the magnetic recording of computer data. A typical hard disk rotates at 3600 revolutions per minute (RPM), and the read/write heads ride over the surface of the disk on a cushion of air 10 to 25 millionths of an inch deep. A hard disk is sealed to prevent contaminants from interfering with the close head-to-disk tolerances. Hard disks provide faster access to data than floppy disks and are capable of storing much more information. Because platters are rigid, they can be stacked so that one hard disk drive can access more than one platter. Most hard disks have between two and eight platters.

hardware

The physical components of a computer system including any peripheral equipment such as printers, modems, and mouse devices.

hardware compatibility list (HCL)

A list of computers and peripherals that have been tested and have passed compatibility testing with the product for which the HCL is being developed. For example, the Windows NT 3.51 HCL lists the products which have been tested and found to be compatible with Window NT 3.51.

HCL

See hardware compatibility list (HCL).

HDLC

See High-level data link control (HDLC).

hermaphroditic connector

A hermaphroditic connector is neither male nor female. For example, IBM cable connectors are hermaphroditic in that two of them can be connected to each other, as opposed to BNC connectors which require both a male part and a female part before a connection can be made.

hertz (Hz)

The unit of frequency measurement. Frequency measures how often a periodic event occurs, such as the manner in which a wave's amplitude changes with time. One hertz equals one cycle per second. Frequency is often measured in kilohertz (KHz, 1000 Hz), megahertz (MHz), gigahertz (GHz, 1000 MHz), or terahertz (THz, 10,000 GHz).

High-level data link control (HDLC)

HDLC is a widely accepted international protocol governing information transfer that was developed by the International Standards Organization (ISO). HDLC is a bit-oriented, synchronous protocol that applies to the Data Link (message packaging) layer of the OSI model. Under the HDLC protocol, data is transmitted in units called frames, each of which can contain a variable amount of data, but which must be organized in a particular way.

hop

In routing through a mesh environment, the transmission of a data packet through a router.

hot fixing

See sector sparing.

HTML
See Hypertext Markup Language (HTML).

Hypertext Transport Protocol (HTTP)
The method by which World Wide Web pages are transferred over the network.

hub
A connectivity component that provides a common connection among computers in a star-configured network. Active hubs require electrical power, but they are able to regenerate and retransmit network data. Passive hubs simply organize the wiring.

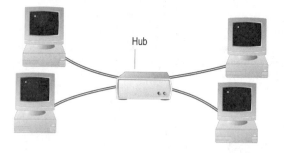

Hub

Hypertext Markup Language (HTML)
HTML is used for writing pages for the World Wide Web. HTML allows text to include codes that define fonts, layout, embedded graphics, and hypertext links. Hypertext provides a method for presenting text, images, sound, and videos that are linked together in a non-sequential web of associations. The hypertext format allows the user to browse through topics in any order. There are tools and protocols that help you explore the Internet. These tools help you locate and transport resources between computers.

I

IDE
See integrated device electronics (IDE).

IEEE
See Institute of Electrical and Electronics Engineers, Inc. (IEEE).

IEEE Project 802
A networking model developed by the IEEE. Project 802, named for the year and month it began (February 1980), defines LAN standards for the Physical and Data Link layers of the OSI model. The 802 project divides the Data Link layer into two sublayers: Media Access Control (MAC) and Logical Link Control (LLC).

impedance
The resistance, measured in ohms, to alternating current flowing in a wire.

Industry Standard Architecture (ISA)
An unofficial designation for the bus design of the IBM PC/XT. It allows various adapters to be added to the system by means of inserting plug-in cards into expansion slots. Commonly, ISA refers to the expansion slots themselves; such slots are called 8-bit slots or 16-bit slots. *See also* Enhanced Industry Standard Architecture (EISA), Micro Channel Architecture.

infrared

Electromagnetic radiation with frequencies in the electromagnetic spectrum in the range just below that of visible red light. In network communications, infrared technology offers extremely high transmission rates and wide bandwidth in line-of-sight communications.

Institute of Electrical and Electronics Engineers, Inc. (IEEE)

An organization of engineering and electronics professionals; noted in networking for developing the IEEE 802.3 standards for the Physical and Data Link layers of LANs.

integrated device electronics (IDE)

A type of disk-drive interface in which the controller electronics reside on the drive itself, eliminating the need for a separate adapter card. The IDE interface is compatible with the Western Digital™ ST-506 controller.

integrated services digital network (ISDN)

A worldwide digital communications network that evolved from existing telephone services. The goal of the ISDN is to replace all current telephone lines, which require digital-to-analog conversions, with completely digital switching and transmission facilities capable of carrying data ranging from voice to computer transmissions, music, and video. The ISDN is built on two main types of communications channels: B channels, which carry voice, data, or images at a rate of 64 Kbps (kilobits per second), and a D channel, which carries control information, signaling, and link management data at 16 Kbps. Standard ISDN Basic Rate desktop service is called 2B+D. Computers and other devices connect to ISDN lines through simple, standardized interfaces.

intermediate systems

Equipment that provides a network communications link, such as bridges, routers, and gateways.

International Standards Organization (ISO)

An organization made up of standard-setting groups from various countries. For example, the United States member is the ANSI, the American National Standards Institute. The ISO works to establish global standards for communications and information exchange. Primary among its accomplishments is the widely accepted OSI reference model.

Internet Protocol (IP)

The TCP/IP protocol for packet forwarding. *See also* Transport Control Protocol/Internet Protocol (TCP/IP).

internetwork packet exchange/sequenced packet exchange (IPX/SPX)

A protocol stack that is used in Novell networks. IPX is the NetWare protocol for packet forwarding and routing. It is a relatively small and fast protocol on a LAN. It is a derivative of Xerox Network System (XNS) and supports routing. SPX is a connection-oriented protocol used to guarantee the delivery of the data being sent. NWLink is the Microsoft implementation of the IPX/SPX protocol.

interrupt request (IRQ)

An electronic signal sent to the computer's CPU to indicate that an event has taken place which requires the processor's attention.

IP

See Internet Protocol (IP). *See also* Transport Control Protocol/Internet Protocol (TCP/IP).

IPX/SPX

See internetwork packet exchange/sequenced packet exchange (IPX/SPX).

IRQ

See interrupt request (IRQ).

ISA

See Industry Standard Architecture (ISA).

ISDN

See integrated services digital network (ISDN).

ISO

See International Standards Organization (ISO).

J

jitter

Instability in a signal wave form over time that could be caused by signal interference or an unbalanced ring in FDDI or Token Ring environments.

jumper

A small plastic and metal plug or wire for connecting different points in an electronic circuit. Jumpers are used to select a particular circuit or option from several possible configurations. For example, jumpers can be used on network adapter cards to select the type of connection through which the card will transmit, either DIX or BNC.

K

key

1. In database management, a key is an identifier for a record or group of records in a data file. Most often, the key is defined as the contents of a single field, called the key field in some database management programs and the index field in others. Keys are maintained in tables and are specially indexed to speed record retrieval.
2. A key can also be the code for deciphering encrypted data.

kilo (K)

One thousand (1000) in the metric system. In computing terminology, because computing is based on powers of 2, kilo is most often used to mean 1024 (2 raised to the 10th power). To distinguish between the two contexts, a lower case k is often used to indicate 1000, an uppercase K for 1024. A kilobyte is 1024 bytes.

kilobit (Kbit)

One thousand twenty-four bits. *See also* bit, kilo.

kilobyte (KB)

One thousand twenty-four bytes. *See also* byte, kilo.

L

LAN

See local area network (LAN).

LAN requester

See requester (LAN requester).

LAT
See local area transport (LAT).

link
The communication system connecting two LANs. Equipment that provides the link, including bridges, routers, and gateways.

local area network (LAN)
Computers connected in a geographically close network, such as in the same building, campus, or office park.

local area transport (LAT)
A nonroutable protocol from Digital Equipment Corporation.

local group
For Windows NT Server, this type of group is implemented in each computer's account database. Local groups can contain user accounts from its own computer, user accounts and global groups from both its own domain and from trusted domains. For Windows NT Server, a group can be granted permissions and rights only for the servers of its own domain.

LocalTalk
Cabling components used in an AppleTalk network. These include cables, connector modules, and cable extenders. These components are normally used in a bus or tree topology. A LocalTalk segment supports a maximum of 32 devices. Because of LocalTalk's limitations, clients often turn to vendors other than Apple for AppleTalk cabling. Farallon PhoneNet, for example, can accommodate 254 devices.

Logical Link Control (LLC) sublayer
The IEEE 802 project divides the Data Link layer into two sublayers. The Logical Link Control (LLC) sublayer is the upper sublayer that manages data link communication and defines the use of logical interface points (called service access points [SAPs]). Computers use these points to transfer information from the LLC sublayer to the upper OSI layers. *See also* Media Access Control (MAC) sublayer.

lost token
Refers to an error condition on a Token Ring network. This error causes an errant station to stop the token, causing a condition where there is no token on the ring.

M

management information base (MIB)
A database or directory containing the names of all the information resources a network management program might need.

MAU
See multistation access unit (MSAU or MAU).

Mb (Mbit)
Usually, 1,048,576 bits; sometimes interpreted as 1 million bits. *See also* bit.

MB
Megabyte or 1,048,576 bytes (2 raised to the 20th power). *See also* byte, megabyte.

Mbps
See millions of bits per second (Mbps).

Media Access Control (MAC) driver
The device driver located at the OSI Media Access Control sublayer. This driver is also known as the network adapter card driver or NIC driver. It provides low-level access to network adapters by providing data transmission support and some basic adapter management functions. These drivers also pass data from the Physical layer to transport protocols at the Network and Transport layers.

Media Access Control (MAC) sublayer
The IEEE 802 standards divided the OSI model Data Link layer into two sublayers. The Media Access Control (MAC) sublayer communicates directly with the network adapter card and is responsible for delivering error-free data between two computers on the network. *See also* Logical Link Control (LLC) sublayer.

medium
The vast majority of LANs today are connected by some sort of wire or cabling which acts as the LAN transmission medium carrying data between computers. The cabling is often referred to as the medium.

megabyte
Megabyte or 1,048,576 bytes (2 raised to the 20th power). *See also* byte, MB.

mesh network topology
Common in WANs, a mesh network connects remote sites over telecommunication links. Meshes use routers to search among multiple active paths (the mesh) and determine the best path for that particular moment.

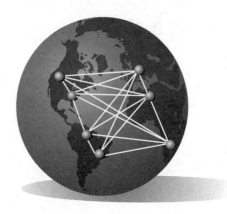

MIB
See management information base (MIB).

Micro Channel Architecture
The design of the bus in IBM PS/2 computers (except Models 25 and 30). The Micro Channel is electrically and physically incompatible with the IBM PC/AT bus. Unlike the PC/AT bus, the Micro Channel functions as either a 16-bit or 32-bit bus. The Micro Channel also can be driven independently by multiple bus master processors. *See also* Enhanced Industry Standard Architecture (EISA), Industry Standard Architecture (ISA).

Microcom Network Protocol (MNP)
The standard for asynchronous data error control developed by Microcom Systems, Inc. The method works so well that other companies adopted not only the initial version of the protocol, but later versions as well. Currently, several modem vendors incorporate MNP Classes 2, 3, 4, and 5.

millions of bits per second (Mbps)
The unit of measure of supported transmission rates on the following physical media: coaxial cable, twisted-pair cable, and fiber-optic cable. *See also* bit.

MNP
See Microcom Network Protocol (MNP).

modem
A communications device that enables a computer to transmit information over a standard telephone line. Because a computer is digital, it works with discrete electrical signals representing binary 1 and binary 0. A telephone is analog and carries a signal that can have any of a large number of variations. Modems are needed to convert digital signals to analog, and vice versa. When transmitting, modems impose (modulate) a computer's digital signals onto a continuous carrier frequency on the telephone line. When receiving, modems sift out (demodulate) the information from the carrier and transfer it in digital form to the computer.

multiplexer (mux)
A device used for division of a transmission facility into two or more channels. It may or may not be a program stored in a computer. Also, a device for connecting a number of communications lines to a computer.

multistation access unit (MSAU or MAU)
The name for a Token Ring wiring concentrator. Also known as a hub.

multitasking
A mode of operation offered by an operating system in which a computer works on more than one task at a time. There are two primary types of multitasking: preemptive and non-preemptive. In preemptive multitasking, the operating system can take control of the processor without the task's cooperation. In non-preemptive multitasking, the processor is never taken from a task. The task itself decides when to give up the processor.

A true multitasking operating system can run as many tasks as it has processors. When there are more tasks than processors, the computer must "time slice" so that the available processors devote a certain amount of time to one task and then move on to the next task, alternating between tasks until all of the tasks are done.

N

name binding protocol (NBP)
An Apple protocol responsible for keeping track of entities on the network and matching names with Internet addresses. It works at the Transport layer of the OSI model.

NDIS
See network device interface specification (NDIS).

NetBEUI (NetBIOS extended user interface)

A protocol supplied with all Microsoft network products. NetBEUI advantages include its small stack size (important for MS-DOS-based computers), its speed of data transfer on the network medium, and its compatibility with all Microsoft-based networks. The major disadvantage of NetBEUI is that it is a LAN transport and therefore does not support routing. It is also limited to Microsoft-based networks.

NetBIOS (network basic input/output system)

An API that can be used by application programs on a LAN consisting of IBM-compatible microcomputers running MS-DOS, OS/2, or some version of UNIX. Primarily of interest to programmers, NetBIOS provides application programs with a uniform set of commands for requesting the lower-level network services required to conduct sessions between nodes on a network, and to transmit information between them.

network

Two or more computers and associated devices that are connected by communications facilities.

network adapter card

An expansion card required to connect a computer to a LAN.

network analyzers

Network troubleshooting tool, sometimes called protocol analyzers. They perform a number of functions in real-time network traffic analysis as well as packet capture, decoding, and transmission. They can also generate statistics based on the network traffic to help create a picture of the network's cabling, software, file server, clients, and interface cards. Most analyzers have a built-in TDR. *See also* time-domain reflectometer (TDR).

network device interface specification (NDIS)

A standard that defines an interface for communication between the Media Access Control sublayer and protocol drivers. NDIS allows for a flexible environment of data exchange. It defines the software interface, called the NDIS interface. This interface is used by protocol drivers to communicate with the network adapter card. The advantage of NDIS is that it offers protocol multiplexing so that multiple protocol stacks can be used at the same time. *See also* open data-link interface (ODI).

Network layer

The third layer in the OSI model. This layer is responsible for addressing messages and translating logical addresses and names into physical addresses. This layer also determines the route from the source to the destination computer. It determines which path the data should take based on network conditions, priority of service, and other factors. It also manages traffic problems such as switching, routing, and controlling the congestion of data packets on the network. *See also* Open Systems Interconnection (OSI) reference model.

network monitors
Network monitors track all or a selected part of network traffic. They examine frame-level packets and gather information about packet types, errors, and packet traffic to and from each computer.

node
On a LAN, a device that is connected to the network and is capable of communicating with other network devices. For example, clients, servers, and repeaters are called nodes.

noise
Random electrical signals that can get onto the cable and degrade or distort the data. Noise is generated by power lines, elevators, air conditioners, or any device with an electric motor, relays, and radio transmitters. *See also* shielding.

non-preemptive multitasking
In non-preemptive multitasking, the processor is never taken from a task. The task itself decides when to give up the processor. Programs written for non-preemptive multitasking systems must include provisions for yielding control of the processor. No other program can run until the non-preemptive program gives up control of the processor.

O

ODI
See open data-link interface (ODI).

ohm
The unit of measure for electrical resistance. A resistance of 1 ohm will pass 1 ampere of current when a voltage of 1 volt is applied. A 100-watt incandescent bulb has a resistance of approximately 130 ohms.

open data-link interface (ODI)
A specification defined by Novell and Apple to simplify driver development and to provide support for multiple protocols on a single network adapter card. Similar to NDIS in many respects, ODI allows Novell NetWare drivers to be written without concern for the protocol that will be used on top of them.

open shortest path first (OSPF)
OSPF is a link-state algorithm derived from the OSI Intermediate System-to-Intermediate System (IS-IS) intradomain routing protocol. Link-state routing requires more processing power as compared to distance-vector routing, but provides more control over the routing process and responds faster to changes. The Dijkstra algorithm is used to calculate routes based on the number of hops (the number of routers that the packet must go through to get to the destination), the line speed, traffic, and cost.

Open Systems Interconnection (OSI) reference model

A seven-layer architecture that standardizes levels of service and types of interaction for computers exchanging information through a network. It is used to describe the flow of data between the physical connection to the network and the end-user application. This model is the best known and most widely used model for describing networking environments.

OSI layer	Focus
7. Application layer	Program-to-program transfer of information
6. Presentation layer	Text formatting and display code conversion
5. Session layer	Establishing, maintaining, and coordinating communication
4. Transport layer	Accurate delivery, service quality
3. Network layer	Transport routes, message handling and transfer
2. Data Link layer	Coding, addressing, and transmitting information
1. Physical layer	Hardware connections

optical fiber

Medium which carries digital data signals in the form of modulated pulses of light. An optical fiber consists of an extremely thin cylinder of glass, called the core, surrounded by a concentric layer of glass, known as the cladding.

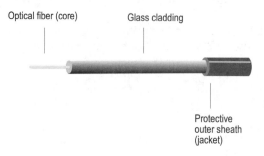

Optical fiber (core)   Glass cladding

Protective outer sheath (jacket)

oscilloscope

An electronic instrument that measures the amount of signal voltage per unit of time and displays the results on a monitor.

OSI

See Open Systems Interconnection (OSI) reference model.

OSPF

See open shortest path first (OSPF).

P

packet
In general usage, a packet is a unit of information transmitted as a whole from one device to another on a network. In packet-switching networks, a packet is defined more specifically as a transmission unit of fixed maximum size that consists of binary digits representing data, a header containing an identification number, source, and destination addresses, and sometimes error-control data. *See also* frame.

Header   Data   Trailer

packet assembler/disassembler (PAD)
A device that breaks large chunks of data into packets, usually for transmission over an X.25 network, and reassembles them at the other end. *See also* packet switching.

packet switching
A message delivery technique in which small units of information (packets) are relayed through stations in a computer network along the best route available between the source and the destination. Data is broken into smaller units and then repacked in a process called packet assembly and disassembly (PAD). Although each packet may travel along a different path, and the packets composing a message may arrive at different times or out of sequence, the receiving computer reassembles the original message. Packet-switching networks are considered fast and efficient. Standards for packet switching on networks are documented in the CCITT recommendation X.25.

PAD
See packet assembler/disassembler (PAD).

page description language (PDL)
PDLs tell a printer how printed output should look. The printer uses the PDL to construct text and graphics to create the page image. PDLs are like blueprints in that they set parameters and features such as type sizes and fonts, but they leave the drawing to the printer.

parity
With computers, parity usually refers to an error-checking procedure in which the number of 1s must always be the same—either odd or even—for each group of bits transmitted without error. If parity is checked on a per-character basis, the method is called vertical redundancy check, or VRC. If checked on a block-by-block basis, the method is called longitudinal redundancy checking, or L/C. Parity is used for checking data transferred within a computer or between computers.

partition
A portion of a physical disk that functions as though it were physically a separate unit.

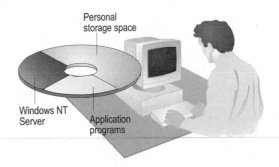

Personal storage space
Windows NT Server
Application programs

PBX Private Branch Exchange (PABX Private Automated Branch Exchange)
A switching network for voice or data lines.

PDA
See Personal Digital Assistant (PDA).

PDC
See primary domain controller (PDC).

PDL
See page description language (PDL).

PDN
See public data network (PDN).

peer-to-peer network
In a peer-to-peer network, there are no dedicated servers or hierarchy among the computers. All of the computers are equal and therefore are known as peers. Normally, each computer functions as both a client and a server.

peripheral
A term used for devices such as disk drives, printers, modems, mouse devices, and joysticks that are connected to a computer and are controlled by its microprocessor.

permanent virtual circuits (PVCs)
PVCs are similar to leased lines that are permanent and virtual except that the customer only pays for the time the line is used. This type of connection service is gaining importance because both frame relay and ATM use it. *See also* virtual circuit.

permissions
See access permissions.

Personal Digital Assistant (PDA)
A term describing a hand-held computer designed to provide specific functions such as personal organization usually including a calendar, note taking, database manipulation, access to a calculator, and communications. Current PDA devices rely on a pen instead of a keyboard or mouse for input. All of a PDA's software is firmware built into the device, and any additional software is generally installed by means of a plug-in PC Card or related device. For data storage, a PDA relies on flash memory instead of disk drives. For communication, a PDA uses cellular or wireless technology that is often built into the system, but that can be supplemented or enhanced by means of a PC Card.

petabyte
See byte.

Physical layer
The first (bottom-most) layer of the OSI model. This layer addresses the transmission of the unstructured raw bit stream over a physical medium (the networking cable). The Physical layer relates the electrical/optical, mechanical, and functional interfaces to the cable. The Physical layer also carries the signals that transmit data generated by all of the higher OSI layers. *See also* Open Systems Interconnection (OSI) reference model.

piercing tap

This is a connector for coaxial cable that pierces through the insulating layer and makes direct contact with the conducting core.

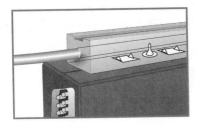

plenum

The short space in many buildings between the false ceiling and the floor above, used to circulate warm and cold air throughout the building. The space is often used for cable runs. Fire codes are very specific on the type of wiring that can be routed through this area.

Plug and Play

An emerging standard from Microsoft, Compaq, Intel, and Phoenix Technologies designed to make computer configuration relatively simple. With Plug and Play, a user would only have to physically plug a board or other peripheral into a computer to complete the connection. The operating system's Plug and Play feature would take care of identifying the peripheral and incorporating it into the system. The user would not have to set any hardware or software parameters or edit any system files.

point-to-point

Point-to-point digital circuits are dedicated circuits that are also known as private or leased lines. They are the most popular WAN communications circuits in use today. The carrier guarantees full-duplex bandwidth by setting up a permanent link from each end point using bridges and routers to connect LANs through the circuits.

Presentation layer

The sixth layer of the OSI model. This layer determines the form used to exchange data between networked computers. At the sending computer, this layer translates data from a format sent down from the Application layer into a commonly recognized, intermediary format. At the receiving end, this layer translates the intermediary format into a format useful to that computer's Application layer. The Presentation layer also manages network security issues by providing services such as data encryption. It also provides rules for data transfer and provides data compression to reduce the number of bits that need to be transmitted. *See also* Open Systems Interconnection (OSI) reference model.

primary domain controller (PDC)

The PDC is the first computer named in a Windows NT Server domain during installation. It contains a master copy of domain information, validates users, and can act as a file, print, and application server. Every domain is required to have one and only one PDC. *See also* domain, domain controller.

Project 802

IEEE defined functionality for the Logical Link Control sublayer in Standard 802.2 and defined functionality for the Media Access Control sublayer and Physical layer in Standards 802.3, 802.4, and 802.5.

802.3 defines standards for logical bus (straight line) networks, such as Ethernet, that use a mechanism called carrier-sense multiple access with collision detection (CSMA/CD). The CSMA/CD protocol regulates network traffic by allowing a broadcast only when the wire is clear and no other computer is broadcasting.

802.4 defines standards for token-passing bus networks. This is a bus layout that uses a broadcast. Every computer receives all the data but only the ones addressed respond to the broadcast. A token that travels the wire determines which computer is able to broadcast.

802.5 defines standards for token-passing ring networks. This is a logical ring network that transmits at either 4 Mbps or 16 Mbps. Even though this is called a ring, it uses a hub and is configured as a star. A token traveling around the physical ring inside the hub determines which computer may send data.

protocol

A set of rules or standards designed to enable computers to connect with one another, and peripheral devices to exchange information with as little error as possible. Protocols exist within protocols as well, all affecting different aspects of communication. Some protocols, such as the RS-232 standard, affect hardware connections.

Other standards govern data transmission, including the parameters and handshaking signals such as XON/OFF used in asynchronous (typically, modem) communications, as well as such data-coding methods as bit- and byte-oriented protocols. Still other protocols, such as the widely used XMODEM, govern file transfer, and others, such as CSMA/CD, define the methods by which messages are passed around the stations on a LAN. Protocols represent attempts to ease the complex process of enabling computers of different makes and models to communicate. Additional examples of protocols include the OSI model, IBM's SNA, and the Internet suite, including TCP/IP.

protocol analyzers

See network analyzers.

protocol driver

The protocol driver is responsible for offering four or five basic services to other layers in the network, "hiding" the details of how the services are actually implemented. The services the protocol driver performs include session management, datagram service, data segmentation and sequencing, acknowledgment, and possibly routing across a WAN.

public data network (PDN)

A commercial packet-switching or circuit-switching WAN service provided by local and long distance telephone carriers.

punchdown block

A wiring terminal, or series of terminals, into which cable can be plugged or "punched down." For environments that require centralized location for all cabling with an ease of making changes, the punchdown block is perfect. Wiring running to the jacks can be more easily organized and maintained.

PVCs

See permanent virtual circuits (PVCs).

PVC (polyvinyl chloride)

The material most commonly used for the insulation and jacketing of cable.

R

RAID

See redundant arrays of inexpensive disks (RAID).

random access memory (RAM)

Semiconductor-based memory that can be read and written to by the microprocessor or other hardware devices. The storage locations can be accessed in any order. Note that the various types of ROM memory are also capable of random access.

However, the term RAM is generally understood to refer to volatile memory, which can be written as well as read.

read only memory (ROM)

Semiconductor-based memory that contains instructions or data which can be read but not modified. *See also* random access memory (RAM).

redirector

Networking software that accepts I/O requests for remote files, named pipes, or mailslots and then sends (redirects) them to a network service on another computer.

reduced instruction set computer (RISC)

A type of microprocessor design that focuses on rapid and efficient processing of a relatively small set of instructions. RISC design is based on the premise that most of the instructions a computer decodes and executes are simple. As a result, RISC architecture limits the number of instructions that are built into the microprocessor but optimizes each so it can be carried out very rapidly, usually within a single clock cycle. RISC chips execute simple instructions faster than microprocessors designed to handle a much wider array of instructions. They are, however, slower than general-purpose CISC (complex instruction set computing) chips when executing complex instructions, which must be broken down into many machine instructions before they can be carried out by RISC microprocessors.

redundant arrays of inexpensive disks (RAID)

A standardization of fault tolerance options in five levels. The levels offer various combinations of performance, reliability, and cost.

repeater

A device that regenerates signals so they can travel on additional cable segments to extend the cable length, or to accommodate additional computers on the segment. Repeaters operate at the Physical layer of the OSI model and connect like networks, such as an Ethernet LAN to an Ethernet LAN. They do not translate or filter data. For a repeater to work, both segments that the repeater joins must have the same media access scheme, protocol, and transmission technique.

requester (LAN requester)

Software that resides in a computer and forwards requests for network services from the computer's application programs to the appropriate server. *See also* redirector.

resources

Any part of a computer system. Users on a network can share computer resources, such as hard disks, printers, modems, CD-ROM drives, and even the processor.

RG-58 A /U

Stranded core coaxial cable. The U.S. military version of this is known as RG-58 C/U.

Stranded wire
(RG-58 A/U)

RG-58 /U

Solid core coaxial cable.

Solid copper
(RG-58 /U)

rights

Authorizes a user to perform certain actions on the system. Rights apply to the system as a whole and are different from permissions, which apply to specific objects. An example would be the right to back up the entire system including the files you do not have permission to access. *See also* access permissions.

ring topology

The ring topology has computers on a circle of cable. There are no terminated ends. The data travels around the loop in one direction and passes through each computer. Each computer acts like a repeater to boost the signal and send it on. Because the signal passes through each computer, the failure of one computer can bring the entire network down. The ring may incorporate features which disconnect failed computers so that the network will continue to function despite the failure. *See also* token passing, Token Ring network.

RIP
See routing information protocol (RIP).

RISC
See reduced instruction set computer (RISC).

RJ-11
A four-wire modular connector used to join a telephone line to a wall plate or a communications peripheral such as a modem.

RJ-45
An eight-wire modular connector used to join a telephone line to a wall plate or some other device. It is similar to an RJ-11 telephone connector but has twice the number of conductors.

ROM
See read only memory (ROM).

router
A device used to connect networks of different types, such as those using different architectures and protocols. Routers work at the Network layer of the OSI model. This means they can switch and route packets across multiple networks. They do this by exchanging protocol-specific information between separate networks. Routers determine the best path for sending data and filter broadcast traffic to the local segment.

routing information protocol (RIP)
RIP uses distance-vector algorithms to determine routes. With RIP, routers transfer information among other routers to update their internal routing tables and use that information to determine the best routes based on hop counts between routers. TCP/IP and IPX support RIP.

RS-232 standard
An industry standard for serial communication connections. Adopted by the Electrical Industries Association (EIA), this recommended standard (RS) defines the specific lines and signal characteristics used by serial communications controllers to standardize the transmission of serial data between devices.

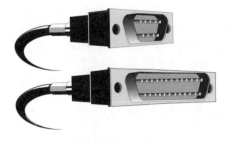
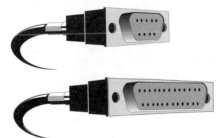

S

SAP
See service access point (SAP).

SCSI

See small computer system interface (SCSI).

SDLC

See synchronous data link control (SDLC).

sector

A portion of the data storage area on a disk. A disk is divided into sides (top and bottom), tracks (rings on each surface), and sectors (sections of each ring). Sectors are the smallest physical storage units on a disk and are of fixed size—typically capable of holding 512 bytes of information apiece.

sector sparing

A fault tolerance system also called hot fixing. It automatically adds sector-recovery capabilities to the file system during operation. If bad sectors are found during disk I/O, the fault tolerance driver will attempt to move the data to a good sector and map out the bad sector. If the mapping is successful, the file system is not alerted. It is possible for SCSI devices to perform sector sparing, but AT devices (ESDI and IDE) cannot.

segment

The length of cable on a network between two terminators. A segment can also refer to messages that have been broken up into smaller units by the protocol driver.

server

A computer that provides shared resources to network users. *See also* client.

server-based network

A network in which resource security and most other network functions are provided by dedicated servers. Server-based networks have become the standard model for networks serving more than 10 users. *See also* peer-to-peer network.

server message block (SMB)

The protocol developed by Microsoft, Intel, and IBM that defines a series of commands used to pass information between network computers. The redirector packages SMB requests into a network control block (NCB) structure that can be sent over the network to a remote device. The network provider listens for SMB messages destined for it and removes the data portion of the SMB request so that it can be processed by a local device.

service access point (SAP)

The interface between each of the seven layers in the OSI protocol stack has connection points, similar to addresses, used for communication between layers. Any protocol layer may have multiple SAPs active at one time.

session

A connection or link between stations on the network.

Session layer

The fifth layer of the OSI model. This layer allows two applications on different computers to establish, use, and end a connection called a session. This layer performs name recognition and the functions, such as security, needed to allow two applications to communicate over the network. The Session layer provides synchronization between user tasks. This layer also implements dialog control between communicating processes, regulating which side transmits, when, for how long, and so on. *See also* Open Systems Interconnection (OSI) reference model.

session management

Establishing, maintaining, and terminating connections between stations on the network.

shell

Software that provides direct communication between the user and the operating system. In Microsoft Windows, Program Manager acts as the shell. In some environments, a shell will reside on a server and allow clients from another environment to access its resources. In the Windows NT environment, for example, a server shell makes it possible for Apple clients to access resources on a Windows NT server.

shielded twisted-pair (STP)

An insulated cable with wires that are twisted around each other with a minimum number of twists per foot. The twists reduce signal interference between the wires, and the more twists per foot the greater the reduction in interference (crosstalk).

shielding

The woven or stranded metal mesh that surrounds some types of cabling. Shielding protects transmitted data by absorbing stray electronic signals, sometimes called noise (random electrical signals that can degrade or distort communications), so that they do not get onto the cable and distort the data.

Shielding

signal bounce

On a bus network, the signal is broadcast to the entire network. It travels from one end of the cable to the other. If the signal were allowed to continue uninterrupted it would keep bouncing back and forth along the cable and prevent other computers from sending signals. To stop the signal from bouncing, a component called a terminator is placed at each end of the cable to absorb free signals. Absorbing the signal clears the cable so that other computers can send data. *See also* terminator.

simple network management protocol (SNMP)

A TCP/IP protocol for monitoring networks. SNMP uses a request and response process. In SNMP, short utility programs called agents monitor the network traffic and behavior in key network components in order to gather statistical data which they put into a management information base (MIB). To collect the information into a usable form, a special management console program regularly polls the agents and downloads the information in their MIBs. If any of the data falls either above or below parameters set by the manager, the management console program can present signals on the monitor locating the trouble and notify designated support staff by automatically dialing a pager number. *See also* management information base (MIB).

small computer system interface (SCSI)

A standard, high-speed parallel interface defined by the ANSI. A SCSI interface is used for connecting microcomputers to peripheral devices, such as hard disks and printers, and to other computers and LANs. SCSI is pronounced scuzzy.

SMB

See server message block (SMB).

SMDS

See switched multimegabit data services (SMDS).

SMP

See symmetric multiprocessing (SMP).

SNA

See systems network architecture (SNA).

SNMP

See simple network management protocol (SNMP).

software

Computer programs or sets of instructions that cause the hardware to work.

SONET

See synchronous optical network (SONET).

spanning tree algorithm (STA)

Because there may be a situation where multiple LANs are joined by more than one path, the IEEE 802.1 Network Management Committee implemented the spanning tree algorithm to eliminate redundant routes. Under STA, bridges pass certain control information between themselves trying to find redundant routes. The bridges determine which would be the most efficient route, use that one, and disable the others. Any of the disabled routes can be reactivated if the primary route becomes unavailable.

SQL

See Structured Query Language (SQL).

STA

See spanning tree algorithm (STA).

stand-alone computer

A stand-alone computer is one that is not connected to any other computers. It is not part of a network.

star topology

In a star topology, each computer is connected by cable segments to a centralized component called a hub. Signals transmitted by a computer on the star pass through the hub to all computers on the network. This topology originated in the early days of computing with terminals connected to a centralized mainframe. The star offers centralized resources and management. However, because each computer is connected to a central point, this topology requires a lot of cable in a large installation, and if the central point fails, the entire network goes down.

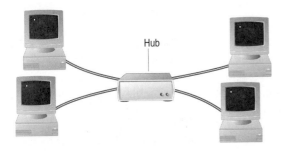

STP

See shielded twisted-pair (STP).

stripe set

A stripe set combines multiple areas of unformatted free space into one large logical drive. In Windows NT, data is written evenly across all the physical disks, one row at a time, in 64K blocks. Because the data is distributed evenly over the drives in the stripe set, all the drives belonging to the stripe set work to perform the same functions done by a single drive in a normal configuration.

This allows concurrent I/O commands to be issued and processed on all drives simultaneously. A stripe set requires at least two physical drives and can use up to 32 physical drives. Stripe sets can combine areas on different types of drives, such as SCSI, ESDI, and IDE drivers.

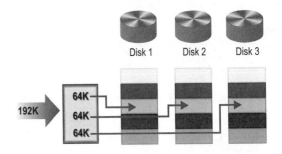

Structured Query Language (SQL)

A database sublanguage used in querying, updating, and managing relational databases. Although it is not a programming language in the same sense as C or Pascal, SQL can either be used in formulating interactive queries or be embedded in an application as instructions for handling data. The SQL standard also contains components for defining, altering, controlling, and securing data.

SVCs

See switched virtual circuits (SVCs).

switched multimegabit data services (SMDS)

A high-speed, switched-packet service that can provide speeds of up to 34 Mbps.

switched virtual circuits (SVCs)

In SVCs, the connection between end computers uses a specific route across the network. Network resources are dedicated to the circuit, and the route is maintained until the connection is terminated. These are also known as point-to-multipoint connections. *See also* virtual circuit.

switching

See packet switching.

symmetric multiprocessing (SMP)

SMP systems, such as Windows NT Server, use any available processor on an as-needed basis. With this approach, the system load and application needs can be distributed evenly across all available processors.

synchronous

Synchronous communication relies on a timing scheme coordinated between two devices to separate groups of bits and transmit them in blocks known as frames. Special characters are used to begin the synchronization and check its accuracy periodically. Because the bits are sent and received in a timed, controlled (synchronized) fashion, start and stop bits are not required. Transmission stops at the end of one transmission and starts again with a new one. It is a start/stop approach, and it is much more efficient than asynchronous transmission. If there is an error, the synchronous error detection and correction scheme simply implements a retransmission. However, because there is more sophisticated technology and equipment involved in transmitting synchronously, it is more expensive than asynchronous transmission.

synchronous data link control (SDLC)

The data link (data transmission) protocol most widely used in networks conforming to IBM's SNA. SDLC is a communications guideline that defines the format in which information is transmitted. As its name implies, SDLC applies to synchronous transmissions. SDLC is also a bit-oriented protocol and organizes information in structured units called frames.

synchronous optical network (SONET)

A fiber-optic technology that can transmit data at more than one gigabit per second. Networks based on this technology are capable of delivering voice, data, and video. SONET is a standard for optical transport formulated by the Exchange Carriers Standards Association (ECSA) for the ANSI.

systems network architecture (SNA)

SNA is a widely used communications framework developed by IBM to define network functions and establish standards for enabling its different models of computers to exchange and process data. SNA is essentially a design philosophy that separates network communication into five layers. Each of these layers, like those in the similar ISO/OSI model, represents a graduated level of function moving upward from physical connections to applications software.

T

T connector

A T-shaped coaxial connector that connects two thinnet Ethernet cables while supplying an additional connector for a network interface card.

BNC T connector

T1 service

T1 is the standard digital line service. It provides transmission rates of 1.544 Mbps and can carry both voice and data.

tap

A connection to a network. This usually refers specifically to a connection to a cable.

TCP

See Transmission Control Protocol (TCP).

TCP/IP

See Transport Control Protocol/Internet Protocol (TCP/IP).

TDR

See time-domain reflectometer (TDR).

Telnet

The command and program used to log in from one Internet site to another. The Telnet command and program gets you to the login prompt of another host.

terabyte

See byte.

terminator

A resistor used at each end of an Ethernet cable to ensure that signals do not reflect back and cause errors. It is usually attached to an electrical ground at one end. *See also* signal bounce.

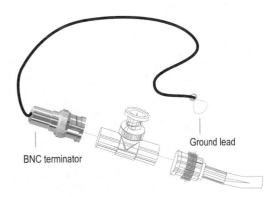

BNC terminator   Ground lead

terminator resistance

The level of resistance in a terminator, measured in ohms. It must match the network architecture specification. For example, Ethernet using RG-58 A/U thinnet cable requires a 50 ohm resistor in the terminator. Terminating resistance that does not match the specifications may cause the network to fail.

thicknet (standard Ethernet)

A relatively rigid coaxial cable about 0.5-inch in diameter. Typically, thicknet is used as a backbone to connect several smaller thinnet-based networks because of its ability to support data transfer over longer distances. Thicknet can carry a signal for 500 meters (about 1,640 feet) before needing a repeater.

thinnet (thin-wire Ethernet)

A flexible coaxial cable about 0.25-inch thick. It is used for relatively short distance communication and is fairly flexible to facilitate routing between computers. Thinnet coaxial cable can carry a signal up to approximately 185 meters (or about 607 feet) before needing a repeater.

throughput

A measure of the data transfer rate through a component, connection, or system. In networking, throughput is a good indicator of the system's total performance because it defines how well the components work together to transfer data from one computer to another. In this case, the throughput would indicate how many bytes or packets the network could process per second.

time-domain reflectometer (TDR)

A troubleshooting tool that sends sonar-like pulses along a cable looking for any kind of a break, short, or imperfection that might affect performance. If the pulse finds a problem, the TDR analyzes it and displays the result. A good TDR can locate a break to within a few feet of the actual separation in the cable.

token

A token is a predetermined formation of bits which permits a network device to communicate with the cable. A computer may not transmit unless it has possession of the token. Only one token at a time may be active on the network, and the token may only travel in one direction around the ring. *See also* token passing, Token Ring network.

token passing

A media access control method in a Token Ring network that involves passing a data frame, called a token, from one station to the next around the ring. *See also* token, Token Ring network.

Token Ring network

On a Token Ring network, computers are situated on a continuous network loop on which a token is passed from one computer to the next. Computers are centrally connected to a hub called a multistation access unit (MAU) and are wired in a star configuration. Computers use a token to transmit data and must wait for a free token in order to transfer data. *See also* token, token passing.

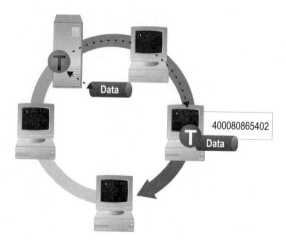

topology
The arrangement or layout of computers, cables, and other components on a network. Topology is the standard term that most network professionals use when they refer to the network's basic design.

transceiver
A device that connects a computer to the network. The term transceiver is derived from transmitter/receiver, so a transceiver is a device that receives and transmits signals. It switches the parallel data stream used on the computer's bus into a serial data stream used in the cables connecting the computers.

Transmission Control Protocol (TCP)
The TCP/IP protocol for sequenced data. *See also* Transport Control Protocol/Internet Protocol (TCP/IP).

Transport Control Protocol/Internet Protocol (TCP/IP)
TCP/IP is an industry standard suite of protocols providing communications in a heterogeneous environment. In addition, TCP/IP provides a routable, enterprise networking protocol and access to the Internet and its resources. It is a Transport layer protocol that actually consists of several other protocols in a stack that operates at the Session layer. Almost all networks support TCP/IP as a protocol.

Transport layer
The fourth layer of the OSI model. It ensures that messages are delivered error-free, in sequence, and with no losses or duplications. This layer repackages messages for their efficient transmission over the network. At the receiving end, the Transport layer unpacks the messages, reassembles the original messages, and sends an acknowledgment of receipt. *See also* Open Systems Interconnection (OSI) reference model.

transport protocols
Transport protocols provide for communication sessions between computers and ensure that data is able to move reliably between computers.

trust relationship
Trust relationships are links between domains that enable pass-through authentication, in which a user has only one user account in one domain, yet can access the entire network. User accounts and global groups defined in a trusted domain can be given rights and resource permissions in a trusting domain even though those accounts do not exist in the trusting domain's database. A trusting domain honors the logon authentication's of a trusted domain.

twisted-pair cable
A cable that consists of two insulated strands of copper wire twisted together. A number of twisted-wire pairs are often grouped together and enclosed in a protective sheath to form a cable. Twisted-pair cable can be shielded or unshielded. Unshielded twisted-pair cable is commonly used for telephone systems. *See also* shielded twisted-pair (STP), unshielded twisted-pair (UTP).

U

UART
See universal asynchronous receiver transmitter (UART).

Uniform Resource Locator (URL)
Provides the Hypertext links between documents on the Web (WWW). Every resource on the Internet has its own location identifier or URL. URLs specify the server to access as well as the access method and the location. URLs can use various protocols including FTP, http, or gopher.

uninterruptible power supply (UPS)
A device connected between a computer, or some other piece of electronic equipment, and a power source, such as an electrical outlet. The UPS ensures that the electrical flow to the computer is not interrupted because of a blackout and, in most cases, to protect the computer against potentially damaging events such as power surges and brownouts. Different UPS models offer different levels of protection. All UPS units are equipped with a battery and a loss-of-power sensor. If the sensor detects a loss of power, it immediately switches over to the battery so that the user has time to save his or her work and shut off the computer. Most higher-end models have features such as power filtering, sophisticated surge protection, and a serial port so that an operating system capable of communicating with a UPS (such as Windows NT) can work with the UPS to facilitate automatic system shutdown.

universal asynchronous receiver transmitter (UART)
A module, usually composed of a single integrated circuit, that contains both the receiving and transmitting circuits required for asynchronous serial communication. Two computers, each equipped with a UART, can communicate over a simple wire connection. The operation of the sending and receiving units are not synchronized by a common clock signal, so the data stream itself must contain information as to when packets of information (usually bytes) begin and end. This beginning of a packet and end of a packet information is provided by the start and stop bits in the data stream. A UART is the most common type of circuit used in personal computer modems.

unshielded twisted-pair (UTP)
A cable with wires that are twisted around each other with a minimum number of twists per foot. The twists reduce signal interference between the wires. The more twists per foot the greater the reduction in interference (crossstalk). This cable is similar to shielded-twisted pair (STP), but lacks the insulation or shielding found in STP cable.

UPS
See uninterruptible power supply (UPS).

URL
See Uniform Resource Locator (URL).

user account
Consists of all of the information that defines a user on a network. This includes the user name and password required for the user to log on, the groups in which the user account has membership, and the rights and permissions the user has for using the system and accessing its resources. For Windows NT, accounts are managed with User Manager. For Windows NT Server, accounts are managed with User Manager for Domains.

UTP
See unshielded twisted-pair (UTP).

V

vampire tap (piercing tap transceiver)
An Ethernet transceiver housed in a clamp-like device with sharp metal prongs that "bite" through thicknet cable insulation and make contact with the copper core. The transceiver's DIX (DB15) connector provides an attachment for an AUI cable that runs from the transceiver to either the computer or a hub or repeater.

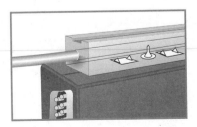

Thick coaxial cable has bands on it every 2.5 meters (8 feet). A vampire tap is inserted into the thick coaxial at each of these bands and an AUI, DIX, or DB15 connector attaches a cable from the tap to the computer or other device to be added to the Ethernet network.

virtual circuit
Virtual circuits are composed of a series of logical connections between the sending computer and the receiving computer. The connection is made after both computers exchange information and agree on communication parameters which establish and maintain the connection, including maximum message size and path. Virtual circuits incorporate communication parameters such as acknowledgments, flow control, and error control to ensure reliability. They can be either temporary, lasting only as long as the conversation, or permanent, lasting as long as the users keep the communications channel open.

volt meter
See digital volt meter (DVM).

volume set
A volume set is a collection of hard disk partitions that are treated as a single partition, thus increasing the disk space available in a single drive letter. Volume sets are created by combining between 2 and 32 areas of unformatted free space on one or more physical drives. These spaces form one large logical volume set which is treated like a single partition.

W

wide area network (WAN)
A computer network that uses long-range telecommunication links to connect the networked computers over long distances.

workgroup
A collection of computers that are grouped for sharing resources such as data and peripherals over a LAN. Each workgroup is identified by a unique name. *See also* domain, peer-to-peer network.

world wide web (WWW)
The World Wide Web (the Web) is the Internet's multimedia service that contains a vast storehouse of Hypertext documents written using the HTML. *See also* Hypertext Markup Language (HTML).

X

X.25
A recommendation published by the CCITT that defines the connection between a terminal and a packet-switching network. A packet-switching network routes packets whose contents and format are controlled standards such as those defined in the X.25 recommendation. X.25 incorporates three definitions: the electrical connection between the terminal and the network, the transmission or link-access protocol, and the implementation of virtual circuits between network users. Taken together, these definitions specify a synchronous, full-duplex terminal-to-network connection. Packets transmitted in such a network can contain either data or control commands. Packet format, error control, and other features are equivalent to portions of the HDLC protocol defined by the ISO. X.25 standards are related to the lowest three levels of the OSI model.

X.400
A CCITT protocol for international e-mail transmissions.

X.500
A CCITT protocol for file and directory maintenance across several systems.

XNS (Xerox Network System)
Protocol developed by Xerox for their Ethernet LANs.

Z

zones
LocalTalk networks can be joined or divided into areas called zones. Two physical networks, for example, can be joined into one logical zone and seen as part of one organization. Conversely, working groups on a single LocalTalk network can be divided into zones to relieve congestion on a busy network.

Index

5-4-3 rule, Ethernet 259, 262
10Base2, Ethernet (thinnet) 77–78, 258–260, 308
10Base5, standard Ethernet
  (thicknet) 78–79, 260–262, 308
10BaseFL, Ethernet 263
10BaseT, Ethernet 86, 256–258, 307–308
10BaseT, transceiver 257
100BaseFX Ethernet media specification 267
100BaseT4 Ethernet media specification 267
100BaseTX Ethernet media specification 267
100BaseVG *See* 100VG-AnyLAN, Ethernet
100BaseX, Fast Ethernet 267
100VG-AnyLAN, Ethernet 176, 229–230, 265–266
802 Project model *See* Project 802

A

Access methods
  choosing (LAN Planner) 250
  contention 229
  CSMA/CA 230
  CSMA/CD
    ANSI specifications 711
    as an access method 229–230
    glossary definition 770
    IEEE 802 category description 175
    IEEE Physical layer protocols 213–214
  demand priority 229–230
  description 223
  token passing
    ArcNet 293–294
    as an access method 228–230
    FDDI 605
    glossary definition 802
    ring networks 42
    Token Ring 277–278
  traffic control on cables 223
  troubleshooting 242
Access permissions
  glossary definition 761
  group permissions 477–479
  overview 475
  resource security 475–477
Access points, wireless networks 106–107

Access, unauthorized, troubleshooting 518–519
Accounts
  group
    creating and deleting, how to (lab) 451–453
    creating 442
    description 441–442
    granting privileges 445
    planning for 441
    types of 443–445
  policies 761
  user
    administrator or supervisor accounts 438
    creating and deleting, how to (lab) 451–453
    creating 434–435
    disabling or deleting 446–449
    glossary definition 805
    guest accounts 439
    key accounts 438
    parameters, setting 437
    passwords 439
    profiles 438
    user information, entering 436–437
ACK (acknowledgment), glossary definition 761
Active
  hubs 44
  window 761
Adapter cards for networks *See* Network adapter cards
Adapter memory, shared, network performance 138
Addresses
  base memory or RAM start address 127–128, 766
  IP 328
Addressing, packets 197
Administration, peer-to-peer networks 17
Administrative Tools Program group,
  Windows NT Server 434, 442
Administrator
  accounts 438
  responsibilities, network management 433
Advanced cable testers 658, 761
Advanced program-to-program communication (APPC)
  protocol 210, 218, 762
Advanced RISC Computing (ARC) 762
AFP (AppleTalk filing protocol) 211
Agent, proxy 684, 762

Algorithms
    Dijkstra 567
    distance-vector 567
    link-state 567
    OSPF (open shortest path first) 567, 787
    STA (spanning tree algorithm) 560, 798
America Online (AOL) e-mail provider 362
American National Standards Institute
    (ANSI) 212, 611, 711, 762
American Standard Code for Information Interchange
    (ASCII) 764
American Wire Gauge (AWG) standard cable
    measurement 98–99, 765
Amplifiers, broadband transmissions 96, 762
Amplifying signals with a repeater 39, 284, 794
Analog
    See also Digital
    connectivity
        dedicated lines 583–584
        dedicated vs. dial-up lines 584
        dial-up lines 582–583
        line conditioning 584
    glossary definition 762
    signals 96, 534–535
    transmission systems 96
Analyzers, network or protocol 659–661, 786
ANSI (American National Standards
    Institute) 212, 611, 711, 762
ANSI specifications 711
Any-to-any connections *See* Packet switching
AnyLAN *See* 100VG-AnyLAN, Ethernet
AOL (America Online) e-mail provider 362
APF (AppleTalk Filing Protocol) 763
API (application programming interface) 763
APPC (advanced program-to-program communication)
    protocol 210, 218, 762
AppleShare
    description 392
    file and print servers 290, 763
    glossary definition 763
    protocol suite 211
AppleTalk
    advantages 288
    AppleShare
        description 392
        file and print servers 290, 763
        glossary definition 763
        protocol suite 211
    DDP (datagram delivery protocol) 211, 566
    EtherTalk 291

AppleTalk *(continued)*
    filing protocol (AFP) 211, 763
    glossary definition 763
    LAN Planner 244, 730
    LocalTalk 289–290, 310, 783
    multivendor environments 392
    overview 288–289
    protocols 218
    Services for Macintosh 388, 392
    TokenTalk 291
    transaction protocol (ATP) 211
    zones 290, 806
Application front end, client/server 400, 777
Application layer, OSI reference model 169, 763
Application programming interface (API) 763
Application protocols
    See also Protocols
    AFP (AppleTalk filing protocol) 211, 763
    APPC (advanced program-to-program
        communication) protocol 210, 218, 762
    AppleTalk and Apple Share protocol suite 211, 763
    DAP (data access protocol) 211
    description 210
    FTAM (file transfer access and management) 210,
        777
    FTP (File Transfer Protocol) 210, 216, 674–675, 777
    glossary definition 763
    NCP (Novell NetWare Core Protocol) 211
    SMBs (server message blocks) 211, 796
    SMTP (simple mail transfer protocol) 210, 216, 366–
        367
    SNMP (simple network management
        protocol) 210, 216, 461–462, 798
    Telnet 211, 801
    X.400 210, 363–365, 715, 806
    X.500 210, 365, 715, 806
Application servers 21
Applications
    network
        See also Network applications
        LAN Planner 423
        troubleshooting 417
    shared
        how to share 382
        overview 382
        requirements 383
        software logs 383
    sharing in a networking environment 10
    troubleshooting 694, 755
ARC (Advanced RISC Computing) 762
Archie protocol 675

Architectures
    client/server 404–405
    data bus 130–131
    layered, OSI reference model
        Application layer 170, 761
        Data Link layer 172–173, 557, 597, 772
        glossary definition 788
        Network layer 172, 570, 786
        overview 169–170
        Physical layer 173, 552, 666–667, 790
        Presentation layer 171, 791
        relationship of layers 169–170
        Session layer 171, 797
        Transport layer 171, 803
    network, selecting (LAN Planner) 307–311, 727
Archive, glossary definition 763
ArcNet 293–294, 310, 764
ASCII (American Standard Code for Information
    Interchange) 764
Async (asynchronous communications) modems 540–542
Asynchronous transfer mode (ATM) See ATM
Asynchronous transmission, glossary definition 764
AT&T e-mail provider 362
ATEC (Authorized Technical Education Center) xli
ATM (asynchronous transfer mode)
    advantages and disadvantages 602
    components 600–602
    glossary definition 764
    overview 599
    technology 599–600
ATP (AppleTalk transaction protocol) 211
Attached Resource Computer Network
    (ArcNet) 293–294, 310, 764
Attachment unit interface (AUI)
    port connectors 79, 133, 261, 764
Attachments to e-mail 361
Attenuation 76, 765
Auditing for security reasons 481
AUI port connectors 79, 133, 261, 765
Authorized Technical Education Center (ATEC) xli
AWG standard cable measurement 98, 765

B

Back end, client/server 401–402, 765
Backbone, Ethernet 261, 765
Backing up data
    glossary definition 765
    server-based networks 25, 639
    using tapes See Tape backup
Backup domain controllers (BDCs) 326, 765
Bandwidth, glossary definition 766
Banyan Intelligent Messaging Service 379
Bar-code routing of faxes 355

Barrel connectors, BNC 39, 81, 258
Base input/output (I/O) ports
    configuring network adapter cards 126
    glossary definition 766
Base memory address
    configuring network adapter cards 124
    glossary definition 766
Baseband transmissions 95, 766
Baselines, establishing 646–648
Basic Rate ISDN 604
Baud rate, modems 538, 766
BBSs (bulletin board services) 664
BDCs (backup domain controllers) 326, 765
Beaconing 608, 658, 767
Bibliography 759
Binary synchronous communications (bisync)
    protocol 543, 767
Binding options, network services 336
Binding process, protocols 209, 767
Bis, international modem standards 537
BISDN (broadband integrated services digital
    network) 599, 611, 768
Bisync (binary synchronous communications)
    protocol 543, 767
Bit, glossary definition 767
BNC
    barrel connectors 39, 81, 258
    cable connectors 80
    glossary definition 768
    T connectors 80, 258, 801
    terminators 81, 258, 801
    thinnet network connection 133
Bottlenecks, network performance 461, 660, 768
Bounce See Signals, bouncing
Bps (bits per second) 538, 768
Bridges
    advantages 561
    broadcast storms 562, 769
    brouters 572, 769
    glossary definition 768
    how they work 557–558
    implementing 561
    LAN Planner 626, 741
    Media Access Control (MAC) layer bridges 557
    overview 556
    remote 560
    routing tables 557–558
    segmenting network traffic 559
    vs. repeaters 561
    vs. routers
        broadcasting 570
        multiple paths 571
        overview 569
    wireless 111–112
British Naval Connector (BNC) See BNC

Broadband integrated services digital network
(BISDN) 599, 611, 768
Broadband network, glossary definition 768
Broadband optical telepoint infrared wireless
networks 109
Broadband Technical Advisory Group, 802.7
category 175
Broadband transmissions 96
Broadcast
   glossary definition 769
   storms
      glossary definition 769
      passed on by bridges 562
      passed on by repeaters 554
      preventing using routers 565
Brouters
   description 572
   glossary definition 769
   routable vs. nonroutable protocols 572
Buffering, RAM, network performance 139
Buffers, glossary definition 769
Built-in groups 443, 769
Bulletin board services (BBSs) 664
Bus mastering, network performance 139
Bus networks
   disrupting network communication 38
   glossary definition 769
   LAN expansion 39
   sending signals 36
   signal bounce 36, 797
   terminators 37, 59, 666, 801
   troubleshooting 59
Busses, description 120
Byte, glossary definition 769

C

C-conditioning, telephone lines 584
Cables
   advanced cable testers 657, 761
   breaking 59–60
   drop 79, 261
   patch, Token Ring LANs 283
   physically securing 473
   transceiver 79, 261
Cabling
   100BaseFX media specification 267
   100BaseT4 media specification 267
   100BaseTX media specification 267
   ArcNet 295
   BNC connectors 80–81, 768
   choosing (LAN Planner) 157–160, 727–728
   coaxial *See* Coaxial
   comparison summary 102

Cabling *(continued)*
   considerations 100–101
   fiber-optic
      cladding 92
      core 92
      description 92–93
      FDDI 608
      overview 92
      Token Ring 284
   IBM system 98–99, 282–283
   limits, LANs 6
   LocalTalk 289–290, 310, 783
   media filters 284
   networks 132–134
   overview 74
   peer-to-peer networks, system for 16
   reusing existing 69
   RG-58 family 78, 794
   standard Ethernet 78, 260, 306
   Token Ring 282–283
   troubleshooting 151, 666–669, 754
   twisted-pair *See* Twisted-pair cables
Cache, glossary definition 770
Capacity of hubs 280–281
Cards, network adapter *See* Network adapter cards
Carrier Sense Multiple Access with Collision Avoidance
(CSMA/CA) 224
Carrier Sense Multiple Access with Collision Detection
(CSMA/CD)
   access method 224–226
   ANSI specifications 711
   glossary definition 770
   IEEE 802 category description 175
   IEEE Physical layer protocols 213
CCEP (Commercial COMSEC Endorsement
Program) 482, 770
CCITT (Comité Consultatif Internationale de Télégraphie
et Téléphonie)
   glossary definition 770
   overview 712–715
   protocol standards 212
   SONET and Synchronous Digital Hierarchy
      recommendations 611
   X.400 363–365
CD-ROMs, setting up course lab files xxviii–xxix
CDDI (copper distributed data interface) 609
CDPD (cellular digital packet data) 115
Cellular digital packet data (CDPD) 115
Cellular networks 115
Central
   file server, glossary definition 770
   processing unit (CPU), glossary definition 770
Centralized computing 396
Certification programs 745
Certified NetWare Engineer (CNE) program 745

Certified Professional program *See* Microsoft Certified
   Professional program
Channel service unit/data service unit (CSU/DSU) 586
Channels, spread-spectrum radio wireless networks 110
Circuits, virtual, packet switching 590, 805
Cladding, fiber-optic cabling, description 92
Client Service for NetWare (CSNW) 390
Client software, network operating systems 319–321
Client solutions in multivendor environments 387
Client/server
   advantages 406
   architecture 404–405
   client, front end, or application 399–400, 777
   computing, description 396–397
   glossary definition 771
   LAN Planner 426, 732
   model, description 398
   process of requesting and receiving information 398–
     399
   program development tools 400
   query tools 400
   search key, on-screen form 399
   server hardware 402
   server, back end, or database server 401, 765
   stored procedures 401
   troubleshooting 421, 756
   user applications 400
Clients
   computers, hardware considerations 26
   description 14
   glossary definition 770
CMIP (common management information protocol) 715
CNE (Certified Netware Engineer) program 745
Coaxial
   cable grades 82–83
   cabling
     considerations 83
     core, description 74–75
     glossary definition 771
     illustrated 75
     overview 74–77
     plenum 82–83, 789
     polyvinyl chloride (PVC) 82, 793
     thicknet (10Base5) 78–79, 260–261, 308, 802
     thinnet (10Base2) 77–78, 258–259, 308, 802
     thinnet vs. thicknet 79
   connection hardware 80–81, 258
   fire codes 82–83
Codec (compression/decompression), glossary
   definition 771
Combination networks 28

Comité Consultatif Internationale de Télégraphie et
   Téléphonie (CCITT)
   glossary definition 770
   overview 713–715
   protocol standards 212
   SONET and Synchronous Digital Hierarchy
     recommendations 611
   X.400 363–365
Commercial COMSEC Endorsement Program
   (CCEP) 482, 770
Common management information protocol (CMIP) 715
Common open software environment (COSE) 712–713
Communications
   asynchronous 540–542
   bus topology
     disrupting 38
     glossary definition 769
     sending signals 36
     signal bounce 36, 797
     terminators 37, 59, 666, 801
   network
     function of packets 192–193
     overview 166
   serial interface
     RS-232 535–536, 716, 795
     RS-422 716
     RS-423 716
     RS-449 716
   servers 22
   synchronous 542–543, 560, 586, 800
   troubleshooting 622–623, 757
Compact disc, setting up course lab files xxviii–xxix
Companies
   large, networks for *See* Wide area networks (WANs)
   small, networks for *See* Local area networks (LANs)
Compressed serial line Internet protocol (CSLIP) 683
Compression/decompression (codec), glossary
   definition 771
CompuServe
   e-mail provider 362
   obtaining Microsoft Certified Professional program
     information xxxviii
Computers
   connected, sharing resources 5
   diskless 482, 774
   stand-alone 4, 798
   troubleshooting 666
Computing
   centralized, description 396
   client/server *See* Client/Server
Conditioning lines 584

Configuring drivers 184
Connecting to network printers 349
Connection hardware
    coaxial cables 80–81, 258
    twisted-pair cables 89
Connectivity
    analog
        dedicated lines 583–584
        dedicated vs. dial-up lines 584
        dial-up lines 582–583
        glossary definition 762
        line conditioning 584
    digital
        CSU/DSU (channel service unit/data service
            unit) 586
        DDS (digital data service) 586
        DS-0 or DS-1 transmission rates 587–588
        E1 service 587
        Fractional T-1 service 587
        glossary definition 773
        ISDN 604, 683, 781
        multiplexing (muxing) 587, 785
        overview 586
        Switched 56 service 588
        T1 service 587–588, 801
        T3 service 588, 601
Connectors
    attachment unit interface (AUI) port 79, 133, 261, 764
    BNC 80, 258, 801
        barrel 39, 81, 258
        cable 80
        glossary definition 768
        terminators 81, 258, 666, 801
        thinnet network connection 133
    DB-15, description 79, 133
    Digital Intel Xerox (DIX) 79, 261, 774
    hermaphroditic, glossary definition 779
    IBM 98, 283
    MIC (media interface connector) 283
    N-series 261
    network 132–134
    telephone
        RJ-11 89, 134, 288, 535–536, 795
        RJ-45 89, 134, 288, 795
Contention
    access method 225, 230
    glossary definition 771
Control information, data frames 172, 253
Control Panel, Microsoft Windows NT Server 184
Controllers, disk See Disk controllers
Controlling traffic on cables 223
Cooperative multitasking 317

Copper distributed data interface (CDDI) 609
Core
    coaxial cable, description 75
    fiber-optic cabling, description 92
Corporation for Open Systems (COS) 715
COS (Corporation for Open Systems) 715
COSE (common open software environment) 712–714
Cost
    peer-to-peer networks 16
    topologies 68–69
Couplers, jack 90
Course
    content overview xxix–xxx
    finding the best starting point xxxii
    hardware and software requirements xxviii
    intended audience of this book xxvii
    prerequisites for taking self-paced training
        course xxvii
    setup information xxviii–xxix
CPU (central processing unit), glossary definition 770
Crashes, server disks 666
CRC, data frames
    Ethernet frame format 253
    glossary definition 771
    packet trailer 195
    simple data frame example 172
    Token Ring format 275
Crosstalk 88, 771
CSLIP (compressed serial line Internet protocol) 683
CSMA/CA 226
CSMA/CD
    access method 224–226
    ANSI specifications 711
    glossary definition 770
    IEEE 802 category description 175
    IEEE Physical layer protocols 212–213
CSNW (Client Service for NetWare) 390
CSU/DSU (channel service unit/data service unit) 586
Cyclical redundancy check (CRC), data frames
    Ethernet frame format 253–254
    glossary definition 771
    packet trailer 195
    simple data frame example 172
    Token Ring format 275

D

D-conditioning, telephone lines 584
Daisy chain, glossary definition 772
DAP (data access protocol) 211

Data
    backing up
        glossary definition 765
        server-based networks 25, 639
        using tapes *See* Tape backup
    bus architecture 130–131
    communications equipment (DCE)
        See also DTE/DCE; Modems
        and DTE equipment 596, 773
        glossary definition 772
    packets 194, 789
    parallel transmission 121
    redundancy
        See also Fault tolerant systems
        server-based networks 26
    sending via network adapter cards 121–122
    serial transmission 120
    sharing in a networking environment 9
    storage warehouse servers, client/server 405
    stream, glossary definition 772
    transmitting via token passing
        ArcNet 293–294
        as an access method 228
        FDDI 606
        glossary definition 802
        ring networks 42
        Token Ring 277–278
Data Access Protocol (DAP) 211
Data communications equipment (DCE)
    See also Modems
    glossary definition 772
Data encryption
    description 482
    glossary definition 776
    key (deciphering) 482, 782
    standards (DES) 482, 772
Data frames
    See also Packets
    description 172
    Ethernet 253–254
    glossary definition 772
    packets 194, 789
    specifying memory 128
    Token Ring format 280
Data Link layer, OSI reference
    model 172–173, 557, 597, 772
Data protection
    fault tolerant systems
        overview 495
        RAID (redundant arrays of inexpensive disks)
            See RAID
        LAN Planner 522–528, 735
    overview 487

Data protection *(continued)*
    tape backup
        implementing 488–490
        installing the backup system 491
        maintaining backup logs 490
        overview 488
        testing and storage 490
    troubleshooting 518, 756
    UPS (uninterruptible power supply) 493–494, 667, 804
Data terminal equipment/data communications equipment
    (DTE/DCE) 596, 773
Database
    management systems (DBMS),
        client/server computing 397, 773
    query language *See* SQL
    server, client/server 401–402
Database server, client/server 765
Datagram delivery protocol (DDP) 211, 566
DB-15 connectors 79, 133
DBMS (database management systems),
    client/server computing 397, 773
DCE (data communications equipment)
    See also DTE/DCE; Modems
    and DTE equipment 596, 773
    glossary definition 772
DCE (Distributed Computing Environment) 719
DDP (datagram delivery protocol) 211, 566
DDS (digital data service lines) 586
DEC, Teamlinks 379
DECnet 218, 566, 773
Dedicated
    lines 545, 560, 583–584
    servers 20, 773
Default gateway, TCP/IP 329
Deleting
    and creating group accounts, how to (lab) 455–456
    and creating user accounts, how to (lab) 453–454
    network adapter card software, how to (lab) 187–188
    or disabling user accounts 450–451
Demand Priority Access LAN,
    100VG-AnyLAN 176, 229, 265–266
DES (data encryption standard) 482, 772
Design of networks *See* Topologies
Designators, drive 320
Designing the layout of networks 34
Destination ID, data frames 172
Device drivers *See* Drivers
DHCP server service 329, 775
Diagrams *See* Topologies
Dial-up lines 545, 584
DID (direct inward dialing) 355

Digital
  See also Analog
  connectivity
    CSU/DSU (channel service unit/data service
      unit) 586
    DDS (digital data service) 586
    DS-0 or DS-1 transmission rates 587–588
    E1 service 587
    Fractional T-1 service 587
    ISDN 604, 684, 781
    multiplexing (muxing) 587, 785
    overview 586
    Switched 56 service 588
    T1 service 587–588, 801
    T3 service 588, 601
  data service (DDS) lines 586
  Equipment Corporation (DEC) *See* DECnet
  glossary definition 773
  Intel Xerox (DIX) connectors 79, 261, 774
  modems 540–543
  signals 92, 95
  volt meter (DVM) 657, 774
Dijkstra routing algorithm 567
DIP (dual inline package) switch settings 124, 774
Direct inward dialing (DID) 355
Direct Memory Access (DMA) 138, 774
Directing packets 197
Directories
  e-mail 362
  sharing
    description 24
    how to (lab) 30–31
Directory services servers, description 22
Disk
  controllers
    ESDI 495, 499, 776
    IDE 181, 495, 499, 781
    SCSI 181, 495, 499, 798
  crashes, servers 666
  duplexing - level 1 RAID 496
  duplicating (mirroring) 496–497, 774
  hard, glossary definition 778
  mirroring - level 1 RAID 496–497, 774
  striping - level 0 RAID 495–496
  striping with ECC - level 2 RAID 497
  striping with large blocks - level 4 RAID 498
  striping with parity - level 5 RAID 498
Disk Administrator, Windows NT Server 500
Diskless
  computers 482, 774
  workstations
    glossary definition 774
    remote-boot PROMs 140
Distance-vector routing algorithm 567
Distributed Computing Environment (DCE) 719

Distributed Management Environment (DME) 719
Distributed queue dual bus (DQDB) 612
Distributed servers, client/server 404–405
Distribution racks, using with twisted-pair cables 89
DIX (Digital Intel Xerox) connectors 79, 261, 774
DMA (direct memory access) 138, 774
DME (Distributed Management Environment) 719
DNS (domain name system) 681–682
Documentation
  bibliography 759
  LAN Planner 700–703, 746
  preparing and maintaining 639
Domain
  See also Workgroups
  controllers
    See also Backup domain controller (BDC);
      Primary domain controller (PDC)
    glossary definition 775
  glossary definition 772
  name system (DNS) 681–682
Downtime, glossary definition 775
DQDB (distributed queue dual bus) 612
Drive designators 320
Drivers
  configuring 185
  glossary definition 775
  installing 184
  Media Access Control (MAC) sublayer 784
  networking software 183
  OSI reference model 182
  planning for (LAN Planner) 244
  protocol, glossary definition 792
  removing 185
  role of 181
  troubleshooting 240, 754
  updating 185
Drop cables 79, 261
DS-0 or DS-1 transmission rates 587–588
DTE/DCE (data terminal equipment/data communications
  equipment) 596, 773
Dual-cable broadband configurations 96
Dual-ring topology 606–607
Dual shielding 75
Dumb terminal, glossary definition 775
Duplex transmission, glossary definition 775
Duplexing disks - level 1 RAID 496
Duplicating disk (disk mirroring) 496–497, 774
DVM (digital volt meter) 657, 774
Dynamic host configuration protocol (DHCP)
  server service 329, 775
Dynamic routers 568

E

E-mail
  attachments 361
  directories 362
  gateways 367–368
  groupware 373
  Internet 674
  LAN Planner 732
  mailboxes 361
  notification 361
  online providers
    AOL (America Online) 362
    AT&T 362
    CompuServe 362
    MCI Mail 362
    Microsoft 362
  overview 360
  reply 361
  return receipt 361
  special features 368
  standards
    communication between standards 367–368
    overview 363
    SMTP (simple mail transfer protocol) 366–367
    X.400 363–365, 715
    X.500 365, 715
  support and training 363
E1 service 587
EB (exabyte) 23, 776
EBCDIC (extended binary coded decimal interchange code), glossary definition 776
ECC stored as parity - level 3 RAID 497
ECSA (Exchange Carriers Standards Association) 611
EIA/TIA wiring standard 568 87
EIS (Electronics Industries Association) 87, 716–717
EISA (extended industry standard architecture) 130, 775
EIU (Ethernet interface unit) 115
Electro-magnetic interference (EMI) 308, 310
Electronic
  mail See E-mail
  scheduling
    group 372
    individual 370
  signals
    See also Signals
    bouncing 36, 797
    free, absorbing 37
    measuring voltage 657
    modems 534–535
    noise, glossary definition 787
    sending on a bus topology 36
    token passing See Token passing

Electronics Industries Association (EIA) 87, 716–717
Electronics Industries Association and the Commercial Building Wiring Standard 87
EMI (electro-magnetic interference) 308, 310
Enable Automatic DHCP Configuration option 329
Encryption
  data encryption standards (DES) 482, 772
  description 482
  glossary definition 776
  key (deciphering) 482, 782
Enhanced Small Device Interface (ESDI) disk controllers 495, 499, 776
Environments
  client/server
    LAN Planner 426, 732
    troubleshooting 420, 756
  mainframe 396
  multivendor
    See also Multivendor environments
    LAN Planner 425–426
    troubleshooting 419, 756
  stand-alone 4, 798
  supported by SMS 467
Error correction code (ECC) 497
ESDI disk controllers 496, 500, 776
Ethernet
  5-4-3 rule 259, 262
  10Base2 (thinnet) 77–78, 258–260, 308, 802
  10Base5 (standard, thicknet) 78–79, 260–261, 308, 802
  10BaseFL 263, 309
  10BaseT 86, 256–258, 307–308
  100BaseX (Fast Ethernet) 267
  100VG-AnyLAN 265–266
  combining thicknet and thinnet 263
  CSMA/CD
    access method 224–226
    ANSI specifications 710
    glossary definition 770
    IEEE 802 category description 175
    IEEE Physical layer protocols 212–213
  features 252–253
  frame format 253–254
  glossary definition 776
  implementation considerations (LAN Planner) 306
  inter-repeater links 259
  Interface Unit (EIU) 115
  network upgrade, troubleshooting 304–305
  overview 252
  performance considerations 268
  segmentation 268, 794
  standard Ethernet cable 78
Ethernet Interface Unit (EIU) 115

EtherTalk 291
Event
    glossary definition 776
    logs 642
Exabyte (EB) 23, 776
Exchange Carriers Standards Association (ECSA) 611
Exchange, Microsoft 376–377
Expandable patch panels, using with twisted-pair
  cables 89, 257
Expanding LANs on bus topologies 39
Extended binary coded decimal interchange code
  (EBCDIC), glossary definition 776
Extended industry standard architecture (EISA) 130, 775
Extended wireless local area networks
    long-range wireless bridges 112
    multipoint wireless connectivity 112

F

FACSys, Optus Software 356
Failures, server disk crashes 666
Fast Ethernet 267
Fault tolerance for hubs, built-in 281
Fault tolerant systems
    implementing 500
    overview 495
    RAID (redundant arrays of inexpensive disks)
        duplexing 497
        glossary definition 793
        level 0 - disk striping 495–496
        level 1 - disk mirroring 496–497, 774
        level 2 - disk striping with ECC 497
        level 3 - ECC stored as parity 497
        level 4 - disk striping with large blocks 498
        level 5 - striping with parity 498
    sector sparing 499, 796
Faxes
    enhancements for fax servers 356
    fax modems, sharing 355–356
    routing 355
    servers 21
    troubleshooting 418–419, 755
FDDI (fiber distributed data interface)
    ATM (asynchronous transfer mode) 599
    beaconing 608, 658, 767
    glossary definition 776
    MANs (metropolitan area networks) 218, 605
    media 609
    overview 605
    token passing 605
    topology 606–607
Fiber channel 601
Fiber distributed data interface (FDDI) *See* FDDI

Fiber-optic cabling
    10BaseFL 263, 309
    cladding 92
    core 92
    description 92
    FDDI 607
    overview 92
    SONET 611
    Token Ring 284
Fiber-Optic Technical Advisory Group, 802.8
  category 176
File and print servers 21
File transfer access and management (FTAM)
  protocol 210, 776
File Transfer Protocol (FTP) 210, 216, 674–675, 776
Filters, media 284
Fire codes, coaxial cables 82–83
Firewall, glossary definition 776
Firmware, glossary definition 777
Flow control, glossary definition 777
Fractional T-1 service 586
Frame
    check sequence *See* CRC, data frames
    glossary definition 777
    preamble, glossary definition 777
    relay 596, 777
Frames, data
    See also Packets
    Ethernet 253–254
    glossary definition 772
    packets 194, 789
    specifying memory 127
    Token Ring format 275
Frequencies
    range of 96
    single 95
Front end, client/server 399–400, 777
FTAM (file transfer access and management) 210, 776
FTP (File Transfer Protocol) 210, 216, 674–675, 776
Full duplex transmission *See* Duplex transmission

G

Gateway Service for NetWare (GSNW) 390
Gateways
    advantages and disadvantages 577
    default, TCP/IP 329
    e-mail 367–368
    glossary definition 777
    how they work 574–575
    LAN Planner 629, 742
    mainframe 576
    overview 574

Gigabyte, glossary definition 777
Global groups 443, 778
Gopher 676, 778
Group
    accounts
        creating and deleting, how to (lab) 451–453
        creating 442
        description 441–442
        granting privileges 445
        planning for 441
        types of 443–445
    permissions 477–478
Groups
    built-in 443, 769
    global 443, 778
    glossary definition 778
    local 443, 783
    special 443
    user 665
Groupware
    e-mail 374
    glossary definition 778
    mixed environments 380
    multimedia 375
    overview 373
    products
        Banyan Intelligent Messaging Service 379
        DEC Teamlinks 379
        Lotus Notes 378
        Microsoft Exchange 376–377
        Microsoft Windows 95 379
        Novell Groupwise 379
    uses for 374
Groupwise, Novell 379
GSNW (Gateway Service for NetWare) 390
Guest accounts 439

H

Handshaking, glossary definition 778
Hard disk
    crashes 666
    glossary definition 778
    partitions, glossary definition 789
Hardware
    and software requirements for self-paced training
        course xxviii
    client/server 406
    compatibility list (HCL) 183, 332, 779

Hardware (continued)
    considerations
        client computers 26
        network operating systems 316–317
        server-based networks 26
        servers 29
    glossary definition 779
    modems 535–536
Hayes modem standard 537
HCL (hardware compatibility list) 183, 332, 779
HDLC (high-level data link control) protocol 543, 779
Header, packets 194, 789
Help, asking for when troubleshooting 655
Hermaphroditic connector, glossary definition 7779
Hertz (Hz), glossary definition 779
Hewlett-Packard Network Advisor 661
High-level data link control (HDLC) protocol 543, 779
Hops 110, 779
Hot fixing, fault tolerant systems 499
HTML (Hypertext Markup Language) 780
HTTP (Hypertext Transfer Protocol) 780
Hub-based networks
    active 44
    advantages 46
    hybrid 45
    passive 44, 279
    troubleshooting 60
Hubs
    See also Multistation access unit (MAU or MSAU)
    capacity 280–281
    description 280
    fault tolerance, built-in 281
    glossary definition 780
    multiport 553
Hybrid hubs 45
Hypertext
    Markup Language (HTML) 780
    Transfer Protocol (HTTP) 780
Hz (hertz), glossary definition 779

I

I/O ports
    configuring network adapter cards 124
    glossary definition 766
IBM
    See also APPC; SNA; Token Ring
    cabling system 98–99
    connectors 98, 283

ICPs (independent content providers) 679
ICR (intelligent character recognition) 355
IDE disk controllers 181, 495, 499, 781
IEEE (Institute of Electrical and Electronic Engineers, Inc.)
    assigning network addresses 121
    Data layer protocols 213
    glossary definition 781
    Physical layer protocols 213
    Project 804
        description 717
        enhancements to OSI reference model 176
        glossary definition 780, 792
        IEEE 802 categories 175–176
        Logical Link Control (LLC) 176, 177, 557, 783
        Media Access Control (MAC) drivers 785
        Media Access Control (MAC) sublayer *See* MAC (Media Access Control)
        OSI protocol suite 218, 564
        overview 175
Impedance
    description 78
    glossary definition 780
Implementation
    network installation (LAN Planner) 737–739
    peer-to-peer networks 17
Independent content providers (ICPs) 679
Industry standard architecture (ISA) 131, 780
Infrared wireless networks
    broadband optical telepoint 109
    glossary definition 781
    line-of-sight 108
    overview 108
    reflective 108
    scatter 108
Input/output (I/O) ports
    configuring network adapter cards 126
    glossary definition 766
Installing
    course lab files ·xxix
    drivers 184
    network adapter cards, how to (lab) 187–188
    network services 334–335
    networks (LAN Planner) 737–739
    protocols 219
    tape backup systems 491
    Windows NT Server
        how to (lab) 338–343
        naming information, server 325
        network adapter card, configuring 328

Installing *(continued)*
    Windows NT Server *(continued)*
        overview 325
        partitioning 327
        responsibilities, server 326
Institute of Electrical and Electronic Engineers, Inc. (IEEE) *See* IEEE
Integrated Device Electronics (IDE) disk controllers 181, 495, 499, 781
Integrated services digital network (ISDN) 604, 684, 781
Integrated Voice/Data Networks, 802.9 category 176
Intelligent
    character recognition (ICR) 355
    MSAUs 307
Intermediate systems, glossary definition 781
International Standards Organization (ISO) 167, 212, 718, 781
International Telecommunications Union (ITU) 212, 537, 611, 713
International Telegraph and Telephone Consultative Committee *See* CCITT
Internet
    Archie protocol 677
    browsers
        Internet Explorer 680, 682
        Mosaic 682
        Netscape 682
    connecting to
        considerations 684
        dial-up accounts 683
        ISDN 684, 781
        proxy agent 684, 762
    CSLIP (compressed serial line Internet protocol) 683
    ICPs (independent content providers) 679
    IP addresses 681
    locating resources
        DNS (domain name system) 681–682
        Internet names 681
    Microsoft site, obtaining Microsoft Certified Professional program information xxxv
    overview 673
    PPP (point-to-point protocol) 683
    Protocol (IP) 211, 566, 781
    services
        e-mail 676
        FTP 674–675
        gopher 677, 778
        Internet sites 678
        news 676–677
        Telnet 678
        World Wide Web (WWW) 674, 806

Internet *(continued)*
    services *(continued)*
        SLIP (serial line Internet protocol) 683
        URLs 681, 804
        Veronica protocol 677
        WAIS 677
Internetwork packet exchange (IPX) protocol
    See IPX (internetwork packet exchange) protocol
Internetwork packet exchange/sequenced packet
    exchange protocol (IPX/SPX) 217, 781
Internetworking, 802.1 category 175
Interrupt request lines (IRQ)
    configuring network adapter cards 125–126
    glossary definition 781
    table of IRQs 126
Inventory management, SMS 464
IP (Internet Protocol) 211, 566, 781
IP addresses 328, 681
IPX (internetwork packet exchange) protocol
    description 211
    frame types 241
    LAN Planner 244–245, 729
    routable vs. nonroutable protocols 566
IPX/SPX (internetwork packet exchange/sequenced packet
    exchange protocol) 217, 781
IRQ *See* Interrupt request lines (IRQ)
ISA (industry standard architecture) 130, 780
ISDN (integrated services digital network) 604, 683, 781
ISO (International Standards
    Organization) 167, 212, 718, 781
ITU (International Telecommunications
    Union) 212, 537, 611, 713

J

Jack couplers, using with twisted-pair cables 90
Jitter, glossary definition 782
Joystick ports vs. AUI network adapter ports 134
Jumpers 128, 782

K

KB (kilobyte), glossary definition 782
Keys
    deciphering data encryption 482
    glossary definition 782
    search key, client/server 399
Kilobyte (KB), glossary definition 782
Knowledge Base, Microsoft 663

L

Labs
    creating and deleting group accounts 451–453
    creating and deleting user accounts 451–453
    deleting network adapter card software 189
    installing network adapter cards 187–188
    installing Windows NT Server 339–341
    sharing directories 30–31
LAN Planner
    See also Local area networks (LANs)
    access methods 246
    bridges 628, 741
    cabling, choosing 157–160, 727–728
    client/server environment 434, 732
    data loss, avoiding 526–527, 735
    documentation 700–703, 746
    drivers 244
    e-mail 732
    Ethernet, implementation considerations 306
    expanding networks 627–630, 740–743
    gateways 630, 742
    implementation process 737–739
    modems 626, 740
    network
        adapter cards, choosing 161, 728
        applications 425
        architecture, selecting 307–310, 727
        performance, managing 526, 736
        topology, choosing 67–68
        type, choosing 64–66, 726
    plan, developing one 724–736
    planning concerns 721–723
    printing 428–429, 731
    protocols, choosing 244–245, 729–730
    repeaters 627, 741
    routers 629, 742
    security, planning 522–527, 733–735
    support
        on-site 744
        post-installation 744–751
        vendor 745
    Token Ring, implementation considerations 306–307
    tools, network troubleshooting 693–699
    topology, choosing the right one 68–69
    training 700–703, 739
    WAN transmission technologies,
        choosing 630–632, 742–743

LANalyzer, Novell 661
LANs *See* Local area networks (LANs)
LAPM (link access procedure for modems protocol) 541
Large networks *See* Wide area networks (WANs)
Laser wireless networks 109
LAT (local area transport) protocol (DEC) 566, 783
Layered architecture, OSI reference model
    Application layer 170, 763
    Data Link layer 172–173, 557, 772
    glossary definition 788
    Network layer 172, 569, 786
    overview 168
    Physical layer 173, 552, 666–667, 790
    Presentation layer 171, 791
    relationship of layers 169–170
    Session layer 171, 797
    Transport layer 171, 803
Leased lines 545
Lessons *See* Self-paced training course
Levels of RAID
    0 - disk striping 495–496
    1 - disk mirroring 496–497, 774
    2 - disk striping with ECC 497
    3 - ECC stored as parity 497
    4 - disk striping with large blocks 498
    5 - striping with parity 498
Line conditioning 584
Line-of-sight infrared wireless networks 108
Link access procedure for modems (LAPM) protocol 541
Link-state routing algorithm 567
Links
    glossary definition 783
LLC (Logical Link Control) 176, 177, 557, 783
Local area networks (LANs)
    AppleTalk *See* AppleTalk
    ArcNet 293–294, 310, 764
    cabling limits 6
    CSMA/CD
        access method 224–225
        ANSI specifications 711
        glossary definition 770
        IEEE 802 category description 175
        IEEE Physical layer protocols 212–213
    description 6, 783
    expanding (LAN Planner) 626–630, 740–742
    expanding on bus topologies 39
    expanding or growing 551
    extended, wireless networks
        long-range wireless bridges 112
        multipoint wireless connectivity 112
        wireless LAN bridges 112
    Token Bus, 802.4 category 175, 213
    Token Ring *See* Token Ring

Local area networks (LANs) *(continued)*
    wireless networks
        access points 106–107
        infrared 108–109, 781
        laser 109
        narrow-band (single-frequency) radio 109
        point-to-point transmission 111, 791
        spread-spectrum radio 110
        transceivers 106–107
        transmission techniques 108–111
Local area transport (LAT) protocol (DEC) 566, 783
Local groups 443, 783
LocalTalk 289–290, 310, 783
Logical Link Control (LLC) 176, 177, 557, 783
Logs
    event 644–645
    security 481
    tape backup, maintaining 490
Long-range wireless bridges 112
Lost token, glossary definition 783
Lotus Notes 378

M

MAC (Media Access Control)
    layer bridges 556
    sublayer
        drivers 784
        enhancements to the OSI model 176
        glossary definition 784
        IEEE protocols 213
        network adapter card drivers 182
Macintosh, Services for 388, 392
Magazines, for support purposes 665
Mail servers, description 21
Mailboxes, e-mail 361
Mainframe
    environment 396
    gateways 576
Maintenance, printers 351
MAN (metropolitan area network) 175, 605, 612
Management information bases (MIBs) 461, 783
Management software 648
Managing networks
    administrator
        accounts 444
        responsibilities 433
    approaches to 638
    backing up the network 639
    baselines, establishing 646–648
    data protection *See* Data protection
    documentation 642
    group accounts
        creating and deleting, how to (lab) 451–453
        creating 446

Managing networks *(continued)*
   group accounts *(continued)*
      description 444–445
      granting privileges 449
      planning for 445
      types of 447–449
   Guest accounts 442
   management software 648
   monitoring performance 461
   network history, maintaining 469
   network monitoring 644–645
   overview 436, 460
   passwords 443
   performance (LAN Planner) 522–528, 736
   preemptive troubleshooting 648
   profiles 441
   security *See* Security
   SNMP (simple network management protocol) 461–
      462
   standardization 641
   Systems Management Server
      inventory management 464
      overview 464
      remote control and network monitor 466
      shared application management 465
      software distribution 465
      supported environments 467
   troubleshooting methodology *See* Troubleshooting
   upgrades and new products 642
   user accounts
      creating and deleting, how to (lab) 451–453
      creating 434–435
      disabling or deleting 446–449
      glossary definition 805
      key accounts 438
   user information, entering 436–437
   user parameters, setting 437
   utilities 644–645
   Windows NT Performance Monitor 458–459
Map *See* Topologies
Mask, subnet, TCP/IP 329
MAU (multistation access unit) 280, 785
MB (megabyte), glossary definition 783
Mbps (millions of bits per second), glossary
   definition 785
MCI Mail e-mail provider 362
MCSE (Microsoft Certified Systems Engineer)
   program 745
Media
   Access Control (MAC) *See* MAC (Media Access
      Control)
   description 14, 784
   filters 284
   interface connector (MIC) 283
Megabyte (MB), glossary definition 783

Memory
   addresses, base 127–128, 766
   cache, glossary definition 770
   RAM *See* RAM
   ROM, glossary definition 793
   shared adapter memory 138
   shared system memory 138
Mesh network topology, glossary definition 784
Message handling service (MHS) 367
Message Transfer Agent (MTA), X.400 364
Message Transfer System (MTS), X.400 364
Metal shielding 75
Methods, access *See* Access methods
Metropolitan area network (MAN) 175, 605, 612
MHS (message handling service) 367
MIBs (management information bases) 462, 783
MIC (media interface connector) 283
Micro Channel Architecture 131, 784
Microcom Network Protocol (MNP) 541, 785
Microprocessor, onboard, network performance 139
Microsoft
   Authorized Technical Education Center
      (ATEC) xxxvi
   Certified Professional program
      intended audience of this book xxvii
      overview xxxiii–xxxiv
      prerequisites for taking self-paced training
         course xxvii
      starting the self-paced training course xxxii
   Certified Systems Engineer (MCSE) program 745
   e-mail provider 362
   Exchange 376–377
   Internet Explorer browser 680, 682
   Knowledge Base 663
   MSDL (Microsoft Download Library) 664
   multivendor environments 390
   NDS (Service for NetWare Directory Services) 390
   NWLink protocol
      description 211, 217
      LAN Planner 244–245, 729
   SMBs (server message blocks) 211, 796
   Systems Management Server
      inventory management 467
      overview 464
      remote control and network monitor 466
      shared application management 465
      software distribution 465
      supported environments 467
   TechNet xxxiv, 663–664
   Windows 95 379
   Windows NT Server *See* Windows NT Server
Microwave systems 115
Mid-split broadband configurations 96

Millions of bits per second (Mbps), glossary definition 785
MIPS processor 23, 331
Mirroring disks - level 1 RAID 496–497, 774
MNP (Microcom Network Protocol) 541, 785
Mobile computing
    cellular networks 115
    microwave systems 115
    overview 114
    packet-radio communication 114
    satellite stations 115
Modems
    async (asynchronous communications) 540–542
    basic functions 534–535
    baud rate 538, 766
    bis 537
    bps (bits per second) 538, 768
    description 534
    digital 542–543, 559
    error control 541
    fax modems, sharing 355–356
    glossary definition 785
    hardware 535–536
    LAN Planner 626, 740
    parity checking 541
    performance 538, 541
    protocols
        bisync (binary synchronous communications) 543, 767
        HDLC (high-level data link control) 543, 779
        LAPM (link access procedure for modems) 541
        MNP (Microcom Network Protocol) 541, 785
        SDLC (synchronous data link control) 543, 800
    remote access 546
    serial 540–542
    sharing fax modems 355–356
    standards
        Hayes 537
        international 537–538
        V series 537–538, 714
    synchronous communications 542–543, 559, 800
    telephone lines
        dedicated vs. dial-up 584
        dedicated 545, 583–584
        dial-up 545, 582–583
        leased 545
        line conditioning 584
        public dial network 545
    terbo 537
    timing schemes 542
MOdulate/DEModulate *See* Modems

Monitoring network performance 768
    bottlenecks 461, 660
    LAN Planner 522, 736
    network history, maintaining 468
    SNMP (simple network management protocol) 461–462
    Systems Management Server
        inventory management 464
        overview 464
        remote control and network monitor 466
        shared application management 465
        software distribution 465
        supported environments 467
    Windows NT Performance Monitor 458–459
Monitors, network, troubleshooting tool 658, 787
Mosaic Internet browser 682
MSAU (multistation access unit) 280, 307, 785
MSDL (Microsoft Download Library) 664
MTA (Message Transfer Agent), X.400 364
MTS (Message Transfer System), X.400 364
Multimedia, groupware 375
Multiplexing (muxing) 588, 785
Multiport hubs or repeaters 552
Multistation access unit (MAU or MSAU) 280, 785
Multitasking, network operating systems 317, 785
Multivendor environments
    client solutions 387
    LAN Planner 425–426
    overview 387
    server solutions 388
    troubleshooting 419, 756
    vendor options
        Apple 392
        Microsoft 390–391
        Novell 391
        overview 389
Muxing (multiplexing) 588, 785

N

N-series connectors 261
Name binding protocol (NBP) 211, 785
Naming information, Windows NT Server 325
Narrow-band (single-frequency) radio wireless networks 109
National Security Agency (NSA) 482
NBP (name binding protocol) 211, 785
NCP (Novell NetWare Core Protocol) 211
NDIS (network device interface specification), glossary definition 786
NDS (NetWare Directory Services) 390
NEST (Novell Embedded System Technology) 355

NetBEUI (NetBIOS Extended User Interface)
  protocol 211, 217, 566, 786
NetBIOS (network basic input/output system),
  glossary definition 786
Netscape Internet browser 682
NetWare
  CSNW 390
  Directory Services (NDS) 390
  GSNW 390
  link services protocol (NLSP) 567
  requesters 390
Netwave Access Point 110
Network
  See also Networks
  accounts, troubleshooting 517, 756
  addresses, network adapter cards 121–122
  Advisor, Hewlett-Packard 661
  analyzers 659–661, 786
  applications (LAN Planner) 425
  applications, troubleshooting 419
  communications
    function of packets 192–193
    overview 166
  design *See* Topologies
  device interface specification (NDIS),
    glossary definition 786
  General Sniffer 661
  glossary definition 786
  history, maintaining 468
  layer, OSI reference model 168, 569, 786
  monitor and remote control, SMS 466
  monitoring 644–645
  monitors, troubleshooting tool 659, 787
  multivendor environments (LAN Planner) 425–426
  multivendor environments, troubleshooting 419, 756
  operations, troubleshooting 417, 755
  performance, troubleshooting 669
  printing (LAN Planner) 428–429, 731
  security
    planning (LAN Planner) 522–527, 733–735
    troubleshooting 517, 756
  security, 802.10 category 176
  support resources
    bulletin board services (BBSs) 664
    MSDL (Microsoft Download Library) 664
    periodicals 665
    TechNet xxxiv, 663–664
    user groups 665
  systems, troubleshooting 693
  traffic, segmenting with bridges 557

Network adapter cards
  binding process 209, 767
  cabling and connectors 132–134
  choosing (LAN Planner) 161, 728
  compatibility 130–134
  configuration options and settings
    base I/O port settings 126
    base memory address 127–128, 766
    interrupts (IRQ) 125–126, 781
    overview 124
    transceiver, selecting 128
  configuring for Windows NT Server 328
  data
    bus architectures 130–131
    preparing 120–121
    sending and controlling 122
  deleting software, how to (lab) 189
  DIP switch settings 124, 774
  drivers 183
  glossary definition 786
  installing, how to (lab) 187–188
  Media Access Control (MAC) driver 214
  network addresses 121–122
  overview 119–120
  performance 138–139
  remote-boot PROMs 140
  servers 139
  Token Ring 289
  troubleshooting 153–154, 754
  wireless 140
  workstations 139
Network Advisor, Hewlett-Packard 661
Network applications
  e-mail *See* E-mail
  groupware *See* Groupware
  scheduling 370–371
  shared
    how to share 382
    overview 382
    requirements 383
    software logs 383
Network General Sniffer 661
Network management
  administrator
    accounts 444
    responsibilities 43 3
  approaches to 638
  backing up the network 639
  baselines, establishing 646–647
  data protection *See* Data protection

Network management *continued)*
  documentation 642
  group accounts
    creating and deleting, how to (lab) 451–453
    creating 442
    granting privileges 445
    planning for 441
    types of 443–445
  Guest accounts 439
  management software 648
  monitoring performance 457
  network history, maintaining 468
  network monitoring 644–645
  overview 432, 456
  passwords 439
  performance (LAN Planner) 525, 736
  preemptive troubleshooting 644, 648
  profiles 438
  security *See* Security
  SNMP (simple network management protocol) 461–462
  standardization 641
  Systems Management Server 464-466
  troubleshooting methodology *See* Troubleshooting
  upgrades and new products 642
  user accounts
    creating and deleting, how to (lab) 451-453
    creating 434-439
    disabling or deleting 446-449
    glossary definition 805
    key accounts 438
  user information, entering 436-438
  user parameters, setting 437
  utilities 644-645
  Windows NT Performance Monitor 458-459
Network News Transfer Protocol (NNTP) 676-677
Network operating systems
  hardware and software coordination 316-317
  installing, how to (lab) 339-341
  multitasking 317, 783
  network services *See* Network services
  network, managing 324
  overview 316
  resource sharing 323–324
  software components
    client software 319–321
    overview 318
    redirectors 319–320, 793
    server software 323–324
  users, managing 324

Network performance
  LAN Planner 526, 736
  monitoring 457
  network history, maintaining 468
  SNMP (simple network management protocol) 461–462
  Systems Management Server
    inventory management 464
    overview 464
    remote control and network monitor 466
    shared application management 465
    software distribution 465
    supported environments 467
  Windows NT Performance Monitor 458–459
Network protocols
  See also Protocols
  DDP (datagram delivery protocol) 211, 566
  description 211
  IP (Internet Protocol) 211, 566, 781
  IPX (internetwork packet exchange) protocol
    description 211
    frame types 240
    LAN Planner 244–245, 729
    routable vs. nonroutable protocols 566
  NetBEUI 214, 566, 786
  NWLink
    description 211, 217
    frame types 240
    LAN Planner 244–245, 729
    Windows NT Workstation and Novell NetWare 390
Network services
  binding options 337
  installing or removing 334–336
  overview 334
  starting automatically or manually 336
Networking
  centralized computing *See* Centralized computing
  client/server computing *See* Client/Server computing
  description 4–5
  overview 14–15
  role of standards 707
  software and drivers 183
Networks
  See also Network
  any-to-any connections *See* Packet switching
  cabling, choosing (LAN Planner) 157–160, 727–728
  choosing the type (LAN Planner) 64–66, 726
  combination 28
  communication on the bus, disrupting 38
  designing the layout 34

Networks *(continued)*
    for large companies *See* Wide area networks (WANs)
    for small companies *See* Local area networks (LANs)
    glossary definition 786
    implementation factors 15
    layered architecture
        Application layer 170, 763
        Network layer 172, 569, 786
        overview 168
        Presentation layer 171, 791
        relationship of layers 169–170
        Session layer 171, 797
        Transport layer 171, 803
    local area (LANs) *See* Local area networks (LANs)
    managing, network operating systems 324
    operating systems *See* Network operating systems
    packet switching
        ATM (asynchronous transfer mode) *See* ATM
        frame relay 597, 777
        glossary definition 789
        how it works 590-591
        virtual circuits 591, 805
        X.25 protocol 595-596
    PDN (public data network) 596, 792
    peer-to-peer *See* Peer-to-peer networks
    performance 138–139
    reasons for using
        application sharing 10
        data sharing 9
        overview 8
        printers and peripherals sharing 8
    selecting topologies, how to 50
    server-based *See* Server-based networks
    services *See* Network services
    topologies *See* Topologies
    upgrading 667
    using more than one operating system 28
    wide area (WANs) *See* Wide area networks (WANs)
    Wireless Networks, 802.11 category 176
    wireless *See* Wireless networks
NLSP (NetWare link services protocol) 567
NNTP (Network News Transfer Protocol) 676-677
Node, glossary definition 787
Noise, glossary definition 787
Non-preemptive multitasking 317, 785, 787
Notes, Lotus 378
Notification of e-mail 361

Novell
    LANalyzer 661
    NetWare
        CSNW 390
        GSNW 390
        requesters 390
        Windows 95-based clients 390
        Windows NT-based clients and servers 390
Novell Embedded System Technology (NEST) 355
Novell Groupwise 379
Novell IPX *See* IPX; IPX/SPX
Novell Netware Core Protocol (NCP) 211
NSA (National Security Agency) 482
Number of users, server-based networks 26
NWLink protocol
    description 211, 217
    frame types 240
    LAN Planner 244–245, 727
    Windows NT Workstation and Novell NetWare 390

O

Object Management Group (OMG) 718–719
OC (optical carrier) levels 611
OC3 SONET 601
OCR (optical character recognition) 355
ODI (open data-link interface), glossary definition 787
Ohm, glossary definition 787
OMG (Object Management Group) 718–719
Onboard microprocessor, network performance 139
Online providers
    AOL (America Online) 362
    AT&T 362
    CompuServ 362
    MCI Mail 362
    Microsoft 362
Open data-link interface (ODI), glossary definition 787
Open shortest path first (OSPF) routing algorithm 567, 787
Open Software Foundation (OSF) 719
Open Systems Interconnection (OSI) reference model
    802 project *See* Project 802
    drivers 183
    enhancements to, by 802 project 176

Open Systems Interconnection (OSI) reference model *(continued)*
   layered architecture
      Application layer 170, 763
      Data Link layer 172–173, 557, 597, 772
      glossary definition 788
      Network layer 172, 569, 786
      overview 168
      Physical layer 173, 569, 666-667, 790
      Presentation layer 171, 791
      relationship of layers 169–170
      Session layer 171, 797
      Transport layer 171, 803
   OSI protocol suite 218, 564
   overview 167
Operating systems
   networks *See* Network operating systems
   peer-to-peer networks 16
   role of software, server-based networks 23
   using more than one in a network 28
Optical
   carrier (OC) levels 610
   character recognition (OCR) 355
   fiber, glossary definition 788
Optus Software, FACSys 366
Oscilloscopes 658, 788
OSF (Open Software Foundation) 719
OSI reference model *See* Open Systems Interconnection (OSI)
OSPF (open shortest path first) routing algorithm 567, 787

P

PABX (Private Automated Branch Exchange), glossary definition 790
Packet assembler/disassembler (PAD) 596, 789
Packet switching
   ATM (asynchronous transfer mode)
      advantages and disadvantages 602
      components 600–602
      glossary definition 764
      overview 590
      technology 599-600

Packet switching *(continued)*
   frame relay 597, 777
   glossary definition 789
   how it works 590-591
   virtual circuits 591, 805
   X.25 protocol 595-596
Packet-radio communication 114
   Packets
   See also Frames
   addressing 197
   components
      data 194
      header 194
      overview 194
      trailer 195
   creating 196
   description 169
   directing 197
   filtering 197
   forwarding 197
   function in network communications 192–193
   glossary definition 789
   network monitors 659, 787
   packet switching *See* Packet switching
   PAD (packet assembler/disassembler) 596, 789
   printing example 199–200
   protocol analyzers 659–651, 786
   troubleshooting 240–241
PAD (packet assembler/disassembler) 596, 789
Page description languages (PDLs) 352, 789
Panels, patch
   Token Ring 284
   using with twisted-pair cables 89, 257
Parallel data transfer 120
Parameters, setting for users 437
Parity
   checking, modems 541
   description 497
   glossary definition 789
   stripe block 498
Partitioning, Windows NT Server 327
Partitions, glossary definition 789
Passing, token
   ArcNet 293–294
   as an access method 228–229

Passing, token *(continued)*
    FDDI 605
    glossary definition 802
    ring networks 43
    Token Ring 277–278
Passive
    hubs 44, 274
    topologies 36
Passwords
    access permissions
        glossary definition 761
        group permissions 477–478
        overview 474
        resource security 475–477
    network management 443
    password-protected shares 474
    troubleshooting 518
Patch
    cables, Token Ring 283
    panels, expandable, using with twisted-pair
        cables 89
    panels, Token Ring 284
PBX (Private Branch Exchange), glossary definition 780
PCI (peripheral component interconnect) bus
    architecture 131
PDAs (Personal Digital Assistants) 114, 780
PDCs (primary domain controllers) 326, 447, 791
PDLs (page description languages) 352, 791
PDN (public data network) 595, 792
Peer-to-peer networks
    administration 17
    cabling system 17
    cost 16
    description 16
    glossary definition 780
    illustrated 16
    implementation 17
    operating systems 16
    peer-to-peer servers vs. dedicated servers 29
    security 18
    server requirements 18
    sharing resources 18
    size 16
    training 18
    troubleshooting 59
    when to use them 17

Performance
    Ethernet 268
    modems 538, 541
    Monitor, Windows NT Server 458 459, 644
    monitoring *See* Monitoring network performance
    network, troubleshooting 668
    networks 138–139
    statistics 644
Periodicals, for support purposes 665
Peripheral component interconnect (PCI) bus
    architecture 131
Peripherals
    client software 321
    description 8
    glossary definition 780
    sharing in a networking environment 9
Permanent virtual circuits (PVCs) 591, 790
Permissions, access
    glossary definition 761
    group permissions 477–478
    overview 475
    resource security 475–476
Personal Digital Assistants (PDAs) 114, 790
Physical layer, OSI reference model 173, 5 69, 666-667,
    790
Physical layout *See* Topologies
Piercing taps 79, 791
Plates, wall, using with twisted-pair cables 90
Plenum
    coaxial cables 82–83
    glossary definition 791
Plug and Play, description 131, 791
Point-to-many-point connections 586, 791
Point-to-point
    glossary definition 791
    protocol (PPP) 683
    synchronous communications 586
    transmissions 111
Policies, security 472–473, 761
Polyvinyl chloride (PVC) coaxial cables 82, 793
Power fluctuations, troubleshooting 667
PPP (point-to-point protocol) 683
Preemptive
    multitasking 317, 785
    troubleshooting 644, 648
Prerequisites for taking self-paced training course xxix
Presentation layer, OSI reference model 171, 791

Primary domain controllers (PDCs) 326, 443, 791
Primary Rate ISDN 604
Print Manager, Windows NT Server 348
Print sharing utility 348
Printers
    See also Printing
    connecting via a network 349
    maintenance 351
    managing remotely 353
    managing users 351–352
    sharing
        how to 347
        managing 351–352
    sharing in a networking environment 9
Printing
    See also Printers
    LAN Planner 423–424, 731
    overview, via a network 346
    packets example 199–202
    PDLs (page description languages) 352, 789
    print sharing utility 348
    troubleshooting 418–419, 755
Private Automated Branch Exchange (PABX),
    glossary definition 790
Private Branch Exchange (PBX), glossary definition 790
Procedures, stored 401
Processors
    Digital Alpha AXP 331
    MIPS 23, 331
    R4000 23, 331
    RISC 23, 331, 762, 793
Profiles, user accounts 441
Program development tools, client/server 400
Project 802
    description 717
    enhancements to OSI reference model 176
    glossary definition 780, 792
    IEEE 802 categories 175–176
    Logical Link Control (LLC) sublayer 176, 177, 557,
        783
    Media Access Control (MAC) sublayer
        bridges 557
        drivers 784
        enhancements to the OSI model 176
        glossary definition 784
        IEEE protocols 212–213
        network adapter card drivers 182
    OSI protocol suite 216, 564
    overview 175
PROMs, remote-boot, network adapter cards 141
Protecting data *See* Data protection

Protocols
    See also specific protocol
    AFP (AppleTalk filing protocol) 211
    analyzers 659–661, 786
    APF (AppleTalk Filing Protocol) 763
    APPC (advanced program-to-program
        communication) protocol 210, 218, 763
    AppleTalk and Apple Share protocol suite 211, 763
    AppleTalk 218, 246, 730, 763
    application *See* Application protocols
    Archie 675
    ATP (AppleTalk transaction protocol) 211
    binding process 209, 767
    choosing (LAN Planner) 244–246, 729–730
    CMIP 715
    CSLIP (compressed serial line Internet protocol) 683
    DAP (data access protocol) 211
    DDP (datagram delivery protocol) 211, 566
    DECnet 218, 566, 773
    description 167
    DHCP 329, 683, 775
    drivers, glossary definition 792
    FTAM (file transfer access and management) 210,
        776
    FTP (File Transfer Protocol) 210, 216, 674–675, 776
    glossary definition 792
    how they work 205
    HTTP (Hypertext Transfer Protocol) 780
    installing 219
    internetworking 216
    IP (Internet Protocol) 211, 565, 781
    IPX (internetwork packet exchange) protocol
        description 211
        frame types 240
        LAN Planner 244–245, 729
        routable vs. nonroutable protocols 566
    IPX/SPX (internetwork packet exchange/sequenced
        packet exchange protocol) 217, 781
    LAT (local area transport) protocol (DEC) 566, 783
    modem
        bisync 543, 767
        HDLC (high-level data link control) 543, 779
        LAPM (link access procedure for modems) 541
        MNP (Microcom Network Protocol) 541, 785
        SDLC (synchronous data link control) 543, 800
    NBP (name binding protocol) 211, 785
    NCP (Novell NetWare Core Protocol) 211
    NetBEUI 211, 217, 566, 786
    network *See* Network protocols
    NLSP (NetWare link services protocol) 567

Protocols *(continued)*
    NNTP (Network News Transfer Protocol) 676–677
    NWLink
        description 211, 217
        frame types 240
        LAN Planner 244–245, 729
        Windows NT Workstation and Novell
            NetWare 390
    OSI protocol suite 218, 564
    OSI reference model *See* Open Systems
        Interconnection (OSI) reference model
    overview 205
    PPP (point-to-point protocol) 683
    removing 219
    RIP (routing information protocol) 567, 795
    routable vs. nonroutable 206, 566, 572, 629
    SLIP (serial line Internet protocol) 683
    SMBs (server message blocks) 211, 796
    SMTP (simple mail transfer protocol) 210, 216, 366–
        367
    SNMP (simple network management
        protocol) 210, 216, 461–462, 798
    SPX (sequential packet exchange) 211
    stacks or suites 208
    standard stacks 209–210
    standards 212–213
    T.30 fax 355
    TCP (Transmission Control Protocol) 211, 803
    TCP/IP (Transmission Control Protocol/Internet
        Protocol)
        description 216
        glossary definition 803
        installing 328–329
        LAN Planner 244, 729–730
    Telnet 211, 678, 801
    transport *See* Transport protocols
    troubleshooting 241, 654
    vendor compatibility 212
    Veronica 677
    X.25 220, 595–596, 715, 806
    X.200 715
    X.400 210, 363–365, 715, 806
    X.500 210, 365, 715, 806
    X.700 715
    XNS (Xerox Network System) protocol 217, 566, 806
Proxy agent, Internet 684, 762
PSTN (public switched telephone network) 582–583
Public data network (PDN) 596, 792
Public dial network lines 545

Public switched telephone network (PSTN) 582-583
Punchdown block, glossary definition 793
PVC coaxial cables 82, 793
PVCs (permanent virtual circuits) 591, 597, 790

Q

Quad shielding 75
Quartet signaling 229
Query tools, client/server 400

R

R4000 processor 23, 331
Rack shelves, using with twisted-pair cables 89
RAID (redundant arrays of inexpensive disks)
    duplexing 496
    glossary definition 793
    level 0 - disk striping 495–496
    level 1 - disk mirroring 496–497, 774
    level 2 - disk striping with ECC 497
    level 3 - ECC stored as parity 497
    level 4 - disk striping with large blocks 498
    level 5 - striping with parity 498
RAM
    buffering, network performance 139
    glossary definition 793
    start address
        glossary definition 766
Random access memory (RAM) *See* RAM
RAS (Remote Access Service), Windows NT 546
Read only memory (ROM), glossary definition 793
Received fax line routing 355
Redirectors 319–321, 387, 793
Reduced instruction set computer (RISC) 793
Redundancy
    See also Fault tolerant systems
    server-based networks 26
Redundant arrays of inexpensive disks (RAID) *See* RAID
Reflective infrared wireless networks 108
Reliability, topologies 68
Remote
    Access Service (RAS), Windows NT 546
    boot PROMs, network adapter cards 140
    bridges 560
    control and network monitor, SMS 466
Remotely managing printers 353

Removing
    drivers 185
    network adapter card software, how to (lab) 187-188
    protocols 219
Repeaters
    advantages and disadvantages 554
    amplifying signals 39, 284
    baseband transmissions 95
    broadcast storms 554, 769
    description 39
    glossary definition 794
    how they work 552-553
    LAN Planner 626, 741
    multiport 553
    Token Ring 284
    vs. bridges 561
Replying to e-mail 361
Requesters (redirectors) 319–321, 387, 793, 794
Requirements
    servers 331
    sharing network applications 383
Resources
    description 8
    glossary definition 794
    security 475–477
    sharing 5
        network operating systems 323–324
        peer-to-peer networks 17
        server-based networks 24
Responsibilities, Windows NT Server 326
Return receipt, e-mail 361
RG-58 family of cabling 78, 794
Rights
    See also Passwords; Permissions; Security
    glossary definition 794
Ring networks
    glossary definition 794
    overview 42
    token passing
        ArcNet 293–294
        as an access method 228
        FDDI 605
        glossary definition 802
        overview 43
        Token Ring 277–278
    troubleshooting 60
RIP (routing information protocol) 567, 795
RISC processor 762, 793

RJ-11 telephone connectors
    glossary definition 795
    modems 535–536
    network adapter cards 135
    Token Ring 283
    twisted-pair cables, 10BaseT 89
RJ-45 telephone connectors
    glossary definition 795
    network adapter cards 134
    Token Ring 283
    twisted-pair cables, 10BaseT 89
ROM, glossary definition 793
Routable vs. nonroutable protocols 209, 566, 572, 628
Routers
    brouters 572, 769
    choosing paths 567
    dynamic 568
    glossary definition 795
    how they work 564-566
    LAN Planner 626, 742
    overview 564
    preventing broadcast storms 565–566
    routing algorithms 567
    routing tables 564-565
    static 568
    vs. bridges
        broadcasting 570
        multiple paths 571
        overview 564
Routing
    algorithms
        Dijkstra 567
        distance-vector 567
        link-state 567
        OSPF (open shortest path first) 567, 787
    faxes 355
    tables
        bridges 556–558
        routers 564–571
Routing information protocol (RIP) 567, 795
RS-232 serial communications interface 535–536, 716, 795
RS-422 serial communications interface 716
RS-423 serial communications interface 716
RS-449 serial communications interface 716

S

SAG (SQL Access Group) 720
SAPs (service access points) 179, 796
Satellite stations 115
Scatter infrared wireless networks 108
Scheduling
    group 372
    individual 370-371
SCSI disk controllers 181, 499, 798
SDLC (synchronous data link control) protocol 543, 800
Search key, client/server 399
Sector sparing, fault tolerant systems 499, 796
Sectors, glossary definition 796
Security
    auditing 481
    data encryption 482, 772, 776
    data protection See Data protection
    diskless computers 482, 774
    group permissions 478–479
    networks, 802.10 category 176
    passwords
        access permissions 476–479, 761
        network management 432
        password-protected shares 474
        troubleshooting 518
    peer-to-peer networks 17
    planning for
        (LAN Planner) 522–527, 733–735
        overview 471, 640–641
        physical security 473
        security levels 471
        setting policies 471–472
        training users 472
    resource 475–477
    server-based networks 24
    virus protection 483
Segmentation, Ethernet 268, 796
Self-paced training course
    content overview xxix–xxx
    finding the best starting point xxxii
    hardware and software requirements xxviii
    intended audience of this book xxvii
    prerequisites xxvii
    setup information xxviii–xxix
Sender ID, data frames 172
Sequential Packet Exchange (SPX) protocol 211

Serial
    communication interface
        RS-232 535–536, 716, 795
        RS-422 716
        RS-423 716
        RS-449 716
    data transfer 111, 120
    modems 540–542
Serial line Internet protocol (SLIP) 683
Server message blocks (SMBs) 211, 796
Server software, network operating systems 323–324
Server solutions in multivendor environments 388
Server-based networks
    backing up data 25, 765
    glossary definition 796
    hardware considerations 26
    illustrated 15
    number of users 26
    overview 20
    peer-to-peer servers vs. dedicated servers 29
    redundancy 26
    role of operating system software 23
    security 25
    sharing resources 24
    specialized servers 21–22
    Windows NT Server features 23
Servers
    application 21
    client/server model See Client/server
    communication 22
    data storage warehouse 405
    dedicated 20, 773
    description 14
    DHCP 329, 775
    directory services 22
    disk crashes 666
    distributed 404–405
    fax 21, 355–356
    file and print
        AppleShare 290, 763
        description 21
    FTP 673–674
    glossary definition 796
    hardware considerations 29
    mail 21
    naming information 325
    network adapter cards 140

Servers *(continued)*
    peer-to-peer vs. dedicated 29
    physically securing 473
    requirements
        network operating systems 331
        peer-to-peer networks 18
    responsibilities 326
    single servers, client/server 404–405
    software, network operating systems 323–324
    specialized 21–22
    Windows NT Server *See* Windows NT Server
Service access points (SAPs) 177, 796
Services for Macintosh 388, 392
Services, network
    binding options 337
    installing or removing 334–336
    overview 334
    starting automatically or manually 336
Session
    glossary definition 796
    layer, OSI reference model 171, 797
    management, glossary definition 797
Setting up *See* Installing
Setup utility 182
Share-level security *See* Passwords
Shared
    adapter memory, network performance 138
    application management, SMS 465
    system memory, network performance 138
Sharing
    applications 10
    data
        description 14
        overview 9
    directories
        description 24
        how to (lab) 30–31
    fax modems 355–356
    network applications
        how to share 382
        overview 382
        requirements 383
        software logs 383
    printers 347–348
    resources
        description 14
        glossary definition 794
        network operating systems 323–324

Sharing *(continued)*
    resources *(continued)*
        peer-to-peer networks 18
        printers and peripherals 8, 14
        server-based networks 24
Shell 319–321, 797
Shielded twisted-pair (STP) cables 88, 797
Shielding
    crosstalk 88
    description 75
    glossary definition 797
Signaling, quartet 229
Signals
    amplifying with a repeater 39, 284, 794
    analog 96, 762
    bouncing 36, 797
    crosstalk 88
    digital 92, 95, 773
    free, absorbing 37
    measuring voltage 657
    noise, glossary definition 787
    quality, reduced by barrel connectors 258
    sending on a bus topology 36
    token passing
        ArcNet 293–294
        FDDI 605
        glossary definition 802
        ring networks 43
        Token Ring 277–278
    transmissions
        baseband 95, 766
        broadband 96
Simple mail transfer protocol (SMTP) 210, 216, 366–367
Simple network management protocol
    (SNMP) 210, 216, 461–462, 798
Simultaneous Peripheral Operation On Line (spool) 346
Single servers, client/server 404–405
Size, peer-to-peer networks 16
SLIP (serial line Internet protocol) 683
Small Computer Standard Interface (SCSI)
    disk controllers 181, 496, 499, 798
Small networks *See* Local area networks (LANs)
Smart hubs 295
Smart multistation access unit (SMAU) 280
SMAU (smart multistation access unit) 280
SMBs (server message blocks) 211, 796
SMDS (switched multimegabit data service) 612, 799
SMP (symmetric multiprocessing) 23, 800

SMS (Systems Management Server)
    inventory management 464
    overview 464
    remote control and network monitor 466
    shared application management 465
    software distribution 465
    supported environments 467
SMTP (simple mail transfer protocol) 210, 216, 366–367
SNA (systems network architecture), glossary
    definition 800
Sniffer, Network General 661
SNMP (simple network management
    protocol) 210, 216, 461–462, 798
Software
    and hardware considerations, network operating
        systems 316–317
    components, network operating systems
        overview 318
        redirectors 319–320, 793
    distribution, SMS 465
    e-mail See E-mail
    FACSys from Optus 356
    glossary definition 798
    groupware See Groupware
    Lotus Notes 378
    management 648
    Microsoft Exchange 3876–377
    network applications See Network applications
    networking and drivers 183
    removing network adapter card software, how to
        (lab) 189
    role of in server-based networks 23
    scheduling 370–372
    server, network operating systems 323–324
    sharing network applications
        how to share 382
        overview 382
        software logs 383
SONET (synchronous optical network) 601, 611, 711,
    800
Spanning tree algorithm (STA) 567, 798
Special groups 443
Spoolers, printing 346
Spread-spectrum radio wireless networks 110
SPX (sequential packet exchange) protocol 211
SQL (Structured Query Language) 398, 799
SQL Access Group (SAG) 720
STA (spanning tree algorithm) 567, 798
Stacks, protocol 209–210
Stand-alone computers 4, 798
Standard Ethernet 78, 260
Standardization in networks 641

Standards
    See also the specific organization
    ANSI 711
    AWG standard cable measurement 98–99, 765
    CCITT 713, 715
    COS 715
    COSE 712–713
    DES (data encryption standard) 482, 772
    e-mail See E-mail
    EIA/TIA 568 wiring standard 87
    EIA 87, 716–717
    IEEE 717
    ISO 718
    modems
        Hayes 537
        international 537–538
        V series 537–538, 714
    networking role 707
    OMG 718–719
    origin of 7068–709
    OSF 719
    protocols 212–214
    SAG 720
Star networks
    glossary definition 799
    overview 41
    star bus variation 48
    star ring or star wired ring variation 49
Start addresses, RAM 127–128, 766
Starting the self-paced training course xxxiv
Static routers 568
Statistics
    performance 644
    usage 644
Stored procedures 401
Storms, broadcast See Broadcast, storms
STP (shielded twisted-pair) cables 88, 256, 797
Stripe set
    See also RAID
    described 495
    glossary definition 799
Striping with parity - level 5 RAID 498
Structured Query Language (SQL) 398, 799
STSs (synchronous transport signals) 611
Subnet mask, TCP/IP 328
Suites, protocol See Stacks, protocol
Supervisor accounts 438
Support
    bulletin board services (BBSs) 664
    MSDL (Microsoft Download Library) 664
    on-site (LAN Planner) 744
    periodicals 665

Support *(continued)*
    post-installation (LAN Planner) 744–751
    TechNet xxxviii, 663–664
    user groups 665
SVCs (switched virtual circuits) 591, 800
Switch settings (DIP) 124, 774
Switched 56 service 588
Switched multimegabit data service (SMDS) 611, 799
Switched virtual circuits (SVCs) 591, 800
Symmetric multiprocessing (SMP) 23, 800
Synchronous
    communication modems 542–543
    glossary definition 800
Synchronous data link control (SDLC) protocol 543, 800
Synchronous optical network (SONET) 601, 611, 711, 800
Synchronous transport signals (STSs) 611
System memory, shared, network performance 138
Systems Management Server (SMS)
    inventory management 464
    overview 464
    remote control and network monitor 466
    shared application management 465
    software distribution 465
    supported environments 467
Systems network architecture (SNA), glossary definition 800
Systems, troubleshooting 693

T

T.30 sub-addressing fax protocol 355
T connectors, BNC 80, 258, 801
T1 service 586–587, 799
T3 service 587, 600
Tape backup
    implementing 488–490
    installing the backup system 491
    maintaining backup logs 490
    overview 488
    testing and storage 490
Taps
    glossary definition 801
    piercing 79, 261, 791
    vampire 79, 261, 805
TCP (Transmission Control Protocol) 211, 803
TCP/IP (Transmission Control Protocol/Internet Protocol)
    description 216
    glossary definition 803
    installing 328–329
    LAN Planner 245, 729–730
TDR (time-domain reflectometer) 657, 658, 802
Teamlinks, DEC 379
TechNet xxxviii, 663–664

Technical Information Network (TechNet) xxxviii, 663–664
Telecommunications
    See also Modems
    troubleshooting 622–623, 757
Telephone connectors
    RJ-11
        glossary definition 795
        modems 535–536
        network adapter cards 134
        Token Ring 283
        twisted-pair cables, 10BaseT 89
    RJ-45
        glossary definition 795
        network adapter cards 134
        Token Ring 283
        twisted-pair cables, 10BaseT 89
Telephone lines
    dedicated vs. dial-up 584
    dedicated 545, 581–582
    dial-up 545, 582-583
    leased 545
    line conditioning 584
    public dial network 545
Telnet 211, 678, 801
Terbo, international modem standards 537
Terminal, dumb, glossary definition 775
Terminators
    See also Signals, bouncing
    BNC 81, 258, 666
    bus topologies 37
    glossary definition 801
    loose 59
    resistance, glossary definition 801
    troubleshooting 666
The Internet *See* Internet
Thicknet (standard Ethernet)
    5-4-3 rule 259
    coaxial cabling, 10Base5 78–79, 260, 308
    glossary definition 802
Thinnet (thin-wire Ethernet)
    5-4-3 rule 259
    coaxial cabling, 10Base2 77–78, 258–259, 308
    glossary definition 802
    vs. thicknet 79
Throughput, glossary definition 802
Time slice 785
Time-domain reflectometer (TDR) 657, 658, 802
Token
    See also Token passing; Token Ring LAN
    glossary definition 802
Token Bus LAN 175
Token passing
    ArcNet 293–294
    as an access method 228

Token passing *(continued)*
  FDDI 605
  glossary definition 802
  ring networks 43
  Token Ring 277–278
Token Ring LAN
  See also Token passing
  cabling 282–283
  data frame format 275
  features 273–274
  fiber-optic cables 284
  glossary definition 802
  how it works 277–278
  hubs (MAU, MSAU, SMAU) 280, 785
  IEEE 802.5 category 175, 711
  implementation considerations (LAN Planner) 306–307
  lost token, glossary definition 783
  media filters 284
  network adapter cards 284
  network, selecting (LAN Planner) 309–310
  overview 273
  patch panels 284
  Physical layer protocol 213
  repeaters 284
  TokenTalk 291
Token, lost, glossary definition 783
TokenTalk 291
Tolerance, fault, built-in for hubs 281
Tools
  See also Utilities
  client/server
    program development 400
    query 400
  LAN Planner 700–703
  troubleshooting
    advanced cable testers 658, 761
    digital volt meter (DVM) 6578, 774
    network analyzers 659–661, 786
    network monitors 659, 787
    oscilloscopes 658, 788
    protocol analyzers 659–661, 786
    TDR (time-domain reflectometer) 657, 658, 802
Topologies
  bus
    communication on the bus 35–37
    disrupting network communication 38
    glossary definition 769
    LAN expansion 39
    overview 35
  choosing the network topology (LAN Planner) 66–67
  choosing the right topology (LAN Planner) 67–68
  cost 67–68
  dual-ring 606–607

Topologies *(continued)*
  existing cabling, reusing 68
  FDDI 605–606
  glossary definition 801
  hubs
    active 44
    advantages 46
    hybrid 45
    passive 44
  mesh network, glossary definition 784
  overview 34–35
  passive 36
  reliability 68
  ring
    glossary definition 794
    overview 42
    token passing *See* Token passing
  selecting, how to 50
  star
    bus variation 48
    glossary definition 799
    overview 41
    ring or star wired ring variation 49
  troubleshooting 59–60
Traffic on a network, segmenting with bridges 557
Traffic on cables, controlling 223
Trailer, packets 195, 789
Training
  content overview xxix–xxx
  e-mail 363
  finding the best starting point xxxii
  hardware and software requirements xxviii
  intended audience of this book xxvii
  LAN Planner 700–703, 739
  Microsoft
    Authorized Technical Education Center (ATEC) xxxvi
    Certified Professional program xxxiii–xxxv
  peer-to-peer networks 18
  prerequisites for taking self-paced training course xxvii
  security issues 472
  setup information xxviii–xxx
Transceiver cables 79, 261
Transceivers
  10BaseT 256-257
  description 79, 261
  glossary definition 803
  selecting, network adapter cards 128
  wireless networks 106–107
Transmission Control Protocol (TCP) 211, 803
Transmission Control Protocol/Internet Protocol (TCP/IP)
  description 216
  glossary definition 803

Transmission Control Protocol/Internet Protocol (TCP/IP)
  (continued)
    installing 328–329
    LAN Planner 245, 729–730
Transmission station identification (TSI) routing of
  faxes 355
Transmission technologies
  advanced WAN
    ATM (asynchronous transfer mode) *See* ATM
    FDDI *See* FDDI
    frame relay 596, 777
    ISDN 604, 684, 781
    LAN Planner 626–632, 742–743
    SMDS 612, 799
    SONET 611
    X.25 protocol *See* X.25 protocol
  WAN
    analog *See* Analog
    digital *See* Digital
    packet switching *See* Packet switching
  wireless networks
    infrared 108-109, 781
    laser 109
    narrow-band (single-frequency) radio 109
    point-to-point 111, 791
    spread-spectrum radio 110
Transmission, asynchronous, glossary definition 764
Transport layer, OSI reference model 171, 569, 803
Transport protocols
  See also Protocols
  ATP (AppleTalk transaction protocol) 211
  description 211
  glossary definition 803
  NBP (name binding protocol) 211, 785
  NetBEUI 211, 217, 786
  NWLink
    description 211, 217
    LAN Planner 244–245, 729
    Windows NT Workstation and Novell
      NetWare 390
  SPX (sequential packet exchange) 211
  TCP (Transmission Control Protocol) 211, 803
Troubleshooting
  access methods 241
  applications 694, 755
  bus networks 59
  cabling 152, 665–667, 754
  client/server environment 420, 756
  communication systems 6212-623, 757
  computers 666
  data security 517, 756
  drivers 240, 754
  faxes 423–424, 755
  hub-based networks 60
  IPX (internetwork packet exchange) protocol 240-241

Troubleshooting *(continued)*
  methodology, structured approach
    collecting information 652–653, 753
    help, asking for 655
    isolating the problem 655
    narrowing down possibilities 654
    possible causes 655
    setting priorities 652
    studying results 655
  multivendor environment networks 419, 756
  network
    accounts 517, 756
    adapter cards 153–154, 754
    applications 419
    operations 417, 755
    performance 669
    systems 693
    upgrades 666
  packets 240–241
  passwords 518
  peer-to-peer networks 59
  power fluctuations 667
  preemptive, in network management 644-645
  printing 418–419, 755
  protocols 241, 652
  ring networks 60
  server disk crashes 666
  timing of problems 696
  tools
    advanced cable testers 658, 761
    digital volt meter (DVM) 657, 774
    network analyzers 659–661, 786
    network monitors 658, 787
    oscilloscopes 658, 788
    protocol analyzers 657–661, 786
    TDR (time-domain reflectometer) 657, 658, 802
  topology problems 59–60
  unauthorized access 518–519
  users affected 694–695
  vendors 694
Trunk segment, Ethernet 260
Trust relationship, glossary definition 803
TSI routing of faxes 355
Twisted-pair cables, 10BaseT
  cabling components
    connection hardware 89
    distribution racks and rack shelves 89
    expandable patch panels 89, 257
    jack couplers 90
    media filters 284
    wall plates 90
  considerations 90
  EIA/TIA 568 87
  glossary definition 803
  overview 86

Troubleshooting *(continued)*
    shielded twisted-pair (STP) 88, 256, 797
    specifications 87
    Token Ring 282–283
    unshielded twisted-pair (UTP) 86–88, 256, 804

U

UA (User Agent), X.400 364
UART (universal asynchronous receiver transmitter),
    glossary definition 804
Unauthorized access, troubleshooting 518–519
Uniform Resource Locators (URLs) 681, 804
Uninterruptible power supply (UPS) 494–495, 667, 804
Universal asynchronous receiver transmitter (UART),
    glossary definition 804
Unshielded twisted-pair (UTP) cables 86–88, 256, 804
Updating drivers 185
Upgrading
    Ethernet networks, troubleshooting 304–305
    networks 642, 667
UPS (uninterruptible power supply) 493–494, 667, 804
URLs (Uniform Resource Locators) 681, 804
USENET 676–677
User accounts
    administrator or supervisor accounts 438
    creating and deleting, how to (lab) 451–453
    creating 434–439
    disabling or deleting 446–449
    glossary definition 805
    guest accounts 439
    key accounts 438
    passwords 439
    profiles 438
    user information, entering 436–438
    user parameters, setting 437
User Agent (UA), X.400 364
User applications, client/server 400
User groups 665
User Manager for Domains 434, 451
User-level security *See* Access permissions
Users
    managing shared printers 351–352
    managing with network operating systems 324
    number of possible, server-based networks 26
Utilities
    See also Tools
    Disk Administrator 500
    network management 644–645
    print sharing 348
    redirector 171
    User Manager for Domains 434, 451
UTP (unshielded twisted-pair) cables 86–88, 256, 804

V

V series modem standards 537–538, 714

Vampire taps 79, 261, 805
Vendor options in multivendor environments
    Apple 392
    Microsoft 390–391
    Novell 391
    overview 389
Vendor support, LAN Planner 745
Vendors, troubleshooting 694
Veronica protocol 677
VG (voice grade) *See* 100VG-AnyLAN, Ethernet
Virtual circuits 591, 805
Virtual private networks (VPNs) 545
Virus protection 483
Voice grade (VG) *See* 100VG-AnyLAN, Ethernet
Voice-grade lines 581–582
Volt meter 655, 774
Volume sets 501, 805
VPNs (virtual private networks) 545

W

WAIS (wide area information server) index search
    system 677
Wall plates, using with twisted-pair cables 90
WANs *See* Wide area networks (WANs)
Warehouse servers, client/server 405
Web (WWW) 674, 806
Wide area information server (WAIS) index
    search system 677
Wide area networks (WANs)
    advanced transmission technologies, choosing
        (LAN Planner) 630–632, 742–743
    analog connectivity
        dedicated lines 583–584
        dedicated vs. dial-up lines 584
        dial-up lines 581–583
        glossary definition 762
        line conditioning 584
    ATM (asynchronous transfer mode)
        advantages and disadvantages 602
        components 600–602
        glossary definition 764
        overview 599
        technology 599-600
    client/server model 405
    creating (LAN Planner) 626–632, 740–743
    description 6
    digital connectivity
        CSU/DSU (channel service unit/data service
            unit) 586
        DDS (digital data service) 586
        DS-0 or DS-1 transmission rates 587–588
        E1 service 587
        Fractional T-1 service 587
        glossary definition 773

Wide area networks (WANs) *(continued)*
    multiplexing (muxing) 587, 785
    overview 586
    Switched 56 service 588
    T1 service 587–588, 801
    T3 service 588
    FDDI
        beaconing 608, 658, 767
        media 609
        overview 605
        token passing 605
        topology 606–607
    frame relay 596, 777
    glossary definition 806
    ISDN 604, 684, 781
    overview 581
    packet switching
        ATM (asynchronous transfer mode) *See herein*
          ATM
        frame relay 597, 777
        glossary definition 789
        how it works 590–591
        virtual circuits 591, 805
        X.25 protocol 595–596
    SMDS 612, 799
    SONET 611
    X.25 protocol 595–596
Windows 95 379, 390
Windows NT Server
    Administrative Tools Program group 434, 442
    Control Panel 184
    Disk Administrator 500
    features in taking advantage of server hardware 23
    groups
        built-in 443, 769
        global 443, 778
        local 443, 783
        special 443
    how to install (lab) 338–340
    installing 325
    naming information, server 325
    network adapter card, configuring 328
    Novell environment 391
    partitioning 327
    Performance Monitor 458–459, 645
    Print Manager 348
    RAS (Remote Access Services) 546
    responsibilities, server 326
    server requirements 331
    TCP/IP installation 328–329
    User Manager for Domains 434, 451
Windows NT Workstation-based clients in Novell
  environment 391

Wireless LAN bridges 111–112
Wireless long-range bridges 112
Wireless networks
    802.11 category 176
    adapter cards 140
    capabilities of 105
    extended local area networks
        long-range wireless bridges 112
        multipoint wireless connectivity 112
        wireless LAN bridges 111–112
    local area networks
        access points 106–107
        infrared 108–109, 781
        laser 109
        narrow-band (single-frequency) radio 109
        point-to-point transmission 111, 791
        spread-spectrum radio 110
        transceivers 106–107
        transmission techniques 108–111
    mobile computing
        cellular networks 115
        microwave systems 115
        overview 114
        packet-radio communication 114
        satellite stations 115
    overview 105
    types of 106
    uses for 105
Workgroups
    See also Peer-to-peer networks
    glossary definition 806
Workstations
    diskless
        glossary definition 774
        remote-boot PROMs 140
    network adapter cards 140
World Wide Web (WWW) 674, 806
WWW (World Wide Web) 674, 806

X

X.25 protocol 217, 595–596, 715, 806
X.200 protocol 715
X.400 protocol 210, 363–365, 715, 806
X.500 protocol 210, 365, 715, 806
X.700 protocol 715
Xerox Network System (XNS) protocol 217, 566, 806
XNS (Xerox Network System) protocol 217, 566, 806

Z

Zones 290, 806

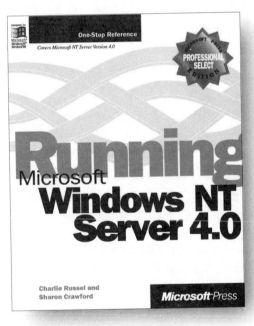

Teach yourself
Microsoft® Windows NT® 4.0
and train for Microsoft Certified Professional exams.

Preparation for Microsoft Certified Professional Exams

Microsoft Windows NT Technical Support Training

Windows NT 4.0 Technical Support Training CD-ROM

Microsoft Windows NT Technical Support Training

Hands-On Self-Paced Training for Windows NT Server Version 4.0

Microsoft Press

With MICROSOFT WINDOWS NT TECHNICAL SUPPORT TRAINING, you can teach yourself to install, configure, optimize, network, integrate, and support Microsoft Windows NT 4.0. And because it's based on Microsoft Official Curriculum, this training packag—along with the information from *Microsoft Windows NT Network Administration Training*—can help you pass the Microsoft Certified Professional exams (70-067 and 70-073) on supporting Microsoft Windows NT Workstation and Microsoft Windows NT Server. You learn through hands-on practice, questions and answers, simulations, videos, and a comprehensive text. It's the convenient, effective way to get the training you want—or to extend the training you've received at a Microsoft Authorized Technical Education Center.

U.S.A.	**$99.99**
U.K.	£93.99 [V.A.T. included]
Canada	$134.99
ISBN 1-57231-373-0	

Microsoft Press® products are available worldwide wherever quality computer books are sold. For more information, contact your book or computer retailer, software reseller, or local Microsoft Sales Office, or visit our Web site at mspress.microsoft.com. To locate your nearest source for Microsoft Press products, or to order directly, call 1-800-MSPRESS in the U.S. (in Canada, call 1-800-268-2222).

Prices and availability dates are subject to change.

***Microsoft*® Press**